CONNECTIVITY
CONSERVATION
MANAGEMENT
A GLOBAL GUIDE

CONNECTIVITY CONSERVATION MANAGEMENT

A GLOBAL GUIDE

(with particular reference to mountain connectivity conservation)

Edited by Graeme L. Worboys, Wendy L. Francis and Michael Lockwood

The World Bank

nature.org

Wilburforce Foundation

publishing for a sustainable future

London • Washington, DC

First published in 2010 by Earthscan

Earthscan Ltd, Dunstan House, 14a St Cross Street, London EC1N 8XA, UK
Earthscan LLC, 1616 P Street, NW, Washington, DC 20036, USA
Earthscan publishes in association with the International Institute for Environment and Development

For more information on Earthscan publications, see www.earthscan.co.uk or write to earthinfo@earthscan.co.uk

ISBN: 978-1-84407-603-1 hardback
ISBN: 978-1-84407-604-8 paperback

Typeset byFiSH Books, Enfield
Cover design by Andrew Corbett

A catalogue record for this book is available from the British Library

Library of Congress Cataloging-in-Publication Data

Connectivity conservation management : a global guide / edited by Graeme L. Worboys, Wendy L. Francis, and Michael Lockwood.
    p. cm.
  Includes bibliographical references and index.
  ISBN 978-1-84407-603-1 (hardback) – ISBN 978-1-84407-604-8 (pbk.) 1. Biodiversity conservation–International cooperation–Case studies. 2. Conservation projects–Management–International cooperation–Case studies. 3. Natural areas–Protection–International cooperation–Case studies. 4. Nature conservation–Case studies. 5. Wildlife crossings–Protection–International cooperation–Case studies. 6. Protected areas–Case studies. I. Worboys, Graeme. II. Francis, Wendy L. III. Lockwood, Michael.
  QH75.C645 2010
  333.95'16–dc22

                                                                                                                              2009022811

At Earthscan we strive to minimize our environmental impacts and carbon footprint through reducing waste, recycling and offsetting our CO_2 emissions, including those created through publication of this book. For more details of our environmental policy, see www.earthscan.co.uk.

This book was printed in the UK by the Cromwell Press Group.
The paper used is FSC certified.

Mixed Sources
Product group from well-managed forests and other controlled sources
www.fsc.org Cert no. TT-COC-2082
© 1996 Forest Stewardship Council

Cover photographs by Graeme L. Worboys illustrating core (embedded) protected areas of large-scale connectivity corridors. From the top left: Wildflower fields, Yellowstone National Park, USA (Yellowstone to Yukon connectivity corridor); Jagungal Wilderness, Kosciuszko National Park, NSW, Australia (Alps to Atherton connectivity corridor); 7234-metre high Langtang Lirung, Langtang National Park, Nepal (Sacred Himalayan Landscape); Eucalypts, South East Forests National Park, NSW, Australia (Alps to Atherton connectivity corridor); Northern Mule-Ears (*Wyehtia ampleixicaulis*) flowers, Yellowstone National Park, USA (Yellowstone to Yukon connectivity corridor); Sub-tropical Rainforest, Lamington National Park, Queensland, Australia (Alps to Atherton connectivity corridor); Sedimentary formations in cloud, Parc Natural de la Muntanya de Montserrat, Spain (Cantabrian Mountains–Pyrénées–Massif Central–Western Alps Great Mountain corridor); Banff National Park, Canada (Yellowstone to Yukon connectivity corridor).

Dedication

We were painfully aware of the two empty places looming large at the November 2006 IUCN World Commission on Protected Areas (WCPA) (Mountains Biome) Papallacta (Ecuador) workshop, which gave rise to this book. Two 'conservation champions', one could even say 'stars' – **Mingma Sherpa** and **Chandra Gurung** – had perished in a tragic helicopter crash on a Himalayan mountain in Nepal just 51 days previously. To them this book is dedicated; with the hope that its usefulness to protected area managers, policy makers and scientists will further the noble work in which they were fully engaged.

Both of them, along with five other World Wildlife Fund (WWF) colleagues and 13 other conservation leaders plus airplane crew, lost their lives that day. They were returning from a ceremony at the remote mountain village of Ghunsa to mark the transfer of the Kangchenjunga Conservation Area to local management. What a shocking and irreparable loss! As one of our IUCN Mountain Protected Areas Network members said: 'Kangchenjunga itself will stand a little bit higher as a memorial, I suspect.'

At the time of his death, **Mingma Norbu Sherpa** was Managing Director of the WWF US Eastern Himalayas Program. He was a pillar of strength and professional courage. He championed the Kangchenjunga tri-national transboundary concept, working long and hard toward the day when India, China and Nepal together would afford secular protection to this sacred mountain, the world's third highest. He is also known and admired for his work to establish a transboundary

complex ranging from the Manas Tiger Reserve in India to the summits of the Himalaya in Bhutan's Jigme Dorji National Park. This altitudinal transboundary corridor is a fantastic vision that has almost become a reality, since Bhutan has established large conservation areas to fill the connectivity voids between these two anchors and Black Mountain and Royal Manas National Parks. Mingma's presentation of this bold scenario in connection with our workshop in the Drakensberg at the IUCN World Protected Areas Congress in 2003 was included in the resulting book entitled *Managing Mountain Protected Areas: Challenges and Responses for the 21st Century*.

I first met Mingma in the early 1980s when he was working with the King Mahendra Trust for Nature Conservation in Nepal. I invited him to share Nepal's experience with involving local communities in Sagarmatha National Park and the Annapurna Conservation Area at a first ever WCPA Mountains Theme/Biome event, a 'Parks, Peaks and People Consultation' in Hawai`i Volcanoes National Park in 1991. Community involvement was one of his passions and successes. By 1991 he had begun to work in Bhutan with WWF, and he also presented a case study on Bhutan's protected areas. At that meeting he became a charter member of our Mountain Protected Areas Network, and remained very active since. Always, whenever connectivity corridors were promoted through WCPA-sponsored meetings and publications, his excellent Bhutan altitudinal corridor was included. Similarly, whenever transboundary conservation areas were 'on the table' his Kangchenjunga activity was featured. His talents and his new work in gap analysis led to his appointment in 2004 to the WCPA Mountain Biome executive team as Deputy Vice-Chair for Conservation. He assisted in planning the Papallacta workshop and prepared a case study for discussion – but his participation in the actual workshop was denied by fate. His case study is included in this volume.

For the last several years, **Chandra P. Gurung** had been Country Representative for WWF Nepal. Of particular interest to the WCPA Mountain Biome, and to this book, was his work in implementing the Terai Arc Landscape. Chandra was with us in the Drakensberg workshop held in conjunction with the 2003 World Congress on Protected Areas, and contributed a concept paper and progress report on the Terai Arc Landscape. This was included in our resulting book *Managing Mountain Protected Areas: Challenges and Responses for the 21st Century*. He also contributed mightily to the section on 'Communities as Partners in Mountain Protected Areas' in the WCPA book *Guidelines for Planning and Managing Mountain Protected Areas* that was the direct synthesis product of that workshop. Chandra had a decisive role in most of our Mountain Biome activities, beginning in the mid-1990s, when he was working on a Ph.D. at the University of Hawai`i. It was there that I met him, and quickly came to respect him, both on and off the tennis court. We had been strong friends ever since.

His fine work on the Annapurna Conservation Area also led to my inviting him to the 'Parks, Peaks and People Consultation' in 1991. At this event, the WCPA Mountain Theme was launched, and the Mountain Protected Areas Network was started with 41 members, including Chandra. He is missed. He also, like Mingma, was expected at Papallacta, and his contribution is included in this volume.

It is an honour to write this dedication to two such valued colleagues and beloved companions. One of the most memorable occasions of my life was the marking of my stepping aside as WCPA Vice-Chair for Mountains Biome. This took place in Durban, South Africa, at the World Congress on

Mingma Sherpa, Keynote speaker, International Mountain Corridors and Peace Parks Conference, Banff, Canada, 2004

Source: Graeme L. Worboys

Chandra P. Gurung
Source: Hum Gurung

Note: Scholarships in honour of our fallen colleagues have been set up for young Nepalis to help them acquire the education needed to become active in the conservation arena. Both of these champions, coming as they did from small rural villages, were assisted by scholarships at several schooling levels. The Mingma Sherpa and Chandra Gurung Conservation Scholarships have been established by the World Wildlife Fund/US. Anyone wishing to honour their memory is invited to make a donation to World Wildlife Fund/US, 1250 24th Street NW, Washington DC 20037, USA. In New Zealand, a memorial fund has been set up in honour of Mingma Sherpa to provide scholarships at Lincoln University (where he received his university education). Donations may be made online at www.fundraiseonline.co.nz/ MingmaNorbuSherpa.

Protected Areas, and was organized with humour and feeling by Graeme Worboys. A highpoint of the celebration was when Mingma, Chandra and two other Nepali colleagues (Pralad Yonzon and Krishna Oli), serenaded me with Nepali love songs. This touched me deeply, and tears still well up when I recall this scene, and think of these two men.

May we boldly carry forward the torch of passion and dedication to mountain conservation, which these two inspiring torch-bearers carried so effectively – although all too briefly.

Lawrence S. Hamilton
Senior Advisor
IUCN WCPA (Mountains Biome)

Contents

List of Figures, Tables, Boxes and Photographs

Figures

Tables

Boxes

Photographs

Acknowledgements

The combined energy of many people from around the world contributed to the development of this book and we gratefully recognize their positive contribution.

Editors

The compilers and editors of the book were:

Graeme L. Worboys, vice chair for mountains and connectivity conservation, the International Union for the Conservation of Nature (IUCN) World Commission on Protected Areas (WCPA), Canberra, Australia
Wendy L. Francis, director, conservation science and action, Yellowstone to Yukon Conservation Initiative, Banff, Canada
Michael Lockwood, senior lecturer, School of Geography and Environmental Studies, University of Tasmania, Australia

Chapter authors

The editors had great pleasure in working with two chapter authors, who were:

Charles C. Chester, adjunct assistant professor, Centre for International Environment and Resource Policy, The Fletcher School, Tufts University, Medford, Massachusetts, USA
Jodi A. Hilty, North America program director, Wildlife Conservation Society, Bozeman, Montana, USA

Case study contributors

The book benefits from 25 outstanding connec-tivity conservation case studies sourced from six (of eight) biogeographic realms of Earth. They are all original contributions specially prepared for this book and written by:

Gill Anderson, Parks Victoria, Bright, Australia; Miguel Angelo Andrade, Pontifical Catholic University of Minas Gerais, Brazil; Rod Atkins, Australian Alps national parks, Australia; Yuri Badenkov, Institute of Geography, Russian Academy of Science, Russia; Keith Bradby, Greening Australia, Australia; E. Buhanga, Uganda Wildlife Authority, Uganda; Liliana Paz B, Executive Director, Fundación Ecohabitats, Colombia; Nakul Chettri, International Centre for Integrated Mountain Development, Nepal; Alex Cortes, Munchique–Pinche macro-corridor, Colombia; Sérgio Augusto Domingues, Associação Cultural Ecológica Lagoa do Nado, Brazil; Barbara Ehringhaus, CIAPM Mountain Wilderness Suisse, Switzerland; Luis A. Ortega Fernandez, Director Protected Areas, Fundación Ecohabitats, Colombia; Marlon Flores, Consultant, Vilicamba-Amboró, Peru and Bolivia; Shaenandhoa Garcia-Rangel, Cambridge University, England; Larry Hamilton, IUCN WCPA (Mountains Biome), Vermont, USA; Robert Hofstede, IUCN South America Office, Quito, Ecuador; Wirato Inung, Gunung Leuser National Park, Indonesia; Hugh Irwin, Southern Appalachian Forest Coalition, North Carolina, USA; Simon Judd, The Wilderness Society, Australia; Yann Kohler, Alpine Network of Protected Areas, Micropolis-Isatis, France; Juan

Carlos Ledezma, Conservation International, Bolivia; Harvey Locke, The Wild Foundation, Colorado, USA; Brendan Mackey, Australian National University, Australia; Josep Mallarach, Fundació Territori i Paisatge de Caixa Catalunya, Spain; M. R. Mariaca, Conservation International, Bolivia; Luis Augusto Mazariegos, The Hummingbird Conservancy, Colombia; Erick Meneses, Conservation International, Peru; Eduard Muller, University for International Cooperation, Costa Rica; I. Owiunji, Wildlife Conservation Society, Kampala, Uganda; N. Pardo, Conservation International, Peru; Candido Pastor, Conservation International, Bolivia; Clea Paz, Conservation International, Bolivia; Brian Peniston, The Mountain Institute-ARO, Kathmandu, Nepal; Guiddo Plassmann, Alpine Network of Protected Areas, Micropolis-Isatis, France; Andrew J. Plumptre, Wildlife Conservation Society, Kampala, Uganda; Ian Pulsford, NSW Department of Environment and Climate Change, Australia; Miquel Rafa, Fundació Territori i Paisatge de Caixa, Catalunya, Spain; Sean Ranger, CapeNature, Rondebosch, South Africa; Sonia Rigueira, Institute Terra Brasilis, Brazil; Bernadino Romano, Universita dell'Aquila Monteluco di Roio, L'Aquila, Italy; A. Rwetsiba, Uganda Wildlife Authority, Kampala, Uganda; Fernando Salazar, Munchique–Pinche macrocorridor, Colombia; Trevor Sandwith, The Nature Conservancy, Arlington, Virginia, USA; Jordi Sargatal, Fundació Territori i Paisatge de Caixa Catalunya, Spain; Eklabya Sharma, ICIMOD, Kathmandu, Nepal; Mingma Norbu Sherpa, formerly WWF, New York, USA; Jordi Surkin, Grupo Nacional de Trabajo para la Participación, Santa Cruz, Bolivia; Sabita Thapa, WWF Nepal, Kathmandu, Nepal; Stephen Trombulak, Middlebury College, Vermont, USA; Jaco Venter, CapeNature, Rondebosch, South Africa; Xavier Viteri, Llanganates–Sangay ecological corridor, Ecuador; Sangay Wangchuck, Department of Forests, Thimpu, Bhutan; James Watson, The Wilderness Society, Australia; Eric Wikramanayake, WWF, New York, USA; Grace Wong, Conservation International, Virginia, USA; Edguard Yerena, Universidad Simón Bolivar, Caracas, Venezeula; Kevan Zunckel, Golder Associates, Durban, South Africa.

Banff 2004 workshop participants

In September, 2004 an international workshop *Protecting the World's Mountain Corridors and Peace Parks* in Banff, Canada, was hosted by the Yellowstone to Yukon Conservation Initiative and IUCN WCPA (Mountains Biome) and sponsored by the Wilburforce Foundation and Fundació Territori i Piasatge de Caixa Catalunya. The workshop involved participants exchanging lessons learned about large-scale connectivity conservation by comparing experiences from places like the Pyrénées, Himalayas, Andes, Amazon, Rockies, Australia and South Africa. During the workshop, participants reviewed and supported an idea to develop a new IUCN book on connectivity conservation management. The plan was to run a workshop in 2006 to consider a number of case studies that could be used as a basis for developing the book. The Banff workshop full-time participants have been listed here in recognition of their positive support and constructive input to the planned contents for the book. Part-time participants also provided support.

John Bergenske, Canada; Jeanette Boleantu, Canada; Casey Brennan, Canada; Rob Buffler, Canada; John Cathro, Canada; David Cherney, USA; Charles C. Chester, USA; Steve Duerr, USA; David Ewing, Canada; Timothy Feher, Canada; Wendy Francis, Canada; Shaenandhoa Garcia-Rangel, Venezuela; Jennifer Grant, Canada; Jeremy Guth, Canada; Cyril Kormos, USA; Cynthia Lane, Canada; Peter Lengyel, Romania; Harvey Locke, Canada; Julia Lynx, Canada; Josep M. Mallarach, Spain; Margo McKnight, USA; Jennifer Miller-Goethals, USA; Laurence A. G. Moss, USA; Carlos Nores-Quesada, Spain; Jordi Palau, Spain; Bob Peart, Canada; Dave Poulton, Canada; Miquel Rafa, Spain; Bart Robinson, Canada; Patrizia Rossi, Italy; Will Roush, USA; Jordi Sargatal, Spain; Mingma Sherpa, Nepal; George Smith, Canada; Gary Tabor, USA; Christine Torgrimson, Canada; Rose Wadsworth, USA; Chukey Wangchuk, Bhutan; Graeme Worboys, Australia.

Participants, 2004 Protecting the World's Mountain Corridors and Peace Parks Conference, Banff, Canada

Source: Florian Schulz; photo copyright Yellowstone to Yukon Conservation Initiative

Papallacta 2006 workshop participants

The workshop first envisioned at the Banff meeting was conducted during the week, 14–17 November 2006 in Papallacta, Ecuador, by the IUCN WCPA (Mountains Biome). The workshop was made possible by sponsorship from the Wilburforce Foundation, The Nature Conservancy, IUCN and the World Bank. The purpose of the workshop was to contribute to a new IUCN connectivity conservation management book by pre-preparing case studies and contributing to the development of two chapters (on lessons learned and future challenges). Thanks to the energy, commitment and enthusiasm of attendees, the workshop was an enormous success. It developed the IUCN WCPA Connectivity Conservation (Papallacta) Declaration, and contributed important connectivity management information for the two chapters. Participants who contributed so positively at the workshop included:

Maria Aillon, The Nature Conservancy, Ecuador; Gill Anderson, Australian Alps Liaison Committee, Australia; Rodney Atkins, Department of Environment and Heritage, Australia; Yuri Badenkov, Russian Academy of Sciences, Russia; Jaime Camacho, Ecociencia, Ecuador; Charles C. Chester, Tufts University, USA; Serena Ciabo, University of L'Aquila, Italy; Roger Crofts, IUCN WCPA, Vice Chair Europe, Scotland; Tatiana Egüez, The Nature Conservancy, Ecuador; Barbara Ehringhaus, CIAPM Mountain Suisse, Switzerland; Mauro Fabrizio, University of L'Aquila, Italy; Elizabeth Fox, Mountain Forum, Nepal; Wendy Francis, Yellowstone to Yukon Conservation Initiative, Canada; Lawrence Hamilton, IUCN WCPA, USA; Jodi Hilty, Wildlife Conservation Society, USA; Robert Hofstede, IUCN-SUR, Ecuador; Hugh Irwin, Coalition for Southern Appalachian Forests, USA; Bruce Jefferies, Conservation planning and management consultant, New Zealand; Harvey Locke, Yellowstone to Yukon Conservation Initiative, Canada; Josep M. Mallarach, Fundació

Participants, 2006 IUCN WCPA Mountains Connectivity Conservation workshop, Papallacta, Ecuador

Source: Linda McMillan

Territori i Paisatge de Caixa Catalunya, Spain; Linda McMillan, IUCN WCPA, USA; Tania Moreno, Universidad De Costa Rica, Costa Rica; Andrew Plumptre, Wildlife Conservation Society, Uganda; Martin Price, Perth College, Scotland; Ian Pulsford, NSW Department of Environment and Conservation, Australia; Miquel Rafa, Fundació Territori i Paisatge de Caixa Catalunya, Spain; Sonia Rigueira, IUCN WCPA, Brazil; Bernadino Romano, University of L'Aquila, Italy; Fausto Sarmiento, IUCN WCPA, USA; David Sheppard, IUCN Secretariat, Gland, Switzerland; Luis Suarez, Conservation International, Ecuador; Jodi Surkin, Conservation International, Ecuador; Xavier Viteri, Conservation biologist consultant, Ecuador; James Watson, The Wilderness Society, Australia; Grace Wong, Conservation International, USA; Graeme Worboys, IUCN WCPA Australia.

Dhulikhel 2008 workshop participants

In November 2008, IUCN WCPA (Mountains Biome) conducted a connectivity conservation workshop in Dhulikhel (near Kathmandu) Nepal in partnership with WWF-Nepal and ICIMOD (International Centre for Integrated Mountain Development). The workshop was part of IUCN's role of facilitating implementation of large-scale connectivity conservation areas. The timing of the workshop fortuitously coincided with the developing (draft) manuscript of the new connectivity management book and feedback was sought on a draft management framework for connectivity conservation. Feedback was generously and positively provided by participants, and it helped to improve the draft framework. The participants in the workshop were:

Farooq Ahmad, ICIMOD, Kathmandu, Nepal; Eng. Latif Ahmad Ahmadi, Environmental Protection Agency, Kabul, Afghanistan; Rod Atkins, Australian Alps national parks, Canberra, Australia; Yuri Badenkov, Russian Academy of Science, Moscow, Russia; Siddhartha Bajra Bajracharya, National Trust for Nature Conservation, Kathmandu, Nepal; Hem Sagar Baral, Bird Conservation Nepal, Kathmandu, Nepal; Shiv Raj Bhatta, National Parks and Wildlife Conservation, Kathmandu, Nepal; Nakul Chettri, ICIMOD, Lalitpur, Kathmandu, Nepal; Galbadrakh Davaa, The Nature Conservancy, Mongolia, Ulaanbaatar, Mongolia; Jamie Ervin, The Nature Conservancy, Vermont, USA; Wendy Francis, Yellowstone to Yukon Conservation Initiative, Banff, Canada; Ghana Shyam Gurung, World Wildlife Fund–Nepal, Kathmandu, Nepal; Bruce Jefferies, Consultant Adviser, Wanaka, Otago, New Zealand; Mr Karma, Ministry of Agriculture Thimphu, Bhutan; Ashiq Ahmad Khan, World Wildlife Fund-Pakistan, Peshawar, Pakistan; Liu Linshan, Chinese Academy of Sciences, Beijing, China; Harvey Locke, Yellowstone to Yukon Conservation Initiative, Montreal, Canada; Michael Lockwood, University of Tasmania, Hobart, Australia; Kathy MacKinnon, World Bank, Washington DC, USA; Marie-Ève Marchand, Canadian Parks and Wilderness Society, Montreal, Canada; Linda McMillan, San Francisco, USA; IUCN WCPA, San Rafael, USA; Krishna Prasad Oli, ICIMOD, Kathmandu, Nepal; Ian Pulsford, NSW Department of Environment and Climate Change, Queanbeyan, Australia; Lesley Pulsford, Environmental Manager, Ainslie, Australia; Trevor Sandwith, The Nature Conservancy, Arlington, USA; Tom Sengalama, Greater Virunga Trans-boundary Secretariat, Kigali, Rwanda; Peter Shadie, IUCN Asia, Bangkok, Thailand; Mingma N. Sherpa, IUCN Nepal, Kathmandu, Nepal; Naw May Lay Thant, Ministry of Forestry, Nay Pyi Taw, Myanmar; Win Naing Thaw, Ministry of Forestry, Nay Pyi Taw, Myanmar; Graeme Worboys, Canberra, IUCN WCPA, Australia; Weikang Yang, Chinese Academy of Sciences, Urumqi Xinjiang, China; Xuefei Yang, Chinese Academy of Sciences, Kunming, Yunnan, China; Tatjana Yashina, Katunskiy Biosphere Reserve, Altai Republic, Russia; Ili Zhang, Chinese Academy of Sciences, Beijing, China; Yuanming Zhang, Chinese Academy of Sciences, Urumqi Xinjiang, China.

Participants, 2008 IUCN WCPA Mountains Connectivity Conservation workshop, Dhulikhel, Nepal

Source: Linda McMillan

Reviewers

This book has benefited from the constructive comments of many reviewers. Most of the case studies were reviewed prior to receipt by the editors. The conceptual framework for connectivity conservation management was reviewed and improved by participants at the IUCN 2008 Dhulikhel workshop. The full text of the book was reviewed by:

Dave Harmon, executive director at the George Wright Society, USA, and Roger Crofts, formerly IUCN WCPA Vice Chair (Europe), Scotland.

We would like to especially thank Roger and Dave for their work. We also thank the following reviewers for their constructive comments and assistance:

Jim Barborak, Conservation International, Costa Rica; Jamie Ervin, The Nature Conservancy, USA; Jodi Hilty, the Wildlife Conservation Society, USA; Fausto Sarmiento, IUCN WCPA, USA; Gary Tabor, Center for Large Landscape Conservation, USA.

Publishing and production

Our special thanks are extended to Rob West, Sarah Thorowgood, Claire Lamont and other staff of Earthscan. We would also like to extend our appreciation to:

Ian Charles of Charles-Walsh Nature Tourism Services for the maps and figures; Harvey Locke, Julia Lynx and the staff of the Yellowstone to Yukon Conservation Initiative, Canmore, Alberta, Canada, who organized the 2004 Mountain Corridors and Peace Parks workshop in Banff; Robert Hofstede and the staff of the IUCN-Sur Office, Quito, Ecuador who helped facilitate the 2006 Papallacta workshop.

Financial support

The preparation and publication of this book would not have been possible without the financial support of the following individuals and organizations:

The International Centre for Integrated Mountain Development (ICIMOD), Kathmandu, Nepal, who helped sponsor the 2008 Dhulikhel workshop and the review process for the management framework – our particular thanks are extended to Nakul Chettri, Eklabya Sharma and Andreas Schild for their assistance; The Nature Conservancy, who helped sponsor the 2006 Papallacta (Ecuador) and 2008 Dhulikhel (Nepal) workshops – special thanks are extended to Maria Aillon, Paulina Arroyo, Silvia Benitez, Ian Dutton, Jamie Ervin and Trevor Sandwith for their help; The Wilburforce Foundation, Seattle, Washington, USA, who helped support the 2004 Banff workshop, the 2006 Papallacta workshop and who contributed to the production of this book – very special recognition and thanks are extended to Gary Tabor and Jennifer Miller; The World Bank, Washington DC, USA, assisted with both the 2006 (Papallacta) and 2008 (Dhulikhel) workshops – special thanks are extended to Kathy MacKinnon, lead biodiversity specialist, Environment Department, World Bank for her help and support. WWF (Nepal) assisted with the running of the 2008 Dhulikhel workshop – our thanks are extended to Jon Miceler and Ghana Gurung of WWF-Nepal.

Copyright permissions

Preface

Nikita Lopoukhine, Chairperson, IUCN WCPA World Commission on Protected Areas

The recent global history of large-scale habitat destruction, fragmentation and degradation has, in most parts of the world, diminished the space for wild species and dramatically modified ecosystems and their natural processes. Marine environments are also profoundly affected as fish stocks are eliminated and bottoms of oceans are dragged beyond recognition. Now human-caused climate change is further deepening the challenges to the survival of many life forms and their habitats, as well as the benefits and values they bring to society. Scientists have provided strong evidence that the Earth is undergoing its sixth great extinction event in the evolution of life on Earth.

The Earth is finite, and it is now abundantly evident that there are limits to how much we humans can pollute, destroy, develop, harvest, populate and modify our environments before the health of our planet is affected and other species impacted. Our children, their children, and generations of the future deserve better. Degraded ecosystems, resource shortages, reduced quality of life, pestilence, conflict and an absence of diverse life forms is an unacceptable future. One critical solution (among many responses needed) is to establish parks (protected areas) and manage them effectively. Parks have effectively protected our animals and plants over time against the pressures of development and human changes.

Parks are a critical investment for life's sake. They are the principal tool of the *Convention on Biological Diversity*'s goal for the conservation of biodiversity on Earth, and additional parks are recognized as a critical action for its Programme of Work for Protected Areas. They also need to be effectively managed. With at least 11 per cent of the Earth's land surface and 1 per cent of its marine environments reserved (as of 2009), progress has been made; but it is not enough. More needs to be done urgently, and organizations like IUCN have a critical role to play.

The conservation of biodiversity is optimized if natural lands or waters that surround protected areas are retained. Natural lands that maintain ecological connectivity between protected areas help to conserve species and retain the integrity of natural habitats and ecosystems. This is especially important given the dynamic of climate-change-caused biome shifts. The alternative of protected areas as islands in a sea of developed lands will mean that many species will be vulnerable to extinction over time.

Connectivity conservation stresses the need for thinking beyond isolated conservation enclaves or islands to a 'whole of landscape' vision of many lands under various tenures and jurisdictions contributing to an integrated approach to conservation. The World Commission on Protected Areas (WCPA), one of the IUCN's six commissions, and the key global expert body on protected areas, strongly endorses large-scale connectivity conservation. It views it as one of the major, strategic responses to climate change available for humans. It is a socially inclusive approach and recognizes the whole society contributing to the conservation effort, which will benefit people as much as it will help wildlife. This effort is an essential investment for sustaining the ecosystem services of terrestrial and marine environments for the 9.3 billion peoples forecast to live on Earth by 2050.

Large-scale connectivity conservation is a major challenge, and it has to include continental scale initiatives if there are to be effective responses to climate change. Opportunities still exist for such connectivity of natural lands and typically they are along major mountain ranges of Earth such as the Andes or the Rockies. Typically, to achieve such connectivity of natural lands, we need to involve many countries working collaboratively, and this means shared visions, cooperation and agreements for the sharing of resources to help achieve the management of connectivity. Concepts such as transboundary protected areas, peace parks and examples of large-scale conservation corridors such as the Yellowstone to Yukon initiative provide examples of how connectivity conservation can be managed at this scale. However, up to now there has been no definitive guide for how this could be achieved.

The purpose of this book is to provide such a guide. IUCN's World Commission on Protected Areas (Mountains Biome) invited connectivity conservation management experts from around the world to a workshop in Papallacta, Ecuador in November 2006. At this workshop, they provided connectivity management lessons that are applicable to a range of different contexts for the world. This book presents and analyses this rich information, and generates a new management framework and guidance for the most important connectivity management tasks. This information is very timely. It provides practical guidance for national and international responses to mitigate the impacts of climate change and biodiversity loss. It introduces a bold new basis for international cooperation and agreement beyond borders, beyond peace parks and transboundary agreements.

I commend this work to you. It is a basis for action!

Nikita Lopoukhine
February 2009

Foreword

Gary M. Tabor, Center for Large Landscape Conservation at Yellowstone to Yukon, Bozeman, Montana, USA

As the human footprint on the planet expands exponentially, biodiversity conservation, ecological processes and the benefits that ecosystem services bestow on humans, are increasingly threatened. Not only do habitat degradation and fragmentation pose direct threats to terrestrial landscape conservation, these threats are now, and will be further, exacerbated by climate change.

Since 1872, when the world's first national park, Yellowstone, was founded, focusing on the creation of defined protected areas has been a pillar of conservation. Whether protected area conservation efforts in the 'Yellowstonian' era considered how larger, surrounding landscapes sustain these natural refugia, or considered how protected areas serve to sustain their surrounding landscapes, is debatable. Much of society views protected areas as natural capital bank accounts, put aside in perpetuity as self-sustaining investments, separate from surrounding land uses. This misperception needs to be addressed; long-term ecological research has now shown that all states of nature are dynamic, particularly with the cascading effects of climate change on the immediate horizon. In this light, protected area conservation requires more vigilant, more adaptive management. Biodiversity conservation can no longer be envisioned as occurring within the boundaries of protected areas alone.

As protected areas become increasingly circumscribed by fragmented lands, as they become, in effect, ecological islands in a matrix of human dominated landscapes, they grow more susceptible to the detrimental consequences of human and natural disturbances. If we expect and desire that protected areas continue to function to sustain and nourish the natural and human world, it is vital that we maintain connectivity in the landscapes surrounding them. Connectivity can be thought of as both a life line linking core protected areas, and as the landscape's circulatory system, facilitating the movement, dispersal and migration of species and the continuity of ecological processes. When connected, core protected areas have more capacity to rebound successfully from the plethora of threats facing landscapes today. Thus, connectivity conservation can be viewed as an opportunity to realize climate adaptation management on the most fundamental level, because connectivity furthers resilience, and resilience, nature's ability to recover from disturbance, means survival for ecological systems.

Ecological resilience will determine how much nature will be affected by the pervasive impacts of global climate change. The Intergovernmental Panel on Climate Change unequivocally states that humans are directly and adversely altering the planet's climate at a pace faster than many of the most sophisticated models predicted (IPCC, 2007a). All species will feel the heat, and survival will be linked to how species are able to respond to changing environmental conditions. In 2009, even the most optimistic models forecast that if greenhouses gas emissions could be reined in today and climate change mitigation efforts optimized, the momentum of global climate change could not be stopped for at least another century. All life on the planet today will be challenged by a future that has no analogue in the past. In this brave new reality, life will persist in flux, with many species going extinct under the impact of human activities, and many ecosystems pushed to the brink of collapse.

All those who seek to maintain connectivity and reconnect fragmented landscapes must face an irrefutable truth: it is easier to conserve existing intact nature than it is to restore fragmented nature. And, just because lands are connected to each other, they are not necessarily fully ecologically functional. Some landscapes have connectivity that is limited to particular functions and species, and so do not possess the degree of connection required to secure fully functioning landscapes. On the other hand, the reality of land use does not always permit partitioning landscapes to maximize optimal core areas and connectivity conservation corridors. Yet, our best hope arises from the reality that connectivity can serve as the architecture for landscape restoration.

All of our conservation investments, all our natural systems, all that nature yields to sustain life and human livelihood, are under threat. If people do nothing, then nothing of nature as we know it in 2009 will be passed on to our heirs. Ultimately, it is the resilience of the human spirit that will unearth our abilities to meet these challenges. Conservation success in a changed world climate requires collective human resolve to create conditions that allow nature to maximize its own resilience. An ideal conservationist-practitioner of the 21st century will be a resilience manager. How, then, can we develop the skills to achieve the effective management of connectivity conservation?

By learning what others have done successfully and what hasn't worked is one way of doing this and this is provided by this book. It is one of its great strengths. The book describes, from first-hand practitioner experience, many inspiring large-scale connectivity conservation initiatives around the globe, and the many lessons learned from managing these areas. This book, however goes much further. It uses these lessons learned to develop a new conceptual framework for connectivity conservation management, a development that is crucial for the effective strategic planning and visioning processes needed for large-scale connectivity conservation by governments, policy makers and practitioners. It is an important development in the conservation management of large, complex natural areas.

Connectivity conservation is not a climate-change adaptation cure-all, but it is a cure that all land managers and policy makers must consider. In our new climate-changed era, species are becoming stressed, some will go extinct, and new ecological assemblages and interactions will form. Connectivity conservation is one of our best strategic response options, and in these uncertain times ahead, we must overcome any potential policy or implementation inertia to help conserve species and our own health and well-being. It is the type of leadership advice that will help conserve species and can provide a better future for the planet.

Gary Tabor
February 2009

List of Acronyms and Abbreviations

AALC	Australian Alps Liaison Committee
ACT	Australian Capital Territory
ALIDES	Central American Alliance for Sustainable Development
AlpArc	Alpine Network of Protected Areas
APE	Appennino Parco d'Europa (Italy)
A2A	Australian Alps to Atherton connectivity conservation corridor
BAPPENAS	Badan Perencanaan Pembangunan Nasional (Indonesia's Central Planning Agency)
BOM	Bureau of Meteorology (Australia)
B2C2	Bhutan Biological Conservation Complex
C.A.P.E.	Cape Action for People and the Environment
CBC	Canadian Broadcasting Corporation
CBD	Convention on Biological Diversity
CCAD	Comisión Centroamericana de Ambiente y Desarrollo
CCAP	Central American Council for Protected Areas
CEPF	Critical Ecosystem Partnership Fund
CFR	Cape Floristic Region
CI	Conservation International
CMA	Catchment Management Authority
CPAWS	Canadian Parks and Wilderness Society
CRC	Corporación Autónoma Regional del Cauca
CREW	Custodians of Rare and Endangered Wildflowers
DAFF	Department of Agriculture Fisheries and Forestry (Australia)
DANIDA	Danish International Development Assistance
DECC	New South Wales (Australia) Department of Environment and Climate Change
DLIA	Discover Life in America
DLUPC	Dehcho (First Nation) Land Use Planning Committee (northern Canada)
DRC	Democratic Republic of Congo
ENGO	environmental non-govermental organization
EU	European Union
EUROPARC	Federation of European Parks

GCBC	Greater Cederberg biodiversity corridor		Royal Government of Bhutan
GEF	Global Environmental Facility	NFA	Northern Forest Alliance (US)
GIS	geographic information system	NFCT	Northern Forest Canoe Trail (US)
GNAB	greater northern Appalachian bioregion	NGO	non-governmental organization
GTZ	German Technical Cooperation Agency	NLWRA	National Land and Water Resources Assessment (Australia)
Ha	hectare		
HKH	Hindu Kush Himalaya (mountains)	NPA	National Parks Association of NSW
HMGN-MFSC	His Majesty's Government of Nepal, Ministry of Forests and Soil Conservation	NPS	National Park Service (US)
		NSW	New South Wales (Australia)
		NWO-WOTRO	Dutch Science Foundation
ICIMOD	International Centre for Integrated Mountain Development	PA	protected area
		PC	Parks Canada
INRENA	Instituto Nacional de Recursos Naturales (Peru)	PERCON	Regional Strategic Programme for Connectivity
IPCC	Intergovernmental Panel on Climate Change	PERFOR	Regional Strategic Programme for Forests
IUCN	International Union for the Conservation of Nature	PERTAP	Regional Strategic Programme of Work in Protected Areas
km	kilometre	PLANECO	Planning in Ecological Networks (Italy)
km²	square kilometre		
K2C	Kosciuszko to Coast	PROMEBIO	Regional Strategic Programme for Biodiversity Monitoring and Evaluation
LRMP	Land and Resource Management Planning		
MAB	Man and the Biosphere programme	PSDF	Provincial Spatial Development Framework (South Africa)
MBC	Mesoamerican biological corridor		
MEAB	Millennium Ecosystem Assessment Board	QLD	Queensland
		RB	Reserva de la Biosfera
MDBC	Murray-Darling Basin Commission (Australia)	RFA	Regional Forest Agreement
		RGB	Royal Government of Bhutan
M-KMA	Muskwa-Kechika Management Area	ROCU	Regional Office Coordinating Unit (Nicaragua)
MOU	Memorandum of Understanding	SAFC	Southern Appalachian Forest Coalition
NCC	Nature Conservancy of Canada	SAMAB	Southern Appalachian Man and the Biosphere (US)
NCD	Nature Conservation Division,	SASEC	South Asia Sub-Regional Economic Cooperation

SCI	Site of Community Interest	UQ	University of Queensland
SERNAP	Servicio Nacional de Áreas Protegidas (Bolivia)	US	United States
		USAID	United States Agency for International Development
SHL	Sacred Himalayan Landscape		
SICA	Central American Integration System	VACC	Vilcabamba–Amboró conservation corridor
SICAP	The Central American Protected Area System	VAS	strategic environmental evaluation
SNV	Netherlands Development Organization	VIA	environmental impact evaluation
SWOT	strengths, weaknesses, opportunities and threats	VIC	Victoria
		VINCA	incidence environmental evaluation
TNC	The Nature Conservancy (US)		
UAESPNN	National Natural Parks Administrative Unit (Colombia)	WCMC	(UNEP) World Conservation Monitoring Centre
		WCPA	(IUCN) World Commission on Protected Areas
UBN	Unsatisfied Basic Needs		
UN	United Nations	WCS	Wildlife Conservation Society
UNDP	United Nations Development Programme	WWF	World Wide Fund for Nature (known as World Wildlife Fund in Canada and the US)
UNEP	United Nations Environment Programme		
		Y2Y	Yellowstone to Yukon
UNESCO	United Nations Educational, Scientific and Cultural Organization	Y2YCI	Yellowstone to Yukon Conservation Initiative

Glossary of Connectivity Conservation Terms

Adequate reserve system

The adequacy of a reserve system is a critical part of the concept of a comprehensive, adequate and representative reserve system referred to in Australia, where adequacy refers to 'the reservation of each ecosystem to the level necessary to provide ecological viability and integrity' (Worboys et al, 2005, p136). A more general characterization of adequacy would also include consideration of the ecological and evolutionary processes underpinning current biodiversity patterns (Watson et al, 2009).

Buffer zones

Buffer zones may be viewed as a shield around the core (protected) area against the direct impact of human activities. They are accepted as areas where a plan of land-use regulations is applied rather than as clearly defined areas that could have legal protection (Jongman, 2004). A buffer zone should be designed to:

- protect local traditional land use;
- accomplish area requirements or shape irregularities of the core area;
- set aside an area for manipulative research;
- segregate core areas for nature conservation from other land uses such as agriculture, recreation or tourism activities;
- manage adverse effects by putting up a barrier for immediate protection;
- locate developments that would have a negative effect on the core area (Jongman and Troumbis, 1995, cited in Jongman and Pungetti, 2004a).

Comprehensive reserve system

A comprehensive reserve system is a critical part of the concept of a comprehensive, adequate and representative reserve system referred to in Australia, where comprehensive refers to including the full range of 'regional' ecosystems within each Australian bioregion (Worboys et al, 2005).

Connectivity (of reserves)

This refers to the ease with which organisms move between particular landscape elements; the number of connections between patches, relative to the maximum number of potential connections (Lindenmayer and Burgman, 2005).

Connectivity conservation

Connectivity conservation is defined using biodiversity conservation criteria, but also includes social and institutional dimensions. Connectivity conservation describes actions taken to conserve landscape connectivity, habitat connectivity, ecological connectivity or evolutionary process connectivity for natural and semi-natural lands that interconnect and embed established protected areas. It may be represented by direct interconnections or by the ecological interconnectedness of disjunct conservation areas. The strong connectedness of people to natural and semi-natural connectivity lands is also recognized. This connection of people (and their groups and institutions) to land, combined with a shared conservation vision and actions such as communication, cooperation, collaboration and partnerships offer significant means for facilitating connectivity conservation outcomes.

Connectivity conservation area

This is a complex of natural and semi-natural lands that are spatially defined as the area subject to a connectivity conservation vision and connectivity conservation management. It potentially includes core protected areas and a range of different landowners, land tenures and land uses.

Connectivity conservation management

This is the process of achieving and maintaining connectivity conservation in response to a clear vision and clear knowledge of conservation needs and priorities through leading, planning, undertaking actions and evaluating performance.

Conservation planning

Conservation planning is the process of locating, designing and managing conservation areas to promote the persistence of biodiversity, one of the main goals of the Convention of Biological Diversity (Bottrill and Pressey, 2009).

Core area

Core areas are natural areas possessing a high level of ecosystem integrity: in most countries they are designated as protected areas and are often managed in accordance with the IUCN definition and guidelines (Dudley, 2008).

Corridor (for wildlife)

A linear strip of habitat of varying lengths or widths that facilitates fauna movement between otherwise isolated patches of habitat (Lindenmayer and Burgman, 2005).

Dispersal

The movement of individuals among spatially separate patches of habitat, including all immigration and emigration events (Lindenmayer and Burgman, 2005).

Ecological connectivity

Ecological connectivity is the connectedness of ecological processes across many scales and includes processes relating to trophic relationships, disturbance processes and hydro-ecological flows (Lindenmayer and Fischer, 2006; Soulé et al, 2006).

Ecological corridors

Ecological corridors are defined functionally to indicate connectivity and as physical structures to indicate connectedness. They are functional connections enabling dispersal and migration of species that could be subject to local extinction and they are landscape structures (other than core areas) varying in size and shape from wide to narrow and from meandering to straight, which represent links that permeate the landscape and maintain natural connectivity (Jongman and Troumbis, 1995, cited in Jongman, 2004).

Ecological integrity

Ecological integrity refers to the condition of an ecosystem where the structure and function are unimpaired by human-caused stresses, and where the ecosystem biological diversity and supporting processes are likely to persist (PC, 1997).

Ecological network

Ecological networks are systems of nature reserves and their interconnections that make a fragmented natural system coherent, so as to support more biological diversity than in its non-connected form (Bouwma and Jongman, 2006). An ecological network is composed of core areas (usually protected), buffer zones and (connected through) ecological corridors (Bischoff and Jongman, 1993, cited in Jongman, 2004).

Ecosystem

Ecosystem means a dynamic complex of plant, animal and micro-organism communities and their non-living environment interacting as a functional unit (CBD, 2008).

Ecosystem approach

The ecosystem approach is a strategy for the integrated management of land, water and living resources that promotes conservation and sustainable use in an equitable way. It is based on:

- the application of scientific methodologies;
- humans being an integral part of many ecosystems;
- using adaptive management to deal with the complex and dynamic nature of ecosystems;

- the integration of conservation land use approaches such as biosphere reserves, protected areas and single species conservation programmes. (CBD, 2008)

Ecosystem services

The ecological services to human societies provided by ecosystems, for example the provision of clean water and air and pollination of crop plants (Lindenmayer and Burgman, 2005).

Evolutionary process connectivity

Evolutionary process connectivity identifies that natural evolutionary processes, including genetic differentiation and evolutionary diversification of populations, need suitable habitat on a large scale and connectivity to permit gene flow and range expansion. Ultimately, evolutionary processes require the movement of species over long distances (Soulé et al, 2006).

Flagship species

A charismatic species that attracts public attention, financial resources or additional conservation efforts to promote the protection of an area or the protection of a suite of other associated taxa (Lindenmayer and Burgman, 2005).

Greenway

Networks of land planned, designed and managed for various purposes, but anyway compatible with sustainable land use (Jongman and Pungetti, 2004b).

Habitat connectivity

Habitat connectivity is the connectedness between patches of habitat that are suitable for a particular species (Lindenmayer and Fischer, 2006).

Habitat corridor

This is a linear strip of vegetation that provides a continuous (or near continuous) pathway between two habitats. This term has no implications about its relative use by animals (Bennett, 2003).

Habitat mosaic

This is a landscape pattern comprising a number of patchy interspersed habitats of different quality for an animal species (Bennett, 2003).

Hierarchical management

This is management by government and by government and private organizations where there are established organizational structures and hierarchical responsibilities for policies and decision making and the implementation of those decisions.

Keystone species

These are species whose addition to, or loss from, an ecosystem leads to large changes in abundance or occurrence of at least one other species (Lindenmayer and Burgman, 2005).

Landscape

This is the combination of ecosystems, plants, animals and ecological processes and abiotic features that interact within a connected and functional ecological network and that allows for the long-term persistence of species (Ervin et al, 2009).

Landscape connectivity

Landscape connectivity is a human view of the connectedness of patterns of vegetation cover within a landscape (Lindenmayer and Fischer, 2006).

Landscape linkage

This is a general term for a linkage that increases connectivity at a landscape or regional scale (over distances of kilometres or tens of kilometres). Typically, such linkages comprise broad tracts of natural vegetation (Bennett, 2003).

Linkage

An arrangement of habitat (not necessarily linear or continuous) that enhances the movement of animals or the continuity of ecological processes through the landscape (Bennett, 2003).

Migration

The regular annual movement of animals between different habitats, each of which is occupied for specific parts of the year; movement of individuals or whole populations from one region to another (Lindenmayer and Burgman, 2005).

Protected area

A protected area is a clearly defined geographical space, recognized, dedicated and managed, through legal or other effective means, to achieve the long-term conservation of nature with associated ecosystem services and cultural values (Dudley, 2008).

Protected area categories

IUCN recognizes six categories of protected areas: Category Ia: strict nature reserve; Category Ib: wilderness area; Category II: national park; Category III: natural monument or feature; Category IV: habitat/species management area; Category V: protected landscape/seascape; and Category VI: managed resource protected area (Dudley, 2008).

Representative reserve system

A 'representative' reserve system is a critical part of the concept of a comprehensive, adequate and representative reserve system, where representative refers to selection of reserves that reflect the variability of the ecosystems they represent (Worboys et al, 2005).

Sector

A sector is any activity that contributes to the economy of a community or country and that has an actual or potential bearing on the effectiveness of an ecological network (connectivity conservation area) (Ervin et al, 2009).

Stepping stones

These are one or more separate patches of habitat in the intervening space between ecological isolates, providing resources and refuge that assist animals to move through the landscape (Bennett, 2003).

Systematic conservation planning

Systematic conservation planning involves the use of explicit and often quantitative objectives, which means that planners and managers must be clear about what they intend to achieve and be accountable for decisions that should make progress toward their objectives. It also involves the principle of complementarity, where systematic methods have identified systems of conservation areas that are complementary to one another in achieving conservation objectives. It usually involves working through a structured, transparent and defensible process of decision making and achieves an integrated system of conservation areas (Bottrill and Pressey, 2009).

Umbrella species

A species whose protection would automatically provide protection for other species or even an entire community (Lindenmayer and Burgman, 2005).

Part I

Setting the Context

1

The Connectivity Conservation Imperative

Graeme L. Worboys

A remarkable conservation land-use revolution occurred at the end of the 20th century and start of the 21st century, with the number of protected areas (PAs) growing from approximately 40,000 in 1980 (Chape et al, 2008) to 113,959 in January 2008 (UNEP-WCMC, 2009). This achievement transpired in response to an international commitment to conserve a representative sample of the natural and cultural heritage of all countries. In the 1990s, in parallel with this effort, the need to conserve the connectivity of natural lands between protected areas also emerged. It had become increasingly evident to many that protected areas, in isolation, may not always be able to protect all of their biodiversity values. 'Island' protected areas were vulnerable to multiple threats, especially the consequences of climate change. A consensus emerged that biodiversity conservation required large-scale interconnected natural landscapes with embedded and interconnected protected areas.

By 2009, as evidence for human-induced climate change became more pronounced and as climate change modelling forecasts demonstrated the ramifications of changes to species and habitats, the interest in connectivity conservation had grown. Scientists such as Andrew Bennett identified the importance of these large-scale connectivity conservation areas:

> linkages also have a role in countering climate change by interconnecting existing reserves and

> protected areas in order to maximise the resilience of the present conservation network. Those linkages [connectivity conservation areas] that maintain large contiguous habitats or that maintain continuity of several reserves along an environmental gradient are likely to be most valuable in this regard (Bennett, 2003).

This book is about managing terrestrial connectivity conservation areas like those described by Bennett. Its primary purpose is to help conserve nature and species on Earth for the long term. Its primary focus is on how to establish and manage these large-scale essentially natural lands to achieve conservation outcomes. It does this by introducing the foundational concepts of connectivity conservation, communicating the experiences and wisdom of connectivity managers, developing a conceptual framework and describing the processes and tasks of connectivity conservation management.

About connectivity conservation

So what exactly is connectivity conservation and what are the common terms that are used in this book? The concept of connectivity described here is based on the biological sciences. Its focus is purely terrestrial (although connectivity conservation is an equally important conservation need for marine environments and deserves similar treatment). Natural connectivity for species in the landscape has a structural component, which relates to the spatial arrangement of habitat or other elements in the landscape, and it has a functional (or behavioural) component, which relates to the behavioural responses of individuals, species or ecological processes to the physical structure of the landscape (Crooks and Sanjayan, 2006b). This description has been refined further to recognize four types of connectivity:

1 *Landscape connectivity*, which is a human view of the connectedness of patterns of vegetation cover within a landscape (Lindenmayer and Fischer, 2006).
2 *Habitat connectivity*, which is the connectedness between patches of habitat that are suitable for a particular species (Lindenmayer and Fischer, 2006).
3 *Ecological connectivity*, which is the connectedness of ecological processes across many scales and includes processes relating to trophic relationships, disturbance processes and hydro-ecological flows (Lindenmayer and Fischer, 2006; Soulé et al, 2006).
4 *Evolutionary process connectivity*, which identifies that natural evolutionary processes, including genetic differentiation and evolutionary diversification of populations, need suitable habitat on a large scale and connectivity to permit gene flow and range expansion – ultimately, evolutionary processes require the movement of species over long distances (Soulé et al, 2006).

The concept of landscape connectivity recognizes that while there may be a continuum of vegetated landscape, it may not include suitable habitat for specific species. There are features that contribute to landscape connectivity and these include wildlife corridors, stepping stones and a matrix of vegetation that has similar attributes to patches of native vegetation (Bennett, 2003; Lindenmayer and Fischer, 2006). It may also involve the conservation of ecological connectivity between lands that are spatially separated. The scientific aspects of connectivity and the language used are discussed in Chapter 2.

The conservation of connectivity is our next consideration. Active conservation involves people and this is where we extend our concept of connectivity conservation to recognize human aspirations and connectedness to land, social values and management institutions. It is about how people feel and value natural, interconnected landscapes. It is about the active involvement of people and organizations in connectivity conservation management: that is, action to conserve landscape, habitat, and ecological and evolutionary connectivity. In a dynamic world of climate change it includes conserving large natural lands that interconnect and often embed (surround) protected areas and help to maintain opportunities for species survival for the long term. Action may also seek to conserve ecologically important linkages across natural and semi-natural lands that are separated by development. Connectivity conservation helps maintain opportunities for species to maintain genetic diversity and resilience and to move, adapt and respond to climate change and to other global change pressures.

The landscape over which connectivity conservation action is being undertaken has been described by this book as a 'connectivity conservation area'. It may include all or some of the features that contribute to landscape connectivity (wildlife corridors, stepping stones and other features). We are using this generic term given there are many different descriptions for landscapes where connectivity conservation is taking place. They have been described (for example) as biolinks, linkages, ecological networks, ecological corridors and connectivity corridors, among many other terms. To assist readers, we define some of these terms (see Chapter 2 and the Glossary), but for reasons of clarity and simplicity we have used the generic term 'connectivity conservation area' (which we may abbreviate to 'connectivity area') in this book. A connectivity conservation area is essentially any natural or semi-natural lands that includes, interconnects and embeds protected areas and where connectivity conservation is a primary objective. In nearly all instances, it is a generic term for lands managed for connectivity conservation.

A connectivity conservation area needs active management and we use the term 'connectivity conservation management' to indicate this. It includes a process of formally recognized management, and recognizes key management functions such as 'planning' that are needed to achieve conservation outcomes. Connectivity manage-

A Trans-Canada Highway 'wildlife crossing', one of many structures that successfully provide Yellowstone to Yukon connectivity conservation across an otherwise dangerous barrier for wildlife

Source: Graeme L. Worboys

ment is guided by a vision and the purpose of management is to achieve conservation of biodiversity. How connectivity conservation is undertaken and what tasks are important provides a focus for this book.

The book takes a strategic approach to connectivity conservation and emphasizes 'large-scale' connectivity conservation areas and their management. This reflects a plan by IUCN WCPA to facilitate the retention of large, natural interconnected lands on Earth (particularly in mountain areas) to help conserve species and the associated archipelago of protected areas for the long term (IUCN WCPA, 2008). These are areas that are tens of kilometres wide (or wider) and hundreds if not thousands of kilometres long.

Ideally, such connectivity conservation areas will have been carefully selected for their strategic conservation benefits and the cost-effectiveness of their management. Their size typically means that they include many protected areas embedded within them and they include, outside of protected area boundaries, many important habitats and functioning ecosystems. The large size

should provide effective connectivity for species between protected areas. By focusing on large-scale areas, we have also tried to avoid some of the questionable conservation benefits of smaller wildlife corridors (Chapter 2). Bennett (2003) comments on large-scale connectivity conservation areas:

> *Linkages [connectivity conservation areas] that maintain the integrity of ecological processes and continuity of biological communities at the biogeographic or regional scale have a more significant role than those operating at local levels. Effective linkages at these scales have a key role in the maintenance of biodiversity at the national level, or at the international level where linkages cross borders between several countries.*

Given that connectivity areas are recognized as being essential to the maintenance of biodiversity, what types of land and land uses are reasonably compatible with connectivity conservation? There are a number of land-use types that may be compatible with nature conservation, provided they are managed with that goal in mind. These are in addition to IUCN Category I-VI protected area lands, world heritage areas, Ramsar wetlands and biosphere reserves that may form the core of connectivity conservation areas. Land tenures include community owned, indigenous, leasehold, Crown or public and private lands. Relative to this ownership, there are also a range of land-use types that need to be considered (Table 1.1).

Table 1.1 Non-protected area lands that may support connectivity conservation

Landownership and land uses that may support connectivity conservation	Notes
Private lands	Natural private lands purchased or managed by philanthropic organizations or private individuals for the purpose of nature conservation
Private lands (restored)	Private landowner restoration of forests and native vegetation on previously cleared lands – the restoration may be sponsored by government grants
Private lands (stewardship)	Lands that benefit from government policies promoting connectivity conservation areas (biolinks or corridors) in the landscape
Private and community lands (NGO stewardship)	Private and other lands (such as community lands) that are subject to NGO stewardship and incentive schemes for restoration and conservation – this may include land purchase and the creation of a conservation covenant over the land title
Private lands (offset schemes)	Conservation values offset through covenants in perpetuity in strategic locations (such as connectivity conservation areas) – for example, the New South Wales Government's biobanking scheme where farmers commit to enhance and protect biodiversity values on their land (DECC, 2009)
Private lands (carbon sequestration)	Private or other lands that are reforested for commercial gain though carbon credit trading schemes
Private lands (ecotourism initiatives)	Private lands where natural vegetation is retained and restoration work is undertaken as part of an ecotourism destination
Private and public lands (water catchment)	Catchment areas that are conserved under regulation, certification or policy for hydroelectric power, drinking water and irrigation – in some cases owners earn a return for providing water, as in the Condor Biosphere Reserve, Ecuador, for example (Echavarria and Arroyo, 2004)
Private lands (catchment stability)	Lands that are conserved to protect catchments from soil erosion and from slope instability, especially in extreme storm events
Private lands (hunting reserve)	Areas that legally protect wildlife for trophy hunting (such as in the Swiss Jura Mountains)
Private lands (recreation park)	Legally protected areas for recreation and wildlife (such as the Dyrehaven Park in Copenhagen)
Private lands (breeding sites)	Areas under voluntary agreements to protect bird breeding sites
Private lands (natural grazing)	Commercial properties that use native animal stock (such as the North American bison (Bison bison)) and native grasslands for their business (such as Ted Turner's ranch in Montana)

Table 1.1 Continued

Landownership and land uses that may support connectivity conservation	Notes
Public lands (forest reserves)	Legally conserved lands either within a designated forest or include an entire forest area under a mechanism not recognized as an IUCN category protected area
Public lands (production forests)	Production forests where codes of practice, rotation cycles, third party certification or other sustainable use forestry management practices provide real opportunities for long-term connectivity conservation areas
Public lands (avalanche control)	Areas legally protected to help protect communities and people from avalanches
Public lands (wildlife corridors)	Lands designated by local or provincial/state authorities as wildlife corridors, such as those established by the Town of Canmore, Alberta, Canada
Community lands (sacred sites)	Sites conserved by voluntary agreement, which may be very location specific or include an entire feature such as a mountain or mountain range (Bernbaum, 1997)
Public lands (cultural sites)	Legally conserved sites, such as Angkor Wat in Cambodia, which protect cultural features and sites as well as biodiversity

Source: Adapted from Dudley and Parish, 2005, p76

Other types of land uses on public or private lands may also be compatible with connectivity conservation under the appropriate conditions. For example, carefully managed grazing by domestic livestock may sustain grassland ecosystems. Innovative best practices in industrial sectors, such as hand-cut seismic lines used in oil and gas exploration, may also maintain the intactness of the landscape.

Connectivity conservation areas are not a substitute for protected areas. The highest priority for nations should be to finalize their reserve systems consistent with the Secretariat for the Convention on Biological Diversity plan of action for protected areas (Dudley et al, 2005). However, it will not be possible to achieve reserve establishment for all natural lands and this is why connectivity areas are an important next conservation initiative for nations. Connectivity areas will include important habitats and provide opportunities for species to move. A large-scale interconnected landscape of natural lands with embedded protected areas provides opportunities for many species to respond to the forecast effects of climate change and other human pressures. Connectivity areas are an integral part of a biodiversity conservation strategy for a nation.

It should be noted that some large remaining intact wild (natural) areas left on Earth such as the Boreal Forests of Canada, the rainforests of the Amazon and other wild lands or wilderness areas are not in themselves connectivity conservation areas. These are very large, undisturbed natural areas that are exceptionally valuable for their functioning ecosystems and the absence of human pressures, and they need to be managed to retain their wildness and wilderness values. However, while such areas are not connectivity conservation areas, they could potentially form core areas for such initiatives, albeit at a massive scale.

I have now described what connectivity areas are (and are not), but how do connectivity areas fit into broad planning schemes of governments? How do they fit into a landscape planning context?

Planning context

Modern governments are challenged to manage increasing demands for a growing variety of land-use activities on a finite land base. Comprehensive, inclusive and transparent land-use planning is a necessary response to these demands. While land-use planning traditionally has included considerations of balancing a variety of land uses and distributing them across the landscape to avoid conflicts and minimize environmental impacts, the conservation of biological connectivity now must be added to land-use planning imperatives.

Some parts of connectivity conservation areas may play important functional roles for communities in local landscapes and may be recognized by land-use planning schemes. The lands may be specifically identified (for example) as water catchment areas, slope protection areas, scenic protection areas, recreation areas and areas reserved for wildlife conservation or special feature protection that are not IUCN Category protected areas. Their connectivity conservation function is clear when they are considered in aggregate. Connectivity areas are also important for national protected area systems planning. The elements of a protected area system master plan have been described (Ervin, 2007) and recognize 'connectivity and corridors' as critical parts of a network of protected areas. A 'representative' reserve system is important, and so is connectivity conservation.

Connectivity conservation areas are therefore important to communities, within land-use planning schemes, and to national systems of protected areas, so where have they been established? What examples may be found around the world?

A global initiative

Connectivity conservation areas have been initiated in many parts of the world. Actions by individuals, communities, non-governmental organizations (NGOs) and governments have helped to establish, plan for and manage them. Many nations on Earth have also instituted connectivity conservation actions. In 2007, IUCN's Asia office completed a preliminary global assessment of the implementation of connectivity conservation initiatives, which is summarized in Table 1.2.

Table 1.2 An indicative global assessment of connectivity conservation initiatives

Region and country examples	Connectivity conservation initiatives
Africa	
Most focus has been on transboundary protected areas particularly in southern and eastern Africa and which have high level political support. In 2007, no country was reported having enabling legislation for connectivity	
South Africa	South Africa has important transboundary and connectivity conservation initiatives in the Drakensberg Mountains (Zunckel, Chapter 4) and the Cape Floristic Region (Sandwith et al, Chapter 4)
Democratic Republic of Congo, Uganda and Rwanda Transboundary protected area and connectivity conservation along the Albertine Rift Valley, with a special focus on the mountain gorilla populations (Plumptre et al, Chapter 4)	
Asia	
Connectivity initiatives are underway in at least ten Asian countries	
Bhutan, India and South Korea	These countries have legal instruments that explicitly enable connectivity corridors (for example, Sherpa et al, Chapter 6)
Nepal	The World Wide Fund for Nature ecoregion programme is driving the Terai Arc Landscape (Nepal) connectivity corridor
Thailand	Has clustered its forest protected areas into 20 areas and is embarking on linking these assemblages (across different tenures)

Table 1.2 Continued

Region and country examples	Connectivity conservation initiatives
South Korea	Has established clear goals for an eco-network on the Korean peninsula
Taiwan	Has initiated steps to interconnect its protected areas as one large connectivity corridor along its central mountain chain (Wang, 2008)
Japan	A commitment was made in 1998 to develop a national scale ecological network

Australia

Biodiversity (connectivity) corridors are recognized in national strategic plans for biodiversity conservation, climate change and the National Reserve System strategy – large-scale initiatives such as A2A (Pulsford et al, Chapter 5) and Gondwana Link (Watson et al, Chapter 5) have been established

Europe

More than 50 countries are involved in some type of connectivity conservation work, and special legislation has been developed in eight countries – in Eurasia, 52 countries have endorsed the Pan-European and Landscape Diversity Strategy, a framework for national conservation of biological and landscape diversity, and ecological networks have flourished where government support is provided

Denmark, Switzerland, Germany and The Netherlands	Ecological networks have been put in place nationally – in The Netherlands, three forms of land management are being employed (protected areas, privately owned land managed for nature conservation purposes and nature development areas)
Spain, France and Italy	The Cantabrian Mountains–Pyrénées–Massif Central–Western Alps connectivity corridor is an important new, large-scale connectivity initiative for Europe (Mallarach et al, Chapter 9)

Latin America

Nearly all countries in the region have developed connectivity conservation initiatives, and over 100 connectivity corridors in 16 countries have been established: more than 20 have been established in three countries or more, and some have been achieving firm progress for ten years or more – the following examples are indicative

Bolivia, Brazil and Venezuela	The three countries have established national connectivity conservation legislation
Colombia, Ecuador and Venezuela	The Andean Páramo connectivity corridor recognizes conservation and management of an ecological archipelago (Hofstede, Chapter 8)
Bolivia–Peru	The Vilcabamba–Amboro connectivity conservation area is located in the tropical Andes hot spot, and directly involves Conservation International in collaboration with national governments (Surkin et al, Chapter 8)
Argentina	Salta Provincial legislation enables connectivity conservation corridors
Ecuador	A connectivity conservation area in the Condor Biosphere Reserve, Ecuador, has been established, which also includes a water-supply finance mechanism (Echavarria and Arroyo, 2004)
Belize, Costa Rica, El Salvador, Guatemala, Honduras, Nicaragua and Panama	The Mesoamerican biological corridor was established in 1994 and extends through eight countries from southern Mexico to Panama, and contains four zones: core areas (368 protected areas), buffer zones, corridors and multiple-use areas (Muller and Barborak, Chapter 8)

Table 1.2 Continued

Region and country examples	Connectivity conservation initiatives
North America	
The most important initiatives have been driven by NGOs in collaboration with communities and governments	
Canada and USA	The Y2Y initiative (Locke, Chapter 7) is well known internationally and has played a leadership role in developing the concept of connectivity conservation
USA	The Southern Rockies Wildlands Network is one of six contiguous networks that the Wildlands Network has developed along the western side of the USA in the Rocky Mountains (Wildlands Network, 2009)
	Connectivity conservation initiatives along the eastern side of the USA and southern Canada including the northern Appalachians (Hamilton and Trombulak, Chapter 7) and the southern Appalachians (Irwin, Chapter 7) have been identified

Source: Adapted from IUCN, 2007

This rising investment by governments and NGOs in connectivity conservation is paralleled by an upsurge in connectivity conservation science and a number of important international policy documents. The *Convention on Biological Diversity* Programme *of Work on Protected Areas* (Dudley et al, 2005) specifically identifies a target for integrating protected areas into broader landscapes by 2015. Establishing and managing connectivity conservation areas (including ecological networks) are part of this target (Dudley et al, 2005). IUCN WCPA's strategic plan and adopted resolutions from the Barcelona 2008 IUCN World Parks Congress also sought to guide the policy and priorities of countries (Box 1.1).

There are also policy review statements that provide further focus for an investment in connectivity conservation. The *Convention on Biological Diversity* 2006 review of experience with 'ecological networks, corridors and buffer zones' identified the importance of ecological networks (connectivity conservation areas), especially for conserving biodiversity (Bennett and Mulongoy, 2006). However, as of 2006 they found that there was limited progress in the actual establishment and management of large-scale connectivity areas.

Potential connectivity conservation areas

I have identified that there is a range of land uses (in addition to protected areas) that may be managed so as to maintain connectivity within the landscape. The degree of naturalness of the land base is also important, since large-scale connectivity is reliant on the retention of natural landscape cover, natural habitats and functioning ecosystems. Some parts of connectivity areas may need to be restored; however, the majority of a large connectivity conservation area (including protected areas) would be expected to be natural. Many of the compatible land-use types (Table 1.1) may be found in such an area.

So where can these large-scale natural areas that interconnect and embed protected areas still be found? They do exist, especially in mountain environments. Many mountain chains run north–south, still retain natural areas and, when combined with many protected areas, provide opportunities to achieve large-scale connectivity conservation. In addition to being essential for the maintenance of genetic diversity, the north–south orientation of these mountains is important during a time of rapid climate change, when species may be forced to move to more suitable aspects, higher latitudes or higher altitudes.

Other mountains may be aligned east–west, and are also important, since conditions may become drier or wetter along these longitudinal gradients causing species to move and adapt. While mountain to mountain connectivity conservation is important, lowland to highland connectivity is also important. Connectivity conservation

---

Box 1.1 Connectivity conservation and international planning

Implementing connectivity conservation is a key strategy for biodiversity conservation in international policy and planning documents, and extracts from two such documents are described here.

Extracts from the Convention on Biological Diversity Programme of Work on Protected Areas (Dudley et al, 2005)

The programme of work emphasizes the importance of protected areas existing in a mosaic of land and water that includes habitat which, if not in a fully natural form, at least provides suitable enough conditions to provide, for example, passage for species and maintenance of ecological processes.

Theme 1: Building protected area systems and the ecosystem approach.

Goal 1.2: To integrate protected areas into broader land/seascapes and sectors so as to maintain ecological structure and function.

Target: By 2015, all protected areas and protected area systems are integrated into the wider land/seascape, and relevant sectors, by applying the ecosystem approach and taking into account ecological connectivity and the concept, where appropriate, of ecological networks.

Activity 1.2.3: Integrate regional, national and sub-national systems of protected areas into broader land/seascapes, inter alia by establishing and managing ecological networks, ecological corridors and/or buffer zones, where appropriate, to maintain ecological processes and also taking into account the needs of migratory species

Activity 1.2.4: Develop tools of ecological connectivity, such as ecological corridors, linking together protected areas where necessary or beneficial as determined by national priorities for the conservation of biodiversity

Activity 1.2.5: Rehabilitate and restore habitats and degraded ecosystems, as appropriate, as a contribution to building ecological networks, ecological corridors and/or buffer zones

Extracts from the IUCN WCPA Strategic Plan 2005–2012 (IUCN WCPA, 2008)

Global change, including climate and socio-economic change, represent an overarching threat to the world's protected areas. To address this, an ecosystem or landscape-scale approach to protected area planning must be applied. This takes a conceptual move from protected areas as 'islands' to protected areas as parts of 'networks' and embedded in landscapes. It also means setting protected areas within a wider matrix of ecosystem-based environmentally sensitive land and water management, supported by the mainstreaming of environmental considerations into various areas of public policy.

Objective: Protected areas more effectively contribute to the conservation of biodiversity, with particular focus on under-represented biomes, especially marine, and on strengthening linkages between protected areas in the land/seascape

Target: By 2008, develop innovative corridor and peace park initiatives in three different regions (Africa, Asia and South America) to link protected areas with surrounding land uses

---

commonly involves mountains, and this book has been developed with input from many mountain connectivity conservation experts, reflecting that there is already a great deal of connectivity management occurring in mountainous areas (Table 1.2). Connectivity conservation management guidelines, however, apply to all terrain types.

Given that connectivity conservation areas are large-scale, need to be managed, typically include a range of land types and uses, and are recognized as an urgent response to climate change, exactly what management responses are needed? What are the forecasts for the future that need to be considered?

Forecast futures

Many experts have described futures applying their judgements to current trends. Recently, scientists from the Intergovernmental Panel on

Climate Change (for example) made a critical prognosis:

> *The resilience of many ecosystems is likely to be exceeded this century by an unprecedented combination of climate change, associated disturbances (e.g., flooding, drought, wildfire, insects, ocean acidification), and other global change drivers (e.g., land use change, pollution, overexploitation of resources)* (IPCC, 2007a).

This depressingly ominous assessment is a consensus statement from more than 1000 conservative scientists. What other future scenarios are experts advising and what detailed forecasts are being made? I provide an assessment here, using two types of information to guide the nature and urgency of connectivity conservation management. First, I summarize the forecast future scenarios developed by the United Nations Environment Programme (UNEP) (2007) to introduce how our world may look in the future. Then, I present, issue by issue, what the world's experts are predicting for a range of environmental and social aspects of Earth for the year 2050.

Four scenarios

Four 'future scenarios' were developed by UNEP (2007). These scenarios are based on key drivers for environmental change, including institutional and socio-economic frameworks, demographics, economic demand, markets and trade, scientific and technological innovation and value systems. The scenarios provide future potential contexts for management that must be anticipated and planned for. Any of the four scenarios may be relevant in the future for any connectivity conservation area. The dominant attributes of the four scenarios are presented in summary form here.

Markets first scenario

Faith is placed in the market to deliver economic advances and social and environmental improvements:

- The role of the private sector is strengthened through legislation and policies.
- There is continued movement to freer trade.
- Nature is commodified.

- Research and development is increasingly dominated by private organizations.
- Investment in developing countries is increasingly direct and includes private donations.
- International trade accelerates.
- Efforts are made to turn ecosystem services into commodities, and the 'commons' shrink.
- Environmental protection progresses slowly, and Kyoto is ineffectively enforced.
- Fossil fuels dominate, and there is little effort to reduce emissions.
- Agriculture intensifies, the use of biofuels increases, natural forests decline, but total forest area increases as a consequence of reforestation efforts.
- Water is privatized, and the percentage of untreated wastewater grows.
- Terrestrial and marine biodiversity continues its downward spiral.
- Shifts in land-use patterns reduce the pressure agriculture places on biodiversity.

This scenario is not good for most life on Earth. Global warming gets worse, natural habitats decrease, ecological functions diminish, pollution of waterways increases and there are many species extinctions. Investments in conservation through the private sector would be welcome, but is likely to be piecemeal and strategic opportunities may be lost. There probably would be limited investment in large-scale connectivity conservation under this scenario.

Policy first scenario

A highly centralized approach is used to balance economic growth and the consequent social and environmental impacts:

- Governments make efforts to deal with major issues such as access to clean water, HIV/ AIDS and climate change.
- There is a more holistic approach to governance – economic growth is pursued relative to its social, economic and environmental consequences.
- It is recognized that uncontrolled markets are limited in their ability to provide the goods and services needed for long-term public welfare, including the maintenance of ecosys-

tem services and the stewardship of non-renewable resources.

- Increased investments are made in health, education and environmental protection.
- Richer nations meet foreign aid targets to poorer countries.
- National governments and international institutions lead in these efforts.
- Perverse subsidies that lead to the overuse of natural resources are reduced.
- Public investments in science and technology grow and increasingly reflect environmental concerns.
- The number of protected areas increases and management is broadly effective.
- Concerted efforts are made to increase energy efficiency and move to low-carbon and renewable fuels.
- Oil and gas dominate fuel supplies, and fuel consumption increases.
- Increased demand for biofuels and food means more land for pasture (at the expense of forests).
- Fresh water concerns are alleviated through increasing supply and reducing demand.
- The total volume of untreated wastewater grows.

Connectivity areas would be expected to benefit from an enhanced national reserve system developed by this scenario. When combined with the additional protected areas, enhanced conservation including large-scale areas may be expected. Additional pressures from polluted wastewater and enhanced climate change would influence how connectivity areas would be managed.

Security first scenario

Security overshadows other values, and much of this scenario is driven by conflict:

- The increased restrictions on migration reduce the movement of people.
- Investments in security, both public and private, grow at the expense of other priorities.
- Many governments hand over public services to private companies to reduce costs.
- Development assistance and foreign investment contracts.

- Broad-based social safety nets deteriorate.
- While governments still play a role in decision making, multinational corporations and other private interests have an increasing influence.
- Little progress is made in reducing corruption in official circles.
- The authority of international institutions declines.
- Public participation and the role of the civil sector are increasingly marginalized.
- Environmental governance suffers, there is no expansion of the protected area networks and environmental services are increasingly the focus of competition and conflict.
- Total energy use increases significantly, with a resurgence in the use of coal causing growth in greenhouse gas emissions, and the planet continues to warm.
- Forests are logged in favour of grazing land, freshwater resources are strained and conflicts over shared resources increase.
- Biodiversity loss is exacerbated by development and climate change, with major losses from conflict in some areas.
- The volume of untreated wastewater and the prevalence of water-borne diseases increase.

Connectivity conservation would not be possible under this scenario. Social conflict poses one of the great challenges for all people on Earth.

Sustainability first scenario

The environmental concerns of Earth are responded to by all members of society:

- Action is taken with or without governments.
- Reforms take place in national and international institutions.
- International trade addresses broader issues other than just economic efficiency.
- The world invests more resources into public and environmental issues, and poorer countries receive improved contributions from richer countries.
- Environmental governance evolves, and more environmentally friendly ways of providing energy and water and services are found.
- More protected areas are established, and there is a larger emphasis on sustainable use and

ecosystem services maintenance within non-protected lands.

- Greenhouse gas emissions are reduced and eventually reversed; and, much later, the effects of climate change recede.
- Total energy use increases, but oil use peaks, coal use declines and renewable energy (such as solar, wind, geothermal and tidal) increases in proportion to total energy.
- Air pollution declines, and wastewater treatment keeps pace with wastewater generation.
- The loss of forest for agriculture declines over time, and water management reduces the growth in water stress.
- Efforts to combat biodiversity loss are significant, with the greatest threats coming from agriculture for food and climate change.

This scenario focuses on a better Earth, and connectivity conservation would provide a key tool to assist this objective.

The four scenarios, one or more of which may apply in different parts of the world at different times, are valuable in 'painting a picture' of the future, but more specific forecasts are also helpful. Four expert reports have been used to obtain more detailed forecasts for the future: Baillie et al (2004), Millennium Ecosystem Assessment Report (2005), Intergovernmental Panel on Climate Change Fourth Assessment (IPCC, 2007b), and United Nations Environment Programme Global Environment Outlook 4 (UNEP, 2007). A summary of their implications is given in Table 1.3.

Table 1.3 Current and forecast global issues for connectivity conservation

Issue	Status	Forecast
World population	In 2007, there were 6.7 billion people, up from 5 billion people in 1987	Global population projections for 2050 are for (low) 7.8 billion, (medium) 9.2 billion and (high) 10.8 billion peoples – the largest absolute growth will occur in Asia and the Pacific
Air quality	In 2007, more than 2 million people per annum died prematurely due to indoor and outdoor air pollution	The UNEP scenarios identify that the total emissions of regional air pollutants decrease by 2050 thanks to improvements to air pollution controls and cleaner energy sources – however, carbon dioxide levels continue to grow
Water quality	In 2007, unsafe water and poor sanitation were the world's second biggest killer of children (after air quality)	The UNEP scenarios identify a wide range of wastewater scenarios for 2050 depending on both how parts of the world are governed and which continent is involved – under the worst UNEP scenario, the volume of untreated domestic and industrial wastewater doubles worldwide by 2050, and the discharge of these waters causes widespread water contamination, worsening health risks and degrading aquatic ecosystems
Water quantity	The period from 1987 to 2007 saw increasing use of water for agriculture, domestic consumption, industrial use and increasing evaporation loss from reservoirs	By 2025, water withdrawals are forecast to increase by 50 per cent for developing countries and 18 per cent in developed ones. In addition, by 2025 about 1.8 billion people will be living in countries or regions with absolute water scarcity, and two thirds of the world's population will be under conditions of water stress

Table 1.3 Continued

Issue	Status	Forecast
Energy consumption, world oil supplies and fossil fuels	By 2007, the global primary energy supply had increased by 4 per cent from 1987, global oil production had stalled and demand (especially from India and China) had increased relative to supply, with prices per barrel of oil increasing significantly; peak oil has been forecast for about 2012 plus or minus five years (APSO, 2008)	Consumption of oil and other fossil fuels is forecast to steadily increase to 2050 – the degree of increase will be dependent on climate change policies and emission standards introduced and enforced
Greenhouse gas emissions	By 2007 there had been an absolute growth in anthropogenic greenhouse gas generation – carbon dioxide levels have risen from 280ppm (from a baseline in the 18th century) to 380ppm	Three different carbon dioxide concentration levels are forecast for 2050 by UNEP depending on their scenario modelling and are (i) highest, greater than 550ppm; (ii) next levels, 540ppm; and (iii) 475ppm under a greenhouse gas reduction scenario
Habitat destruction and fragmentation	Between 1990 and 2005 the global forest area shrank by 0.2 per cent per annum	UNEP scenario modelling shows major losses in biodiversity by 2050 in all scenarios due to broad-scale land-use changes, with Africa, Latin America and the Caribbean showing the greatest losses, followed by Asia and the Pacific – resilient, well-connected ecosystems are identified as suffering fewer ill effects from climate change than fragmented, overexploited ecosystems
Land degradation	Overexploitation of land is a critical issue – between 1991 and 2003, there was an absolute decline in net primary productivity of land across 12 per cent of the global land area, and this affected about 15 per cent of Earth's peoples – this resulted in about 800 million tonnes of carbon not being fixed from the atmosphere	In 2050, UNEP scenario modelling identifies rainfall erosion risk increasing by 50 per cent for areas that receive increased precipitation and is greatest for agricultural areas
Desertification	Drylands cover about 40 per cent of terrestrial Earth, and in 2007 supported about two billion people: desertification is determined by socio-economic and biophysical factors and no quantitative data was available	UNEP scenario modelling identifies that changes in arid areas will be relatively small due to climate change, but human pressures are likely to increase impacts on arid lands
Climate change (temperature)	By 2007, the Earth's temperature had increased by 0.74 degrees Celsius over the last 100 years	The IPCC forecasts temperatures to increase by between 2 and 4 degrees Celsius by 2100 and UNEP's scenario modelling identifies average temperature increases between 1.7 and 2.2 degrees Celsius at 2050

Table 1.3 Continued

Issue	Status	Forecast
Climate change (precipitation)	Evidence shows that precipitation patterns have changed worldwide as a result of climate change: global land precipitation has increased by 20 per cent since the beginning of the 20th century and it is not a uniform increase; more intense and longer droughts have been experienced since the 1970s particularly in the tropics and subtropics	In the northern hemisphere, IPCC modelling identifies increased subpolar and decreased subtropical precipitation over North America and Europe, while subtropical drying is less evident over Asia; in the southern hemisphere, subtropical drying is more prominent, while projections for tropical areas are more uncertain, although the monsoons of southern Asia are forecast to increase their rainfall
Climate change (extreme weather)	Since the 1950s there has been a 2 to 4 per cent increase in heavy precipitation events in the mid to high latitudes – at the start of the 21st century, there has been an increasing frequency of severe droughts, floods, severe storms and multiple recordbreaking extreme hot weather days (Ochoa et al, 2005)	IPCC forecasts that hot extremes, heatwaves and heavy precipitation events will continue to become more frequent, intense storms will become more frequent, and tropical cyclones especially will become more frequent and intense, and will track further pole-ward
Snow and ice	Since 1987, continental ice sheets and mountain glaciers have continued to melt and retreat. Permafrost is thawing at an accelerating rate, and the maximum area of seasonally frozen ground has decreased by 7 per cent since 1900	Melting ice is forecast to raise the sea level with ramifications for the 60 per cent of the global population that lives 100 kilometres from the coast, and perennial streams previously fed by tropical and subtropical mountain glaciers become intermittent and potentially ephemeral
Sea-level rise	The total 20th century sea-level rise has been estimated to be 17cm relative to the pre-industrial era	The estimated average sea-level rise for future scenarios by UNEP for the year 2050 is 30cm relative to the pre-industrial era – in 2008, based on new data, many consider this to be too conservative an estimate
Ecosystem function	Since 1987, ongoing, and in many cases accelerating, declines and losses in biodiversity have decreased the capacity of ecosystems to provide services: for half of the world's 14 biomes, 20–50 per cent of their surface areas have been converted to cropland. 50 per cent of inland water habitats are estimated to be transformed for human use, 60 per cent of the largest rivers have been fragmented by dams and impacted by water withdrawal and the fragmentation of ecosystems is increasingly affecting species	According to the Millennium Ecosystem Assessment, the degradation of ecosystem services could grow significantly worse during the period to 2050, with the most important drivers for change being habitat change, overexploitation, invasive alien species, pollution and climate change – a cause of this exploitation is increased population and demand for energy and food

Table 1.3 Continued

Issue	Status	Forecast
Species extinctions	In 2007, species extinction rates were 100 times greater than the baseline rate identified by the fossil record, and of the groups assessed, 30 per cent of amphibians, 23 per cent of mammals and 12 per cent of birds were threatened in 2007	Baillie et al (2004) identifies that it is feasible that extinction rates will increase to the rate of 1000 to 10,000 times background rates over the coming decades and UNEP scenario modelling identifies global temperature increases have a profound influence on the survival chances of many of the world's species up to 2050 and beyond
Poverty	In 2007, most regions of the world had made progress on meeting the Millennium Development Goal of reducing extreme poverty and hunger – those in poverty had deceased from 1.2 billion people to 1.0 billion people by 2002	All four of UNEP's scenarios identify reduction in poverty and hunger at the global level, though there are problems in Latin America, the Caribbean and Africa, and Africa, Asia and the Pacific have the highest numbers of malnourished peoples
Armed conflict	Since 1945, the number of interstate conflicts has been low and the number of civil conflicts remains the greatest concern, although the number of peace keeping missions was at an all-time high in 2007 – eight million people have died directly or indirectly from war in Africa since 1960, and in 2005 there were an estimated 11.5 million refuges, asylum seekers and stateless persons and 6.6 million internally displaced persons	One of UNEP's (four) scenarios for the future identifies an increased focus on security and increased armed conflict, with direct impacts on environmental management and biodiversity conservation – under this scenario, guns are readily available, unsustainable hunting takes place and militias seek resources from protected areas, protected areas are looted for meat, timber and minerals, and there is no environmental management

Source: Baillie et al, 2004; MEAB, 2005; IPCC, 2007b; UNEP, 2007

All four reports identify major changes for the planet for the period to 2050. This includes a 40 per cent increase in the number of people, serious changes to the climate, resource shortages and the sixth great extinction of species on Earth. The challenges posed for nature conservation and specifically protected areas and connectivity conservation in the 21st century are thus formidable. There is an imperative for connectivity conservation initiatives for they are one part of a conservation response that can help create better futures.

An imperative for connectivity conservation

[W]e applaud the growing community of scientists, environmental activists, planners, land managers and politicians who are working on behalf of the world's citizenry to prevent further fragmentation, to restore connectivity at all scales, and in the end to make the world healthier for all of its inhabitants (Hilty et al, 2006, p274).

Leadership in the manner Jodi Hilty has described is vital in the face of the forecast global outlooks, and action is needed urgently since negative changes are happening so quickly. Thankfully there has been a 'call to action' from many national and international leaders who believe that a do nothing option is not good enough for this generation and future generations. Many have targeted the big issues such as the root causes of most greenhouse gas emissions. Additional positive responses may be anticipated, and some actions are already underway. Leaders will want to keep ecosystems and ecological services intact to help maintain clean water supplies and clean air for people. They will want to conserve their nation's species and protect the finest of their lands in a representative and completed protected area system. They will also want to climate-proof their remarkable wildlife as much as possible and initiate, with the help and support of the community, large-scale connectivity conservation of nature in an effort to provide opportunities for species movement and survival. Connectivity conservation can be expected to be part of national responses to climate change and other potential changes forecast. It will help conserve a nation's protected areas. It will help conserve those large remaining interconnected natural lands that cannot, for whatever reason, ever be part of the protected area system. It is a positive and immediate response to climate change.

National leaders will also have many supporters and individual champions who wish to assist. There is an imperative for connectivity conservation in strategic locations around the world and a commitment to achieving this. The IUCN WCPA Connectivity Conservation Declaration is a testimony to this type of commitment (Box 1.2). The declaration is also a significant milestone in the evolution of thinking on connectivity conservation by its practitioners.

Origins, purpose and structure of this book

The idea for this book originated at an international conference convened in Banff in September 2004 by the Yellowstone to Yukon Conservation Initiative and the Mountains Biome of the IUCN WCPA. The book's content and themes were further developed at a conference held in September 2005 in Planes de Son, Spain, under the auspices of the WCPA and the Fundació Territori i Paisatge de Caixa Catalunya. In November 2006, IUCN WCPA's Mountains Biome convened a workshop of connectivity conservation managers and experts at Papallacta, Ecuador. A key purpose of this workshop was again to advance the preparation of this book. Invited participants contributed in three ways. First, they prepared case studies for their connectivity conservation areas. Second, at the workshop they contributed 'lessons learned' for managing connectivity conservation and guidance for future connectivity conservation challenges. Third, they developed the IUCN WCPA Connectivity Conservation Declaration (Box 1.2). The second and third contributions enabled us to develop a draft framework for connectivity conservation management, which we presented at a November 2008 meeting of connectivity managers in

Antisana Mountain, a protected area within a connectivity conservation area, near Papallacta, Ecuador

Source: Graeme L. Worboys

Box 1.2 The IUCN WCPA Connectivity Conservation Declaration

In November 2006, IUCN's WCPA Mountains Biome convened a workshop of connectivity conservation managers and experts in Papallacta, Ecuador. Over the four days of the workshop, the group systematically developed (among other tasks) the *IUCN WCPA Connectivity Conservation Declaration*, a statement that has reinforced the importance of strategically conserving and managing large natural areas that interconnect protected areas. The *Declaration* text was facilitated by Dr Martin Price, and it was adopted unanimously by participants. The *IUCN WCPA Connectivity Conservation Declaration*, which was initially referred to as the *Papallacta Declaration*, describes the purpose and function of connectivity conservation, a rationale for its implementation and management (especially in mountains) and a call to action to implement the concept. The Declaration is relevant to all connectivity conservation areas.

The IUCN WCPA Connectivity Conservation Declaration

Mountains provide freshwater to more than half of humanity and are major centres of global biological and cultural diversity and sources of inspiration and spirituality. Maintaining the integrity of mountain ecosystems is vital for the well-being of current and future generations. Yet mountains have low resilience and high vulnerability, and are therefore under serious threat from land transformation, infrastructure development, environmental degradation and climate change.

The maintenance and restoration of ecosystem integrity requires landscape-scale conservation. This can be achieved through systems of core protected areas that are functionally linked and buffered in ways that maintain ecosystem processes and allow species to survive and move, thus ensuring that populations are viable and that ecosystems and people are able to adapt to land transformation and climate change. We call this proactive, holistic, and long-term approach 'connectivity conservation'.

Connectivity conservation in and around mountain areas is essential to achieve the goals of the Programmes of Work on Protected Areas and on Mountain Biological Diversity adopted by the 7th Conference of Parties to the Convention on Biological Diversity (Kuala Lumpur, Malaysia, February 2004) and the Plan of Implementation of the World Summit on Sustainable Development (Johannesburg, South Africa, September 2002).

Accomplishing these goals requires the support, involvement, cooperation and leadership of people who live and recreate in, derive economic benefit from, manage, study, gain spiritual inspiration from and appreciate mountain environments.

Therefore, we urge communities, governments at all levels, non-governmental and intergovernmental organizations, businesses, religious groups and academic and research institutions to take coordinated action to engage in connectivity conservation in and around mountain regions. This will ensure that mountains continue to supply ecosystem services and many other benefits to humanity, including:

- *the ability for ecological, hydrological, social and economic systems to respond to climate change;*
- *reliable supplies of water and renewable energy;*
- *reduced risks of downstream natural disasters;*
- *effective responses to local, regional and global impacts of habitat fragmentation and species loss, particularly in protected areas;*
- *the alleviation of poverty and the promotion of more sustainable economic activity;*
- *cultural diversity, spiritual and community values;*
- *shared understanding and peaceful cooperation across internal and international boundaries.*

We, the participants at the Workshop on Mountain Connectivity Conservation Management (Termas de Papallacta, Ecuador, November 2006) commit ourselves to work with all relevant stakeholders to engage in connectivity conservation in and around the mountain regions of the world, for the benefit of our planet and humanity.

(Signed by all workshop participants)

Dhulikhel, Nepal. Comments from meeting participants were influential in shaping our thinking for the material presented in Chapter 11. Overall, the book comprises 12 chapters which are broadly structured into three parts.

Setting the context

Following this introduction, *Chapter 2* introduces the science of connectivity conservation. The authors present an overview of important contributing theories, scientific debates and current views about connectivity conservation. It reinforces the importance of large-scale connectivity conservation as a means of helping to conserve species at a time of climate change. *Chapter 3* provides considerations for authorities, planners and managers to help them to achieve successful connectivity conservation management.

Applied connectivity conservation management: Case material

Connectivity conservation management is being undertaken in nearly all of Udvardy's (1975) eight biogeographic realms of Earth, and case material from six of these is presented in this book. A range of different examples are presented in each realm. The lessons learned from the case material are analysed and used to develop the management framework for connectivity conservation presented in the third part of the book.

Chapter 4: Africotropical realm. The greatest concentrations of flora on Earth, the richest concentration of primates for Earth and an area of high mountain species richness are described by the three African case studies. The three large-scale connectivity conservation areas include the Cape Floristic Region of southern South Africa, the Maloti-Drakensberg Mountains of South Africa and Lesotho, and the Albertine Rift Valley of the Democratic Republic of Congo, Rwanda and Uganda, the home of the mountain gorilla (*Gorilla beringei*).

Chapter 5: Australian realm. For Australia, a biodiversity hot spot in south-west Western Australia, the greatest concentrations of Australia's species (east coast) and the highest mountains with their important catchments are described. The connectivity areas include: 'Gondwana Link' (south-west Western Australia); 'A2A', the

Australian Alps to Atherton, which extends for 2800km along the east coast; and the 'Australian Alps' project, which interconnects and involves cooperative management for 11 protected areas across two states and a territory.

Chapter 6: Indomalayan realm. The immense area of the high mountains of the Himalaya, including the highest mountain on Earth, Mount Everest, and the Himalaya biodiversity hot spot, the species-rich connectivity corridors of Bhutan (a hot spot) and connectivity conservation in northern Sumatra (also a hot spot) are described. The three case studies include the Sacred Himalayan Landscape, the Bhutan biological corridors and tropical rainforest connectivity in northern Sumatra.

Chapter 7: Nearctic realm. Western and eastern North America are represented by three case studies. On the west, the species rich Yellowstone to Yukon connectivity conservation corridor extends some 3200km north–south along the Rocky Mountains and across the USA–Canada border. On the east coast, case studies describe the conservation network in the southern Appalachian mountains, an ecologically rich area that escaped massive ice sheets, and the ecologically diverse greater northern Appalachians, which extend across the USA–Canada border.

Chapter 8: Neotropical realm. The case studies from central and South America describe connectivity conservation for rich and varied landscapes. The Mesoamerican biological corridor describes connectivity management from southern Mexico through seven other countries southwards through Panama. Mountains feature prominently, with case studies describing rich ecosystems and ecological hot spots, including the Andean Páramo corridor (Venezuela, Colombia, Ecuador and northern Peru), the Vilacamba–Amboro conservation corridor (Peru and Bolivia), the Serra do Espinhaço Biosphere Reserve (Brazil), the Munchique–Pinche macro-corridor (Colombia), the Llanganates–Sangay ecological corridor (Ecuador) and the interconnected protected areas in the Venezeulan Andes that help to conserve the Andean spectacled bear (*Tremarctos ornatus*).

Chapter 9: Palaearctic realm. The ecologically rich Altai mountains, 'the heart of Asia', and their connectivity with four countries, China,

Kazakhstan, Mongolia and Russia, are described, as are the European Alps. Connectivity within the European Alps, such as the Cantabrian Mountains–Pyrénées–Massif Central–Western Alps Great Mountain corridor (Spain, France and Italy) and the Apennines from the Alps to the Mediterranean (Italy) are also presented. Connectivity within and across the Alps are also described (the European Alps, the Mont Blanc Massif and an ecological network for the European Alps).

Chapter 10: Case material: The Papallacta, Ecuador 2006 workshop. Connectivity management practitioners developed additional lessons learned at the Papallacta workshop, and these have been analysed as supplementary information to the case studies. This chapter presents this information, and also provides a summary of the most important connectivity conservation management lessons learned.

Synthesis

In *Chapter 11*, we analyse the rich empirical case information and develop a conceptual framework for connectivity conservation management. We then use the framework to present the principal management actions needed for implementing 15 priority connectivity management tasks. Drawing again on the Papallacta workshop session, in *Chapter 12* we offer a brief account of important challenges and opportunities for the connectivity conservation.

The scope of connectivity conservation management is broad, and includes a diversity of subjects and disciplines. It is also a relatively new profession, with many management practices evolving ahead of adequate theoretical underpinnings. This book is the first of its kind for connectivity conservation management. The focus of the book is practical and conveys the lived experience of many connectivity conservation practitioners working in six of the Earth's eight biogeographic realms (Udvardy, 1975; Worboys and Winkler, 2006a). It has been prepared to provide guidance for managing large-scale connectivity conservation areas and is developed for a wide audience of professional people and stakeholders. Connectivity areas or parts of connectivity areas are managed by governments, NGOs, communities, indigenous groups, private organizations and individuals, and at different spatial scales, and the book includes an audience of managers from many different backgrounds. We hope politicians, policy makers, planners, students (future managers) and members of the community may also benefit from the information provided in this book. The management framework (for example) provides an orderly (planned) process of establishment, management, implementation and evaluation of connectivity conservation areas, and is intended to assist both connectivity managers and support organizations with funding and resourcing allocations and management.

2

Connectivity Science

Charles C. Chester and Jodi A. Hilty

The scientific study of connectivity conservation dates from the 1970s, and considerable attention and controversy has attended their benefits and costs in the subsequent decades (Simberloff and Cox, 1987; Hilty et al, 2006). Yet with the 2006 publication of five major treatises synthesizing the role of connectivity conservation in biodiversity conservation (Anderson and Jenkins, 2006; Bennett and Mulongoy, 2006; Crooks and Sanjayan, 2006a; Hilty et al, 2006; Lindenmayer and Fischer, 2006), it is probably fair to say that the science of connectivity ecology has only recently come into its own. It should also be said that these publications were hardly the first to synthesize the myriad issues surrounding connectivity conservation, with two important examples being the contributions by Graham Bennett (Bennett, 2004) and Andrew Bennett (Bennett, 2003). Given the dual deleterious trends of increasing habitat fragmentation and climate change, biologists, scientists and managers have increasingly turned to the potential of connectivity conservation areas in protecting biodiversity. Indeed, it may only be a matter of time before 'connectivity ecology' becomes as familiar an endeavour as, say, 'forest ecology'.

The term connectivity is a measure of the extent to which plants and animals can move between habitat patches, as well as the extent to which non-local ecosystem functions associated with soil and water processes, for example, are maintained. Landscape features such as corridors, greenbelts and habitat 'stepping stones' are physical structures that are a means for achieving connectivity. Unfortunately, 'corridor' has become widely used to describe connectivity areas – unfortunately because it is a term that carries many different connotations, and semantic confusion has arisen over what exactly constitutes a corridor. Biologists, conservationists, land managers and the general public are very likely to have substantially different concepts in mind when they convene to talk about 'corridors'. A corridor has been defined as 'any space, usually linear in shape, that improves the ability of organisms to move among patches of their habitat', and 'spaces in which connectivity between species, ecosystems, and ecological processes is maintained or restored at various levels' (Anderson and Jenkins, 2006, p4; Hilty et al, 2006, p50). Dobson et al (1999, p132) define connectivity corridors to be 'large, regional connections that are meant to facilitate animal movements and other essential flows between different sections of the landscape'. Along with such definitions, scientists have parsed the broad concept of a connectivity corridor into a number of different typological schemes, five prominent examples of which are summarized in Box 2.1. In comparing these categorical frameworks, what is important to note is that they do not necessarily contradict each other, but rather that they simply provide a tangible demonstration that there are many different ways to think about the roles and functions of corridors in connectivity conservation.

Box 2.1 Alternative definitions of 'corridor'

Scientists and conservationists have put forth numerous definitions of 'corridor'. While these definitions usually do not directly conflict, they generally reflect different aspects of the same phenomenon. To clarify the situation, several attempts have been made to define, outline and categorize the various types of corridors. The following summarizes five such approaches. In comparing these five approaches, not only does it become clear that 'corridor' connotes many shades of meaning, but that there are significantly different ways to conceptualize how corridors function.

1   Broad yet overlapping groups of corridors
*   Biodiversity corridor: large-scale landscape linkages covering hundreds to thousands of square kilometres.
*   Biological corridor: same as 'biodiversity corridor'.
*   Corridor networks: systems of corridors running in multiple directions.
*   Dispersal corridor: corridors that promote the movements or migrations of specific species or groups of species.
*   Ecological corridor: corridors that maintain or restore ecological services on which biodiversity conservation depends; alternatively used as a synonym for 'biodiversity corridor'.
*   Habitat corridor: a linear strip of native habitat linking two larger blocks of the same habitat.
*   Movement corridor: same as 'dispersal corridor'.
*   Wildlife corridor: same as 'dispersal corridor'. (Anderson and Jenkins, 2006)

2   Two basic types of corridors
'An alternative and simpler' distinction was identified by Anderson and Jenkins (2006):

*   Linear corridors, which establish or maintain relatively straight-line connections between larger habitat blocks and extend over distances of up to tens of kilometres.
*   Landscape corridors, which maintain or establish multidirectional connections over entire landscapes and can encompass up to thousands of square kilometres.

3   Distinctions made between different types of habitat corridors based on their origin
*   Disturbance habitat corridors, which include roads, railway lines, cleared utility lines, and other linear disturbances.
*   Natural habitat corridors, which included streams and riparian zones typically following topographic or environmental contours.
*   Planted habitat corridors, which include farm plantations, windbreaks, and shelterbelts, hedgerows, and urban greenbelts established by humans.
*   Remnant habitat corridors, which include roadside woodlands ('beauty strips'), linear stretches of unlogged forest within clearcuts, and undisturbed habitats between protected areas.
*   Regenerated habitat corridors, which were formerly cleared or disturbed linear strips where vegetation has regrown, such as fencerows and hedges (Bennett, 2003).

4   Three broad kinds of landscape corridor
*   Linear corridors such as a hedgerow, forest strip or river, which are types of minor connectivity within an interlinked landscape.
*   Stepping stones or arrays of small patches of habitat that individuals use during movement for shelter, feeding and resting.
*   Interlinked landscape matrices, which are various forms that allow individuals to survive during movement between habitat patches (Bennett and Mulongoy, 2006).

Box 2.1 Continued

5   Planned and unplanned corridors
- Unplanned corridors, which are landscape elements that enhance connectivity but exist for other reasons.
- Planned corridors, which are established for both biological connectivity and other reasons, including:
    - greenways, which are areas set aside for recreation, culture and ecosystem services;
    - buffering riparian zones, which are vegetated areas adjacent to creeks, and are sometimes retained in human domi-nated landscapes;
    - corridors for individual species conservation, which are required through mandated management plans for rare and endangered species;
    - corridors that enhance community integrity and which are promoted to protect biotic community integrity or suites of species moving among protected areas across large regions (Hilty et al, 2006).

Ecological connectivity can be defined as 'the extent [spatial and temporal] to which a species or population can move among landscape elements in a mosaic of habitat types' (Hilty et al, 2006, p90). Connectivity can be categorized according to the scale over which it operates (Dobson et al, 1999): (i) connectivity between isolated habitat patches; (ii) connectivity at the landscape mosaic scale; and (iii) connectivity at the large or regional (many countries) scale. Importantly, the idea of connectivity focuses equal attention on both the connection itself (the corridor) and on what is being connected. In most cases, particularly for the purposes of this book, what is being connected are 'core areas' of habitat that in many cases are reserved as protected areas. A protected area is 'a clearly defined geographical space, recognized, dedicated and managed, through legal or other effective means, to achieve the long-term conservation of nature with associated ecosystem services and cultural values' (Dudley, 2008, p8). Core habitat areas may also be unreserved natural lands that continue to be little impacted by humans.

Within the broad sweep of a connectivity conservation area, management must also consider 'gaps' where connectivity has been broken or disrupted. Human settlement, agriculture, infrastructure (roads, pipelines, electricity transmission lines, dams and so on), mines and intensive forestry are some of the main sources of breaks in natural connectivity. A connectivity conservation area may thus be understood as a predominantly natural area comprising:

- a core of protected areas, as well as, in some cases, currently unreserved lands;
- extensive natural and semi-natural lands that provide linkages (corridors) and/or embed core areas;
- generally smaller areas of developed or degraded lands that create gaps in connectivity and could therefore be targeted for restoration or rehabilitation works (Figures 2.1 and 2.2).

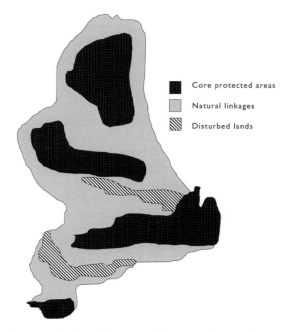

Core protected areas

Natural linkages

Disturbed lands

Figure 2.1 Schematic representation of a connectivity conservation area

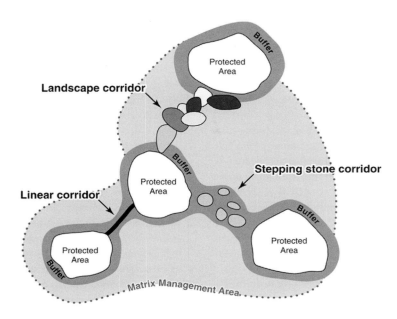

Figure 2.2 Linear, stepping stone and landscape corridors linking core areas

Source: Bennett, 2004

The maintenance and where necessary restoration of connectivity, described in this book as 'connectivity conservation management', largely consists of those land-use planning and on-ground actions necessary for achieving the integrity and resilience of natural lands that interconnect protected areas and other large remaining natural areas. Even though connectivity conservation areas are but one means of achieving connectivity, they are without question the most important in the 'connectivity toolbox' of conservationists (Hilty et al, 2006). For the purposes of this book, biodiversity conservation can be said to be the broad mission towards which connectivity conservation managers are striving. In turn, connectivity conservation is the particular goal that leads to achievement of the mission. Finally, a connectivity conservation link, such as an area that interconnects established protected areas, constitutes the particular strategy that accomplishes the goal.

Under this framework, the case studies in this volume (Chapters 4 to 9) have the same mission of biodiversity conservation. The goal is also the same, with some form of connectivity being necessary for long-term biodiversity conservation. But in terms of strategy, the constant looming problem remains how to retain, restore or even establish connectivity between natural areas, and this will vary dramatically between locations, or even within large areas where significant progress in implementing connectivity conservation has already occurred. Each area brings with it a unique (situational) set of opportunities and management problems. Consequently, it is important at this level of analysis to consider carefully the multifarious character of these landscape components collectively called 'connectivity conservation areas'.

Island biogeography, metapopulation theory and landscape ecology

To understand why there are so many variations on the definition of corridor, and why connectivity conservation area is the preferred concept for the purpose of this book, it is helpful to look back at its intellectual foundations in two intertwined realms: wildlife conservation and the biological sciences. This is a useful distinction, albeit one that overlooks the innumerable biologists who consider themselves conservationists and the vast majority of conservationists who have a better-than-average understanding of biology. In the case of the latter, conservationists have long recognized that habitat is disappearing, and that what remains is becoming more and more fragmented. Although accurate assessment of habitat alteration has typically been piecemeal, field observations have long raised warning flags of the consequent widespread extirpations and possible extinctions. The principal response to this challenge has been the establishment of protected areas, of which there were 113,959 in January 2008 (UNEP-WCMC, 2009). Yet even while protected areas can now be found in 233 countries and territories, conservationists have strongly intuited that even this apparently impressive number of protected areas is insufficient to protect the Earth's biodiversity. Major efforts are being made by many nations to achieve comprehensive and representative reserve systems (Dudley et al, 2005), and connectivity areas that embed, interconnect and enlarge protected areas are critical in maintaining the ecological viability and integrity of populations, species and communities (Sattler and Glaznig, 2006). Therefore, the idea of 'wildlife corridors' simply makes intuitive sense, at least to the typical conservationist.

Importantly, the intuition of conservationists has been largely borne out by the investigations of biologists. In the 1960s, prominent sociobiologist and biodiversity conservationist Edward O. Wilson, along with his colleague, Robert MacArthur, formalized the theory of island biogeography. This theory held that the number of species on marine islands was directly related to two primary factors: the size of the island and proximity of the island to the mainland (MacArthur and Wilson, 1967). Over the course of the following decades, many biologists attempted to apply the theory to habitat 'islands' in a terrestrial context (such as mountain tops and isolated wetlands), as well as to protected area design. Yet despite progress made in understanding

how and why species are distributed, biologists generally came to recognize that the theory of island biogeography was far less applicable in a terrestrial context than in a marine one (for a recent critique of the theory of island biogeography as applied to landscape conservation, see Franklin and Lindenmayer, 2009).

Turning from island biogeography, biologists began to focus on the study of connected and unconnected populations, with a single population being loosely defined as a group of individuals of the same species living at the same time in the same area. After a half century of investigation along these lines, this work had been collectively subsumed under the theory of metapopulations (Hanski, 1998). Metapopulations, in turn, have been defined as 'systems of isolated population units that periodically go extinct ('blink out') and are re-established ('blink on') by dispersing individuals from other units' (Dobson et al, 1999, p151). Whereas the theory of island biogeography had focused on the total number of species, metapopulation theory focused on the fate of a single species. In so narrowing their focus, biologists could use metapopulation theory to think about 'populations of populations'. That constituted a conceptual breakthrough inasmuch as it treated individual populations (rather than an entire species), as generally discrete units. Biologists distinguished between various types of metapopulations and identified various metapopulation processes, with the most important of these being dispersal (to which we will return).

Unlike island biogeography, metapopulation theory explicitly recognized that population interactions between habitat patches were highly dynamic, and that the barriers between individual populations may or may not be entirely impermeable. But metapopulation theory has had its own critics. Some, including Anderson and Jenkins (2006), pointed out that metapopulation theory had little empirical evidence to show for it. Dobson et al (1999) summarized one broad critique in noting that 'most species in nature are not as structured as metapopulations in the original sense' and that the original scientific concept of a metapopulation had become so diluted as 'to denote almost any system of populations whether or not they blink out periodically'. This meant that the concept had little predictive ability and was not likely to be applicable to particular conservation problems.

Despite these critiques, the original idea of metapopulations provided a broad framework for understanding how connectivity corridors might function. In order to describe the dynamic processes involved with metapopulations, biologists borrowed three 'especially useful' terms from the field of landscape ecology, which were 'matrix', 'patch' and 'corridor' (Forman, 1991, p71). The matrix was originally defined as the dominant landscape type (such as forest, city or residential development), which in turn is determined according to three factors: the greatest total area; the highest level of connectivity; and the strongest control over dynamics (such as seed dispersal, herbivory, keystone predation and pollutant deposition) (Forman, 1991, p277).

Patches were originally conceived of as landscape elements both different from and within the matrix. Notably, ecologists today generally take a more nuanced approach, placing patches within a matrix composed of various types of natural and human-created communities (rather than a single dominant landscape type). Finally, corridors were defined as 'a strip of a particular type that differs from the adjacent land on both sides' within the matrix (Forman, 1991, p38). As described above, conservation biologists have expanded on that definition.

With connectivity corridor ecology emanating from these three compelling fields of island biogeography, metapopulation theory and landscape ecology, it is not difficult to understand why so many scientists have become drawn to the subject. But far more pressing than mere scientific curiosity have been the conservation implications of connectivity corridors. Namely, scientists have recognized connectivity corridors as a realistic tool for protecting biodiversity in a world where the landscape matrix is increasingly dominated by the loss and fragmentation of habitat due to anthropogenic influences. Furthermore, connectivity corridors enable a suite of biological processes that can be summarized in the single word 'movement', although the phrase 'effective movement through the landscape' would be more accurate. Movement includes daily peregrinations,

various types of dispersal, nomadism, seasonal migrations and migrations during extreme events (such as drought). It is the facilitation of movement that constitutes the essential *raison d'être* underpinning connectivity conservation areas.

With this evolution of thinking, ecologists have identified two primary components of connectivity (Mackey et al, 2009). The first is structural or landscape connectivity (Lindenmayer and Fischer, 2006), which is the arrangement of vegetation cover and habitats and is based on the connectedness of vegetation in the landscape. It does not consider the movement of organisms or processes in the landscape. The second is called functional connectivity, and is the behavioural response of individuals, species or ecological processes, and it can be subdivided into habitat connectivity and ecological connectivity (Mackey et al, 2009). Habitat is the subset of physical environmental factors that permit an animal (or plant) to survive or reproduce. Habitat connectivity is the connectedness of habitat patches for a particular species (Lindenmayer and Fischer, 2006). Ecological connectivity recognizes the connectedness of ecological processes across multiple scales (Crooks and Sanjayan, 2006b; Lindenmayer and Fischer, 2006), and 'includes processes related to trophic relationships, disturbance processes and hydro-ecological flows' (Mackey et al, 2009). Evolutionary connectivity, defined as 'the connectedness required by spatially dependent evolutionary processes', can also be added to these definitions. Mackey et al (2009) describe this point further: 'to be successful, measures in biodiversity protection must attend to the conditions necessary for continuing evolution, particularly the potential for adaptation to changing environmental conditions and for speciation'.

Biologists have long argued that effective movement through the landscape is necessary for a number of important demographic and genetic processes. Demographic processes include the colonization of new or recovered habitat and the recolonization of habitat where species have been extirpated. Genetic processes include the maintenance of allelic (one of the alternative forms of a gene) diversity within populations, which can both create greater resilience to changing environmental conditions and decrease the risk of inbreeding depression (the decreased vigour in terms of growth, survival or fecundity that follows one or more generations of inbreeding) (Rosenberg et al, 1997, p679). Effective movement via functioning effectively managed and natural connectivity conservation areas means that individuals are not alienated or displaced from habitat that has been altered or fragmented to the extent that it is no longer useable, nor deterred or killed by impediments such as road traffic, which is a particularly important consideration for many mammals, including large carnivores. Finally, effective movement can also entail the evasion of predation and disease.

Effective movement through the landscape does not cover all of the reasons why connectivity areas are important. Most significantly, they offer potential protection to biodiversity from the effects of climate change, especially through their function of retaining landscape connectivity of natural lands at a time of climate-caused shifts in biomes (see Heller and Zavaleta (2009) for a review). Connectivity areas can also be beneficial by constituting an increase in or the retention of habitat itself, and thus it can sometimes be difficult to distinguish between core protected areas and connectivity areas (Dobson et al, 1999). Related to habitat protection are various ecosystem services such as catchment protection, water filtration and pollution control (including carbon sequestration). In agricultural regions connectivity conservation areas can provide habitat for important pollinator species, limit pesticide drift, and control populations of pest species by maintaining populations of natural predators. Connectivity areas can also provide recreational opportunities for people and can serve as barriers to the expansion of sprawling urban areas.

Scientific debate over the value of corridors

Scientists also debate about the functional advantages and disadvantages of corridors (and especially smaller wildlife corridors). It is useful to quickly visit this historical scientific debate, since it helps to reinforce a need to be careful about terms used and the need to focus, with connectivity conservation work, on large-scale areas.

Do we know that wildlife corridors will help protect biodiversity if we establish and protect them? By the early 1980s, a number of biologists were answering in the affirmative, basing their arguments on the tenets of island biogeography. They not only argued that corridors make eminent theoretical sense, but also cited indications, if not empirical evidence, that corridors work, and even noted that corridors represent an 'established wildlife management technique in some regions' (Harris, 1984, p141). Yet in the ensuing decade, corridors became the subject of considerable contention in the world of conservation biology. Despite the now familiar litany of their potential benefits, multifarious arguments were made against corridors, or more specifically against the idea that corridors can only have positive effects for conservation. A considerable amount of ink would be poured over the issue, generating a 'corridor controversy' that saw much vitriolic academic wrangling. In their overview of this debate, Anderson and Jenkins (2006) note that it has focused on three primary issues: the scientific evidence for corridor functions; the positive and negative effects of corridors; and the cost-effectiveness of corridors. Hilty et al (2006) delved into more specific issues and catalogued 30 potential disadvantages of corridors or causes of failure that have been identified by conservation biologists.

Both of these reviews, however, are congruent with what appears to be a general consensus among conservation biologists – that is, the potential problems do not negate the benefits or even the necessity of corridors:

> *Singly or collectively, these factors can cause corridor projects to fail or be diminished in their effectiveness. Do they add up to a denial of the importance of or efforts to achieve a better-connected world? They do not. While we have attempted to present these possible difficulties as strongly as possible, we believe that in the vast majority of cases the benefits of a corridor will outweigh the negativities* (Hilty et al, 2006).

Given this growing consensus, it is appropriate to interpret the potential drawbacks not as justification to exclude the protection or establishment of a corridor, but as a standard checklist of issues to take into account when designing, establishing and managing a corridor (Hilty et al, 2006, p148). Such a checklist would include the following considerations:

1 The physical structure of corridors should minimize edge effects such as increased levels of predation and parasitism.
2 Corridors should be established to minimize competition between indigenous biota and exotic and native invasive species.
3 Corridors should not lead to the dilution of locally adapted genes.
4 Corridors should not allow local populations to be overwhelmed by immigrants.
5 Where populations are small and lack immunity, corridors should not allow for the spread of infectious diseases.
6 Any connectivity conservation area established needs to be of strategic social, economic and political importance; it needs to be carefully designed; and it needs active management to retain the values and functions for which it was established. Because corridors will often be placed in areas of high economic value, the opportunity costs associated with establishing and maintaining corridors must be evaluated (for example, whether it would be more effective to enlarge core areas to achieve adequate biodiversity conservation).

Another long-standing debate among biologists and conservationists has been the requisite dimensions of corridors. The appropriate minimum dimension of a corridor will, of course, depend on the species involved. Generally, the smaller the target species, the smaller the corridor needed. Scientists have also identified that 'the home range requirements of carnivores, primates, and ungulates scales allometrically with body size' (Dobson et al, 1999). This means that certain species will require extremely large corridors for effective movement. Ultimately the generic question of whether corridors work 'may be sterile because the answers are indubitably yes, no, maybe, or sometimes' (Dobson et al, 1999). The efficacy of corridors 'depends on a number of factors, including the character of the matrix, the particular species involved, which individuals are moving, the time of year, the degree of movement required to connect populations and many others' (Dobson et al, 1999).

So far, we have largely described the debate over corridors in theoretical terms, an approach that is historically accurate since so much of the debate rested on propositions, hypotheses and models. However we also need to ask the question: What of the empirical evidence for corridors? Until only recently, comparative reviews of corridor analyses were ambiguous. For example, a seminal review by Beier and Noss (1998) found that a majority of relevant studies published between 1980 and 1997 did not provide conclusive evidence regarding any benefits resulting from corridors. Nonetheless, they did argue that there was sufficient evidence from a select number of well-designed studies that generally supported 'the utility of corridors as a conservation tool' (Beier and Noss, 1998, p1249). Furthermore, whatever weaknesses there were in the case for corridors, they also pointed out that: 'No study has yet demonstrated negative impacts from conservation corridors' (Beier and Noss, 1998, p1249). Since their 1998 article, empirical evidence on corridors has been generally encouraging. In particular, two studies conducted at the Savannah River Site in the USA found strong net benefits of corridors (Tewksbury et al, 2002; Damschen et al, 2006). The more recent study concluded that:

> By providing experimental evidence that corridors increase the number of native plant species in large-scale communities over a wide range of environmental conditions, we show that corridors are not simply an intuitive conservation paradigm; they are a practical tool for preserving biodiversity (Tewksbury et al, 2002, p12923).

The IUCN World Commission on Protected Areas has responded to the weight of scientific opinion supporting the efficacy of connectivity conservation by identifying large-scale connectivity conservation as a key strategic action, with a focus on mountain areas (IUCN-WCPA, 2005) (Box 2.2).

Box 2.2 Mountains: IUCN's strategic focus for large-scale connectivity conservation

From space, a view of Earth reveals scores of cragged mountain ranges criss-crossing the continents. From low ground, mountains dominate the landscape wherever they are found. From either perspective, the human eye cannot help but be drawn to high mountain terrain. It is not surprising, then, that mountain views have inspired myriad forms of cultural lore and traditions, revealing a widely shared cultural reverence for the high country through the assignation of divine, sacred and protected status for mountains worldwide.

Mountain ranges have also directly influenced the patterns of settlement and movement by both humans and wildlife. They act variously as barriers to movement, as sources of seasonal resources at different elevations, and as navigational reference points. In the first case, mountain chains serve as a limit to the range of a number of species and populations, which in our case are often described as 'geopolitical boundaries'. As food resources, seasonal migration up and down mountains enables the sustenance of larger populations, be they of the domestic cow (*Bos taurus*) or the wild grizzly bear (*Ursus arctos horribilis*), than could otherwise exist. For other species, humans included, mountain terrain not only provides navigational assistance, but also directly influences travel routes: birds, for example, use the updraft from mountains to assist their long seasonal migrations.

Although the human footprint expands over more than 80 per cent of the land area in the world (Sanderson et al, 2002a), montane regions have to a significant degree escaped much of this anthropogenic transformation. Historically, many of the world's earliest protected areas were established in mountain environments. Some argue that these early efforts reflected romantic sensibilities over the sublimity of nature as manifested in lofty peaks, as well as the fact that such lands were hardly useful for any practical purpose beyond tourism (Runte, 1987; Purchase, 1999). Others rejoin that the practical benefits of mountain conservation were well understood early on (Marsh, 1864 [1965]; Lowenthal, 2000). Yet this simplistic dichotomy between the concept of preservation (that is, prohibiting any human use of the landscape that would degrade it) and the concept of conservation (where biodiversity protection is but one aspect of land management) was far less contradictory than mutually supportive in early political and policy debates over 'nature protection'.

Today, regardless of myriad exhortations for the integration of 'preservation' and 'conservation', the distinction remains intact, as can be detected in a review of the handful of extant globally focused mountain conservation initiatives. On the one hand, a number of these initiatives focus directly on the preservation of mountain landscapes and biodiversity; on the other, a number of initiatives focus on sustaining the human environment in the mountains, with biodiversity protection typically included as one component of a broader environmental mission. While these two worlds overlap significantly in terms of substance, ongoing debate reigns as to where and when humans should and should not be part of the conservation equation (Chapin, 2004).

Over the years, ecologists have accumulated a plethora of information on mountain ecology, much of which has become highly relevant to the mountain corridor concept. For instance, mountain chains were found to host a high degree of endemism (species found nowhere else on the planet) due to unique geological features, assorted hydrological regimes, natural barriers, differing aspects and varying elevations, which all contributed to a greater potential complexity of habitats. Mountain regions also often retain species that were once more widespread, but are now only found in montane regions due to human-induced habitat change or persecution in low-lying areas. But even as they act as 'natural' refuges, mountain systems are arguably more fragile than many other ecosystems. Harsher climates at higher elevations mean that primary production is slower, which in turn makes recovery from perturbations a longer process. Steeper slopes mean that logging, road-cutting and other activities are likely to cause greater erosion. Further, because some endemic species have relatively small ranges, even habitat alteration that is confined to a relatively small area can imperil populations and species.

Evidence has accumulated that many of the major challenges of mountain conservation across the globe do share some similar characteristics. Most notably, humans have always tended to settle the most fertile valley bottoms, and this includes mountain valleys. Most mountain protected areas were created to protect the higher and less fertile elevations (Scott et al, 2001). Yet the very productivity that makes valleys so attractive to humans also indicates their importance both for resident species and for species that rely on those areas temporally, particularly in terms of wintering range. Scientists have documented that human occupation has affected biotic composition and survivorship in these mountain valleys directly through land-use change (Hansen et al, 2002) and by creating movement barriers for some species (Epps et al, 2005). As a result,

> ### Box 2.2 Continued
>
> species movement through and among mountain ranges may be diminished or even lost (Berger, 2004). Pollution drift into mountains, resource extraction and grazing are some other common threats that plague many mountain ecosystems as well (Lavergne et al, 2005). In addition, future efforts to protect mountain ecosystems will consider global climate change as well, which is known to have a greater immediate impact on higher elevations and latitudes (IPCC, 2007b, c).
>
> Looking over this growing understanding of mountain ecosystems, it would not take a great deal of ecological insight to surmise that connectivity conservation areas could be important for mountain ecosystems. In fact, because many mountain environments are still relatively undisturbed and because there are proportionally many more protected areas associated with them, there is greater potential for continental-scale connectivity conservation along major mountain chains of the world. This is why IUCN's World Commission on Protected Areas has focused on these areas as an opportunity to mitigate the effects of climate change through connectivity conservation.

Connectivity conservation and climate change

Can connectivity conservation areas provide a 'solution' to the problem of climate change? This is hardly an original notion. By 1991, Hobbs and Hopkins (1991, p282) were able to state that: 'One commonly touted solution to the problems of habitat fragmentation in the face of greenhouse-driven climatic change is to establish connectivity conservation corridors to provide for migration.' And a year later, in the first major volume dedicated to the effects of global warming on biodiversity, Peters (1992, p24) argued that: 'Corridors along altitudinal gradients are likely to be most practical because they can be relatively short compared with the longer distances necessary to accommodate latitudinal shifting.' Notably, the same year a more critical look at the use of corridor as a response to 'global warming' would be published by Simberloff et al (1992).

Since these early publications, discussion of climate change and corridors has been intimately linked. The proposition still remains largely untested, and there is little evidence that corridors can protect biodiversity from the effects of climate change. Yet as Hilty et al (2006, p112) summarize in general terms, 'it is hard to imagine any realistic alternative that would be conducive to species persistence'. This issue is further described by Mansergh and Cheal (2007):

> *Under changed climate, populations of species may respond in two broad ways or a combination of these at the same time. Firstly, a species may adapt to changed conditions within the existing range through phenotypic plasticity or evolution... In the absence of adaptation, populations may contract to refugia or go extinct within the present range. Secondly, a species may migrate to keep pace with shifting climatic range (Bennett et al, 1992). This option is only available if suitable habitat matrices are, or become available, that allow such movement... Each species can adapt only within the potential available to it ... and in interaction with its biotic community. The relative magnitude of in-situ adaptation (including contraction) versus migration remains unknown for any species.*

Despite these unknowns, it is hard to think of any alternative to connectivity conservation, reasonable or unreasonable. Translocation? Genetic manipulation? Controlling greenhouse gas emissions to a safe level? Connectivity conservation areas appear to be our best comparatively reasonable hope for protecting biodiversity in the long term (Box 2.3).

Box 2.3 Mountains, climate change and connectivity conservation

When Rob Buffler, Executive Director of the Yellowstone to Yukon Conservation Initiative (Y2Y) was asked what Y2Y planned to do about the challenge of climate change, his immediate response was that 'Y2Y is a response to climate change.' His point goes straight to a basic premise within the conservation community: the best response to climate change is to give biodiversity the ability to move in accordance with changing habitat conditions. From this standpoint, it is but a short jump to the idea that corridors present us with promising method for enabling such movement. Y2Y is fundamentally about ensuring that a vast mountain landscape carries sufficient biological connectivity to protect biodiversity in the long term. Unfortunately, it is in the long term that the looming problem of climate change threatens to become a severe obstacle to effective biodiversity conservation in mountain regions. Dating back to the 1950s (Körner, 2000), scientific research on climate change in the mountains has given weight to this concern, and several noteworthy studies are highlighted here.

By 2007, the Intergovernmental Panel on Climate Change (IPCC) had published four assessment reports on the effects of climate change on Earth in the years 1990, 1996, 2001 and 2007. Its Second Assessment Report (Beniston and Fox, 1996) included an extensive review of the effect of climate change on mountain systems, and subsequent reports reaffirmed these findings. According to the 1996 report:

> The projected decrease in the extent of mountain glaciers, permafrost and snow cover caused by a warmer climate will affect hydrologic systems, soil stability and related socio-economic systems. The altitudinal distribution of vegetation is projected to shift to higher elevation; some species with climatic ranges limited to mountain tops could become extinct because of disappearance of habitat or reduced migration potential. Mountain resources such as food and fuel for indigenous populations may be disrupted in many developing countries. Recreational industries, of increasing economic importance to many regions, also are likely to be disrupted (IPCC, 1996).

Research in the subsequent decade on climate change in mountain regions has not significantly changed this basic assessment. However, the 2001 Assessment Report (IPCC, 2001) includes an extensive coverage and analysis of the worldwide phenomenon of glacial retreat, and a subsection on ecosystem services points out that conforming with general climatic trends, climate change is likely to have a greater effect on mountain regions at higher latitudes.

At the same time that climate change in the mountains constitutes a considerable threat to biodiversity, there are some important 'comparative caveats' to consider. For example, not all mountain species will be affected by climate change; some species have even been shown to remain in the same mountain sites despite thousands of years of 'natural' climate changes. Furthermore, it is important to note that although climate change is likely to be a particular threat to species living in alpine zones, mountains are also potentially capable of affording greater habitat flexibility to many mountain species. Some evidence, for example, points to bird species in mountains as being more likely to withstand climate change than bird species on the plains (Peterson, 2003). Another consideration, put forth in the IPCC's Third Assessment Report, is that 'direct human impacts on alpine vegetation from grazing, tourism, and nitrogen deposition are so strong that climatic effects on the goods and services provided by alpine ecosystems are difficult to detect' (Gitay et al, 2001, p241; see also Körner, 2000). However, a recent initiative in Australia has found that altitudinal shifts can be accurately measured through statistical sampling techniques that focus on mean altitudinal range rather than range boundaries (Shoo et al, 2006).

Despite these caveats, climate change remains a tremendous threat to mountain biodiversity. For example, using extensive time-series evidence to investigate plant responses to climate change, a team of scientists working in the European Alps found that 'there is no doubt that even moderate warming induces migration processes, and that this process is underway'. It is a process, they argue, that 'may cause disastrous extinctions in these environments' (Grabherr et al, 1994). The threat appears to be particularly strong for montane cloud forests due to the combined phenomena of reduced cloud contact and increased evapo-transpiration, both of which 'could have serious conservation implications, given that these ecosystems typically harbour a high proportion of endemic species and are often situated on mountain tops or ridge lines' (Still et al, 1999, p608). These concerns were borne out by Pounds et al (1999, p611), who found that population crashes of 20 anuran species (frogs and toads) found in a tropical mountain environment 'probably belong to a constellation of demographic changes that have altered communities of birds, reptiles and amphibians in the area and are linked to recent warming'.

Box 2.3 Continued

There is also the threat that climate change could occur so rapidly that many plant species would simply be unable to spread to higher elevations. And even if they are able to spread, there remains the question of whether they could survive the presumably harsher annual temperature variations at such altitudes. In such a bleak scenario, if the plant species were not able to spread to higher elevation or more northerly latitudes, the end result could be widespread extirpation and even extinction.

Conclusion

Scientists and ecologists have generally defined the concept of connectivity as the extent to which a species or population can move among landscape elements in a mosaic of habitat types. Large-scale connectivity conservation includes landscape, habitat, ecological and evolutionary process connectivity, and connectivity conservation areas include the interconnection (and potentially embedding) of key protected areas or refugia areas. With the threat of climate change, an increased attention to connectivity largely results from a belief that the retention of natural environments between such protected areas offers species the best possible chance for survival in the long term. Despite limited empirical evidence available in 2009 that supports this, there does not appear to be any feasible alternatives that would provide similar benefits for species conservation. Large-scale connectivity conservation is a precautionary strategy that provides an insurance policy for many species to move and to adapt at a time of climate change.

3

Scoping the Territory: Considerations for Connectivity Conservation Managers

Michael Lockwood

The purpose of this chapter is to canvas the diverse matters that need to be considered by connectivity conservation managers. By 'managers', I mean organizations and individuals who have governance powers that shape and direct connectivity conservation policies, decisions and actions, as well as planners and implementation personnel (staff and partners) who work with their guidance or under their direction. Some actors, such as government conservation agencies, may be governance authority, planner and implementer. Some non-governmental organizations (NGOs) undertake planning and implementation, but may not have a governance role. Private landholders, who can also be NGOs, are implementers, sometimes planners and have a governance role through their property rights, which are often circumscribed by higher-level authorities. Community groups may also be planners and implementers, and may have governance responsibilities over common-property. NGOs and community groups often also have governance responsibilities authorized under joint management agreements. These various arrangements are further considered in the third section of the chapter.

Some of the topics surveyed in this chapter are widely recognized. Others, while well known within a particular discipline, may have only limited recognition outside of it. The presentation is based on the premise that connectivity conservation is more likely to be successful if all managers are aware of and understand the complex array of considerations presented here; both how they relate to their own sphere of influence and activity, as well as those of others involved in connectivity conservation.

The selection of topics considered in the chapter was influenced by Moore et al (2006) account of community capacity for achieving conservation outcomes, as well as by the editors' experiences in protected area and natural resource management. I review each of the topics based on a reading of the literature from a variety of environmental sub-disciplines within the natural, social, economic and policy sciences. It is not my intention to thoroughly cover each of the topics raised – that would of course be impossible – rather I attempt to summarize the core considerations to which connectivity conservation managers need to be alert.

Natural considerations

The essential biophysical characteristics of connectivity identified by conservation ecologists have been described in Chapter 2. In this section, I interpret these characteristics in terms of three core considerations for connectivity conservation: resilience, adaptivity and sustaining productive capacity.

Resilience refers to the amount of change or disturbance that can be absorbed by a system before it is reconstituted into a different set of processes and structures (Gunderson and Holling, 2002). Resilient systems have the capacity to buffer against minor change and respond to major perturbations. When change occurs, resilience allows a system to either renew itself or undergo reorganization so that essential components, such as species, or dynamic relationships, such as ecosystem processes, are maintained (Berkes et al, 2002; Gunderson and Holling, 2002). Systems with high *adaptivity* are 'able to re-configure themselves without significant declines in crucial functions in relation to primary productivity, hydrological cycles, social relations and economic prosperity' (Folke et al, 2002, p7). Adaptive capacity is the ability of a system, region or community to actively respond (mitigate or take advantage of) to the actual or predicted effects of change (IPCC, 2001). The opposite is the case with vulnerable systems. Systems lacking resilience have little ability to adapt to change. This fragility can lead to system breakdown, and as sources of resilience are eroded, through fragmentation of ecosystems for example, species and human livelihoods become threatened (Folke et al, 2002).

Resilient systems thus have adaptive capacity – that is, the ability to contend with new and emerging circumstances without foreclosing options or losing their essential character. Key attributes of ecological resilience and associated adaptive capacity include:

- genetic, species, ecosystem and functional diversity, and the heterogeneity of this diversity within landscapes;
- the amount of variability that can be accepted by one of the critical processes necessary for ecosystem functioning (such as hydrological, geomorphological and biological processes and the interactions between them), so that the self-organizational capacity of the system is maintained;
- the extent to which such critical processes interact and overlap, so that local failures in one function can be compensated for, and perhaps corrected by, the responses of another;
- the variety of ecosystem functions that provide for reorganization following disturbances (Bengtsson et al, 2002; Folke et al, 2002; Nunes et al, 2003).

Adaptation options for enhancing ecosystem resilience include changes in management processes, practices or structures to reduce antici-

pated damages or enhance beneficial responses. Planned adaptation to manage change depends on awareness that conditions are about to change or have changed, and an understanding of which strategies may be suitable to meet management goals (Julius and West, 2008). The purpose of adaptation strategies is to reduce the risk of adverse outcomes through activities that increase the resilience of systems (Tompkins and Adger, 2004). This implies that connectivity authorities need to shift away from policies that aspire to control change in systems, and move towards those that accept uncertainty, seek to build the capacity of systems to cope with, adapt to, and shape change. Rigid governance, planning and management approaches can compromise resilience and hasten breakdown of socio-ecological systems (Folke et al, 2002). Adaptive connectivity conservation strategies that can contribute to natural resilience include:

- reducing human-caused stresses such as habitat fragmentation that hamper the ability of species or ecosystems to withstand change;
- adequately protecting representative areas of all species and ecosystem;
- protecting and where necessary replicating multiple examples of each species population and ecosystem, to absorb disturbance, spread risk, and maximize the potential for self-reorganization;
- rehabilitating degraded ecosystems;
- protecting or establishing refugia that can assist the recovery of other areas (Julius and West, 2008);
- providing suitable 'spaces' into which species may be able to move in the face of threats such as climate change.

Adaptive management goes beyond simple avoidance of error and stresses intentional learning from experience. Kay et al (1999) distinguish between passive and active approaches. Passive adaptive management involves systematic review of management activities, while active adaptive management includes the former but is more deliberate in learning about the managed system. Active adaptivity is an experimental approach to management where policies become hypotheses, management projects become the experiments to test them (Gunderson et al, 1995), and where experimentation, embracing complexity, inclusiveness and learning are the defining values (Allan and Curtis, 2005).

Connectivity conservation, and the network of core protected areas that will typically be encompassed within a connectivity area, have a key role in *sustaining the productivity* of natural systems that is essential to sustain human livelihoods. People directly harvest and mine products from natural areas. Livestock grazing, timber and non-timber forest products (medicines, food plants, thatching, animal fodder), fishing and subsistence hunting are important activities that are dependent on the continued productivity of these natural areas (Chapman et al, 2006). Use of natural resources is particularly important for local and indigenous communities. Many of the goods and services provided by natural lands can make a contribution to preventing or alleviating poverty (Borrini-Feyerabend et al, 2004).

People also indirectly benefit from the services that natural areas provide. Ecosystem services flow from natural assets (soil, biota, water systems and atmosphere) to support human activities and lifestyles that take place both within and outside natural areas. For example, wetlands can help remove pollutants from water, thereby ensuring that downstream flow can be extracted for domestic uses. The agricultural industry depends heavily on many ecological processes, including soil formation and nutrient cycling. Common instances of agricultural failure after ecosystem alteration include soil loss after excessive tree removal, as well as population explosions of pest species once the habitat for their predators has been removed (Cork and Shelton, 2000). In general, terrestrial natural areas provide a number of ecosystem service benefits, including:

- climate regulation through carbon sequestration, regulation of albedo and other processes;
- hydrological benefits associated with controlling the timing and volume of water flows and maintaining or improving water quality for uses such as domestic, agricultural and industrial consumption, recreation and fisheries;

- protection of and habitat for useful predators, pollinators and dispersal agents;
- reducing sedimentation, thereby avoiding damage to downstream infrastructure such as reservoirs, hydroelectric power stations, irrigation pumps and canals;
- maintaining soil and land productivity;
- disaster prevention through watershed protection reducing the risk of flooding and landslides (Georgieva et al, 2003).

Factors that are increasing pressures on the productivity of forest, grassland, wetland and coastal resources include: local economic development aspirations; globalization and neoliberal policies of developed country governments that facilitate entry of corporations to appropriate assets and opportunities in developing countries; changing land uses and landscapes; population growth and climate change (Barber et al, 2004; MEAB, 2005; Igoe and Brockington, 2007). In addition, breakdown of traditional norms has eroded the willingness and capacity of some communities to maintain sustainable practices (Alcorn, 1993). On the other hand, Hess (2001) cites numerous examples of the sustainability of local and indigenous land-use practices, and argued that such practices justify recognition of community access rights.

Connectivity conservation managers need to understand these values, influences and tensions so that their policies and activities support both the resilience of natural systems and the supply of benefits they deliver to human communities. The concepts of resilience and adaptivity also have application in the design of institutional arrangements for connectivity conservation. Connectivity initiatives need to have institutions capable of jointly sustaining the productivity of natural areas for human use and protecting or re-establishing ecosystem resilience. Developing such capacity is both pragmatic in terms of achieving connectivity outcomes, and a moral recognition of the intrinsic value of wild nature, as well as the duties human beings owe each other to secure livelihoods and uphold human rights (a matter I consider further in the fourth section).

Institutional considerations

Connectivity conservation mangers need to have a clear understanding of the institutional setting in which they operate: the organizations that enable collective action, the governance arrangements that are created by them and control how they operate, the instruments they use to achieve their desired outcomes, and the managerial approaches they bring to bear to achieve conservation outcomes. Within an organization, understanding of these elements can promote effective design and implementation of governance responsibilities, as well as intelligent selection of appropriate management instruments. By looking outside their own circumstances and understanding the wider institutional setting in which they operate, including the roles and methods adopted by other organizations and individuals, managers can critique, learn from, develop respect for, and seek to influence the institutional setting of connectivity conservation. Such endeavours are essential for developing institutional adaptivity and resilience.

Organizations are the collective structures that act as vehicles for the policies and actions needed to develop and deliver services and products. When operating effectively, they provide consistent direction, cohesive action and continuity of effort. Connectivity conservation organizations include:

- governments and their agencies responsible for protected areas, natural resource management, tourism, agriculture, forestry, fisheries and water;
- conservation-oriented NGOs operating at international, national and local scales;
- natural resource-based private companies and representative bodies;
- governing bodies of indigenous and mobile peoples;
- local-level community-based organizations that may provide representation or have collective land-management responsibilities;
- consortia, partnership-based or private organizations specifically set up to facilitate and coordinate connectivity conservation management.

Some of these organizations provide the structural platform for making strategic and operational conservation decisions, including design and delivery of instruments that directly achieve land management outcomes, or enable land managers to participate in conservation programmes. Others may be affected by conservation actions, or make decisions and take actions that impact on conservation concerns. As connectivity conservation is attempting large-scale action, and is operating in a highly complex environment, partnerships between two or more of these organizations are usually required. Some partnerships will be long term and established through formal agreements such as memoranda of understanding or contracts. Others will be more informal and perhaps ephemeral, as parties seek to work together on a particular matter and then go their separate ways.

A prerequisite for effective connectivity management is establishing and maintaining good *governance* across a diversity of landscape-scale ownership and responsibility arrangements (UNEP, 2002). It is fundamental to securing the political and community support essential to the development of a connectivity system (Ostrom, 1990; Borrini-Feyerabend et al, 2006). Governance means the structures and processes that determine how power and responsibilities are exercised, how decisions are made, and how stakeholders have their say (Graham et al, 2003).

Governance has assumed particular significance under the conditions of uncertainty and open-endedness that prevail in relation to environmental matters (Stoker, 1998), so that the tasks of governing affect the distribution of power, public decision making, and stakeholder engagement in complex ways. Consequently, governance has taken on a number of features distinct from conventional government. Key among these is an increase in interdependencies among a wide range of participants. These interdependencies have necessitated greater interaction among diverse actors from different territories, at multiple scales. To regulate activities and facilitate decision making and problem solving, a range of horizontal arrangements for governing are emerging, among them policy networks, partnerships and communicative forums. Actors engage in cooperation, coordination and communication that involve collaboration among agencies of public government, private sector businesses and groups in civil society, and may combine formal and informal governmental arrangements. A range of collaborative governance instruments is being used to integrate and coordinate decision making, including multi-level, multi-sectoral and multi-organizational partnerships, 'joined up' government and policy networks (Lockwood et al, 2009). Potential governance arrangements for conservation connectivity include:

- public governance (for example, legislated or state-managed protected areas, or public finance of conservation activities with associated accountability and performance requirements);
- collaborative governance (that is, partnership-based governance in which one party has primary authority, often a government partner);
- joint management (that is, partnership-based governance in which power is shared);
- private governance (for example, conservation measures taken by landholders enabled through their property rights);
- community-based conservation (through, for example, customary norms and laws developed and enforced by local and indigenous communities) (Borrini-Feyerabend et al, 2006).

Contemporary connectivity governance is thus characterized by collaborative arrangements such as networks, partnerships and deliberative forums, used to coordinate and guide decision making. This work is accomplished through formal institutions of government and informal arrangements among government and non-government actors from the private sector and civil society. The term 'new governance' (Howlett and Rayner, 2006) has emerged as a descriptor for this mode of governing. The findings of Davidson and Lockwood (2008), among others, suggest that such partnership-based governance arrangements constitute a means of addressing complex problems of coordination and integration; they provide a framework by which actors at multiple scales can communicate with each other; and they can foster goodwill and trust to address issues and facilitate solutions to entrenched problems. As well, they can

engender improved downward accountability particularly by central governments to other scales of government. Successful partnerships have a basis in trust and mutual understanding among the parties, a shared sense of purpose and a sense of the equitable distribution and exercise of power (Breckenridge, 1998; Curtis and Lockwood, 2000).

Notwithstanding the potential of new governance modes to drive more equitable and sustainable forms of development and conservation, some analysts question their representativeness and democratic credentials, their aptitude for coordination, as well as their inclusiveness and transparency (Bauer, 2002; Swyngedouw, 2005; Wallington and Lawrence, 2008). Their potential to advance problem-solving capacity and generate efficient outcomes may be at the expense of core values of legitimacy and accountability, as well as the capacity to govern (Peters and Pierre, 2004). Such considerations mean that connectivity conservation organizations need to pay serious attention to the requirements of good governance. Good environmental governance can be represented by eight principles: legitimacy, transparency, accountability, inclusiveness, fairness, capability, integration and adaptability (Lockwood et al, 2009).

Legitimacy requires that a governing body has valid authority to undertake its responsibilities, and that those in authority act with integrity and have a genuine commitment to delivery of their responsibilities. Validation can be conferred by democratic mandate, or earned through stakeholders' acceptance of a governing body's authority. Legitimacy also encompasses the notion of subsidiarity, which requires that power be devolved to the lowest level at which it can effectively be exercised. *Transparency* requires that decision-making processes are visible to stakeholders, that the reasoning behind decisions is clearly communicated, and that relevant information about the governance and performance of a governing body is ready available. *Accountability* requires that responsibility for decisions and actions is unambiguously allocated, and that the designated organization or individual accepts these responsibilities and demonstrates how they have been met.

Inclusiveness requires that opportunities are available for all stakeholders to participate in and influence decision-making processes and actions. *Fairness* requires that the distribution of responsibilities to individuals and organizations is commensurate with their potential or obligation to assume them, that governance authorities respect and give attention to stakeholders' views, that there is consistency and absence of personal bias in decision making, and that consideration is given to the distribution of costs and benefits arising from decisions.

Capability requires that a governing authority has the skills, leadership, experience, resources, knowledge, plans and systems that enable delivery of responsibilities. *Integration* requires alignment of priorities, plans and activities across governing bodies, as well as connection and coordination vertically across different levels of governance (international, national, state/provincial, local) and horizontally between governing bodies at the same governance level. *Adaptability* requires that governing bodies incorporate learning into decision making and implementation, anticipate and manage threats, opportunities and associated risks, and systematically reflect on individual, organizational and system performance.

Attempting to meet these principles poses a number of challenges for connectivity conservation governance authorities. Legitimacy, integration and inclusion in the new governance arrangements are of particular concern. Decentralization may result in fragmented, unrepresentative and undemocratic institutions and processes (Ribot, 2002; Agrawal and Gupta, 2005), and while potentially empowering those who have been without an effective voice, can also make it more difficult for non-local interest-holders to effectively express their values and have them considered in decision-making processes. It is contrary to good governance if the legitimate empowerment of local interests disenfranchises non-local conservation advocates. Poor governance can also open up strategic opportunities for resource-based industries to co-opt management and satisfy distant private interests, at the expense of local communities and conservation outcomes. Internationally, decentralization of governance has often yielded economic, social and cultural bene-

fits to local and indigenous communities (Borrini-Feyerabend et al, 2006), but the consequences for biodiversity conservation have been inconsistent, with both positive (for example, De Oliveira, 2002) and negative (for example, Wells and McShane, 2004) outcomes reported.

Government agencies, particularly in developed countries, generally have well-established public participation processes that, while they may be inclusive, often offer limited opportunities for stakeholders to influence decisions and actions. For some agencies, the extent to which decision-making processes are visible to stakeholders, and the reasoning behind decisions, may also warrant attention. While annual reports are standard, and 'state of the parks' reports are developed by some protected area agencies, the ready availability of relevant performance information may be lacking. Often only limited attention is given to the distribution of costs and benefits arising from decisions. And while advances have been made, the culture and processes for incorporating learning into decision making and implementation, and systematically reflecting on individual, organizational and system performance, are incomplete. Inadequate finance is likely to be a major constraint on the ability of governing bodies to deliver on their responsibilities, leading to a capacity deficit. In many jurisdictions too, the systems for information management are underdeveloped, restricting the ability of governing bodies to effectively embrace accountability and adaptability requirements. Many of these issues are even more pronounced in developing countries.

NGOs, community-based and private governors face particular challenges in validating their legitimacy to assume responsibility for achieving public good outcomes, as their opportunities for securing stakeholders' acceptance are limited, and they lack the democratic mandate of state agencies. Nielsen (2006), for example, investigated participatory processes managed by two intermediary NGOs working with four different indigenous community-based conservation projects located in the Mesoamerican biological corridor. Participants were not representative of their communities, and participation was primarily in the initial decision making and early implementation phases of the projects, but was not ongoing. The results suggested a need for strengthening trust, respect, transparency and sustained dialogue. Adams and Hutton (2007, p168) note that large NGOs and 'the scientists, intellectuals and supporters from whom they draw their vision and strength, have remarkable power to define and delineate nature, to determine who can engage with it and under what rules, and to divide landscapes into zones that structure rights and access'.

Such observations suggest that some conservation NGOs may need to take active steps to prevent or, as far as is possible within their sphere of influence, redress power imbalances that may undermine the fairness of connectivity conservation initiatives. Many of the major NGOs are, of course, well aware of and responding to such issues. Nonetheless, important concerns continue to be raised about the specific roles played by NGOs in some conservation initiatives. In the Mesoamerican biological corridor in Central America, for example, an emphasis on market-based instruments and the power of large international conservation NGOs have led to claims that local people have been marginalized, inequities between the rich and poor reinforced, and international conservation NGOs benefit while local environmental groups struggle to survive (Grandia, 2007).

Community-based organizations and private managers often find it difficult to provide opportunities for all stakeholders to participate in and influence decision-making processes and actions, and the latter may give little consideration to the distribution of costs and benefits arising from decisions. Transparency can also be an issue, as revealing decision-making processes to stakeholders is not common practice for community groups or private landholders. Furthermore, information about governance and performance may be limited or restricted in distribution. In some arrangements, it may be unclear to whom NGOs, community groups and private landholders are accountable, although where these actors receive public funds through state or national agency programmes, financial and performance accountability may be comparatively well defined. Compared with government agencies, adaptability is often regarded as a strength of NGOs and private sector organizations. Nonetheless, establishing themselves as learning organizations able to effectively incorporate new knowledge into decision making and systematically reflecting on individual, organizational and system performance remains a challenge.

A diverse array of *instruments* is available to connectivity conservation organizations for pursing their objectives. Before the emergence of the current neo liberal regimes of governance, regulatory instruments, often referred to as 'command and control' measures, were favoured by governments to carry out environmental policy. Community environmental concern, particularly between the late 1960s and the early 1980s, led many governments to develop extensive bodies of environmental regulation, which are still largely in place. Such regulations are often established through legislation. Regulations can attempt to:

- prohibit or regulate action (such as stopping or restricting resource extraction);
- require action (such as environmental impact assessment of development proposals or preparation of recovery plans for threatened species);
- establish processes (such as public participation in the preparation of land management plans);
- establish the structure, powers and responsibilities of organizations and their employees (many public environmental agencies are established through legislation);
- establish the structure and operating rules for markets in natural resources such as water or production 'externalities' such as carbon;
- set standards (such as extraction rates for renewable resources that are based on sustainable yield);
- establish land tenure (the boundaries and governance of public protected areas are generally established through legislation) (Lockwood and Kothari, 2006).

Regulations provide a protection and management capability that is often critical for achieving conservation objectives. They provide a measure of stability and surety that can support long-term investments and actions. Young et al (1996) also note that regulatory instruments provide an essential safety net. If other policy approaches such as market-based or voluntary instruments were to fail, then there is always the deterrent of regulation to reduce the likelihood that undesirable behaviour results in environmental damage. Regulatory measures alone, however, are insufficient. Poor implementation and enforcement of regulations may occur. Administrators could know too little about the situations faced by individual firms or landholders, and as a result may impose inappropriate and costly constraints on them. Poorly conceived regulations can also impose unfair burdens on local communities. Regulations can conflict, be overly complex, lack flexibility and responsive capacity, and fail to recognize local needs and aspirations (Hodge, 1991; Pennington, 2000).

Economic instruments, which act through market processes and other financial mechanisms, can create incentives for rational resource use and protection. Economic instruments include: creating markets for natural resources such as water, or for trading the rights to produce externalities such as greenhouse gases; offering incentives for reducing environmental degradation; and placing financial burdens on resource users. Economic measures can reduce environmental destruction and promote conservation by increasing returns from conservation activities and increasing the cost or lowering the return to activities that damage ecosystems.

Market approaches such as carbon trading systems can be designed to place a value on protecting current repositories of stored carbon and provide an incentive for vegetation plantings that sequester carbon from the atmosphere. In a connectivity conservation area, such market systems can enable landholders to offset the costs of protecting natural lands and enable them to undertake revegetation works, although in the latter case specific permit or contract conditions are required to ensure that plantings are directed towards re-establishing indigenous plant species.

Users of natural resources such as water and timber often do not pay the full costs associated with their production. Many natural resources are under priced. Governments have often not attempted to recover all the costs they face in producing the resource. For example, irrigation subsidies have primarily involved water prices that do not provide an adequate rate of return for investments made in public infrastructure such as dams, weirs, pipelines and channels. In some cases, prices have not been set high enough to cover the government's operating costs. Reducing or eliminating subsidies encourages resource users to reduce their consumption or make more effective use of current allocations. Such measures can encourage sustainable resource use within a connectivity conservation area.

Economic incentives in the form of grants and subsidies encourage and assist landholders to adopt conservation management practices. Such payments, supported by a formal agreement or contract, can enable landholders involved in connectivity conservation to, for example, fence off areas to control livestock, control weeds or feral animals, and undertake revegetation works. Stewardship payments can also be used to recognize the role that private landholders play in providing public good outcomes by offsetting the opportunity costs of protecting land within a conservation corridor.

While such market-based and incentive instruments have an important contribution to make towards connectivity conservation, there are good reasons for managers to be careful about their design and application. The use of economic instruments may create tensions with the good governance requirements of inclusion and fairness. Some landholders, whether for cultural reasons or because of their personal disposition, do not take up opportunities to access economic incentives, and unless other means are also utilized, may be excluded from participation. Establishing markets over natural resources can also be exclusionary in that there will always be winners and losers when resource rights are allocated. Where such allocations are made, as they often are, based on existing economic and political power, they can serve to reinforce disadvantage. The competitive environment that best suits the effective operation of economic instruments can similarly reinforce existing disadvantage. Care must be taken therefore that the use of economic instruments to achieve connectivity conservation objectives does not exacerbate unfair distributions of opportunity and resources.

Voluntary measures such as partnership agreements are another important instrument for connectivity conservation. They can take the form of a 'Memorandum of Understanding', which sets out the purposes of the agreement and the roles and responsibilities that are accepted by each party. Such voluntary instruments are typically of low administrative cost, high community and political acceptability, and can be designed to be inclusive and fair (Young et al, 1996). Management agreements are another option. Essentially, a management agreement is a contract between a landholder or community and a third party regarding the use and management of their land. This third party can be a government agency, local government, NGO or trust. Management agreements can be binding or non-binding. Agreements that bind the landholder either for a fixed period or in perpetuity may be registered on a title to land, or be prescribed in a licence agreement or contract. Non-binding agreements are voluntary in nature and fundamentally rely upon ongoing landholder support and participation. In recognition of the costs incurred by the landholder for adopting conservation management, management agreements can be used in conjunction with economic incentives or stewardship payments.

As indicated above, inclusive engagement and attention to a fair sharing of power and resources are two precepts of good governance. To achieve these, good communication between proponents and participants in connectivity conservation, as well as with other stakeholders who may be affected, is fundamental, as is the deployment of appropriate means by which people can engage with and influence connectivity decisions and actions. Communication is also a crucial instrument for seeking community support for connectivity initiatives, accounting for performance, and informing stakeholders of decisions made and actions taken. As well as underlying most aspects of organizational functioning, communication processes are also necessary for the formation of the capacities associated with social capital (Hazelton and Keenan, 2000) that are considered in the next section.

The *managerial approach* adopted by organizations influences people's management values and philosophy and the way they work. With the private sector, there is a focus on profit, providing a service to customers, and the efficiency and effectiveness of delivery of services. Performance monitoring is dominant, and rewards are given for individual performance achievements. Connectivity conservation management objectives may be part of the mandate of a private enterprise, but will generally be subordinate to trading profitably. As they become more professionally oriented and entrepreneurial, large NGOs and community-based organizations are adopting many of the practices used by private firms, but instead of a profit focus their activities are often directed by building the status and well-being of their organization concurrently with achieving their connectivity conservation mission. For those that receive significant philanthropic or government funding, strategic direction, planning, research and accountability processes tend to be closer to public sector approaches (see below). Smaller NGOs and community-based organizations are largely reliant on volunteers contributing their time and energy. Rewards may be through personal satisfaction and public recognition rather than remuneration and power. As a consequence, their managerial approach tends to be more informal, with accountability and line-management procedures less well developed. Nonetheless, such organizations still need to conduct their financial affairs with due probity, be clear about the roles taken on by office bearers and volunteers, and agree on procedures for setting direction and making decisions.

For government conservation organizations around the world, the dominant management approach is called New Public Management (McLaughlin and Osborne, 2002). New Public Management is a marriage between economic theories and a variety of private sector management techniques that have been introduced into the public sector. The approach includes strengthening the prerogatives of managers, measuring performance, increasing competitive pressures and cost-cutting. It has also seen the introduction of managerial initiatives such as decentralized wage bargaining, individual employment contracts, total quality management, performance-based pay, downsizing and contracting out (O'Donnell et al, 1999). This approach is set within a context of government priorities and social justice objectives. However, some critics argue that the influence of New Public Management is waning, as it tends to reduce capacity for collective action, increase institutional and policy complexity, thereby inhibiting effective social problem solving, and makes it more difficult for citizens to understand and access appropriate means to represent their interests (Dunleavy et al, 2006). Connectivity conservation authorities should be alert to such concerns and, where possible, seek to influence managerial approaches so that they fit more comfortably with the principles of good governance.

In summary, the institutional considerations for successful connectivity conservation include: strong and diverse institutions, including governments, NGOs, landholder and community-based bodies and partnership organizations; governance regimes that are legitimate, transparent, accountable, inclusive, fair, integrated, capable and adaptive; employment of a diverse range of regulatory, economic, voluntary and communication-based instruments; and understanding of the primary managerial motivations for success within different organizations as they work towards the larger connectivity conservation vision. Successful connectivity conservation is thus likely to be institutionally complex and feature multi-centred governance arrangements and deployment of multiple policy and management instruments in a manner that reinforces their respective strengths and compensates for their weaknesses. Such complexity can also contribute to the resilience of the socio-ecological system in which the connectivity initiative is embedded.

Financial considerations

Financial sustainability is the ability to secure sufficient, stable and long-term financial resources, allocate them in a timely manner and in an appropriate form, cover the full costs of connectivity initiatives and ensure that management is effective and efficient (Emerton et al, 2005). Achieving connectivity conservation can be costly. Land may need to be purchased, financial incentives made available, organizations and governance structures established, engagement programmes implemented, education and information materials developed and on-ground management actions undertaken. Adequacy of financial resources is an important aspect of successful partnerships and collaborative efforts (Cropper, 1996; Leach and Pelkey, 2001), which are a key feature of connectivity conservation initiatives.

Establishing a sufficient financial base, and buffering against the failure or reduction in any one source, will typically require access to a diversity of sources. A stable funding base may include:

- government funding;
- grants from development banks and development agencies;
- endowments, sinking funds and/or trusts;
- debt-for-nature swaps;
- private sector payments for access, use and services;
- local communities' in-kind contributions;
- investments by NGOs;
- philanthropic donations by individuals or companies;
- business enterprises established by connectivity conservation organizations (Lockwood and Quintella, 2006).

A significant proportion of lands that are the subject of connectivity conservation initiatives may be managed by government agencies, and have a heavy reliance in government funds derived from taxation revenue. Funding to government land management agencies is typically provided through annual appropriations from national and sub-national treasuries. Governments often also provide the funds needed to implement conservation incentive programmes and local economic development programmes.

Many opportunities exist for connectivity conservation organizations to develop constructive partnerships with the private sector. A growing number of business sectors are seeing opportunities in partnership with protected areas and the communities that surround them. For example, payment for potable water has potential to become an important source of revenue for connectivity conservation. In this case, the partner may be municipalities, private companies where water services have been privatized, or the agricultural sectors if the water is used for irrigation.

A wide range of international conservation organizations, among them WWF, Conservation International, The Nature Conservancy and IUCN, offer funding for technical assistance and partnerships for the development and implementation of innovative connectivity conservation management. The Conservation Finance Alliance is particularly important, as it brings together a diverse membership for the purpose of developing and implementing sustainable finance solutions as well as providing financial training and capacity building.

Private donors are a major potential source of support for connectivity conservation management. In developing countries these sources, which include individual donors, foundations and corporations, are particularly important. However, there has been a tendency for support to be directed more towards specific projects with limited time-horizons, rather than long-term investment in ongoing management requirements. Fiscal incentives in the form of tax exemptions for donations supporting conservation (and other allowed charitable activities) are important to encourage the development of private philanthropy. In the US, for instance, this kind of legislation has resulted in the growth of a wide range of foundations created by wealthy individuals and corporations for the purpose of funding a range of charitable initiatives. It has also encouraged individuals to give personal gifts for their preferred causes. Their contributions have not only supported the management of public and private protected areas in the US, they have also helped US-based conservation organizations to support many conservation efforts overseas (Lockwood and Quintella, 2006).

Many developing countries have a relatively small philanthropic community. In these areas, partnership with NGOs from wealthier countries can leverage funding from individuals, foundations and corporations. These partnerships can take many forms and the specific nature of the transfer of funds can be regulated by tax legislation in the donor country. These types of partnerships are very common and have produced significant accomplishments for the conservation of biodiversity and the effective management of protected areas. However, as noted above, care must be taken to avoid inequitable distributional effects that can arise from such investments.

Just as a diversity of funding sources can be important for financial capacity, a range of methods can contribute to the financial sustainability for connectivity conservation. Governments can impose taxes to generate revenues and to discourage activities that are detrimental to the environment. For instance a tourism fee, collected at the airport, has been adopted by Belize to fund its Protected Area Conservation Trust. Costa Rica, in the late 1990s, established a fuel tax to support carbon sequestration and forestry projects. Investment funds can generate stable and predictable income flows. Sinking funds involve a specific amount of money, the capital, which is invested, typically in a variety of financial instruments. All the income and dividends earned from the investment, in addition to the capital, are then expended on relevant projects. As with the sinking fund, in an endowment the capital is invested in a variety of financial instruments, but only the income and dividends are spent for project support. This ensures that the principal of the fund remains untouched, and ideally would increase to retain its real value against inflation (Lockwood and Quintella, 2006).

Connectivity conservation areas provide a range of ecosystem services that benefit people outside their boundaries, such as potable and irrigation water, water for hydroelectric power, carbon sequestration and retention. For example, the quality of many cities' water supply is in part due to the watershed protection afforded by protected areas some distance from these cities. About one third of the world's largest cities obtain a significant portion of their drinking water directly from protected lands (Dudley and Stolton, 2003). Undisturbed watersheds provide higher quality water with less sediment and fewer pollutants. Such services are often taken for granted, in part because the beneficiaries are generally not required to pay for them. However, if they were no longer provided, communities, companies and indeed whole economies would suffer and even collapse completely. Payments for environmental service provision help ensure a continuity of supply by generating funds to enable proper protection and management of the land and waters from which these benefits derive. In the water supply example, downstream users can be asked to pay for the services they receive from protected watersheds upstream, as has occurred in Costa Rica, for example, where a hydroelectric company signed a contract with the Monteverde Conservation League to pay for ecological services provided by the protected area managed by the League (IUCN, 1998).

The spatially extensive and multi-organizational character of connectivity conservation means that managers are well-placed to build a sustainable financial capability by tapping into diverse funding sources. To realize this potential, well-developed business planning, marketing and fund-raising capacities are required. To maximize their efficiency and effectiveness, partners in a multi-organizational connectivity initiative may have to coordinate their individual business and accounting systems. Good governance is also important to engender confidence amongst potential donors that their investments will be well managed and directed towards agreed outcomes. However, while a business orientation is important, the drive to build organizational capacity and attract large public and private investments can lead to 'empire building', where the status and power of an organization, rather than the outcomes being sought, begin to drive business practices and decisions. Attention must also be given to the local impacts of conservation investments. In many developing countries, connectivity conservation is financed largely through international institutions and private donors from developed countries, and funds are often channelled through and managed by the major conservation NGOs. This places a responsibility on these NGOs and supporting governments to be scrupulous in their observation of good governance, in particular principles of inclusion and fairness, so that nature conservation achievements are not at the expense of social justice.

Social and individual considerations

Connectivity conservation is critically dependent on people working together. At the 'grass roots'

level, individual landholders and local communities are major contributors to conservation works and management, in some cases assisted by NGO and government local staff and volunteers. Effective planning and governance requires concerted effort from all parties at all scales, from the local to the international. Social capital and human capital provide useful frameworks for understanding factors that are likely to explain why and how people work together (Putnam, 1993; Moore et al, 2006). Understanding such factors can assist managers develop and sustain the social and individual capacities needed to make connectivity conservation work.

Social capital, which has been described as the 'glue that holds people together' and the 'lubrication that assists our "business"' (Macbeth et al, 2004, pp504, 512), includes trust, connectedness, sense of place and leadership (Pretty and Ward, 2001). Interaction and connections develop shared norms, trust and reciprocity that in turn foster cooperation to achieve common ends (Ecclestone and Field, 2003). Capacities possessed by particular individuals within an organization or community, such as commitment, knowledge, skills and experience (sometimes referred to as human capital), are also important. Both social and human capital have been found to be strong predictors of participation in, and support for, conservation programmes (Falk and Kilpatrick, 2000; Anderson et al, 2002). Communities where these capacities are particularly evident have been demonstrated to be more able to respond to conservation initiatives (Pretty and Smith, 2004). Individuals associated with communities with high levels of social capital tend to have the confidence to invest in collective activities, knowing that others will do likewise, and they are also less likely to engage in self-interested actions that degrade resources and have negative collective outcomes (Pretty, 2003).

Social interactions only make sense when they are directed towards *purposeful community activities* (Falk and Kilpatrick, 2000). A clear vision and well-defined and agreed goals and objectives are important as they are correlated with organizational and individual commitment, motivation and achievement of outcomes, with this relationship being particularly evident in institutional arrangements based on partnerships (Brinkerhoff, 2002). Cropper (1996) also discusses the benefits of a clearly expressed, explicit statement of purpose, as both a statement of identity that helps collaborative organizations to clarify commitments and as a means to control against 'directional drift'. Direction (visions, goals, objectives, plans) has been identified as an important factor in successful protected area–tourism partnerships, and inadequacies in this regard were identified as an important source of partnership failure (Moore et al, 2008a, b). The same is likely to be true for partnerships between connectivity conservation organizations and individuals.

Trust is an important dimension of social capacity (Moore et al, 2006). Trust creates a sense of community and makes it easier for people to work together. Trust reduces transaction costs so that instead of having to invest in monitoring others, individuals are able to trust them to act as expected (Pretty and Smith, 2004). Investing in social relationships and building trust between stakeholders assists group mobilization and associated processes of self-organization and learning (Folke et al, 2005). Trust is defined by Leach and Sabatier (2005, p234) as 'knowing that one's fellow stakeholders are likely to negotiate honestly, are worthy of respect, and are sufficiently honourable and competent to keep any promises they make'. Two forms of trust are distinguished in the literature – trusting based on personal experience and trust based on a general community norm. Putnam (2000) values the latter more highly in terms of its contribution to social capacity, as it is not restricted to a relatively small circle of friends and colleagues with whom we frequently interact, but extends across larger communities of interest.

Reciprocity (exchanges of goods and knowledge of roughly equal value and the continuing of such relations over time) increases trust and contributes to the development of long-term obligations between people, which helps in achieving positive environmental outcomes (Pretty, 2003). Recognition of different perspectives is also an important stepping stone towards trust. Connectivity partners and affected communities need not necessarily share the same values but should at least value and respect their differ-

ences. In order to avoid misunderstandings, miscommunication and unproductive conflict, managers need to understand social and historical differences between organizations and communities operating within a connectivity conservation area (Poncelet, 2004). Trust is both a pre condition and product of such interactions.

Networks (interconnected groups of people with common interests or purposes) are a core element of social capacity. A network provides individuals with benefits such as social support and greater access to information, including lower search costs. Networks can also help to develop and consolidate trust and social norms, which in turn build community coherence and collective ability to act towards common purposes. Networks support the spread of new ideas, which can promote processes of social learning that improve understanding of biodiversity and sustainability issues. When people are well connected in groups and networks, and when their knowledge is sought, incorporated and built upon during planning and implementation of conservation and development activities, then they are more likely to sustain stewardship and protection over the long term (Pretty and Smith, 2004). Networks are central to the development and maintenance of new governance relations, norms and institutions that can lead to positive conservation outcomes. The persistence and stability of governance systems depend on the distribution of benefits from networks and the extent to which the system commands legitimacy and trust among stakeholders (Adger et al, 2005). The networks of relationships and trust that develop through interaction enhance governance resilience and adaptivity (Manson, 2001).

Networks vary in their degree of formality, spatial scale and extent of their vertical and horizontal connectivity. Horizontal networks, such as those between neighbouring landholders, tend to be relatively informal and possess high levels of trust and cohesion. Vertical networks across local, national and international scales may require a more concerted effort to build the trust and cohesion necessary to make them functional. While some cross-scale networks can be empowering for local groups, interventions by powerful stakeholders such as governments have the potential to undermine trust in resource management arrangements by disempowering other stakeholders. Adger et al (2005) cite the example of Tobago fisheries management where government regulators and planners retained a 'gatekeeper' role throughout negotiation of co-management responsibilities, while local stakeholders remained effectively outside of such processes. This initial distribution of network linkages skewed the power relations between the groups involved, so that the cross-level linkages controlled by these powerful players undermined trust in shared management arrangements. Adger et al (2005) concluded that the key is to identify those network linkages that build social capacity and avoid those that have the potential to undermine trust.

Connectivity conservation requires *leaders* who can build trust, manage conflict, assist the development of linkages and partnerships between actors, compile and generate knowledge, and mobilize support for change (Folke et al, 2005). Lundblad (2003) distinguishes between three types of leader: change agents, opinion leaders and champions. A change agent is often an 'outsider' who has sufficient status and trust to encourage innovation, often in association with opinion leaders. Opinion leaders are important figures in communication networks, and have an influence that can derive from their expertise and competence, but also from the degree to which they appeal to community norms (which, although often positive, can in a negative sense also tap into fears and prejudices). Opinion leaders are often high status individuals who are better connected outside their community than other community members, more cosmopolitan and more innovative. A champion, on the other hand, is important in securing commitment, fomenting excitement and spearheading new initiatives. In a partnership context, champions are entrepreneurial advocates who are acknowledged by partners and stakeholders to have legitimacy to act on their behalf (Brinkerhoff, 2002). While leadership is commonly identified as a success factor in achieving conservation outcomes, excessive dependence on the leadership provided by a particular individual makes partnerships or individual organizations vulnerable. This problem can be alleviated by connectivity conservation organizations implementing succession plans for key personnel as well as training and mentoring programmes.

Tensions are often evident between the pursuit of legitimate local *aspirations* for securing an acceptable quality of life, and non-local conservation agenda, which may also enjoy wide acceptance and support from democratic processes. Connectivity conservation will not be fair or effective without simultaneously addressing issues of local livelihoods and poverty. Connectivity conservation management therefore often needs to be part of a wider sustainable development agenda. In pursuing conservation outcomes, managers need to respect agreed norms of entitlement associated with human rights and social justice. Social justice can be understood as the right of individuals and communities to self-representation and autonomy, participation as equal partners throughout policy processes, and political, economic and cultural self-determination (Taylor, 2000; Brechin et al, 2002). Rights to self-determination are supported by Article 1 of the UN International Covenant on Civil and Political Rights: 'All peoples have the right of self-determination. By virtue of that right they freely determine their political status and freely pursue their economic, social and cultural development.' Under Article 27, ethnic, religious or linguistic minorities should not be denied the right, in community with the other members of their group, to enjoy their own culture, to profess and practice their own religion, or to use their own language.

Some conservation programmes have increased poverty by denying or reducing community access to resources traditionally used for survival and livelihoods. Borrini-Feyerabend et al (2004) cite the example of the Karrayu, a pastoral group living in Africa's Rift Valley. In 1969, following the establishment of a national park, the Karrayu were displaced from the park, reducing their lands from 150,000 to 60,000ha, breaking the traditional rotational grazing pattern and causing hardship for the community, as well as serious degradation in the remaining area outside the park. On the other hand, conservation programmes, in preventing or remediating environmental degradation, can also combat poverty by sustaining or increasing resource productivity (Box 3.1) and providing employment opportunities.

Connectivity conservation managers often face a difficult task attempting to achieve two objectives, nature conservation and social justice, that at times can seem irreconcilable. Well developed social capital – social connectedness, trust, shared norms and reciprocity – significantly increases the likelihood that this challenge can be met while staying true to the principles of good governance, particularly legitimacy, inclusion and fairness.

Places, including natural areas, motivate our actions and are central to our attempts to make sense of the world (Sack, 1992). An initially undifferentiated space becomes a 'place' as we become familiar with its biophysical characteristics, encounter it as a setting for personal, social and spiritual experiences, and as a result endow it with meaning and value (Relph, 1976; Tuan, 1977). Place is 'space that is special to someone' (Vanclay, 2008, p3). Key concepts that assist an understanding of the relationship between people and places are *sense of place*, and the subsidiary concepts of place attachment, place dependence and place identity (Jorgensen and Stedman, 2001).

A concise and precise definition of 'sense of place' has proved to be elusive. It is a response to environment that is simultaneously individual and relational: intimately connected to self and community identity and experience; it is visceral, emotional and cognitive, being made by and constituting sights, sounds, smells, thoughts and feelings (Vanclay, 2008). Place attachment can be more precisely identified as the bonding of people to places, and is usually associated with a strong emotional connection. Attachment to place generally requires long and deep experience of, and involvement with, a particular place (Relph, 1976). Place dependence refers to the functional relationships individuals or communities have with places through their capacity to directly or indirectly satisfy physical or psychological needs. Place identity is sense of belongingness or symbolic connection through which a subjective sense of self is constructed and expressed in terms of a person's relationship to the settings that comprise day-to-day life (Stokols and Shumaker, 1981; Proshansky et al, 1995; Jorgensen and Stedman, 2001).

Box 3.1 Community conservation in Nagaland State, India

Nagaland State of India bordering Burma is occupied by 16 tribal communities, each culturally and geographically distinct from the other. Unlike other parts of India, nearly 90 per cent of the land is under community ownership and 85 per cent is still under forest cover. Originally hunter-gatherers, these communities have developed an intricate land-use system, with land distributed between shifting cultivation, settled agriculture and forest reserves to meet food, fruit, fuel, timber and other requirements. Wild meat is an integral part of the tribal culture. Most families own guns and go hunting nearly every day. Easy availability of guns and non-implementation of wildlife protection laws led to unsustainable hunting. Increasing population and heavy dependence on timber and forest produce for livelihood has also affected forest quality. During the late 1980s and early 1990s the effects of these activities began to manifest themselves in the drying up of water resources, declining availability of wild foods, and declining populations of wild animals. In 1988, the Khonoma Village Council in Kohima district declared 2000ha of forest and grassland as the Khonoma Nature Conservation and Tragopan Sanctuary. Rules were formulated to strictly ban hunting in the reserve, and over the whole of Khonoma's 135 square kilometre territory, to stop all resource uses in the sanctuary area, and to allow only a few ecologically benign uses in the buffer area.

In the same district, the village council of Sendenui resolved to set aside an area of about 1000ha after some discussions initiated by the village youth concerning the decline in wild animal populations. The village has issued its own wildlife protection act, with rules and regulations for the management of the sanctuary. In neighbouring Phek district, several villages have taken up conservation measures. In 1983, the Luzaphuhu village Student's Union had resolved to conserve a 500ha patch of forest land above the village as a watershed. In 1990, they declared another 250ha a wildlife reserve, with hunting strictly prohibited. As well as having nature conservation benefits, such measures are helping sustain important food and water resources.

Source: Adapted from Pathak, in Kothari (2006)

Some place meanings translate into strong emotional bonds that influence attitudes and behaviours. As a component of self-identity, place identity enhances feelings of belonging to one's community (Relph, 1976), thereby fostering community cohesion and capacity to act towards collective goals. Vaske and Kobrin (2001) found that place identity was significantly related to environmentally responsible behaviour. A well-developed sense of place can support long-term commitment to endeavours such as connectivity conservation. Attachment motivates people to protect the integrity of places, and in particular those properties and qualities of a place that are the foundation of attachment, dependence and identity.

Awareness of people–place relationships is often central to understanding community identity, and can enhance land managers' capacity to address important landscape meanings and place-specific values in their decision making (Williams and Vaske, 2003). As sense of place is developed when people interact with the associated social and physical characteristics in the environment, these characteristics of connectivity conservation areas deserve special attention because they contribute to place identity and ultimately to self identify, health, sense of community and sense of place (Hull et al, 1994). By encouraging an individual's connection to a natural setting, environmentally responsible behaviour can be facilitated and 'outsiders' can be made aware of and maintain values while they participate in desired activities (Vaske and Kobrin, 2001).

Many areas that are the subject of connectivity conservation initiatives include places with significant cultural values. Culture

consists of webs of significance woven by humans, in which we are all suspended. Places occur where these webs touch the earth and connect humans to the world. Each place is a territory of significance, distinguished from adjacent and from larger or smaller areas by its name, by its particular environmental qualities, by the stories and shared memories connected to it, and by the intensity of the meanings people give to it or derive from it. ... where communities have deep roots and intense meanings, it seems that their places often fuse culture and environment,

and this fusion is then revealed in striking cultural landscapes (Relph, 2008, pp311–312).

Cultural values may be seen in a place's physical features, but can also be associated with intangible qualities such as people's associations with, or feelings for, a place (Lennon, 2006). Human society has, through interaction with nature, forged identity, tradition, lifestyle and spirituality. For many communities, natural areas are closely associated with deeply held historical, national, ethical, religious and spiritual values. A particular forest or river may, for example, have been the site of an important event in their past, the home or shrine of a deity, the place of a moral transformation or the embodiment of national ideals (MEAB, 2005). Many mountains have spiritual meaning. Examples given by Hamilton (2000) include:

- mountain forests in the Yunnan prefecture of Xishuanbanna in China are largely intact because of the reverence the Dai people have for these dwelling places of their ancestors' spirits;
- Hawaii's Volcanoes National Park, wherein the volcano goddess Pele, creator and destroyer by her lava flows, is both feared and loved;
- the sacred peak of Gauri Shanker in Nepal, which embody the lord Shankar and his consort Gauri.

Wirikuta, sacred natural site to the Huichol (Wixarika) people who live in the valleys of the Mexican Sierra Madre Occidental, is now included in a 140,211ha reserve that protects key biodiversity elements of the Chihuahuan Desert, including endemic and endangered cacti and relict forests (Acha, 2003). Such sites are essential to the vitality and survival of traditional cultures. For communities, identity is in part formed by connection with such places. Community histories are often ingrained with stories and memories in which such places are a central element. Natural areas can also foster understanding between traditional and modern societies, or between distinct cultures (Putney, 2003). All these features constitute a significant element of the 'glue' that imparts cohesion and meaning to communities. They therefore constitute an important aspect of community capacity, proving the stability and unity of purpose needed to undertake and sustain conservation action. Connectivity conservation areas provide opportunities to keep alive or conserve the cultural values that give a sense of identity, connection and meaning.

Many people in developed countries, especially those living in urban areas (including many champions of connectivity conservation), lead highly mobile lives, and may not spend long enough in one place to develop the depth of association with a particular local place, especially a 'home' place, that is characteristic of indigenous communities and cultures. On the other hand, mobility and opportunity may also engender complex, diversified and expansive ways of experiencing and constructing places. One example is the vision being championed in this book, of large-scale spaces, made into places through connections, extant and built, that impart integrity and resilience to the natural and human communities that reside within them.

Seen in this way, connectivity conservation is an exercise in making very large places, requiring a breadth of vision and understanding that has perhaps only recently become possible. Good governance and respect for social justice require that this grand new place-making effort must respect and support local places. Conservation arguments based on a duty to protect the intrinsic value of nature or a responsibility to maintain opportunities for future generations need to be reconciled with human rights and social justice. While contest cannot and should not be avoided – differences between local and non-local will be, in most cases, inevitable, and consensus unlikely – it is how the parties approach the table, the understandings and attitudes they bring, and the behaviours when they are there, that are important. Contests must be fair, they must be inclusive and they must be legitimate. Connectivity conservation must include a nested sense of place that is 'simultaneously local and extended' (Relph, 2008, p320).

Effective connectivity conservation requires deployment of a formidable array of *knowledge, skills and experience* and associated capacities of acquisition, storage, management, analysis and deployment. The capacities identified by the United Nations Development Programme,

presented by Hough (2006, pp168–169), provide a useful indication of the broad domains that require attention.

Capacity to conceptualize and formulate policies, legislations, strategies and programmes. This category includes analysing broader societal conditions that may affect needs and performance in a conservation connectivity area, developing a vision, long-term strategizing, and setting of objectives. It also includes conceptualizing broader sectoral and cross-sectoral policy, legislative and regulatory frameworks, including synergies between them. It further contains prioritization, planning and formulation of programmes and projects.

Capacity to implement policies, legislation, strategies and programmes. This category includes process management capacities that are essential in the implementation of any type of policy, legislation, strategy and programme. It also includes execution aspects of programmes and projects – that is, connectivity conservation area management. It includes mobilizing and managing human, material and financial resources, and selection of technologies and procurement of equipment.

Capacity to engage and build consensus among all stakeholders. This category includes issues such as mobilization and motivation of stakeholders, creation of partnerships, awareness-raising and developing an environment in which government, civil society and the private sector can work together, stakeholder identification and involvement, managing of large group process and discussion, including mediation of divergent interests, as well as the establishment of partnerships and other collaborative mechanisms.

Capacity to mobilize information and knowledge. This category pertains to the mobilization, access and use of information and knowledge. It includes issues such as effectively gathering, analysing and synthesizing information, identifying problems and potential solutions, as well as consulting experts and peers. It further covers specific technical skills that are related specifically to the requirements of protected areas, including the capacity to carry out scientific and technical assessments.

Capacity to monitor, evaluate, report and learn. This category pertains to the monitoring of progress, measuring of results, codification of lessons, learning and feedback, and ensuring accountability. It also covers aspects such as reporting. It naturally links back to policy dialogue, planning and improved management of implementation.

Developing the social and human capacities required for successful connectivity conservation is clearly a long-term project for managers. Persistence, commitment and integrity are essential, as is a willingness to learn and apply the lessons afforded by experience. The diverse elements of social and human capital described in this section provide an indication of the factors that need to be considered.

Conclusion

The natural, institutional, financial, social and individual considerations outlined in this chapter suggest that connectivity conservation is an attempt to manage a complex socio-ecological system that is beset with 'wicked problems'. A complex socio-ecological system is characterized by multiple interrelationships and interdependencies between natural and human systems, and their components, which manifest at multiple scales and levels (Berkes et al, 1998). Wicked problems (Rittel and Webber, 1973) involve stakeholders with competing values and goals, encounter uncertainties and incomplete knowledge, lack consensus on either problem definition or solutions, have fragmented institutional settings, and suffer from inequities in the distribution of power (Roberts, 2000; Davidson et al, 2006). All these characteristics ring true for connectivity conservation. While this analysis highlights the magnitude of the challenge, Chapters 1 and 2 clearly demonstrate the importance of success, while Chapters 4 through 9 confirm that success is possible. In this context, the literature on complex systems and wicked problems, together with the 14 considerations outlined in this chapter, suggest four broad, interrelated strategies for connectivity conservation leaders:

1   Encourage fair and inclusive collaborative interactions between all actors. Capacity to resolve problems will be aided by open communication processes, generation of mutual trust, deliberation, and application of local and technical knowledge. As momentum builds, political, community and financial support will be easier to obtain.

2   Establish a clear vision and sense of purpose. Outcomes to be sought include shared understandings, innovation, ownership and collective mobilization of effort that is directed towards joint achievement of large-scale nature conservation and sustained productivity.

3   Cultivate a flexibility to adapt, openness of decision making and a learning culture. There is a need for continuous adaptation through experimentation. Adaptive learning processes enable convergence of problem perspectives and so reduce uncertainty and build resilience.

4   Develop multi-centric governance structures, with authorities that possess legitimacy commensurate with their powers and responsibilities, able to deliver level-specific (local, regional, national, international) outcomes. Organizations need to pursue just distributions of benefits and costs and have well-defined upward and downward accountabilities. Institutional settings need to be appropriate for the varied local and extended places of connectivity conservation. (Berkes et al, 1998; Holling, 2001; van Bueren et al, 2003; Lachapelle and McCool, 2005; Lebel et al, 2006)

While the complexities and difficulties raised in this chapter make it inevitable that some connectivity conservation initiatives will fail to live up to expectations, at least for a period of time, each of the case examples described in the next chapters exhibit elements of success. In the spirit of adaptive improvement, the considerations outlined here may assist the identification of lessons that can be learned from such cases, and help inform approaches to new connectivity conservation initiatives.

Part II

Applied Connectivity Conservation Management: Case Material

Wendy L. Francis (principal editor)

The rich experience of connectivity conservation managers is presented in Chapters 4 to 10. In Chapters 4 to 9, we showcase examples of some of the most innovative and successful conservation connectivity initiatives occurring around the globe, many of which have been influenced or inspired by the Yellowstone to Yukon conservation initiative (Chapter 7) and other early international corridors. From the Himalayan Mountains to the páramo grasslands of the Andes, from the European Alps to the mountain ranges of southern Africa, and from Central America to eastern Australia, scientists, conservationists, government agencies and communities have recognized the urgent need to preserve connectivity between protected landscapes. In Chapter 10 we then present key findings from the IUCN Papallacta, Ecuador 2006 Workshop, synthesize the lessons learned from the case material, and identify generic connectivity management functions and tasks.

Most, if not all, of the case studies refer to initiatives that are occurring in transboundary mountain environments. There are several reasons why mountain ecosystems are good candidates for large-scale connectivity conservation endeavours. Their rugged topography means that mountain landscapes often have avoided the types and intensities of fragmenting activities that have altered much of the Earth's more accessible environs. For similar reasons, mountainous regions also tend to be less populated than lowland areas.

As a consequence, opportunities to maintain or restore connectivity between protected areas often are greater in high elevation zones. Although these case studies emphasize mountain examples, connectivity conservation efforts are ongoing in many other global ecosystems, including grasslands, boreal and hardwood forests and oceans.

The projects exemplified in the case studies are at various stages of implementation. The complexity of developing and executing connectivity conservation initiatives, including the challenges of absent political will, insufficient resources, community opposition or indifference and lack of scientific information, means that some initiatives take longer to implement, or become mired somewhere between the vision and planning stages. The range of efforts described below provides examples of each stage and offer insights into the advantages and challenges of large-scale connectivity conservation endeavours.

The case studies that follow were written in late 2006. Many activities have occurred, partnerships have been established, programmes have been implemented and successes have occurred since that time. Nonetheless, the case studies remain important examples of the range of connectivity conservation efforts and the lessons that can help inform connectivity conservation management practice. The case studies have been ordered according to Udvardy's (1975) biogeographical realms (Figure 4.1).

Together, Chapters 4 to 10 provide the empirical data to underpin a framework for connectivity conservation management, which we develop and present in Chapter 11.

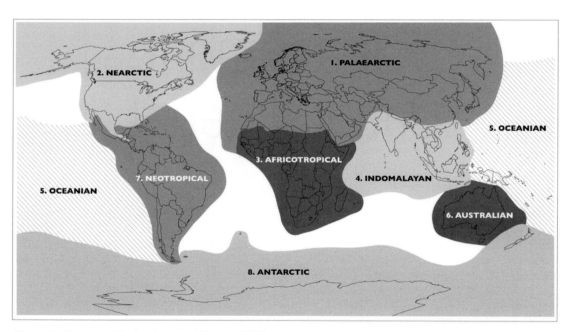

Figure 4.1 Biogeographical realms from Udvardy (1975)

4

Africotropical Connectivity Conservation Initiatives

The Africotropical realm comprises Africa south of the Sahara desert, with Madagascar and neighbouring islands forming a distinctive subregion. Madagascar and the Seychelles are old pieces of the ancient supercontinent of Gondwana that broke away from Africa millions of years ago. The realm includes large freshwater lake systems; large areas of wetlands such as the upper Nile; a large tectonic geological feature, the Great Rift Valley; high mountains such as Mount Kilimanjaro (5595m) and Mount Kenya (5200m); and high mountain ranges such as the Mountains of the Moon and the Drakensberg. The Africotropical realm includes many protected areas, and 1.29 per cent of its area has been inscribed as world heritage. This chapter presents three connectivity conservation case studies from the Africotropical realm.

Young elephants (Loxodonta africana), South Africa

Source: Graeme L. Worboys

Joining the dots: Stewardship for connectivity conservation in the Cederberg Mountains, Cape Floristic Region, South Africa

Trevor Sandwith, Sean Ranger and Jaco Venter

Setting

South Africa's Cape Floristic Region (CFR) at the southern tip of Africa is widely regarded as one of the world's richest hot spots of biodiversity (Myers et al, 2000). Its complex landscape of mountains and lowlands and underlying geology and hydrology is at the heart of this diversity, which led to representative portions of the area being listed as a United Nationsl Educational, Scientific and Cultural Organization (UNESCO) serial world heritage site in 2005. In addition to its spectacular diversity and high proportion of threatened species, the CFR demonstrates the ongoing ecological and biological processes associated with the evolution of the distinctive plants known locally as 'fynbos'. Such processes include complex adaptive responses to fire, pollination and seed dispersal leading to active speciation and adaptive radiation.

The CFR is characterized by its extensive coastline and coastal lowlands influenced by hinterland coastal and inland mountains, which trend east–west on the southern Cape coast, and north–south on the west coast (including the Cederberg mountains). Rainfall patterns are driven by oceanic high pressure systems as they interact with the landmass and the sea temperatures, notably the cold upwelling currents of the Benguela system on the west coast. The result is a complex mosaic of microhabitats, microclimates, edaphic and disturbance conditions in both mountain and lowland sites.

The history of colonization and mercantile exploitation of the Cape as a strategic way-point on the sea route between Europe and the east has made its mark on the social and political history of the subcontinent and has irreversibly impacted its biodiversity. In particular, large-scale exploitation of arable soils for wheat and wine production has resulted in the fragmentation of lowland habitats to critical proportions (Rouget et al, 2003). This can be contrasted with the relatively intact mountain ecosystems, although they are moderately impacted by invasive alien species and fire mismanagement affecting watershed services to the region. The result is a highly fragmented landscape with few remaining natural linkages between the mountains and the sea. Coupled with this is the skewed landownership of South Africa's apartheid history and enormous and persistent disparities in wealth and economic opportunity of the region's peoples. On the whole, whereas the state is in control of most of the mountain catchment areas, it is private and mainly white landowners who manage the highly fragmented lowlands. Intensive and extensive agriculture is the biggest land use (79 per cent) in the Western Cape and is one of the largest employers (11.3 per cent), yet it contributes only 5.2 per cent to the gross regional product. By way of contrast, tourism contributes 11.6 per cent of employment and 10.7 per cent to the gross regional product (Western Cape Department of Environmental Affairs and Development Planning, 2005).

This detailed background is crucial to understanding the way in which governmental and non-governmental organizations (NGOs) are approaching connectivity conservation and development goals in the CFR. South Africa's goals for reconstruction and development include the reconciliation of its diverse population and the restoration of equity and participation in every aspect of society and the economy. Dominating conservation policy and practice in the region is

the drive to mainstream the region's undoubtedly significant biodiversity and scenic beauty into the reconstruction and development of the post-apartheid society, while achieving the national conservation targets established through the Millennium Development Goals (UN Millennium Project, 2005) and South Africa's National Biodiversity Strategy and Action Plan. Perhaps the most ambitious and far-reaching approach being undertaken is the development of landscape-scale connectivity corridors designed to mitigate the impacts of historical fragmentation of habitats and land uses while addressing regional sustainable development goals. In South Africa's Cape Action for People and the Environment (C.A.P.E.) programme, no fewer than seven of these landscape-scale corridors are currently being planned and implemented, representing one of the most significant conservation and development investments at a large scale in the history of the CFR (Lochner et al, 2003). This approach is exemplified by the Greater Cederberg biodiversity corridor (GCBC) on the Cape West Coast (Figures 4.2 to 4.4).

The connectivity conservation initiative

Since the adoption of South Africa's Constitution in 1994, a process of policy and law reform has been undertaken to redress the inequalities of the past. Significant among these has been the National Spatial Development Perspective, adopted by government in 2003 following the World Summit on Sustainable Development. It addresses the changing spatial economy and, in particular, provides guidance for coordinating planning and policy at national, provincial and local government levels. Principles of bioregional planning underpin the Western Cape's Provincial Spatial Development Framework (PSDF) that promotes land-use planning and management to promote sustainable development (Western Cape Department of Environmental Affairs and Development Planning, 2005).

A landmark reform is that the PSDF fully incorporates the biodiversity priorities generated by systematic conservation planning methods in the development framework, and recognizes the dependence of the built and socio-economic environments on the underlying natural resource

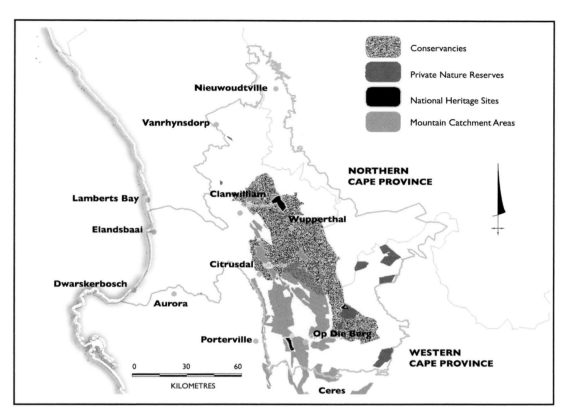

Figure 4.2 The Greater Cederberg biodiversity corridor

base. Institutionally, elected local government has been empowered to apply these development principles in district and local municipalities, taking principled decision making to the most local level feasible. However, translating these progressive policies into practice is not without its challenges, since the necessary understanding and capacity among citizens and public representatives has yet to be developed. In particular, authorities at both national and provincial levels operate in sectoral isolation and processes of decision making are reactive and fraught with conflict between developers, landowners, government agencies and the general public.

The GCBC can be regarded as a pathfinder in this progressive enabling environment that mobilizes government, NGOs and the public at large to forge progress towards the policy goals (Ashwell et al, 2006). The origin of the GCBC lies in the Cape Action Plan for the Environment, which employed defensible and systematic conservation planning methods to determine conservation priorities for the first time in the whole CFR (Driver et al, 2003). This approach took into account both the pattern of biodiversity across the regional landscape, as well as the ecosystem processes required to maintain biodiversity in the long term. In addition, the conservation plans incorporated levels of disturbance and threat to generate information layers that described the irreplaceability and hence conservation significance of the entire CFR in the face of development pressures and predicted patterns of climate change. Necessarily coarse, these conservation plans revealed opportunities for the establishment of protected areas and conservation corridors that would meet acceptable targets for the persistence of these ecosystems and the species they contain. The GCBC was identified as one of the options that would link ecosystems from the

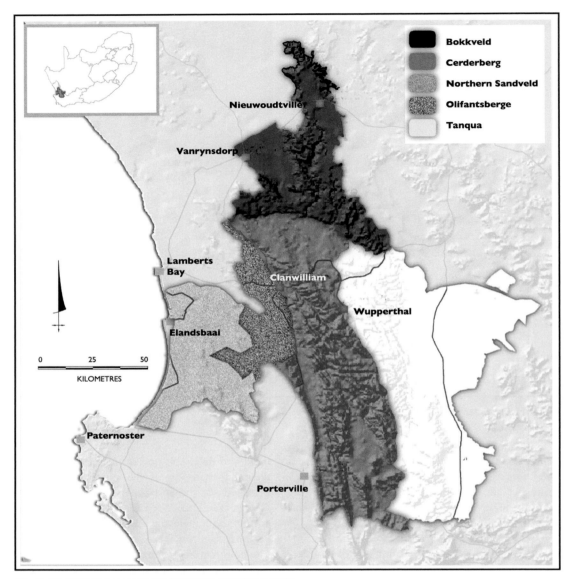

Figure 4.3 Protected areas in the Cederberg planning domain

mountains to the sea while offering the potential to address the threats of global climate change and the challenges of sustainable development.

Specific threats in the GCBC planning domain include the impacts of alien invasive species and fire mismanagement. Fynbos ecosystems are fire prone, and require burning at specific intervals to promote resprouting and seed germination. However, more significant in the GCBC,

has been the complete transformation of extensive areas through the recent cultivation of potatoes and rooibos tea. A recent mapping exercise revealed that in a total study area of 234,258ha, 31 per cent of the area had been transformed by 1989, with an additional 5 per cent by 2001. The rate of transformation is alarming; in the latter 12-year period it amounted to 2.7ha/day. The scale of the physical impact is illustrated graphically in

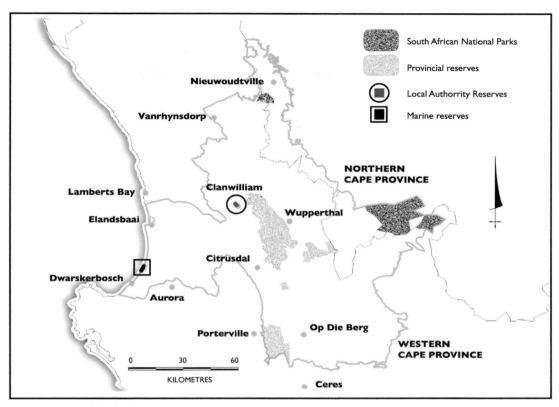

Figure 4.4 Private conservation measures in the Cederberg

Figures 4.5 and 4.6. Proximate causes of this change are also significant; generally, it is ground-water resources that are being exploited for irrigation purposes. In a region where rainfall ranges from 100mm/year to 500–750mm/year in the mountains, this had predictable impacts on groundwater resources. Over-extraction occurred in six sub-catchment areas, and recorded water shortages and salt water intrusion resulted in the coastal zone. Changes in water tables are impacting wetlands, freshwater springs and estuaries and their associated biodiversity in the GCBC.

Communication of these concerns among authorities and local stakeholders alike resulted in a call for action, both to take progressive steps toward achieving connectivity conservation, and also to verify existing information and obtain a better understanding of the ecological, social and economic issues. A second iteration of conservation planning helped to ground-truth the

situation in the corridor at a much finer scale of resolution. This resulted in a refined map of conservation priorities in the planning domain (Figure 4.7). These priorities were described in terms of categories listed in the South Africa *National Environmental Management: Biodiversity Act* (Act No. 10 of 2004), paving the way for the application of the law for their protection. A more explicit description of conservation priorities and options at a scale of 1:10,000 and based on cadastral information (legal land parcel and property boundary data) enabled engagement with implementation at the level of the relevant municipalities and landowners, whereas previously only a generalized relationship between priorities and practice could be established.

Consistent with the overall pattern of biodiversity across the CFR, the pattern of biodiversity in the GCBC domain includes high gamma diversity – that is a rapid turnover of species along

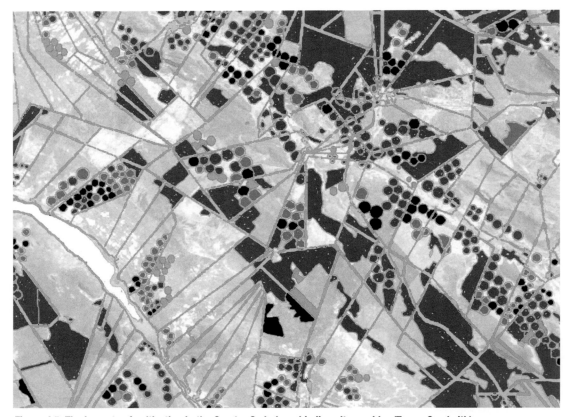

Figure 4.5 The impacts of cultivation in the Greater Cederberg biodiversity corridor (Trevor Sandwith)

the geographical gradient. This renders it impossible to concentrate conservation measures in a tightly defined spatial unit, even if ecosystem processes are not included. A corridor design is the only viable option for meeting conservation targets across the regional landscape. A significant implication of this is the confirmation that it is not possible for government alone to provide an efficient solution to protection, making it essential that the existing owners and land managers are involved in conservation measures in an extensive approach. Although conventional connectivity conservation planning has aimed to achieve highly efficient conservation solutions, an emergent outcome of this extensive corridor approach is that it can involve large numbers of people in concerted actions and they can include not only the powerful government agencies but the very people who can support and benefit from the

arrangement, namely the landowners and the workers who depend on these areas for their livelihoods.

Connectivity conservation management

Ensuring that a strategy can be implemented and achieve 'results on the ground' is crucial for successful connectivity conservation outcomes. One often hears a plea for more effective conservation management practices that mobilize local action rather than elaborate conservation strategies and action plans that fail to be implemented. However, a false dichotomy is created when the effort is one-sided. Effective connectivity conservation management in practice is rarely achieved unless there is a sound planning framework and the application of agreed principles by all stakeholders. It is true also that plans without effective local action and management are unlikely to

Figure 4.6 Patterns of land transformation in the Sandveld (Trevor Sandwith)

achieve conservation outcomes. The solution lies in ensuring that all of the critical success factors are in place and co-managed. In this section, the close and ongoing relationship between planning and implementation will be highlighted, and the management tools that complement strategies and action plans will be emphasized.

The development of the GCBC has employed a number of conservation management tools that have been piloted and tested more generally throughout the C.A.P.E. programme. These include two broad categories, namely area-wide planning and conservation stewardship.

Developed in the agricultural sector and akin to the Australian model for Landcare, area-wide planning is a comprehensive process that integrates social, economic and ecological considerations in defined agricultural development areas. In principle, it ensures that local landowners identify and address the natural resource management issues

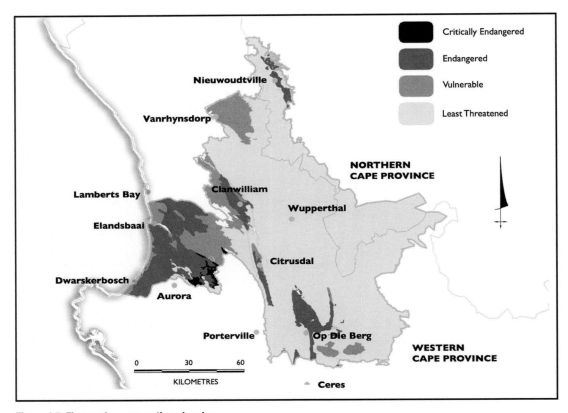

Figure 4.7 Fine-scale conservation planning

that face them, drawing on their own extensive knowledge of local conditions, experience with different land-use practices, observed changes over time and perceptions of opportunities and threats for the future.

The process followed in the GCBC included the following steps.

Establishing local area-wide planning committees

These provide an interactive forum for the sharing and dissemination of knowledge. In the GCBC, the inputs to the area-wide planning process were the C.A.P.E. programme broad-scale conservation plans and the GCBC fine-scale conservation plans that identified priorities in a systematic way. These were ground-truthed by an extensive understanding of the local landscape and patterns of transformation for agriculture developed by nature conservation and agricultural extension

staff over many years. These motivated individuals, private sector representatives and government officials were members of a task team that emerged from concerns regarding the transformation of the sandveld. A combination of science and local knowledge thus enabled the identification of two broad corridor options, the Sandveld corridor (east–west) and the Cederberg corridor (north–south). An important result was a growing cooperation among relevant stakeholder groups and individuals who are situated in these corridors, thereby ensuring broad support for both the purpose and feasibility of corridor establishment.

Compiling a database of individual properties

Using an electronic database of all properties making up the corridor and the most recent orthophotos and conservation plans, an extensive programme of visits to properties was undertaken to gather more information. In particular, the purpose was to assess landowner willingness to participate. Whereas there are potentially many options for the location of specific corridors, the approach adopted in the early phase was to work where it was possible and feasible to make significant progress. If landowners in a particular area were unwilling to cooperate, it was less efficient to work there. Instead, such landowners were the focus of awareness generation activities. In tightly knit farming communities, information spread rapidly and the identification of local champions and opinion leaders resulted in rapid exchange and dissemination of information and effective leadership.

Confirming priorities by governance structures

Local consensus on the emerging priorities was rapidly confirmed by discussion and decision making by the relevant authorities (in this case CapeNature, the provincial nature conservation authority) and the Greater Cederberg Biodiversity Corridor Steering Committee.

Compiling detailed information on corridor properties

Working closely with individual landowners, agricultural and nature conservation extension staff compiled relevant information about the land-use practices on the properties concerned. Using 1:10,000 orthophotos, information about the existing status and use of the property, including infrastructure, cultivation, wetlands and other natural habitats, was captured. Second, the landowners' proposals for future agricultural development were mapped. This information was supported by maps of recent fires and the extent of alien invasive species. Finally, an assessment was made of the potential for the property to contribute to the corridor. Areas of incompatibility both within and between neighbouring properties were discussed and resolved where possible. (The important point here is that the voluntary commitment by landowners to contribute to the corridor provides the platform for stewardship negotiation down the line; it is the common ground on which the future stewardship partnership is based.)

Assessment of feasibility for inclusion in corridor and stewardship arrangements

Each property was assessed as a prospective corridor site, depending on:

- the property's contribution to biodiversity targets in the corridor;
- its connectivity (linkage to compatible portions of adjacent properties and overall corridor axis);
- the level of threat to connectivity, development pressures, invasive alien or fire mismanagement threat or incompatible surrounding land uses;
- landowner willingness to cooperate.

Confirmation of inclusion

Consensus was reached among agriculture and nature conservation authorities regarding the compatibility of agricultural resource conservation and nature conservation priorities on each property. Once satisfied, the property was identified as suitable for the application of stewardship options (see below). The suite of conservation stewardship tools used in the development of the GCBC was developed through the piloting and testing of incentives for conservation stewardship among landowners and communities across the CFR. The system was built on a tradition of landowners who, over many years, became involved in the establishment and management of conservancies, private nature reserves and natural heritage sites. It sought to establish the designation of these sites as components of the protected area system and also to grow and expand stewardship beyond the traditional participants.

Incentives for conservation stewardship

Emanating from work conducted by the Botanical Society of South Africa, the research focused on the factors that would encourage landowners to conserve biodiversity in productive landscapes, and on the identification of legal, financial and social incentives for conservation. Important incentives for landowners included assistance with fire and alien plant management and advice on conservation management. A landmark decision, facilitated by the Botanical Society, was the government's inclusion of a legislative provision for tax rebates for properties where landowners designated portions as protected areas under the relevant laws. However, research indicated that the fiscal incentives to take land out of production, to set further land aside for conservation or to incur costs in conservation management would be unlikely to compete with the overwhelming financial returns from productive use of the land. In the GCBC, for example, the benefits of potato production exceed the conservation values by several orders of magnitude. More significant was an appeal to the sense of personal commitment and responsibility of the landowners as custodians of rare and threatened species on their own properties.

Conservation stewardship protocols also benefited from the parallel development of enabling laws and on-the-ground piloting and testing. Legal support for conservation stewardship came from the promulgation of comprehensive legislation for protected areas in South Africa under the *National Environmental Management: Protected Areas Act* (Act No. 57 of 2003). Under this law, protected areas on private land can be designated if they meet specific national standards and have the consent of the landowner. The standards include the conclusion of management plans and management agreements for the specific protected areas. A suite of stewardship options were developed as a result where greater levels of protection, benefit and assistance are provided to landowners coupled with increasing levels of binding commitment and limitations to property use by the landowner. In practice, three options exist – contract nature reserves, biodiversity management agreements/ cooperation agreements and conservation sites (Figure 4.8) – the provisions of which are compared in Table 4.1.

Once a property has been identified as the possible subject for the use of conservation stewardship options through Custodians of Rare and Endangered Wildflowers volunteers (Box 4.1), environmental assessment outcomes, Landcare area-wide planning or another source, agriculture or nature conservation extension staff members approach the landowner with the suite of steward-

Fynbos habitat, Cape of Good Hope, Table Mountain National Park near Cape Town, South Africa

Source: Graeme L. Worboys

Table 4.1 Comparison of stewardship options

Option	Contract nature reserves	Biodiversity management agreements	Conservation sites
Land-use designation	Protected area	No formal designation	Registered as conservation site with nature conservation agency
Protection mechanism	Landowner consent to assignment of a management authority	Landowner enters into management agreement	Landowner agrees to registration of site
Duration	30 years +	10 years +	As agreed
Management mechanism	Adoption of management plan	Adoption of management plan	Management plan not required but advised
Zoning mechanism	Rezoning by local authority involving restrictions on development rights	An option for rezoning	No rezoning
Implementation mechanism	Conclusion of protected area management agreement	Conclusion of biodiversity management agreement	Application for designation of conservation site
Legal mechanism	Notarial deed of servitude over title restricting use	No notarial deed of servitude	No notarial deed of servitude
Nature of protection	No mining or prospecting is permitted	Incompatible land-uses not permitted	No land-use limitations
Tax treatment	Municipal property rates exemption	No property rates exemption	No property rates exemption
Financial benefit	Substantial assistance to landowner for nature conservation management	Eligibility for assistance with nature conservation management	Eligible for professional advice, help with preparation of farm plans

ship options. The steps in the process include:

1   Providing information on the costs and benefits of each of the options to the landowner.
2   Completing all of the relevant property information.
3   Preparation of a management plan for the property.
4   Preparation of a draft Protected Area Management Agreement, Biodiversity Management Agreement or Conservation Site Application.
5   Submission of landowner consent for the assignment of a management authority.
6   Obtaining approval of the provincial and national nature conservation authorities.

7   Conclusion of agreements and application by the landowner and by the relevant authority.
8   A public participation process whereby the intent to designate a contract nature reserve is published for public comment and stakeholders are provided with opportunities to comment.
9   Submission of the package of agreements to the provincial or national minister to initiate the process of designation under the *Protected Areas Act*.
10 Drafting and registering of notarial deed of servitude.

In addition to this property-by-property process, groups of properties can also become involved in

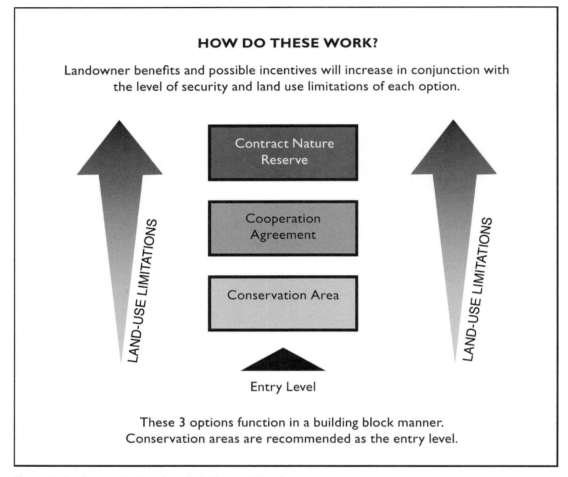

Figure 4.8 Land stewardship options, limitations and benefits

---

Box 4.1 Mobilizing volunteers: Custodians of Rare and Endangered Wildflowers

One of the techniques to promote volunteerism was the Custodians of Rare and Endangered Wildflowers project (CREW). CREW mobilized groups of volunteers in several local areas across the CFR. For example, in the Nieuwoudtville area of the GCBC, CREW focused on enabling linkages between research and development practitioners interested in the unique flora, and local communities desperate for employment and educational opportunities in this remote rural area. The CREW protocol is simple, yet robust. Using existing interest or community groups and identifying champions within these, CREW provided training programmes and site-specific materials to help groups identify rare, endemic and threatened species in the local area. Access was provided to essential resources such as aerial photographs, Geographical Information System (GIS) maps and herbarium records. Support was provided for project development and to access small grant funding for projects. In particular, after field surveys had verified the existence of species of concern, CREW was able to work with specific communities to develop *in situ* and *ex situ* species recovery programmes supported by ongoing monitoring and awareness-building at the local level. The information generated by CREW volunteers fed directly into conservation stewardship and area-wide planning processes.

Protea (Protea sp.) Botanic Gardens, Cape Town, South Africa

Source: Graeme L. Worboys

a collective management arrangement, such as a conservancy, and the whole suite of properties designated by the relevant minister as a Protected Environment after the relevant consents and agreements have been reached.

Benefits and accomplishments

A consideration of the benefits of connectivity conservation, or of participation in connectivity conservation, is crucial if the process is to be sustained and replicated. At this early stage in the development of the GCBC, the early benefits and promise of future benefits influenced authorities, landowners and stakeholders alike to participate. While an explicit identification of the costs and benefits of corridor development has not been conducted, a socio-economic study was planned during 2007 to better understand the impact on landowner decisions of the various land-use options available. Qualitatively, benefits that have accrued or that are likely to accrue are as follows.

The biodiversity corridor has provided multiple benefits for conservation, including:

- identification of biodiversity priorities at the level of individual properties enabled the prioritization of sites for conservation action and landowner participation;
- biodiversity agreements for four properties were concluded by 2006, adding 9000ha to the conservation estate;
- biodiversity management plans were in place for four properties, ensuring improved management of the biodiversity heritage;
- biodiversity agreements on 15 properties were planned for the Sandveld corridor and seven properties were planned for the Cederberg corridor.

Benefits for governance of the corridor include the following:

- The Greater Cederberg Biodiversity Corridor Steering Committee was established, has been operating satisfactorily since 2003 and has provided a platform for government and civil society stakeholders to interact, share concerns and reach consensus, resulting in a marked improvement in relationships among the authorities and between authorities and stakeholders in the region.
- A Sandveld Task Team was established to communicate about, seek solutions to and resolve differences regarding the way forward for this specific subregion.
- A Sandveld Action Plan was prepared and submitted to the provincial minister for approval.

Authorities and institutions also benefited:

- Agriculture, water affairs and nature conservation officials began to work together in a much greater spirit of cooperation after the GCBC aligned their goals and work programmes.
- Former antagonistic approaches resulting in poor decision making were replaced with regular forums for joint decision making supported by a draft Memorandum of Understanding that was developed as one of the first legally binding inter-sectoral cooperation agreements.

- Greater capacity was developed among agricultural and nature conservation extension workers to understand and apply the provisions of the new biodiversity and nature conservation laws.
- A means to combine the best components of area-wide planning with conservation stewardship was piloted, setting the stage for the adoption of these guidelines across the region.

Benefits also accrued to landowners, communities, farm workers and the agricultural sector:

- Landowners who individually were unable to address the underlying causes of loss of productivity and depletion of groundwater resources found a collective platform to understand and develop coordinated responses.
- Efforts to involve the agricultural and tourism sectors in the development of best practice guidance resulted in the adoption of progressive principles for sustainable practices – for example, the Rooibos Council's adoption of biodiversity guidelines, and also settled differences among stakeholders and critics.
- Assessments of properties in the context of conservation and development corridors generated optimism regarding the development of other enterprises on farms to bolster the flagging agricultural economy and sustain and increase employment opportunities.
- Agri-tourism products, including tourism and heritage routes, were planned and poverty-relief funding and other project funding was directed into the planning and management of new tourism products involving local communities.
- Increased capacity of landowners to effectively manage biodiversity was facilitated through the development of management plans and management partnerships.

Finally, there were benefits in the form of increased knowledge and information:

- Previously coarse conservation plans were refined into sophisticated and defensible fine-scale plans detailed to the level of individual properties.
- Gaps in information regarding the distribution and status of threatened species were filled, enabling species recovery plans to be developed, herbarium records to be improved, 'lost' species to be rediscovered, and new species to be identified and described.
- Sequential mapping of land-use transformation over a 12-year period gave a clear indication of rates of change.

Lessons learned

The GCBC is a programme in progress, epitomizing the notion that the best learning is derived from *in situ* experience as the proponents of the corridor encounter and deal with the emerging issues. In broad terms, the lessons of the GCBC, of area-wide planning and of conservation stewardship in this context include the following.

Knowledge and information sharing facilitate landowner engagement

One of the most encouraging aspects of this experience with implementing stewardship was the willingness of landowners and authorities alike to participate. The programme demonstrated that knowledge and information as well as communication are keys to success. On the one hand, it is encouraging to note that incentives for stewardship are not limited to financial rewards. On the other hand, it quickly was realized that facilitating stewardship requires skilled and deft handling of a complex social programme, supported by a relatively stable institutional setting, as well as experienced and committed staff.

A cooperative approach that welcomes diverse actors has multiple management benefits

The GCBC is guided by a Steering Committee, Project Coordination Unit and Task Teams where specific issues are championed. The gathering of a diverse group of stakeholders involving government and civil society can be regarded as a significant achievement in its own right, and its latent potential as an active strategic learning vehicle has yet to be fully captured. A review of the Steering Committee functioning indicated that greater emphasis could be given to exploring emergent issues, surfacing questions and drawing conclusions that directly impact on planning and further action (Community Development Resource Association, 2006) and making this new interactive style of conservation governance structure a distinctly 'social enterprise'.

The pace of progress toward connectivity conservation outcomes must match the capacity of participants

An important lesson is that even though the methods promise good returns for conservation and involvement, this has stretched the capacity of the organizations and individuals involved. A fine balance has to be achieved between encouraging active progress and ensuring that the back-up processes are in place to meet the expectations and commitments made. The programme has shown how resources among organizations can be pooled, how agreed processes can result in more efficient and effective responses by several organizations working together and how the capacity of the wider stewardship community can be harnessed.

New tools are still needed to encourage and promote landowner participation

The programme has shown that a well-organized approach will yield quick returns. However, a question remains regarding the scaling up of this approach over a much wider area and involvement in the long term. There remains a need to influence change in the way in which landowners perceive the value of biodiversity on their properties and in how new opportunities for compatible land-use activities can be initiated and promoted. In this regard, changes are required to the prevailing set of incentives and disincentives that impact landowner behaviour in the long term. Further research is required into the economic incentives for changes in land use and the influences of the fiscal and regulatory environment.

Conclusion

The GCBC can be regarded as a complex biological and social experiment in the new South Africa. In particular, it has harnessed the scientific research heritage of the CFR to enable some of the most progressive and systematic connectivity conservation planning in the world. Perhaps more importantly, it is being implemented in the social and economic context of a landscape undergoing rapid change, where despite the expressed goals of sustainable development, the means to achieve this are quite elusive. Through a combination of well-planned and -executed methods of participatory planning and the application of stewardship tools, the GCBC makes a significant contribution to developing practice in connectivity conservation management. However, its real value as a case study is closely linked to the deliberate process of establishing the programme within a robust governance and institutional framework. It is reflexive and flexible, enables learning by doing, is responsive to the local context and is resonant within the broader C.A.P.E. programme.

Acknowledgements

This case study is based on the seminal work by Mark Botha and Chris Martens who established the conservation stewardship programme in the CFR. Further perspectives and lessons learned have been drawn from Domitilla Raimondo and Ismail Ebrahim of the CREW project and from Cape Flats Nature under the leadership of Tanya Goldman and Zwai Peter. These pioneers and their voluntary co-workers have helped to design and promote new ways to engage people in connectivity conservation activities.

Conserving connectivity in the Greater Virunga Landscape

Andrew J. Plumptre, Deo Kujirakwinja, Isaiah Owiunji, Edgar Buhanga, Deo Mbula and Aggrey Rwetsiba

Setting

The Greater Virunga Landscape (1,310,000ha, Figure 4.9) straddles the international boundary of the Democratic Republic of Congo (DRC), Rwanda and Uganda. This connectivity conservation area highlights transboundary collaboration within a politically explosive, highly threatened landscape that truly came 'from the bottom up'. Main achievements can be measured as the continued conservation of species such as the mountain gorilla (*Gorilla beringei beringei*) and successful cross-border camaraderie. The Greater Virunga Landscape is formed by 12 contiguous or neighbouring protected areas: Virunga National

Park (DRC); Volcanoes National Park (Rwanda); Mgahinga Gorilla, Queen Elizabeth, Rwenzori Mountains, Kibale and Semuliki National Parks; Kasyoha-Kitomi, Rwenzori and Kalinzu Forest Reserves; and Kyambura and Kigezi Wildlife Reserves (Uganda). Virunga and Rwenzori parks are world heritage sites, Queen Elizabeth National Park is a biosphere reserve and Lake George, which is surrounded by Queen Elizabeth on three sides, is a Ramsar site. Bwindi Impenetrable National Park, also a world heritage site, used to be contiguous with a controlled hunting area in the DRC that linked to Virunga National Park, but this connection has been lost over the years to

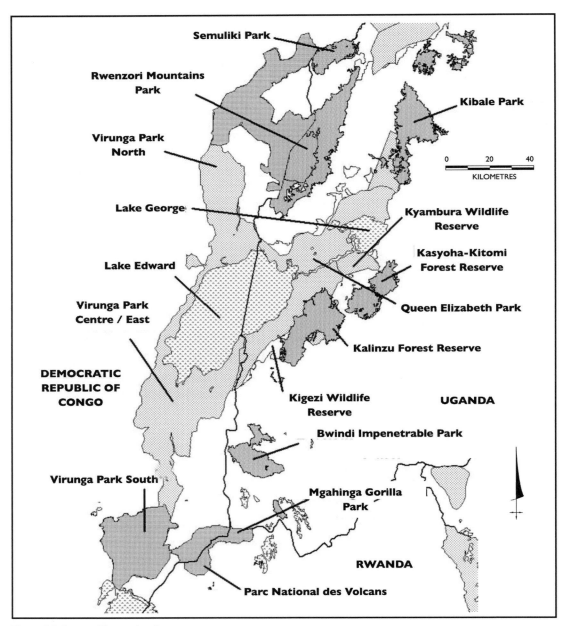

Figure 4.9 Greater Virunga Landscape

encroachment for land. The parks and wildlife reserves in the Congo are managed by the Institut Congolais pour la Conservation de la Nature, in Rwanda by the Office Rwandais de Tourisme et Parcs Nationaux and in Uganda by the Uganda Wildlife Authority (formerly Uganda National Parks and Game Department), and the forest reserves in Uganda by the National Forest Authority. The Mikeno sector (south-east) of Virunga National Park, Mgahinga Gorilla National Park and Volcanoes National Park are all part of the Virunga Volcanoes Massif.

As a result of the varied altitude (from 600 to 5100m) and habitats (from glaciers and bare rock to alpine habitats, montane and medium altitude forests and savanna and wetland habitats), this landscape contains more vertebrate species than any other contiguous landscape in Africa and possibly the world (Plumptre et al, 2003). It also contains a high number of endemic species (those found only in the Albertine Rift) as well as globally threatened species (Table 4.2). Virunga National Park (Le Parc National de Virunga) was Africa's first national park, created in 1925 and at that time included the Volcanoes National Park (Parc National des Volcans) in Rwanda. The forested areas in Uganda were protected as forest reserves in the early 1930s and Queen Elizabeth Park was created in 1952. Rwenzori Mountains, Semuliki, Kibale, Bwindi Impenetrable and Maghinga Gorilla National Parks were converted from forest reserves in the early 1990s.

Connectivity exists between protected areas that are adjacent to each other across the international borders and also between those within Uganda. In the past, elephants would migrate from the south to the north of this landscape and further north in Uganda towards Sudan and between Kibale Forest and Rwenzori National Park (Wing and Buss, 1970). Many of these connections have been severed by increasing human population expanding to farm the fertile land in this region and many of the protected areas now exhibit a hard edge between the natural habitat and farmland. As a result, much of this migration has been halted. However, within the landscape it is still possible for species to move between protected areas, although in some areas these corridors are very narrow. For instance the corridor linking Queen Elizabeth Park to Virunga Park north of Lake Edward has an enclave formed by a fishing village that narrows it further. This is also true west of Lake George (Figure 4.9). The corridor between Kyambura Wildlife Reserve and Kasyoha-Kitomi Forest is very narrow (about 30m at its narrowest) and yet elephants, chimpanzees and other species still move through it according to local people (Nampindo and Plumptre, 2005).

For much of the time that these protected areas have existed, they have been managed as separate protected areas without much attention paid to their connectivity. In Uganda there are also connectivity issues between different protected areas. There was some informal cross-border collaboration between Virunga and Queen Elizabeth parks in the 1970s, when poaching of wildlife was intense in Uganda and resources available to parks staff were limited. At that time the Institut Congolais pour la Conservation de la

Table 4.2 Number of species of vertebrate and plant taxa recorded in the Greater Virunga Landscape

Taxon	Species richness	Endemic species	Threatened species
Mammals	278	30	22
Birds	871	31	16
Reptiles	134	12	1
Amphibians	84	21	10
Fish	81	56	?
Plants	3180	246	27

Nature gave support to the Uganda National Parks through gifts of fuel, vehicle tyres and other equipment. None of this was formalized, however. Suggestions were made in the late 1980s (D'Huart, 1989) to promote cross-border collaboration between Queen Elizabeth National Park and Virunga National Park, but for the most part this remained a suggestion only.

War started in the Virunga Volcanoes region in late 1990, when the Rwanda Patriotic Front invaded Rwanda from the Ugandan side. This continued with intermittent peace talks up to the Rwandan genocide in 1994. Following the genocide, intermittent rebel activity continued to occur from bases in the DRC into Rwanda, and to a lesser extent into Uganda, up to 2001/2002. Uganda and Rwanda nationals were involved in helping to overthrow President Mobutu of what was then Zaire and installing Laurent Kabila as president of the newly named Democratic Republic of Congo in 1996. Fighting continued with Ugandan and Rwandan military based in DRC for several more years up to the early 2000s. A separate rebel group opposing the Ugandan Government, the Allied Democratic Front, was based in the Rwenzori Massif from 1997 to 2002 and was pushed west into the lowland forest in Virunga National Park by the Ugandan Defence Forces.

The connectivity conservation initiative

In 1991 the Mountain Gorilla Project, which had been operating in Rwanda to support conservation of the gorillas in the Volcanoes park, expanded its activities and became the regional International Gorilla Conservation Programme. With its main focus on the mountain gorilla, the Programme aimed to conserve the natural movements of this species between the three countries. One of its main activities was to promote cross-border collaboration between the three countries in the Virunga Volcanoes Massif. A process was developed that brought together park wardens from each country to plan joint activities together and encouraged regional communication and regional meetings with other conservation NGOs and protected area authorities. This process continued with regular training of wardens and joint planning meetings despite the fact that the

three countries have been at war with each other to different extents (Lanjouw et al, 2001).

In 2003, the Wildlife Conservation Society (WCS) began supporting a process of transboundary collaboration between Uganda and the DRC for the other protected areas in the Greater Virunga Landscape, north of the Virunga Volcanoes. This initiative used a similar process to the one developed by the International Gorilla Conservation Programme, which worked with wardens and NGOs in those parks to address issues pertinent to the region. However, the conservation issues were very different between the two areas of intervention. In the Bwindi and Virunga Volcanoes region, the issues concerned poaching of gorillas for infant trafficking, crop raiding by gorillas, gorilla health monitoring, (until recently) the presence of armed rebel groups in the Virunga Volcanoes, the need to work with the Rwandan, Congolese and Ugandan military and the snaring of ungulates for meat. In the Queen Elizabeth, Rwenzori, Semuliki and Virunga areas the issues were illegal wildlife/ wildlife products trade, including ivory trade, poaching of animals for meat with guns, timber trade across the border from the DRC to Uganda, the presence of rebel groups in the north of the Virunga park, encroachment by people looking for land and over-fishing on Lake Edward.

Much of the transboundary collaboration was informal, working with protected area authorities at the site level. This is because it was impossible to obtain agreements at a higher level while the countries had political differences. Recently the International Gorilla Conservation Programme funded a process to develop a Memorandum of Understanding (MOU) between the protected area authorities and subsequently the respective ministries of the three countries to formalize the transboundary collaboration with a tripartite agreement. The process for the development of the MOU and agreement looked at a conceptualized continuum of potential transboundary collaboration ranging from zero collaboration at one end to the management of one transboundary protected area at the other extreme of the continuum (Sandwith et al, 2001). Protected area authorities and subsequently ministries then discussed where along this continuum they felt most comfortable.

Most felt that a transboundary park was too ambitious at the time, and were more comfortable with management at a landscape scale through collaboration, while recognizing the territorial integrity of protected areas in each country. It is possible that with time this position will change as collaboration continues. In 2005, the protected area authorities led a process to develop a transboundary strategic plan for most of the Greater Virunga Landscape (excluding the forest reserves, as they are not on the international borders).

Transboundary conservation in the Greater Virunga Landscape grew organically. Initially its focus was on mountain gorillas in the 5 per cent of the landscape that contains this species. One of the first activities implemented by the WCS was an assessment of landscape species in the Greater Virunga Landscape. Landscape species are those that usually live at low density, range over large areas, tend to be impacted by human activities and require larger land bases in order to survive than can be contained within most protected areas (Sanderson et al, 2002b). The process looked at a large list of potential species but whittled these down to 13. These were thought to be the species that most needed management at the scale of the landscape and that together occurred throughout most of the habitat types in the landscape. Collectively the chosen 13 were likely to be threatened by most of the major threats in the landscape (Plumptre et al, 2007). Lions (*Panthera leo*) were one of the species that was most threatened and needed management at a landscape scale. At the time there were between 100 and 150 lions in Queen Elizabeth National Park (Dricuru, 1999) and an unknown number in Virunga Park, although heavy poaching of prey species and lions themselves has probably reduced their numbers in the recent past. It was clear that this species, one of the main attractions for tourism and hence revenue generation, required management at a larger scale than the individual protected areas. Other species included apes (mountain gorilla and chimpanzee (*Pan troglodytes*)), ungulates (elephants (*Loxodonta africana*), buffalo (*Syncerus caffer*), hippopotamus (*Hippopotamus amphibious*), Rwenzori duiker (*Cephalophus rubidus*) and sitatunga (*Tragelaphus spekei*)), carnivores (leopards (*Panthera pardus*), golden cats (*Felis aurata*)) and birds (crowned eagle (*Stephanoaetus coronatus*), lappet-faced vulture (*Torgos tracheliotus*) and lesser flamingo (*Phoeniconaias minor*)). In collaboration with Institut Congolais pour la Conservation de la Nature and the Uganda Wildlife Authority, the WCS supported research on some of these species to better understand their movements between the three countries.

Much of the connectivity in this landscape already existed within the boundaries of the protected areas. However, some of the existing corridors were very narrow and research examined options for expanding these, either through land purchases or conservation easements, or encouraging wildlife-friendly crops such as tree plantations alongside the corridor areas to increase their effective width (Nampindo and Plumptre, 2005; Nampindo et al, 2006).

Connectivity conservation management

In the initial stages of transboundary collaboration it was impossible to work between ministries or governments because of the political situation in the Great Lakes region of Africa. As a result, the collaboration grew from the grass roots level rather than starting at a higher level under the legal, policy and implementation framework of relevant international and regional treaties or multilateral environmental agreements such as the Bonn Convention on the *Conservation of Migratory Species* and the *Convention on Biological Diversity*. In some ways the political situation was fortuitous because by working bottom up several benefits subsequently have been observed. Park wardens soon came to understand the benefits of collaborating and communicating between themselves about threats to conservation, and soon saw benefits in having 'friends' across the border when they needed to tackle threats that emanated from a neighbouring protected area. As a result, the wardens have subsequently promoted the collaboration to their staff at headquarters and they in turn have promoted collaboration to their respective ministries.

Throughout the landscape the protected area authorities and the NGOs realized the need to work with other stakeholders in the region. Around the Virunga Volcanoes and Bwindi, many resources were put into working more closely with local communities through integrated conservation and development programmes. A trust fund was established for Bwindi and Mgahinga parks, from which 60 per cent of the interest was used to support development projects and income generating activities within the communities adjacent to these parks. Around Queen Elizabeth, Rwenzori and Virunga parks an effort emerged to work with the military, police, judiciary, customs and immigration officials to tackle some of the main threats to conservation in these areas from poaching activities. The importance of involving these other stakeholders cannot be over emphasized. For instance, one of the problems park wardens faced in the Rwenzori, Semuliki, Kibale and Queen Elizabeth National Parks was that poachers that were arrested were usually fined less than the value of the meat with which they had been caught. As a result there was no disincentive to continued poaching. A regional meeting held to look at this issue highlighted the value of these animals in terms of the tourism revenue they generate for Uganda. As a result the police and judiciary started giving stiffer penalties within the legal range allowed.

Regional workshops and meetings were facilitated (financially and technically) by either the International Gorilla Conservation Programme or the WCS (depending on geographical location). Agenda for the workshops were decided during wardens' meetings or at previous workshops by participants who were present, but they generally aimed to tackle issues that were relevant to current management needs. Where experience was lacking, the International Gorilla Conservation Programme or the WCS would bring in experts who could help with training: examples include conflict resolution, planning for insecurity and wildlife trade. These helped to build the skills of both the protected area and NGO staff attending the meetings. Wardens meetings allowed more detailed discussions of threats to the parks and the sharing of more sensitive information.

While initially the transboundary collaboration was driven by the NGOs, it steadily changed until the International Gorilla Conservation Programme and the WCS were playing the role of

facilitators of the process with the protected area authorities making all the management decisions. The only constraints to this were the limits of the NGOs' funding; however, with long-term planning it was possible to raise funds for necessary activities. This process culminated in the development of a transboundary strategic plan, which was driven by the three executive directors of the government agencies – the Institut Congolais pour la Conservation de la Nature, the Office Rwandais de Tourisme et Parcs Nationaux and the Uganda Wildlife Authority.

The threats to the conservation of this landscape constantly evolve and the responses need to be flexible as a result. While the military activity was a major concern in 15 years that ended in 2006, it was declining and peace was hoped for in the DRC. Illegal settlement of people in the Virunga National Park was a major issue that needed to be addressed because it was reducing the functionality of existing corridors. About 20,000 encroachers settled in Virunga Park in the early 2000s, almost blocking the corridor north of Lake Edward between the Congo and Uganda. It was only with help from the collaboration in Uganda that these people were moved back into Uganda. There were still people settled in the corridor to the west of Lake Edward that links the southern and northern parts of Virunga Park and, at the time of writing, this corridor was no longer functional. Institut Congolais pour la Conservation de la Nature and its NGO partners were trying to work with local political leaders to reopen this corridor.

Benefits and accomplishments

The general benefits of transboundary conservation have been summarized elsewhere (Sandwith et al, 2001; van der Linde et al, 2001; Wilkie et al, 2001). In this specific case study, there have been many benefits from the collaboration and improved coordination between the countries. One of the main benefits has been the ability to work with neighbouring protected area authority staff to control the actions of their militaries in the protected areas. Parks staff have been threatened or at risk when entering the parks at times because of the presence of military from another country. Clear communication about the movements of parks staff has prevented incidents of 'friendly fire'. As a result it has been possible to patrol the parks for illegal activities despite the presence of armed groups. Other benefits are as follows:

- The friendships and camaraderie that develop between parks staff across borders reinforced to their desire to help each other resolve threats that were transboundary in nature.
- In the past poachers knew they could flee across the border and that the parks staff couldn't follow; now, jointly planned patrols along the borders significantly reduced illegal hunting of wildlife. This was much easier to implement in the lowland areas than in the mountain blocks of the Virunga Volcanoes and particularly the Rwenzori Massif because of the more difficult terrain.
- The regional meetings also benefited the three countries because they were used to provide training to protected area staff and helped to bring people who were at different educational/experience levels up to a similar level of skills. It also reduced the costs of training in the three countries by bringing people together to one training session.
- Meetings between wardens also helped to reduce suspicions between countries, as parks staff realized the issues that each protected area was dealing with. This reduction in suspicion was extremely important and was what catalysed further collaboration.
- While research on movements of landscape species across borders is still in its infancy, it was clear that elephants and lions moved across the Ishasha river that separates Virunga and Queen Elizabeth National Parks. Research was underway to identify where the important crossing points were and how the animals' movements may be influenced by human activities. These results will be used to help manage in a way that encourages animal movements.
- Tourism to mountain gorillas is constrained by the habituated groups that cross international borders. Agreements that existed between the Congo and Rwanda to allow tourists to cross the border while tracking the gorillas were being revisited at the time of writing. Visits to the gorillas are the major tourism attraction in

this landscape at present, and generate a large proportion of the revenues.
- Awareness created among other law enforcement agencies such as the police, judiciary, customs and military helped to reduce illegal activities across borders.

Lessons learned
Personal relationships can enhance connectivity conservation success

One of the important lessons is the value of bringing people from different protected areas together to create and build friendships. The social hours after a workshop often are as important as the workshop itself. Once camaraderie develops between protected area staff, it is much easier to implement collaboration and coordination between sites. It is important to maintain these friendships even when there are issues that cause friction between the countries.

Local authorities can help promote management actions at higher levels

Managing the politics was difficult at times, primarily at the local level because it is often at this level that illegal activities occur and can be linked to local political leaders. It often proved useful to employ the knowledge of these illegal actions by an adjacent country to help the protected area authorities put pressure on their local political leaders to stop them. Examples include when local leaders in Rwanda encouraged people to enter the Virunga Park in the DRC to cultivate land. Pressure from the parks staff in Rwanda and international concern soon moved the encroaching people back into Rwanda.

Species needs provide a rationale for connectivity conservation

There is a need to provide good reasons why the connectivity in landscapes such as these is needed. The landscape species approach can help people conceptualize the need to think about managing for connectivity and why certain species may need to be actively managed. It also can be used to help justify the maintenance or rehabilitation of corridors and the need for research on these species.

A neutral arbiter can smooth over power imbalances between agencies

While the transboundary collaboration now could be managed solely by the protected area authorities with financial support from NGOs or donors, there still is a role for a neutral party to help maintain equality between different institutions. There can be a tendency for the better funded institution to dominate at meetings because the levels of funding increase staff confidence and the ability to implement plans. Yet in this region, history shows that there have been shifts of status over the years. In the 1970s and 1980s, Uganda was the poorer cousin while Rwanda and the DRC were doing well. In the 1990s, Rwanda was the poor cousin and the Congo had more resources. It is therefore important for all parties to remember this and try to make sure neutrality is maintained.

Education about large landscape needs led to support for connectivity conservation

Support to the transboundary collaboration was given in the belief that it would help retain and support connectivity conservation within the Greater Virunga Landscape. The fact that the landscape is now discussed at meetings is already leading to planning at a protected area level that includes looking at the connectivity with other areas. Regional meetings that have identified landscape species have helped managers to understand better the need for landscape management and why connectivity research is needed. Ongoing research is looking at the connectivity between sites in the landscape, particularly in the areas where corridors are at their narrowest. Therefore, illustrating the values and importance of the larger landscape and arguing the need to maintain connectivity led to a better understanding of the need for research on corridor use and design. By involving managers in planning the research, the results are much more likely to lead to management action being taken. It is also important to do this with the donor community if funds are to flow to support the landscape management. The United States Agency fo International Development (USAID) has been very receptive to conservation at a landscape scale and has helped to target funds from development

projects to corridor areas around Queen Elizabeth Park in Uganda as well as supporting transboundary collaboration between the protected area authorities.

A 'bottom-up' approach can facilitate connectivity conservation success

The bottom-up approach to transboundary collaboration, while dictated by political factors, seems to have been very successful. The collaboration in the Greater Virunga Landscape avoided some of the problems that have been faced in other transboundary areas where the approach was top-down. Political support by the protected area institutions in the field was quick, and as a result it was fairly easy to work on agreements at higher levels because of the appreciation of the value of the approach. However, the bottom-up approach cannot continue for too long before the importance of agreements and support from higher levels soon becomes apparent. Issues such as staff moving across international borders, sharing radio frequencies between parks and sharing resources all require higher level agreements before they can be implemented. The formal agreements are necessary to move further along the continuum towards the collaboration and management of one protected area. However, it is the informal collaboration between staff on the ground that is most important in making the whole thing happen.

Conclusion

The Greater Virunga Landscape is still highly threatened. Oil exploration within the Albertine Rift may come to parts of this landscape, mining for lime and gold are real possibilities in the near future and the large-scale encroachment of parts of Virunga National Park still leave this protected area very vulnerable. Each individual protected area on its own will struggle to provide the rationales to tackle these threats and to minimize any impacts if they go ahead. However, together, as Africa's and possibly the world's most biodiverse landscape, they stand a better chance of maintaining their ecological integrity. Transboundary collaboration will be one of the tools that helps maintain this integrity.

Maloti–Drakensberg Transfrontier Conservation and Development Programme: A South African perspective

Kevan Zunckel

Setting

The Maloti and Drakensberg mountain ranges form the eastern and southern portions of the boundary between the Kingdom of Lesotho and the Republic of South Africa. The Maloti Mountains are in the northern portion of this transfrontier conservation area and lie between the district of Butha-Buthe in Lesotho and the Free State Province in South Africa. The Drakensberg Mountains run the full length of the boundary between the district of Mokhotlong in Lesotho and the province of KwaZulu-Natal in South Africa, and the districts of Qachas Nek and Quthing in Lesotho and the province of the Eastern Cape in South Africa.

The full extent of the Maloti Drakensberg Mountain bioregion is approximately 5,200,000ha, with the contributions from both countries being almost equal. The total length of the international boundary within the bioregion is approximately 730km. These figures were to be revised once detailed vegetation surveys had been completed in the second half of 2007.

Topographically, the bioregion differs significantly between the two countries. In Lesotho, the Maloti Mountains form a continuous landscape of rounded mountains dropping off into deep valleys, which drain the country into the Senqu (Lesotho) and Orange (South Africa) Rivers to the south-west. In South Africa, the Drakensberg Mountains are predominantly sheer basalt cliffs, which drop off from the international boundary into the sandstone foothills. These are deeply incised by numerous eastward flowing rivers. In the north of the bioregion, the ranges are at their highest, with altitudes exceeding 3000m; while in the south the average height of the peaks is generally below this level. The Drakensberg range is also more dramatic in the north in comparison to the south (rainfall and temperature are also slightly higher).

An illustration of this is the uThukela Falls, which drop almost 1000m and are claimed to be the second highest waterfall in the world. Another feature is Thaba Ntlenyana ('The Beautiful Little Mountain') in Lesotho, which, at 3482m, is the highest point in Africa south of Mount Kilimanjaro.

Kniphofia caulescens, Maloti Mountains, Lesotho

Source: Greig Stewart

Lesotho is classified as one of the least developed countries in the world, while South Africa is comparatively economically strong, thus providing a context of significant difference. Socially there are similarities between Lesotho and South Africa's Free State Province where Sotho is the dominant culture. A greater diversity occurs elsewhere in South Africa where the Zulu culture dominates in the KwaZulu-Natal Province and the Xhosa culture is prevalent in the Eastern Cape Province.

The economic context in Lesotho is generally rural and there is little commercial activity that is significant enough to render the population self-sufficient. Some mining activities and textile manufacturing offer opportunities, and taxes on the earnings of migrant labour contribute significantly to the state coffers. Years ago, when the Kingdom of Lesotho extended across the Caledon River into the rich maize-growing areas that are now part of the Free State Province in South Africa, the country had greater economic diversity. Cross-border dynamics are still influenced by this history. The economy in the South African portion of the bioregion is more established and diverse, and the agricultural and tourism sectors dominate. Agriculture includes both extensive and intensive livestock farming and crop production.

Tourism plays a major role in South Africa with a well established industry where supply currently exceeds demand. Lesotho, on the other hand, is poorly developed in this regard and has huge potential for growth.

More recently the concept of payment for ecosystem services is beginning to emerge as a distinct opportunity. Lesotho is already selling water to South Africa through the Lesotho Highlands Development Authority under a bilateral agreement between the two countries. Through this initiative the country also is self-sufficient in terms of energy supply through the hydroelectrical systems associated with the Katse Dam. More direct economic benefits from this arrangement still need to manifest themselves in Lesotho. The same opportunities exist in South Africa and are being explored at the time of writing.

The earliest record of land use is that of Stone Age hunter-gatherers (the Bushman or San) whose legacy of globally significant rock art remains an important archaeological feature of the bioregion. A pastoral system was introduced by the Iron Age Bantu-speaking nations who began to move into the area in the late 17th century. Together with white settlers who arrived in the 1830s, the Bantus eventually reduced the numbers of San so significantly that it is popularly believed that they were exterminated from the area by the 1880s. The original occupation of land in South Africa for agricultural purposes was limited to the foothills of the escarpment, with much of the rugged terrain remaining Crown land that could be hired for grazing.

A communal land tenure system dominates in Lesotho, with most of the area being under subsistence agriculture with extensive livestock grazing and crop production. The extreme winter temperatures accompanied by frequent snow mean that these activities are seasonal, with large portions of the bioregion being accessed only in summer. Protected areas in Lesotho are the formally proclaimed Sehlabathebe National Park (6795ha), the Bokong Nature Reserve (1953ha) and the Ts'ehlanyane National Park (5394ha).

Communal area, Mnweni Valley, northern Drakensberg

Source: Kevan Zunckel

With the different topography in South Africa, more of the bioregion is accessible, but the extremes between winter and summer also place seasonal limitations on utilization. Land tenure in South Africa is now diverse with state, private and communal ownership all being evident.

State-owned land in South Africa is in the form of formally protected areas including a world heritage site (uKhahlamba Drakensberg Park), two national parks (Golden Gate Highlands and Qwa Qwa) and a series of provincial nature reserves (Sterkfontein Dam, Coleford, Ntsikeni and Malekgalonyane). All of these have their own history and were proclaimed at different times, but the most significant is the uKhahlamba Drakensberg Park World Heritage Site (242,813ha), which has it origins in the recognition of the area as a significant water catchment. Its establishment history is rich, with initial proclamation beginning in 1903 and progressing into the 1980s through the use of a variety of statutes.

Both Lesotho and South Africa are under democratic governance systems, although Lesotho still has an active monarchy. Although much of Lesotho's governance emanates out of its capital city of Maseru, there is a recently introduced system of local governance through district council structures. Traditional authority is recognized through the inclusion of traditional leaders in these structures.

South Africa introduced a local government system after it achieved democracy in 1994, with the country's nine new provinces being divided into numerous district and local municipalities to which implementation responsibility has been devolved. The provincial structures provide support to the local municipalities, with national departments providing the policy and legal frameworks. As with Lesotho, traditional authorities are also recognized and are included in decision-making processes.

The connectivity conservation initiative

While this portion of the international boundary between Lesotho and South Africa is well placed ecologically (that is, they are on an international watershed), the two countries share many common interests in the bioregion. Mostly these are cultural, economic and social, and it is on this

basis that officials from Lesotho approached what was then the Natal Parks Board (now Ezemvelo KZN Wildlife) in the early 1980s to discuss the possibility of collaborative management. These initial discussions grew to include other decision makers in South Africa and led to the signing of the Giant's Castle Declaration in 1997. In that document the key land managers recorded their collective agreement that the bioregion contained features of international significance and committed themselves to manage the area collaboratively.

This new collaboration led to a two-year project-preparation phase in 1999 and 2000, with a view to acquiring international donor funding for the implementation phase. Phase 1 was closely followed by the signing of an MOU at Sehlabathebe National Park in Lesotho in June 2001. On the strength of this MOU, grant agreements with the World Bank were then signed in July 2002 by the Ministry of Environment, Gender and Youth Affairs (now known as the Ministry of Tourism, Environment and Culture) in Lesotho and the Department of Environmental Affairs and Tourism in South Africa. These agreements were instrumental in securing funding from the Global Environmental Facility for a five-year implementation phase, which began with the establishment of two project coordinating units in the beginning of 2003.

The vision of the implementation phase was to: 'establish a framework for cooperation between Lesotho and South Africa to ensure the protection and sustainable use of the natural and cultural heritage of the Maloti–Drakensberg Mountains for the benefit of present and future generations'. The original rationale for the establishment of the Maloti–Drakensberg Transfrontier Conservation and Development Area (Figure 4.10) is expressed in the declaration that decision makers made at a workshop held at Giant's Castle in September 1997. The declaration reads as follows:

In recognition of the grandeur and magnificence of the Lesotho Highlands and the KwaZulu-Natal Drakensberg, the rich and unique biodiversity of these mountains, the singularity of their geological history, their importance as a source of water, the unparalleled richness of their cultural history and rock art, their potential as a major tourism focus for

Southern Africa and the desirability of a cohesive land use plan, joint management and control to initiate sustainable development and alleviate poverty in the area, it was unanimously resolved that the workshop endorse the need for the establishment of the Transfrontier Conservation and Development Area and work together towards its establishment and maintenance.

From the above rationale it is clear that the vision always has been at the landscape level and the goal to conserve the full suite of biodiversity and cultural sites. In addition to this, the concept of ecological functionality is reflected in the declaration's reference to uKhahlamba Drakensberg Park being recognized as a wetland of international importance through the Ramsar Convention. An emphasis has been placed on enhancing the conservation status of the formally protected areas that occur within the bioregion as well as conserving the connectivity between these.

As a brief indication of the richness of the natural resources of the bioregion, the Drakensberg Alpine Centre has 2520 angiosperms (flowering plants) recorded, of which 37 per cent are southern African endemics and 13 per cent are local endemics with very limited distribution ranges. To put this into context, the Drakensberg Alpine Centre is recognized as that portion of the bioregion that is generally above 1800m, which is approximately 4,000,000ha or 77 per cent of the bioregion. These figures could well increase if surveys were extended to the full extent of the landscape.

This unique bioregion has some 119 plant and animal species that are threatened and are listed in the *IUCN Red List of Threatened Species* (Baillie et al, 2004). Some of these threatened species are the Drakensberg cycad (*Encephalartos ghellinckii*), various lilies and orchids, and birds such as the bearded vulture (*Gypaetus barbatus*) and the Cape vulture (*Gyps coprotheres*). Forty-one out of the 43 southern African endemic bird species breed in this bioregion. Thirty-two of these are endemic to the bioregion. There are 11 endemic mammal species in the area. The area is also considered to be one of eight major centres of diversity for reptiles and amphibians in southern Africa, there being about 40 endemic species present. These levels of diversity and endemism coupled with the existence of the largest concentration of rock art and paintings in sub-Saharan Africa led to the declaration, in December 2000, of one of the largest parks in the bioregion, the Ukhahlamba-Drakensberg Park, as a world heritage site.

Northern Drakensberg

Source: Kevan Zunckel

Drakensberg Mountains, South Africa

Source: Graeme L. Worboys

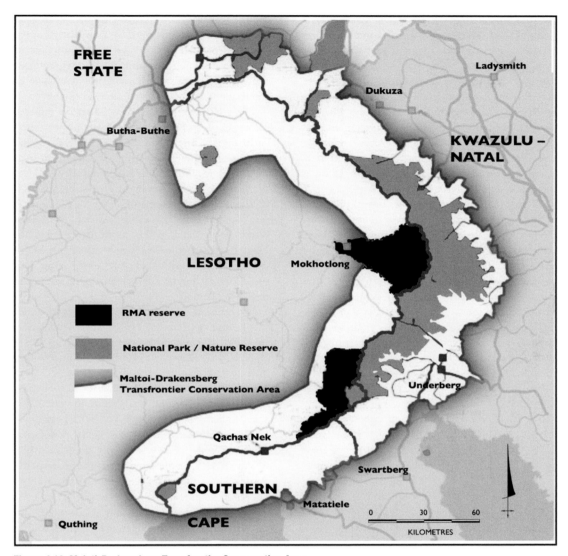

Figure 4.10 Maloti-Drakensberg Transfrontier Conservation Area

If one were to put forward a species that epitomizes the transfrontier nature of this initiative, it is the bearded vulture. In recognition of the endangered status of this flagship species, a population and habitat viability assessment recently has been completed with specialists from both countries collaborating to determine the conservation measures required. These will be captured in a 20-year conservation and development strategy and five-year action plan (described below). All the levels of collaboration required to maintain this initiative as a whole will be necessary for this species on its own.

Connectivity conservation management

The current instrument of agreement between the two countries (the MOU) establishes a bilateral steering committee, which is co-chaired by the Permanent Secretary of the Ministry of Tourism, Environment and Culture from Lesotho and the Director of Transfrontier Conservation Areas of the Department of Environmental Affairs and Tourism in South Africa. The committee is comprised of the members of the respective national coordination mechanisms (the project coordinating committees). The long-term nature of this initiative is recognized by the bilateral steering committee and there is agreement that the current leadership structures will be entrenched in an updated and upgraded international agreement. The latter will also bring a ministerial committee into being.

Two of the main deliverables of this phase are a 20-year strategy and a five-year action plan for the next phase. In recognition of these, it has been accepted that the existing MOU needs to be updated to reflect the findings of the current phase. In the course of so doing, it is likely that the membership of the South African project coordinating committee will be increased, as it currently is dominated by conservation agencies and requires a more diverse representation from the agriculture, cultural heritage and tourism sectors. In addition to this national structure, interdepartmental working groups need to be established at the provincial level.

A South African statute, namely the *Intergovernmental Relations Framework Act* (No. 13 of 2005), calls for organs of state to coordinate their actions through the compilation of implementation protocols. The Eastern Cape Province already has established the Eastern Cape Implementation Committee, which preceded this legislation, while work is still needed to achieve this in the other two provinces.

The planning deliverables from this phase of implementation have already been mentioned and it is envisaged that these will introduce a five-year iterative planning process complete with monitoring and evaluation strategies.

The approach that was taken during this phase was largely based on systematic conservation planning principles and processes (that is, the identification and setting of conservation targets to ensure sufficient representation of ecosystem elements). It is also attempting to integrate all other relevant information through the use of GIS technology. The latter was used to capture spatial data for the disciplines of cultural heritage, livelihoods, security, economic aspects and ecological services. This was enhanced by a qualitative interpretation of each layer as well as the outcome of the collective interpretation of the integration of these. This exercise will provide the substance of the strategy and action plan referred to above.

The planning process was based on existing information. However, as this was the first time such an extensive planning exercise was carried out for the bioregion, there were significant gaps that had to be filled with additional surveys. One of these was the assessment of vegetation, which is the foundational information layer for the systematic conservation planning process. With the resources available to the coordinating unit, this exercise proved to be extremely valuable, exceeding the robustness of any preceding effort and providing a product of high integrity for future land-use planning.

Essential to any planning process is stakeholder involvement and in this regard all relevant specialists within the implementing agencies were engaged and actively involved. In addition to this, both countries implemented a broader stakeholder involvement strategy relevant to their own circumstances. Lesotho was able to be very inclusive of all the communities within its portion of the bioregion due to the relatively low population figures (approximately 200,000 people), while South Africa had to take a more targeted approach, as there are more than two million people in its portion.

In terms of partnerships and alliances, it is also relevant to mention the approach taken to implementation during this phase. Early on it was realized that, in order for the initiative to be sustainable and for the key implementing agencies to take ownership of it, these agencies would have to be integrated into every aspect of implementation. In this regard the coordinating units have seen themselves as facilitators of the various processes inherent within implementation, applying the available resources in a way that supports existing agencies, initiatives, NGOs and other groupings already working and having an interest in the bioregion. It has been an objective of the project coordinating units since the outset to develop the relevant partnerships and alliances to such an extent that they (the coordinating units) are no longer required. The role of the project coordinating units will be absorbed by the key implementing agencies, and a small unit will remain to assist with the logistics of coordinating and monitoring implementation of the five-year action plan.

Externally the initiative has links with other southern African transfrontier conservation areas through the Department of Environmental Affairs and Tourism's Transfrontier Conservation and Development Area Directorate and the Peace Parks Foundation, an NGO that coordinates an annual learning conference for people involved in transfrontier conservation areas. More recently, the office of the Southern African Development Community has recognized that it may be able to play a role in coordination, both within and between these transfrontier initiatives. It remains to be seen how this may develop and add value to existing structures.

Initially the approach to communications differed between the two countries. Lesotho immediately launched into a process of making people aware of the initiative, whereas in South Africa a low profile was maintained well through the first two years of this phase in an attempt to minimize the creation of unrealistic expectations amongst stakeholders. Since March 2005, a joint communication strategy was applied with public relations expertise procured and a quarterly newsletter published and widely distributed. In addition to the latter, the service provided by the public relations professionals included the placement of news articles with the general media, the production of a monthly electronic newsletter, and the provision of any other services such as the production of project banners.

From a marketing perspective, the initiative has gained a very high profile through the identification of all the southern African transfrontier conservation areas as preferred tourism destinations for the 2010 Soccer World Cup. More specifically, a significant amount of effort has been put into developing an overall tourism brand for the bioregion. In this regard, the relevant tourism agencies in both countries signed an MOU binding them to work towards this end.

In general the most obvious threats to this area have to do with unsustainable land-use practices, such as the injudicious use of fire as a grassland management tool and overstocking, which leads to overgrazing and soil erosion, all of which impacts on the integrity of the grassland and associated biodiversity. Another threat is the irreversible transformation brought about by mono-specific cultivation such as maize and timber. More recently the threat of property speculation and development is emerging, with wealthy people taking up residence in second homes on golf and equestrian estates. Mostly this is occurring on agricultural land, where farmers are vulnerable to the promise of a greater financial return from their land than can be obtained by growing crops. Cultural heritage resources are also under threat from direct pressures brought to bear by visitors to some of the sites, whether tourism related or from traditional healers collecting material for their own purposes.

Perhaps the greatest threat is the socio-political circumstances that are vast and complex, with both countries having inherited legacies of the colonial era. These have impacted specifically on Lesotho as has already been mentioned, namely the loss of productive land to South Africa. South Africa has had its own challenges, exacerbated by the long reign of the apartheid government. Even though the new democracy is more than ten years old, there are legacies that will remain and continue to impact on the bioregion. More specifically these have to do with settlement policies that placed people in areas that are now unable to sustain them.

The devolution of responsibility to local government is proving problematic in South Africa and could be the same in Lesotho. What is clearly evident in South Africa is that the local government bodies do not have the multidisciplinary capacity to manage the large tracts of land under their jurisdiction. Since 1994, an emphasis has been placed on economic growth with a view to empowering previously disadvantaged people. While this is understandable, local government has been driving this agenda with little to no regard for environmental consequences. South Africa has a world class suite of environmental and nature conservation legislation, but this has not been supported by the institutional structures necessary for successful implementation. Lesotho is in the process of revising its legislation and it is hoped that the current institutional fragmentation will be addressed as this new legislation is inter-preted, but they have similar problems with implementation.

Closely related to the socio-economic status of many of the people of the bioregion is the prevalence of illegal movements across the inter-national boundary. The reasons for these movements are many, and are predominantly asso-ciated with illegal activities such as the theft of livestock and the smuggling of drugs (predomi-nantly *Cannabis*) as well as the illegal employment of Lesotho nationals by South African farmers. None of these security issues was identified as a threat that needed to be addressed when this phase of the initiative was planned. However, it was quickly recognized that such challenges could not be ignored as they are having an increasingly serious impact on numerous aspects of resource management in the bioregion.

In view of these threats, as they relate to the international boundary and the need for a trans-frontier programme of this nature, it is critical to reiterate that the majority of the approximately 730km long boundary is on an ecological divide, namely the edge of the Drakensberg escarpment. The preliminary outcome of the vegetation surveys carried out during this phase clearly illus-trate this, with areas of similarity being only in the north, where the Caledon River forms the inter-national boundary, and in the south, where the topography is less extreme. The motivation for collaboration is thus more related to the manage-ment of these undesirable socio-economic dynamics and the need to enhance economic collaboration than it is on ecosystem management. Coordination especially is needed around tourism development and the possibility of introducing the concept of payment for environmental services, with a focus on water catchment management.

In realization of this, it was proposed that the updated agreement between the two countries be phrased in a way that does not limit the initiative to a particular geographical entity; rather that the extent of the dynamics that require management will determine the degree of effort. The focus will be on actions necessary to secure the integrity of the natural and cultural resources of the bioregion and the scope of these actions will be determined by the dynamics they are aimed at addressing.

This is a critical aspect, as the delineation of the bioregion and the actual area of implementa-tion has been a topic of serious discussion between the countries since the beginning of this phase. Considering the history and contextual differences, Lesotho citizens are sensitive to South African takeovers and this initiative has been perceived as exactly this by some. As it is, the current area of implementation is a small fragment of the actual bioregion and was justifiably chal-lenged early on in this phase. A compromise was reached when the bilateral steering committee accepted the need to allow planning and survey work to extend to the full extent of the bioregion. Subsequent phases will not be constrained by the boundary of the bioregion and the geographical extent of the work will be determined by the scope of the issues that threaten the bioregion.

Benefits and accomplishments

Current and potential benefits from the initiative include:

- collaboration around the conservation of globally significant natural and cultural heritage resources through improved land-use management strategies;
- improvement of the management of and link-ages between a network of effectively managed protected areas and formalized private landowner agreements;
- securing ecosystem functionality of an area that is of extreme strategic significance in terms of the delivery of ecosystem services, predominantly water;
- collaboration around the securing of econo-mic development opportunities with an emphasis on attempting to create parity between the two countries; this would initially be focused on nature-based tourism, and would need to diversify and look towards the payment for ecosystem services as a potential innovative approach;
- collaboration around the management of the security issues in order to establish and main-tain an enabling environment for all of the above to be realized.

Lessons learned

International multi-stakeholder projects are often complex

- Contextual differences must be recognized as early as possible and all role players must be sensitized to these.
- When working with funding facilitated through the World Bank, it is essential that all concerned are fully familiar with the bureaucratic requirements as far as financial and procurement management are concerned; many frustrating and unnecessary delays were experienced during this phase, which will impact on the integrity of the final outcomes.
- A stakeholder involvement strategy must be established as soon as possible and implemented faithfully.

Setting priorities and allowing adequate time are essential to success

The complexities and dynamics of the bioregion were under estimated and the project design should either have allowed for a longer period of time for this phase of implementation, or should have been scaled down to focus on actions that could be replicated.

Building support for collaborative effort takes time

- Extensive bilateral negotiations and preparatory work provided a solid base for the current phase of implementation.
- Where external funding is concerned, expectations within all stakeholders must be managed well, especially within the key implementing agencies, which needed to be reminded that the project is not additional work but a more efficient way of carrying out their existing legal mandate.
- Apparent progress had to be slowed in order to ensure that the key implementing agencies were on board and taking ownership, in order to facilitate the sustainability of the initiative.
- The capacity of the implementing agencies needed to be assessed upfront in order that the vision, goals and objectives were more meaningful and realistic.

Conclusion

The Maloti–Drakensberg Transfrontier Conservation and Development Programme is laudable because it ambitiously goes beyond the scope of using a network of protected areas to achieve its conservation and development objectives. It recognizes the need to integrate conservation land-use strategies into the private and communal land tenure systems in addition to the protected areas. It also recognizes that the possibility of expanding the current protected area network through the acquisition of additional land is unlikely and that the emphasis must be 'off reserve'.

The vision for this phase was realized with a solid framework of collaboration established. The prognosis for the 20-year strategy and five-year action plan for the next phase being implemented is thus very good. This is particularly encouraging considering the difficulties that have been experienced and that have been worked through by the stakeholders and implementation teams. This initiative is certainly no different from any of the other transfrontier or transboundary efforts discussed in this volume, in that it takes clear vision and strong drivers to get them established and to keep them going.

5

Australian Connectivity Initiatives

This realm is dominated by Australia. The Great Dividing Range of eastern Australia provides steep upland environments in comparison to the larger expanses of flat terrain in central Australia. During the ice ages, sea levels were lower, exposing the continental shelf that links Australia to New Guinea and some of the islands of Asia, allowing land animal transfers. The Australian realm includes many protected areas with 0.91 per cent of its area inscribed as world heritage. Australia is one of 17 mega-biodiverse countries of Earth – of 22,000 species of plants, 85 per cent are found nowhere else, and 1350 of its terrestrial vertebrate species are also endemic. This chapter presents three connectivity conservation case studies from Australia.

Eastern Grey Kangaroos (Macropus giganteus), New South Wales, Australia

Source: Graeme L. Worboys

Australian Alps national parks: Enhancing connectivity through cooperation across borders

Gill Anderson and Rod Atkins

Setting

The Australian Alps are located in the south-eastern corner of mainland Australia, stretching from Canberra through the Brindabella Range in the Australian Capital Territory (ACT), the Snowy Mountains of New South Wales (NSW) and the Victorian Alps (Figure 5.1). They are a mountainous biogeographical region in a predominantly dry and flat continent, and contain Australia's highest peaks together with unique alpine and sub alpine ecosystems.

The region consists of extensive undulating plateaus, ridges and peaks surrounded by a dissected landscape of steep slopes, escarpments and deep gorges. The plateaus are characterized by broad shallow valleys and gentle slopes rising to rounded or flattened mountain tops. In New South Wales, much of the undulating plateau landform is still intact while in Victoria there are a number of smaller isolated plateaux dissected by escarpments, deep gorges and river valleys. The

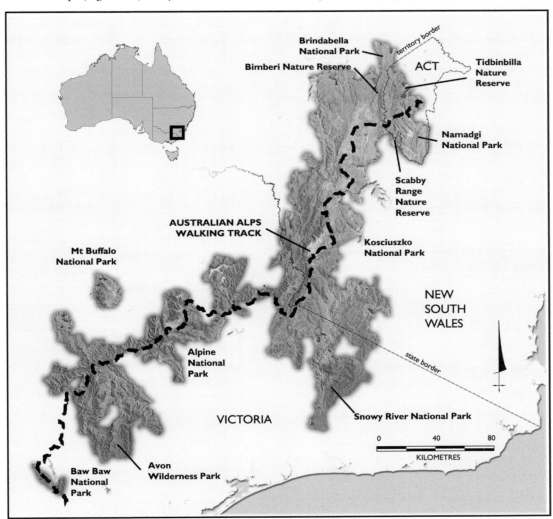

Figure 5.1 Australian Alps national parks

Australian Alps contain plants and animals found nowhere else in the world, as well as significant landscapes, and Aboriginal and historic places. They are a highly valued recreational resource for many Australians, and are the headwaters of some of Australia's most important rivers (the Murray, Murrumbidgee and Snowy Rivers), supplying snow-melt waters for the maintenance of ecological processes and communities, domestic use, industry, irrigation and hydroelectric production in NSW, Victoria, the ACT and South Australia.

The connectivity conservation initiative

Unlike many nations, the Australian Government is not responsible for managing all national parks. The states of Victoria, NSW and the ACT are individually responsible for legislation, policy setting and management of the Australian Alps national parks and protected areas (Alps parks) within their jurisdictions. Together with the Australian Government, they have combined their efforts to ensure that management of the Alps parks reflects a single biogeographical unit across state and territorial jurisdictions. This coordinated management and conservation of the Alps parks is the subject of a Memorandum of Understanding (MOU) between the Australian, NSW, ACT and Victorian Governments (Table 5.1).

Table 5.1 Protected areas of the Australian Alps National Parks Co-operative Management Program

Protected area	Responsible agency
Victoria	Parks Victoria
Alpine National Park	
Snowy River National Park	
Avon Wilderness	
Mount Buffalo National Park	
Baw Baw National Park	
New South Wales	NSW National Parks &
Kosciuszko National Park	Wildlife Division,
Brindabella National Park	Department of
Scabby Range Nature Reserve	Environment &
Bimberi Nature Reserve	Conservation
Australian Capital Territory	Environment ACT
Namadgi National Park	
Tidbinbilla Nature Reserve	

The prolonged work of several individuals within the different park management agencies responsible for Alps protected areas led to the first formal gathering of Alps parks staff in October 1985. This meeting brought together policy makers, planners and managers from four park organizations 'to discuss strategies and priorities for co-operative planning and management for national parks and other protected areas in the Australian Alps' (Davies, 1986).

The vision of the Australian Alps National Parks Co-operative Management Program (the Alps Program) is of 'agencies working in partnership to achieve excellence in conservation management of natural and cultural values and sustainable use through an active programme of cross-border co-operation'. This vision has been implemented through the MOU, which requires that participating governments and agencies develop a programme that provides for:

- consultation in the preparation of management plans or in amendments to existing plans, such that management plans provide for complementary policies and management practices;
- consultation in the formulation of regulations for the management of the Alps parks and the enforcement of those regulations;
- collaboration on matters of research including resource data collection;
- exchange of information, ideas and expertise relevant to protecting the values of the Alps parks;
- cooperative management training for Alps parks staff;
- consultation with Aboriginal communities and fostering of their participation in the management of the Alps parks;
- opportunities for community education, interpretation and awareness of the values of the Alps parks;
- opportunities for public participation in the management of the Alps parks;
- complementary recreation management policies;
- monitoring the use of and public awareness about the Alps parks;
- recognition of the bioregional, national and

international significance of natural and cultural values of the Alps parks.

Connectivity conservation management

The protected areas that make up the Alps parks are found within the South Eastern Highlands and Australian Alps bioregions (Thackway and Cresswell, 1995). While these biogeographic regions are naturally interconnected, the cooperative management programme builds on this to realize the benefits of connectivity conservation management. The Alps Program has strong leadership at a number of levels from ministerial (the relevant government ministers sign the MOU) to the heads of the park agencies and to heads of parks and their senior staff. Under the MOU the agencies have also agreed to maintain a coordinating group called the Australian Alps Liaison Committee (AALC). Each agency is represented on the committee by a senior manager. The function of the AALC is to facilitate the development, coordination, and implementation of the Alps Program. A number of groups have functional roles in the Alps Program (Figure 5.2) and they include:

- the Australian Alps Ministerial Council, which involves the state, territory and national government ministers responsible for the Alps parks, and is responsible for high-level intergovernmental relationships and the MOU;
- the Heads of Agencies group, which meets annually to consider strategic issues and to give direction to the AALC on policy, priority areas and emerging issues;
- the AALC, which facilitates the development, coordination and implementation of the Alps Program including through strategic planning (AALC, 2004) – its members include a senior officer from each of the participating agencies in NSW, Victoria and the ACT and one from the relevant Australian Government department (such as Parks Australia);
- AALC working groups, which advise the Liaison Committee on specific matters and assist with the implementation of the Alps Program by developing new projects in key result areas outlined in the strategic plan, by recommending priority projects for AALC funding and by delivering the projects.

Working group members are drawn from each of the Australian Alps agencies with a mixture of both operational and planning staff. The working groups in 2006 were Natural Heritage Working Group, Cultural Heritage Working Group, Visitor Recreation and Facilities Working Group and Community Awareness Working Group. The Alps Operational Group (Australian Alps park managers) meets and advises the AALC on the annual work programme and a number of operational matters.

The Alps Program is based upon a strategic plan that is developed and reviewed by staff every three years. A number of key result areas have been identified in the plan. They provide a framework for the Alps Program and this in turn contributes to individual agency objectives and outcomes for their respective Alps parks.

A financial contribution is made by each participating agency to assist in achieving the MOU vision and the objectives of the strategic plan. Financial management generally is vested with the agency that is providing the Alps Program Manager position, with this responsibility rotated from one Alps agency to another every three years. The AALC allocates funding to annual cooperative works programmes. These programmes are determined by funding project proposals responding to the key result areas of the strategic plan that are submitted by Alps parks staff. Agreement to implement the strategic plan is based upon agency resources and priorities; but traditionally each agency makes a substantial annual financial contribution.

The key connectivity conservation management partnership is between the three protected area management agencies that have responsibility for policy and operational management of the Alps parks in Victoria, New South Wales and the ACT as well as the Australian Government department responsible for the environment. There are also collaborative partnerships with a range of external organizations and community groups, the strength of which varies from year to year depending upon priority projects and issues. Alliances with these organizations provide evidence of the growing profile and relevance of the Alps Program. In 2006, some operating examples of alliances included work with:

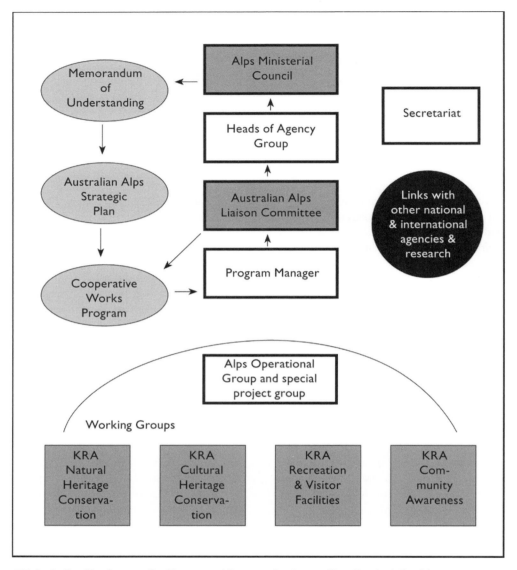

Figure 5.2 Australian Alps Co-operative Management Program structure and functional relationships

- Aboriginal traditional owner groups and communities;
- Australia International Council on Monuments and Sites;
- alpine resorts and resort boards;
- National Parks Associations of Victoria, NSW and ACT;
- VicWalk, Canberra and NSW bushwalking clubs;
- Australian Network for Plant Conservation;
- Royal Society for the Prevention of Cruelty to Animals (NSW) and Bureau of Animal Welfare in the Victorian Department of Primary Industries;
- the Co-operative Research Centre for Sustainable Tourism;
- Victorian Department of Sustainability and Environment, Tasmanian Parks and Wildlife Service and alpine management boards and resort lessees;

- Leave No Trace Australia;
- IUCN World Commission on Protected Areas Mountains Biome group.

Marketing and media management is an important part of the Alps Program. This key result area is facilitated by the Community Awareness Working Group, and it is the role of the Group to ensure that the public is aware of, and has access to, information about the Alps parks and their unique mountain landscapes, catchments and natural and cultural values. Whenever the opportunity arises, the actions and behaviours needed to protect these values and the objectives and achievements of the cooperative management programme are promoted by a number of media including the Australian Alps website (www.australianalps.environment.gov.au), the *News from the Alps* seasonal newsletter, interpretive displays, publications, workshops, conferences and the media. The working group is assisted with these tasks by the Alps Program Manager. A number of publications and products have also been developed that enhance a visitor's enjoyment and understanding and encourage protection of the Alps parks. These include:

- map and touring guide to the Australian Alps that promotes the Alps as a single interconnected tourism destination that crosses state and territory borders (AALC, 2005);
- *Wild Guide* to the native plants and animals of the Australian Alps;
- *Australian Alps Education Kit* and a guide, *Cool Ideas for the Alps*, which provide information and activities for teachers, students and tour operators;
- *Care for the Alps – Leave No Trace* brochure and promotional products, such as water bottles and bookmarks, to assist visitors.

The Alps MOU states that agencies will cooperate to 'provide opportunities for public participation in the management of the Alps parks'. Two of the terms of reference for all Alps Program working groups reinforce this commitment by requiring consideration of the perspectives of Aboriginal people in contributing to the outcome for their key result area; and a focus on the knowledge needs of the agencies and their staff, as well as those of the community.

A number of projects demonstrate how the Alps Program has worked closely with indigenous communities and the broader community. Aboriginal traditional owner and custodian advice and involvement (for example) has been included in projects such as mentoring participants in an indigenous interpretation training and employment programme and has provided cultural heritage information for use on park signs and displays.

Community conservation groups and bushwalking clubs have been involved in cross-border strategic planning for the Australian Alps walking track management work. The tourism industry was involved in frontline workshops. These community awareness training courses were aimed at increasing knowledge of the Australian Alps, interpretation methods and networking. Catchment management authorities and other land management organizations from around the Alps sponsored a practical identification guide, *Alps Invaders: Weeds of the Australian High Country* (Hosking et al, 2006), to promote public support for AALC's weed management and eradication campaign.

Working with scientists and experts has been an important aspect of all projects facilitated by the AALC and working groups. The Working Group for Natural Heritage Conservation in particular concentrates on improving understanding and enhancing management of the flora and fauna, ecological processes and natural communities of the Alps parks. It employs the full rigour of scientific research and monitoring in its work. More recently the Alps Program (in partnership with the IUCN World Commission on Protected Areas Mountains Biome) ran a series of annual science management workshops that have explored the implications of research (of key subjects such as fire and climate change) for park managers and how science and management can work more closely together.

The performance of the Australian Alps Cooperative Management Program is evaluated annually by the AALC and its working groups. The evaluation focuses on the outcomes for each of the key result areas of the strategic plan and is based on the following criteria:

Participants at an Australian Alps Science-Management workshop on fire management

Source: Graeme L. Worboys

- The key result area is supported by, and relevant to all of the involved agencies.
- The outcome for the key result area remains valid and relevant in its scope and applicability to the Alps parks.
- There is evidence that the required outcome for the key result area is being achieved.
- The completed project contributed directly or indirectly to the conservation of significant values of the Alps parks.
- The target users were aware of the project's results, had access to the project and found the project relevant and useful.

Towards the end of each financial year the Alps Operational Group independently reviews the year's programme in relation to the five criteria (above) and makes recommendations on the direction of the following year's programme. The AALC prepares an annual report, which provides an assessment of the success of the MOU, the Alps Program and the implementation of the strategic plan through the annual work programme. It includes the performance evaluation reporting against key results areas required by the strategic plan. The report is submitted to the Heads of Agencies Group, the ministers responsible and other key stakeholders, and is made available to the public.

Benefits and accomplishments

Prior to the establishment of the MOU, each park agency, and at times each park, had its own way of responding to the challenges of mountain park management. Communication between park managers was ad hoc and rarely added value to the long-term resolution of common issues. With the establishment of the Alps Program, many connectivity conservation benefits have been derived and some of these are described below (by key result areas of the strategic plan).

A culture of cooperation and goodwill has been established and maintained among the agencies responsible for connectivity conservation management in Australia's Alps. Networking, formal and informal links and the ability to share information, knowledge and experiences (especially by specialists) have been enormously beneficial. It has resulted in (among many other things) a reduction in duplication of effort. The Alps Program works as a facilitator and provides access to a great body of knowledge for use by individuals and agencies. Consistency of approach is another benefit. Uniform and coordinated planning approaches, management policies, visitor advice and compliance activities across borders are continually pursued and have been achieved for many areas.

The Alps Program has generated a number of strategic documents that facilitate a coordinated approach to natural heritage management across the two states and one territory of the Alps. The

significant natural values of the Alps parks (for example) have been defined, with this statement being widely used as a basis for planning, research and operational management (AALC, 2006). The AALC generated a study, *Protecting the Natural Treasures of the Australian Alps* (Coyne, 2001), which identified more than 1300 significant natural features in the Australian Alps and nearly 100 threats to their survival. In 1998, it sponsored an identification guide to facilitate public support for weed eradication and management that was revised in 2006 (Hosking et al, 2006).

The Alps Program funded many projects dealing with pest animal species, including wild dogs, foxes, pigs, deer and feral horses. It facilitated wild dog workshops for field staff and adjacent land managers, and spent considerable effort on the control, management and potential eradication of feral horses. For the wild, free-ranging feral horses, there was a need for consistent approaches to monitoring and control. To assist, a major study

Watson's Crags, Kosciusko National Park, Australian Alps

Source: Graeme L. Worboys

was commissioned (Dawson, 2005) and this estimated a baseline population of about 5000 wild horses for the Australian Alps in 2001.

Fires were another major issue and in response to the fires of the summer of 2002/2003 that burnt approximately 68 per cent of the Alps parks (Worboys, 2003; Gill et al, 2004) a number of projects were initiated to encourage collaboration in facilitating recovery (and greater understanding) of the Alps ecosystems and natural communities. These projects included: (i) monitoring and analysis of the burnt fire ecology plots that were established prior to 2003 and previously unburnt; (ii) establishment of an Expert Scientific Committee to review and make recommendations regarding the response of the Alps agencies to the 2003 fires; and (iii) facilitating workshops involving scientists and staff looking predominantly at the research and monitoring undertaken since the 2003 fires and the lessons learned or implications for on-the-ground management.

The start of the 21st century has witnessed increased awareness and respect for the Aboriginal values and heritage of the Australian Alps. In addition, there is improved engagement and involvement between Alps parks staff and Aboriginal peoples with connections to the mountains. In 2005, at the Australian Alps First Peoples' Gathering, over 60 traditional owners and Aboriginal custodians from around the Alps signed a treaty agreeing to work together towards achieving greater involvement in park management. The Alps Program continues to work with traditional owners to implement the directions established at the Gathering.

The cultural heritage of the Alps is also important, and a research strategy has been developed, based on key Australian historic themes, to help to identify the national heritage significance of the Alps parks. This has been facilitated by partnerships with universities undertaking research on both indigenous and non-indigenous cultural heritage to respond to identified knowledge gaps. There are many historic sites in the Australian Alps. In order to raise awareness levels of cultural heritage issues, the AALC has organized a number of staff training activities. In 1996, *Cultural Landscape Management Guidelines* (Lennon and Mathews, 1996) were prepared for identifying,

assessing and managing cultural landscapes in the Alps parks. There are many historic mining sites in the Alps and a *Mining Heritage Conservation and Presentation Strategy* was completed (Kaufman, 2002). A study called *Mountains of Science* produced a *Thematic Interpretation Strategy for Scientific Sites of Cultural Significance in the Australian Alps* (Macdonald and Haiblen, 2001).

The Australian Alps are usually thought of by Australians (and others) as a single biogeographic entity of national significance. There is also potential for these outstanding values to achieve national heritage listing, and this status was formally being assessed in 2007. This informal and potentially formal social recognition of the Australian Alps as one interconnected park reinforces the concept of connectivity conservation from the perspective of people in the community.

For the Alps parks managers, there is increased recognition of the customer services needed by visitors, and a suite of visitor information tools (maps, publications, signs and displays) that promote enjoyment, appreciation and sustainable use has been produced. A range of very successful *Care for the Alps – Leave No Trace* brochures has been distributed. Much effort has also been devoted to raising the awareness and knowledge of those working in the tourist industry. An *Australian Alps National Parks Tour Operators' Manual* (Gibbs and Mackay, 1994) provided background information about the natural and cultural values of the Alps and park management issues. Training programmes and workshops have also been run for commercial tour operators. Frequent community awareness training courses have been held for Alps parks public contact staff and the local tourist industry staff. This involved rangers, park workers and visitor centres staff. These 'Frontline of the Alps' courses were aimed at increasing knowledge of the Australian Alps, increasing staff skills, providing interpretation methods and encouraging networking between visitor information staff.

Each of the Alps parks provides particular recreation opportunities and visitor facilities. However, there are some initiatives that are Alps wide, and one important activity has been the provision of cross-border, non-commercial tourist and recreational facilities. Particularly important are the various recreational trails, for walking, horse riding, mountain bike riding and cross-country skiing. Recreational trails workshops have dealt with such issues as construction materials for walking tracks, erosion control and drainage, maintenance and the need for an Alps parks-wide trails strategy. The Australian Alps have a long tradition of horse riding, and a cross-border horse riding management strategy (Gibbs, 1993) achieved consistency for the conditions and practices required of recreational horse riders by Alps parks staff. Backcountry recreation management was an early concern, involving activities such as ski-touring, canoeing, bushwalking and mountain biking. In 1995, an Australian Alps National Parks *Back-Country Recreation Strategy* (Nixon and Mackay, 1995) was completed, which again provided a consistency of approach.

Capacity building for Alps parks staff has been very effective. Coordination of many areas of training and research has occurred and has resulted in the enhancement of management expertise and performance. It has also avoided duplication of training across the Alps parks agencies. Workshops aimed at best practice management have provided training for feral animal control, waste management and the maintenance of historic huts. These have been provided annually and bring together staff and experts to share experiences and knowledge.

Lessons learned

The Australian Alps National Parks Co-operative Management Program extends connectivity conservation management across two Australian bioregions and three separate state and territorial administrations. It involves a total of 11 protected areas that span 1.6 million hectares and lie between 200m above sea level and Australia's highest mountain at 2228m (Crabb, 2003). This example of a connectivity conservation initiative is particularly valuable because it is a combination of transboundary protected area management and connectivity conservation action at a landscape scale that is managed solely by government agencies. The key lessons learned are as follows.

Community engagement and partnerships are essential

Engaging and working with the community

helped to ensure the long-term survival of the programme. Collaboration continues with a number of groups covering a wide range of programme areas such as indigenous cultural heritage, research and monitoring, community awareness of climate change and tourism opportunities.

Success depends on good communication

Maintaining staff and community support for the programme depended predominantly upon good communication on a number of levels including: (i) the dissemination of, and access to, information about programme research, strategy development and project outcomes and their implications for management; (ii) the internal communication about individual agency staff and new initiatives, the benefits of the programme and how to get involved and the working groups and their achievements; and (iii) external communication that increased community awareness and appreciation of the values of the protected areas and support and involvement in the Alps Program.

Establish governance mechanisms that facilitate connectivity conservation

The governance of the Alps Program provided numerous valuable lessons for others. Its great strength was that it worked effectively at critical but different levels of organizations. At the strategic level, the Ministerial Council and Heads of Agencies forums ensured that politicians and heads of agencies were well briefed and had input into transboundary land-use management while working within a federated Australia constitutional framework that jealously guarded state rights. The carefully worded MOU and the inclusiveness of public recognition of success helped maintain the cooperative involvement.

At the tactical level, the AALC's careful implementation of the agreed Alps Strategic Plan, the shared responsibility for managing the programme and the due process of project proposal, annual evaluation of performance and annual reporting provided a sound administration framework for the programme. The permanent programme leader position was critical. While only one individual, it was a full-time role that provided secretariat-style services that maintained the momentum of the Alps Program.

At the operational level, the Alps Program provided opportunities to resource connectivity conservation initiatives not otherwise available. It also ensured that staff competency for responding to key threats and connectivity management needs were at a national best practice level given the quality and frequency of the cooperative training. In addition, many used the programme as an opportunity to press for the highest common denominator, as they did in terms of potential initiatives for national heritage listing, world heritage listing and even the concept of one park (a futuristic concept for a single park for the entire Australian Alps).

Provide staff support and encourage networking

A major strength of the programme was the agency people who were involved. Overall, the commitment and dedication to the conservation of the Alps parks was very strong. Given the relative remoteness and small groups in which many staff worked, facilitating bonds between like-minded people and added peer support was an important function of the Alps Program. It provided a bioregional (landscape scale) context for the work that was conducted at the site level. This appreciation of context helped to facilitate connectivity conservation initiatives.

Commit to adequate ongoing funding and resourcing

The funds available through the annual work programme provided opportunities for rangers and other staff to initiate projects that might not have been possible in their own agencies. The freedom and opportunity to get things done was highly valued.

Promote achievable, stimulating and relevant initiatives

It is particularly important, in the early stages of any new connectivity programme, to identify a pilot project that both encapsulates the overall strategy and is relatively easily achieved. This will have ongoing benefits. Implementing a management report on long distance walking trails through the Australian Alps (for example) provided a tangible example of cross-border

cooperation and connectivity management for staff and community members. Lessons learned in running a transborder pest species programme found it was wise (after Hayes, 1995, cited in Crabb, 2003) to:

- insist that projects have an identifiable benefit for the majority of parties;
- ensure that research projects have identifiable on-ground benefits for management;
- continue monitoring and reporting on the outcome of projects after the on-ground work is completed;
- ensure regular reporting on projects;
- encourage staff to initiate projects that are of direct benefit to them – which fosters a sense of ownership of the project;
- ensure that all staff of the agencies are informed of the programme and its results;
- encourage projects that lead to a sharing of knowledge and skills across agencies;
- build skills of local staff by encouraging their involvement in projects carried out by others in their park.

Australian Alps to Atherton connectivity conservation corridor

Ian Pulsford, Graeme L. Worboys and Gary Howling

Setting

The Australian Alps to Atherton (A2A) connectivity conservation corridor is a vision to help conserve and manage 2800 north–south kilometres of Australia's natural lands and species for the long term. The vision involves a diverse array of people and communities in responding to climate change to enhance the resilience of some of the continent's most biologically diverse and environmentally significant lands. It recognizes scientific advice concerning the management of this precious and unique biodiversity and the extraordinary species richness and high endemicity of eastern Australia's habitats and ecosystems; and it provides a national strategic focus for improved and more sustainable land management. The vision for A2A respects the cultural importance of lands and recognizes the utmost economic and

Kangaroo Range, Great Dividing Range, Kosciuszko National Park, NSW, part of A2A

Source: Graeme L. Worboys

social significance of conserving water catchments and the ecosystem services they provide for over 50 per cent of Australia's 21 million peoples at a time of climate change.

Australia is the world's oldest and flattest continent. While dominated by arid and semi-arid grasslands and woodlands, better watered lands and their associated forests and rainforests can be found to the far north, south-west, east and in Tasmania (Worboys et al, 2005). On the eastern margins of Australia, two very old, mountainous and sometimes more subtle undulating landscapes are found. These are the Great Dividing Range and Great Escarpment of eastern Australia (Ollier, 1982). The Great Divide separates coastal (easterly) flowing streams from inland (westerly) draining waters in eastern Australia. The Great Escarpment mostly lies to the east of the Great Divide. It is usually an abrupt, dissected landscape

feature many hundreds of metres in altitude, which separates tableland environments from the coast. It extends north–south from East Gippsland in Victoria to north of Cairns in Queensland, although it may also be obscure in places and totally absent in others (Worboys, 1996).

Collectively these features have been described as the great eastern ranges. The New South Wales (NSW) Department of Environment and Climate Change officially recognised the NSW section of A2A as the Great Eastern Ranges connectivity corridor (DECC, 2008). The two features extend for more than 2800km north–south for most of the length of the eastern Australia, and through 21 degrees of latitude. During human existence, these natural features, which extend from the Australian Alps in Victoria to Atherton in Queensland, have always been naturally vegetated. They include a diverse array of habitats along their length. The A2A connectivity conservation corridor (Figure 5.3) in 2009 still essentially retained its landscape connectivity for 2800 kilometres. Nonetheless, some parts are fragmented through clearing, there are highway crossings at some locations, some parts are tenuously interconnected and there are other natural areas under threat from further clearing and fragmentation. Climate change threatens all of A2A.

The landforms and ecosystems of A2A are old, in fact, very old. The origins of the elevated A2A lie in the Cretaceous Gondwana supercontinent some 80 million years ago commensurate with the creation of the Great Dividing Range (White, 1994; Johnson, D., 2004). It existed 50 million years ago when basalt lavas flowed over the Great Escarpment near Nerriga in southern NSW (Johnson, D., 2004). Its evolving ecosystems have been interconnected from these times. Forty-five million years ago, after the break-up of Gondwana, Australia was isolated from other continents and migrated northwards from southern latitudes to its present location. It was a giant Ark of life during this migration and included its own distinctive evolutionary and adaptive processes and unique ecological settings (White, 1994; Lindenmayer, 2007; Mackey et al, 2009). It was (essentially) tectonically stable with periods of volcanicity. Immense periods of time, the slow movements north and Earth's climate fluctuations were the key evolutionary change factors.

The ecosystems of A2A experienced climatic and evolutionary changes to their ancient Cretaceous Gondwanan flora and fauna. This included the establishment of continent-wide rainforests during the early Tertiary and then the drying and modernization of Australia's flora, with the contraction of rainforests to moister island refugia along A2A, in the mid to late Tertiary (White, 1994). The very recent past witnessed quite variable climates including an intense cold and dry period just 30,000 years ago, some glaciation in the Australian Alps then warming, the development of woodland and forest vegetation communities and the retention of the older rainforests along A2A (White, 1994). Many examples of these older flora and habitats are still found along A2A and contribute to its high species diversity and high endemicity.

A2A extends through 21 degrees of latitude and includes spectacular scenic lands amongst more rounded hilly terrain. The terrain is a refreshing contrast to Australia's more expansive flat landscapes. A2A includes Australia's highest mountains and its highest peak, the 2228m Mount Kosciuszko and, along its length, many dissected escarpment landscapes and deep gorges. This includes some of Australia's highest waterfalls such as Queensland's Wallaman Falls (305m) and NSW's Wollombi Falls (220m). There are limestone gorges and cave systems such as at Jenolan

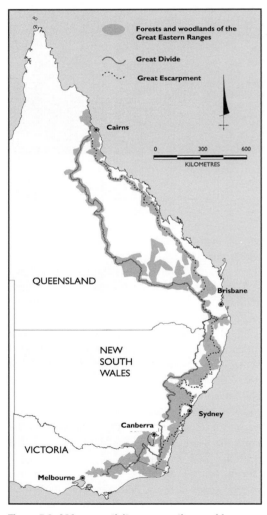

Figure 5.3 A2A connectivity conservation corridor

Palms, sub tropical rainforest, Lamington National Park, Queensland, part of A2A

Source: Graeme L. Worboys

and Bungonia (NSW) and Buchan Caves in Victoria. Large grand granite dome landscapes are found at Girraween and Bald Rock on the Queensland–NSW border and old volcanic landscapes feature prominently at the Atherton Tablelands and the Tweed Volcano (Queensland) and at Mount Warning, Ebor, Dorrigo and Barrington Tops (NSW). Spectacular sandstone cliff-escarpments, waterfalls and 'pagoda' lands are found in the large natural areas to the north, west and south of Sydney, NSW.

Australia is one of the 17 biologically megadiverse countries of the world. It has the world's largest number of endemic vertebrate species (1350) due to its long evolutionary isolation (Lindenmayer, 2007) and many of these species are concentrated along A2A (The Allen Consulting Group, 2005) making it one the most

biodiverse areas for the country (Mackey et al, 2009). A2A includes 14 of Australia's 85 bioregions, which range from Australia's winter snow covered alpine areas to the tropical rainforests of far north Queensland.

Preliminary estimates indicate there are at least 1235 species of animals found in A2A of which 152 (23 per cent) are endemic (Williams et al, 2006). It includes areas with the highest concentration of bird species in Australia, with 429 species in south-east Queensland and 428 species in north-eastern NSW. This biodiverse area also includes the richest concentration of Australia's mammal species, amphibians and snakes and one of the two great concentrations of Eucalyptus and Acacia (Commonwealth of Australia, 2002; DECC (Department of Environment and Climate Change), NSW, 2008). A2A includes an estimated

8250 species of vascular plants (Williams et al, 2006), which is about 36 per cent of Australia's total and 26 per cent of these are endemic (Williams et al, 2006). There are many ancient, relict plants including the Gondwanan species, Wollemi pine (*Wollemia nobilis*), Antarctic beech (*Nothofagus moorei*) and ribbonwood (*Idiospermum australiense*).

A2A is special to people. Aborigines have been present in Australia for at least 40,000 years (Mulvaney and Kamminga, 1999), and A2A contains spiritual places and 'Country' that include song lines, ancient traditional pathways, trade routes, resources and relics that are highly significant for many Aboriginal peoples. Its often dramatic landscapes are an important part of the 'Australian story' for many Australians.

A2A is a significant area for biodiversity conservation and an archipelago of protected areas has been established along its length including three world heritage areas (the Wet Tropics, Gondwana Rainforest and Greater Blue Mountains areas). Many sites along A2A are recognized refugia areas, biodiversity hot spots or centres of endemism and many are formally protected for this reason. In NSW, it is estimated that 37 per cent of A2A has protected area status (excluding privately owned reserves) and the balance of the natural lands includes 12 per cent as state forests, 4 per cent as crown land and 48 per cent as private land.

The A2A connectivity conservation corridor includes these important protected areas. They are embedded within this large natural landscape and it ensures that protected areas are interconnected with natural lands. A2A's 2800 kilometre length of landscape connectivity is on average tens of kilometres wide. Its terrain is complex and includes often abrupt changes in altitude, aspect and geology and there are many different habitats. Its large size provides opportunities for habitat, ecological and evolutionary connectivity for species inside and outside of the established reserve system (Bennett et al, 2006; Hilty et al, 2006; Mackey et al, 2007, 2009).

The connectivity conservation initiative

The origins of A2A date back to the 1990s, but its connectivity conservation design has been under-

pinned by 80 years of protected area established during the 20th century, pioneered by conservationists, visionaries and governments in three states and the ACT. Action for a connectivity corridor was directly linked to a long-standing conflict between conservation and timber industry interests in NSW's South East Forests in the 1990s, during an era of particular partisan state government politics, tense state and federal politics, competing government departments and direct action by conservationists, including forest blockades. There was a need for major Australian forestry reform and it was an intense and turbulent time.

To help resolve tensions, the Australian National Forest Policy was agreed to by Australian governments in 1992, and this helped to establish a comprehensive regional assessment process for the south-east in 1995 (DAFF, 1999). It led to the signing of the Regional Forest Agreement (RFA) between the NSW and Australian Governments in 1999. The RFA decision-making process was guided by sophisticated tools including the C-Plan conservation planning system (Barrett, 2005; Pressey et al, 2009) using irreplaceability and complementarity principles for forestry and conservation land-use decisions. Park professionals were also guided by early connectivity conservation thinking championed by Professor Larry Hamilton of the IUCN World Commission on Protected Areas and others and this also influenced thinking about conservation design principles. All inputs ultimately contributed to the establishment of a 'Comprehensive, Adequate and Representative' reserve system including a new South East Forests National Park launched by the NSW Premier, The Honourable Mr Bob Carr and Minister for the Environment, The Honourable Mr Bob Debus in 1997 (Worboys, 2005a). This new park, when combined with Victoria's Coopracambra National Park, achieved 150 north–south kilometres of interconnected protected areas along the Great Escarpment where previously there had been an archipelago of smaller protected areas embedded in a landscape of state-owned production forests.

This conservation milestone was announced internationally in Montreal, Canada, in 1996 at a workshop convened by IUCN (Worboys, 1996). Like Yellowstone to Yukon, another formative vision presented at this workshop (see Chapter 7), the NSW speech announced a grander vision for Australian connectivity conservation for 1000km of NSW's Great Escarpment lands (Worboys, 1996). It was a step towards full recognition of an A2A connectivity conservation corridor.

The A2A vision, which extended the connectivity conservation corridor from just 1000km of NSW to over 2800km, was first published in 2004 (Pulsford et al, 2004). It recognized the national benefits of conserving these critical lands and identified its strategic national importance as an adaptive response to climate change. Importantly, there was strong political support for the connectivity conservation concept. At about this time, the NSW National Parks Association launched its Eastern Links conservation corridor, reinforcing the conservation importance of the A2A connectivity area (NPA, 2002). The then Minister for the Environment, The Honourable Mr Bob Debus provided strong leadership for the A2A vision and, at a November 2006 meeting of the Environment Protection and Heritage Council of Australia and New Zealand, he presented a proposal to establish the Australian Alps to Atherton connectivity conservation corridor. The proposal was positively received and environment ministers from the Commonwealth, NSW, Queensland, Victoria and the ACT agreed to cooperate and establish a working group to further develop the concept. It was the start of a transborder partnership supported by the state and Australian governments. With the support of the other states and territory, Minister Debus took this initiative one significant step further.

On Saturday, 24 February 2007, Minister Bob Debus announced to the *Sydney Morning Herald* newspaper that the NSW Government would help facilitate A2A connectivity conservation in Australia as a major adaptive response to climate change and, specifically for NSW, that the Environment Trust had allocated $7 million over three years to help establish the NSW section of A2A, the Great Eastern Ranges. The A2A connectivity conservation corridor had officially been born.

A2A is an essential investment for the people and governments of Australia:

- It is an adaptive response to climate change-caused biome shifts and aims to help conserve over 8257 vascular plant and 1235 animal species and the richest concentrations of wildlife in Australia. Many of these species are endemic and many are already vulnerable and endangered. It recognizes habitat conservation requirements for lands beyond protected area boundaries. In a climate-changed world, it is a strategic Australian investment to help conserve landscape connectivity, ecological services and species.
- A2A helps provide essential natural ecological services for 93 per cent of Australia's east coast population and 74 per cent of its total population (approximately 20 million) – potable water is supplied to 16 plus impoundments that service four capital cities and multiple impoundments serve hundreds of towns and cities along the east coast (Barrett, 2009).
- Climate change forecasts (IPCC, 2007b) identify a high probability for less rain for eastern Australia for at least 14 degrees of latitude and as far north as Brisbane and beyond. Data for the last 50 years has demonstrated this trend is already occurring and is pronounced (BOM, 2008). Every litre of water delivered from the catchments of A2A becomes more valuable with time. It is in the interests of all governments to achieve high quality natural conditions for its A2A catchment areas at a time of biome shifts. Connectivity conservation investments help achieve this.
- A2A is especially important to many indigenous peoples. It has been 'Country' to Aboriginal nations for at least 40,000 years (Mulvaney and Kamminga, 1999) and includes multiple dreaming tracks, pathways and sacred sites. A natural A2A helps retain these special values.
- A2A is the source of stories, adventures and histories for many Australians. It includes the routes of many early explorers. It is a tourism destination for visitors and recreationists and includes the 5330km Bicentennial National Trail. Conserving its natural integrity helps to retain these special values.
- The A2A connectivity conservation corridor is already globally significant as an emerging

large-scale adaptive response to climate change. It is Australian leadership demonstrating connectivity conservation and transboundary responses to climate change for species and ecosystem conservation. It is providing inspiration and motivation for many, even at this early stage in its development.

- A2A emerges at a time of global economic instability, climate change and urban expansion, and it reflects an increasing awareness by the community of the importance of large-scale responses to large-scale issues. It is at a time when large-scale collaborative responses are central to conservation delivery by governments.

Connectivity conservation management

A2A consists of protected areas, state forests, crown lands, indigenous lands, private leasehold and privately owned lands. Many protected areas are found along the Great Divide and Great Escarpment and some large-scale connectivity conservation protected areas have been established. These include the Australian Alps parks and protected areas from East Gippsland in Victoria to the Hunter Valley in NSW, including the Greater Blue Mountains World Heritage Area. North of the Hunter Valley and Queensland, sections of A2A include an archipelago of protected areas including two world heritage designations, the Gondwana and Wet Tropics sites. Natural lands of other tenures are found interconnecting these protected areas and comprise the balance of A2A.

Steps towards national agreement for establishing a coordinated A2A initiative have been progressing slowly and steadily to 2009. An Australian interstate agency working group is responsible for developing and providing advice on A2A to the Environment Protection and Heritage Council and Natural Resources Management Ministerial Council (Figure 5.4). The working group commissioned and approved a key report by independent scientists that identified the scientific basis for an A2A connectivity conservation corridor (Mackey et al, 2009). The report provides the scientific basis for governments to implement A2A connectivity conservation and its management.

In 2009, A2A connectivity conservation management in NSW had advanced furthest of all of the states and the ACT. It had established a number of operating governance arrangements including: (i) a Great Eastern Ranges advisory sub committee for the Environmental Trust, the funding organization for the NSW Great Eastern Ranges initiative (Figure 5.4); (ii) a science and technical advisory group; (iii) collaborative research partnerships; (iv) pilot connectivity projects partnerships with about 60 organizations in northern NSW, the Hunter Valley and south of Canberra; and (v) a community forum. A small Great Eastern Ranges secretariat had been established to manage the initiative and, as part of its work, it prepared a business plan, a budget and a communication and community involvement strategy.

Habitat destruction, fragmentation, climate change, fire, weeds and introduced animals are the greatest threats facing A2A. Some of the key causes are population growth and development, which results in clearing of native vegetation for urban expansion, transport, utilities mining, agriculture and industrial development. Amenity migrants ('sea changers') are a relatively new phenomenon that are urbanizing some natural areas such as the Australian Alps (Buckley et al, 2006). Future impacts from climate change are forecast to: (i) reduce the freshwater quantity and quality in eastern Australia with consequent increased costs to consumers and businesses (Young et al, 2006); (ii) accelerate the decline of ecosystems accompanied by an accelerating rate of extinction of plant and animal species (IPCC, 2007b); (iii) cause changes to fire regimes due to more frequent, longer, hotter and drier summers and more intense storm events (The Allen Consulting Group, 2005); and (iv) cause disturbance and changes to ecosystems, biome shifts and potentially invasions from alien plant and animal species and diseases. All of these threats need active management.

In NSW, a number of mechanisms including incentives are available to landowners and some have been used to encourage connectivity conservation action. These include voluntary conservation agreements (negotiated by government agencies and NGOs), stewardship payments, use of carbon credits, establishing biodiversity

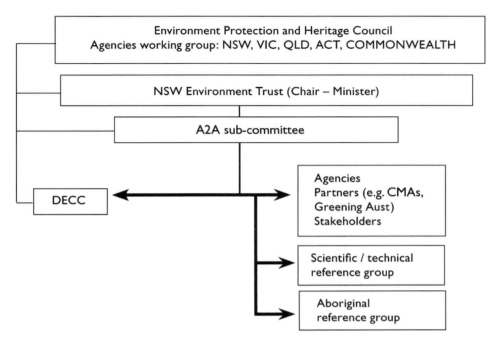

Figure 5.4 A2A governance: An Australian interstate agency working group

Note: NSW, New South Wales; VIC, Victoria; QLD, Queensland; CMA, Catchment Management Authority.

banks, property vegetation plans and investment in revegetation programmes by government, industry and private individuals. Many partnerships are being established. Bush Heritage Australia, for example, a national, private, not-for-profit conservation organization, is working collaboratively with NSW Department of Environment and Climate Change and has purchased and established a private protected area as a 'stepping stone' in the critical Kosciuszko to Coast (K2C) connectivity corridor between A2A and NSW south coast protected areas. Many public forums have been conducted, including a science forum, a community open day and public meetings. Future programmes include a community visioning process, a community forum and opportunities to provide advice for how long-term A2A governance is achieved. Community awareness education programmes are also programmed.

Benefits and accomplishments

Conserving and managing the natural landscape connectivity of A2A, with its rich habitats and ecosystems inside and outside of protected areas, is the most cost-effective and ecologically sound way of helping to conserve many plant and animal species for the long term, conserve water supply catchments and provide clean air.

A2A is the only opportunity for large-scale north–south (21 degrees of latitude) connectivity conservation involving 14 bioregions and interconnecting areas of Australia's greatest concentrations of fauna and flora. It is an area where reserve 'representativeness' is generally adequate in an archipelago of protected areas along A2A, but where reserve 'adequacy' is less satisfactory. Climate change and biome shift are significant threats to some of Australia's richest concentrations of species. A2A connectivity conservation helps to maintain the adequacy of the nation's reserve system in eastern Australia at a time of rapid changes to habitats, ecosystems and ecological processes. Given the large number of endangered and threatened species within A2A, connectivity conservation action could help Australia to achieve the global target of 'a significant reduction of the current rate of biodiversity loss by 2010'.

A2A helps to conserve ecosystem services and, in particular, water. The east coast of Australia historically received reasonably reliable rainfall and A2A includes catchments for 63 of Australia's major easterly and southerly flowing rivers. These rivers are the domestic water supply sources for Australia's four east coast capital cities, Brisbane, Canberra, Melbourne and Sydney (NLWRA, 2002); coastal towns and 93 per cent of Australia's east coast population of approximately 15 million benefit from this (Barrett, 2009; Mackey et al, 2009).

The A2A catchments provide other benefits. For westerly flowing and diverted rivers, the Australian Alps is one of the most important and reliable catchments for the Murray Darling River Basin with its towns and irrigation areas. Water from the Australian Alps through the Hume Weir and to the Murray River contributes 37 per cent of the total inflow during normal years and 42 per cent during dry years (MDBC, 1990). For easterly flowing rivers in far north Queensland, a natural A2A helps to maintain the quality of water flowing to the Great Barrier Reef, both through normal run-off times and during major tropical cyclone events.

A2A conservation initiatives complement other landscape conservation and natural resource management actions in response to impacts to Australia's rural environments including droughts, soil loss, rising salt, water shortages, habitat decline and declining agricultural productivity. For Aboriginal peoples, voluntary agreements for connectivity conservation stewardship and partnerships may help maintain spiritual connections with 'Country' and may be important for employment, health and welfare of Aboriginal communities.

Lessons learned

Connectivity has existed for 80 million years

A2A has (effectively) been naturally interconnected from the end of the Cretaceous to the Recent. The connectivity corridor and its fauna and flora have experienced major evolutionary changes, multiple climate changes, and recently, from the Pleistocene to Anthropocene, significant

climate change that witnessed glaciation in the high peaks 30,000 years ago to sea-level rises and warmer (present) climates from 6000 years ago. The majority of Australia's modern fauna survived these changes (Mackey, 2007). The key lesson is that many of Australia's fauna and flora, given the opportunity, can adapt to, evolve, cope (phenotypic plasticity) or move with climate change. The lands of A2A are a grand story of migration and dispersal over the millennia and at grand geographic scales. Contemporary A2A connectivity conservation and its effective management will help to retain these options for Australian species in the 21st century despite the threat of rapid global warming caused changes.

It is important to manage for four types of connectivity conservation

Retaining A2A landscape connectivity preserves options for fauna and flora species. Depending on the location and the characteristics of species, it may: (i) provide cover and opportunities for movement; (ii) include suitable habitat; (iii) provide functioning ecosystems; and (iv) provide opportunities for evolutionary interactions and adaptations. Australia has extreme natural climate variability (from droughts to flooding rains) and 535 vertebrate species are known to be dispersive as an evolutionary adaptation (Mackey, 2007). Their life strategy depends on geographically extensive networks of habitat patches. A2A plays a conservation role for many of these species. For others, seasonal migrations will be important. For less dispersive species A2A potentially will play an even bigger conservation role as biome shifts occur.

Size matters

Spanning 21 degrees of latitude A2A is a large (continental) -scale connectivity conservation corridor. Coarse climate change forecasts for eastern Australia identify temperature increases and east coast drying indicatively spanning at least 14 degrees of latitude across three states and a territory (IPCC, 2007b). A2A is a strategic national adaptation response to climate change and provides water catchment conservation management to help sustain future water supplies for 50 per cent of Australians.

Responding to climate change: People want to help

A2A is for many people the climate change response with which they want to be involved. The simple but effective name helps. People understand A2A. They know where it starts and finishes, the immensity of the geography involved and how their circumstances relate to it. They intuitively understand and relate to concepts like 'large-scale', 'connectivity corridor' or 'integrated activities' and their direct relationship with wildlife conservation at a landscape scale. They find A2A visionary and motivating, and desire to help.

One size does not fit all

The communities and partners involved with A2A are as varied and diverse as the landscapes found along the length of the eastern ranges. Of the five 'regional' partnerships established in NSW no two are alike. In the Hunter Valley, they include representatives from heavy industry, tourism and community groups whereas the Slopes to Summit has an academically focused collaboration. This diversity demonstrates the importance of not having a prescriptive approach for developing partnerships. It is more important to focus on the A2A goals and allow local people to determine the best way to engage in the process.

Government leadership

In Australia, governments have a key role in working in partnership with the community by supporting and facilitating large-scale connectivity conservation initiatives. Species conservation needs a national response. The National Reserve system in Australia provides a critical conservation core, whose viability can be supported by large-scale connectivity conservation areas. A2A is one of these, and leadership is needed by five governments, community groups and industry to help achieve this.

Acknowledgement

The authors would like to recognize the enormous contribution of the Hon. Mr Bob Debus MP, former NSW Minister for the Environment and Attorney General who facilitated the formalization, national and international recognition, official announcement and NSW implementation of the A2A corridor in Australia.

Ecological restoration in Gondwana link (south-western Australia): A convergence of thought and action

James E. M. Watson, Simon Judd, Brendan G. Mackey and Keith Bradby

Setting

Australia faces two critical conservation challenges. First, there is an urgent need to conserve threatened species and ecosystems in heavily cleared and fragmented landscapes. Second, it is essential to keep intact country that has yet to be subject to broad-scale land clearing and related developments. Meeting both of these challenges makes it imperative that protected areas are systematically designed and are embedded within a broader landscape matrix where land management facilitates biodiversity conservation goals that cannot be met from protected areas alone. In both cases, conservation planning is needed on a regional basis. Unfortunately, governments have been tardy in taking up this challenge and, in response, various civil society initiatives have emerged to fill the conservation void. The aim of this case study is to describe two parallel civil society responses to meeting this challenge: The WildCountry programme of The Wilderness Society of Australia and the Gondwana Link collaboration.

The Wilderness Society of Australia is an NGO whose mission is protecting, promoting and restoring wilderness and natural processes across Australia for the survival and ongoing evolution of life on Earth. The Wilderness Society launched the WildCountry programme (hereafter WildCountry) to promote the long-term conservation of Australia's biodiversity (Recher, 2004). WildCountry was inspired by the American Wildlands Project (Foreman, 2004). A volunteer council of conservation scientists was formed to help develop a sound scientific basis for WildCountry. The central philosophy of WildCountry science is the importance of large-scale and long-term ecological processes that drive and enhance connectivity between ecosystems and species (Soulé et al, 2004; Mackey et al, 2007; and see Box

5.1 below). In the WildCountry context, connectivity draws attention to large-scale phenomena and processes that contribute to the maintenance of landscape ecological function. Connectivity is understood to be vital for many ecological processes such as food sources for nomadic species and the location of refugia during times of drought. As such, WildCountry science aims to integrate continental scale, ecological and evolutionary time-span considerations of ecosystem processes into conservation planning at national, regional and local scales. WildCountry science also recognizes the impact of rapid climate change and the need to incorporate this reality into conservation systems.

As the WildCountry vision promotes a landscape-wide approach to conservation, the work of The Wilderness Society Australia must necessarily involve collaboration with all organizations, communities, governments and individuals with responsibilities for land stewardship in a region. It also means that cross-tenure and multi-stakeholder approaches to conservation are needed to build upon, and complement, the anchors provided by the existing protected area network. Therefore, WildCountry reflects the need for (i) a significant improvement in the protected area network and off-reserve management; (ii) community engagement to catalyse and sustain 'coalitions of the willing' capable of developing and implementing conservation assessment, planning and action; and (iii) recognition that assessments, plans and management must be based on scientific considerations designed to ensure the long-term conservation of biodiversity. An important difference between a WildCountry approach and the existing protected area network is the theme of unifying and linking and not excluding

---

Box 5.1 WildCountry scientific connectivity considerations

The following points are taken from Soulé et al (2004) and Mackey et al (2007):

- *The conservation requirements of highly interactive animals* – a good example is the dingo. There is good evidence that a healthy dingo pack may regulate feral cats and foxes. This in turn may reduce predation on so-called critical weight (that is, smaller) marsupials.

- *The conservation requirements of dispersive animals* – many animals (in fact about 350 of Australia's bird species) travel large distances, between seasons or from year to year, often to find scarce food and other habitat resources.

- *Adaptation to climate change* – human use of fossil fuels along with land clearing is causing rapid climate change. Plants and animals persist even in the face of rapid climate change by evolving, dispersing to more suitable locations or taking refuge.

- *Ecological fire regimes* – fire has been part of the Australian environment since the continent broke free of Antarctica some 60 million years ago and began its slow drift northwards. Ecologically, what is important is not a single fire event but the pattern of fire experienced in a region over time, so-called fire regimes. All Australian plant species are adapted to persist through particular fire regimes.

- *Hydro-ecology* – water is the main environmental resource limiting landscape productivity in Australia. Rainfall is both limited and highly variable from year to year. This variability has been a major selective force on the evolution of Australia's plants and animals. Environmental assessment needs to consider the special relationships between the surface/groundwater resources and the vegetation cover, and the significance of this for animal habitat.

- *Spatially dependent evolution* – one way new species evolve is by animals dispersing through the landscape and establishing new populations. These populations can then become isolated from the other populations of the species. Over time, the new, isolated population can develop a sufficiently different genome that it becomes a new species. So, in the long term, over evolutionary timescales, it is important that humans do not place in the landscape barriers to species dispersal.

- *Coastal zone fluxes* – land and marine environments are linked through the flow of water, nutrients and organisms, such as the movement of fish from coastal catchments to near coastal marine ecosystems. What happens in costal catchments therefore affects near-coastal marine ecology.

degraded lands from conservation initiatives (Mackey et al, 2007).

The WildCountry programme only recently moved beyond the vision stage and was starting to be incorporated into conservation planning around the country. As such, there were no appropriate WildCountry activities that could be useful for the practical aims of this book. However, civil collaborations in Australia were conducting effective conservation actions that encompassed the large-scale, long-term WildCountry vision. These actions relied on the need for action and were not waiting for the science to drive their planning. In the rest of this case study, we provide a description of the Gondwana Link collaboration, outline how this effort fits well within the WildCountry vision, describe how WildCountry science has contributed to this collaboration and outline the lessons learned from its efforts to date.

Gondwana Link is a loose collaboration between several NGOs, including Australian Bush Heritage Fund, Fitzgerald Biosphere Group, Friends of Fitzgerald River National Park, Green Skills, Greening Australia, The Nature Conservancy and The Wilderness Society Australia. It commenced independently of WildCountry and is a prime example of civil society forming a 'coalition of the willing' to restore and protect one of the world's biodiversity hotspots – the Southwest Australian Floristic Region (Hopper and Gioia, 2004). The Wilderness Society of Australia was a founding member and is committed to the shared vision because of the obvious synergies with its WildCountry programme.

The Gondwana Link vision is being implemented in south-west Australia, which is recognized as one of the world's top 25 biodiversity hotspots (Hopper et al, 1996; Myers et al,

Wildflowers, south-west Western Australia

Source: Graeme L. Worboys

2000). This region is home to over 8000 plant species, more than 48 per cent of which occur nowhere else on Earth. Despite this high diversity and endemism, much of the area has been devastated by activities associated with agricultural development. Programmes and incentives generated by the Western Australian government until the early 1980s meant that the local farming community was encouraged to clear at least 400,000ha a year of vegetation (Rijavek, 2002). Unfortunately, the process was very effective, and in the past 40 years more than ten million hectares of south-western Australia unique vegetation communities have been cleared.

Across the 850km Gondwana Link pathway, eight distinct operational areas have been identified (Figure 5.5). In this chapter, we focus on one of these operational areas. The Fitz-Stirling

Operational Area (hereafter Fitz-Stirling) is so called because it sits between the Fitzgerald River National Park and Stirling Range National Park. In this case study, we examine how the work in the Fitz-Stirling has been catalytic in establishing the wider project and document some of the important lessons so that the key elements of the intent and approach may be applied elsewhere.

The connectivity conservation initiative

The Fitzgerald River and the Stirling Range National Parks are both floristic hot spots (Hopper and Gioia, 2004). The Fitzgerald River National Park is approximately 330,000ha in size, and contains 1800 plant species, of which 110 species are confined to the park. The Stirling Range National Park is 115,000ha in size, and contains over 1500 plant species, of which 78

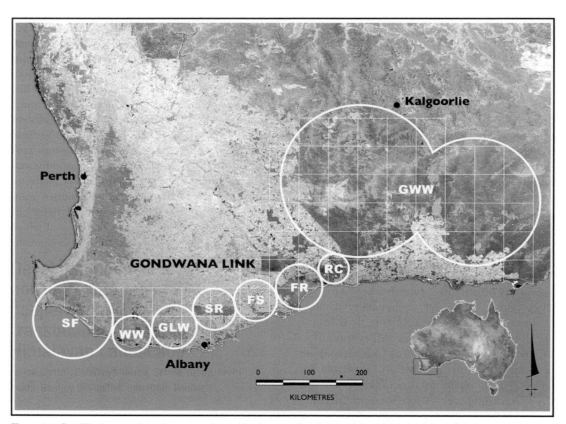

Figure 5.5 Satellite image of south-western Australia showing Gondwana Link and its eight operational areas

Note: SF = Southern Forests; WW = Walpole Wilderness; GLW = Gondwana Link West; SR = Stirling Range National Park; FS = Fitz-Stirling; FR = Fitzgerald River National Park; RC = Ravensthorpe Connection; GWW = Great Western Woodlands

species are endemic to the park. The two national parks include remnants of mountain ranges, a product of erosion. At 1050m, the Stirling Range is the highest mountain chain in south-western Australia, while Fitzgerald River contains a series of low quartzite ranges (400m high at their highest point). Both national parks encompass extensive sand heaths and rocky areas that were considered mostly unsuitable for agriculture and therefore largely spared from land-clearing processes, although attempts were being made into the mid-1980s to clear parts of what is now Fitzgerald River National Park (Bradby, 1991).

Over the last four decades, the area between the two national parks has fared less well. Much of the landscape has been cleared since the 1950s, which has left the remaining habitat fragmented and in ecological decline. The Fitz-Stirling area has a Mediterranean type climate and its characteristically rich flora have evolved due to a complex set of ecological processes operating at a range of scales over a fine-scale mosaic of soil and landforms (Hopper et al, 1990). These processes have been operating continuously since the area was last glaciated, some 250 million years ago. Unfortunately, there were virtually no ecological surveys done in the area before large-scale clearing commenced, and the degree of detailed biological knowledge remains minimal today. Nevertheless, recent work by Hopper and Gioia (2004) has identified the southern section of the Fitz-Stirling area as being as significant a floristic hot spot as either of the two adjacent national parks. As our knowledge of the area increases, no doubt the botanical importance of the Fitz-Stirling will increasingly be appreciated.

The Fitz-Stirling area is an extremely important refuge for many vertebrate species. There have been numerous rediscoveries across the region of formerly widely distributed mammal species, including the dibbler (*Parantechinus apicalis*), Shortridge's native mouse (*Pseudomys shortridgei*) and Gilbert's potoroo (*Potorous tridactylus gilbertii*). There is also increasing recognition that some of the region's animals, such as the western mouse (*Psuedomys occidentalis*), black-gloved wallaby (*Macropus irma*), square-tailed kite (*Hamirostra isura*), western ground parrot (*Pezoporus wallicus flaviventrus*), western whipbird

Banksia, south-west Western Australia

Source: Graeme L. Worboys

(*Psophodes nigrogularis oberon*), tammar wallaby (*Macropus eugenii*) and carpet python (*Morelia spilota imbricata*) have become (or are becoming) regionally extinct or rare elsewhere. Twelve species of mammal, seven species of bird and one reptile that occur in the Fitz-Stirling are considered threatened on a state and/or federal level (IUCN, 2006).

The current reserve system does not include sizeable patches of many of the Fitz-Stirling vegetation assemblages and will almost certainly not provide sufficient habitat for many of the region's vertebrate species to persist in the longer term. For example, Robinson (1997) found that only 2 per cent of four unique woodland associations were found in reserves and less than 10 per cent of three other vegetation communities were found within the parks. The clearing of native ecosystems has resulted in the severing of broad-scale ecological connections between the wetter forests and the drier inland that surrounds the region. This loss of connectivity is likely to impact upon the movement of many species in response to both climatic shifts and temporally variable seasonal or habitat resources.

Both the broader Gondwana Link vision (see www.gondwanalink.org for more information) and the more specific work underway in the Fitz-Stirling grew from community recognition of both need and opportunity. A shared vision was developed around fundamental concepts such as an appreciation of the high levels of biological richness, localized endemism in the area, concern for the damage caused during the preceding decades of land clearing and a need to counter the impacts of salinity, fragmentation and ongoing agricultural practices. Key members of the groups concerned recognized that ecological systems work only across whole landscapes. They also saw that the levels of funding for ecological management in south-western Australia were so low, when compared to the need, that only a programme that restored ecological resilience to the system and addressed the sources of ecological problems, rather than their symptoms, was worthwhile.

The Gondwana Link approach was to build on each participating group's core strengths, through a loose consortium that had its benefits in individual relationships as much as in organizational arrangements. The Wilderness Society's contribution to this coalition of the willing was to employ a scientist to work with the Gondwana Link Coordination Unit. The work helped to develop a sound scientific basis for work in the Fitz-Stirling. The position provided for a two-way flow of information and a scientific discourse that helped develop WildCountry science as much as it guided on-ground conservation work. WildCountry collated data and produced tools that were needed to make the task of filling the conservation void a little easier. The Wilderness Society of Australia also offered a small grants programme that assisted community groups in doing WildCountry and Gondwana Link style collaborative projects continent wide.

The resources of the collaborating organizations were put to work with the aid of The Nature Conservancy's (TNC) Conservation Area Planning approach (Low, 2003; TNC, 2007). A functional landscape plan for the Fitz-Stirling region was produced. This was the result of an iterative process and the plan, which was quick and easy to produce, consisted of TNC's spreadsheet and supporting documentation. The plan was not a static blueprint but a dynamic process subject to ongoing revision as information became available (Low, 2003). Gondwana Link was the perfect expression of what WildCountry was trying to achieve. It included some of the richest and best national parks on the continent and ecological restoration on a grand scale (Figure 5.6), but, most of all, both the WildCountry effort and the Gondwana Link focused on ecological function or process. To this end, organizations promoting the Gondwana Link developed the following characteristics of what they consider a functional landscape.

The collaboration agreed that a functional Fitz-Stirling landscape would allow:

- biophysical connection between bushland areas to enable viable fauna populations to be maintained;
- biophysical connection between bushland across the landscape that enables migratory and nomadic species to continue their life histories;
- the maintenance of seasonal food supplies to support viable fauna populations;
- nesting habitat to be protected so that existing fauna survives and previous fauna is restored to the greatest degree possible;
- freedom from stream pollution and streams with those hydrological characteristics that underpin the original ecological systems;
- the provision of freshwater in the landscape needed for key species, to underpin the original ecological systems and to maintain refugia;
- reversing or slowing the process of accelerated landscape xerification;
- genetic permeability to enable continued evolution of the area's diverse plant assemblages;
- trophic regulation by predators that favour indigenous species and systems over introduced species;
- for critical mass in specific plant and animals communities to enable longer term survival and ongoing evolution;

Figure 5.6 Direct seeding as part of broad-scale ecological restoration in the Fitz-Stirling operational area of Gondwana Link – the mountains of the Stirling Range National Park can be seen in the background

Source: Barry Heydenrych

• fire regimes that do not degrade the natural values of the landscape.

The collaboration generated a number of specific restoration targets to achieve this functional landscape.

Connectivity conservation management

Work to establish the Gondwana Link commenced formally in August 2002, with the appointment of a coordinator. In December that year, the Australian Bush Heritage Fund purchased Chereninup Creek Reserve (an 877ha property that included 60ha of cleared land). By July 2006, over 5300ha had been secured within the Fitz-Stirling area. This was achieved by a mixture of outright purchase and incentives for existing landholders to fence and covenant their habitat on their land.

The collaborating groups contributed in different ways. For example, the Australian Bush Heritage Fund purchased over 2000ha of bushland across the area, while Greening Australia drove the revegetation of large areas, having achieved almost 1000ha on farms and especially purchased properties. This included Australia's largest ecological replanting project to date: 600ha on a property co-owned with Bush Heritage. TNC provided a range of specialist skills, including conservation planning and also fund-raising and business management. The local Fitzgerald biosphere group organized incentive payments for covenanting and linked existing farmers into the revegetation efforts. These examples show that the Gondwana Link collaboration encompassed a genuinely holistic approach; there was engagement between a range of organizations, communities and individuals with a focus on conservation, and it was directed by science that looked at the broad-scale ecological processes that drive the ecosystems within and beyond the Fitz-Stirling area.

One of the reasons for the success of the Fitz-Stirling work was that lessons from previous conservation attempts were not forgotten. Local

Community revegetation at Australian Bush Heritage Funds' Chereninup Reserve

Source: Craig Keesing

landholders and groups had been involved with various conservation efforts since the early 1970s, and farmer groups had been working on more sustainable land management approaches since the early 1980s (Bradby, 1991). In 1999 a locally based effort to develop the Gondwana Link commenced; but after this lapsed, members of the local community sought assistance from a wider range of environmental NGOs. Consequently the benefits of a multi-group, multi-stakeholder collaboration became increasingly evident as momentum developed.

There were also other factors apart from the convergence of interests across a number of NGOs that led to a successful programme. The collaboration was able to gain momentum in the same period that restrictions were put on land clearing, thus removing a major negative influence on both the landscape and people's morale. TNC, which was in the early days of establishing its Australia programme, gave critical financial and moral support, and channelled donor funds into the first property purchase. Donor funds were also made available to support the establishment of a Gondwana Link Coordination Unit with a full-time position (the Gondwana Link Coordinator)

who could focus solely on building the collaboration between the parties and the local landholders. These different opportunities were critical early steps in giving the Gondwana Link vision some tangibility and energy.

Once momentum had started, it became critical that it was maintained. Two key objectives were to make sure that the Gondwana Link Coordination Unit remained small, while the groups grew in capacity, and to generate a solid working collaboration between the participating NGOs. As the NGOs were quite diverse and fulfilled very different niches across the spectrum of Australian environmental groups, this was a difficult task. It was found that a rigid organizational structure across the range of groups was clumsy and time-consuming. After considerable discussion a more inclusive, loose model of collaboration was developed that was found to be more effective. A simple set of informal guidelines were developed whereby groups agreed to:

- work cooperatively and share information;
- minimize formal joint decision making;
- have no joint legal accountability;
- foster inclusivity;

- maintain a focus on ecological outcomes, recognizing that these will be lasting only if achieved with respect to social outcomes.

At the same time, a set of ten principles was adopted to guide all the activities within the Gondwana Link (Box 5.2). These principles would be constantly refined as part of the desire to improve operational effectiveness. Gondwana Link became more than a broad-scale landscape restoration programme or a conservation area design. It was also a process that fostered and encouraged activities in the landscape that produced outcomes favourable to the persistence of the region's indigenous species.

Benefits and accomplishments

The Gondwana Link works not only at different spatial scales but also with respect for the cultural and social diversity of the landscape. The activities conducted in the Fitz–Stirling are guided by broad collaborative principles, so not only is each individual action valuable in its own right (a good thing) but broader landscape-scale conservation benefits also logically flow. In carrying out Gondwana Link activities, ecological resilience and functionality is retained in a way that relates directly to cultural and social health and resilience. This also helps to ensure that conservation activities are accepted and generally supported by the local agricultural community.

Box 5.2 Gondwana Link principles

1 Gondwana Link activities must be relevant to the ecological needs of the landscape and be directly linked to measurable and readily demonstrated ecological benefits (outcomes).

2 Gondwana Link activities must significantly reduce the impact (or likely impact) of overwhelming current and future threats to natural systems and to ecological processes. Currently, threats are identified and strategic actions are determined and evaluated by the functional landscape planning process. The planning process is ecologically based, open and participatory and is informed by the best available scientific and community knowledge.

3 Gondwana Link activities occur across a range of land-uses, tenures and social systems to effect lasting change. Individuals, groups and organizations undertaking activities must do so cooperatively and in a coordinated manner. They must also respect and support the coordination process. One Gondwana Link activity must not compromise another.

4 Gondwana Link activities should aim to restore connectivity and natural resilience to our natural ecosystems. Resilient ecosystems will not need intensive management intervention in the longer term. Connectivity conservation (at all scales and for all organisms) is central to the vision's thinking.

5 An activity that results in the loss of native vegetation or habitats (e.g. creek systems, wetlands, estuarine or marine systems) cannot be a Gondwana Link activity. The protection of native vegetation and habitat is always preferable to revegetation.

6 Gondwana Link restoration activities should demonstrate consolidation and/or extend native vegetation across the Link, preferably from bushland remnants, and cannot be replacements for native vegetation cleared elsewhere.

7 Individual habitat restoration projects should be designed and undertaken as incremental and opportunistic progressions towards our larger goal. They should be developed to contribute as much as possible to maintaining the ecological processes essential for the retention of functioning landscapes and avoid the creation of ecological sinks.

8 Gondwana Link activities are those that, where appropriate, combine indigenous, local and scientific knowledge and which are carried out with respect to the diversity of the environment and cultures across the Link.

9 Commercial enterprises that maintain the health of the landscape and/or do not compromise natural ecological processes can be included as Gondwana Link activities.

10 Ecological restoration that assists in the renewal or persistence of associated indigenous cultural practices may be called a Gondwana Link activity. A landscape may be ecologically degraded such that little of the pre-contact ecosystems persist, yet the country may still hold significant cultural value to an indigenous community. Eco-cultural restoration should also adhere to the principles above but must include consultation and advice from the traditional owners.

While resources and staff time remain focused on ecological outcomes, work has also progressed on diverse activities such as art exhibitions and installations, recording oral knowledge and supporting efforts by the indigenous Noongar community to reconnect with Country.

Lessons learned

The work in Fitz–Stirling has been pivotal in the consolidation of the Gondwana Link collaboration, in teasing out the implications of achieving landscape-scale change through such a cooperative approach, and in mobilizing the resources to support the work. A number of key lessons follow.

Good organizational and personal relationships are essential

The collaboration found that there were too many problems associated with formal agreements, especially when there was not a solid understanding of and respect for all the other players. There have been issues where strongly divergent views had to be worked through, and only mutual respect made progress possible.

Strategic opportunism is important

Diversity across the collaboration helped numerous opportunities to be embraced, a process that has been enhanced since late 2005 by a deliberate decision not to pursue tight organizational agreements across all the groups.

Detailed scientific planning can follow the action, initially at least

Many programmes are slowed by lengthy planning processes, which consume considerable time and resources. In Fitz-Stirling, valuable momentum was gained by letting organizations collaborate in a loose sense, and letting the science catch up. TNC's planning tool was found to be an excellent and adaptive shortcut to the heart of the science needed to further focus operations, with the functional plan developed for the region after a number of properties were purchased (not to the detriment of the collaboration!). It also was found that, perhaps like many damaged systems, the Fitz-Stirling environment responded to opportunity and that, by removing the threats, providing opportunities and enhancing natural resilience

through restoration efforts, some welcome ecological surprises resulted.

Flexibility is essential

The first four years were ones of great change, with many important elements becoming apparent only as the work progressed. For some of the NGOs involved, this required fundamental changes to how they undertook their core business.

The development of a consistent vision is crucial

Because of the difficult financial circumstances in which they operate, it is easy for NGOs to be lured away from their core direction by the availability of different sources of money, as a consequence of which their vision changes considerably over time. The simplicity and appeal of both the larger Gondwana Link vision, and its subset in Fitz-Stirling, was of great value in ensuring that the core focus was maintained, and that funding streams were drawn in behind that vision.

Visions gain significant horsepower when they start being implemented in a tangible way

Gondwana Link projects an ambitious vision, but the rapid purchase and restoration of properties in Fitz-Stirling provided tangible demonstration of the achievability of the vision. By concentrating on achieving significant land-use change, rather than further elaboration of the vision itself, significant extra resources were mobilized.

Benefits arise from coupling conservation theory and practice

Conservation protection and restoration is a practical activity that is catalysed by a vision of what the future can be and sustained by the passion of the people, communities and organizations involved. However, in the long term, conservation practice must achieve the desired ecological and evolutionary outcomes. Conservation theory can help ensure that strategic conservation planning and on-the-ground action is directed towards protecting and restoring the most important targets and outcomes, and that actions work synergistically towards agreed large-scale and long-term targets. However, the benefits from coupling conservation theory and practice flow both ways. Conservation theory usually develops, like all scientific theory, incrementally but with the occasional giant leap courtesy of new thinking. To be scientific, theories must be testable and tested. Regionally-scaled long-term restoration efforts like Gondwana Link provide crucial field data for testing conservation theory. Interpreting the practical relevance of the WildCountry connectivity principles in the Fitz-Stirling region both helped validate WildCountry science theory and highlighted areas where the principles were limited and further research was needed.

6

Indomalayan Connectivity Initiatives

The Indomalayan realm extends from the Hindu Kush range of Afghanistan through the Indian subcontinent and south-east Asia to southern China, and through Indonesia as far as Java, Bali and Borneo. It also includes the Philippines and Japan's Ryukyu Islands. East of Borneo lays the Wallace line, which separates the Indomalayan realm from the Australian realm. The Indomalayan realm has the highest mountains on Earth imme-diately to its north, and includes major rivers such as the Ganges and the Brahmaputra, volcanic landscapes, rainforests, mangrove forests and coral reef systems. This chapter presents three connec-tivity conservation case studies from the Indomalayan realm. As these initiatives are largely in their formative stages, the lessons from them are preliminary, and in some instances raise future challenges rather than provide firm conclusions.

Langtang Lirung (7234m), Langtang National Park, Nepal, part of the Sacred Himalayan Landscape connectivity conservation area

Source: Graeme L. Worboys

Creating biological corridors for conservation and development: A case study from Bhutan

Mingma Norbu Sherpa, Sangay Wangchuk and Eric Wikramanayake

Setting

Bhutan is a small country clinging to the southern slopes of the Himalayan Mountains. It retains most of its natural habitat, primarily because of its small human population, and strong ethical, cultural, economic and national policy considerations. However, in recent years, the country has begun to become more exposed to regional and global market forces and other external cultural influences, eroding these values and increasing the threats to biological resources. The population of Bhutan is increasing rapidly (RGB, 1999) and with it the demand for land for economic activities such as farming, grazing and trading.

Recognizing the importance of forest conservation to maintain environmental integrity, the Royal Government of Bhutan committed to maintain at least 60 per cent of the country under intact forest cover. The foundation for this will be the system of protected areas that covers over 26 per cent of the country, with an additional 9 per cent within habitat linkages. This system of linked protected areas, known as the Bhutan Biological Conservation Complex (B2C2), was bequeathed as a Gift to the Earth by the people of Bhutan in November 1999. The challenge became how to maintain those linkages so they could be effective corridors for species and ecological processes.

In this case study, we describe the steps taken to plan and implement the B2C2. Although the implementation is still in an incipient stage, we discuss the significance of the B2C2 to conservation and development for Bhutan, as well as to the global community, to make it a true Gift to the Earth.

Bhutan's geographic position along the eastern Himalayan mountain range places it squarely in the ecotone of two zoogeographical realms — the Indo-Malayan and the Palaearctic. The monsoon rains that sweep inland from the Bay of Bengal are funnelled along the Ganges River valley and deluge the eastern extent of the Himalayan range during the summer months, to make the eastern Himalayas biologically richer than the drier western extent. Bhutan, situated at the mouth of the funnel, bears the brunt of the monsoon rain. Because of this geographic position and the extreme, abrupt altitudinal variations and complex topography, the country harbours a diverse biodiversity represented within several distinct ecosystems that range from alluvial grasslands to savannas along the southern foothills to rich subtropical and temperate broadleaf forests in the mid-hills, and subalpine conifer forests and Himalayan alpine meadows in the upper slopes, just below the snow and ice covered mountain peaks along its northern borders. The known species include an inventory of over 5500 vascular plant species, 178 mammals, and 770 birds (RGB, 2002a). However, it is very likely that comprehensive surveys will increase the numbers among these and other taxonomic groups such as reptiles, amphibians, fishes and insects for which data are lacking.

The diverse assemblages of flora and fauna in the south are comprised of Indo-Malayan species. The tropical flora includes many species, such as *Dipterocarpus*, *Shorea* and *Terminalia* trees, climbing figs and other lianas and epiphytic orchids. Vertebrates here include many of the Indo-Malayan species such as Asian elephants (*Elephas maximus*), tigers (*Panthera tigris*), wild water buffalo (*Bubalus bubalis*), gaur (*Bos taurus*), hornbills (*Buceros* spp.), cobras (*Naja* spp.) and geckoes (various spp.). The northern Palaearctic realm contributes plant species characteristic of the higher elevations, including conifers like *Piceae, Abies* and *Larix*, deciduous broadleaf species such as *Betula, Alnus* and *Salix* and diverse alpine forbs such as *Potentilla* and *Pedicularis*. Palaearctic mammals include snow leopard (*Uncia uncia*), red panda (*Ailurus fulgens*), wolf (*Canis lupus*) and ungulates such as the takin (*Budorcas taxicolor*) and blue sheep (*Pseudois nayaur*) (WWF and ICIMOD, 2001). The alpine scrub and meadows up to an altitude of 4500m consists of dense shrubberies of juniper (*Juniperus*) and an array of rhododendron species as well as several, such as *Rosa, Lonicera, Cotoneaster, Potentilla, Meconopsis* and *Primula*, which have their global centres of biodiversity in the eastern Himalayas.

Because of its rich biological heritage, Bhutan is included in several global measures of biodiversity. It lies within a Global 200 ecoregion complex (Olson and Dinerstein, 1998), a biodiversity hot spot (Myers et al, 2000), important bird areas (Stattersfield et al, 1998), and a centre of plant diversity (WWF and IUCN, 1995). Thus, its biological wealth is considered to be a global conservation priority (Wikramanayake et al, 2001).

With over 70 per cent intact forest cover, especially in the mid-elevation temperate broadleaf and mixed conifer forest ecoregions, Bhutan represents one of the best opportunities for conservation of eastern Himalayan biodiversity. Over the past decade, conservation efforts in Bhutan have also undergone a paradigm shift. The initial protected areas system that was dominated by biologically depauperate rock and ice was transformed into a conservation landscape consisting of protected areas and habitat linkages, which is representative of the biodiversity of the country and the eastern Himalayan ecoregions. This landscape was designed to conserve biodiversity in its broadest sense, including species, communities, and processes (Franklin, 1993).

The connectivity conservation initiative

Until 1995, Bhutan's protected areas system was dominated by vast areas of rock and ice in the large parks along the northern border (Figure 6.1A). Thus, the most important and biologically diverse ecosystems in the mid- and lower hills were under-represented. In 1995, there was a significant redesign of the protected areas system. Two protected areas, Thrumshing La National Park and Jigme Singye Wangchuck National Park (first known as Black Mountains National Park) were enlarged to capture more intact broadleaf and subalpine forests. Two others, Sakteng Wildlife Sanctuary and Toorsa Strict Nature Reserve, were added to the mid-hills. Jigme Dorji National Park, which extended across the northern border of the country, was truncated to exclude large areas of rock and ice, but extended southwards to capture alpine grasslands and subalpine forests (Figure 6.1B). The eastern region of the original Jigme Dorji National Park was also extended southwards to include conifer and broadleaf forests and

renamed the Bumdeling Wildlife Sanctuary. This new system, which covers about 26 per cent of Bhutan, was more representative of the county's ecosystems and the biodiversity contained in them.

Then a system of corridors that linked the protected areas was identified from satellite images, based on available intact and contiguous habitat that excluded larger human settlements, and on the likelihood that they will not be prioritized for other land uses (Figure 6.1C). However, subsequent surveys to verify and document the biodiversity and conservation importance of these linkages revealed the presence of tigers at almost 3000m – elevations substantially higher than previously documented in the Himalayas (WWF, 2001). This prompted further tiger surveys, which found additional evidence of tiger presence outside of the protected areas, and a subsequent revision of the linkages to include potential tiger corridors and facilitate tiger movement between the protected areas (McDougal and Tshering, 1998).

Snow leopard surveys further north provided the basis for additional revision to corridors between the northern protected areas. North–south linkages were also modified to better ensure the maintenance of ecological processes along the elevation gradients, such as seasonal bird migrations and hydrological processes. In 2006, the resulting B2C2 covered almost 35 per cent of the country, and consisted of five national parks, two wildlife sanctuaries, one strict nature reserve and 12 corridors covering 15,230 square kilometres (Figure 6.1C; Table 6.1).

The vision for the B2C2 is to manage a landscape of protected areas and corridors to conserve the natural biodiversity of Bhutan in harmony with the values and aspirations of the Bhutanese people. The goal is to conserve the biodiversity, soils and watersheds of the landscape by integrating conservation and sustainable development for the livelihoods of the people.

The B2C2 was confirmed as a priority landscape for conservation of eastern Himalayan biodiversity during a regional analysis (WWF and ICIMOD, 2001). Bhutan offers the best opportunities for conserving large, unfragmented areas of the globally important eastern Himalayan

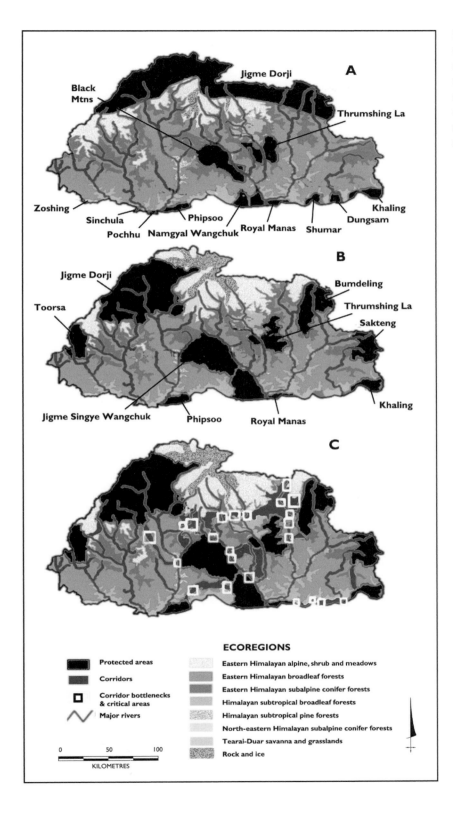

Figure 6.1 The evolution
of the protected areas
system in Bhutan:
(A) Protected area
system prior to 1995;
(B) Revised protected
areas; (C) Protected
areas and corridors

Table 6.1 Protected areas and corridors within the Bhutan Biological Conservation Complex

Name	Length (km)	Area (km²)	Zones	Significant wildlife
Torsa to Jigme Dorji	30	147	conifer and alpine	takin, blue sheep, musk deer, red panda, snow leopard
Jigme Dorji to Black Mountains	56	275	conifer and broadleaf	musk deer, red panda
Black Mountains to Jigme Dorji	55	601	conifer and broadleaf	takin, musk deer, red panda, blue sheep, tiger
Black Mountains to North corridor	20	549	conifer and broadleaf	musk deer, red panda, tiger, snow leopard
North corridor	76	663	conifer and alpine	takin, musk deer, red panda, tiger, snow leopard
Thrumsing La to North corridor	16	142	conifer and broadleaf	red panda, tiger
Kulong Chhu to North corridor	54	119	conifer and broadleaf	musk deer, tiger
Thrumsing La to Kulong Chhu	17	79	broadleaf and conifer	musk deer, red panda, tiger
Black Mountains to Thrumsing La	40	385	broadleaf to conifer	tiger
Phipsoo to Royal Manas	51	376	broadleaf	tiger, gaur, elephant
Khaling to Sakteng	32	160	broadleaf to conifer	tiger, gaur (unsurveyed)
Royal Manas to Khaling	49	212	broadleaf	tiger, gaur, elephant, rhino

temperate broadleaf and mixed conifer forests, since these forests are extensively converted and fragmented elsewhere in the region. Therefore, the ecological processes that depend on habitat continuity within ecoregions and contiguity among adjacent ecoregions along the altitudinal gradient – such as seasonal bird migrations and hydrological processes – which have been disrupted in most other places in the eastern Himalaya, are still intact in Bhutan.

All the major rivers that descend the Himalayan mountains join the Ganges and Brahmaputra Rivers, both of which eventually join and flow out into the Bay of Bengal. The northern headwaters of these rivers assure a perennial water supply to downstream human and ecological communities. Therefore, conservation of Bhutan's river systems also has a positive effect on the downstream ecological processes and the lives and livelihoods of people in Bhutan and further downriver in India and Bangladesh.

Connectivity conservation management

Although the biological corridors in the B2C2 were identified and given official recognition by the government, development and implementation of clear management guidelines had not been completed by 2006. The Nature Conservation Division within the Ministry of Agriculture, in collaboration with other line ministries and local government bodies, including park managers, divisional forest officers and Dzongkhag (district) forest officers, was mandated with conservation and management of the B2C2 system. From 2003, with funding from Global Environmental Facility (GEF) and WWF, the Nature Conservation Division had an ongoing programme to carry out biodiversity and socio-economic surveys, along with stakeholder consultations in the parks and corridors. With the limited capacity of the government, management of biological corridors was expected to be a gradual process with a need for careful and long-term planning, training, and awareness-raising, along with pilot activities in selected areas.

The conservation strategy in the corridors was to consist of conservation-friendly land-use options that ranged from forest management units, community forestry and traditional agricultural practices. However, because most corridors lay along steeper sloped terrain and along mountain ridges where forestry practices and forest clearing was prohibited, land-use practices that entailed resource exploitation would be limited in extent. Instead, maintaining the intact forests was to be the primary option throughout most corridor areas. The initial priorities for conservation interventions were 21 critical bottleneck areas (Figure 6.1C), where corridor width was restricted to less than 2km due to land uses such as roads and farms, causing connectivity to be tenuous.

The forest resource policy of the government supported and promoted sustainable natural resource exploitation. Since a large segment of Bhutan's population was dependent upon forest products, the government recognized the need for sustainable management of its forests. It also recognized that intact forests were linked to its economic mainstays: tourism, hydropower and timber. By 2006, gross revenue from tourism was expected to exceed US\$21 million (RGB, 2002b). Bhutan's up market tourism industry, which promoted a Himalayan experience, was based on a pristine and intact environment. Bhutan also saw the export of hydroelectricity to neighbouring India as an important future economic potential. In 1997, at the start of the 8th Five Year Plan, taxes and dividends from the hydropower sector contributed to 45 per cent of government revenue (RGB, 2002b). The government expected to capitalize on a potential 30,000MW of hydro-electricity, and set a target to achieve 100 per cent rural electrification by 2020.

Therefore, Bhutan's development policy and aspirations were dependent on maintaining environmental integrity. Realizing this, the government made a commitment to maintain at least 60 per cent intact forest cover. The Bhutan Biological Conservation Complex met over half of this target, and provided the foundation for this conservation goal. Since steep topography made most of Bhutan's land area unsuitable for agricul-

ture and large settlements, conservation of an additional 25 per cent of land area as forests was not an unattainable target, especially since it was in Bhutan's economic interests to do so.

Over the next ten years, threats to corridor habitats will be identified and conservation strategies will be developed and implemented in all corridors. Corridor management plans will include various land uses and land management regimes and classifications such as agriculture, pasture, forest types and degree of expansion of human settlements that can be permitted within corridors. It will also indicate the legal status of the land uses within the corridors. Implementation of the management plan will be concurrent with the issuance of a legal notification to the general public on the status of the corridors. The legal status of the corridors will be derived from the *Forest and Nature Conservation Act* 1995, wherein power is conferred on the Ministry of Agriculture to declare such conservation areas.

The designated corridors have been classified into three categories based on their width and intactness, and will require different management options:

1   *Intact corridors* connect protected areas and allow the potential exchange of species between otherwise isolated protected areas to ensure long-term viability and continuing evolution of the natural biota. No new development should be approved in these corridors that can potentially sever or restrict the corridor to less than 2km in width. Forest Management Units to meet local demands for timber and firewood can be permitted in these corridors, provided they are managed according to sustainable harvest regimes.

2   *Critical bottlenecks* are small sections within designated corridors that have vulnerable constrictions where gene flow is potentially curtailed below safe levels and where the further spread of human activities might completely sever natural habitat connections. Such areas will require immediate attention to prevent further degradation, along with restoration work to broaden the habitat connection where possible.

3   *Critical corridors* are corridors or corridor sections or sites that have specific conservation significance because of high biological values, their role as stepping stones or their vulnerability to existing threats. These areas include major passes on east–west highways, such as Dochu La and Pele La. These sites need special attention to protect the forest and watershed from erosion, road development and overgrazing by domestic livestock.

Preliminary survey results show that the habitat is still in good condition in most of the designated corridors. Socio-economic surveys have indicated that most corridors are free of dense human habitation. The original corridor delineation strove to avoid large human settlements. However, there are 50 villages comprising 1000 households concentrated in the lower valleys of several corridors. Biological and socio-economic surveys have been conducted in the three major corridors linking Thrumsingla with Manas and Jigme Singye Wangchuck National Parks, and the information gathered will be used to prepare management plans. The surveys indicated that most residents have a per capita income below the national average. These people depend heavily on forest resources for fuel wood, which is used for cooking and heating. The low human densities and their dependency on forest resources are considered opportunities for conservation.

Benefits and accomplishments

In 2002, the Royal Government of Bhutan and WWF initiated a gateway community programme in five communities within the corridors to guide local natural resource management, support local economic empowerment, support and strengthen local governance and improve local health and education. The objectives of these pilot community development projects – in Phobjikha, Ura, Kunga Rabten, Shingneer and Daliphangma – were to improve directly the lives of Bhutanese villagers in the heart of the corridors and reduce their dependence on forest resources. It was hoped that such a strategy would increase support for stewardship, thereby stabilizing the habitat for such vanishing species as the tiger, snow leopard and red panda (RGB, 2002b).

Surveys have shown that tigers occur in both corridors that connect Thrumshing La with Jigme Singye Wangchuk and Royal Manas National Parks (McDougal and Tshering, 1998). This represents the only confirmed occurrence of tigers above 3000m. In accordance with Bhutan's national tiger action plan (Bhutan Nature Conservation Division, 2005) the Nature Conservation Division and WWF have established a tiger compensation fund to provide compensation for livestock depredation by tigers in the corridors. Despite the fund, five to ten tigers are killed by local inhabitants each year in retaliation for livestock losses.

Four protected areas, Thrumshing La, Jigme Dorji, Jigme Singye and Royal Manas, already have five-year management systems in place. These efforts were supported by GEF, Danish International Development Assistance (DANIDA), Netherlands Development Organization (SNV), WWF, Bhutan Trust Fund and the MacArthur Foundation. The core of the Bhutan Biological Conservation Complex comprises Thrumshing La, Jigme Singye Wangchuck and Royal Manas National Parks. Therefore, these were prioritized for management planning. WWF and GEF supported conservation management of Thrumshing La National Park and its buffer zone, and the two biological corridors that connect Thrumshing La National Park with Royal Manas National Park and Jigme Singye Wangchuck National Park (Figure 6.1C). Management plans were developed for both Royal Manas National Park and Jigme Singye National Park, but the former was not implemented because of an unstable security situation. However, in 2004 this situation was resolved, and WWF was poised to resume support to repair park infrastructure and revise the management plan.

Conservation management of the Bhutan Biological Conservation Complex had only begun and much work remained to be done. The strategic management options for the immediate future were to implement conservation and sustainable development activities in full partnership with the district, gewog (village) administration and local community-based organizations, along with local and international NGOs and donor agencies. Returning economic benefits from natural resource management, ecotourism and other alternative income generation schemes to the local people to uplift their livelihoods was an important component of the B2C2 strategy.

At the same time, management of protected areas was to be strengthened, since poaching and unsustainable harvest of non-timber forest products were fast becoming a major problem. Transboundary conservation opportunities with India were to be pursued, since several protected areas along the southern and eastern borders were adjacent to existing Indian protected areas or abutted intact habitat that linked with Indian protected areas.

The B2C2 is an ambitious and important conservation model in Asia for creating a landscape where people and wildlife can coexist. Achieving the goals of this programme will contribute greatly to a global conservation effort, and establish Bhutan as one of the world's most innovative countries in wildlife conservation and community-based natural resource management. With over 70 per cent intact forest cover, especially in the mid-elevation temperate broadleaf and mixed conifer forest ecoregions, Bhutan represents one of the best opportunities for conservation of eastern Himalayan biodiversity. A combination of government commitment, international support and local engagement has resulted in the establishment of a network of interconnected protected areas that represent 35 per cent of Bhutan's land area, covering over 15,000km^2.

Lessons learned

Conservation efforts must go hand-in-hand with economic opportunities

As in many mountainous countries, Bhutan's rural people are dependent on natural resources for their economic well-being. Management planning for the B2C2 is accommodating the needs of local people for forest products and revenue from tourism, and the need of the country for hydroelectric generation.

Conservation of headwater areas has multiple benefits

All of the major rivers that descend from the Himalayan Mountains eventually join the Ganges and Brahmaputra Rivers, both of which join and flow out into the Bay of Bengal. The northern headwaters of these rivers assure a perennial water supply to downstream human and ecological communities. Therefore, in addition to protecting the biodiversity of Bhutan's Himalayan environments, conservation of Bhutan's river systems also has a positive effect on the downstream ecological processes and the lives and livelihoods of people in Bhutan and further downriver in India and Bangladesh.

Political will is essential to large-scale connectivity conservation

The Royal Government of Bhutan has committed to maintain at least 60 per cent of the country under intact forest cover. This has made it possible to implement a significant system of core protected areas encompassing 26 per cent of the country, linked by corridors covering another 9 per cent that are managed for the conservation of key species. Recognizing the need to ensure that diverse ecosystems and their species assemblages were included, the government redesigned the protected areas system, eliminating some high-elevation areas in order to include more biologically rich lower elevations. Such a strategic approach to protected areas design by government agencies is rare.

The support of international agencies is often necessary for successful outcomes

A number of international agencies and organizations have facilitated the creation of the B2C2. WWF and GEF supported biodiversity and socioeconomic surveys, along with stakeholder consultations in the parks and corridors. Meanwhile, WWF, GEF, DANIDA and SNV supported the implementation of management plans in four of B2C2's national parks.

A science-based approach is required for effective corridor design

Bhutan's system of corridors was identified from satellite images, based on available intact and contiguous habitat that excluded larger human settlements, and on the likelihood that they would not be prioritized for other land uses. When subsequent surveys revealed the presence of tigers at almost 3000m, further tiger surveys found additional evidence of tiger presence outside of the protected areas. This prompted a subsequent revision of the linkages to include potential tiger corridors and facilitate tiger movement between the protected areas. Snow leopard surveys further north provided the basis for additional revision to corridors between the northern protected areas. North–south linkages were also modified to better ensure the maintenance of ecological processes along the elevation gradients, such as seasonal bird migrations and hydrological processes.

A combination of top-down and bottom-up approaches can provide the greatest protection for connectivity

Bhutan legislation provided the legal framework for corridor management plans. They designated appropriate land management regimes and land uses that could be permitted within corridors. At the same time, a community-based programme guided local natural resource management, supporting local economic empowerment, supporting and strengthening local governance and improving local health and education. These community development efforts improved directly the lives of Bhutanese villagers in the heart of the corridors and reduced their dependency on forest resources while gaining support for stewardship, thereby stabilizing the habitat for vanishing species. Returning economic benefits from natural resource management, ecotourism and other alternative income generation schemes to the local people to uplift their livelihoods was an important component of the B2C2 strategy.

Developing conservation corridors and regional cooperation in the transboundary Sacred Himalayan Landscape

Nakul Chettri, Eklabya Sharma, Sabita Thapa, Yeshi Lama, Sangay Wangchuk and Brian Peniston

Setting

The Hindu Kush Himalaya (HKH) mountains are spread over an area of 4,300,000km². With diverse land-use types and rich in culture, the region sustains about 150,000,000 people with different class, caste and ethnicity. Sustainable use of resources and conservation is culturally embedded in traditions and practices of many indigenous communities living in the region (Ramakrishnan, 1996; Xu et al, 2005). The sacred knowledge and sacred places scattered over the HKH region have been very effective in biodiversity conservation (Xu and Melic, 2007). These religious and traditional practices linked to the worship of sacred space and maintenance of biodiversity is the testimony of functional landscapes that gave the region its cultural heritage. In terms of biodiversity, the HKH region hosts two of the world's 34 biodiversity hot spots, namely the Himalaya and Indo-Burman hot spots, endowed with a rich variety of genetic, species and ecosystem diversity of global importance with a high degree of threat (Mittermeier et al, 2004).

In recognition of this global significance, the region's member countries, namely Afghanistan, Bangladesh, Bhutan, China, India, Myanmar, Nepal and Pakistan, are signatories to the 1992 *Convention on Biological Diversity*. Between them, they have established 358 protected areas covering a wide range of habitats across the region and many other concrete steps have been taken to make biodiversity conservation effective and integrated. However, the majority of the protected areas are still isolated as conservation islands with a protectionist approach, ignoring the human dimension and cultural aspect embedded in the landscape dynamics. They are scattered without natural connectivity between the existing protected areas or the countries. Interestingly, quite a few of these protected areas are transboundary in nature, demanding an integrated approach for effective conservation through regional cooperation (Pei and Sharma, 1998; Sherpa et al, 2003; Sharma and Chettri, 2005).

Realizing this imperative, WWF Nepal and the International Centre for Integrated Mountain Development (ICIMOD) in 1997 initiated regional conservation initiatives on key transboundary areas of the eastern Himalayas. Even before this, the Government of Nepal, The Mountain Institute and ICIMOD initiated transboundary study and cooperation at the local level between Nepal and the Tibetan Autonomous

Region of China in the Mount Everest complex (Sherpa et al, 2003). The initiatives considered the geopolitical and ecological importance of the region and were based on the premise that effective conservation of important transboundary landscapes is possible only through regional cooperation (Rastogi et al, 1997; Sherpa et al, 2003). This developed a niche for further research and consultations. From numerous consultations, research and review processes the Kangchenjunga Complex was unanimously identified as one of the most critical biodiversity conservation areas in the eastern Himalayas (Yonzon et al, 2000; WWF and ICIMOD, 2001; CEPF, 2005). Since 2002, this recommendation was taken further by ICIMOD, which advocated for developing conservation corridors between the existing protected areas and across the political boundaries of three countries (Figure 6.2), namely Nepal, India and Bhutan

(Sharma and Chettri, 2005; Chettri and Sharma, 2006). In 2004, further collaboration amongst WWF Nepal, ICIMOD, The Mountain Institute, IUCN Himal Program, IUCN Nepal and the Nepal Ministry of Forest and Soil Conservation conceptualized the Sacred Himalayan Landscape to address the conservation of biodiversity and cultural integrity (HMGN-MFSC, 2005; Gurung et al, 2006).

The connectivity conservation initiative

The proposed Sacred Himalayan Landscape (Figure 6.3) is a conceptualized vision for a transboundary landscape that captures the alpine meadows, grasslands and temperate broadleaf and conifer forests of the eastern Himalaya and a vast majority of sacred sites. It covers an area of 39,021km², of which about 73.5 per cent falls in Nepal, 24.4 per cent falls in Sikkim India and the

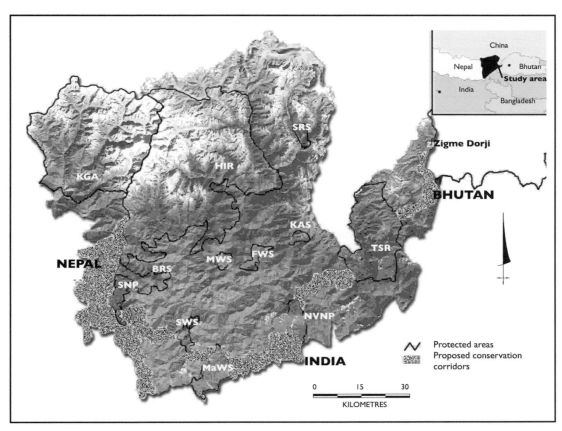

Figure 6.2 Kanchenjunga transboundary landscape with proposed conservation corridors

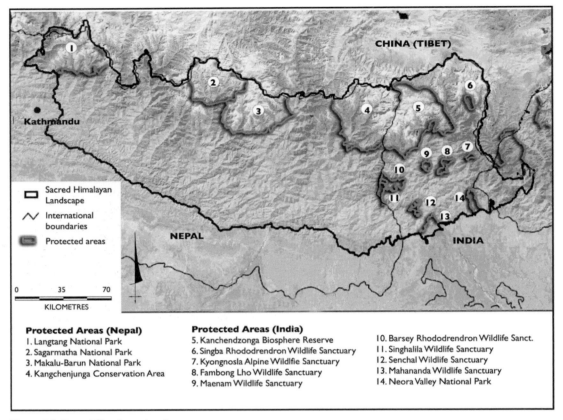

Protected Areas (Nepal)
1. Langtang National Park
2. Sagarmatha National Park
3. Makalu-Barun National Park
4. Kangchenjunga Conservation Area

Protected Areas (India)
5. Kanchendzonga Biosphere Reserve
6. Singba Rhododrendron Wildlife Sanctuary
7. Kyongnosla Alpine Wildlfie Sanctuary
8. Fambong Lho Wildlife Sanctuary
9. Maenam Wildlife Sanctuary

10. Barsey Rhododrendron Wildlife Sanct.
11. Singhalila Wildlife Sanctuary
12. Senchal Wildlife Sanctuary
13. Mahananda Wildlife Sanctuary
14. Neora Valley National Park

Figure 6.3 Sacred Himalayan Landscape

remaining 2.1 per cent falls in Bhutan. It extends from Langtang National Park in central Nepal through the Kangchenjunga region in Sikkim and Darjeeling in India to Toorsa Strict Nature Reserve in western Bhutan. It includes two of the WWF Global 200 ecoregions (Olson and Dinerstein, 2002) and lies within the Himalaya biodiversity hot spot (Mittermeier et al, 2004), a testament to the global significance of its biodiversity. Beside this, the landscape has many sacred mountains, lakes, forests, streams, relics, monasteries, temples and so on, and is peopled with communities having strong spiritual faith and conservation ethics (Ramakrishnan, 1996; Xu et al, 2005). Hence, the transboundary nature of the cultural landscape presents an excellent opportunity for cooperation among the countries in the region for effective conservation and also for meeting obligations under international agree-

ments such as the *Convention on Biological Diversity* and the *Convention on Migratory Species* (Pei and Sharma, 1998).

Landscape-level biodiversity conservation is an evolving concept (Smith and Maltby, 2003; Faith, 2005; Locke and Dearden, 2005). More than preserving isolated patches of sustained wilderness in the form of protected areas, the focus is now on maintaining landscape integrity and connectivity, and on viewing and conserving ecosystems as part of larger agro-ecological and socio-cultural landscapes (McNeely, 2004; Canova, 2006). Therefore, the conventional approaches call for a thorough re-contextualization and reorientation of the familiar precepts of biodiversity conservation (Sheppard, 2000). Taking a cue from recent international processes and declarations on biodiversity conservation like the *Convention on Biological Diversity*, the World Summit on Sustainable

Development and the Durban Accord, the global community started seeing ecosystems as part of larger biomes, and ecological landscapes made up of several such biomes including anthropogenic, or man-made, systems impacting on biodiversity (Balasinorwala et al, 2004). There are many such landscapes in the Himalaya that are transboundary in nature and the interdependence at this level is so strong that any change influencing one system in one country would automatically impact on the neighbouring one (Chettri and Sharma, 2005).

In recent years, the eastern Himalaya witnessed a number of such landscape-level initiatives for biodiversity conservation (Sherpa et al, 2003; Sherpa et al, 2004). There are many critical ecoregions and transboundary complexes that are of global importance (Chettri and Sharma, 2005). The area surrounding Mount Kangchenjunga is one of the richest landscapes in the Himalayan region and one of the world's most critical centres of biodiversity (Yonzon et al, 2000; WWF and ICIMOD, 2001). Due to its strategic location between Nepal, India, Bhutan and China, transboundary cooperation is necessary to make conservation efforts effective (Pei and Sharma, 1998; CEPF, 2005). During the past several years, many consensus-building processes on regional cooperation for this critical transboundary area were initiated (Rastogi et al, 1997; Sharma and Chettri, 2005) that led to envisioning a greater transboundary landscape in the form of the Sacred Himalayan Landscape (HMGN-MFSC, 2005; Gurung et al, 2006).

The Sacred Himalayan Landscape comprises five of the 19 ecoregions of the eastern Himalaya and provides a home for about 7000 flowering plants, including more than 400 orchids, over 60 rhododendrons, above 350 wild edible plants and hundreds of high-value medicinal plants (Wikramanayake et al, 2001). Among this vast floral diversity, a significant proportion is endemic to the region (Shrestha and Joshi, 1996; WWF and ICIMOD, 2001). The fauna in this landscape is diverse and rich. The whole landscape is considered to be a contiguous habitat for many flagship species that are of global importance. Over 100 species of mammals have been reported within the protected areas of this landscape, including more than 50 species of conservation importance (CEPF, 2005). Similarly, over 550 species of birds and 600 butterflies have also been found in the landscape (Yonzon et al, 2000).

Our analysis revealed that the Sacred Himalayan Landscape is an extended habitat, beyond political as well as protected area boundaries, for many charismatic and endangered species such as snow leopard (*Uncia uncia*), blue sheep (*Pseudois nayur*), Himalayan tahr (*Hemitragus jemlahicus*), goral (*Naemorhedus baileyi*), serow (*Capricornis sumatraensis*), takin (*Budorcas taxicolor*), red panda (*Ailurus fulgens*), Himalayan musk deer (*Moschus chrysogaster*) and tiger (*Panthera tigris*). Interestingly, during the course of the initiative's participatory research, it was revealed that there are a number of contiguous habitats outside the protected areas with the potential for developing corridors, as there was substantial evidence of the use of such areas by a number of key species. Therefore, the areas lying outside the designated protected areas appeared to be equally important for conservation of biodiversity by providing connectivity for the long-term population viability of such species. Thus, development of corridors through protection in Bhutan and through rehabilitation in Nepal and India will provide the necessary connectivity between the protected areas spread across this transboundary landscape.

Connectivity conservation management

During the last three decades, efforts to conserve biodiversity in impoverished regions have gradually begun to shift away from law enforcement and use restrictions towards more participatory approaches emphasizing equitable and sustainable use of natural resources (Sharma and Chettri, 2005; Chettri and Sharma, 2006). This change in approach was important in the remote border areas of the Sacred Himalayan Landscape, where biodiversity was concentrated, where poverty tended to be pervasive, and where the reach of development programmes was often limited.

The strategy to create habitat links between protected areas in the Sacred Himalayan Landscape was built upon recommended strategies (Yonzon et al, 2000; WWF and ICIMOD, 2001) and the priorities of national governments for landscape-level conservation. The *Nepal*

Biodiversity Strategy (HMGN–MFSC, 2002) clearly emphasizes the need to establish conservation linkages between the Kangchenjunga Conservation Area and Makalu Barun National Park. Likewise the National Biodiversity Strategy and Action Plans of Bhutan (Anonymous, 2002) and India (MEF, 2004) also emphasize the need for a landscape-scale approach, connectivity and transboundary cooperation for effective biodiversity conservation. As a result, in 2002, ICIMOD with its partners put into action the landscape approach to biodiversity conservation by developing corridors within a transboundary conservation landscape in the Kangchenjunga complex, including lands from eastern Nepal, the State of Sikkim and Darjeeling District of India and western Bhutan (Sharma and Chettri, 2005). This initiative was further nurtured with a strategic process to conceptualize the Sacred Himalayan Landscape in collaboration with other key partners (Figure 6.4). Two sets of strategic process were followed, one for regional cooperation amongst Nepal, Bhutan and India and another for developing strategic plans within each of these countries (Table 6.2). Following the recommendations of various consultations, in 2004 a consortium of partners under the leadership of the relevant ministries and departments from the three countries (Nepal,

India and Bhutan) initiated steps towards feasibility assessments at local and national levels for the development of the Sacred Himalayan Landscape and conservation corridors. ICIMOD, partnering with the Department of Forests in Nepal, Sikkim and West Bengal and the Nature Conservation Division of the Ministry of Agriculture in Bhutan, along with a number of local NGOs, worked on a feasibility assessment and participatory planning for developing corridor linkages between protected areas in the Kangchenjunga complex (NCD, 2005). The Mountain Institute worked towards building capacity for joint forest management and enterprise-based conservation initiatives in Sikkim's protected areas and livelihood-based conservation approaches in the habitat corridors outside the Kangchenjunga Conservation Area in eastern Nepal. The WWF initiated programmes to strengthen protected area management by communities in the Kangchenjunga Conservation Area of Nepal and in Sagarmatha National Park and buffer zones through capacity building of the Management Council. IUCN worked to address deforestation of sensitive habitats by promoting local community development in the Tinjure Milke Jaljale Area, which links Kangchenjunga Conservation Area and Makalu Barun National Park. This partnership, under the auspices of the

Table 6.2 Strategic planning processes in the Sacred Himalayan Landscape

Regional level	National level
Step 1: Developed rationale for regional cooperation based on conservation importance of biodiversity of the area through consultative process.	Step 1: Institutionalized the process through forming task force/steering committees.
Step 2: Conceptualized landscape with mission, vision and objectives.	Step 2: Redefined vision and goals through consultative workshops at national and district levels and identified potential conservation corridors.
Step 3: Mobilized stakeholders for realization on importance of transboundary landscape for socio-economic development and biodiversity conservation.	Step 3: Analysed key contextual factors through participatory research.
Step 4: Organized inception workshop to identify priority thematic areas of interventions.	Step 4: Developed detail corridor development strategies and action plans.
Step 5: Facilitated research for recommended thematic areas.	Step 5: Developed strategic documents for the proposed landscape shared by each participating country.
Step 6: Organized policy dialogue based on the research outputs and developed a draft policy framework.	

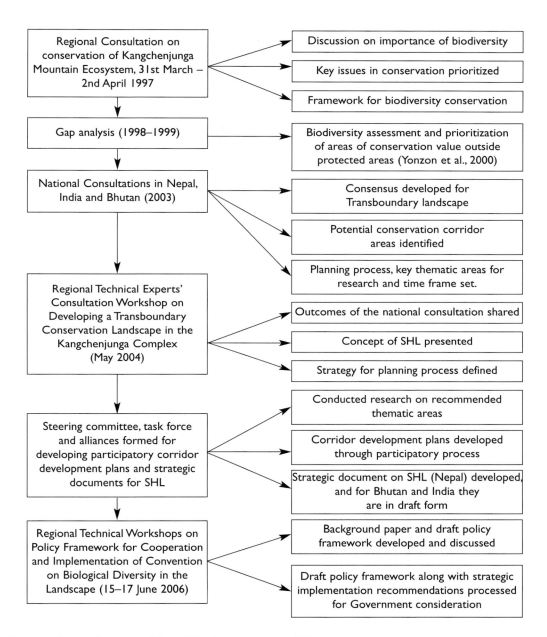

Figure 6.4 Process flow chart of Sacred Himalayan Landscape (SHL)

Sacred Himalayan Landscape, enabled participating agencies and organizations to strategize and harmonize current and future interventions involving multiple stakeholders in order to work towards a common vision, rather than intervening haphazardly across the landscape without larger conservation goals.

Benefits and accomplishments

Biological corridors are generally designed in an effort to overcome problems associated with island biogeography. So called 'islands' are created when distinct areas are placed into an environmental protection plan while the surrounding environment is subject to the deleterious effects of the human-induced pressures of 'no' management. Corridors that connect individual protected areas embed the zone of management into a larger context, and a landscape approach to management requires the land-use matrix to maintain those ecosystem processes necessary for the preservation of regional biodiversity. Fortunately, the protected areas in this Himalayan landscape have not yet suffered from the island syndrome. The Sacred Himalayan Landscape initiative will help in long-term conservation planning to avoid the island syndrome in the future. However, the matrices in the Sacred Himalayan Landscape and the ecological systems are complex and their services in terms of benefit to human beings are diverse and numerous.

Most of the ecological zones of the landscape are extended habitat for many charismatic Himalayan species. It recently was learned that substantial proportions of red panda and snow leopard habitats are found outside the existing protected areas (Wikramanayake, 2005). The Sacred Himalayan Landscape provides contiguous habitat for many such charismatic species due to its natural continuity with the vast Quomoloangma Nature Reserve in Tibet (China) in the north and with the Bhutan Biological Conservation Complex to the east. The conservation value of these charismatic species will be significantly enhanced when environmentally managed corridors link them (Yonzon et al, 2000; Sharma and Chettri, 2005; Chettri and Sharma, 2006). Moreover, the proposed landscape also captures more biodiversity than existing smaller and scattered protected areas because of the beta-diversity effect. In this context the Governments of Bhutan, India and Nepal have already initiated processes for developing strategic documents to enhance the conservation corridor concept.

Ecosystem health is essential to maintain the integrity of biodiversity values and their services to mankind (Costanza et al, 1997). Therefore, understanding the negative and positive effects of land use for conservation of biodiversity and its relation to ecosystem services needs a landscape perspective (Tscharntke et al, 2005). Created by interactions of living organisms with their environment, ecosystem services support the inhabitants of the Sacred Himalayan Landscape by providing clean air and water, decomposing waste, pollinating flowers, regulating climate and supplying a host of other benefits. The mountain water towers and the cascading streams, diverse forest types and agro-ecological practices within the landscape play an important role in hydrological processes, nutrient dynamics and economic development in the region (Sharma, 1997). These many ecological goods and services sustain the livelihoods of millions of people living in the area as well as support thrice the population downstream with associated economic benefits. With the formation of the Sacred Himalayan Landscape, conservation efforts for these water towers could be linked to global initiatives with local, regional and global leverages.

The societal integrity of the different ethnic groups is still strong in the landscape. The local communities have long-standing traditions of conservation and restrained resource use guided by conservation ethics, customary laws and traditional rights (Rai et al, 1994; Ramakhrishnan, 1996; Jha, 2002; Pant, 2002). Many of the key areas of the landscape such as Mount Everest, Mount Kangchenjunga and Mount Zhumolari are sacred to the local people. They are the owners and co-managers for considerable forested lands and had been instrumental in conserving natural and domestic biodiversity, both inside and outside the protected areas. Traditional natural resources management systems, such as Shinggi Nawa among the Sherpas of Nepal, Dzumsa among Lachungpas and Na Zong Nyo among Lepchas of Sikkim, are some of the effective traditional conservation measures that are seen to address 'sustainability' of resources and maintain the resilience of natural systems. These practices are also a vehicle for transferring indigenous knowledge and practices with a clear message of conservation ethics. Thus, conservation is culturally enforced within many of the indigenous groups of the landscape. This reflects the strong link between biological resources and human needs. However, these practices are fading slowly due to various driving forces, leading to numerous conservation challenges. There is a vast opportunity to revitalize practices that might retain cultural values while contributing to conservation goals.

The location of the Sacred Himalayan Landscape across four national boundaries is an important asset for the region's geopolitics. The contiguous habitat and open border situation make the landscape an ideal place for cooperation for biodiversity conservation. As signatories to the *Convention on Biological Diversity*, especially the Mountain Biodiversity Programme (Sharma and Acharya, 2004), all of these countries are committed to promote an ecosystem/landscape approach to conservation and to establish regional and transboundary collaboration in conservation. Bhutan and Nepal, being land locked countries with limited arable land for increasing populations, have a high potential for bilateral cooperation with India in trade, research and monitoring, information and technology sharing for mutual benefits.

The Sacred Himalayan Landscape has a high potential for tourism development. Many of the potential tourism destinations, such Mt Everest and the Kangchenjunga Conservation Area of Nepal, Sikkim and Darjeeling of India and Zumolari trek of Bhutan, have a high potential for cross-border ecotourism. The South Asian Sub-Regional Economic Cooperation (SASEC) group has already identified the region as a potential tourism destination and developed a tourism development plan (SASEC, 2004). This provides a strong basis for cooperation by the countries signatory to the *Convention on Biological Diversity* in managing biodiversity over transboundary landscapes to fulfil their global commitments. In this context, biodiversity conservation at regional scales can take advantage of complementarity in ways that promote regional sustainability (Faith and Walker, 2002). Thus, there is a strong regional basis for developing a transboundary landscape to address global conservation and sustainable development goals.

Lessons learned

The Sacred Himalayan Landscape has diverse land-use types encompassing varied cultures, traditions, conservation priorities and policies. Such a scenario brings complexities and to bring all these stakeholders into one platform to discuss a common goal for mutual benefits was a great challenge and a time-consuming process.

The involvement of local communities is critical to success

Human accelerated pressures are the most important factor that leads to habitat degradation and is equally challenging for conservation. No other option remains but to broaden the focus of conservation by including the people in the larger landscape. With this realization local communities were considered as a central pillar in the Sacred Himalayan Landscape planning process. It was also learned that people are willing to come forward for conservation, provided some alternative economic options are available. Their participation seemed to increase when community empowerment in decision making was strengthened.

Spiritual and cultural practices can support conservation efforts

A strong cultural identity to the landscape, especially where natural features and process are incorporated into spiritual beliefs, can strengthen conservation efforts. Traditional natural resources management systems such as Shinggi Nawa among the Sherpas of Nepal, Dzumsa among Lachungpas and Na Zong Nyo among Lepchas of Sikkim are some of the effective traditional conservation measures that are seen to address sustainability of resources and maintain the resilience of natural systems. These practices were also a vehicle for transferring indigenous knowledge and practices with a clear message of conservation ethics. Thus, conservation was culturally enforced within many of the indigenous groups of the landscape, facilitating acceptance of the Sacred Himalayan Landscape approach.

Multiple organizations and agencies must be included from the outset

The Sacred Himalayan Landscape process considered extensive participatory and consultative measures from its initial inception phase. This was found to be very critical and provided the lesson that multi-stakeholder partnership and support from government agencies are crucial for success in such initiatives.

Mountainous, transboundary regions provide many opportunities for conservation

The Hindu Kush Himalaya constitutes a major biogeographic boundary between the subtropical and tropical flora and fauna of the Indian subcontinent and the temperate-climate Palaearctic ecozone. The HKH region hosts two of the world's 34 biodiversity hot spots, namely the Himalaya and Indo-Burman hot spots, endowed with a rich variety of genetic, species and ecosystem diversity of global importance with a high degree of threat. The proposed Sacred Himalayan Landscape is a conceptualized vision for a transboundary landscape that captures the alpine meadows and grasslands, temperate broadleaf and conifer forests of the eastern Himalaya and a vast majority of sacred sites. During the course of the initiative's participatory research, it was revealed that there are a number of contiguous habitats outside the protected areas with the potential for developing corridors, as there was substantial evidence of the use of such areas by a number of key species. Thus, development of corridors through protection in Bhutan and through rehabilitation in Nepal and India will provide the necessary connectivity between the protected areas spread across this transboundary landscape.

National and international commitments help to engage government participation

Government commitments to biodiversity conservation can provide a rationale for and help to anchor large-scale connectivity conservation efforts. As signatories to the *Convention on Biological Diversity*, especially the Mountain Biodiversity Programme, all these countries are committed to promote an ecosystem/landscape approach to conservation and to establish regional and transboundary collaborations in conservation. The Nepal Biodiversity Strategy clearly emphasizes the need to establish conservation linkages between the Kangchenjunga Conservation Area and Makalu Barun National Park. Likewise the National Biodiversity Strategy and Action Plans of Bhutan and India also emphasize the need for a landscape-scale approach, connectivity and transboundary cooperation for effective biodiversity conservation.

A coordinated approach fosters effective actions

Having a large-scale vision provides a context for strategies, toward the achievement of which individual organizations and agencies can contribute meaningful activities. The large-scale vision and strategies help to link together individual efforts and ensure that they collectively help to accomplish connectivity conservation. In this case, government agencies and NGOs in four different countries were able to coordinate diverse efforts toward the goal of connecting landscapes between and improving management within protected areas in the Sacred Himalayan Landscape. This partnership, under the auspices of the Sacred Himalayan Landscape, enabled participating agencies and organizations to strategize and harmonize current and future interventions involving multiple stakeholders in order to work towards a common vision, rather than intervening haphazardly across the landscape and without larger conservation goals.

Conclusion

The Sacred Himalayan Landscape is an important repository of biodiversity. However, human population is dispersed all over the landscape, making it impossible to separate physically forests and other natural ecosystems from the human influence. Many local people who are largely dependent on natural resources for their livelihoods heavily influence the sustainability of protected areas. Therefore, it has been apparent that protected areas alone cannot meet the demands of conservation; the surrounding matrix of the landscape and addressing human needs and aspirations are critical. It is important that people who depend on the region for their survival are benefited from conservation activities if conservation is to be made truly sustainable.

The initiatives taken by Sacred Himalayan Landscape partners have already brought some positive steps towards regional cooperation for effective biodiversity conservation. Efforts to conserve biodiversity in the region have gradually begun to shift away from law enforcement and use restrictions towards more participatory approaches emphasizing equitable and sustainable use of natural resources. The Sacred Himalayan Landscape initiative revealed that the conservation of biodiversity in ecosystems straddling international borders not only renders services to nature, but also constitutes an opportunity to strengthen processes for socio-economic development among the cooperating countries. Therefore, the landscape approach to conservation seems to be ideal to enable the three countries sharing the Sacred Himalayan Landscape to benefit from the resources they share. It also enhances transboundary cooperation between the countries to meet their obligations under international agreements such as the *Convention on Biological Diversity*.

Acknowledgements

The authors are thankful to the cooperating Governments of Nepal, India and Bhutan for their leadership in and support of conservation. Technical support provided by Gokarna Thapa of WWF Nepal and Birendra Bajracharya of ICIMOD are acknowledged. Financial support received from the MacArthur Foundation helped to conceptualize the landscape approach. The authors are thankful to all the partners from Bhutan, India and Nepal who have contributed to this initiative. The reviewer's comments from Professor Xu Jianchu of ICIMOD and Dr G. S. Rawat of the Wildlife Institute of India helped us to revise and bring many new thoughts to this case study.

Establishing tropical rainforest connectivity in northern Sumatra: Challenges and opportunities

Wiratno Inung

Setting

Indonesia is an archipelago of more than 17,000 islands extending 5000km along the equator and spanning two major biogeographical realms, Indomalaya and Australasia, as well as several distinct biogeographical provinces. The western islands of Sumatra, Borneo, Java and Bali, lying on the Sunda Shelf, were joined to mainland Asia at times of lowest sea levels during the Pleistocene epoch. Similarly the eastern province of Papua and the Kai and Aru Islands on the Sahul Shelf were once connected to Australia. While the species composition varies from west to east, the flora remains dominantly Malaysian throughout the archipelago. Faunal distributions more closely reflect ancient land connections, with placental mammals in the west and marsupials in the east.

At 1800km long and 400km wide, Sumatra is the fifth largest island in the world. It contains an extraordinary wealth of natural resources and habitat diversity. The Bukit Barisan Mountains form the backbone of the island. The majority of this mountainous area is included in nature reserves and national parks. The western slopes are very steep, while the eastern side slopes gradually to the plains and swamps of eastern Sumatra, which include some of the most important wetlands in Indonesia. The island was almost completely forested until the end of the 19th century. Today, approximately a quarter of the original jungle remains.

Sumatra is one of the richest islands in the world in terms of its biodiversity and is classified as one of the 25 hot spot areas in the world identified by Conservation International. This great wealth is due to Sumatra's large size, its diversity of habitats, and its past links with the Asian mainland. It has perhaps 10,000 plant species, at least 17 endemic genera of plants and some unique and spectacular species, such as the largest (*Rafflesia arnoldii*) and the tallest (*Amorphophalus titanium*) flowers in the world (Whitten et al, 1997). Sumatra is also rich in term of its faunal diversity. The island has at least 201 species of mammal and 580 species of bird (Whitten et al, 1997). Nine species of mammal are endemic to mainland Sumatra and a further 14 species are endemic to the isolated group of Mentawai islands. Sumatra has 15 other species confined only to the Indonesian region, including the Sumatran orangutan (*Pongo abelii*). It is the last place on Earth where Sumatran elephants (*Elephas maximus sumatrensis*), rhinoceros (*Dicerorhinus sumatrensis*), tigers (*Panthera tigris sumatrae*), clouded leopards (*Neofelis diardi*) and orangutan (*Pongo abelii*) are all found. The island also harbours 22 species of Asian mammals found elsewhere in Indonesia. In addition, Sumatra is extremely rich in bird diversity.

Of its 580 species, 465 are resident and 21 are endemic.

In Sumatra, much of the remaining forest is on the hills and mountains along the western backbone of the island, some of which is of sedimentary origin and some of which is volcanic (such as the highest mountain, Mt Kerinci, at 3804m). There are also major areas of forest on the deep peat swamps of the eastern margin. The steep hills of the northern tip of the island have abundant forests, and further south is the huge volcanic caldera now occupied by Lake Toba. To the west are the biologically and anthropologically unique Mentawai Islands. In the south are some large rivers which, together with the island's abundant natural resources, have been the foundation for major industrial developments. In the far south there is very little forest left.

Sumatra and Kalimantan are the two main islands targeted for commercial timber exploitation. Forestry has been one of the development pillars of Indonesia since 1970. The modern and large-scale forest exploitation in Indonesia started in 1967, when the government passed two pieces of legislation designed to generate as much foreign exchange as possible to support national development. A programme to establish forestry land-use plans was initiated in the 1980s by the Ministry of Forestry and approved by all development sectors.

The first period of commercial logging was characterized by a focus on infrastructure and investment. In the beginning, local entrepreneurs controlled 80 per cent of the timber concessions, with the rest controlled by foreign companies. However, by 1990 foreign interests controlled almost 80 per cent of national timber concessions (Dephutbun, 1999).

In 1967, Indonesia produced 4,000,000m³ of logs, mostly for the local market. By 1979, Indonesia had become the biggest log-exporting country in the world, with almost 41 per cent of the world market in a trade worth US$2.1 billion (Forest Watch Indonesia, 2001). Indonesia was also the largest plywood-exporting country in the world (Dephutbun, 1999).

In 2004, there were 120,400,000ha of land declared as forest land with 110,000,000ha regulated for defined uses, including conservation forest (23,000,000ha), protection forest (29,000,000ha), limited production forest (16,000,000ha) and production forest (28,000,000ha). According to Sumatran Ministry of Forestry, by 2002 approximately 60,000,000ha had been deforested.

The number of timber concessions decreased from 560 units in 1990 to 270 units in 2002. In the late 1990s, nine large companies controlled the majority of forest concessions in Indonesia. The amount of allowable timber cut declined during that period from 27,000,000m³ to 23,800,000m³. It declined by a further 5,800,000m³ in 2004. However, the low level of quotas issued by the government, coupled with the high demand for timber in the regional and global markets, mean that illegal logging is widespread. It is estimated that 65 per cent of the timber supply in the year 2000 came from illegal sources (Mattews, 2002).

Throughout Indonesia, there has been a dramatic loss in natural habitats, and the archipelago is likely undergoing an extinction crisis. The richest habitats across Sumatra are under the greatest pressure. Population explosion, agriculture expansion, particularly oil palm, and exploitation of other biological and physical resources have put increasing pressure on the forest. For example, the fragmentation of habitat and the high rate of forest loss (58 per cent forest loss) in Riau province has led to increasing elephant–human conflict and decreases in the elephant population from between 1000 and 1600 in 1985 to between 350 and 430 in 2003 (Fadli, 2006). The status of habitat coverage in Sumatra in the 1990s, based on BAPPENAS (1993) is given in Table 6.3.

Surveys have confirmed that Sumatran montane and lowland forests have disappeared at an alarming rate. By the mid-1990s, Sumatran montane forest had lost an average of one third of its original extent, whereas between two thirds and four fifths of lowland forests had disappeared (Whitten et al, 1997). Extraction of timber, rattan, fisheries and other biological resources has made major contributions to the national economy, but has not been managed in a sustainable manner. Other key factors threatening forest biodiversity include:

• illegal logging;

Table 6.3 Changes in habitat areas in Sumatra

Habitat	Original area (km²)	Remaining area (per cent)	Protected areas (km²)	Protected areas (per cent)
Forest on limestone	31,079	59	3280	10.5
Freshwater swamp	36,948	18	560	1.5
Heat forest	10,900	18	0	0.0
Ironwood forest	1320	33	80	6.0
Lowland evergreen rainforest	229,218	31	8075	3.5
Montane rainforest	54,500	68	9345	17.1
Mangrove forest	13,529	29	365	2.6
Peat swamp	84,952	50	71	3.4
Semi-evergreen rainforest	5280	17	50	0.9
Tropical pine forest	215	60	500	15.5

- plantation establishment to supply the pulp and paper industry;
- oil palm plantation development and associated clearing, especially by fire;
- mining;
- inappropriate agricultural and estate development;
- fuel wood collection;
- illegal hunting and wildlife trade;
- road construction;
- war and civil conflict;
- introduction of exotic species (Wiratno, 2002, 2006).

The connectivity conservation initiative

Given the above economic and industry context and the multitude of threats to forest biodiversity in Sumatra, establishing connectivity conservation is an urgent priority. The promotion of corridor or connectivity concepts is a new approach in Indonesia. This concept is appropriate to be implemented in Sumatra due to the fact that fragmentation of natural habitat, caused by various development activities, is occurring at an alarming pace.

In 2003, Conservation International Indonesia introduced the concept of connectivity conservation at the landscape level in the northern part of Sumatra. The goal is to connect the fragmented habitat from Aceh in the west to Angkola in the east via the Seulawah–Leuser–Angkola corridor. The fragmented habitat in the northern part of Sumatra can be seen in Figure 6.5. Conservation International Indonesia plans to establish a huge complex of 4,600,000ha, consisting of Seulawah Heritage Forest (1,400,000ha), Leuser Ecosystem (2,500,000ha), Western Toba Watershed (250,000ha) and Angkola Lowland Wilderness (400,000ha) (Figure 6.6).

The key species that are a focus for conservation across this corridor are the endangered Sumatran elephant and orangutan. However, the connection also will conserve a wide range of other fauna diversity, thousands of plant species and environmental services such as watershed and soil protection. The continuum of connectivity will start from protected areas (national parks, wildlife sanctuaries and strict nature reserves), to protected forests, limited production and production forests, agriculture lands, estates, community

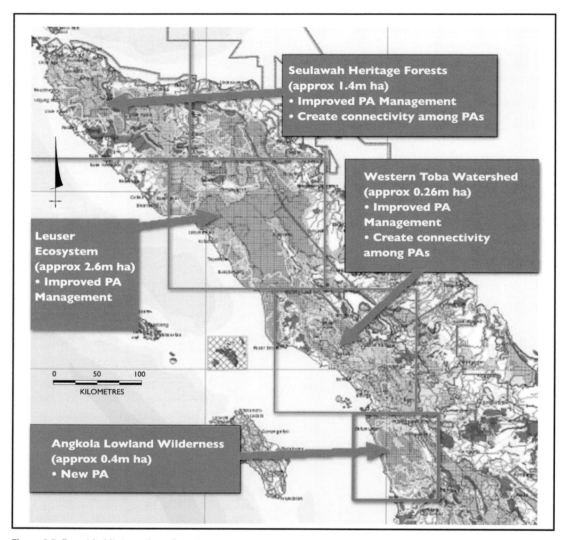

Figure 6.5 Forest habitat, northern Sumatra

forestry lands and freshwater ecosystems. Connections will cross provincial and district borders and will address the issue of managing entire watersheds.

The northern Sumatran corridor is in its infancy. The visionary map of 4,600,000ha of conservation connectivity has been discussed with partners, but the commitment among the interested parties remained unachieved at the time of writing. Beginning in 1997 in the Leuser Management Unit, for example, the Leuser International Foundation initiated the connectivity between Leuser National Park and a surrounding buffer area that covers approximately 2.6 million hectares of protection forest, limited production forest, production forest and agricultural as well as estate land. Leuser National Park was declared a UNESCO world heritage site in 2004. Unfortunately, there are still many weaknesses and unclear commitments between the parties at the district, provincial and national levels. It seems that the single organization, the

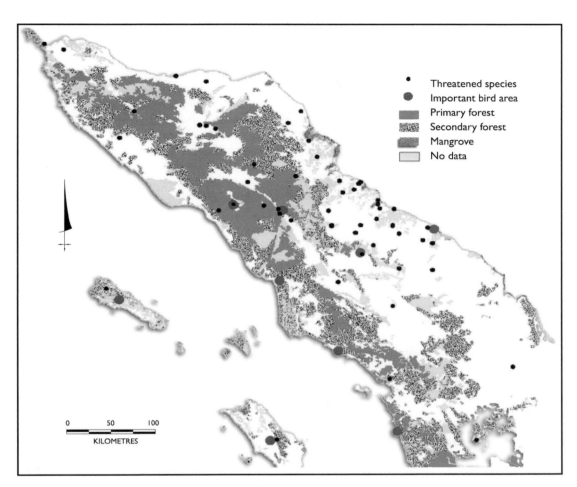

Figure 6.6 Proposed Seulawah–Leuser–Angkola corridor

Leuser International Foundation, was unable to establish the strong commitment necessary. However, we can learn from its experiences. The key elements in establishing and implementing this vision are described next.

Connectivity conservation management

Connectivity in northern Sumatra covers a wide range of land-use practices governed, variously, by local, district, provincial and national administrations. There is no example of the necessary cross-sectoral collaboration required to implement this concept of connectivity. In Indonesia, decentralization has led to increasing authority at the district level without an accompanying redistribution of expertise, capacity and infrastructure. Conflict between districts concerning natural resource management has substantially increased. There has also been a significant increase in the number of new districts. Before the decentralization era (1997), Aceh (now called Nanggroe Aceh Darussalam) consisted of ten districts. Since then the number has doubled to 20. The new districts are characterized by a lack of human resources, weak leadership and a lack of infrastructure and financial support. Mostly, they rely upon forest resources or mining as the only ready source of revenue. Qualified and strong leadership is needed to empower the administration at the district and provincial level to support the concept of connectivity to manage 4.6 million hectares area of various land-use categories across two provinces and administrative units of more than 25 districts.

Effective multi-stakeholder partnerships are one of the key requirements for successful connectivity establishment. In the case of the northern Sumatra corridor, the key partners are district governments, provincial governments and local, national and international NGOs (including Fauna Flora International, Leuser International Foundation, Friends of the Earth Indonesia, Conservation International Indonesia, Sumatran Orangutan Conservation Programme, Orangutan Information Center and many local NGOs). Key challenges in bringing these groups together are differences concerning roles and responsibilities, the lack of a common vision and divergent views on priority setting and funding. There is a need to establish a strong oversight body that includes representatives of all interested parties. In this respect, the role of government is very strategic to facilitate the process and avoid domination by particular interests, particularly in decision-making processes. Scaling up environmental issues through connectivity management efforts will increase global support in the form of expertise and financial resources for practicing better natural resource management.

Developing the northern Sumatra corridor requires working with multi-layered partnerships. Some of the strategic and prime stakeholders are local communities living in the buffer zone of the corridor. By developing micro-economic initiatives in the buffer zone, their level of dependency on extractive industries can be moderated. At the same time, communities can benefit from environmental services in the form of protection of upland ecosystems and their contribution to downstream agricultural productivity. Thus, local communities need to be involved at the beginning of the process of corridor design. Local communities may come to participate in forest patrolling and monitoring activities, helping to prevent illegal activities such as poaching, encroachment and logging. In the case of Aceh, the role of community informal leaders is obvious. They are the decision maker at the community level.

In Indonesia, environmentally related issues are not generally considered as a strategic priority for politicians. However, this is changing, and there is a trend among politicians at the district level to support conservationists. For example, the 2004 creation of the Batang Gadis National Park in Mandailing Natal District, north Sumatra, illustrates how important the role of politicians can be. Political support at the district and provincial levels can be an important element in advancing the concept of connectivity.

The concept of connectivity conservation requires multidisciplinary expertise. Scientists can provide the technical design and justification for each corridor and its connectivity. The northern Sumatra corridor consists of various environments, such as montane forest ecosystems, lowland tropical rainforest ecosystems, freshwater, mangroves, agricultural lands, forest gardens, community forests and smallholder and large-scale rubber and oil palm estates. Scientists can help determine the distribution of important habitats for key species across these various environments. The distribution of focal species such as Sumatran elephant, orangutan, tiger and rhinoceros is among the strategic information to be considered in designing the connectivity conservation networks.

Benefits and accomplishments

By using the connectivity conservation concept, environmental issues can be addressed by various stakeholders at many levels. Connectivity conservation provides many environmental benefits that range from intangible values associated with biodiversity to more direct benefits such as watershed protection and its contribution to water management, soil erosion control, flood prevention and soil fertility protection. Better management of resources in the upstream forest ecosystem within a northern Sumatra corridor will contribute to better protection of environmental service provision to downstream activities.

For example, the Leuser Ecosystem, including Gunung Leuser National Park, supplies water for four million people living in Nanggroe Aceh Darussalam and north Sumatra. At least nine districts depend upon Gunung Leuser National Park for domestic and irrigation water, soil fertility and flood control. A study done by Beukering et al (2003) estimated the total economic value of Leuser Ecosystem at US$7.0 billion (deforested scenario), US$9.5 billion (conserved scenario) and US$9.1 billion (sustainably managed scenario). This is an example of the economic value of conserving Leuser as part of a conservation network.

Connectivity will bring better communication and partnerships across the key stakeholders of governments, the private sector, NGOs, civil society, scientists, universities, practitioners and the media. As a result, environmental issues can begin to be addressed across sectoral and institutional boundaries. Links between theoretical understandings and practical experiences can also be established.

Developing connectivity will increase community awareness and collective action. Strong societal awareness can lead to effective civil society control over natural resource management policies and practices at all levels. This social capital is one of the pillars of good environmental governance at district, province and national levels.

Lessons learned

A unity of vision and purpose is necessary

In Sumatra, differences between NGOs concerning roles and responsibilities, lack of a common vision and divergent views on priority setting and funding hampered efforts to kick-start the connectivity conservation initiative.

Strong leadership is essential to success

Developing connectivity across 4.6 million hectares requires strong leadership and consistent commitment from key parties – governments, private sectors, NGOs, communities, scientists, practitioners and media. A long-term participatory process that is supported by policy at all levels is needed to secure the commitment to achieve a common vision. Central government should play a pivotal role in developing favourable policies

and programmes and in monitoring and evaluation. New legislation for Nanggroe Aceh Darussalam that stops the issuance of logging permits in Ecosystem Leuser is an example of an appropriate policy to support development of the corridor. Central governments should establish overarching regulations to provide for connectivity as a tool to implement sustainable conservation and responsible development.

Fragmented decision making is a barrier to connectivity conservation

In Indonesia there is no example of the necessary cross-sectoral collaboration required to implement this concept of connectivity. Decentralization has led to increasing authority at the district level without an accompanying redistribution of expertise, capacity and infrastructure. Conflict between districts concerning natural resource management has substantially increased. There has also been a significant increase in the number of new districts. The new districts are characterized by a lack of human resources, weak leadership and a lack of infrastructure and financial support. Mostly, they rely upon forest resources or mining as the only ready sources of revenue.

An integrated approach is necessary

There is a need to support local governments in preparing land-use plans in relation to their neighbouring districts in the context of landscape or ecosystem approaches. There is a need for an extended process of mentoring key partners (local government, NGOs, private sectors, media and community) to secure their commitment to spatial plans. The concept needs to be supported by consistent national policy. A good example of a new initiative can be easily destroyed by one permit issued by a central government to allow extractive and large-scale activities such as open pit mining, oil palm plantation, pulp and paper industries or timber concession. Consistent policy back up should come from all levels.

7

Nearctic Connectivity Initiatives

The Nearctic covers most of North America, including Greenland and the highlands of Mexico. It was separated from South America for tens of millions of years, and evolved very different plant and animal lineages. A former land bridge across the Bering Strait between Asia and North America allowed many plants and animals to move between these continents, and the Nearctic shares many plants and animals with the Palaearctic. Major mountain chains are found (the Appalachians and the Rockies) along with major freshwater lake systems (the Great Lakes) and wetlands such as the Everglades. Many of the outstanding natural areas of the Nearctic are protected areas and 0.92 per cent of its area is inscribed as World Heritage. This chapter presents three connectivity conservation case studies from the Nearctic.

Bull Elk (Cervus elaphus), Yellowstone National Park, Yellowstone to Yukon Conservation Initiative

Source: Graeme L. Worboys

Conservation network in the southern Appalachian mountains

Hugh Irwin

Setting

The southern Appalachian region has been delineated in a variety of ways over the last century (Wilson, 1902; SAMAB, 1996). While the exact extent has varied somewhat, the region has generally been interpreted to encompass mountainous portions of the south-eastern and mid-Atlantic United States from Alabama to the southern reaches of Pennsylvania. For the proposed conservation network, the northern boundary for the region is considered the southern extent of permafrost during Pleistocene glaciation. The south-western extent includes the mountains and canyons at the edge of the ridge and valley and the north-western Alabama section of the Cumberland Plateau.

In order to represent the important aquatic components of biological diversity and the critical contribution mountain headwaters play in the rich aquatic diversity throughout the south-east, the boundary of the region was drawn to include the extent of headwater watersheds. This delineation of the southern Appalachian region encompasses an area of 28,327,995ha (Figure 7.1).

The southern Appalachian region is one of the most biologically significant ecoregions in the United States. Scientists are beginning to document and understand the surprising extent of this

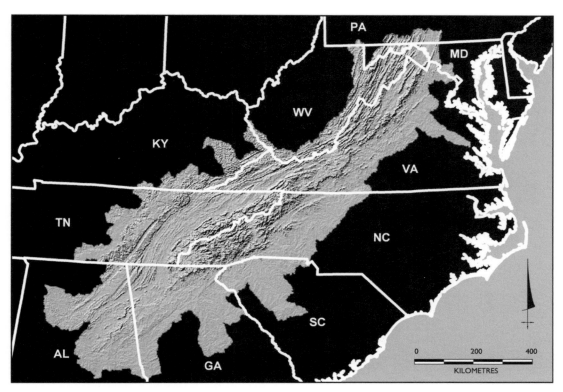

Figure 7.1 Southern Appalachian region in the mountainous portion of eight states, from Alabama to Virginia

biological diversity. The All Taxa Biodiversity Inventory being conducted in Great Smoky Mountains National Park by Discover Life in America (DLIA) seeks to inventory all species of plants, animals, fungi and protozoa found in the park. DLIA scientists estimate that less than 10 per cent of a projected 100,000 species, excluding bacteria, have been identified in Great Smoky Mountains National Park (Kaiser, 1999). An intensive species inventory is underway in this relatively small portion of the region, and discoveries of new invertebrates, nonvascular plants, fungi and protozoa are expected to be particularly successful (Sharkey, 2001). As of October 2006, 5317 species had been documented – 4666 new species for the park and 651 species new to science (DLIA, 2007).

The southern Appalachian region has served as a biological refuge through much of the Earth's history. The southern Appalachian mountains are some of the oldest on Earth, forming over 260 million years ago (Pittillo et al, 1998). They have been sculpted by repeated cycles of uplift and erosion, continental collision and separation. The southern Appalachians have been continuously vegetated at least since the Cretaceous extinction of species 65 million years ago. Most areas of North America and the world have been covered by seas or scoured by glaciers within this time period. This extended history of continuous evolution, in conjunction with favourable climatic and geologic conditions, has allowed the region to play a primary role as a refuge for species during periods of climate change.

Humans are thought to have inhabited the south-east portion of North America for at least 17,000 years. During the early periods, Native Americans made their subsistence from hunting game and gathering herbs from the surrounding mountains' abundant resources (Hatley, 2001).

There is evidence that early Native Americans extensively hunted North American mega fauna (such as mammoths (*Mammuthus imperator*), mastodons (*Mammut americanum*), camels (*Camelops hesternus*) and horses (*dinohippus* spp.)) at the end of the Pleistocene. Some researchers have concluded from this evidence that Native Americans played a role in the extinction of these species due to over-hunting (Alroy, 2001). This conclusion has been disputed by other researchers (Grayson, 2001).

Eastern North America recently has been established as a centre of independent plant domestication by Native Americans (Smith, 1992). Human population densities only reached significant numbers when farming became a major component of the economy after approximately 900 AD. During this farming period, Native Americans made their primary settlements in the river valleys of the region, clearing and farming the rich soils found along the rivers. There is considerable disagreement about population numbers, particularly in the more remote and mountainous areas of the southern Appalachians. During this farming period Native Americans influenced the ecological dynamics of the region. Using fire to clear land where they farmed, they tended to work within the dynamics of the ecological processes of the region rather than destroy those processes (Hatley, 2001).

The first settlers of European descent to arrive in the region exploited the wildlife extensively for pelts and cleared land for farming. At first their numbers were few and their tools were relatively primitive, but soon a growing population of settlers with rifles, axes, traps and slash-and-burn agricultural practices began to kill off and displace important elements of the region's diversity. Beavers were trapped to very low numbers by the early 1800s. The last buffalo in the southern Appalachians was killed in 1797; the last elk (*Cervus canadensis*) died in 1854 (Bass, 2000). The wolf (*Canis lupus*) and cougar (*Puma concolor*), because of their secretive natures, held on into the 20th century before they were eliminated as an ecological presence. Even bear (*Ursus* spp.) and white-tailed deer (*Odocoileus virginianus*) were driven to the brink of extinction.

Clearing of forests in the stream valleys and lowlands opened the landscape to extensive agricultural use. An increasing population and shortage of flat land forced farms to more marginal and erosion-prone lands in the mountains. During the late 1900s, the use of increasingly more efficient technologies allowed logging efforts to threaten forests in the most remote and sensitive areas of the mountains. By the turn of the 20th century rapacious logging had wrought such devastation that the entire nation began to take notice.

Protection and restoration of the southern Appalachians began more than 100 years ago, when devastating floods and wildfires resulting from large-scale clear-cutting prompted cries of alarm locally and nationally. President Theodore Roosevelt's *Message from the President*, authored by Secretary of Agriculture James Wilson (1902) gave official voice to the leading conservationists of the day. Witnessing the unbridled exploitation of forests that created enormous wealth for a few while leaving economic and ecological destruction in its wake, regional leaders decided that actions were needed to protect sensitive mountain areas of the region to prevent flooding and the destruction of natural resources.

To halt the onslaught and repair the damage, a handful of visionary citizens initiated a movement and made their voices heard in Washington. As a result, the first national forests of the eastern United States were established in 1911. Great Smoky Mountains National Park followed in 1934 and Shenandoah National Park was established a year later. Current conservation efforts have their roots in this century-old tradition of protecting and restoring the southern Appalachian forests. This history also helps to explain the prevalence of protected reserves in the upland areas of the region where protection efforts were first focused. Much of the region's lowland areas were in established agricultural use and were not a focus of the early conservation efforts. As development and urbanization have proceeded in the region, many of the more marginal and sensitive agricultural areas have been allowed to return to forest. Many of these areas are of importance in establishing conservation connectivity within the region, and these areas are receiving increased conservation attention.

The first decades of the 20th century witnessed a race between the gathering momentum of protection and the ongoing destructive forces. By the 1930s, most areas had been either acquired as public lands or logged. Logging companies were experiencing difficulty accessing merchantable trees and started closing operations. Many of these operations moved to the Pacific North-west (Wear and Greis, 2002). Acquisition of national forest lands continued with the addition of these already logged lands. Although accessible areas were extensively logged during this period, significant areas were spared. Recent surveys (Yost et al, 1994; Messick, 2000) demonstrate that significant old growth survived this period, mainly in inaccessible areas where logging operations were unprofitable or unfeasible or in areas that were acquired before logging operations reached them.

In the decades following the 1930s came a period of recovery. The lack of mature, marketable timber, along with an operating mandate within the US Forest Service to promote the recovery of the southern Appalachian forests, combined to halt the commercial-scale logging and begin a period of recovery. But after World War II, the process of recovery was interrupted. The post-war economic boom spurred a demand for timber just as many trees on national forest lands were approaching commercial maturity. These forces triggered another cycle of heavy logging from the 1950s until the early 1980s.

By that time, environmental and conservation groups had formed, in response to a variety of environmental challenges, and these new NGOs worked to suppress this increase in logging. At the same time, the wilderness protection effort was gaining momentum. The US Wilderness Act, which established the nation's Wilderness Preservation System, became law in 1964. At first, the Forest Service refused to consider areas in the eastern US for wilderness recommendations, insisting that previous logging and other uses had 'disqualified' all eastern forest candidates (Frome, 1989). Then the Eastern Wilderness Areas Act of 1975 confirmed the legitimacy of wilderness designation in the eastern US, and several wilderness areas were designated within the southern Appalachians. New areas have since been added to the wilderness preservation system in the region, amounting to 202,343ha or 9 per cent of its national forest ownership; an additional 32,375ha of wilderness have been designated in national parks and a majority of the 211,000ha Great Smoky Mountains National Park is managed as wilderness. Other legislative categories, including national recreation area and national scenic area, have been applied to sections of national forest in the southern Appalachians.

Cataloochee, southern Appalachians

Source: Hugh Irwin

The connectivity conservation initiative

Protecting and restoring the biological diversity and ecological health of the southern Appalachians will require the collaboration of many groups and individuals. And the full recovery of the region's species and their networks of relationships will take decades – if not centuries – to accomplish.

The success of this effort depends on the intelligent management of large core areas of habitat, much of which are already in public ownership. The most critical of these lands are those that retain a high degree of their natural ecological function. These areas provide the healthy and stable sanctuaries from which recovery and restoration can proceed. They can also furnish the best reference data to guide the recovery of more-damaged ecosystems. Key conservation lands include forests with few or no roads, tracts of old-growth forest, biological hot spots and critical watersheds, all of which must be wisely managed over the long term to protect and enhance their natural value.

Using these conservation building blocks, the Southern Appalachian Forest Coalition (SAFC) and its member groups have identified landscape-scale conservation areas throughout the southern Appalachian region. These large areas, if offered strategic protection and restoration, can serve to protect both individual native species and complex ecological processes. Their health can be further enhanced through robust landscape connections between these areas and by securing adequate representation of habitat types. The success of this work depends on promptly securing the integrity of those core areas that have the highest degree of ecological integrity (Figure 7.2).

Two major problems confront the conservation management of public lands in the southern Appalachians and assuring their connectivity. The first is inadequate protection. The initial period of responsible stewardship after national forests were established was followed by several decades of intense road building and logging. Within both

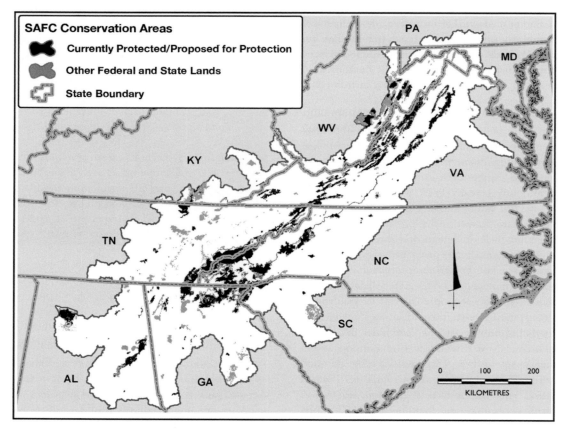

Figure 7.2 Significant public land holdings in the southern Appalachians form the basis for landscape-scale conservation areas

the US Forest Service and the US Congress, there are efforts to return to such intense management even though it fragments core areas of habitat and severely reduces their effectiveness. Second, public agencies have devoted little energy to finding the means to connect existing reserves through corridors that would allow essential movement of wildlife.

Connectivity conservation management

SAFC is a network of national, regional and local non-governmental conservation organizations whose goal is to provide guidance toward renewed ecological health for the southern Appalachian region. SAFC conducted analysis and mapping over a ten-year period to develop a vision and a plan for a connected conservation network in the southern Appalachians. This process involved extensive consultation with scientists, building of partnerships with a broad diversity of organizations and developing good working relationships with government agencies.

The context in which SAFC undertook the design of a long-range plan for a connected conservation network for the southern Appalachians was a fertile one. The region had a long history of conservation protection. There was a well-developed network of public lands in the region. The region is the site of an international biosphere reserve and Great Smoky Mountains National Park, a world heritage site (UNESCO, 2006; Box 7.1). Federal agencies had undertaken an extensive assessment of the region during the 1990s that resulted in the Southern Appalachian Assessment (SAMAB, 1996). SAFC partnered with The Nature Conservancy (TNC) and the Association for Biodiversity Information (now NatureServe) to develop ecoregional conservation plans for the Southern Blue Ridge ecoregion (TNC and SAFC, 2000) and Cumberland and Southern Ridge and Valley ecoregion (TNC, 2003). These studies provided the scientific basis for biodiversity conservation in the southern Appalachian region. The biological significance of the southern Appalachian region was widely appreciated and numerous governmental and non-governmental organizations adopted an agenda to conserve the region. Numerous international, national, regional, state and local organizations endorsed SAFC's

conservation vision, joining well-known scientists, writers and politicians in their support of this vision of protecting and restoring the southern Appalachians.

Securing core areas of habitat in the southern Appalachians will require protecting a variety of conservation lands. Fortunately, the region is rich in such lands. By 2006, conservation protection efforts had been ongoing in the region for over a century. A solid base of natural areas was in public ownership. Approximately 34 per cent of the land within the mountainous core of the southern Appalachians, the Southern Blue Ridge, was in public ownership (TNC and SAFC, 2000). While the Cumberland and Southern Ridge and Valley portions of the southern Appalachians had proportionally less public land (approximately 7 per cent), active efforts were ongoing to place more of these lands in public ownership and in conservation easements (TNC, 2003). A majority of the acreage considered to be biologically significant sites was in public ownership, so protecting these public lands was especially important (TNC and SAFC, 2000). The maintenance of biological diversity and ecological integrity should be the overriding guiding principle on these public lands.

SAFC identified existing and recoverable landscape-scale conservation areas throughout the southern Appalachians. Figure 7.3 shows the landscape conservation areas that had been identified. These areas were designed to take advantage of existing conservation building blocks including:

- currently protected natural areas;
- unprotected natural areas;
- old-growth areas;
- biological hot spots;
- aquatic watersheds;
- high-priority areas for public acquisition;
- conservation easement areas;
- cultural and heritage areas.

Management of these components to achieve their highest conservation potential will help to establish and restore landscape-scale conservation areas in much of the region.

Within these landscape conservation areas SAFC identified 1.13Mha of existing public lands

Box 7.1 Connectivity management around Great Smoky Mountains National Park

There is broad agreement that Great Smoky Mountains National Park is the premier natural reserve in the southern Appalachians. At 211,000ha, it is the largest and best protected reserve in the region. With over 29 per cent of its forests never logged (Messick, 2004) and with numerous rare and endemic species, it protects a large proportion of the region's biodiversity. The National Park is also significant because it is the largest protected area in the region and connects to adjacent landscape reserves, forming the beginning of a well-connected reserve system at the centre of the region. Preserving and enhancing landscape connections between Great Smoky Mountains National Park and adjacent reserves was a high priority for the success of the southern Appalachian regional conservation network.

From some standpoints these landscape connections were in relatively good shape. Adjacent public lands in close proximity to Great Smoky Mountains National Park provided good habitat and physical connections to other landscape conservation areas. There was also wide recognition of the importance of providing corridors for animals (such as black bear (*Ursus americanus*) and neo-tropical migrant birds) to move between Great Smoky Mountains National Park and nearby conservation areas.

However, private lands around Great Smoky Mountains National Park were under intense pressure from second-home development, urbanization, sprawl and road building. This process was destroying buffer habitat that had been used by animals in the past and was fragmenting the natural habitat around the National Park into numerous smaller patches.

The encroaching development highlighted the importance of protecting the existing connectivity to adjacent public lands. Two major roads had been proposed along the edges of Great Smokey Mountains National Park. The North Shore Road would be within the south-eastern boundary of the park. This road proposal, which had been a remote possibility for decades because of a federal road commitment to the local government, was given new life through federal funding in recent years. There was little doubt that the road would be environmentally destructive. Wildlife habitat, rare plants and important aquatic habitat would be directly impacted by the road. The integrity of landscape connections to adjacent public lands would also be degraded. A politically influenced environmental analysis raised fears among many conservationists that this road would be approved for construction. SAFC and other groups fought approval of this road for several years. Recent changes in federal political representation from North Carolina, the affected state, have all but removed this threat, and efforts are underway to permanently solve the issue by changing the agreement between the federal and local governments.

Another major highway recently was proposed that also could affect the south-eastern boundary of Great Smoky Mountains National Park. This highway would be a four-lane, divided interstate highway that would sever existing intact landscape connections between the National Park and the adjacent Unicoi Mountains Reserve and the Nantahala Mountains Reserve. There was widespread opposition to approval of this highway, but powerful political and economic interests lined up in support of the road. SAFC and other conservation groups organized a coalition to oppose approval of this road in order to preserve the landscape connections of Great Smokey Mountains National Park to adjacent conservation areas and to conserve the integrity of the mountain landscape.

On the north-eastern boundary of Great Smoky Mountains National Park, Interstate Highway 40 for decades had degraded the connectivity between the National Park and the adjacent Bald Mountains. This highway inhibited black bear and other animal movement between the two conservation areas. SAFC proposed mitigation measures to provide crossing structures for animal movements across this highway barrier. This type of mitigation had been implemented in other parts of the world and the United States. It will likely be years before this mitigation is implemented, but there is no technical obstacle to its realization.

These efforts were specifically targeted at preserving and enhancing connectivity around Great Smoky Mountains National Park. It will take this type of detailed attention to connectivity issues throughout the southern Appalachian mountains to preserve and enhance a functioning and connected regional conservation network.

that it proposed for permanent protection. These lands, added to 405,000ha of existing wilderness and lands managed as wilderness were the key elements to maintaining and restoring the biological and ecological integrity of these large landscape conservation areas. The effectiveness of these lands as functioning conservation core areas would be enhanced by additional acquisitions,

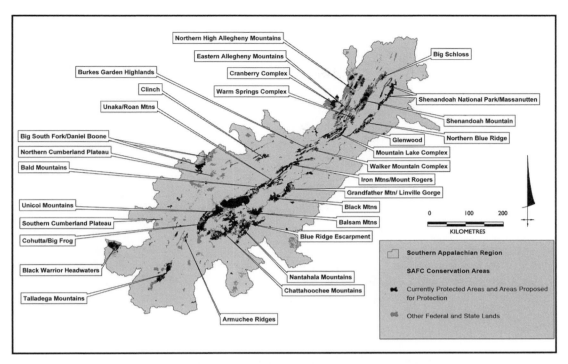

Figure 7.3 Relatively intact or recoverable landscape conservation areas in the southern Appalachians

conservation easements, ecological management of remaining public lands, establishment of functional corridors and mitigation of man-made barriers to connectivity.

Since roads are the conduits for both direct and indirect fragmentation, the absence of roads is one of the primary prerequisites for connectivity conservation. In order to evaluate the conditions of the region's conservation areas and to evaluate the potential for connectivity between them, SAFC identified and analysed remaining roadless areas in the southern Appalachians (Figure 7.4). SAFC adapted the methodology used by the Pacific Biodiversity Institute (Morrison, 2001) to identify roadless areas greater than 404.7ha (1000 acres) throughout the southern Appalachian mountains. These areas were categorized by size on the conservation biology principle that larger areas generally provide greater ecological value than smaller areas. The areas ranged in size from the 404.7ha minimum to more than 110,074ha, with their distribution heavily weighted to the

smaller sizes. This roadless area analysis verified that landscape conservation areas identified by SAFC contained some of the most significant clusters of roadless areas, particularly larger roadless areas.

To enable landscape conservation areas to function as a regional conservation network, there must be ecological linkages between the areas (Figure 7.5). This requirement is a challenge to fulfil in a region that has been fragmented and developed as much as the southern Appalachian mountains. However, there currently remain many viable connections across the landscape, and in the long term the potential for connectivity is great – if we as a culture understand its value and give it the high priority it deserves. SAFC has assessed connectivity between roadless areas for its value to large wide-ranging predators that need big territories and depend on connections across the landscape. Larger roadless blocks (generally greater than 10,117ha) were assumed to provide primary habitat and were considered to be 'source

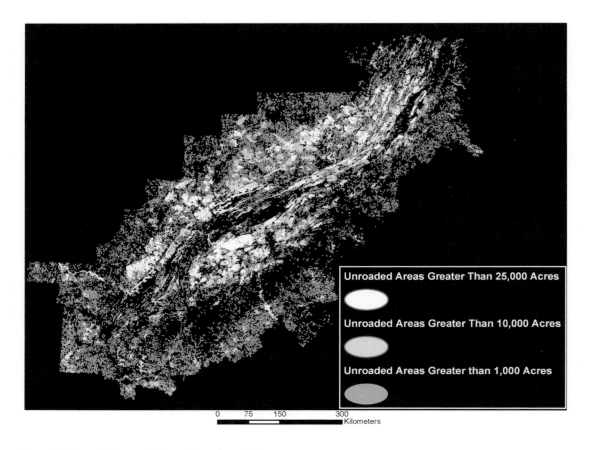

Figure 7.4 Unroaded areas in the southern Appalachians

areas' for such animals. Potential landscape connections between these largest areas were considered primary connectivity while connections between the largest roadless areas and a second tier of unroaded areas between 404.7ha and 10,117ha were considered secondary connectivity. A GIS analysis modelled the routes that would incur the least biological cost for animal movements.

The connectivity analysis helped to visualize potential connectivity between landscape conservation areas. The condition of these landscape connections varied. Some functioned as landscape connections; some could function with key conservation initiatives to improve their conditions; others would require extensive conservation groundwork, including the establishment of wildlife crossing structures over or under high-

ways. In most cases considerable conservation work, including conservation acquisitions, easements and road redesign was required to secure the integrity of the connections into the future.

The implications of the roadless area identification and connectivity analysis in an otherwise fragmented landscape were clear. In order to maintain and enhance the ecological performance of conservation areas on a regional basis, roadless blocks should be maintained and even expanded whenever possible. Conservation protection, acquisition and easement priorities should be established, taking regional connectivity into account. The connectivity between conservation areas should be strengthened as well by mitigating the fragmenting effects of major roads using designs that allow freer passage for wildlife. Landscape and regional analysis to retain and

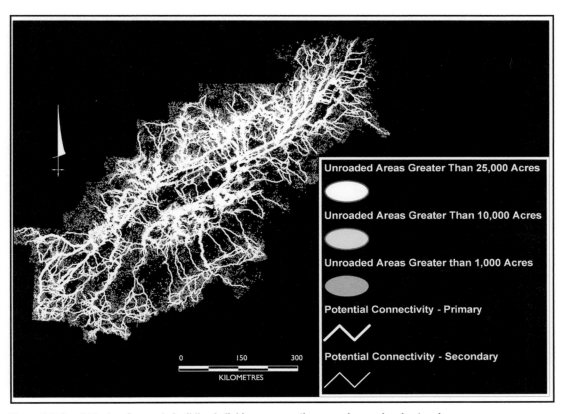

Figure 7.5 Small blocks of unroaded wildlands linking conservation areas in a regional network

augment wildlife linkages should become a regular part of conservation planning in the future.

Benefits and accomplishments

Five hundred years ago the southern Appalachian region was a rich and resilient landscape. A tremendous amount of ecological destruction occurred from that time until the present. However, much of the biological diversity and many of the ecological processes survived. The groundwork established by conservationists over the last century was just a beginning, and the task of recovering the ecosystems of the region is immense. It would be easy to turn away from these tasks because they seem too difficult or politically unrealistic. SAFC's conservation vision for a system of connected conservation areas in the southern Appalachian mountains is a long-range plan. It is a vision that may take as long to

fully realize as the 500 years it has taken to alter the landscape, but there are no fundamental barriers to its realization.

SAFC's connectivity conservation vision was extremely useful as a framework to analyse conservation issues, discuss these issues with other organizations and begin to make progress on a regional network of connected natural areas. Until the connectivity conservation vision was proposed, the scope of conservation issues and the potential for recovery had been artificially constrained. For over a century there had been a failure to address the region's conservation issues at a sufficiently large scale and to envision what regional connectivity recovery would entail. The connectivity conservation vision for the southern Appalachians provided a framework to start addressing these issues on a regional basis and to propose specific plans to move toward its imple-

Unicoi Mountains, southern Appalachians

Source: Hugh Irwin

mentation. The conservation vision provided goals and criteria to assess project proposals, restoration actions and local decisions. It also guided proactive strategies and tactics that contributed to the accomplishment of regional connectivity conservation objectives.

There are many examples of the benefits of approaching connectivity conservation issues from a context of building a connected network of natural areas. Within such a framework, conservation acquisitions or increased management protection was persuasive not only because it contributed to local conservation efforts but also because it moved the region closer to a system of interconnected natural areas. For example, a new highway proposal may have minimal impact on a specific natural area. However, when analysed in a landscape and regional context it is obvious that the highway will have severe impacts on the corridors between natural areas. This context provided a fresh framework for analysing and documenting the environmental costs of the proj-

ect. The conservation vision made it apparent that the environmental impacts were not isolated to individual natural areas but had landscape and regional implications. Similarly, providing landscape linkages across existing infrastructure can seem expensive when considered from a local perspective. However, when considered on a landscape and regional basis, these expenses can start to be persuasive for their landscape and regional benefits.

Lessons learned

Government agency support for NGO-led initiatives can be slow to appear

The vision of consolidating existing public reserves and establishing corridors across the landscape had been well received within the conservation NGO community, by several state agencies and many individuals in the public. These goals also received support from individuals within federal public agencies. However, the official position of these public agencies, such as the

US Forest Service, which manages the largest share of public land reserves, did not acknowledge the feasibility or desirability of these goals. The lack of support from these crucial federal partners highlighted the remaining work in building support within these arenas.

Building a broad base of support at the outset of a connectivity conservation initiative can lead to long-term benefits

SAFC put considerable focus on building partnerships and broad support for the regional conservation vision. This proved to be a very good investment. These alliances enabled the coalition to maintain the conservation gains that already occurred and even make advances in some cases. Over 200 influential groups and individuals endorsed SAFC's conservation vision. The broad alliances in which SAFC invested in early in the process (such as businesses, scientists, political leaders and recreation groups) provided access to groups and audiences that it otherwise would have had difficulty reaching.

Repeating the connectivity conservation vision and presenting it in different lights help to maintain long-term support and focus

It was necessary to keep the conservation vision fresh and to present it in a variety of ways in order to keep the focus on its utility and relevance. The tendency was for government agencies, other NGOs and the public to revert to treating conservation issues in a regional vacuum, as though the connectivity conservation vision had not been presented as a viable option. This tendency was countered by searching for new applications in which to apply it, different contexts in which to present it and new audiences to learn its utility.

Recruiting young people can help to ensure future success

Outreach efforts were focused on young adults, particularly those coming out of universities in the conservation field. Emphasis was placed on recruiting interns to work on different aspects of conservation planning. The success of this long-term project will depend on future generations to carry on the work and reach for possibilities that

were not yet clear. Investment in these future conservationists may be the most important investment.

Having clear goals and objectives help to guide connectivity conservation management efforts

The clear goals coming out of a regional vision served very well during difficult times for conservation. The work and plans that were articulated in the conservation vision made it easier to set priorities and place resources where they had the best lasting benefit. For instance, roadless areas were very important components in the regional conservation network. SAFC placed considerable resources and effort in defending and securing these areas. This prioritization resulted in keeping these areas secure and even increased their protection in some cases.

Clear goals and objectives enable the incorporation of new opportunities into connectivity conservation strategies

Additional avenues opened for making conservation gains. When the conservation vision was published in 2002, the Coalition had not fully anticipated the shift in focus and funding that would become available to the US Forest Service for forest restoration. This focus on restoration projects opened up opportunities to address the abuses of past logging projects, to rehabilitate streams, to address invasive exotic species and to remove unneeded and problem roads. This experience highlighted the importance of being alert to emerging opportunities.

Implementing conservation connectivity management at a large scale is a long-term endeavour

When SAFC proposed a southern Appalachian regional network of interconnected natural areas, it was understood that this would be a multi-generational project. When SAFC began developing a conservation plan for the southern Appalachians in the mid-1990s, there was considerable support within agencies and in the political arena for this type of regional approach. The speed with which environmental protections eroded between 2000 and 2008 under a different political administration came as a surprise. Significant resources have gone toward maintaining past conservation accomplishments as opposed to promoting new conservation initiatives. This reinforced the perception that establishing a regional conservation network was a long-term project and temporary setbacks needed to be absorbed while continuing to plan for enduring progress.

Greater northern Appalachian bioregion

Lawrence S. Hamilton and Stephen C. Trombulak

Many fledgling conservation corridor initiatives in mountains are not yet coordinated in an effective way. This is especially true in large ecoregions, particularly when they cross major political boundaries. The greater northern Appalachian bioregion (GNAB) was struggling to achieve such integration and thus may offer lessons on fitting together several smaller initiatives to promote connectivity in a single mountain range. Work in the GNAB was made even more important by its neighbouring initiative, the Southern Appalachian Forest Coalition (Irwin, this chapter). Together with the Southern Appalachian Forest Coalition, the initiatives described below would encompass the eastern spine of the United States and Canada, complementing work in the western spine, such as the Yellowstone to Yukon Conservation Initiative, the Southern Rockies ecosystem project and the Sky Islands wildlands network.

Setting

The GNAB was meant to include the northern part of the Appalachian Mountains as they stretch northward from south-eastern New York through Quebec's Gaspé Peninsula, as well as important western extensions into Tug Hill and the Adirondack Mountains of New York State (Figure 7.6). As a distinct geological feature, the Appalachian Mountains run some 2400km from Quebec and New Brunswick in the north to Alabama in the south, and were uplifted from 320 to 450 million years ago. The much younger Adirondack Mountains were uplifted only 20 to 40 million years ago. The entire bioregion was ice-covered and shaped by the most recent Pleistocene glacier, which began to retreat some 19,000 years ago. The mountains tend to be rounded with U-shaped valleys, and glacial bowls (cirques) are prominent on higher mountains. Mount Washington, New Hampshire, the highest mountain in the bioregion, achieves 1917m. Lowlands are covered with glacial sediments and have many wetlands and lakes.

The region has relatively cold winters and humid summers. The frost-free season is generally less than 90 days, and average annual snowfalls of over three metres are common. It is a well-watered region, with annual precipitation (predominantly in the summer) ranging from 900 to 1700mm per year (Schnelling et al, 1992).

The northern Appalachian region is the source of many of the major rivers of the north-eastern US and Canada's maritime provinces. These were important settlement and transportation routes for both the Native Americans and the colonizing Europeans, and remain critical to the life and economy of the whole area today. The most well-known waterways are the Delaware, Hudson, Mohawk, Richelieu, Connecticut, Androscoggin, Penobscot, Allagash, St. John and Restigouche rivers and Lake Champlain. Their importance as a source for freshwater throughout the region cannot be overemphasized.

The northern Appalachian region is highly diverse ecologically due to its humid temperate climate, varied elevation, steep slopes and north-east–south-west orientation of mountains. Although there are a few relatively small alpine tundra zones on the highest summits of the Adirondack, Green and White Mountains and on Mounts Katahdin and Cadillac in Maine, the vast majority of the region is forested. The slopes, valleys and associated lowlands are largely part of a grand mosaic of three different closed-canopy forest types: Appalachian oak, northern hardwood (predominantly maple (*Acer* spp.), beech (*Fagus grandifolia*) and birch (*Betula* spp.)) and boreal (predominantly spruces (*Picea* spp.), fir (*Abies* spp.) and pine (*Pinus* spp.)). All three of these forest types have been extensively modified during the more than 300 years of European colonization. Extensive forest clearing for agriculture and timber harvesting, introduction of exotic pests, near-extinction of some tree species (such as

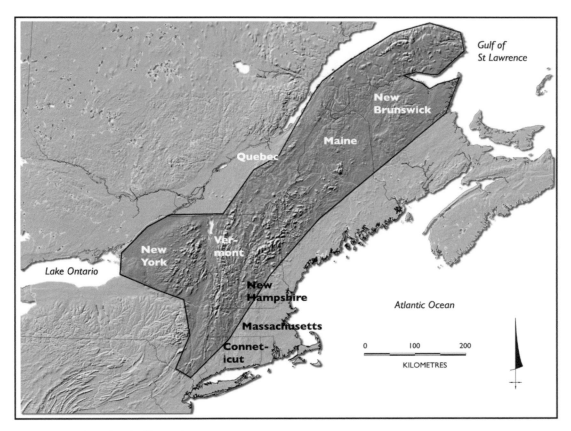

Figure 7.6 Northern Appalachian region

American chestnut (*Castanea dentata*)), and extirpation of some animal species have all taken their toll.

While there has been an impressive recovery of forest cover throughout the region relative to historic lows during the mid- to late 19th century, the communities of animals that once inhabited the region have been dramatically altered. This is most readily seen among the mammals. Some species, like the mountain lion (*Puma concolor*), wolf (*Canis lupus*) and wolverine (*Gulo gulo*) have been regionally extirpated. Others, like the lynx (*Lynx canadensis*) and pine marten (*Martes americana*) have been reduced beyond the point of ecological effectiveness. Some native species (such as white-tailed deer and beaver (*Castor canadensis*)) have increased far beyond natural levels of abundance and some exotics (such as coyote (*Canis*

latrans)) have become numerous, all with unfortunate consequences for regional ecological health.

The socio-political context of the bioregion is extremely complex. Numerous stakeholders, each with different perceptions of its mission and constituency, need to be involved in implementing comprehensive strategies for connectivity. The GNAB encompasses all or parts of six US states and two Canadian provinces, resulting in a diverse mix of land-use histories, cultural traditions and economic patterns.

Landownership is perhaps the most diverse factor affecting conservation here. In portions of the region, a significant amount of the land is publicly owned. For example, the Adirondack Mountains are largely protected in the Adirondack Park, which was delineated in 1892 (Hamilton et al, 1982). Of the 2.3Mha inside of the park's proclamation boundary, one million are publicly owned as 'forever wild', and managed for ecological and recreational values. Similarly, in the Acadian Mountain section of Quebec and New Brunswick, 37 and 45 per cent respectively is provincial (Crown) lands (WCS, 2006); however, the vast majority of them are leased for timber harvesting.

Public land makes up a smaller portion of the rest of the region. Such public lands as the Green Mountain (Vermont) and White Mountain (New Hampshire) National Forests and Baxter State Park (Maine) notwithstanding, the bulk of the land in the bioregion is privately owned. It is estimated that 85 per cent of the Northern Forest (the northern extents of New York, Vermont, New Hampshire and Maine) is privately owned (NFA, 2005). Yet, even private ownership here is characterized by diversity. For example, ownership in Maine has historically been dominated by large timber or paper companies. While large areas have been logged over the last 200 years, the area has remained largely forested. However, a significant amount of land previously owned by forest-products companies has recently been bought by development corporations for liquidation and amenities development (Hagan et al, 2005). Efforts to alter this process have been instituted by The Nature Conservancy (TNC), partnering with state and national land trusts and state and federal governments, in purchases or conservation easements. At least four of these ranging in size from 10,522 to 162,000ha have been implemented in the bioregion (TNC, 2006).

In contrast, private ownership in Vermont, New Hampshire, Massachusetts, Connecticut and southern Quebec, made up largely of small-parcel, non-industrial ownerships, resulted in large-scale conversion of forestland to agriculture and settlement.

Such diversity in ownership makes the region a patchwork of management jurisdictions and objectives. In some parts of the bioregion, particularly in the New England states, local governments exert a great deal of actual and philosophical control on conservation initiatives, posing a serious challenge to regional-scale connectivity projects. In other parts, such as Maine and New Brunswick, corporations have either outright or de facto control over the land (through ownership or lease), posing a different set of challenges. Everywhere, state and provincial governments own land – in the case of New York, substantial amounts – and have the capacity, at least in theory, to implement initiatives on those lands for conservation purposes. Both federal governments own strategic lands, particularly in mountain regions in Vermont, New Hampshire, Quebec and New Brunswick, the inclusion of which is essential for region-wide connectivity conservation.

At the conclusion of the French and Indian Wars (1763), Europeans pushed into the Appalachians. The period 1770–1870 witnessed heavy exploitation of the forest lands of the GNAB. In the boreal forests, unregulated logging, even on Crown lands in Canada, gave no attention to regeneration, and fires often followed. The conifers that would float were cut and rafted down the rivers, and built a strong wood economy. Pulpwood cutting for paper entered the scene at the turn of the 20th century. Logging continues today on a reduced scale, with more sustainable harvesting practices becoming increasingly common. In the Appalachian oak/northern hardwood forests, much land was cleared for agricultural use. Southern New Hampshire, Vermont and Massachusetts were mostly cleared land by 1860. However, the US Civil War, transcontinental railways and the collapse of the wool market led farmers to move off the land in large numbers. In the next century, regrowth of forests occurred, so that by the mid-1950s 84 per cent of New Hampshire was forested (Watson, 1967) and by 1980, 75 per cent of Vermont was forested (Klyza and Trombulak, 1999). Agriculture has continued, mainly as dairy farming in the valleys, so today there is a mosaic of farms and forests. The commercial tapping of the sugar maple is the basis for a very significant maple syrup products industry. Further, while large forest industry continues its decline, a smaller-scale, value-added artisanal hardwood products industry increases. White-tailed deer, moose (*Alces alces*) and rabbit (*Sylvilagus floridanus*) populations responded to forest recovery, along with recreational hunting. Beaver, turkey (*Meleagris gallopavo*) and fisher (*Martes pennanti*) were successfully reintroduced and coyotes have made their appearance and proliferated. There is some call for the reintroduction of wolf and encouragement of remnant populations of mountain lion and lynx needed to restore ecological balance.

With the growth of urban centres, increased affluence and increased leisure time, the region increasingly became a magnet for outdoor recreationists. The explosion in recreation activity came after World War II. Hiking, swimming, camping, fishing, canoeing, hunting and skiing in the recovered forest became increasingly popular, especially in the national forests and state forests and parks established on the land abandoned during and following the Great Depression. These visitors to rural and forested areas assisted greatly to stabilize a declining rural economy. As other improvements in outdoor recreational equipment occurred, cross-country skiing, mountain biking, snowmobiling and wilderness backpacking boomed, more recently followed by snowboarding and kayaking. Unfortunately, the development of off-road, all-terrain vehicles engendered an often conflicting use of wild lands. Provision of a mix of recreational opportunities became the major function of much public land, replacing wood production. Icons of recreational opportunity in the bioregion are the International Appalachian Trail, located along the spine of this mountain system, and the 1190km Northern Forest Canoe Trail (NFCT) (completed in 2006) that stretches from the Central Adirondacks through Vermont, Quebec, New Hampshire and into northern Maine (NFCT, 2006).

Ecological connectivity along the mountains of the GNAB plays a critical role in maintaining large-scale ecological health in eastern North America. Because of the general north–south orientation of the Appalachians, entire biomes shift location with major changes in climate, such as during the most recent glacial retreat. Although the region is now largely dominated by boreal and northern hardwood forests, the ebb and flow of plant communities through this region in response to climate change has been remarkable. In a world projected to warm substantially, plant and animal species are expected to make dramatic northward shifts in their geographic ranges (Iverson et al, 1999), yet their ability to do so will depend largely on the extent of habitat connectivity across the landscape.

Connectivity is also critical for ecological health over short timescales. Numerous native species have been extirpated or severely reduced in the bioregion. Although large mammalian carnivore species are most notable, numerous other taxa have been similarly affected, such as turtles, snakes, frogs and passerine birds. While not all instances of population decline or extirpation are due to decreased connectivity, many species are significantly hurt by habitat fragmentation, particularly by roads and urban sprawl. Large-lot residences increasingly occupy field and forest, creating a Swiss cheese of gaps in rural landscapes. Large blocks of private forest are increasingly parcelled into numerous small lots, encouraged by a perverse taxation system. The increasing number and variety of ownerships of land makes the connectivity conservation job harder.

Nonetheless, the GNAB is the largest repository of wild lands in the north-eastern US and maritime Canada. Thus, for both the maintenance of populations across their natural ranges of abundance and of the region's responsiveness to environmental change, connectivity conservation is crucial in the bioregion.

The connectivity conservation initiatives

The region's large size, cultural diversity, international boundary and language differences have made it difficult for people residing in the GNAB to recognize the region's ecological coherence, let alone the need for a concerted approach to maintaining ecological health. There is, as yet, no widely shared vision of an interconnected GNAB.

Yet many of the residents in the region have a fairly sophisticated awareness of the importance of maintaining natural areas and of linking them together; thus, a number of separate initiatives developed over the years, which taken together represent the beginnings of a connectivity network. We provide here a brief sketch of these initiatives, their objectives and programmes. At the outset, we emphasize that these initiatives are largely in their formative states, and as yet no major effort has been made within the region to unite them into a unified vision. Ultimately, we believe that such unification will be necessary.

While this may seem unrealistic, we are encouraged by the example of the Yellowstone to Yukon Conservation Initiative, with over 280 members and 74 different groups (Tabor and Locke, 2004) either supporting or working on the linkage with great success.

The Appalachian Trail

One of the earliest visions of a connecting (though narrow) corridor along the spine of the Appalachians was that of the Green Mountain Club (Vermont), which in 1931 completed the Long Trail 438km along the summits of the Green Mountains to the Canadian border (Green Mountain Club, 2006). This was the inspiration for the Appalachian Trail, and indeed the two trails coincide for 161km in southern Vermont. After this, the Appalachian Trail heads east to the White Mountains of New Hampshire and then to Mount Katahdin in Maine (Figure 7.7). The Appalachian Trail Conference was formed in 1925 by individuals and clubs that worked to win federal status as America's first natural scenic trail, pushed federal and state governments to acquire land through which the Trail passes and created some 3475km of footpaths, campsites and shelters. Three to four million people hike some part of the Trail each year, and more than 300 hike the entire length. While the Trail itself is only a few metres wide, and hardly qualifies as a biotic corridor for climate adaptation, migration and gene flow, the Conference is broadening its vision to include acquisition and conservation of land adjacent to the Trail. Moreover, in 1999 an international extension of 1110km was inaugurated (Hughes, 2002). This extension runs from Mount Katahdin north through New Brunswick and Quebec, passing through Mount Carleton Park, Gaspesie National Park (a Quebec provincial park) and Forillon National Park to Cape Gaspé.

Northern Forest Alliance

The Northern Forest Alliance (NFA) – a membership organization of 43 conservation, recreation and forestry organizations – emerged during the early 1990s to represent forest conservation interests in the Northern Forest, a region of primarily boreal forest running from New York's Tug Hill Plateau, across the Adirondacks, through

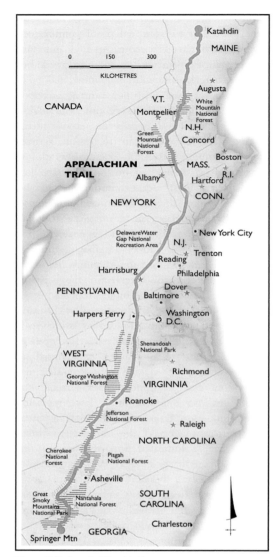

Figure 7.7 Appalachian Trail

northern Vermont, New Hampshire and Maine (Figure 7.8). The members of the Alliance share a threefold vision: permanently protected wildlands, sustainably managed forests and strong and vibrant local economies and communities. The Alliance identifies priority projects in these three arenas, focusing most of its attention on the protection of existing wildlands. It lobbies state and federal governments for funding to support actions in these priority arenas.

Figure 7.8 Northern forests of north-eastern US

The Nature Conservancy; the Nature Conservancy of Canada (NCC)

TNC, NCC and similar organizations work (with partners) to conserve at least 10 per cent of the world's biodiversity. Within the GNAB, they are among the few organizations that have an action plan to promote connectivity conservation on an ecoregional basis. Under the initiative called Conservation by Design, these organizations develop portfolios of priority conservation areas within ecoregions. The northern Appalachian boreal forest and the Lower New England/ Northern Piedmont ecoregions are the principal areas involved in the GNAB, plus a small (Catskills) part of the High Allegheny Plateau. A few examples may suffice as illustrative of TNC and NCC actions on the ground. In Vermont, there are some 68,625ha of conserved lands, including 44 preserves owned and managed by TNC, totalling some 7247ha; the jointly owned (with Vermont Land Trust) 10,632ha Atlas

Timberlands; and easements on 10,316ha (TNC, 2004). In addition, it provides up front funds to buy key areas that are then transferred (with conservation restrictions) to partners such as the Green Mountain National Forest or Vermont Agency of Natural Resources. TNC regional activity is increasingly important as forest industries of the Northern Forest divest their large land holdings to development companies. A recent conservation easement was negotiated in Maine, covering 162,000ha of former Plum Creek forest holdings (TNC, 2006). On an ecoregional scale, TNC's eastern regional office and the NCC's Atlantic and Quebec offices are playing important roles in the realization of a conservation design for the GNAB through their recently developed northern Appalachian/Acadian ecoregion conservation assessment. This initiative includes the identification of numerous priority conservation areas throughout the GNAB as well as their associated linkages.

Wildlands Network (formerly Wildlands Project)

The Wildlands Network, founded in 1991, is a North America-wide effort to design and implement an ecological reserve network of protected wildlands. One of the 25 project areas where it plays a role is in the Greater Laurentian region, comprised of New York, New England, Quebec, New Brunswick, Nova Scotia and Prince Edward Island, which broadly overlaps the GNAB. It uses as a main criterion for protection and restoration efforts the predicted habitat for three focal species: wolf, lynx and marten. Mapping wildlife habitat connections that should be protected or restored is done in cooperation with TNC, NCC, Two Countries, One Forest and Wildlife Conservation Society (US and Canada). The Wildlands Network has also spawned a project to link the Adirondack Park north and westward to Algonquin Provincial Park in Canada (Quinby et al, 2000), hoping to accommodate wolf recolonization in the Adirondack Mountains. It has recently produced a Network Design for the Greater northern Appalachians (from Adirondacks to Acadia), following a series of regional expert workshops and using TNC data and assistance (Reining et al, 2006).

Two Countries, One Forest

Two Countries, One Forest formed in 2001 as a confederation of over 50 organizations, researchers and foundations working on conservation and restoration of the northern Appalachian/Acadian ecoregion. Organizations that have played key roles include TNC, NCC, the Wildlife Conservation Society (Canada), the Wildlands Network and the Canadian Parks and Wilderness Society. The focus of the organization is on conserving the natural beauty, native species and ecosystems of the northern Appalachian/Acadian ecoregion while maintaining economically and culturally vibrant local communities.

Two Countries, One Forest has identified four corridor areas that are thought to be critical for long-term ecological health in the GNAB: Tug Hill to Adirondack Mountains, Adirondack Mountains to Green Mountains, Berkshire Mountains through Green Mountains into Quebec and the St. John River valley (connecting Maine, New Brunswick and Quebec). Of these, the Vermont–Quebec linkage is currently the focus of a new initiative for transboundary connectivity conservation. A coalition formed by the NCC, the Appalachian Corridor, Forest Watch, the Wildlands Network and the Northeast Wilderness Trust seeks to develop a conservation plan that will protect land and allow for transborder connectivity between the Green Mountains in Vermont and its northward extension into the Sutton Mountain area of southern Quebec. A meeting in December, 2006 near Sutton brought several other organizations on board, to plan for a strategy in this area.

Northeast Wilderness Trust

Created in 2001 with headquarters in Boston, Massachusetts, this regional body covers all states in the GNAB and is patterned after state and national land trusts. It promotes the permanent dedication of wilderness lands by purchase of or easements on private lands, or having wilderness designation on state or federal lands. It is a fundraising organization that mounts targeted gift campaigns for selected areas, including areas where restoration can enlarge or connect wildlands. A priority project for the Trust is the Split Rock Wildway, intended to connect the High Peaks region of the Adirondack Park with the western shore of Lake Champlain, an important component of what will hopefully become a major east–west region of connectivity through northern New England.

Wildlife Conservation Society

Within the greater northern Appalachian bioregion, the Wildlife Conservation Society has a focus area in the Adirondack Park. One of its regional projects is the Adirondack Conservation and Communities Program, which seeks to develop wildlife-based strategies for conservation of large, wild ecosystems that are integrated into wider landscapes of human influence. Although largely focused on the park, this effort supports the Two Countries, One Forest initiative by providing community-based conservation support for the transboundary Northern Forest area. The Adirondack Park is a vital component of a functional system of connected reserves in the bioregion. Thus, the work of the Wildlife Conservation Society to improve the ecological health of the Adirondacks is a major contribution to regional connectivity conservation.

Shawangunk Ridge Biodiversity Partnership

Situated east of the Catskill Mountains in New York and close to the Hudson River, the low mountains of the Shawngunk Ridge constitute an important stepping stone of connectivity between the Catskills and the Berkshire Mountains in Massachusetts, which are part of the main spine of the Appalachians. The Shawngunks also link to the highlands region that is the focus of efforts by the Highlands Coalition (see below), by linking to the series of state parks in the Taconic Range and the Pallisades of the Hudson River. The Ridge extends south to become the Kittatinny Mountains in New Jersey and Blue Mountains in Pennsylvania. Sparked by TNC, the Partnership was formed in 1997 as an 11-member consortium of organizations to study biodiversity and wildlife habitat, protect key natural features and habitats,

encourage compatible uses of the Ridge and improve management effectiveness on public and private lands.

The Highlands Coalition

By promoting awareness and communication among organizations, the Highlands Coalition focuses on the mountainous backdrop to Philadelphia, New York City, Newark and Hartford in a belt that stretches from the northern border of Maryland, through Pennsylvania, southern New York and Connecticut to Massachusetts' Berkshire Mountains (Figure 7.9). It issues a newsletter entitled *Higher Ground* to keep various agencies and organizations informed about land and water conservation accomplishments of some 100 groups. It was instrumental in securing passage of the 2005 *Highlands Conservation Act*, which provides federal funding for a regional study aimed at conserving the highlands' critical lands, freshwaters and recreational opportunities. It will play an increasingly important role in bridging the northern and southern Appalachian initiatives.

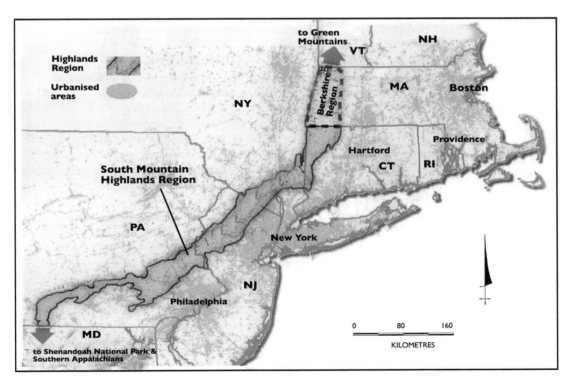

Figure 7.9 Highlands region

Lessons learned

Collaborative efforts characterize connectivity conservation approaches

This overview of the connectivity conservation initiatives in the GNAB highlights a common theme in approaches taken to promote connectivity in this region. Initiatives tend to involve coalitions of existing conservation groups that work together to implement a specific project. Even organizations that have identified their own set of connectivity initiatives participate in coalitions to advance the implementation of those or other connectors. This tendency to work cooperatively grows from important political and ecological realizations among conservation organizations in the GNAB:

- Connectivity conservation <u>any</u>where in the region is enhanced by connectivity conservation <u>every</u>where in the region.
- Achieving connectivity conservation throughout the region is more complex than can be achieved by any one group alone.
- It will require the conservation of many kinds of lands (wild reserves, sustainable forests and nature-friendly agriculture).
- It will require restoration or 'rewilding'.

Unfortunately, the art of effective management of coalitions has yet to be perfected. As a result, all coalitions must invest the time to learn how to move forward on projects that may not be owned (and therefore branded) by any single organization. Other organizations that focus on conferences and publications for raising awareness about the northern forest in general, such as the Northern Forest Center, have a significant contribution to make in promoting connectivity.

The absence of key players hampers connectivity conservation efforts

Despite the emergence of conservation coalitions in the GNAB, many organizations responsible for the management of public lands and waters are not yet major participants. In this region, agencies such as Parks Canada, the US Forest Service, US Fish and Wildlife Service and all of the relevant state and provincial agencies ultimately need to come together with the NGOs described above to implement a region-wide, integrated system of ecological reserves that includes adequate consideration of intra- and inter-regional connectivity. While individual biologists in the land-administering agencies recognize the need for connectivity and cohesion, the decision-making levels have not yet adopted the vision of a GNAB, and connectivity conservation within it. Moreover, there is often a tension between these agencies and the NGOs. Even within the NGO community there are sometimes serious schisms, as between snowmobiling associations, wilderness advocates, organized sporting groups and farmers' organizations. Outreach and education is sorely needed for all of these groups and for the general public as well. One vehicle with great potential is *Northern Woodlands*, published by the Center for Woodlands Education. It is respected by professionals, laity, environmentalists and the forest industry as having a balanced coverage of forest land-use issues in New York and New England. It is poised for major expansion and wider distribution.

Bold leadership is essential for large-scale connectivity conservation success

But if connectivity conservation within the GNAB, let alone connectivity to other bioregions, is to be achieved, there is a pressing need for some sort of transnational umbrella organization, rooted in the science of conservation biology and education, which can provide a coordinating role among the various players. Sustaining connectivity among collaborative groups and communities is vital to achieving coordinated, science-based, landscape-scale conservation connectivity. We see great potential for Two Countries, One Forest to fulfil this role since it encompasses a large part of the GNAB, has a science working group (headed by the junior author), works with organizations in both the US and Canada, and is specifically focused on achieving on-the-ground conservation. Time will tell if it or some other group entirely will accomplish this important coordinating task.

Yellowstone to Yukon connectivity conservation initiative

Harvey Locke

Setting

The Yellowstone to Yukon (Y2Y) region is a vast landscape of mountains and valleys that forms the backbone of north-western North America. The Yellowstone to Yukon Conservation Initiative is a citizen-led connectivity conservation endeavour encompassing the entire Y2Y region. It promotes and implements a vision for maintaining the natural values for an iconic region of the US and Canada. The Y2Y effort has many facets, as it is at once a region, a vision, a social movement, an organization and a symbol of connectivity conservation efforts. It is evolving constantly. It has inspired extraordinary contributions to conservation from many people and organizations.

Y2Y is divided politically into two countries, two provinces, two territories and five states. Extending 3200km from Wyoming's South Pass at 42 degrees latitude in the US to the Peel River watershed in the Yukon and Northwest Territories at 66 degrees north in Canada, it is characterized by high mountains, large cold rivers, and vegetation ranging from sage steppe to arctic alpine (Figure 7.10).

Altitude, latitude, geology and geomorphology combine in Y2Y to create a landscape that often has remarkable similarities across this vast distance. The mountains tend to be oriented in parallel ranges that run north–south. Almost the entire region was glaciated during the Wisconsin Ice Age, which was at its maximum about 18,000 years ago, and during earlier (Pleistocene) glacial events. Mountain building has principally occurred through large uplifted masses of sedimentary rock that have been thrust in an easterly direction, as in the Canadian Rockies, or through volcanism, as in Yellowstone. Notable batholiths occur in central Idaho, the Bugaboos of British Columbia, Wyoming's Cirque of the Towers, and the Cirque of the Unclimbables in the South Nahanni River watershed of the Northwest Territories. The latter three are all world class rock-climbing destinations.

Old Faithful Geyser, Yellowstone National Park

Source: Graeme L. Worboys

The distribution of plant communities varies with latitude and elevation. In Wyoming's Wind River Range is found Gannet Peak (4183m), the highest mountain in the Y2Y system. The vegetation gradient encountered there ranges from sage steppe to high alpine mountains with glaciers. Grasslands are found in dry valleys and along the east side of the mountains from Yellowstone north to the area at the latitude of Banff, Alberta. These areas are often snow free in winter due to warm Chinook winds. As one goes further into the mountains, interior Douglas-fir (*Pseudotsuga menziesii*), trembling aspen (*Populus tremuloides*) and lodgepole pine (*Pinus contorta*) forests dominate, which yield to higher elevation forests of Engelmann spruce (*Picea engelmannii*), subalpine fir (*Abies lasiocarpa*) and Lyalls' larch (*Larix lyallii*). These latter forests experience heavy snowfall that remains on the ground for eight months of the year.

In dry valleys in the western part of the same region there are ponderosa pine (*Pinus ponderosa*) forests, but mostly the climate is wetter and milder

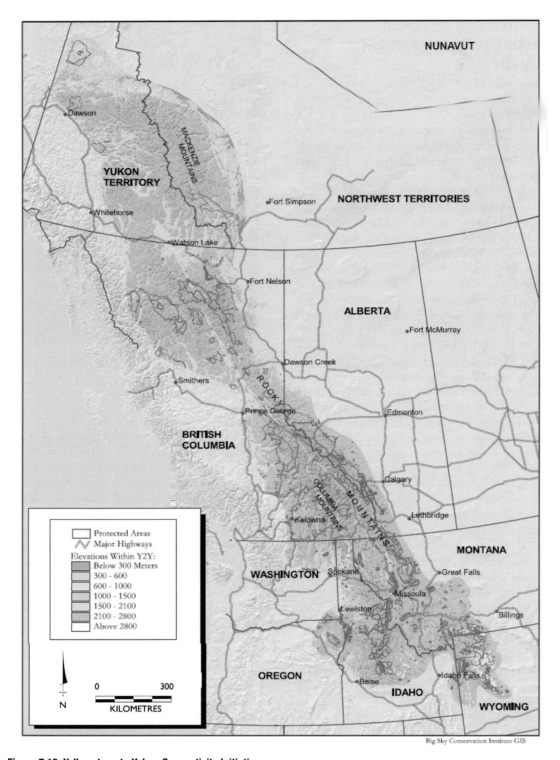

Figure 7.10 Yellowstone to Yukon Connectivity Initiative

so there are lush forests of western red cedar (*Thuja plicata*) and hemlock (*Tsuga heterophylla*) (reminiscent of the temperate rainforests of the Pacific Coast) and large stands of western larch (*Larix occidentalis*). At the northern end, the mountains support boreal, Arctic and some Beringian refugee species (Beringia refers to an area that was not glaciated during the most recent ice ages). There is a wide variety of spectacular wildflowers throughout the region.

The Y2Y region is notable for its role as the headwaters of western North America. The mountains give rise to: the Green River (the major tributary of the Colorado River, which drains into the Gulf of Baja California on the Pacific Ocean); the Columbia, and Fraser, which flow into the Pacific Ocean; the Yellowstone-Missouri and Saskatchewan-Nelson, which flow into the Atlantic Ocean; and the Athabasca, Peace, Liard and Peel Rivers, all of which drain into the Arctic Ocean through the Mackenzie River. These are all major rivers by international standards.

This water tower role for the Y2Y region is not only due to orographic effects, but also due to the presence of glaciers in the high peaks, especially in the vicinity of Banff and Jasper National Parks in the Canadian Rockies and in the Columbia Mountains of British Columbia. Lesser but still important glacial remnants are also found in the Wind River Range, Wyoming, in Glacier National Park, Montana, and in the Selwyn Mountains of the South Nahanni watershed, Northwest Territories. The cold rivers to which they give rise support the most significant cold water fish resource in North America, including Pacific salmon species, west slope cutthroat (*Oncorhynchus clarki*), bull trout (*Salvelinus confluentus*) and Arctic grayling (*Thymallus arcticus*).

In terms of large mammals, the two greatest concentrations of large varieties of carnivores and ungulates in North America occur in the region on the relatively snow-free areas of Yellowstone National Park's northern range and on the east slope of northern British Columbia's Muskwa-Kechika Management Area (Laliberte and Ripple, 2004).

These areas still support robust predator–prey relationships. The same species are distributed throughout the region at lesser densities with some regional variations in species. For example there are bighorn sheep (*Ovis canadensis*) and elk (*Cervus elaphus*) in the south in contrast with thin horn sheep (*Ovis dalli*) and caribou (*Rangifer tarandus*) in the north.

While species richness is generally greater in the south, biodiversity reaches its apex along the Canada–US border in the vicinity of Waterton-Glacier International Peace Park and the adjoining Flathead Valley in south-east British Columbia. Here is the largest concentration and greatest variety of large carnivores in the North American continent including Canada lynx (*Felis lynx*), bobcat (*Felis rufus*), wolverine (*Gulo gulo*), grey wolf (*Canis lupis*) and grizzly bear (*Ursus arctos horribilis*). In addition, there are a wide variety of vascular plants including boreal, Arctic, Pacific, American Cordilleran and prairie plants (Konstant et al, 2005).

Black bear (*Ursus americanus*), Yellowstone National Park

Source: Graeme L. Worboys

The Y2Y region can be divided into three from a landscape condition point of view (W. L. Francis, 2003, pers. comm.). The 'Wild North' from the Mackenzie Mountains to the Peace River contains some of the wildest and largest unroaded areas left on Earth. This is a function of remoteness and lack of agricultural productivity more than conscious

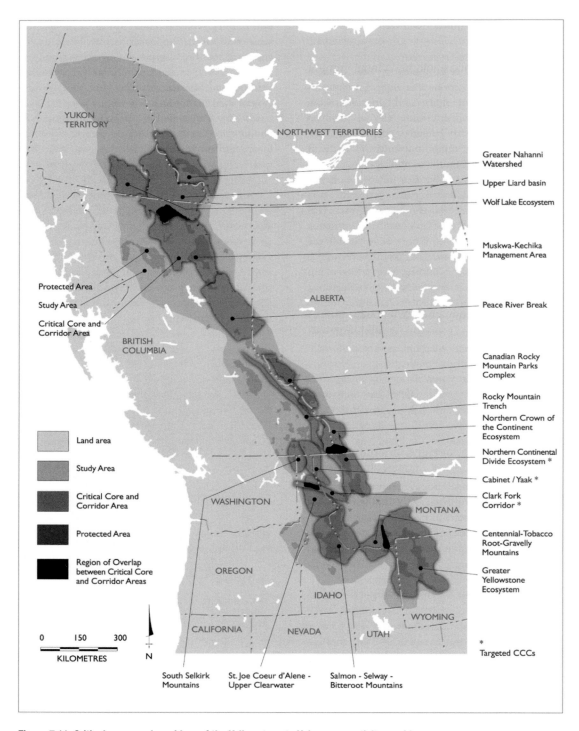

Figure 7.11 Critical cores and corridors of the Yellowstone to Yukon connectivity corridor

Note: CCC = Connectivity Conservation Corridors

policy. There are few protected areas here except in the Muskwa–Kechika Management Area of British Columbia. Development pressures on these wild areas, particularly energy and mining exploration and production, are increasing rapidly. The 'Central Region' from Jasper National Park to the Clark Fork River in Montana is more heavily fragmented by human activities but has many large protected areas (Figure 7.12). This region still supports robust populations of carnivores that are connected genetically, though some linkages are under serious pressure from human development along highways. The 'Fragmented South' extends from the Clark Fork River to South Pass, Wyoming. In this region some species have been extirpated from some of their range notwithstanding a large network of protected areas. The genetically isolated population of grizzly bears in Yellowstone National Park is a major conservation concern. This area has seen successful wolf reintroduction with animals sourced from the Wild North region.

The Y2Y region is home to aboriginal people who are called First Nations in Canada and Native Americans in the US. The Wild North is occupied by Gwichin (Northwest Territories) and Gwich'in (Yukon) (two distinct groups), Dene (several distinct groups) and Beaver people. The Central Region has a diversity of ethnic groups including Interior Salish, Stoney, Blackfoot and Ktunaxa (Kootenai). In the Fragmented South, Native American groups include Crow, Nez Perce, Shoshone and Arapahoe.

Most regional residents are of European ethnic descent varying from seven generations of occupancy to new arrivals. There are small communities across the region but they are widely spaced. No city in the region exceeds 100,000 in population and less than five exceed 50,000. Two smaller urban concentrations (Billings, Montana, and Boise, Idaho) with populations above 100,000 are found along the edge of the region but their 'footprint' is primarily local. However, Calgary, Alberta, on the edge of the Canadian Rockies has

Forests, Greater Yellowstone Ecosystem, Yellowstone National Park

Source: Graeme L. Worboys

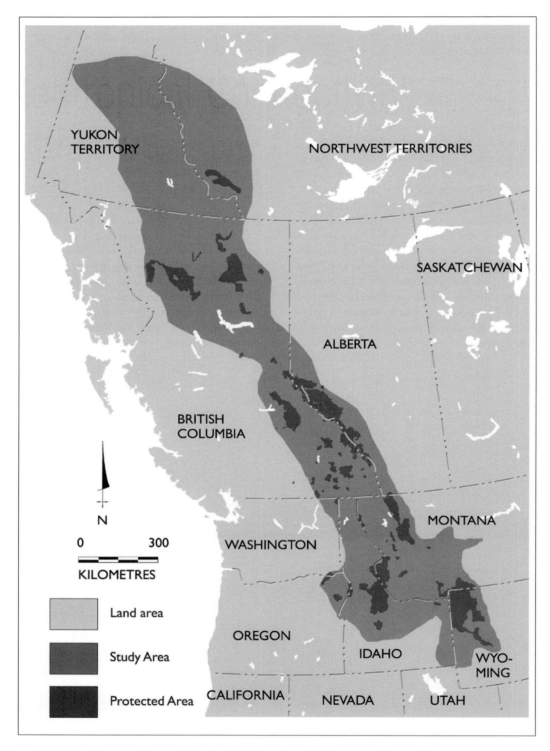

Figure 7.12 Protected areas of the central part of the Yellowstone to Yukon connectivity corridor

almost one million people and its 'footprint' is very large. Regional impacts are due to Calgary being the headquarters of the oil and gas industry and a source of people buying second homes in the scenic areas of Alberta, British Columbia and north-western Montana and Idaho. Further, because the Y2Y region is an exporter of raw materials, the global prices of commodities affect land use tremendously, with pressure on wild areas increasing when prices are high. The region also is influenced by people who live outside its boundaries and who love the landscape, fishing or wildlife of the area.

In historical times (since the mid-1800s), the Y2Y region has been characterized by two competing land uses: protected areas and resource extraction. Some of the world's largest, oldest and most iconic protected areas are found here including Yellowstone (established 1872) and Banff (established 1885) national parks, the Bob Marshall Wilderness and Waterton-Glacier International Peace Park. These places of exceptional natural beauty support an important tourism industry and an amenity migrant-based economy (Moss, 2006). Indeed, the Y2Y region boasts one of the largest international networks of IUCN Category I and II protected areas as well as several natural world heritage sites, including two of the first to be so designated. Nahanni National Park Reserve and Yellowstone National Park were both inscribed as world heritage sites in 1978. Further, Yellowstone, Banff and Nahanni protected areas enjoy cultural icon status in their respective countries and Yellowstone is probably the most famous protected area in the world.

The summer tourism industry in the region is centred around protected public lands, especially national parks like Banff and Yellowstone, which respectively draw annually 3.3 million (PC, 2007b) and 2.8 million (NPS, 2006) national and international visitors. A significant tourism infrastructure is associated with these tourism magnets. There is also an important downhill ski industry that attracts global clientele to Banff, Fernie, Sun Valley and Jackson Hole and national market skiers to Big Sky, Kimberly, Whitefish, Bridger Bowl and Kicking Horse. The world's largest helicopter skiing industry operates in the mountains of southern British Columbia.

On the other hand, the Y2Y region has a long history of significant resource extraction industries including the fur trade in the 19th century, mining and forestry in 20th century and, more recently, energy development. The abandoned copper mines in Butte, Montana, and the silver and lead zinc mines of British Columbia were among the world's largest. The Yukon Gold Rush is the stuff of legend. The state motto for Montana is 'oro y plata' or 'silver and gold'. The many dams on the Columbia River and the W.A.C. Bennett Dam on the Peace River are among the world's largest water impoundments and electricity generating facilities. The oil and gas industry along the east slope of the Canadian Rockies on the Alberta Plain is globally significant and the gas industry in Wyoming's Green River Basin is also important. The timber industry in the high precipitation areas of western Montana, Idaho and British Columbia has been of global significance, especially during the period of cutting old-growth forest, which is largely over. Cattle ranching has been an important traditional use in dry interior valleys and along the east slope of the Rockies from Wyoming to south-west Alberta. Sheep grazing has been locally important in Wyoming. Another important factor is the transportation network. National highway and railway transportation systems bisect the region's few biologically productive low-elevation valleys with the potential to fragment the landscape.

The connectivity conservation initiative

The name Yellowstone to Yukon Conservation Initiative was given to the strategic connectivity conservation initiative extending from Yellowstone National Park, US, to the Yukon in northern Canada. It is built on both old and new foundations and is rooted in culture and biology. Its mission states (Y2Y, 2007):

> *Combining science and stewardship, Y2Y seeks to ensure that the wilderness, wildlife, native plants, and natural processes of the Yellowstone to Yukon region continue to function as an interconnected web of life, capable of supporting all of the natural and human communities that reside within it, for now and for future generations.*

The initiative has set its own measure of success:

'when ... residents of the Y2Y region take it for granted that their long-term personal, spiritual, and economic well-being is inextricably connected to the well-being of natural systems' (Y2Y, 2002). From the outset, it was anticipated by its founders that it may take as long as 100 years to achieve the Y2Y vision.

The Y2Y idea touches on the ancient wisdom of the traditional peoples of this region. To First Nation peoples this mountain corridor was the ancient route of travel that enabled humans to populate the interior of North America at the end of the Wisconsin Ice Age. Some of them already had a name for the region: the Dene call it the 'People's Trail' (Porter, 2002); the Blackfoot call it the 'Old North Trail'. The great wildlife artist Carl Rungius travelled from Yellowstone to the Yukon at the turn of the 20th century to paint the images that defined North America's large mammals for a public concerned with their conservation. For years tourists from around the world have been making trips from Yellowstone to Banff and on up to the Yukon along the Alaska Highway. For millions of other people who have never had a chance to visit and never will, Yellowstone, the Yukon and the Canadian Rockies in between fire the imagination as global symbols of wild beauty and adventure in nature.

The modern origins of the Y2Y idea are complex. The phrase 'Yellowstone to Yukon' as an organizing principle for conservation efforts along North America's Rocky Mountains was first written in 1993 (Locke, 1994) but it did not appear out of thin air. Findings of biologists made possible by the use of modern technologies like animal radio collars and satellites showed the vast and previously unrecognized scale of animal movements in the region. The broad theoretical ideas of conservation biology that had been developed in the 1980s, especially the importance of connectivity between wildlife populations to prevent their extinction and the limitations of geographically restricted protected areas as a conservation tool, were essential ingredients. The effort by The Wildlands Project to bring these ideas into land-use planning was important (Soulé and Terborgh, 1999). Many, many people already had been thinking along similar lines. The expression 'Yellowstone to Yukon' simply gave voice to

widely held thoughts that were waiting to be crystallized, and a thorough review of the many faceted origins of Y2Y was compiled by Chester (2006).

The formal Y2Y effort was initiated in 1993 by non-governmental wilderness and wildlife organizations and conservation biologists. The Canadian Parks and Wilderness Society (CPAWS) and The Wildlands Project (now the Wildlands Network) organized the first meeting and provided important services to the broad-based group. When the Y2Y initiative began, the connectivity region existed in fact but not on paper. The initial preparatory tasks for the first meeting were to write a discussion paper that linked the landscape together and to commission a map that showed Yellowstone and the Yukon on the same page perhaps for the first time.

To move ahead with conservation at this scale, it was necessary to establish human ties across an international border that had previously been a psychological and informational barrier. So the Y2Y community developed an atlas of physical and cultural resources that showed the unified integrity of the region (Willcox et al, 1998). Over time and through many face-to-face meetings, a community of people emerged who think and work together north–south along the grain of the landscape instead of confining themselves within national mental frameworks. The Internet (which was an emergent technology at the time) was an indispensable tool, as was a grand gathering in 1997 (enabled with the funding support of the North American Fund for Environmental Cooperation) that brought together hundreds of people from all over Canada and the United States. This created a sense of participation in a shared endeavour with the result that conservationists began working together more cooperatively, supporting each others' ventures, seeing how everyone's work across the region contributed the greater whole of which they formed a part. Individual organizations ranging from wilderness advocates, to wildlife conservation groups, to private land trusts each set to work to assemble their piece of the whole landscape puzzle.

The collaboration gradually moved from community building and specific projects, to forming an organization called the Yellowstone to

Yukon Conservation Initiative (Y2YCI), incorporated in both Alberta and Montana in 2000. At the same time, both within the region and in cities like Ottawa, Boston, New York and Seattle, many NGOs and philanthropic foundations developed formal Y2Y programmes aligned with the vision but independent of Y2YCI.

From the time the Y2Y idea was first articulated in 1993 and then immediately refined and embraced by a broad community of biologists and conservationists, it struck a deeply resonant chord with conservation leaders and other people around the world. It provided a glimmer of hope for species conservation and protection in a world increasingly impacted by humans. The idea of an interconnected series of parks and wilderness areas that could be designed in a way that allowed both people and animals to thrive across this vast and exceptional landscape made immediate sense to people and they wanted to help. The interest in the Y2Y vision from local, regional, national and international media exceeded our wildest dreams. Bart Robinson, hired in 1996 as the first coordinator of what would become Y2YCI, compared the enormous interest to 'being at the centre of the "Big Bang"' at the origin of our universe. In addition to the conservation groups and foundations that aligned their programmes with the vision, many independent efforts locally and internationally were spawned by the Y2Y idea.

Among the remarkable things that emerged were the extraordinary individual efforts that came to the Y2Y endeavour, often unsought. People were simply inspired by the Y2Y vision and found ways to help. Caroline Underwood raised funds in Germany to produce an hour-long episode of CBC Television's *The Nature of Things* with David Suzuki that ran on television across North America (CBC, 1997). Ernie Labelle, a senior government relations person in Washington DC, took the idea to the editor of *National Geographic* magazine and the result was the first book on Y2Y (Chadwick, 2000). Karsten Heuer, a young park warden and biologist from Alberta heard of the idea and decided to walk from Yellowstone to the Yukon and share his findings about the viability of the idea from a wildlife habitat perspective. Huge media interest and a best-selling book followed (Heuer, 2002). Singer-songwriter Walkin' Jim

Stoltz of Montana also walked the distance and returned with songs of the Y2Y landscape that he took to regional classrooms. Josh Burnim, a college student in Idaho walked the Sawtooth to Selkirks part of the region and carried the Y2Y message to local communities.

Banff Filmmaker Guy Clarkson's four-part high definition television series *Shining Mountains* (Raven, 2005) features Yellowstone to Yukon, and was shown at the Cannes Film Festival and on television in North America, Europe and Asia. Florian Schulz, a young German nature photographer devoted ten years of his life to documenting the wild animals and geography of this vast region which resulted in a spectacular book, *Yellowstone to Yukon: Freedom to Roam*, featuring his photography and essays by some of North America's leading conservation writers (Schulz, 2005). An extensive North America speaking tour followed. Eleanor Sterling of the American Museum of Natural History in New York curated a photo exhibit on Y2Y that opened in 2006 to which 11 photographers from North America and Europe donated their work.

Several philanthropic foundations were initially introduced to the Y2Y idea by Ted Smith and Gary Tabor of the Henry P. Kendall Foundation in Boston. Subsequently, under the leadership of Gary Tabor, the Wilburforce Foundation opened a Yellowstone to Yukon field office in Bozeman, Montana, the first of its kind in North America.

The importance of thinking about Y2Y as an interconnected region began to appear in publications related to national parks management in Canada (Locke, 1997; PC, 2000; Dearden and Rollins, 2002) and in many books about conservation and environment (Soulé and Terborgh, 1999; Wilson, 2001; Suzuki and Dressel, 2002; Nelson et al, 2003; Bennett, 2004; Anderson and Jenkins, 2006). School teachers and college professors across the continent began including Y2Y in their courses. Several master's degree and doctor of philosophy theses were completed about Y2Y at universities across North America. One thesis resulted in a book *Conservation Across Borders* (Chester, 2006) that provides an excellent history of the development and evolution of the Y2Y effort until 2004.

Over many years other talented individuals including David Johns, Bart Robinson, Ray Rasker, Louisa Willcox, Bob Peart, Wendy Francis, Bob Ekey, Barb Cestero, Ed Lewis, Christine Torgrimson, Jeremy Guth, Rob Buffler, Troy Merrill and many others devoted themselves to building an ever evolving organization to serve this innovative concept across a vast bi-national geography and two culturally different countries. For the past 15 years it has been my privilege to work with them and carry the Y2Y idea to audiences across North America and around the world. However, these are but a few of the many things that have been done by so many that relate to the Y2Y effort.

Connectivity conservation management

Y2Y is several things: it is a geographical region; a vision; a social movement; and an organization. It is also a symbol of connectivity conservation efforts. Large-scale conservation initiatives around the world have started to use catchy alliterations that built on the resonance of 'Yellowstone to Yukon' including Algonquin to Adirondacks (Canada and US); Alps to Atherton (Australia); Baja to Bering (Mexico, US and Canada); and the Cantabric–Pyrenees–Massif Central–Alps initiative (Europe). Media stories about connectivity conservation initiatives and other published papers often reference the Y2Y corridor as the exemplar of the connectivity conservation idea (Dean, 2006; Mitchell, 2006.

A conscious effort has been made to engage First Nations and Native Americans in the Y2Y effort. Two important meetings were organized: the first brought together indigenous people from all sides of the Mackenzie Mountains to discuss large-scale conservation. The second brought to Banff indigenous people from the length of the Y2Y corridor to provide guidance as to how best to engage them in the Y2Y vision. This resulted in a formal policy for indigenous peoples' engagement that was embraced by First Nations and led to the inclusion of Native Americans on the Y2YCI board. First Levi Holt of the Nez Perce Tribe and Peter Westley of the Stoney Nakoda First Nation and subsequently Dick Baldes of the Shoshone Tribe actively served on the board. Y2YCI staff continue to engage actively with Native Americans and First Nations across the Y2Y landscapes.

Efforts of Canadian First Nations are making major contributions to the implementation of the Y2Y vision. The Kaska conservation initiative of the Kaska Dene of northern British Columbia and southern Yukon is consistent with the Y2Y vision and they have signed a Memorandum of Understanding to work on Y2Y with CPAWS (Porter, 2002). The Kaska Dene were key to the inclusion of the Kechika in the Muskwa-Kechika Management Area, part of Y2Y. The Dehcho people of the Northwest Territories have developed a visionary plan for their 214,000 square kilometre territory along the Mackenzie River and in the Mackenzie Mountains area that they wish the Canadian Government to adopt. It is a development plan that calls for strict protection (while preserving traditional aboriginal harvesting) of over 60 per cent of the area with the majority of the balance of the lands to be in special management zones. The plan includes a proposal to expand Nahanni National Park Reserve to protect the entire South Nahanni watershed and adjacent karstlands (DLUPC, 2006). This would create an exceptional 3,500,000ha national park. This park expansion was the subject of a large national outreach campaign in Canada on which conservationists and the Dehcho worked together (CPAWS, 2006) and led to a formal prime ministerial commitment to greatly expand the park (Harper, 2007).

The phenomenon of Y2Y also attracted a negative response from anti-conservation forces. The attacks varied from characterizing the effort as one that would exclude all people from the Rocky Mountains to a United Nations conspiracy to impose 'one world government' on freedom-loving Americans. The Forest Alliance of British Columbia asserted that it would mean an end to all resource extraction and issued a spurious report asserting a catastrophic level of job loss. The John Birch Society, a reactionary, right wing, American organization (Wikipedia, 2007), suggested it was part of an agenda to create 'eco-gulags'.

The backlash was effective within some communities that were dependent upon traditional resource extraction economies. It also frightened some groups, particularly on the US side of the region, away from affiliating themselves publicly with Y2Y. It also caused the Y2Y collaborative to explicitly incorporate a reference to healthy human communities in its message (which had previously emphasized nature over people).

There were likely three things that motivated the backlash. First, some traditional industries, notably open-pit coal mining, had no interest in there being a public agenda that would compete for land use in the regions they had traditionally dominated. Second, the traditional extraction industries, notably logging, were experiencing severe economic conditions that led to lay offs and mill closures, which created feelings of vulnerability in affected communities. The cause was the elimination of large trees in public forests and the slow rate of reforestation but it was convenient to blame environmental interests. Third, wolf recovery and reintroduction, particularly in the US northern Rockies, created fears among cattle ranchers for their livestock. Even compensation programmes did little to address deeper cultural loathing of this predator. As one rancher said 'Even if you pay him for it, I never met a rancher who raised a cow to feed a wolf' (R. Jennings, 2006, pers. comm.). The backlash was abetted by inadvertent lack of care in the choice of words used by some Y2Y supporters to describe the initiative, which fed anti-environmentalist suspicions. It was also augmented by efforts to portray Y2Y supporters as outsiders.

The backlash was not a factor in communities that had more diverse economies based on tourism and amenity migration such as Jackson Hole, Wyoming, where the Chamber of Commerce under the leadership of Steve Duerr incorporated Y2Y into its strategy for marketing its brand (Jackson Hole Chamber of Commerce, 2006). But conservation is not a matter of convenience and large-scale efforts like Y2Y cannot confine themselves to places where a cultural welcome mat has been laid out for conservationists.

An interesting illustration of how backlash was dealt with comes from the East Kootenay region of southern British Columbia. Situated adjacent to the US, it is a key linkage in the Central Region of the Y2Y corridor. Simply put, if Y2Y

did not succeed at this location, the Y2Y connectivity concept would fail.

Despite the strong resource extraction based economy and pro-development supporters in the East Kootenay (the federal member of parliament once said that Y2Y stood for 'four legs good, two legs bad') connectivity conservation successes were achieved. National conservation groups like CPAWS were undeterred, framed their work in a Y2Y context, and set about advocating for the expansion of Waterton-Glacier International Peace Park into the Flathead Valley of British Columbia and for conserving connectivity across critical sections of Highway 3 in the Elk Valley. This action successfully brought the largest forestry company in the southern part of the region, Tembec (an international forestry company) to the table. Tembec adjusted its forestry plans for the Flathead Valley and negotiated the sale of low-elevation lands for wildlife linkages of continental scale connectivity conservation significance. The Nature Conservancy of Montana and the Nature Conservancy of Canada were engaged to secure these private lands. The money to pay for the land was successfully raised across North America, thanks especially to the wide reach of and support for the Y2Y vision. There were simply no local resources available to acquire lands of this value.

Wildsight (formerly the East Kootenay Environmental Society), a credible conservation group (based on the deep regional roots of its leadership) in the East Kootenay region, chose to publicly frame its work within the Y2Y context. It also benefited from the increased resources that the Y2Y vision had brought to this previously overlooked area. Through time the combined effect of these efforts and the changing demographics of the region caused the impact of the backlash to diminish in importance. In 2004, Y2YCI organized a conference on 'International Mountain Corridors' to visit this region as part of its deliberations, and hosted public meetings so that the idea of connectivity conservation and continental scale corridors could be seen as one of international interest as opposed to a scheme unique to the region.

There has also been considerable engagement around mutual areas of interest with the Ktunaxa peoples who have an important land claim over the area. Less effective to date has been direct outreach by Y2YCI staff and contractors to hostile constituencies like coal mining and local hunting groups.

Though opponents remain, large-scale visions like Y2Y can yield large-scale results that are not possible from operating solely in a local context. Critical connectivity conservation outcomes in the East Kootenay region would have been lost if there had been a retreat due to the backlash. The lesson from the East Kootenay is to stay the course and work with locally credible conservation leaders while maintaining the broader perspective that comes from articulating clearly and publicly a vision for large landscape conservation.

There is an economic tension in the Y2Y region. The primary economic activities come from either traditional resource extraction with its associated impacts on the environment including mining, logging, hydro dams, and oil and gas extraction, or the new amenity migration economy (Moss, 2006) and tourism, which are based on conservation and the quality of the environment and which also have negative impacts on connectivity and habitat security for wildlife. There are also culturally valued activities like cattle ranching, which have less economic importance but significant symbolic importance.

Some resource extraction industries are interested in engaging with conservation groups, and some, most notably the mining sector, are not. Some cattle ranchers have engaged successfully with conservation land trusts that enable them to maintain their lifestyle while ensuring their lands maintain native grasslands and support wildlife's seasonal needs.

Others convert their land to housing subdivisions to realize capital. People engaged in the amenity migration economy are very receptive to conservation but ironically often have a taste for building houses on small acreages that fragment important areas for wildlife connectivity while their recreational activities can impact wildlife security.

The amenity migration economy merits more discussion for it is less well known but is a significant economic force in the Y2Y region. First described in a Y2Y context in *The New Challenge* (Rasker and Alexander, 1998), it is a phenomenon

of modern communications and attractive communities located near beautiful natural environments. Due to airports and the Internet, people can now pursue their economic goals by engaging in global commerce from settings of their own choosing or can bring their personal capital (such as retirement funds and stock market investments) with them to new settings. It is a global phenomenon that is particularly present in mountain regions (Moss, 2006). Amenity migrants tend to be well educated and entrepreneurial and the amenity migration economy is responsible for most of the new jobs and economic growth in the US portion of the Y2Y region (Rasker et al, 2004). It is also significant in some communities in Canada like Canmore, Alberta, and Invermere, British Columbia. Amenity migrants like protected nature and thus one economist has determined that a new protected area could also stimulate economic activity in an area previously dependent on resource extraction (Johnson, J., 2004).

Y2Y advocates have pointed out that protecting nature is good for business due to the amenity migration economy. This is persuasive to some audiences. But to people with no connections outside their communities and with no educational or work experience that would enable them to engage with the broader world, it is not a compelling alternative to resource extraction in their home town. This is particularly the case among middle-aged and older males for whom the traditional resource extraction model has been the norm and has provided high wages to those with modest levels of education.

The Y2Y region is remarkable because it has been colonized by prosperous industrialized cultures yet it has mostly maintained its full range of pre-industrial wildlife species (though often reduced in their distribution and abundance). In the Fragmented South and the Central Region, this remarkable conservation success is due to two things that pre-date Y2Y: first, the presence of large national parks that are nature sanctuaries with effective warden services protecting them; second, wildlife management laws dating from the early 20th century that have been enforced on all public and private lands. On the US side, these laws were importantly supplemented by the *Endangered Species Act* of 1970, which protected grizzly bears and wolves. In the Wild North, the health of the landscape is primarily due to its remoteness rather than any deliberate public policy.

If it were not for these important pre-existing building blocks, the Y2Y conservation initiative would not likely have come about. No large landscape conservation initiative will succeed in saving all species including large predators and wild grazers unless there is a core of IUCN Category I, II and/or IV protected areas, which may be supported by Category V areas, as well as effective regimes that protect wildlife in some way on the rest of the landscape.

The Y2Y vision has been assisted by some native species reintroductions completed by public agencies to restore depleted or extirpated populations. Over the years, elk from Yellowstone were reintroduced to Banff, plains bison (*Bison bison*) were reintroduced to British Columbia's northern Rockies, and trumpeter swans (*Cygnus buccinator*) have been reintroduced to the Blackfoot Valley in Montana. Wolves from Canada were reintroduced to Idaho and Yellowstone. This is not to say that all is well. Non-native sport fish introduction has had a severe impact on native fish and lake ecology in the Fragmented South and the Central Regions of Y2Y. Exotic diseases like blister rust have severely impacted whitebark pine (*Pinus albicaulis*) populations.

Climate change has reduced natural controls on the mountain pine beetle *(Dendroctonus ponderosae)*, which is spreading rapidly and causing dieback in pine forests throughout the Y2Y region except the Wild North. Global warming is also causing species to migrate north, up slope and around mountain aspects where landscape conditions permit (Hall and Fagre, 2003; Welch, 2005). Habitat fragmentation threatens to make islands out of the core areas in the Central Region and has already isolated core areas in the Fragmented South. No network of large officially protected core areas is in place in the Wild North, which faces increasing development pressures. Y2Y is a strategy to respond to these realities by framing a positive vision of restoration (Fragmented South), maintaining and improving current conditions (Central Region) and protection in advance of industrial development (Wild North).

One of the most daunting self-imposed tasks for Y2Y was to scientifically determine what conservation efforts would meet the vision of:

wilderness, wildlife, native plants, and natural processes of the Yellowstone to Yukon region continuing to function as an interconnected web of life, capable of supporting all of the natural and human communities that reside within it, for now and for future generations (Y2Y, 2007).

An outcome of the first meeting in 1993 was the commitment by several participants to a multi-authored special issue of *Conservation Biology* on the state of knowledge of large carnivore conservation in the Rocky Mountains, which was coordinated by Dr Tim Clark of Yale University and Dr Reed Noss, the journal's editor (Clark et al, 1996).

An initial ambitious plan to produce a 'conservation area design' or detailed blueprint for an adequate system of protected areas, buffer zones and corridors across the region ran into practical problems. The Wild North was so wild that there were little data to work with and most theory had no application there because it had been developed for fragmented landscapes. For the Central Region and the Fragmented South, while the conceptual foundation calling for connectivity among core protected areas became more and more accepted, the theory for applied reserve designs was in its infancy and changing as Y2Y developed.

The concept of a core protected area surrounded by a buffer zone had been developed years before by the UN's Man and the Biosphere Programme. The essential new addition was connectivity. But connectivity can mean a narrow strip one metre wide or a continental scale migration depending on the species. Methods and models changed rapidly. Another basic question was: 'What conservation goals were appropriate: survival of minimum viable populations or abundance?'

The Y2Y region is also home to several research universities, independent researchers, government agencies and NGOs with research or analytical capacity who were active simultaneously with the Y2Y collaborative. Thus the available knowledge was growing all the time. And this led to another important question: 'Who should do the work and develop the conservation strategies?' Should it be the staff and contractors of the Y2Y collaborative, local NGOs, universities or more locally based researchers?

To help answer these questions, Y2Y Science Coordinator Marcy Mahr organized a 1999 workshop chaired by leading conservation biologist Michael Soulé and grizzly bear biologist Stephen Herrero, which brought together some of the most prominent conservation biologists in western North America. In the end, a focal species approach based on modelling was taken. The species included carnivores, birds and fish. It was also determined that the best focus for the Y2Y collaborative that would add value to all the other efforts would be to answer questions that were inherent at the Y2Y scale rather do local field-based research. To ensure that regional efforts that fed the connectivity vision continued, Wilburforce Foundation, of its own volition, created the Y2Y Science Grants Program to engage researchers and NGO partners in questions of connectivity at regional scales. From 1999 to 2006, this programme provided 86 grants for scientific research to 42 different NGOs with more than $1.5 million spent over the eight years. The science work the Y2Y collaborative initiated took far longer than anticipated. However, by 2001 there was enough information to begin to prioritize efforts. By 2006, the carnivore work was largely complete, the bird work was nearing completion and the fish work was underway.

In 2007, the *Y2Y Grizzly Bear Conservation Strategy* has guided the identification of 12 priority areas within the Y2Y landscape, the protection or restoration of which is essential to connectivity among continental bear populations. Y2Y staff members are convening collaborations of environmental non-governmental organizations (ENGOs), researchers and government agencies to identify and implement strategies to address specific challenges to connectivity for grizzlies. Where grizzly connectivity conservation is insufficient to ensure the protection of biodiversity as a whole, projects aimed at protecting or restoring connectivity for other key species also are undertaken.

Because it is a social movement, the Y2Y vision was pursued by many groups simultane-ously with over 200 groups having formally adopted it. Many accomplishments resulted from work undertaken by those Y2Y supporters. This approach of many actors in collaborative pursuit of a common vision has often proven to be very effective but it is not systematic.

Y2YCI was incorporated by the many supporting groups in 2000 as a formal NGO. It provides strategic guidance by facilitating and connecting the Y2Y efforts, commissioning necessary research, catalysing conservation action, building the capacity of local NGOs, attracting new funding to the region, and ensuring that no key area is overlooked. It also promotes the Y2Y vision throughout the continent. Y2YCI is supported by over 200 organizations, has directors from across North America and in 2006 had a permanent staff of ten who were supported by five principal contractors. It had offices in Canmore, Alberta; Bozeman, Montana; and Sun Valley, Idaho. It solicits funds and has a membership (Y2Y, 2006).

To ensure that no critical connectivity areas essential to the Y2Y vision were missed, Y2YCI originally identified 17 priority areas that were later reduced to 12 priority areas, based on its leading-edge work to identify areas necessary for grizzly bear conservation. It then completed an assessment of threats, opportunities and conservation capacity for each of the priority areas. Where there is sufficient capacity Y2YCI supported the work done by others. Where there was a critical area in urgent need of attention Y2YCI entered the field, initiated the work, attracted resources, built local capacity and then stepped away (Y2Y, 2006; Figure 7.12).

The first area to be addressed through this process was in the Central Region just north of the Canada–US border along Highway 3 in the Rockies and Purcell Mountains of British Columbia and their southern extension to the Cabinet Mountains in northern Montana. It included the Crowsnest Pass region of Alberta and is partially located in the previously discussed East Kootenay region of British Columbia. Grizzly bear modelling by Troy Merrill commissioned by Y2YCI helped identify this as a key area of continental scale concern. There was also near unanimity among large carnivore biologists that the Canadian portion contains the two critical linkages to connect carnivore populations in the US to the large wild gene pool in the Y2Y Central Region and the Wild North. If this linkage were severed, all the US populations would be at risk. Similarly, the isolated population of grizzly bears in the nearby Cabinet Mountains of northern Montana was at serious risk of extinction if it remained disconnected from others (US Fish and Wildlife Service, 2006). But if the connection north were restored, not only would its future be more secure, it could form a lifeline for recolonization of vacant but viable grizzly habitat in Idaho (US) and ultimately provide a basis for restoring population connections to Yellowstone (Merrill, 2005).

With increased staff capacity at Y2YCI in 2007, other critical areas began to be addressed. The Peace River Break area of northern British Columbia, for example, cuts across the Rockies between the Wild North and the Central Region, providing connectivity between the protected cores of the Muskwa-Kechika Management Area and Jasper National Park. It is under tremendous pressure from hydroelectric development, coal mining, coal bed methane extraction, forestry and oil and gas drilling. Y2YCI staff have made several forays to the area to establish partnerships with local ENGOs and First Nations people. The goal is to establish a collaborative strategy for actions that will preserve the connectivity of the region.

Benefits and accomplishments

The Y2Y vision and the efforts of conservationists to align with it began changing conservation results almost immediately. Articulating publicly the scale of conservation activities needed to maintain healthy wildlife populations at the Y2Y scale enabled changes in public policy. By 2006, two outstanding outcomes inspired by Y2Y were the establishment of the Muskwa-Kechika Management Area and the creation of two multi-million dollar highway overpasses for wildlife in Banff National Park.

The northern Rockies of British Columbia is one of the few remaining large, natural and wild areas of Earth. It is an area of spectacular beauty with no permanent human settlements that has a continuing tradition of aboriginal use. A vast

block of wilderness of over six million hectares in area, these northern Rockies have very large mammal populations as well as robust native fish populations. At the time the Y2Y idea was launched, it had 50 contiguous undeveloped watersheds draining into the Muskwa or Kechika Rivers, major tributaries of the Liard River.

In the early 1990s, the Government of British Colombia, as part of its *Provincial Land Use Strategy*, initiated a regional Land and Resource Management Planning (LRMP) process. The process was cooperative and consensus-based, involving people who represented varying perspectives from industry to conservation to cultural and spiritual values. Conservationists George Smith (CPAWS) and Wayne Sawchuk, both of whom had attended the first Y2Y meeting in 1993, brought connectivity conservation ideas from that meeting to the LRMP processes that were to determine land use in the northern Rockies of British Columbia (Sawchuk, 2004).

After many years of negotiation, the land and resource planning table members in Fort Nelson and Fort St. John, and later in Mackenzie, reached consensus on land use in the Muskwa-Kechika area. They agreed that the area was unique because of its size, unroaded condition, its cultural, ecological and geographical diversity and that it should be managed as a special management area. The result was the formal creation of an innovative land-use designation under the *Muskwa Kechika Management Area (M-KMA) Act* 1998. Under this Act, 6.4 million hectares of land were designated for varying levels of protection, conservation and use, described as follows:

> the management intent for the Muskwa-Kechika Management Area is to maintain in perpetuity the wilderness quality, and the diversity and abundance of wildlife and the ecosystems on which it depends while allowing resource development and use in parts of the Muskwa-Kechika Management Area (Muskwa-Kechika Management Board, 2006).

The M-KMA includes protected areas where resource extraction is prohibited (25 per cent of the area), and special management zones where resource extraction may occur, but based on higher environmental standards than elsewhere in the province. A public advisory board was appointed by the premier of British Colombia to provide advice to government on planning and land-use management, and a trust fund was established to fund projects. The *M-KMA Act* and management plan required the development of five 'local strategic plans' would provide direction to ensure appropriate management of activities and intensities of development for wildlife, oil and gas, recreation and forestry. The establishment of the M-KMA was an early breakthrough for Y2Y; however, the British Columbia Government changed in 2001 and in 2006 had been showing signs of undermining this innovation.

Canada's Banff National Park is one of the oldest and most famous national parks in the world and is the most heavily visited park in Y2Y. Located in the Y2Y Central Region it has a large amount of tourism infrastructure, which is concentrated in the low-elevation Bow Valley. This broad valley cuts across the north–south grain of the Rockies and has been used by people to move east–west for 11,000 years. It now hosts the Trans-Canada Highway and the Canadian Pacific Railway, the two busiest transportation arteries in Y2Y. The Bow Valley is also home to large carnivores including grizzly bears and wolves, as well as several ungulate and weasel species. Thus there were many vehicle and train collisions with wildlife before mitigation efforts were undertaken.

In the 1980s, to reduce the number of animals killed in association with doubling the lanes of traffic from one to two in each direction, Parks Canada erected fences on one stretch of the highway. Underpasses for wildlife were built in an effort to mitigate the barrier these fences would pose to animal movements across the valley. These underpasses were effective for ungulates but much less so for carnivores.

In the mid-1990s, Parks Canada proposed to continue expanding the highway through the park, with the same mitigations. By reference to the Y2Y region, conservationists were able to raise the concern that poor mitigation for carnivores was not merely a local issue but rather an issue of continental scale connectivity. If the highway

Banff National Park; part of the Yellowstone to Yukon connectivity corridor

Source: Graeme L. Worboys

became a 'Berlin wall of biodiversity' it could cut North American large carnivore populations in two and put the populations in the southern part of Y2Y at risk. This raised national media attention with the result that additional funds were appropriated to build two 50-metre wide overpasses for the highway.

By 2004, there were 24 highway wildlife crossing structures of various kinds in place along the 45km of fenced and twinned sections of the highway in Banff's Bow Valley (PC, 2004). More will be installed as doubling of the highway continues. These varied crossing structures have proven much more effective for the full range of species than underpasses alone and are now widely studied by people from around the around the world (Center for Transportation and the Environment, 2006). Monitoring from 1997 to 2003 by Parks Canada of wildlife use of 23 underpass and overpass structures revealed 48,682 individual wildlife passages, and this included cougars (*Felis concolor*) (197 times), wolves (254 times), black bears (*Ursus americanus*) (166 times) and grizzly bears (86 times) (PC, 2007a).

Similar wildlife crossing structures have been adopted on highways in other parts of the Y2Y region. The Kootenai-Salish people of Montana responded to a request to expand a highway across their reservation by insisting on road mitigations for wildlife like those found in Banff. They were successful, and the structures are under construction during 2006 including the additional innovation of burying the road for a stretch (US Department of Transportation, 2002). NGOs are working on analogous efforts on highways in the Crowsnest Pass area of Alberta, the Bozeman Pass area of Montana, the MacArthur Lake area of Idaho and the Togwotee Pass of Wyoming. Each of these involves highways that fragment big blocks of public land that have high wildlife-habitat values.

Perhaps the greatest validation of the Y2Y effort are early indications that maintaining and restoring connectivity guided by continental-scale thinking results in the return of sensitive wildlife species. In the mid-1990s, prompted by citizen and NGO outcry against the rampant pace of commercial development in Banff National Park, a new management plan was implemented. One of the plan's imperatives was the removal from the Bow Valley of an enclosure for bison, a small air strip, and a group of buildings used as a camp for military cadets that were thought to constitute a barrier to wildlife connectivity in the valley (PC, 1997). Almost immediately after these obstacles were removed, use of this portion of the Bow Valley by wolf packs greatly increased.

More recently, in September 2007, a hunter in north central Idaho, US was surprised to find that a bear he had shot was a grizzly bear, rather than a black bear. The last grizzly had been documented in that area in 1946 (Backus, 2007). Biologists say the bear migrated 140 miles south and crossed two major highways to explore the northern fringes of an ecosystem that experts have been expecting bears to discover on their own for years (Ridler, 2007). The migration of this bear across the 'no man's land' of northern Idaho holds out great hope for the restoration of the species to high quality, but vacant, grizzly habitat in this part of the Y2Y system.

The Y2Y region is already feeling the effects of climate change. Glaciers are receding rapidly, with predictions that Montana's Glacier National Park will lose all its glaciers by mid-century (Hall and Fagre, 2003). But the Y2Y region appears likely to bear the burden of climate change better that most parts of western North America due to its mountainous topography, which allows species to migrate upslope in response to warming, around slope in response to drying and northwards thanks to connectivity. In 2004, Y2Y Board member Bob Peart assembled a group of leading climate experts to help develop a strategy to respond to climate change. They stressed the Y2Y region's key importance as a refuge in the face of rapid climate change. Climate forecast models suggest it will be one of the few areas that maintain temperate forest cover (R. Hebda, 2004, pers. comm.). The glaciers of the Central Region will be one of the few reliable sources of freshwater in western North America with implications as far-reaching as the freshwater balance in the delta areas of the Arctic, Atlantic and Pacific Oceans (T. D. Prowse, 2004, pers. comm.). However, much remains to be done to develop an appropriate strategy to respond to climate change in the Y2Y region.

Retreating Athabasca Glacier, Columbia Ice Field, Banff National Park

Source: Graeme L. Worboys

Lessons learned

A large-scale vision yields large-scale results

The Y2Y grand vision has had greater impact than could have been achieved by responding, in isolation, to the individual conservation initiatives along the Y2Y landscape. It has also inspired multiple individuals to volunteer their time and resources to contribute to the connectivity conservation cause. The many individual, organizational and institutional efforts that are contributing to connectivity conservation within the Y2Y landscape are too numerous to inventory, and many are unknown to Y2YCI. Importantly, the organizational structure, activities and administration of Y2YCI has provided opportunities for such initiatives to happen. Beyond North America, the Y2Y vision has inspired people to initiate connectivity conservation action in their own countries.

More hands on deck are better than just a few, but coordination is needed

Because it is a social movement, the Y2Y vision is pursued by many groups simultaneously with more than 200 groups having formally adopted it. This approach of many actors in collaborative pursuit of a common vision has often proven to be very effective but is not systematic. An organization like Y2YCI that serves as a catalyst and facilitator is useful to ensure that attention is paid to the big picture and that no key areas are overlooked. At the same time, once the grand vision of connectivity in the Y2Y system was unleashed, it was impossible to control. Spontaneous activities emerged everywhere in the system that have contributed to advancing the large-scale agenda. Attempting to control these efforts would have stifled much of that creativity and energy. Rather, a more successful strategy was to 'let go' of control and let everyone who wanted to claim the Y2Y agenda as his or her own.

An informed, inspired and supportive community is a powerful ally

Strategic investments were made by Y2Y organisers to ensure that communities were well informed, and if possible supportive, including First Nations and Native American communities and some pro-development focused communities (to minimize any backlash). The provision of accurate information, based on highly credible research was an important part of this investment but is not always enough to calm concerns. In the face of very strong push back in some communities, it was very important to stay the course and continue to provide accurate and credible information. Over time, this created space for supportive community members to emerge and express their support.

Healthy environments mean healthy people

Connectivity conservation is not just about wildlife. Maintaining healthy environments through connectivity conservation helps to maintain healthy ecosystems and the life support systems needed by people, including clean air and clean water. This is an important message that, if conveyed earlier as part of the Y2Y campaign, might have avoided some of the backlash from resource industries and communities.

Clear, accurate and readily available printed and electronic information for people is essential

The printing of simple but clear location maps and the provision of an *Atlas of Physical and Cultural Resources* for Y2Y demonstrated the uniform nature of the corridor across the US–Canada border and helped to promote the concept of connectivity. Readily accessible information helped empower people to understand the Y2Y vision.

A mobilized, supportive and integrated research contribution is critical

Y2Y established outstanding partnerships with researchers, and their input directly contributed to the grand conservation vision and the identification of strategic areas requiring conservation attention. Collaboration with researchers was, and still is, a vital partnership for Y2Y. Investments by philanthropic organizations helped to consolidate a very active research programme.

Partnerships with philanthropic organizations were a key factor of success

Successfully working with key funding partners has been critical. Y2Y has inspired some key philanthropic partnerships, and their continued participation has been based on high quality, interpersonal and professional working relationships. Not only has Y2YCI benefited from this support, but dozens of partner NGOs and researchers throughout the region have seen their budgets for Y2Y-related research and initiatives grow since advent of the Y2Y vision.

Establish a governance mechanism under common law, which facilitates citizen-driven connectivity conservation

The incorporated society established by the Y2Y initiative provides a governance mechanism, through its board of directors, that provided opportunities for employing staff, for receiving gifts and charitable grants, and for providing a formal contribution to government processes or Court proceedings. Y2Y stewardship was facilitated thanks to the broad range of representatives on the board. A formal organizational structure also allowed for the development of strategies and activities leading toward fulfilment of the Y2Y agenda.

Use, to advantage, any supportive land-use types, legislation and government policies

If it were not for important pre-existing building blocks of large protected areas with adequate protection and universal wildlife laws, the Y2YCI would not likely have come about. No large landscape conservation initiative will succeed in saving all species including large predators and wild grazers unless there is a core of well-managed IUCN Category I, II and/or IV protected areas, which may be supported by Category V areas, as well as effective regimes that protect wildlife in some way on the rest of the landscape.

Use economic instruments as a tool to support connectivity conservation

Natural scenic amenity is a powerful attractant to many urban people wishing a lifestyle change and is consequently an important economic tool. The conservation of natural values, a core part of the Y2Y vision, helps to maintain these landscapes in a natural condition, which attracts amenity migrants. Amenity migrants bring with them their wealth and spending power, and consequently provide an economic benefit to rural environments. Y2YCI has used this trend as an economic benefit to help argue the case for the Y2Y vision. Such migrants also bring their values with them, which often are compatible with connectivity conservation, strengthening the constituency of support for conservation efforts.

Link the needs of iconic species and connectivity conservation

Y2Y focused on both people (social issues) and species (nature conservation), but in choosing the very large home range of the wolf, and the extensive pattern of movement of the grizzly bear amongst other iconic species, the message of continental-scale connectivity conservation needs was successfully marketed to the greater community.

Establish priorities for action

The scale of the Y2Y landscape has made deciding where to focus Y2YCI's limited resources often daunting. Some wildlife connectivity locations were more important than others, and research identified a number of these for Y2YCI. These critical 'choke' points, established generally because of development pressures, became a focus for conservation efforts, and even the acquisition of land.

Develop a management structure that is representative

Y2YCI's staff was overseen by a board of directors, and efforts were made to ensure that it included a cross-section of representative people, including First Nations and Native American landowners. This was no mean feat given the 3000km length of Y2Y. This was an important step, given the role of the Y2YCI board in establishing priorities. Over the decade of Y2YCI's evolution, the attributes of its governing personalities have shifted significantly. The original board of directors, formally constituted in 2000, but operating informally since 1996, was composed exclusively of environmental activists and scientists. As the organization matured and its needs changed, the board has evolved to have a broader set of skills, including financial management and major giving

capacity, with less of an emphasis on science and activism.

Identify local champions and stay the course

A powerful approach adopted by Y2Y was to work with highly credible local champions to facilitate the Y2Y vision for their 'local' section of Y2Y. This strategy helped to provide credibility for the Y2Y concept amongst their local communities. Forces hostile to conservation had often led a backlash to the Y2Y concept in places. Critical conservation outcomes would have been lost if there had been a retreat due to such backlash. The lesson is to stay the course and work with locally credible conservation leaders while maintaining the broader perspective that comes from articulating clearly and publicly a vision for large landscape conservation.

Create responsive and supportive management

Y2YCI delegates mutually agreeable tasks to its constituent members and this was shown to be a very successful model. Where additional resources were needed locally, they were provided by Y2YCI, but on an interim basis until more local capacity was built.

Establish priority areas for connectivity conservation action

Priorities for conservation action were established for the 3000km Y2Y corridor. Once identified, these areas were subject to more detailed 'conservation capacity' assessments and the development of collaborative conservation agenda to guide the work of Y2YCI and partner groups.

Purchase lands of critical strategic importance

Y2YCI has demonstrated the effectiveness of working with partners to negotiate with private companies and individuals for the purchase of lands of critical significance in maintaining the Y2Y connectivity vision. Y2YCI's ability to target key areas was based on good science; it was facilitated by organizations with the competency to negotiate land purchases, and it was supported by national fund-raising appeals that relied on public knowledge, sympathy and support for the Y2Y vision.

Use freehold land covenants to maximize the purchasing power of the available funds

Y2YCI's collaborating land trust organizations like the Nature Conservancy of Canada, use a technique of rural freehold land purchase and conservation easements in critical locations. Conservation easements are an agreement with the landholder that the rural characteristics (and connectivity conservation attributes) of the property are retained and subdivision or other developments are precluded. If a landholder prefers to sell, following purchase, the land trust covenants the property title with a conservation easement. The property is then resold, which then mobilizes the original investment monies to continue this work.

Government efforts complement the Y2Y vision

Momentum generated by the Y2Y vision also influenced planning and investment strategies by governments. Plans of management for parks such as Banff National Park have been influential in facilitating connectivity for wolves around and through Banff townsite and major overpass structures for wildlife have assisted animal movement across the Trans-Canada highway. Although slow to formally recognize it as an organizing principle, governments were complementing and extending the Y2Y vision.

Use powerful media tools to facilitate Y2Y connectivity conservation

The communication power of computers and the Internet was embraced by Y2YCI. Other electronic media such as television and radio and the print media through books, journals and magazines were used very successfully to extol the virtues of continental-scale conservation. Y2Y champions including celebrities and adventurers also helped sell the positive message.

8

Neotropical Connectivity Initiatives

The Neotropical realm includes South America, Central America (including the Mexican lowlands and Florida) and the Caribbean. The dominant mountain spine, the Andes, extends north–south from the northern hemisphere almost to Antarctica, and includes high mountains, volcanoes and large icefields. The realm includes one of the great rivers of the world, the Amazon. South America was originally part of Gondwana and shares many plant and animal lineages with Gondwanan continents, including marsupials and the Antarctic flora. The Neotropical realm includes many protected areas, and 1.28 per cent of its area has been inscribed as world heritage. This chapter presents seven connectivity conservation case studies from the Neotropics.

High altitude Páramos, Cayamba-Coca Ecological Reserve, Andes, Ecuador

Source: Graeme L. Worboys

Mesoamerican biological corridor

Eduard Muller and Jim Barborak

Setting

The Mesoamerican biological corridor (MBC) is an eight-country initiative from southern Mexico to Panama to conserve biological and ecosystem diversity while fostering sustainable social and economic development. The MBC consists of a land-use planning system that maintains the inter-connectivity of protected areas, and establishes buffer zones where forms of sustainable natural resource use may occur (Figure 8.1). The MBC initiative is based on the conviction that long-term biodiversity conservation can be achieved only with the reduction of rural poverty and through strengthening the economic viability of countries in the region (CCAD, 2002).

The Mesoamerican region comprises the seven Central American countries (Belize, Guatemala, Honduras, El Salvador, Nicaragua, Costa Rica and Panama) plus the five southern-most states of Mexico (Campeche, Chiapas, Quintana Roo, Tabasco and Yucatán). The total area of Mesoamerica is close to 76,000,000ha, which corresponds to approximately 0.51 per

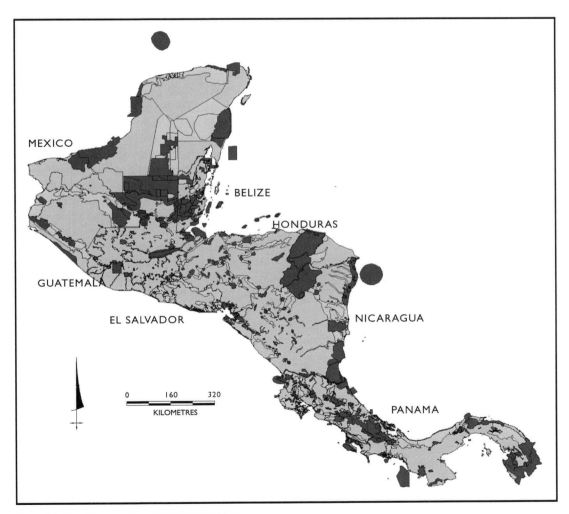

Figure 8.1 The Mesoamerican biological corridor

cent of the world's land surface. In the year 2000, the MBC covered approximately 30 per cent of the region, interconnecting the Central American Protected Area System with buffer and multiple-use zones (Mendieta and Vinocour, 2000). By 2001, the MBC had increased to 42 per cent, encompassing an estimated 32,110,300ha, of which 48.7 per cent corresponded to legally declared protected areas, 3.9 per cent to proposed protected areas and 47 per cent to connectivity areas. By 2003, the surface of declared protected areas had increased by 26.2 per cent and that of connecting areas by 43 per cent. This increase was due to the revision of the proposed areas in every country, which led to new national corridors, and to better mapping (McCarthy and Salas, 2003).

The Mesoamerican region is very diverse both naturally and culturally. Its narrow shape, serving as a bridge between North and South America, is surrounded on one side by the Caribbean Sea, with the world's second most important coral barrier reef, and on the other by the Pacific Ocean. A central mountain chain rises throughout the region to the 4211m height of the Tajamulco volcano in Guatemala. In this relatively small territory is found between 7 per cent and 8 per cent of the planet's biodiversity in 206 ecosystems (SICAP, 2003), three biomes, 20 life zones and 33 ecoregions (Dinerstein et al, 1995). The region boasts more than 60 vegetation forms and close to 350 landscapes, ranging from cloud forests with over 7500mm of annual rainfall to semi-arid regions with only 400mm of rainfall. In terms of number of species and endemism, it is considered to be the second most important hot spot after the Tropical Andes (CI, 2004a). Central America has 4715 endemic plants and 451 endemic vertebrates. It is estimated that close to 70 per cent of the vascular flora of the high mountains of Guatemala is endemic (D'Arcy, 1977). Aside from this high endemism, there is a high agro-biodiversity; the region is the centre of origin of many domesticated crop species. There are still found here many primitive varieties of beans, maize, cocoa, cotton, tomatoes and others.

Cultural diversity is just as rich. Central America is a cultural bridge, the place where the Maya-Nahuatl and Chibcha cultures met. Presently, the region is inhabited by 32 different ethnic and indigenous groups that communicate in 29 languages (CI, 2004a).

The connectivity conservation initiative

The Mesoamerican region has a long conservation history. A first regional meeting took place in 1973 to discuss conservation of natural and cultural heritage. In 1989 the Central American Commission for Environment and Development (CCAD) was established as the main environmental organ of the Central American Integration System (SICA).

The need to unite strategic ecosystems for conservation purposes was first addressed in Central America at the Second Central American Meeting on the Management of Natural and Cultural Resources held in Guatemala in October 1987. In 1990, the Wildlife Conservation Society and the Caribbean Conservation Corporation, led by Mario Boza, launched the Paseo Pantera project, which aimed at establishing a biological corridor running from the Darien in Panama to the Selva Maya forest in Mexico, Guatemala and Belize. The project addressed the need to unite the region through different biological corridors in order to guarantee species conservation, thus the name of Paseo Pantera – Path of the Panther. It based much of its vision on joint efforts between the countries, setting a new agenda for conservation in Mesoamerica.

In 1992, at the XII Summit of Central American Presidents in Managua, the Agreement for the Conservation of Biodiversity and the Protection of the Priority Protected Areas in Central America was signed. This first normative instrument states the need to establish biological corridors to unite the Regional System of Protected Areas of Central America. In order to guarantee this, the Central American Council for Protected Areas (CCAP) was established within the CCAD. In 1994, the Central American Alliance for Sustainable Development (ALIDES) was established as a political strategy to promote peace, consolidate democracy and protect the environment. ALIDES specifically mentions the need for integrated sustainable management of the territories to guarantee the conservation of biodiversity, and the establishment of biological corridors is one of the specific objectives of the

Alliance. At the XVIII Meeting of the Central American Commission for Environment and Development in October 1995, a joint declaration between the governments of Central America and Mexico was signed with the goal of promoting cooperation in sustainable use and conservation of natural resources and the environment in priority areas of the MBC. In December of 1995, the Global Environment Facility gave the CCAD a project development grant of US$340,000 to develop a proposal for the MBC. In February 1996 the Tuxla II Summit was held in San Jose as a follow-up to a first meeting held in Tuxla Gutierrez, Mexico in 1991. This officially included Belize and Mexico, with special reference to its five southern states, in the Central American sustainable development initiative, thus giving birth to the MBC.

During the 1990s, several corridor initiatives were initiated in the individual countries (Garcia, 1996). In 1995, Costa Rica, with the leadership of Randal Garcia, conducted the Gruas project that resulted in land-use planning aimed at the conservation of at least 90 per cent of the country's biodiversity. This document identified the possible corridors necessary to guarantee connectivity between protected areas. Godoy and Cardona (1996) presented a similar proposal for Guatemala. From 1998 to the year 2000, a Global Environmental Facility/World Bank project was conducted in Panama with a total of US$12.8 million, aimed at conserving the Atlantic forests of the Mesoamerican biological corridor of Panama (World Bank, 1998). In total, large sums were made available to the region for many different corridor projects.

Finally, the Global Environmental Facility grant led to the fusion of the national biological corridor proposals into a single document and the first regional geographic information system (GIS) map was created. When funding for the project was approved in 1999, the CCAD established the Mesoamerican biological corridor Regional Office Coordinating Unit (ROCU) in Managua, Nicaragua. This unit was to work with the technical liaisons that were designated in each of the eight countries to plan, coordinate, monitor and evaluate strategic policies and actions for the MBC implementation. In April 2000 funds totalling US$16,600,000 were made available by Global Environmental Facility, the UN Development Programme (UNDP) and the German Technical Cooperation Agency (GTZ). Since this initial grant, the MBC has received support from many different sources including World Bank, Interamerican Development Bank, bilateral cooperation, big international NGOs and also national allocations. By the year 2001, a total of US$888 million had been invested directly and US$4.5 billion indirectly in the MBC (Interamerican Development Bank, 2001).

The MBC has progressed in scope, structure and philosophy. The initial proposal of the Paseo Pantera project had a strong biological focus. Later developments lead to a strong social and economical focus, which makes it difficult to satisfy expectations due to the complexity of socio-economic and political problems in the region's countries. The MBC project officially ended in 2006, giving way to several new projects with the goal of consolidating the MBC: PERTAP (Regional Strategic Programme of Work in Protected Areas); PERCON (Regional Strategic Programme for Connectivity); PROMEBIO (Regional Strategic Programme for Biodiversity Monitoring and Evaluation); and PERFOR (Regional Strategic Programme for Forests).

Mesoamerica's population is close to 45 million people and is growing rapidly – at over 2 per cent per annum from 1995 to 2000 and is expected to double by 2025. Of these, 22 per cent live in coastal areas and 70 per cent are on the Pacific slope. Nearly 60 per cent live in poverty, 15 million of them in extreme poverty, especially in rural zones.

Civil wars, natural disasters and political instability have hampered socio-economic development. Hurricane Mitch alone caused more than US$5 billion in losses (CI, 2004a). Traditionally, the region's economies were based on agriculture and cattle production. Over the last two decades industry, commerce and especially tourism have become important components of the economy.

Deforestation has been declining over the years; nevertheless it still is significant. During the 1981–1990 period, Central America and Mexico were losing close to 1.1 million hectares per year due to deforestation, the equivalent of 1.5 per cent per year. In the 1990–1995 period deforestation rates decreased slightly but still amounted to a total of 2,284,000ha at a rate of 388,000ha per year (Rodriguez, 1998).

Poverty has been linked to natural resource degradation; however, a very significant factor has actually been related to other non-poor sectors and to governmental and international policy. During the 1970s and 1980s, bilateral and multi-lateral agencies supported the expansion of cattle production with low-interest loans. Existing legislation at the time considered primary forest as unused land and there were many incentives that led to deforestation for appropriation of land. The multinational banana companies and other monocultures such as palm oil also had an important role in deforestation activities. Today in many parts of Costa Rica the largest threat to forest cover is illegal clear-cutting of forest by large pineapple multinationals. Over weekends and longer holidays, when the ministry inspectors are not working, these companies devastate large surfaces of land illegally, burying the trees to hide the evidence, draining wetlands with deep canals and working the soil to the very edges of the rivers. Recently a new threat has arisen, namely the construction of vacation homes for rich foreigners. This real-estate boom, initially affecting mostly coastal zones, is now spreading widely throughout all Mesoamerican countries. In the near future, land use for biofuels likely will pose an even greater threat to conservation.

The peace processes that began in the 1980s with the signing of the Esquipulas and then Tuxtla agreements produced favourable conditions for realigning the region's development, this time based on the principles of peace, freedom and democracy. A new generation of pluralist governments restored the rule of law and rebuilt democratic institutions. This lay the groundwork for injecting new life into the idea of integration, starting with a common strategic vision. As mentioned earlier, the year 1989 marked the signing of the Central American Commission for Environment and Development Charter. Its purpose is to strengthen regional cooperation among national bodies responsible for managing natural resources and the environment. During the early 1990s, the peace process in Central America was consolidating itself. By 1991 the Central American Integration System was established. At the same time, parallel to the Rio Summit of 1992, several processes were started in the region, resulting in the establishment of new regional institutions.

The MBC is a complex system of protected areas and the connectivity between them. The final design originated from a series of studies conducted at the country level where connectivity possibilities, conservation gaps, development trends and other factors were analysed, resulting in detailed maps of possible corridors. These maps were later combined at a regional scale. Many other initiatives complemented the design. Lambert and Carr (1998) conducted a Meso-american corridor suitability analysis using GIS data layers (roads, hydrography, political boundaries, population centres, topography, Holdridge life zones, indigenous areas and forest/non-forest cover) derived from a variety of sources and map scales. A suitability analysis was performed at a four square kilometre resolution to define a 'least cost' proposed corridor between Mexico and Colombia. The authors concluded that the study was a preliminary effort with great potential to assist in the prioritization of a proposed corridor, and refinements and higher resolution data (at 1:250,000) were recommended for more detailed regional corridor analysis.

Remaining forest cover was one of the main factors influencing corridor design. A study conducted by Sader et al (2000) revealed that 80.4 per cent of forest remained in the proposed corridor, while the forest cover outside the corridor was only 30.8 per cent. Forest clearing within the MBC was only 0.26 per cent while outside the proposed corridor it was 1.44 per cent.

Connectivity conservation management

Mesoamerica has a total of 626 protected areas encompassing 16.4 million hectares. Most of these areas are small. Data from 507 areas show that 68.8 per cent are less than 10,000ha, and only four areas representing 0.8 per cent are greater than 500,000ha. This evidences the importance of connectivity conservation between these areas. Many of these areas are not functioning properly and only about 50 per cent of them (not counting

Guatemala) have some management instrument. A vast majority does not have adequate staffing – many don't have any staff at all. Only 33 per cent of the protected areas have a permanent management presence and not necessarily in adequate numbers. Few protected areas have staff members that work outside of the limits of the protected area, resulting in limited work with the local communities. Staffing at the central offices is not much better. For example, in Belize only two people from the forestry department are in charge of the protected areas there, and in Panama there are six people at the central offices with three dedicated to the protected areas system.

One important aspect is that there are 51 protected areas on the borders between countries. Of these, 32 have official declaration and 23 are bi-national areas. Most of the protected areas in the region have communities living in them, both indigenous and campesino (peasant farmers). This has led to important efforts to establish co-management processes. By 2005, 31.7 per cent of the declared protected areas had some form of local participation in their management and this number is expected to increase rapidly (IUCN, 2005).

For the design of the MBC, four land-use zones were defined: core zones, buffer zones, corridor zones and multiple-use zones. Buffer zones surround the core areas and have the function of buffering the impact of human activities so that they don't impact directly the protected areas. Most of these buffers are privately owned. It is difficult to regulate land use in the buffer zones. Alternative sources of economic benefit, including ecotourism, must be presented to local communities in order to conserve functioning buffer zones. The payment for environmental services, mostly for water production but also for carbon fixation, has come to play a very important role in providing income and incentives to local people to conserve the forest cover in the buffer zones.

Corridor zones are also usually privately owned and frequently are encroached to some extent by agricultural practices. As with the buffer zones, efforts are made to have farmers use more ecologically friendly practices. Examples are the use of live fences (trees instead of posts for pinning

wires for cattle pastures), the maintenance or restoration of river margins with native vegetation, reforestation with native trees or the use of agroforestry, where trees are mixed with pastures or crops in order to assure biodiversity-friendly environments and landscapes while providing livelihoods for local people.

Multiple-use zones are devoted to more intense human use, including settlements and intensive agriculture. These areas form a mosaic of different land uses. Efforts are made to maintain or restore biodiversity capability to these areas. As with the two other zones, the existence of technical assistance and incentives to local farmers to establish better practices is fundamental.

The MBC is a complex network that brings together international, national and local initiatives. To address these complex issues, an institutional structure was designed (Figure 8.2). This structure is dependent on other regional processes within the Central American Integration System. The CCAD, which is headed by the Council of Ministers for the environment and natural resources, is the main institution in charge of the corridor. The Commission is responsible for the harmonization of the region's policies with regard to the environment and natural resource management. The presidency of the council rotates within the seven countries every six months. The Commission established a Regional Office Coordinating Unit in Managua, Nicaragua. This unit is in charge of coordinating the different countries' efforts to achieve an integrated regional strategy. The Commission is assisted by advisory groups such as the Biodiversity Technical Committee and the Central American Council of Protected Areas.

This structure allows the CCAD to exert political influence, generate synergies, upscale activities and overcome any asymmetries. It acts to catalyse, facilitate, harmonize and integrate the region's environmental policies, which would not be possible through only national actions. Strategic regional actions are established in the Environmental Plan for the Central American Region, which has three areas of focus: biodiversity and forests, water and management of agricultural production.

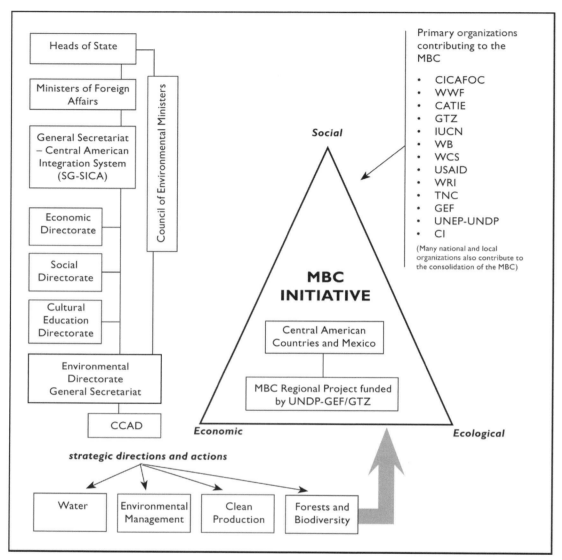

Figure 8.2 Institutional structure of the Mesoamerican biological corridor initiative

Notes: CICAFOC, The Central American Community Agro-Forestry Indigenous and Peasant Co-ordination Association; CATIE, Tropical Agricultural Research and Higher Education Center; WB, World Bank; WRI, World Resource Institute

Benefits and accomplishments

After the adoption by Central America of the *Convention on Biological Diversity* (CBD) in 1992 and the Protection of Priority Wilderness Areas (prior to the CBD), the Central American Protected Areas System was established based on the National Protected Area Systems. The Central American Protected Area System is a well-consolidated environmental integration initiative and is composed of 557 legally established protected areas covering close to 25 per cent of Central America's territory. The Mesoamerican Biodiversity Strategy was formulated in 2003 (CCAD, 2003).

At national levels there is one official liaison with the MBC within each country's ministry of

Box 8.1 The San Juan–La Selva biological corridor

This corridor was started in Costa Rica in 2001 in order to halt the disappearance of the great green macaw (*Ara ambigua*) and the almendro tree (*Dipteryx panamensis*), its main food source. Besides these emblematic species, the manatee (*Trichechus manatus*), the jaguar (*Felis onca*) and approximately 6000 species of vascular plants, 515 birds, 139 mammals, 135 reptiles and 80 amphibians will be protected in this rich and unique ecosystem. The biological corridor forges connections between forest patches of the Central Volcanic Range and La Selva Biological Station in the North, with the Barra del Colorado Wildlife Reserve and Tortuguero National Park on the Caribbean Coast of Costa Rica and through the south-east of Nicaragua, with the Indio-Maíz Biological Reserve, Punta Gorda and Cerro Silva.

The corridor initiative has an executive committee that represents 29 members from 19 local, national and international organizations that are involved with this project. These organizations contribute their experience and vision and join efforts with civil society, the Ministry of Environment and Energy and local governments. Incentives were created for landowners in the zone to conserve and restore their forests, where a wide range of systems are receiving payments for environmental services. Knowing that only a unified force will be able to maintain the natural richness of this region, including the great green macaw, a strong effort has made for this bird to become a source of pride for the inhabitants of this area (Chassot et al, 2005).

the environment. The liaison's activity is to coordinate efforts with the many local initiatives that are taking place. In Costa Rica alone there are 33 local initiatives for connectivity conservation. Each one varies in complexity, stakeholders, structure and even viability. The San Juan–La Selva biological corridor, for example, is composed of 19 organizations from Costa Rica, involving the Ministry of the Environment, local NGOs, local governments and scientific institutions (Box 8.1). It connects to a transboundary corridor: San Juan–La Selva–El Castillo. A bi-national committee was created to manage this initiative.

The inclusion of private reserves has proven of great importance for the consolidation of local corridors. Many private reserves have well-conserved forests or are dedicated to the restoration or regeneration of forest cover. In the mid-1990s, Costa Rica and Guatemala founded their national networks of private reserves and a few years later the other countries established similar national networks. The Costa Rican network comprises over 140 private reserves covering more than 100,000ha of protected area, mostly primary forests (Costa Rica Network of Private Reserves, 2006).

According to Miller et al (2001), effectively planning and implementing the MBC will require that several strategic challenges be addressed, including:

- reconciling stakeholder interests;
- fostering democratic governance and enabling civil society participation;
- catalysing information for participatory decision making;
- clarifying the function of MBC land-use categories;
- addressing property rights and land-tenure issues;
- capturing benefits from ecosystem goods and services;
- harmonizing institutional and legal frameworks and promoting inter-sectoral cooperation;
- setting investment and management priorities.

Today, the MBC still faces many of these challenges, but the administrative structure has consolidated itself, allowing the eight countries to meet and jointly plan and evaluate progress. The generation of several projects mentioned above to give continuity to the MBC initiative is proof of this willingness to work together. The implementation of the payment for environmental services, initially in Costa Rica, then Mexico and lately with projects emerging within the other countries has opened a new window of opportunities. The same goes for the official recognition and incentives linked with private protected areas, which are growing in number and extension.

Lessons learned

After more than ten years of existence, the MBC still faces many of the challenges identified by Miller et al (2001). Nevertheless, the large number of local initiatives is proof that the importance of connectivity has been understood by local groups. A viable institutional and legal framework allows for more effective conservation processes. Harmonization of laws and policies has also played an important role in making a regional approach more viable (Rodriguez, 2006).

An inclusive approach is required

One of the most important lessons refers to the need to include all sectors of society. A governmental approach alone would not have allowed this initiative to consolidate itself as it is today (Rodriguez, 2006). There is a need not only to include all stakeholders from the beginning but to make them true partners, and leave open the possibility to include sectors that initially weren't involved. Stakeholders range from local communities, private sector, NGOs, especially the local ones, educational institutions, to local governments and central government agencies. Inter-sectoral cooperation is essential, requiring special efforts to coordinate activities between and within institutions.

Involve local communities

Local communities must play a strong role in decision making from the very beginning. This requires efforts to generate capacity at the local level to have well informed communities for adequate decision-making processes. Strong communication and education programmes are necessary. Involvement of children from the beginning is very important, since they quickly become strong partners and influence their parents to change practices.

A coordinating actor is necessary

There is a need for a strong coordinating role, dedicated and with sufficient funding to assure operation in the mid-term and broad regional coordination. This must go together with strengthening and empowerment of local organizations in order to achieve success at the local level.

Outreach and education are critical

A strong campaign for environmental education and sensitizing of local communities must take place from the beginning. It is important that it is adjusted to the different local conditions and needs and is most effective when local groups are involved in the process.

Management must occur at the appropriate scale

Management at a landscape level is also vital. The use of watershed management at an international level such as the San Juan River between Nicaragua and Costa Rica has led to integrated strategies.

Benefits must be generated for local actors

The generation of tangible objectives, such as a clean and permanent water supply is fundamental for the involvement of different stakeholders. Water is one of the main concerns today for local communities and the relationship between water supply and conservation of forest cover is clearly understood by them.

Innovative approaches are required

The development of tools such as payment for environmental services is important to stimulate participation. The economic benefit of these instruments is, at the moment, lower than the revenues produced from agriculture or cattle production, but do represent an alterative income source. The altruism of the campesinos is strong enough in many cases for them to be willing to accept a lower income if nature is conserved. Economic valuation of natural resources has started to set the baseline to create conditions for financial sustainability for the environmental agenda and sustainable development. It is important for the population to perceive these economic values until it becomes the best defender (Rodriguez, 2006). Efforts must also be made for the diversification of economic activities. The generation of ecotourism initiatives and the linking of them to other productive and service sectors results in added value and a higher possibility for success.

Acknowledgements

The information presented in this case study has been summarized from many different documents. For more in-depth information see the overview written by Kenton Miller, Elsa Chang and Nels Johnson, *Defining Common Ground for the Mesoamerican Biological Corridor* (Miller et al, 2001).

Ecosystem approach applied to international connectivity: The Andean Páramo corridor

Robert Hofstede

Setting

The Páramo is a natural, high-altitude non-forest ecosystem, covering approximately 3,500,000ha in the tropical Andes extending across Venezuela, Colombia, Ecuador and northern Peru, from 11° North to 8° South (Luteyn, 1992; Figure 8.3). The Páramo is an ecological archipelago, distributed along the highest parts of the northern Andes. It is characterized by high biological, cultural and landscape diversity. The Páramo is the most biodiverse high mountain non-forest ecosystem in the world (Smith and Cleef, 1988). Its vegetation is dominated by characteristic giant stem rosettes (*Coespeletia lutescens*), basal and acaulescent rosettes, shrubs, prostrate herbs and bunch grasses. Several well recognized emblematic animal species live in Páramo (Ramsay, 1992). The Páramo forms a perfect example of a biome wherein connectivity is a key attribute of its biogeographical history, its present appearance and its ecological and social importance, as well as for its management and conservation.

The history of neo-tropical vegetation begins approximately 100 million years ago, when the South American continent separated from Gondwana. South America remained isolated until it was connected again to North America

Páramo landscape with Espeletia stem rosettes, Los Nevados, Colombia

Source: Robert Hofstede

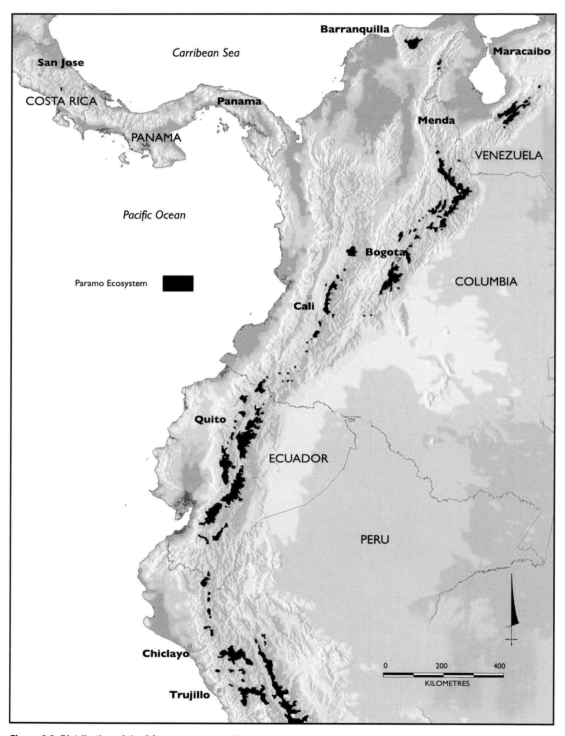

Figure 8.3 Distribution of the Páramo ecosystem in the northern Andes

through the Panama isthmus (approximately ten million years ago). After this, during the Miocene epoch, several holarctic taxa entered the continent and the Andes began to arise (Gentry, 1982). It was not until the Pliocene or later that the northern Andean region attained its present altitudes. During this period (four to five million years ago) there was abundant volcanic activity, at which time elevations above the tree line came into being accompanied by associated speciation and radiation events (Simpson, 1986; Schuchmann et al, 2001). The upper Andean forest and Páramo belts evolved more or less simultaneously in the early Pleistocene (two to four million years ago), and an early Páramo vegetation (protopáramo) was present consisting of species of the families *Poaceae*, *Cypereceae*, *Asteraceae* and *Ericaceae*, among others (Van der Hammen and Cleef, 1986). During the Pleistocene epoch, genera of north temperate origin (such as *Alnus* and *Quercus*) entered the Andean forest, evidencing a next phase in connectivity between the northern and tropical cool biomes (Luteyn, 1999).

During the later years of the Quaternary epoch, glacial and interglacial periods continued to alternate, with some short but severe cold periods interspersed with warmer and wetter periods. The result of this process of past climatic changes and the associated lowering and rising of altitudinal belts and the narrowing and widening of the area occupied by Páramo was that Páramo patches were connected and separated repeatedly (Van der Hammen and Cleef, 1986; Luteyn, 1999; Wille et al, 2002). It is expected that during colder periods, during which the Páramo occupied larger areas, connectivity resulted in the fast expansion of species ranges over the Andes, while during warmer periods, many Páramo areas were separated resulting in species niche contraction and speciation events driven by the dynamic process of local isolation with occasional dispersal between them (Jørgensen and Ulloa, 1994; Roy et al, 1997). As a result of these climatic events, the present Páramo flora have many tropical as well as boreal elements, with genera that are relatively common (Sklenar et al, 2005) but a high endemism at the species level (Luteyn, 1992).

Today, the Páramo forms an ecological archipelago, distributed along the highest parts of the northern Andes, like a 'chain of pearls' (Balslev, 2001). In total, it occupies approximately 3,500,000ha. The northernmost Páramo areas are the isolated complex at the Sierra Nevada de Santa Marta, in Colombia, and the small areas on top of the Talamanca mountain range in Costa Rica. Due to their isolation, both have a specific flora and fauna. The Páramos in the Colombian western Cordillera form isolated small patches that might have been connected in the past (Hofstede et al, 2003).

In the Mérida Range (Venezuela), the Páramo ecosystem forms a large connected corridor. Since geologically this area is the oldest part of the northern Andes, this is probably where most of the tropical elements of the Páramo flora originated and dispersed southwards during glacial periods (Van der Hammen and Cleef, 1986). From Tamá (the transborder Páramo between Colombia and Venezuela) down to the Sumapaz massif (south of Bogotá), there is a large and, in many areas, connected Páramo complex that covers the Colombian eastern Cordillera. The Colombian central Cordillera, its southern continuation in the Colombian Massif and the entire Ecuadorian Cordillera form one large mountain range, fully of volcanic origin. This range has variable maximum altitudes, and there are large but separated complexes of Páramo (for example, los Nevados, Las Hermosas, the Colombian Massif and the transborder complex between Nariño and Carchi). On the Ecuadorian eastern mountain range, or Cordillera Real, the largest connected complex of Páramos is found from the Cayambe Volcano down to Sangay National Park, interrupted only by the Chambo River valley (Ambato). In the Ecuadorian Western Cordillera, large but separated Páramo complexes are found around Cotacachi, Pichincha, Ilinizas and Chimborazo volcanoes. In southern Ecuador, where the Andes are older and consist of heavily glaciated metamorphic geology, a large separated Páramo complex is found west of the city of Cuenca (El Cajas). The southernmost Páramo extension is a connected, but very narrow, Páramo covering the lower and wet Páramo of the Cordillera de Sabanilla down to the Huancabamba depression, which is generally considered as the biogeographical limit between the northern and central Andes (Duellman and Wild, 1993; Jørgensen and Ulloa, 1994). South of the Huancabamba valley, a similar but more seasonal ecosystem continues, locally known as Jalca.

The present natural pattern of connectivity and separation is being disrupted or altered by human impact. In several areas, Páramo habitats disappeared after being transformed into productive grassland, annual crops (such as potatoes) or industrial non-native plantations (such as pines). This artificial separation caused the interruption of natural larger Páramo complexes (Castaño, 2002; Etter et al, 2006). On the other hand, large-scale burning of Páramo and Andean forest caused a downward movement of Páramo vegetation, taking over areas that previously had been covered by Andean forest (Ellenberg, 1979; Lægaard, 1992). This artificial lowering of the tree line caused an extension of the Páramo biome ('paramization') and increased connectivity in certain areas. However, this connectivity and the resulting possibility of species distribution have limited positive effect for enhanced distribution of the native flora. Because these areas are used for extensive animal husbandry, including repeated burning, most valued Páramo plant and animal species disappeared from these areas (Hofstede et al, 2002).

Connectivity in the Páramo supports its role as a biological corridor for many of its most important inhabitants, both animal and plant species. The Andean bear (*Tremarctos ornatus*) roams the corridor and the associated cloud forests from the Cordillera de Mérida in Venezuela down to northern Argentina (Kattan et al, 2004). The condor (*Vultur gryphus*), which can easily travel 150km per day, will fly only over zones of Páramo and farmland that are uninterrupted by urban areas. The mountain tapir (*Tapirus pinchaque*) operates across a mosaic of Páramo and forest (Downer, 1996). Many of the endemic birds of the Páramo are dependent upon remnant patches of *Polylepis* that provide food and shelter for them throughout the entire high Andes. The floristic symbol of the northern Páramos, *Espeletia* is one of the best examples of diversification and adaptive distribution in a novel environment. The genus *Espeletia* contains about 130 species

endemic to the northern tropical Andes between Venezuela and Ecuador (Cuatrecasas, 1958). The seeds are wind dispersed but lack wings or hairs, so their colonization has been a slow process and must depend upon intact stretches of Páramo.

The environmental conditions, their position on top of the Andes, as well as their deep, high organic soils, give the Pàramo a vital role in the regulation of Andean hydrology (Buytaert et al, 2006). This vertical connection is possibly their single most important ecological role. In almost the entire northern Andes, all people living in the interandean valleys (approximately 50 million individuals) use water originating from Páramo catchments for consumption, for electricity generation and for irrigation. Conservation issues in the Páramo naturally connect biodiversity and water regulation objectives (Mena, 2002).

There have been settlements in the highlands of the Andes probably for over 15,000 years (Eckholm, 1975). Although most settlements were at lower altitudes, there is much evidence that the Páramo was used for many different purposes during the pre-Colombian period. Originally, Páramo landscapes probably had religious and mystic importance, for occasional hunting and gathering and for transport (Reichel-Dolmatoff, 1982; Schjellerup, 1992; Recharte and Gearheard, 2001). There is evidence of direct use of Páramo for over 1400 years in Venezuela and over 800 years in Colombia, mostly for tuber crops and as crop-storage areas (Van der Hammen and Cleef, 1986). In the southern part of the Páramo, more intensive use occurred after the Inca colonization, which expanded their infrastructure over Páramo areas and introduced extensive livestock husbandry and intensive agriculture (including irrigation) into the Ecuadorian and Peruvian highlands. Incans also deliberately introduced ethnic groups from other regions of the Empire (known in Quechuan as *mitimaes*) to the northern countries as a manner of suppression and colonization (Ramón, 2000). After the Spanish conquest, the situation changed drastically, as large herds of sheep, cattle and horses were introduced and the Páramo was used on a large scale by Spanish haciendas for maintaining these animals. This affected principally those Páramo areas of moderate climate, relatively good access and with stronger Spanish dominance (for example, central Ecuador and the high plain of Cundinamarca-Bogotá). In Venezuela, because of its proximity to the Caribbean ports, the high Andes were intensively used for wheat crops (Hervas Ordóñez, 1994; Recharte and Gearheard, 2001).

After independence from the Spanish, at the beginning of the 19th century, there was little change for the Páramo. Although the haciendas came to be owned by nationals and they produced less wool for Europe, there still was a great demand for beef and potatoes for the increasing American market. Drastic changes occurred in the middle of the 20th century, when land and agrarian reform policies in all northern Andean countries divided extremely large haciendas and unclaimed land (many of these in Páramo) among smallholders and (indigenous) farmer communities. Among the

consequences of the agrarian reforms was the spatial redistribution of the small landowners (*minifundistas*) towards the steep hillsides and the highlands (Commander and Peek, 1986). Combined with internal migration (due to drought or violence in other areas), this resulted in a colonization of the Páramo, a fast upward movement of agriculture into Páramo, permanent settlements and an intensification of animal production in the lower Páramo belts (Monasterio, 1980; Hess, 1990). This period also formed the basis for a modern identification of Andean indigenous groups with the Páramo environment (Ramón, 2000; Recharte and Gearheard, 2001).

The cultural history of the Páramo and the present significant presence of people living in and depending on the Páramo have resulted in a drastic modification of the Páramo landscape. Cattle

Heavily modified Páramo landscape, with small-scale intensive agriculture encroaching into overgrazed tussock grassland, Tungurahua, Ecuador

Source: Robert Hofstede

grazing, combined with extensive fires, have cleared forest remnants, lowered the natural forest line and homogenized the Páramo landscape (Hofstede, 1995; Verweij, 1995; Sklenar and Ramsay, 2001). Páramo areas that are more intensively used, particularly for potato cultivation (in all Páramo areas) and for garlic (Venezuela) and pine (Ecuador and Peru) are completely modified and, if overused, degraded. Overgrazing and erosion has resulted in severely degrading about half of all Páramo area that is currently under use and the resulting low productivity has brought about poverty and socio-economic instability. This local poverty has forced people to colonize other, formerly unused Páramo areas. In this way, poverty results in intense land use and further degradation. Hofstede et al (2002) calculated that only 30 per cent the Ecuadorian Páramo (the inaccessible and extremely wet or cold areas) are in relatively natural conditions, another 30 per cent is modified into more monotonous tussock grassland and up to 40 per cent is transformed into artificial grasslands, crops, pine plantations or degraded. This situation obviously impacts the landscape's overall biodiversity value, it impacts connectivity between different natural areas and it impacts the single most important feature of Páramo: its capacity for hydrological regulation.

Although human presence has caused large-scale ecological damage to the Páramo, the connectivity of people with the Páramo, and its transformation into a cultural landscape, forms a basis for its survival as well. Many people – possibly up to 450,000 in Colombia and Ecuador (Hofstede et al, 2003) – live directly in the Páramo and use it as their life space. Indigenous groups identify with the Páramo and, for many, their cultural or theological values include the care of their natural environment. City-dwellers connect to the Páramo as a recreation area, to enjoy clear air, marvel the landscape or merely hike in a natural environment. The Páramos of Mérida and around the snow-capped mountains in Colombia and Ecuador, in particular, are traditional tourist attractions. The construction of a funicular in Quito to the Pichincha Páramo increased the visitor count to this area to over 50,000 per month (*El Comercio*, 2006). Finally, the importance of the Páramo for water regulation is being recognized increasingly by the population in general and has created more respect for this once unknown landscape. These relationships of the Páramo landscape to both rural and urban populations increase the possibility to create a social basis for Páramo conservation.

The connectivity conservation initiative

Effective conservation of the Páramo requires an adequate understanding of the long-term trends underlying land use in the highland regions. Unfortunately, at this time there are not enough livelihood alternatives for Páramo farmers, so advancing agriculture will increasingly affect the remaining intact area. At present, there are a number of local conservation projects in the Páramo whose interventions have managed to slow down somewhat the rate of Páramo transformation at several sites. However, these projects are site specific and have relatively little national impact because: (i) they do not or cannot include all social, historical, political, institutional, economical and biogeographic aspects within their conservation efforts; (ii) the large variability in the mentioned aspects results in a different situation in every single Páramo area, hence replication and upscaling of conservation efforts are very difficult; and (iii) they normally lack a clear trans-sectoral vision so decision makers for agriculture, public works and finance are not impacted (Mena, 2002; Hofstede et al, 2003). As a result, the conservation of Páramo as an ecosystem, its international corridor function and its importance as a water harvesting area for several major watersheds is still highly threatened in the absence of a regional Páramo conservation effort.

Recognizing the ecological and social importance of Páramo at different scales (from local to global), the four Andean countries with Páramo and several NGOs agreed on an international strategy for the conservation of this highly strategic and vulnerable ecosystem. This initiative (Proyecto Páramo Andino) is currently receiving the highest amount of foreign investment (from Global Environmental Facility through the United Nations Environment Programme) ever for a single Páramo conservation project. This project recognizes that the major threats to Páramo biodiversity are the direct result of social actors that live in and use the natural resources within the Páramo, and of external demands for its environmental goods and services. But effective biodiversity conservation in the Páramo is difficult due to underlying causes that pertain to other levels and sectors. These underlying causes include: (i) excessive reliance on classical agriculture; (ii) disarticulation of local, regional and national planning and execution efforts; (iii) weak inter-sectoral policy coordination promoting ecosystem management; (iv) lack of policies and policy instruments at all scales; (v) lack of an effective international conservation strategy for transboundary ecosystems and watersheds; (vi) limited expertise and capacity at all levels; (vii) underestimation and loss of traditional knowledge and practices; (viii) lack of public awareness about this marginalized ecosystem; and (ix) lack of adequate information to support decision making.

The Páramo biome is a perfect example of where an ecosystem approach is appropriate for its connectivity conservation. Particularly, the presence and direct dependence on Páramo environmental services of a large rural and urban population requires an approach where people are considered as a fundamental part of the ecosystem (Hofstede, 2006). The recognition of the dynamic interrelation of nature conservation and rural development proved to be the key to a successful conservation experience in the Páramo. Through an ecosystem approach, the conservation of the Páramo recognizes the diverse and highly dynamic situation caused by human impact and climate change, combined with social and political instability (Pirot et al, 2000). Through the Grupo Páramo and the Proyecto Páramo Andino (Hofstede and Mujica, 2002; Mena, 2002) partnerships were established in the entire Páramo region, at international, national and local levels, between farmers, civil society organizations, the private sector and governmental institutions of different sectors. These partnerships were the main facilitators of a mid-term integrated management programme, which recognized and promoted participation of all stakeholders, that analysed and promoted connectivity processes at different scales (site, watershed, regional and national) and that included activities in investigation, policy development, communication and hands-on management.

Connectivity conservation management

During an execution period of six years, the Proyecto Páramo Andino will concentrate on removing the barriers linked to the major threats for the conservation of the Andean Páramo. Conservation and sustainable use of the Páramo will require a diversified set of responses at different levels tailored to the differentiated threats and opportunities to be found across countries and regions both in the Páramo and in its buffer zones. The project recognizes that the Páramo is a transboundary ecosystem over four countries with a corridor function for many key elements of its biodiversity. This project provides a regional Andean response to the threats. The root causes for land degradation in the areas included in this project are similar across the political and physical borders. A regional, multi-country coordinated effort that is directed at mitigating land degradation is the only sustainable approach to addressing the problems in the area. Applying an ecosystem approach helped integrate Páramo connectivity conservation and management efforts across national borders, ecosystems and life zones and focused on the role of the Páramo as the origin of international watersheds.

The major goals of the initiative will be accomplished by connecting *in situ* conservation of Páramo biodiversity with the sustainable use of the Páramo's resources through equitable participation of those stakeholders responsible for its stewardship. Specifically, this means that in the four countries the project will: (i) implement examples of good practice, including zoning, conservation strategies and productive activities compatible with biodiversity conservation in a series of critical sites; (ii) support institutions at different governmental and non-governmental levels to adopt key policies to support conservation and sustainable use, including codes of conduct for different sectors; (iii) strengthen the technical capacity of inhabitants, field technicians and local governmental and non-governmental organizations to sustainably use and conserve the Páramo; (iv) increase awareness and information about the importance of the Páramo among key decision makers and the rural and urban population; and (v) generate a replication strategy for the project, applicable to other areas and scales at the Andean level.

Benefits and accomplishments

The planned interventions will have several widespread benefits. The aims are to reduce the advance of agricultural activities presently encroaching on the Páramo and to mitigate other threats, thus conserving biodiversity and improving water regulation by the Páramo. The project will strengthen an enabling environment through improved policies that support Páramo conservation and the sustainable use of its resources, enhance farmers' and other users' capacity for using environmentally friendly productive processes, strengthen local and national governments' abilities for decision making, and raise public awareness about the importance of the Páramo. The most tangible results will be secured through a series of ten representative project sites. The best lessons thus gained will be replicated in other sites and at a larger scale, hence promoting substantial support for Páramo conservation and policy development at different levels (local, national and Andean). After the project, all stakeholders (such as executing organizations, local and national governments, local NGOs and farmer communities) will be considerably strengthened in their capacity to sustain long-term Páramo management and will be working in an international exchange and coordination network for Páramo conservation.

   This approach also will deliver several domestic benefits. Biodiversity conservation is achieved through a combination of *in situ* conservation planning and agricultural systems that have a lower environmental impact and higher economic profit (Llambi et al, 2005). The latter helps to increase local incomes by which the project brings about an improved quality of life and social services for mountain communities. The generally improved land use (conservation areas and low-impact agriculture) in the Páramo zone will result in stabilizing or even improving water availability and quality. In summary, mitigating threats to biodiversity will enhance the protection of the natural base for agricultural production and lead to conservation and sustainable use of the Páramo, all of which will contribute to strengthening local and national economies and support the eradication of poverty at the project sites.

Lessons learned

Human connectivity conservation can lead to biological connectivity conservation

The connectivity of people with the Páramo, and its transformation into a cultural landscape, forms a basis for its survival as well. Many people live directly in the Páramo and use it as their life space. Indigenous groups identify with the Páramo and, for many, their cultural or theological values include the care of their natural environment. City-dwellers connect to the Páramo as a recreation area, to enjoy clear air, marvel the landscape or merely hike in a natural environment. The Páramos of Mérida and around the snow-capped mountains in Colombia and Ecuador, in particular, are traditional tourist attractions. The centuries long and continuing connection of people to the Páramo provided a wealth of potential supporters for a connectivity conservation initiative that will provide social and economic as well as conservation benefits.

Connectivity conservation in multi-use landscapes requires an inclusive vision

Prior efforts at Páramo conservation had had little impact at the appropriate scale because not all interests were engaged and their founding visions were too narrow. The recognition of the dynamic interrelation of nature conservation and rural development proved to be the key to a successful conservation experience in the Páramo.

Natural attributes lend weight to connectivity conservation efforts

The natural connectivity of Páramo landscapes lends itself well to a connectivity conservation-focused management regime. The Páramo's role as the source of drinking water, hydroelectric power and irrigation for millions of inhabitants also provided a key rationale for its conservation. Conservation issues in the Páramo naturally connect biodiversity and water regulation objectives.

A multidisciplinary, large-scale approach facilitates connectivity conservation

Understanding the complexity of the geographical, ecological, social and political setting of a transboundary landscape is the basis for adequate management. Taking into consideration the multiple benefits and various interests of the Páramo for different human groups, an approach that connects management activities at different scales, that tackles both the underlying causes and the direct threats and that includes direct beneficiaries in the management of the ecosystem is a feasible way of attaining conservation of the Páramo, its biodiversity and its environmental services as well as providing the local population with a basis for sustainable livelihoods. The ecosystem approach is apt to be applied to this complex reality, in which a dynamic and adaptive management, based on academic knowledge, practical management examples and continuous debate to attain an optimal balance between different interests, can be a model applied to other ecosystems in similar conditions.

Large-scale ecosystems require large-scale connectivity conservation regimes

The Páramo system is spread throughout the northern Andean mountains. It took the commitment of four countries and numerous NGOs to begin the formulation of goals and strategies for Páramo conservation. Partnerships were established in the entire Páramo region, at international, national and local levels, between farmers, civil society organizations, the private sector and governmental institutions of different sectors. These partnerships were the main facilitators of a mid-term integrated management programme that recognized and promoted the participation of all stakeholders, which analysed and promoted connectivity processes at different scales (site, watershed, regional and national), and that included activities in investigation, policy development, communication and hands-on management. A regional, multi-country coordinated effort that is directed at mitigating land degradation was the only sustainable approach to addressing the problems in the area.

Successful connectivity conservation involves local stakeholders

The activities being implemented through Proyecto Páramo Andino include connecting *in situ* conservation of Páramo biodiversity with the sustainable use of the Páramo's resources through the equitable participation of those stakeholders responsible for its stewardship.

Connectivity conservation initiatives must address root causes of ecosystem decline

Proyecto Páramo Andino identified the origins of destructive practices and implemented programmes to reverse them. Promoting best land-management practices, supporting institutional policy development and adoption, building capacity of local inhabitants and land managers, undertaking public outreach and exporting skills and lessons to other areas were key strategies aimed at overcoming destructive practices.

Acknowledgements

The author based this case study on his experience from two decades of work in the Páramo ecosystem. This was supported by, among others, the University of Amsterdam, the Dutch Ministry of Foreign Affairs, the Dutch Science Foundation (NWO-WOTRO), IUCN and the Global Environmental Facility. The Proyecto Páramo Andino is executed by CONDESAN, Ecociencia, Universidad de los Andes, The Mountain Institute, Instituto Alexander von Humboldt and the Universities of Amsterdam and Wisconsin, in collaboration with many local partners. Barbara Ehringhaus and Francisco Cuesta are acknowledged for their comments on previous versions of this case study. Good management of the Páramo ecosystem is not possible without continuous collaboration from their inhabitants, and therefore the Páramo farmers are acknowledged for continuously pursuing a sustainable future.

Integrating protected areas and landscapes: Lessons from the Vilcabamba–Amboró conservation corridor (Bolivia–Peru)

Jordi Surkin, Marlon Flores, Juan Carlos Ledezma, M. R. Mariaca, Erick Meneses, N. Pardo, Candido Pastor, Clea Paz and Grace Wong

Setting

The Vilcabamba–Amboró conservation corridor (VACC) is a mountainous landscape located primarily in the Tropical Andes hot spot, which is the most biodiverse region on Earth, containing about a sixth of all plant life in less than 1 per cent of the world's land area (Mittermeier et al, 1997). A smaller portion of the VACC also falls within the Amazon Wilderness Area. It follows the Andes from north-west to south-east and extends from the Vilcabamba region in central Peru to the Amboró National Park in eastern Bolivia (Figure 8.4). It totals more than 30 million ha of which 14 are in Bolivia and 16 in Peru, including 19 protected areas totalling 13 million ha (CEPF, 2001; Salas et al, 2006).

This corridor has a tremendous altitudinal variation (from 200m to more than 6000m) and includes the entire Yungas ecoregion, part of the south-western Amazonian ecoregion, the sub-Andean and pre-Andean forests and inter-Andean dry forests. It plays an essential role in the regulation of ecosystem functions and hydrological processes at a regional level (CEPF, 2001).

The VACC has extremely high levels of biodiversity and endemism, with world records for taxa such as butterflies and birds. It is home to approximately 6000 species of plants, including *Polylepis* forests in Peru and Bolivia and more than 3500 vertebrates (Mittermeier et al, 1997; CEPF and CI, 2003a). Manu National Park in Peru alone has more than 1000 birds and 10 per cent of global avifauna (Forno et al, 2006). At the present, the VACC is home to 8 per cent of the threatened species in the Andes and has a total of 145 globally threatened species (Table 8.1).

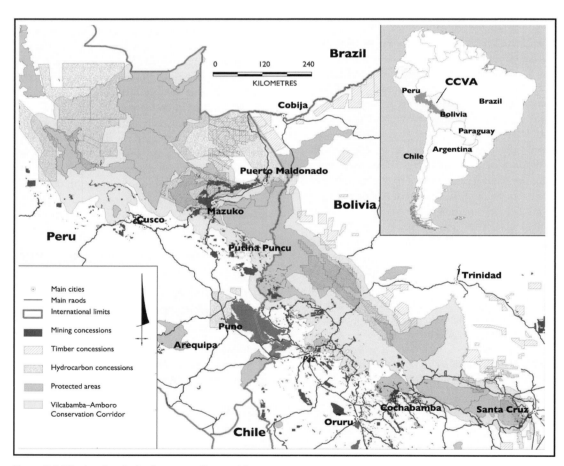

Figure 8.4 Vilcabamba–Amboró conservation corridor

Table 8.1 Globally threatened species that require corridor-scale action

Scientific name	Class	Status	Requires large area	Dependent on intact ecological processes
Atelopus tricolor	Amphibia	Vulnerable		Yes
Bufo quechua	Amphibia	Vulnerable		Yes
Hyloscirtus charazani	Amphibia	Endangered		Yes
Telmatobius marmoratus	Amphibia	Vulnerable		
Telmatobius sibiricus	Amphibia	Endangered		Yes
Telmatobius verrucosus	Amphibia	Vulnerable		
Telmatobius yuracare	Amphibia	Vulnerable		
Agriornis andicola	Avifauna	Vulnerable		
Alectrurus tricolor	Avifauna	Vulnerable	Yes	
Ara militaris	Avifauna	Vulnerable	Yes	
Culicivora caudacuta	Avifauna	Vulnerable	Yes	
Dendroica cerulea	Avifauna	Vulnerable	Yes	
Leptosittaca branickii	Avifauna	Vulnerable	Yes	
Primolius couloni	Avifauna	Endangered	Yes	
Inia geoffrensis	Mammalia	Vulnerable	Yes	Yes
Oreailurus jacobita	Mammalia	Endangered	Yes	Yes
Priodontes maximus	Mammalia	Vulnerable	Yes	
Pteronura brasiliensis	Mammalia	Endangered	Yes	Yes
Speothos venaticus	Mammalia	Vulnerable	Yes	
Tapirus terrestris	Mammalia	Vulnerable	Yes	
Tremarctos ornatus	Mammalia	Vulnerable	Yes	
Trichechus inunguis	Mammalia	Vulnerable	Yes	Yes
Podocnemis unifilis	Reptilia	Vulnerable	Yes	Yes

Source: IUCN, 2006

The corridor is characterized by cultural diversity, poverty and a growing population. In the highlands the main indigenous groups are the Quechuas and the Aymaras, while in the lowlands there are more than 20 ethnic groups. Throughout the corridor there are numerous indigenous territories or reserves, including some for uncontacted groups. In 2001, the population living inside the corridor was approximately 424,000 people on the Bolivian side and 683,000 on the Peruvian side. The population densities are 13.4 inhabitants per square kilometre in Peru and 5.35 on the Bolivian side (Ministerio de Economía y Finanzas de Peru, 2001).

Biodiversity loss has been fuelled by various economic activities. The main cause of such processes is forest conversion to agricultural land or pasture. In the Amazonian lowlands, the agricultural frontier has expanded rapidly since the relocation of poor, highland migrants began in the 1980s. Both historically and currently, legal and illegal logging have been important economic activities (CEPF, 2001). Much of the corridor lies under mining or oil and gas concessions. In Bolivia there has been little exploration and production. However, in Peru in recent years the massive Camisea Gas Project was implemented inside the VACC (Chauvin, 2003). More recently, nature tourism has gained strength in and around Tambopata and Madidi (Soriano et al, 2006).

The connectivity conservation initiative

The VACC arose from a long history of cooperation between Peru and Bolivia. In the late 1980s, the Tambopata–Candamo reserved zone was established by the Peruvian government along the Bolivian border. This was an important first step towards establishment of the corridor. In 1993, both governments signed a cooperation agreement under the framework of the Amazon Cooperation Treaty. This was a key starting point for government institutions and private organizations to promote a Tambopata–Madidi transborder conservation complex, during much of the 1990s (CEPF and CI, 2003a). In February 1999, there was a meeting on conservation in the border area, which resulted in a letter of intent to support bi-national conservation. This meeting was organized by Servicio Nacional de Áreas Protegidas de Bolivia (SERNAP) and Peru's Instituto Nacional de Recursos Naturales (INRENA) and included participation of other government institutions as well as Conservation International and other NGOs. Corridor design began with an August 2000 internal Conservation International meeting. Development of the basic corridor implementation strategy took place in 2003. This strategy was developed through national and bi-national workshops, with participation of governmental entities, protected area administrators, NGOs and local actors (CEPF and CI, 2003a).

This corridor is the result of bi-national political processes led by government institutions (SERNAP, INRENA and others) in close collaboration with NGOs and local organizations. This collaboration has been the key to ensuring a degree of acceptance of the corridor in many spheres.

Governmental structures on both sides are improving policy frameworks and capacities. SERNAP and INRENA do not have adequate internal policies to regulate natural resource use (in both countries) or land tenure (in Bolivia) in protected areas. This is particularly important given overlapping land and resource access rights on both sides of the border, which cause high levels of social conflict. Most protected areas have a low level of management effectiveness, due to underfunding, understaffing and lack of adequate infrastructure (O'Phelan and Argandoña, 2001).

The VACC was one of the earliest corridors in which Conservation International had an active role. Its original boundaries were drawn by mapping existing protected areas and placing a 20km buffer around them (Gisbert, 2007, pers. comm.). The design process was based on the early definition of a corridor as:

> a mosaic of parks, reserves and sustainable use areas, which is managed to: 1) ensure the survival of the largest spectrum of species and habitats in the region, and 2) contribute to regional sustainable development, by means of its biological richness and environmental services (CEPF and CI, 2003b).

Here we see some commonalities with the definition currently being utilized by Conservation International, but also notable differences such as no emphasis on globally threatened species (CI, 2004b, 2005). Thus, until recently, the focus has been more on conserving the greatest spectrum of species possible in an area with globally important biodiversity (Mittermeier et al, 1997; Forno et al, 2006).

To identify the scientific gaps more rigorously and refine the strategic planning for the VACC, Conservation International and its Bolivian partners initiated two scientific studies in 2004 and 2005. The first study focused on development of a common vision and definition of the technical arguments behind the corridor approach (Ibisch et al, 2007). A second study sought to identify priority conservation gaps in the corridor and at the national level on the basis of three variables (Araujo et al, in press): representation, functionality of ecosystems and viability. These two studies served to identify species richness, endemism, conservation priorities (based on the IUCN list of globally threatened species) and the state of conservation suitability (for example, extent of habitat fragmentation or degradation) as well as the social feasibility of protecting these areas and species.

In the VACC's landscapes, connectivity has two distinct and somewhat unique meanings. Due to the existence of large complexes of forested area already dominated by well conserved protected areas (Figure 8.4), one objective is to *maintain* connectivity within these complexes. Conservation actions in these areas include proactive land-use planning and policy engagement with stakeholders at all levels to divert potential threats and prevent fragmentation. Where the landscape is more fragmented, the objective is to *create* connectivity within the blocks of natural habitats and protected areas in the corridor, to ensure the long-term viability of species. Conservation action in these areas includes the promotion of biodiversity-friendly practices such as agroforestry systems.

The VACC is home to a large number of globally threatened species, which require action primarily at the site or protected area level. Within the VACC, we focus on a smaller set of species that specifically require large-scale conservation action. Planning for these species is currently being revised and improved through the two studies mentioned above as well as a preliminary analysis of the requirements of these species being led by Conservation Inernational-Bolivia and the Center for Applied Biodiversity Science. As information on habitat requirements and needs is refined and developed, connectivity planning will focus more on these species.

Connectivity conservation management

This section begins with a brief discussion of the main threats, and then turns to the main strategic planning actions that Conservation International and its partners implemented to promote biodiversity-friendly economic alternatives in the VACC. These are the planning actions that enable the two types of connectivity mentioned above.

The main threats in the VACC are (i) unsustainable agriculture and natural resource use driven by poverty and unsustainable development policies; (ii) insufficient participation in protected area management; (iii) weak policy frameworks and governance of natural resources and conservation; (iv) high population growth; and (v) mining and hydrocarbon development. Recently, the expansion of road infrastructure has become a significant threat as well (Fleck et al, 2006). On the Peruvian side, the construction of the Interoceanica Sur highway, linking Brazil with the Peruvian coast, is under way and will affect numerous protected areas such as Tambopata. It will also pass through sensitive ecosystems and impact more than 12 ethnic groups (Dourojeanni, 2006; Surkin, 2006).

Between 2005 and 2006, Conservation International-Bolivia implemented a project to develop a land-use plan for the Municipality of Apolo, which includes several protected areas in the VACC. While Bolivia has certain unique characteristics, this experience still provides key insights into how to integrate protected areas into the local socio-political context and generate a more sustainable land-use matrix.

The process was implemented through a series of steps (Figure 8.5) including (i) collection and systematization of existing biophysical and socio-economic information; (ii) development of an integrated assessment, based on biophysical and socio-economic characteristics of the municipality, resulting in an agro-ecological zoning plan; (iii) development of a soils-use plan based on the agro-ecological zoning plan as well as the results of participatory workshops; (iv) a proposed land-occupation plan based mainly on social and economic characteristics; (v) a proposed land-use plan that incorporates information from the soils-use plan and land-occupation plan; and (vi) a participatory validation of the land-use plan by the municipality and stakeholders (CI, 2006a).

It is important to highlight key aspects of this process. A concerted effort was made to ensure that the land-use plan combined technical and participatory information. The agro-ecological zoning, for example, is based on current and potential land uses as well as constraints and limitations identified through technical and

Buff-tailed Coronet Hummingbird (*Boissonneaua flavescens*), in Ecuador Cloud forest, part of a private protected area that interconnects natural land in the Andes

Source: Graeme L. Worboys

participatory analyses. Once it is approved by the local authorities, the agro-ecological zoning results in the soils-use plan (CI, 2006a; Flores, 2007, pers. comm.). Local participation is also important in ensuring that there is a greater appropriation of and consensus on the land-use plan. In July 2006, the land-use plan officially became municipal policy.

The VACC has numerous traditional tourism locations such as La Paz in Bolivia and Cuzco and Machu Picchu in Peru. As such, tourism has always been an important economic activity in the corridor, with 1,057,621 visitors in 2005 to Cuzco. More recently, nature tourism has become increasingly important in the VACC, with over

13,000 visitors to the municipality of Rurrenabaque (2004) and 5000 to Madidi National Park in 2005 (based on data from SERNAP and the municipality of Rurrenabaque).

This tourism has been closely connected to protected areas and is a key strategic component of connectivity planning. On the Bolivian side, the ecotourism strategy for the VACC has involved work at various levels. At the local level, the focus has been on communities and the development of products that incorporate self-management. At the departmental level, these local actions are connected to regional policies, through governmental departments. National-

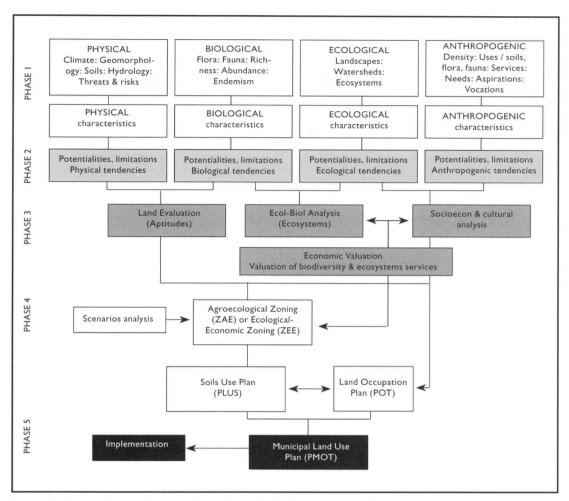

Figure 8.5 Phases of the development of a land-use plan for the Municipality of Apolo

level actions have involved close coordination with the Vice-Ministry of Tourism, in order to improve the legal and structural conditions for tourism development. Local-level actions, in and around protected areas, would not succeed in contributing to the mitigation of threats to biodiversity and improvement of local livelihoods without work at these other levels.

What follows is one example of a community-based ecotourism enterprise implemented in the corridor; this site-specific activity is, as noted above, part of a corridor-wide strategy. During the 1990s, the indigenous community of San Jose de Uchupiamonas, located inside Madidi National Park, began to view ecotourism as an economic activity that could reduce out-migration and improve local livelihoods. As a result, in 1999 Conservation International began to provide technical and financial support for the Chalalan community ecotourism business enterprise. This project went on to thrive, as a result of additional support from the community, NGOs and the Inter-American Development Bank (Pastor, 2003).

This project has incorporated an integrated approach that combines ecotourism, sustainable agriculture and craft production. Ecotourism interventions focused on training, construction of infrastructure and marketing. Project members were trained in environmental interpretation, food and beverage preparation and marketing. Training was implemented through exchanges, workshops and field visits. Infrastructure was built including a lodge, bar, interpretation hall and ecological paths. A heavy emphasis was placed on marketing Chalalan through participation in international fairs, promotional materials, a web page, visits by international media and inclusion in international travel books. These actions were complemented by the implementation of sustainable agroforestry and animal husbandry systems (Pastor, 2003). Finally, to generate additional income for local families, a craft production proj-

ect was implemented to sell masks to tourists (Pastor, 2007, pers. comm.). As a result of these actions and strong commitment by the community, today Chalalan is a self-sustaining ecotourism business, with 50 per cent of its stock belonging to community members and the other 50 per cent to the community organization that runs it (Pastor, 2003).

Given the large number of indigenous territories and area in the VACC, work with this population has been extremely important. Through a partnership with Wildlife Conservation Society, Conservation International supported the development of a management plan for the Reserva de la Biosfera(RB)–TCO (indigenous lands) Pilon Lajas (Bolivia) (Figure 8.6) (WCS, 2006). The methodology for this process (Figure 8.7) was based on steps identified in SERNAP's guide for the development of

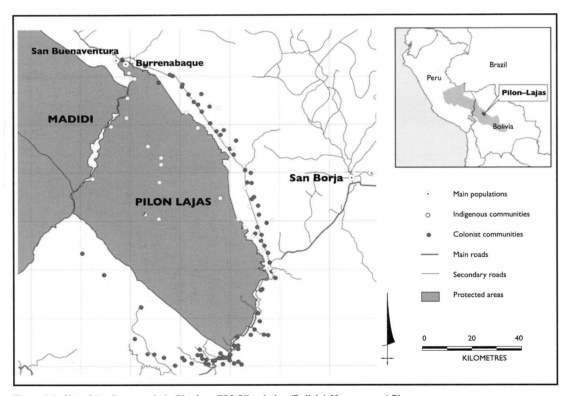

Figure 8.6 Site of the Reserva de la Biosfera-TCO Pilon Lajas (Bolivia) Management Plan

Note: TCO, Territorio Communitario de Origen (Indigenous Territory)

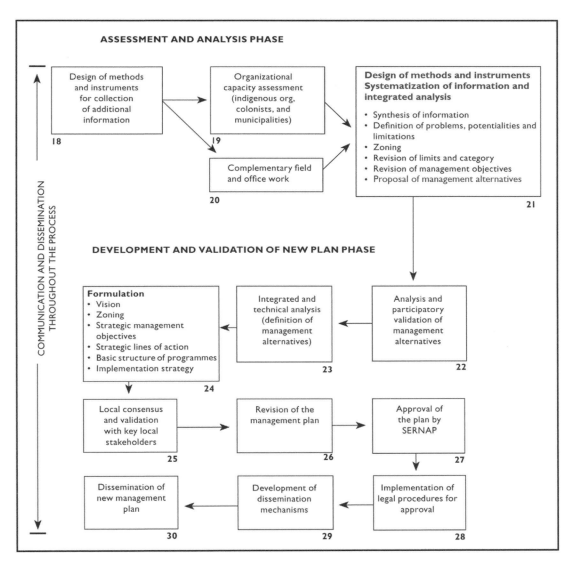

Figure 8.7 Key steps in development of the management plan for the RB-TCO Pilon Lajas

protected area management plans (SERNAP, 2002). Below we highlight some of its most relevant components.

From the beginning, this plan was intended to be both a livelihood plan and a management tool for the protected area and local population. For this reason, it was developed with the active participation of the indigenous groups that live inside the area, colonist communities surrounding the protected area, municipalities and the

protected area management committee. Indigenous people and park guards (from both local indigenous and colonist communities) were provided with training on the planning process and methodology, so that they could be active members of the planning team. Their role was to ensure community participation and help communicate more effectively, especially with non-Spanish speakers of the indigenous population. Participatory mapping was used to identify current and desired types and locations of different land uses of indigenous and colonist communities. In turn, this information, especially on indigenous land uses, was fundamental in the design of the protected area zoning plan (WCS, 2006). In fact, the planning team ensured that agricultural production areas, hunting sites and other important areas of indigenous use were zoned so as to allow such activities to continue.

Communications strengthened the corridor and centred on numerous key corridor-wide actions. A strategy was developed and implemented, with the participation of key actors from both countries, including Peru's Instituto Nacional de Recursos Naturales and Servicio Nacional de Areas Protegidas de Bolivia, in order to inform the public and private sectors about the VACC and explain its benefits. This strategy included the development of promotional materials such as brochures and a documentary film titled *Treasures without Border*, which reached millions in both countries (Salinas, 2006). Journalists were provided with training courses, which involved visits to protected areas, to help them appreciate the corridor, biodiversity and the value of protected areas (Mariaca, 2007, pers. comm.). Finally, communications strategies for key protected areas were developed through the participation of protected area staff and key local stakeholders (Salinas, 2006).

To communicate to indigenous and poor peasant communities, Conservation International-Bolivia utilized an informal educational tool called 'the green tent', an actual tent with drawings of environmental or conservation issues. These materials were developed through consultation with local communities and incorporated local cultural beliefs and practices (Tarquino, 2006). To implement the green tent, park guards in the Reserva de la Biosfera-TCO Pilon Lajas, Carrasco National Park and other national parks were trained. These guards, with support from Conservation International, travelled with the tent to communities and schools, to educate community members, children and politicians about biodiversity, conservation and the VACC.

Transboundary coordination has been at the heart of the VACC. In November 2003, a bi-national technical committee was formed in the

context of the Conservation and Development in the Tambopata-Madidi Complex project financed by the International Tropical Timber Organization and implemented by Conservation International. The members of this committee included the directors of protected areas in the Tambopata-Madidi Complex, representatives of Servicio Nacional de Areas Protegidas de Bolivia, Perú's Instituto Nacional de Recursos Naturales and Conservation International. The bi-national technical committee was a space for coordinating actions within the VACC, exchanging information and making decisions tied to conservation and development processes in the corridor. As such, it generated proactive conservation action for connectivity maintenance in the corridor and the bi-national complex.

Between 2002 and 2004, various actions were taken to strengthen transborder coordination in the Tambopata-Madidi complex. In April 2002, the directors of Bahuaja Sonene, Tambopata and Madidi protected areas met and signed a coordination agreement to conduct joint patrols and training and greater information exchange. In May 2003, technical staff, directors and local actors from these same protected areas held a workshop to ensure compatibility between their respective management plans. In this meeting, agreements were reached to carry out joint research, monitoring and tourism development. These activities led to a June 2004 workshop to develop the strategy for the Tambopata-Madidi complex, with participation of 92 representatives from different sectors in both countries (Salinas, 2006).

Transboundary coordination also involved the exchange of experiences between key actors. Local community members from both countries living in and around protected areas participated in training and exchange workshops on themes such as sustainable systems of agriculture and animal husbandry, agricultural extension and monitoring of hunting and fauna (Salinas, 2006).

Benefits and accomplishments

The connectivity actions discussed above have been implemented primarily to ensure improved conditions for biodiversity conservation. In this section, we discuss some of the other benefits of these actions, but before doing so we want to briefly examine some of the key broader scale benefits. For one, the VACC helps to guarantee the maximum connectivity of habitats, particularly across altitudinal gradients, which will be important for species migration in the context of climate change. Some studies have also demonstrated that, taking into account factors such as climate regulation, water services, control of erosion and others, a hectare of tropical forest is worth between US$1170 and $4052 in terms of ecosystem service (Costanza et al, 1997; Ibisch and Choquehuanca, 2003). More specifically, important environmental services (especially water purification) for the population in both countries as well as in the VACC are directly linked to the functions of forests in the corridor, including capture of precipitation, maintenance of water quality, water regulation and prevention of erosion (Ibisch et al, 2007). However, it is still necessary to develop mechanisms to transform such valuations from theory into practice.

While it is still too early to know the full benefits of the municipal land-use plan in Apolo, evidence to date suggests that there already have been some clear and tangible benefits. The zoning plans for protected areas and indigenous territories in the municipality have been integrated into the land-use plan, as have conservation issues. Doing so has contributed to increasing local understanding of the importance of protected areas and conservation. Because the plan identifies solutions for land-use conflicts and the information it contains can help improve municipal development planning, conditions have also been improved for a mosaic of biodiversity-friendly land uses that favour connectivity (CI, 2006b). This process is currently being replicated in other municipalities in the corridor and an effort is underway to explore its applicability in Peru as well. As a result, the Apolo land-use plan will produce a beneficial multiplier effect throughout the VACC and make a valuable contribution to improving conditions for biodiversity conservation

Chalalan has been highly successful. Between 1999 and 2002, the community members secured a total of US$118,374 in income from employment generated by Chalalan. The enterprise has invested close to US$10,000 in social benefits for

the community, such as school supplies, improvement of school infrastructure, purchase of agricultural products and titling of their communal lands (Pastor, 2003).

There have also been notable biodiversity conservation benefits. Today, community members are much more aware that they are responsible for caring for biodiversity, especially because without it they would lose income from ecotourism. In the area surrounding the ecolodge, the presence of fauna is increasingly evident. The use of crop rotation systems has also contributed to a decreased expansion of the agricultural frontier (Pastor, 2003).

The lessons learned from Chalalan have been replicated in similar projects throughout the corridor. These include indigenous community-based ecotourism in San Miguel, El Chairo, Kausay Wasi and Turismo Ecológico Social (Figure 8.8). These projects will reach financial sustainability in a shorter time, because they incorporate lessons from the Chalalan experience.

The territorial planning process in Pilon Lajas has given the indigenous population a planning instrument that reflects their needs, ensures sustainable use, prevents further incursion by colonists and promotes the conservation of biodiversity. In this sense, it has provided the local indigenous organizations and the protected areas administration with a tool that will strengthen their capacities to manage the area that is critical for biodiversity in the VACC. The high level of participation by local stakeholders has served to create a sense of ownership of the plan, which is one reason it was easily approved by the management committee in August 2006, and helped improved local perceptions of the Reserva de la Biosfera-TCO, especially in colonist communities.

In the short term, journalism training appears to have stimulated more and better coverage of environmental issues. Through communications and environmental education, Conservation International and its partners have achieved a greater consciousness about conservation, protected areas and the VACC at all levels. In other words, public opinion towards the corridor has improved and decision makers are now more aware of conservation issues. Environmental education work in and around protected areas has

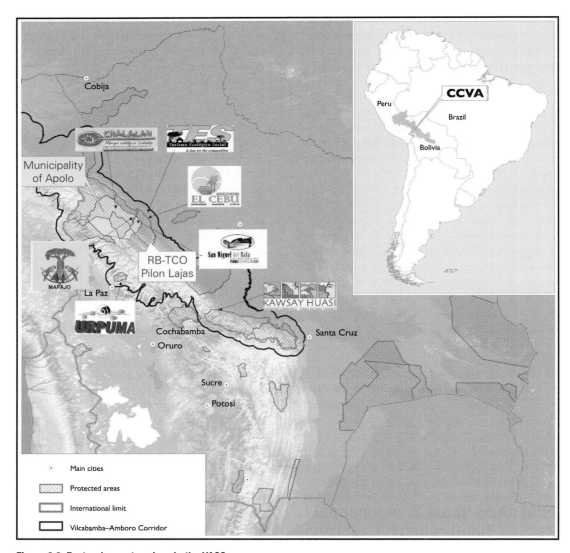

Figure 8.8 Ecotourism enterprises in the VACC

served to change the image of protected areas and park guards. In some parks, park guards are now viewed as friends and a source of support rather than police.

Transboundary coordination has been fundamental in the consolidation of the corridor. However, due to the political nature of these processes, it has been difficult to see clear benefits in the short term. Those benefits that have been evident include the establishment and strengthening of the Tambopata-Madidi complex, through improved coordination between protected areas in the border region.

Lessons learned

Involving indigenous people in planning helps ensure positive outcomes

The development and establishment of indigenous territoriality is a key opportunity for connectivity conservation throughout the corridor. Instruments for protected area and indigenous territorial planning can be compatible.

Communication and environmental education must accompany implementation

Communications can only be successful with ongoing and continued support, because results only become evident in the long term. Protected areas need to budget for communications and environmental education activities.

Coordination between responsible managers across departmental boundaries is essential

One of the biggest challenges is to integrate corridor planning into policies and planning instruments, from local to national levels, as well as the agendas of partners. In Bolivia, the VACC has given local actors such as municipalities a sense of responsibility for conservation action. The full involvement of all actors in corridor planning and implementation processes is fundamental. The VACC will be more effective when there is greater inter- and intra-sectoral coordination, especially with development-oriented partners.

Ecotourism initiatives generate local support for connectivity conservation efforts

Community-based ecotourism projects need to incorporate a value chain approach as well as a heavy emphasis on training to be successful. An alliance with the private sector and government institutions is a key factor in the success of community-based ecotourism projects.

Local land-use planning also provides multiple benefits

Municipal land-use planning can serve to harmonize connectivity conservation efforts with the needs and objectives of communities. The Apolo municipal land-use plan was a valuable means to integrate protected areas into local planning and the surrounding landscape as well as increase local knowledge of the importance of conservation.

Cooperation across national boundaries strengthens conservation opportunities

Bi-national coordination requires a clear understanding of the dynamics of international relations as well as socio-economic and political realities on both sides. The exchange of experiences is a great way to strengthen transboundary coordination. A bi-national corridor is not simply the sum of actions or activities in two countries.

Acknowledgement

Some of the information contained in this case study is based on the results of a systematization of experiences in the VACC workshop held on 8–9 August 2006 in La Paz, Bolivia.

Serra do Espinhaço Biosphere Reserve

Miguel Angelo Andrade, Sérgio Augusto Domingues and Sônia Rigueira

Setting

The Espinhaço Mountain Range represents the largest and most continuous Precambrian orogenic belt of Brazil's territory, serving as a watershed divide between the São Francisco river basin and the river basins that drain directly into the Atlantic Ocean. The range extends in a north–south direction, over a length of approximately 1200km. In Minas Gerais State, the Espinhaço Range has a north–north-west orientation, following approximately the meridian 43° 30´. The altitude is quite variable. Along the 1000km of the cordillera, alternating elevations of 1000 and 1500m, with peaks reaching up to 2070m, allow for an enormous diversity of climate and rainfall conditions.

Although one might think so from the range-like succession of its mountains, the Espinhaço is not a single block. There is a discontinuity in northern Minas Gerais, which divides the cordillera into two segments – the north and south Jequitinhonha regions. Due to the vast surface area occupied by it and its direct relations with different geographies, the Espinhaço Range constitutes an important reference point for understanding the geological evolution of Brazil's south-east and central-east regions.

The Espinhaço Range represents a unique region in its bio geographical aspects. It encompasses three Brazilian biomes of high ecological relevance: Caatinga, Cerrado and Atlantic Forest. The latter two are included in the list of global biodiversity hot spots (Mittermeier et al, 1999). In the northern portion, 'caatinga' areas are

Espinhaço mountain range at Serra do Cipó

Source: Miguel Andrade

characterized by dry forest ecosystems, and xero-phyte vegetation (*Cactaceae*) interspersed with 'cerrado' areas are the dominant feature. Plant and animal species that are common to both biomes occur in this portion of the Espinhaço Cordillera. It should be noted that these areas show a rela-tively low level of human occupation, when compared to the southern portion.

The more central region is characterized by the domain of the 'Cerrado' *sensu stricto*, in the low areas, with the portions situated above 1000m being dominated by rupestrian fields. Amidst this landscape, forest patches are found along the margins of streams. At the higher elevations of the Espinhaço Range, within the Cerrado Biome, a unique phytophysionomy dominates. It is a type of rocky field, the so called 'campos rupestres'. In general, they occur at altitudes above 900m, on a rugged relief, overlying rock outcrops, in areas with fine, sandy soil or acidic, shallow, gravel-like soil, poor in nutrients and organic matter and with a low water-retention capacity. The vegetation

layer is predominantly composed of a continuous herbaceous stratum and small sclerophyllous, ever-green bushes.

Although only a small number of areas have been intensely inventoried, it is estimated that approximately 3000 plant species can be found in the campo rupestre. Related to Cerrado plant endemism, 30 per cent of the taxa are estimated to be exclusive to the campos rupestres, which would represent approximately 1000 to 2000 endemic species. A high level of endemism is also observed in the fauna as a whole: endemic birds, mammals, amphibians, reptiles and fishes have also frequently been recorded.

The campo rupestre is an extremely fragile ecosystem as it has very low resilience. Should the delicate link between this vegetation and the soil be broken, spontaneous regeneration will rarely occur. As a result of this fragility, a large number of ravines, grooves and 'voçorocas' (gullies) result-ing from mining activities can be observed throughout the Espinhaço Range.

Notwithstanding their high biodiversity and conservation importance, several of the campo rupestre species are facing extinction due to the impacts of a variety of human activities. The factors affecting the campos rupestres have become increasingly severe over the past few years. Cattle production, favoured by the existence of natural pastures, is currently the main economic activity in all regions of the Espinhaço Range. Burning methods used by locals to renew the herbaceous vegetation have accelerated the destruction of these areas. In addition to these, impacts such as mining, planting of exotic species, increasing real-estate speculation, the growth of predatory tourism and the extraction of species of ornamental value also have been contributing to the destruction of the campos rupestres.

Pursuant to its main phytophysionomic identity, the area of the proposed Serra do Espinhaço Biosphere Reserve comprises the largest occurrence of campos rupestres in Brazil, for which reason its conservation should be a priority. However, the springs from which arise the main tributaries of the largest drainage basins in Minas Gerais – Doce River, Jequitinhonha River and São Francisco River – are intimately related with the interfluvia found along the entire length of the crests on which these ecosystems occur. This region also plays a key role in national connectivity, through one of the most important watersheds of south-eastern Brazil – the Doce, Jequitinhonha and São Francisco basins. Thus, conservation of the area's landscape elements requires a strategy to be applied at a large landscape scale.

For the Espinhaço Range as a whole, 357 threatened species have been included in the *List of Species Threatened with Extinction in the Flora of Minas Gerais*. According to Giullietti et al (1987), at the Serra do Cipó, there are 1590 species of plants registered in an area of approximately 200 square kilometres. Giulietti et al (1987) comment that a large part of the Espinhaço Range is occupied by campos rupestres, where the largest number of endemic species has been concentrated, corresponding to about 30 per cent of its flora. The same authors also affirm that a large number of those endemic species are confined to one or a few mountain ranges.

Everlasting species harvested locally for ornamental purposes

Source: Miguel Andrade

In addition to its natural beauty, this region harbours cultural assets such as several colonial towns dating from the 18th century, as well as traditional artistic and religious elements. Remnant cities from the early colonization at Minas Gerais State, such as Diamantina, Congonhas and Ouro Preto have been nominated as cultural world heritage sites by UNESCO. They boast a series of rich art and tradition clusters, making up a genuine cultural kaleidoscope. In this area, towns and villages are found that keep the largest homogeneous complexes of baroque and colonial architecture in Brazil, the heirs to the gold and diamond cycles, as well as important sites of prehistorical human presence. The Espinhaço is also the site of several tourism circuits, among them the 'Estrada Real' (Royal Road), which has become a major state government project in this region.

The Espinhaço is undoubtedly one of the richest and most diverse regions in the world. The extent of its area and its biological, geomorphological, historical and cultural importance justify the urgent implementation of measures aimed at the conservation of connectivity within this mountain complex.

The connectivity conservation initiative

An effective conservation planning strategy for the Espinhaço Range was urgently needed. In 2005, under the leadership of the Minas Gerais state government, in association with several other

Colonial town Ouro Preto, southern end of the Espinhaço Range

Source: Miguel Andrade

institutions, UNESCO, through its Man and the Biosphere programme, declared the Serra do Espinhaço Biosphere Reserve, first phase. This phase considered only its southern portion. A second phase was already under discussion between the governments of Minas Gerais and Bahia states, as the future area to be declared encompasses both states.

In addition to helping to ensure the protection of an area of great significance, the creation of the Serra do Espinhaço Biosphere Reserve can become a focus for the establishment of dialogue between politicians, developers and other actors in the region who seek a balance between conservation and development and enduring, effective public policies. The Serra do Espinhaço Biosphere Reserve covers an area of 3,076,457ha. Figures 8.9 and 8.10 show its location and zoning, as

proposed in the document that led to its creation.

The Core Areas as mapped cover an area of 204,522ha distributed over 33 protected areas under the management responsibility of the federal and state governments. Considering the size of the Espinhaço Range, this is relatively small in both number and size of protected areas. Protected areas under municipal management and private reserves are not taken into account in these figures. The potential to increase substantially the total area of the Core Zone is great once these are considered.

The declared Serra do Espinhaço Biosphere Reserve area includes lands within 53 municipalities. As all the cities were kept out of the declared area, within the biosphere reserve there are around 640,000 inhabitants living in rural lands divided as: core zones – 347 inhabitants;

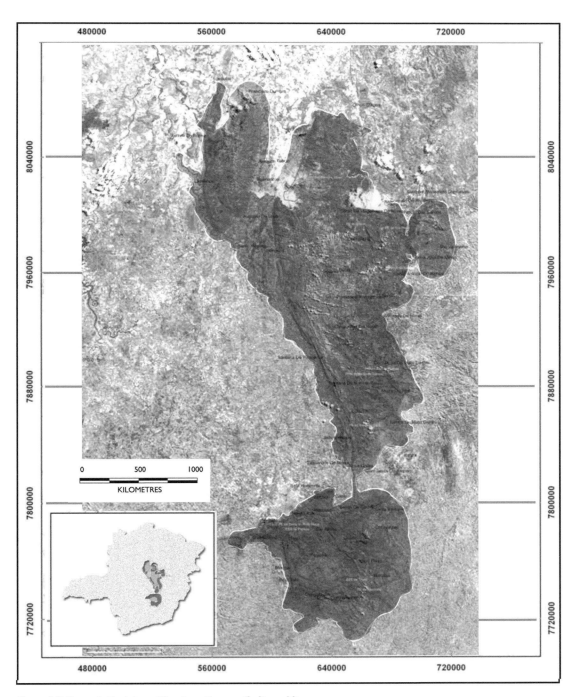

Figure 8.9 Serra do Espinhaço Biosphere Reserve limits and its zones

buffer zone – 345,250 inhabitants and transition zone – 297,138 inhabitants (IBGE, 2000). The southernmost portion of the Serra do Espinhaço Biosphere Reserve includes part of the Iron Quadrilateral. This region is the richest part of the country in mineral diversity. More than 20

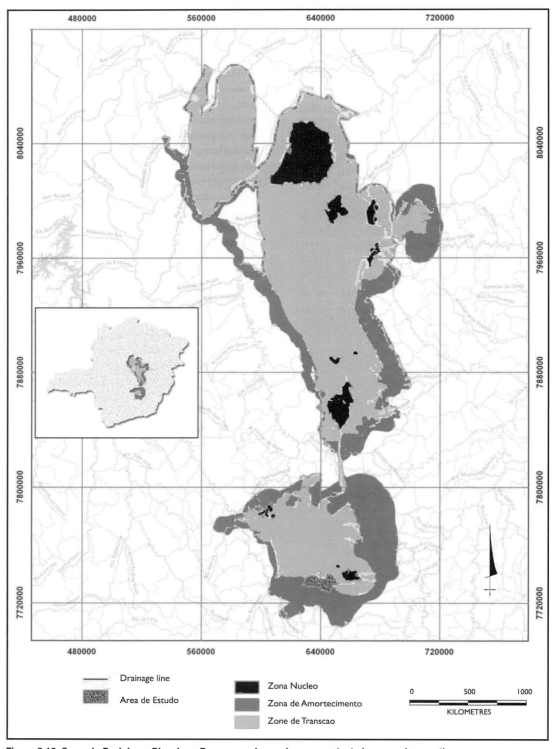

Figure 8.10 Serra do Espinhaço Biosphere Reserve zoning and a new protected area under creation

different minerals can be found there. Most of them are of great economic relevance. Several mining developments are ongoing in this region and many others are under development. Mining is one of the major challenges that conservation faces in this reserve.

The zoning (Figure 8.10) was developed considering the interests of multiple sectors and the establishment of partnerships for conservation of the natural aspects of the Espinhaço Range. Priority was placed on the connectivity of landscape elements, such as vegetation remnants, ecological corridors, orographic groups and drainage basins. The management strategy is to monitor and control actions pertaining to sustainable development, creating a policy under which the biosphere reserve stands as a reference for regional and national planning.

Connectivity conservation management

Taking the landscape approach as a premise, a large-scale co-management approach is necessary to secure the implementation of the biosphere reserve. The starting point is quite challenging and it relies mainly on organizing the already existing information to inform strategic follow up. The most important strategies are described here.

There are many professionals, institutions, stakeholders, agencies and so on based in the region that must be linked together in order to guarantee a participatory process and to optimize the desired results of the conservation and development of the region. A well-balanced representation at the senior management level brings efficiency and transparency to the reserve implementation process. There is an immense amount of data about this region, but it must be organized as a tool to promote conservation. This will help to ensure connectivity within the region, especially regarding the campos rupestres, by subsidizing new research needs, management effectiveness and monitoring, environmental education and public awareness efforts, development and public policies implementation. Results expected are the enlargement of the protected area system in the region, support of implementation and management of already existing protected areas and subsequent participatory and technical planning seminars.

Considering that any biosphere reserve is a portion of land with multitudinous interests and that the overlapping of different objectives and functions is quite common, the potential for conflicts is great. Mapping the most serious conflicts is a starting point to solving them. There are different planning scenarios for this region and the Serra do Espinhaço Biosphere Reserve emerged as an opportunity to bring them together in line with the biosphere reserve concept. However, to ensure an effective management policy for this region, these planning scenarios must be incorporated into linked public policies that are flexible, to accommodate changes over time in order to ensure connectivity conservation, cultural and development objectives.

Already existing knowledge was enough to deliver environmental education and public awareness in the region. The involvement of key actors in this effort was fundamental to ensure its success due the size of the region. Communication tools are most important to spread information and bring actors together around the conservation and development of the region. The integration and strengthening of institutions and professionals working within the region was fundamental to ensuring the satisfactory delivery of conservation and development actions and in order to guarantee the implementation of public policies in the medium term.

There is a great diversity of interests and actions within the Serra do Espinhaço Biosphere Reserve. In order to have a well-represented management committee, a carefully balanced group was chosen to form its first membership. It is composed of 13 governmental institutions, nine non-governmental institutions, three institutions from the private sector and three universities. They cover an array of perspectives from the natural, cultural and development interests.

The southern portion of the Espinhaço Range is marked by a highly diverse area, both in terms of biodiversity and minerals. Previous studies undertaken in the state aiming at the establishment of priority areas for conservation appointed this region as one having the most interest to conservation considering some of its fauna and flora groups. This region is located within the so called 'Quadrilátero Ferrífero' (Iron Quadrilateral), although more than 20 different minerals can be found there, most of economic interest. Several mining requests were addressed to the government, as shown on Figure 8.11, showing that development pressure in this region is quite high, as well as the need to conserve its diversity.

From both cultural and natural perspectives, and considering its importance to development and the economy, this area will become a model for planning and implementing biosphere reserve strategies following the statement found within the document *The Sevilla Strategy for Biosphere Reserves* (UNESCO, 1995).

In this region of the Serra do Espinhaço Biosphere Reserve, there is a quite significant mosaic of five protected areas (Figure 8.12). Of those, four are IUCN Category I and II and one is Category V. All together they cover an area of around 26,000ha. Although of a relatively small size, these protected areas conserve important portions of land in this region.

As a strategy to improve the core zones of the biosphere reserve and to guarantee connectivity among important Atlantic Forest and campos rupestres areas, new protected areas are recommended in this region. A study undertaken in this region proposed the creation of one state park and three private protected areas. These areas will improve by 50 per cent the already existing protected land in this region and are located in the extreme south of the range, as shown on Figures 8.10 and 8.12. Their creation will also:

- contribute to the preservation of connectivity between the already existing protected areas and other important conservation areas not yet included under any formal conservation agreements;
- support ongoing ecological processes in a very low resilience area;
- guarantee water supply to the population of Ouro Branco city and to local industries;
- minimize the pressure towards the transformation of the land by mining industries (Figure 8.11 shows the formal requests for new mines at the National Department of Mineral Production in this region);

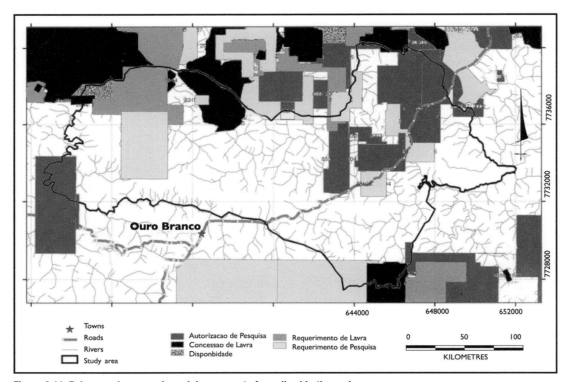

Figure 8.11 Polygons show ongoing mining requests formalized in the region

- stop urbanization speculation in a highly scenic and fragile area;
- provide ecotourism potential to the local population and its visitors;
- support the implementation of public policies in the region, such as the Estrada Real tourism project;
- contribute to the already existing mosaic of protected areas, bringing new categories and new forms of land management into the conservation toolbox.

Both the state of Minas Gerais and local landowners agreed in principle to such protected areas and the paperwork was put in place. Implementation was to occur by the end of 2006. The State Forestry Institute is the agency responsible for the protected areas at the state level. It is also responsible for the coordination of the Serra do Espinhaço Biosphere Reserve Committee. Under this responsibility are the studies towards creating management plans for several protected areas along the Espinhaço Range.

At least six plans are under development. These plans will be of great value, considering that they are applicable within the Serra do Espinhaço Biosphere Reserve Core Zone.

A high technology web page was under development as a tool for communication and database implementation. It was to be available to the general public as a facility to obtain information regarding the Espinhaço Range and the importance of the biosphere reserve, at different levels. The web page was to be designed to be accessible by different publics, in an interactive and easily managed way, with well-organized information. The language to be adopted must reflect Serra do Espinhaço Biosphere Reserve concepts, philosophy and objectives. This web page's main objectives were to:

- inform various audiences about the biosphere reserve's creation;
- support communication between partners and other biosphere reserves;

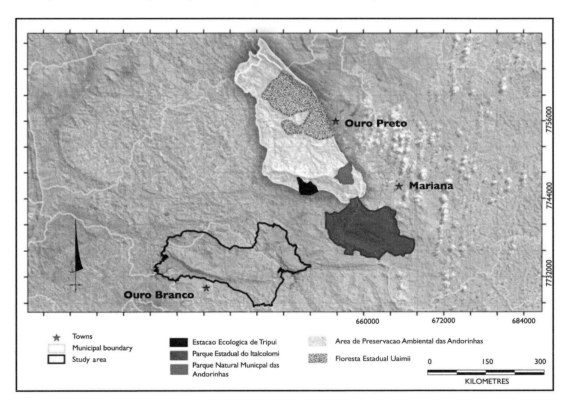

Figure 8.12 Protected areas at the southernmost portion of the Serra do Espinhaço Biosphere Reserve

- explore features that could bring benefits to the Serra do Espinhaço Biosphere Reserve, helping to build it as an important planning and management unit, with an emphasis on the ecological, cultural, technological and infrastructure aspects.

Among the available on line services, the most important are: an on line newsletter; reference documents available for download; zoning information; information regarding the protected areas within the region; information about tourism routes; and a virtual library. The first version of this web page was expected to be available to the general public starting in January 2006. There are many other activities under way in the Serra do Espinhaço Biosphere Reserve region, which must be surveyed and integrated into the management system. This will optimize the efforts towards the effective implementation of this reserve; as well it will guarantee biodiversity and cultural conservation and the sustainable development in the region.

Lessons learned

The fewer jurisdictions involved, the more readily connectivity conservation can occur

The southern portion of the Serra do Espinhaço was the first to receive biosphere reserve declaration. Its boundaries are entirely within the state of Minas Gerais. The northern portion straddles the boundaries of Minas Gerais and the state of Bahia. Negotiations involving two state governments were more complex and, thus, more time-consuming.

Linking ecological and cultural values can strengthen conservation efforts

In addition to its global ecological significance, the Serra do Espinhaço region harbours cultural assets such as several colonial towns dating from the 18th century, as well as traditional artistic and religious elements. In this area, towns and villages are found that keep the largest homogeneous complexes of baroque and colonial architecture in Brazil, the heirs to the gold and diamond cycles, as well as important sites of pre-historical human presence. Remnant cities from the early colonization at

Minas Gerais State, such as Diamantina, Congonhas and Ouro Preto have been nominated as cultural world heritage sites by UNESCO. They boast a series of rich art and tradition clusters, making up a genuine cultural kaleidoscope. The Espinhaço is also the site of several tourism circuits, among them the 'Estrada Real' (Royal Road), which has become a major state government project in this region. Preserving these cultural assets and the opportunity for economic activity through tourism projects provided an additional impetus for creation of the biosphere reserve.

International rankings support connectivity conservation

The inclusion of two of the Serra do Espinhaço natural regions on Mittermeier's list of global biodiversity hot spots helped to make the case for protecting this unique and vulnerable region.

Connectivity conservation must occur at the same scale as geophysical processes

The springs from which arise the main tributaries of the largest drainage basins in Minas Gerais – Doce River, Jequitinhonha River and São Francisco River – are intimately related with the interfluvia found along the entire length of the crests on which these ecosystems occur. This region also plays a key role in national connectivity, through the one of the most important watersheds of south-eastern Brazil – the Doce, Jequitinhonha and São Francisco basins. Thus, conservation of the area's landscape elements required a conservation strategy to be applied at a large landscape scale.

The scale and scope of management must reflect the scale of the landscape

Taking the landscape approach as a premise, a large-scale co-management approach was necessary to secure the implementation of the biosphere reserve. The starting point was quite challenging and it relies mainly on organizing the already existing information to inform strategic follow-up.

The involvement of multiple actors is necessary for connectivity conservation success

From the outset of this initiative, governments at all levels, NGOs, industries and communities were involved. Zones within the biosphere reserve were designated with the input of multiple sectors, with the goal of maximizing conservation of connectivity for multiple species and processes. A well-balanced representation at the senior management level brought efficiency and transparency to the reserve implementation process. Early involvement ensured that both the state of Minas Gerais and local land owners agreed in principle to new protected areas within the biosphere reserve.

Connectivity conservation offers opportunities for sustainable development

In addition to helping to ensure the protection of an area of great significance, the creation of the Serra do Espinhaço Biosphere Reserve became a focus for the establishment of dialogue between politicians, developers and other actors in the region who seek a balance between conservation and development and enduring, effective public policies. The need for a rational set of management policies for the biosphere reserve also helped to harmonize a diverse set of local management policies.

Publicly accessible information facilitates connectivity conservation

The biosphere reserve's website will make a wide array of information available to managers, businesses, communities and individuals, both inside the reserve and around the globe.

Articulating local visions to build macro-corridors: The Munchique–Pinche example

Luis Alfonso Ortega Fernandez, Liliana Paz B., Luis Augusto Mazariegos, Alex Cortes and Fernando Salazar

Setting

Colombia is located in the north-western corner of South America and physically connects Central and South America. Colombia can be divided into four geographic regions: the Andean highlands, consisting of the three Andean ranges and intervening valley lowlands; the Caribbean lowlands coastal region; the Pacific lowlands coastal region, separated from the Caribbean lowlands by swamps at the base of the Isthmus of Panama; and eastern Colombia, the great plain that lies to the east of the Andes Mountains. Near the Ecuadorian frontier, the Andes Mountains divide into three cordilleras that extend north-eastward almost to the Caribbean Sea and connect to Venezuela. These complex series of geographic regions make Colombia one of the most diverse of countries and a strategic region for both land and ocean connectivity.

In 1959, Colombia initiated the process of declaring and establishing natural national parks. These parks increased in number through the years until reaching 52 currently protected areas that represent 10 per cent of the total national territory. Multiple proposals for the establishment of corridors use the declared natural parks as nuclei. The first one to be declared was a biosphere reserve in 1979 (UNESCO-MAB, 1979).

Although the idea of establishing corridors dates back to the 1980s, the first proposed and documented corridor in Colombia was the Naya corridor, between the Munchique and Farallones National Parks (Negret, 1990). This initiative would later give origin to the Munchique–Pinche corridor project (Ortega and Gomez, 1998).

Since 1992, with the UN *Convention on Biodiversity* and with the signing of the Biodiversity Law in Colombia in 1995 (Law 165 of 1995), many corridor proposals flourished, with a vision to include more than just connectivity between parks. Corridors to include biological, environmental and multicultural connectivity appeared, all based on territorial planning as a reference frame.

In 1992, with the appearance of the Environmental Law and the establishment of the Ministry of the Environment, regional environmental authorities and various research institutes, there was an increase of collective interests in knowledge, value and management of national biodiversity. Equally, a new Law of Territorial Land Use was passed in 1997, which emphasized the identification of natural areas of municipal interest. All of these elements, combined with the existence of national parks and a proposal of community involvement promoted in 1995 by the National Natural Parks Administrative Unit (UAESPNN), were the basis for the proposal of national conservation corridors.

After 1980, with the formation of the Association for Rural Development in Nariño, and the creation of the Network of Reserves of the Civil Society in 1991, many local conservation initiatives and land-use establishments were promoted. These national, regional and local initiatives were the basis for institutionalizing a defined strategy of a Regional System of Protected Areas coordinated by UAESPNN. The initiative is currently in development with the participation of institutions, NGOs and indigenous, Afro-American and peasant communities in the areas of influence of conservation processes.

The connectivity conservation initiatives

In the present case study two elements are presented: macro-corridors (national and bi–national connectivity) and local connectivity (municipal level). The main macro-corridors are briefly described and the local experience of the Biological and Multicultural Munchique–Pinche corridor (Munchique–Pinche corridor) is presented as a way to build connectivity 'bottom up'. Based on the above characteristics, the Colombian government and various NGOs proposed the creation of biological connectivity corridors to maintain biodiversity (Table 8.2)

The Munchique–Pinche corridor is located in south-west Colombia in the Choco region in the Valle de Cauca department. It encompasses 360,000ha of which 47,000 are part of the Munchique National Park, 3000 are within natural reserves (Tambito, Proselva Foundation and Proaves), 2400 are within Indian reservations and 120 have been prioritized for conservation and are currently under formation (Ortega and Gomez, 1998).

The decision to establish corridors was based on results obtained in studies that pointed towards the need for conservation and management of the different ecosystems in the country. The main studies were: Biogeographic Units of Colombia (Hernández-Camacho et al, 1992); Caribbean and Latin American Ecoregions (WWF and World Bank, 1996); General Map of Colombian Ecosystems (Etter, 1998); Map of Colombian Andes Ecosystems ((Rodriguez et al, 2004); and Strategic Regional Ecoregions (Ministerio del Medio Ambiente, 2000). In 2005, Fandiño-Lozano and van Wyngaarden published the book *Prioridades de conservacion biológica para Colombia*, which is a tool for the design of connectivity. These studies, added to the accelerated environmental deterioration (as threat) and the existence of national natural parks (as opportunity), and offered support to the identification and protection of high priority conservation areas through the establishment of corridors. Decisions for establishing corridors were based on: high priority areas for conservation; decreasing pressures on

Table 8.2 Macro-corridor initiatives in Colombia

Corridor name	Scale	Purpose
Choco–Manabi	Bi-national (Colombia–Ecuador)	Biodiversity conservation of the Choco hot spot
Norandean	Bi-national (northern part of the eastern cordillera in Colombia and Andes of Mérida in Venezuela)	Biodiversity conservation in the Tropical Andes hot spot
Trans Amazonean	International (Colombia–Peru–Brazil)	Cultural and biodiversity conservation of the Brazilian, Peruvian and Colombian Amazon.
Los Cocos–Malpelo–Galapagos	International (Costa Rica–Panama–Colombia–Ecuador)	Conservation of marine ecosystems and coastal habitats in the Tropical Western Pacific

ecosystems; community involvement in conservation; and land-use planning.

Conservation in Colombia is undoubtedly a difficult process if one takes into account social and economic variables. One of the main reasons is the great level of social inequality that is caused by the accelerated deterioration of natural ecosystems and the advancement of the agricultural frontier, the existence of illegal crops, the presence of armed groups and the lack of incentives for conservation.

On the other hand, the new focus on the active participation of local communities has generated new 'conservation allies'. This will guarantee the long-term survival of the processes built upon local and regional inputs that are then projected to a national level. No process at a national scale, such as the macro-corridors, will be successful unless it involves and recognizes the dynamics of local communities and includes sustainable development strategies compatible with each region and ethnic group. Although the will to conserve exists within community and local organizations, it is necessary to implement economic alternatives that act as an incentive and are seen as a benefit of conservation.

In the specific case of the Munchique–Pinche corridor, this initiative emerged with the support of various organizations such as the University of Cauca-Inderena, the Global Environment Facility (GEF), Conservation International, the British Council, the Proselva Foundation and the Corporación Autónoma Regional del Cauca (CRC) (Negret, 1990). Later, due to social problems, this proposal was unviable and a geographic variation to the south of the original corridor was proposed (Ortega and Gomez, 1998). The CRC included this proposal in its corporate plan, declaring this area as strategic for the Valle de Cauca department. The proposal was presented to the GEF and was approved through the World Bank. The project is being executed by the Center for Research of Sustainable Productive Agricultural Systems, the Proselva Foundation and the Western Indigenous Authorities. At the same time, CRC and UAESPNN continue with the identification, promotion and establishment of a regional system of protected areas.

Various elements contributed to an understanding that the establishment of the Munchique–Pinche corridor was both possible and necessary: the biological richness, the conservation status of the area, the existence of baseline information, the backing of institutions and communities, the existence of protected natural areas, the interest of governmental authorities and a group of NGOs already working together.

The Corporación Autónoma Regional del Cauca identified the Munchique–Pinche corridor as a priority given the current trends. This area has multiple attributes that favour conservation: (i) it is very important for the generation of water; (ii) it has the only Páramos in the south of the cordillera; (iii) there is important biodiversity with a high number of endemic species; (iv) it is located in a forest reserve and national park; and (v) it is one of the last Choco areas with possibilities for establishing connectivity. Another element that weighed heavily in this decision was the presence of multiple conservation processes at a local scale that provide for long-term social sustainability.

The Munchique–Pinche corridor is located in two geographic regions in the same cordillera: one in the western slope corresponding to the Choco region and the second on the eastern slope that corresponds to the Andean region. The Choco biogeographic region is covered with extensive forests in very good conservation state. Intervening areas are located in the lower areas of the basin where historically logging and mining exploitation has occurred (Ortega and Gomez, 1998). The Andean region has been more heavily altered, since this area has been populated since pre-Columbian times by Indian tribes, followed by the arrival of the Spanish conquistadors. This has favoured the expansion of agriculture and other land uses in these areas, which has resulted in the loss of 85 per cent of the forest cover (Etter and van Wyngaarden, 2000). Currently these conditions of land use are maintained, but there is an increase of agriculture, both legal and illegal, and mining in the Choco region.

The political context for conservation is founded on: normative tools that favour the creation of protected areas; scientific capacity that allows for decision making; local communities willing to get involved in local projects; and possibilities to leverage local processes to influence national initiatives. Even though armed groups and an ongoing conflict existed in the region, the political context in which the Munchique–Pinche corridor was developed was favourable. This was due to the participation of the various organizations already mentioned. The connectivity design was conceived at three levels:

- ecosystems – connectivity between subxerophytic enclaves and high Andean ecosystems, including subandean, andean and Páramo ecosystems;
- land use – connectivity around established communities;
- political – connectivity between municipalities, environmental authorities and departmental authorities, through planned territorial development.

For the Munchique–Pinche corridor, from a physical point of view, the connectivity must occur on three levels:

- conservation – connectivity between healthy and pristine ecosystems;
- sustainable development – strategic areas to achieve connectivity in which sustainable productive systems must be established, and others in which natural rehabilitation and isolation must be implemented;
- cultural – identifying the customs, ancestral productive systems and traditions to create stronger bonds within communities and to promote regional identity.

The area's several municipalities and ethnic groups had been planning according to political boundaries and not from an environmental perspective. The implementation of the corridor was an opportunity to give the area a new environmental plan to address the complex needs of communities and of biodiversity. Important species around which monitoring, conservation and management activities are being developed include Andean bear (*Tremarctos ornatus*), puma (*Puma concolor*), pacarana (*Dinomys branickii*), white-tailed deer (*Odocoileus virginianus tropicalis*), Chestnut-bellied flowerpiercer (*Diglossa gloriosissima*), dark-backed wood quail (*Odontophorus melanonotus*), baudo guan (*Penelope ortoni*), cauca guan (*Penelope perspicax*),

harlequin poison dart frog (*Dendrobates histrionicus*), blue-bellied poison frog (*Minyobates minutus*), green poison frog (*Minyobates viridis*), *Espeletia marnixiana* and South American oak (*Quercus humboldtii*).

Connectivity conservation management

Connectivity management in the Munchique–Pinche corridor is developed through: identifying the environmental processes of local communities; joint identification of environmental supply and demand; participative zoning not limited by administrative boundaries (ecosystemic focus); implementation of a communication strategy; cooperative agreements to comply with management zoning; and joint preparation of project portfolios by regional environmental authorities; the above under the approval and backing of the appropriate environmental authority.

The creation and implementation of the Munchique–Pinche corridor will be led by the regional environmental authorities that have included this area in their zoning plans as a priority. The legal rights and rules have been communicated throughout the communities, which has allowed for a dynamic process and has generated local community leaders that have promoted this initiative.

The Cauca department of the CRC undertook an analysis to identify strategic ecosystems that would benefit from an integrated planning approach. The upshot of that process was the Munchique–Pinche corridor, which involves all the different actors (i.e. environmental, governmental, municipal, ethnic and social authorities) that directly contribute to the necessary zoning and management of the corridor. The corridor will also be contributing to a national zoning plan by being an example of management and territorial order.

There are two levels at which organizing takes place. At the institutional level, the CRC and the Colombian National Natural Parks Administrative Unit signed several agreements to identify, promote and establish conservation areas. This guarantees a national institutional presence alongside the local conservation processes, also defining normative elements that provide stability to the areas and configure the corridor. At the community level, workshops and training sessions defined in the institutional agreements were carried out to help in the establishment and management of the protected areas within the corridor.

Alliances with social organizations, municipal authorities, local universities, national research institutes and national and international NGOs were possible through the implementation of the Munchique–Pinche corridor project. Financial partners included the Global Environment Facility/World Bank, Proselva Foundation, the Foundation Center for the Investigation of Sustainable Systems of Agricultural Production, Asociación de Autoridades Indígenas del Occidentes del Cauca, Corporación Autónoma Regional del Cauca and the Colombian National Natural Parks Administrative Unit.

The main marketing tool was to hold multiple workshops with the local communities, not only to promote the initiative but also to create an ownership of the corridor by them. Also, the CRC included this area in its strategic plan, thereby publicizing this initiative through its various channels. Furthermore, the Global Environment Facility project included the use of Internet, printed matter and multimedia as marketing and media management tools.

In order to explain the management of the corridor, environmental zoning and regulations, workshops and meetings were carried out with the local community and organizations. To complement these, social cartography exercises were held to define the different management corridor zones to identify strategic goals, plans and projects and establish the roles and competences.

Local universities and NGOs such as Ecohabitats Foundation and the Hummingbird Conservancy joined the initiative through the environmental authority that approves and regulates research permits and processes. The scientific community was involved in the construction of a baseline, design and execution of a monitoring plan for biodiversity in the area of interest.

The main threats to the establishment of connectivity in the Munchique–Pinche corridor are:

- slow processing by the local authorities to declare areas as a priority for conservation to allow for connectivity;
- lack of productive alternatives that are compatible with conservation;

- lack of management and planning strategies for potential mining and road infrastructure in the area.

Connectivity management is assured through conservation networks, known as Local System of Protected Areas, in which the CRC and the National Natural Parks Administrative Unit coordinate their development, and the local authorities and organizations consolidate the connectivity system. Additionally, Ecohabitats Foundation and the Hummingbird Conservancy implemented a rapid assessment programme to evaluate and monitor the state of forests in the area.

Benefits and accomplishments

The main environmental benefit is the conservation of one of the richest, most biodiverse and threatened ecosystems on the planet, the Choco biogeographic region. With this action, ecological processes are protected throughout an important altitudinal gradient connecting an inter-Andean valley and the Pacific coast. From an economic point of view, the protection of the corridor guarantees the generation of water for more than 12 municipalities, the supply of water for hydroelectric projects in the Pacific basin and the regulation of flows for navigation and tourism. As for social benefits, this connectivity gives the opportunity to local communities to create a new territorial order not based on political boundaries, which can bring new options to the area.

The case of the Munchique–Pinche corridor, in its design, implementation and sustainability as advanced by environmental authorities, institutions and NGOs is an example of how to consolidate environmental, social, economic and political connectivity through a new focus on territorial planning.

Lessons learned

The key lesson was that connectivity conservation is best secured by working from the bottom up, that is, from a local level to a national or international level. To guarantee a sustainable social and cultural process, one must involve the local communities and regional environmental authorities from the earliest design stages. If not, the establishment of a corridor may cause a negative reaction from the community, as they may feel their legal rights are being violated. When local communities feel they are proponents of the process, there is a positive disposition to contribute with local visions and to foresee the future benefits of establishing conservation areas. Furthermore, for this corridor or connectivity to have institutional sustainability it is important to take into account the priorities and plans established by environmental authorities, specially the regional ones. To obtain credibility in the establishment of a corridor, one must identify local conservation initiatives that provide valuable experiences and promote appropriate management strategies.

Successful connectivity conservation requires the alignment of many actors and opportunities

Various elements contributed to an understanding that the establishment of the corridor was both possible and necessary: the biological richness, the conservation state of the area, the existence of baseline information, the backing of institutions and communities, the existence of protected natural areas, the interest of governmental authorities and a group of NGOs already working together.

Local leadership ensures implementation

The process enabled regional environmental authorities to embed connectivity plans and elements in their local zoning regimes. This fostered leadership at the local level for the implementation of connectivity conservation. Because the vision and mechanisms for its implementation were well communicated to local communities, leaders emerged as the corridor's champions.

Local capacity building can help ensure appropriate management for conservation

In this case, workshops and training sessions, defined in the institutional agreements, were carried out to help in the establishment and management of the protected areas within the corridor.

Watershed protection provides an economic rationale for connectivity conservation

The protection of the corridor guarantees the generation of water for more than 12 municipalities, the supply of water for hydroelectric projects in the Pacific basin and the regulation of flows for navigation and tourism.

A congruence of elements is necessary for success

The political context for conservation is founded on: normative tools that favour the creation of protected areas; scientific capacity that allows for decision making; local communities willing to get involved in local projects; and possibilities to leverage local processes to influence national initiatives. Even though armed groups and an ongoing conflict existed in the region, the political context in which the Munchique–Pinche corridor was developed was favourable. This was due to the participation of the various organizations already mentioned.

Local involvement and support was necessary for conservation connectivity outcomes

Another element that weighed heavily in the successful implementation of the corridor was the presence of multiple conservation processes at a local scale that provided for long-term social sustainability.

Llanganates–Sangay ecological corridor, Ecuador: Good conservation practice at a local scale

Xavier Viteri

Setting

The ecological corridor is located in central eastern Ecuador, an area typified by tropical evergreen mountain forest and Páramo belonging to the mountain forest of the central eastern Andes Cordillera of the Northern Andes Ecoregion. This natural corridor of 42,052ha connects two national parks – the Llanganates and the Sangay.

Llanganates National Park, located at the eastern cordillera of the Andes, comprises 219,700ha, was created in 1996, and ranges in elevation from 1200 to 4571m above sea level. The Llanganates Cordillera presents a geological composition different from the rest of the Andes – metamorphic, sedimentary (limestone) and volcanic rocks. This uniqueness allows the Llanganates to have special ecological conditions. Because of the variety of ecosystems in the Llanganates, important species diversity has emerged. The habitat heterogeneity allows a low dominance and a high species rarity (Benítez et al, 2000). Up in the Llanganates Cordillera, rumour has it, the Incas hid their treasure when Spanish conquistadors invaded more than 400 years ago (Anhalzer, 1998). Treasure hunters have so far failed to find the hoard. But botanical adventurers have uncovered a different kind of wealth, an ecological El Dorado of orchids found nowhere else on the planet.

Located to the south of Llanganates National Park, Sangay covers more than 517,765ha, was created in 1979, and ranges in elevation from 900m to 5319m – from piedmont tropical evergreen forest to perpetual snow at the Altar peaks. In 1983, Sangay was declared a natural world heritage site by UNESCO. The upper elevations of this park include vegetation typical of the Andes while the lowlands evidence vegetation shared with the tropical lowlands and Andean vegetation. The park is home to two indigenous communities (Quichua and Shuar), who have little or no access to basic services and so rely on surrounding natural resources for their livelihoods.

Both national parks are home to pumas (*Felis concolor*), ocelots (*Leopardus pardalis*), condors (*Vultur Gryphus*), endangered spectacled bears (*Tremarctos ornatus*) and mountain tapirs (*Tapirus*

Tungurahua, Llanganates–Sangay ecological corridor

Source: Xavier Viteri

pinchaque). Trees like alder (*Alnus acuminata*), myrtle (*Myrtaceae* spp.) and cedar (*Cedrela* spp.) are also examples of the biodiversity found here. A width of approximately 22km separates the two national parks.

The connectivity conservation initiative

In the year 2000, Natura Foundation – an Ecuadorian NGO – and a group of regional experts identified a natural strip between two national parks as part of the 65 most important areas for conservation in the Northern Andes Ecoregion. This project, funded by WWF, is part of its campaign to identify the 200 most important ecoregions of the world. From March to December 2001, Natura Foundation with WWF funds developed a project to identify and design the potential ecological corridor between Llanganates and Sangay National Parks. A team of national and international experts, the latter coming from Texas Tech University, worked in the field to test the validity of the corridor for some animal species. These two teams performed both ecological and genetic studies and outstanding results were found. The field results allowed the development of a spatial model using GIS software to design the corridor. Social studies were also carried out in the area. Once the field studies were completed, and having gathered important data on the biodiversity of the corridor, WWF proposed to provide the ecological corridor with international recognition using the Gift to the Earth, an initiative to promote legal protection for those areas considered globally important for their biodiversity.

If the corridor was going to receive international recognition, Natura Foundation needed to develop a strategy to accomplish the Gift to the Earth goals and worked side by side with national and local authorities, as well as farmers. The NGO worked with three local municipalities – Baños, Mera and Palora – developing ordinances to declare a local protected reserve. Campesinos, local authorities and national authorities were all determined to declare a local reserve and all of them received the international recognition. Thus, in December 2002 Llanganates–Sangay ecological corridor was recognized as the 81st Gift to the Earth in the world and the second one in Ecuador (after the Galapagos Island).

More than 70 per cent of the total corridor surface is native vegetation, with 14 per cent of the total being pasture, crops and small towns. Most of the native vegetation is typical of tropical mountain forest (including cloud forests) and a small percentage is Páramos. More than 2000 people inhabit the ecological corridor. An average of 64 per cent of those inhabitants were living with Unsatisfied Basic Needs (UBN – an index to measure poverty), when the Ecuadorian national average UBN is 61.3 per cent (Viteri, 2004). According to León (2002), landowners have lands of different sizes, some of them with farms of 8–10ha, others of 80–100ha and others 30ha. Most landowners have titles to their property.

Agriculture, livestock and tourism were found to be the main local activities. Due to unprofitable agricultural and livestock activity, local people had been incorporating different occupations by selling fruits and other refreshments, and by building small tourism businesses. Close to the corridor area is the city of Baños, considered the fourth most important city for national and international tourism in Ecuador, with ecotourism being the main activity.

Three main agricultural products are produced in the corridor area: naranjilla, (*Solanum quitoensis*), tree tomato (*Cyphomandra betacea*) and babaco (*Carica* spp.). None of these products was found to be profitable, but in some way farmers commercialize their products using wood to build boxes. It was found that campesinos use agrochemicals to improve their crops. Raising livestock is an unprofitable activity for farmers settled in the corridor and cattle represent an expensive business due to, among other factors, the inaccessibility of the terrain. Some farmers maintain a few cattle that are sold when extra income is needed.

During the process of identifying a local protected reserve (prior to obtaining the international recognition of Gift to the Earth), the author and his colleagues worked for about two months with the Environmental Ministry of Ecuador to explore the best alternative for establishing the Llanganates–Sangay ecological corridor as a protected area.

The concept of ecological corridors was not contemplated within Ecuadorian laws; therefore, it was not feasible to establish a corridor legally as such. However, objectives and management tools for creating what is known technically as a corridor existed within Ecuadorian laws. In this sense, the area connecting the Llanganates and Sangay National Parks could be administrated and managed as an ecological corridor under the terms recognized in Ecuador's Forestry Law for Natural Areas and Wildlife.

The Special Law of De-centralization allowed local governments to manage the natural resources of those areas that required protection for their particular characteristics. Through this means, municipalities and provincial councils in Ecuador could achieve the protection of important areas under their jurisdiction, in coordination with the national authority, the Environmental Ministry of Ecuador.

At the time of writing, a new law, the Special Law for Conservation and Sustainable Use of Biodiversity, was under consideration by the Ecuadorian Congress. This law would unify and update the old Ecuadorian laws for conservation and management. The concept of ecological corridors appears within one of the chapters of this amalgamated and streamlined draft legislation.

Once all legal alternatives for corridor protection were studied, participants carried out an exercise to determine the best management category in order to develop a management plan for the Llanganates–Sangay ecological corridor. Since the main objective of the corridor was 'conservation and sustainable use of its natural resources', the corresponding management category was 'protected area with managed resources' (IUCN Category VI) (Bajaña and Viteri, 2002). The management plan was agreed upon with local authorities and other local entities. Thereafter, municipal ordinances were drafted to be discussed and approved within their respective municipalities. Finally, the area of the ecological corridor was declared a protected reserve.

Within its 200 Global Ecoregions project, the World Wildlife Fund identified the Northern Andes as one of the ecoregions most important to protect. The Northern Andes Ecoregion extends throughout the Andes of Venezuela, Colombia and Ecuador and ends in northern Peru, where the natural depression Huancabamba appears (Kattan et al, 2000). The Northern Andes Ecoregion is in fact a complex of 14 ecoregions of more than 48 million ha. More than 1500 bird species and 500 species of frogs inhabit the Northern Andes Ecoregion (Kattan et al, 2000).

After a series of studies, WWF and its associates identified 65 priority areas for conservation in the Northern Andes Ecoregion Complex (Palminteri et al, 2001). Eleven of the 65 sites occur in Ecuador, not including the protected areas already declared by the government. One of those 11 sites constitutes a natural strip that connects two important natural parks: Llanganates and Sangay. Two ecoregions are present in this natural corridor: mountain forest of the Real Cordillera and northern Andean Páramos.

Once the area of the potential corridor was identified, Natura Foundation at first secured funding to determine the location and functionality of the corridor. Thereafter, and with the purpose of receiving the Gift to the Earth international recognition from WWF, the same organization helped to declare a local protected area with the final goals of minimizing fragmentation, improving land-use practices and maintaining connectivity between habitats at a time of climate change.

During March and December of 2001, a team of two biologists, an anthropologist and a geographer conducted field work to determine the preliminary movements of birds and mammals between Llanganates and Sangay National Parks. The biologists determined richness, abundance and diversity of species patterns for the study area (Box 8.2).

The anthropologist raised the issue of social and economic studies of the potential corridor, and the geographer – using data provided by the biologists – made a spatial model of the corridor. Later, a team of biologists from Texas Tech University joined the national team to determine gene dispersion of some mammal populations. During the study, the national team found 101 mammal species, with bats being the most diverse group (55 species). Twenty-one species of mammals were threatened in some way (Fonseca et al, 2003), and 11 bird species were threatened (Loaiza and Morales, 2002). Scientists also found some patterns of movement between the two

---

Box 8.2 Orchid diversity in the Llanganates–Sangay ecological corridor

Lou Jost is a local scientist interviewed by Fred Pierce for WWF in 2002, at the time of the corridor's public announcement. Jost gave up life as a quantum physicist to take up botany. He had spent the last six years living in the Ecuadorian Andes, collecting dozens of new orchid species in the remote cloud forests and valleys. The valley and the mountains that surround it have more endemic orchids than anywhere else on the planet. 'This region really is special,' he says. Why? The Pastaza river valley is the deepest, straightest valley in the eastern Andes. Every afternoon a hot, wet wind blows up the valley from the Amazon. It brings huge volumes of moisture that evaporate to form near-permanent clouds over the precipitous mountain ridges that flank the valley.

'Each ridge has its own microclimate in the clouds,' Jost says. 'The first ridge west of the rainforest is the wettest and windiest. The next is slightly less wild and wet. But every one offers a unique environment, and that usually means unique orchids.'

In these wet, sunless environments, dozens of species of tiny, delicate orchids have evolved. 'Each species seems to specialize in a particular combination of rain, mist, wind and temperature,' he says. 'High in the clouds, you can come across whole areas of forest smothered in a single species of orchid that probably exists nowhere else on Earth. It is an amazing experience.'

Jost has identified 90 orchids unique to the valley during his six years' study. 'There is nowhere like it and I see no sign that the discoveries will stop,' he says. One day, he found four new species of *Teagueia* orchids in a single patch of moss on Mount Mayordomo. That one find raised the number of known *Teagueia* species from six to ten. And since that day, he has found another 16 long creeping *Teagueia* orchids on the mountain.

No cloud forest is like any other – and for orchids that makes all the difference. 'Subtle climate variables are the driving force behind the evolution and survival of endemic species among Andean orchids; and not just orchids. This pattern holds for all the plant families in the Andes with high endemism.' Some might see that as good news for the survival of plant biodiversity here if, as expected, the planet warms in the coming decades. Many endangered plants may be better at seeking new territory than botanists previously thought. But the bad news is that if they are so picky about climate, will they find anywhere suitable to go?

---

national parks for brocket deer (*Mazama rufina*), collared peccary (*Pecari tajac*) and white-lipped peccary (*Tayassu pecari*).

Genetic results showed that with some species, particularly those at higher elevations, there seemed to be a potential Andean migration route through the eastern Andean corridor. In contrast, the lower-elevation species appeared to be using the Rio Pastaza as a riverine migration route toward higher elevations in the Andes mountains (Haynie et al, 2006).

Biological variables obtained in the field were input into GIS software to create a model. Multivariate statistical analyses were used to create the modelling, with the objective of having the best routes to define the ecological corridor (Novoa, 2002). The final result was the creation of the ecological corridor map (Figure 8.13). The corridor is 7km wide at its narrowest point and 21km at its widest.

Connectivity conservation management

Having physically designed the corridor, the author and his colleagues identified the key actors necessary for determining its actual management as a protected area. Strategic allies were found in the municipalities. Mayors of the cities of Baños, Mera and Palora embraced the idea of working towards the declaration of a protected reserve. Baños city is close to the corridor and many national and international tourists travel along the Baños–Puyo road. Having a declaration of Gift to the Earth would attract more tourists and bring benefits to local people settled along and within the ecological corridor.

Having the necessary political approval, including the presidents of the local parochial boards (the lowest political division category in Ecuador), the environmental NGOs worked with farmers through workshops teaching organic and sustainable agriculture. A workshop to identify

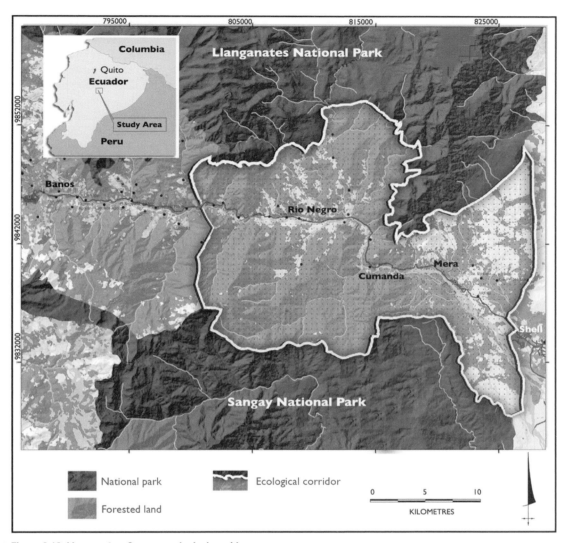

Figure 8.13 Llanganates–Sangay ecological corridor

threats to the Llanganates–Sangay ecological corridor was also developed, with invitations going to government, NGOs and other local actors (for example, local scientists, tourism agencies and farmers). The idea of these workshops was to create a growing confidence and consciousness about the potential benefits of the corridor idea. Of particular usefulness was the participation of a foreign and respected botanist, who justified the importance of declaring a local protected area between the two national parks.

At the same time, the mayors of the three communities were preparing drafts of ordinances to declare a protected area. These ordinances were approved in their respective jurisdictions. Later, the ordinances appeared in the Official Record of the State, declaring the area of the ecological corridor a Conservation and Ecological Reserve.

In the end, increased media management at the local, national and international level was necessary to increase knowledge of the corridor and the achievement of the Gift to the Earth recognition. Local, national and international interviews were published in different media, and an article about the corridor's Gift to the Earth status was published on the WWF website.

Another key requirement in the declaration of the protected reserve noted above was to create a management plan for the corridor. Local actors participated in the design of the management plan. The main objective of this plan was to assist in the conservation and sustainable management of the natural resources and ecosystems of the Llanganates–Sangay ecological corridor. Five management programmes were identified: biodiversity protection; sustainable management of natural resources; tourism development; communication and environmental education; and administrative and financial strengthening. Each programme included objectives, norms, main activities to be developed, indicators, verification tools, hypotheses, actors, resources and a prioritization of activities. The participation of all actors at all levels was expected for the management plan (Bajaña and Viteri, 2002).

Given this expectation, an administrative structure was suggested. Since the Llanganates–Sangay ecological corridor was the union of conservation efforts of three municipalities with autonomy in natural resources management within their respective territories, they all contributed to meeting regional objectives. This situation suggested that the administrative structure be decentralized, so that the three municipalities could execute their activities corresponding to their jurisdictions in an independent but coordinated way, with the goal of having a viable corridor where municipal boundaries intersected.

The recently completed hydroelectric dam on the San Francisco River threatens the future of the ecological corridor, since the project alters water flow in the Pastaza watershed. Due to a recent eruption of the Tungurahua volcano, local campesinos are moving in towards the corridor area, which might cause fragmentation of natural habitats within the corridor. The expansion of agriculture and/or the conversion of natural habitats to pasture land also threaten biodiversity within the corridor.

Benefits and accomplishments

The protected area includes portions of the top-priority Global 200 ecoregions. These forests are among the richest tropical mountain forests on Earth, with an outstanding number of species, many of them endemic. The spectacled bear is the only bear species in all of Central and South America, and is found primarily the northern Andean mountain forests. This ecoregion is home to an incredible variety of plants and animals, including mountain tapirs – the smallest tapirs in South America – pumas, endangered Andean condors (*Vultur gryphus*) and sword-billed hummingbirds (*Ensifera ensifera*) – to name but a few. These forests also contain 86 species of palm, including two found nowhere else on Earth – the feather palm and the endangered wax palm (*Ceroxylon andiculum*). In order to preserve this unique biodiversity, local governments were encouraged to make a commitment to creating a high-level public platform to search for funds. A Gift to the Earth publication on the web might bring possibilities for calling attention for future funding.

More than 2000 people living within the corridor benefited by the declaration of a local protected reserve. At the time of writing, through the WWF programme on 'Poverty Reduction through Improved Natural Resources Management', additional efforts were in place to contribute to the conservation of the area due to the Llanganates–Sangay ecological corridor being part of the Pastaza River basin. Project implementation also prioritized this area for the implementation of its conservation with selected communities.

As part of the democratic process at the beginning of 2005, local authorities were replaced. This required renewed efforts to promote the management plan of the Llanganates–Sangay ecological corridor as a tool for defining strategic interventions and projects for their planning efforts.

Lessons learned

International recognition can help foster success

In this case, the potential for international recognition through inclusion in WWF's Gift to the Earth programme helped encourage local communities to become involved in the corridor management planning process.

Early communication with all relevant parties is essential

Dialogue is a very important tool to achieve agreements; the capacity of working in multidisciplinary teams was an important element for the success of the project. The creation of a management committee as an initial strategy to follow up and execute the management plan was considered fundamental; unfortunately, changes of local authorities delayed this process. It was important to establish an informed participation process from the beginning. In short, the development of a communication strategy in which all actors participated was fundamental. Establishing strategic alliances was imperative; in this sense the political actors in the process were decisive.

Connectivity management can benefit local populations

Residents and communities in the Llanganates–Sangay ecological corridor were struggling with marginal agricultural and resource exploitation activities. They were able to see the protection and international recognition of the corridor as a source of more sustainable economic activities, thus fostering their support and involvement.

Look for natural opportunities

The narrow width (22km on average) between two existing national parks provided the opportunity for envisioning and working to promote connectivity conservation. Ecological and genetic studies proved the viability of the landscape and helped to attract international interest and funding for corridor development.

Flexible management arrangements can accommodate local conditions

Since the Llanganates–Sangay ecological corridor was the union of conservation efforts of three municipalities with autonomy in natural resources management within their respective territories, they all contributed to meeting regional objectives. This situation suggested that the administrative structure be decentralized, so that the three municipalities could execute their activities corresponding to their jurisdictions in an independent but coordinated way, with the goal of having a viable corridor where municipal boundaries intersected.

The management process never ends

As municipal leadership changed in the affected communities, it was necessary to renew the process of local education and capacity building so that support for the corridor would continue.

Science is an essential tool for connectivity conservation implementation

Scientific methods that tested the functionality of the corridor were decisive in the success of the project. Ecological and genetic information in the Llanganates–Sangay ecological corridor case helped to justify to international donors the importance of declaring a local protected area.

Conclusion

The Llanganates–Sangay ecological corridor is part of the northern Andes ecoregion and is considered one of the 65 most important sites to be conserved in this ecoregion. The Llanganates– Sangay ecological corridor harbours an important biodiversity representation of the eastern cordillera of the Andes and is a place in which lowland species and Andean species converge. The Llanganates–Sangay ecological corridor location between two national parks favours connectivity conservation between these parks. Local people benefit from the presence of a feature internationally recognized as a Gift to the Earth, especially with the introduction of ecotourism. Traditional practices (intensive agriculture) are being changed to other more sustainable activities favouring the existence and maintenance of the ecological corridor.

Implementation of an interconnected system of protected areas in the Venezuelan Andes

Edgard Yerena and Shaenandhoa Garcia-Rangel

Setting

The Venezuelan Andes are comprised of two mountain ranges, the Cordillera de Mérida and the Colombian Cordillera Oriental (Figure 8.14). The Sierra de Perijá is a subdivision of the latter; the Macizo de Tamá range is a subdivision of the former. Each branch is of different geological origin and has different physiography, separated one from another by lowlands or depressions. Only the Mérida Cordillera is the focus of this case study, being the largest of the above mountain ranges, with an area of nearly 36,000km^2 and a 400km south-west–north-east axis. Altitudes range from piedmont, around 200–500m above sea level, up to 4980m (La Marca, 1997).

Conservation of Andean landscapes by means of protected areas started in 1952, when Sierra Nevada National Park was established. Uniqueness of landscapes and protection of watersheds were the rationales for designating this and subsequent national parks, scattered along the Andean landscape. By 1985, five national parks had been designated, three of them within Mérida Cordillera. At the time, there was no connectivity conservation vision or plan (see 4, 9 and 11 in Figure 8.15). At about the same time, the Venezuelan National Park Service started to receive submissions from planners trained in conservation biology and geography who were aware of the need for a large landscape perspective in conservation planning.

Since pre-European times, the Andes have been one of the most populated areas in what today is Venezuela. By the time Spaniards first arrived in the Andes, the estimated human population was about 847,000, a number reached again only in the 1950s (Naveda, 2005). Land use was intensive in valleys and terraces with a sub-humid climate, leaving the outer humid and hyper-humid Andean slopes facing the Orinoco Llanos and the Maracaibo Lake basin mostly untouched by humans. Europeans also brought cattle, sheep and goats, using Páramos (alpine meadows) as well as deforested areas as pasture land. Pre-European and colonial period agriculture was based mainly on horticulture. Coffee plantations introduced by the early 19th century were a major factor in modifying some of these forested slopes, mainly between 700 and 1500m in elevation, in areas close to towns. It was only by the mid-1920s that paved roads first traversed the cordillera across some of these slopes, opening the inner portions

of the Andes region to the rest of the country (Méndez and Méndez, 1996).

The social structure of Andean populations, although based on the previous Amerindian culture (Méndez and Méndez, 1996), was transformed by Europeans and generated an Amerindian-European syncretism. The 21st century economy is based mainly on agriculture and related services, with small- to medium-scale production units in the hands of family landowners. This is a major socio-economic characteristic of the Venezuelan Andes. Large portions of land in hands of private landlords are rare or non-existent. Some community land-use rights for cattle ranching, derived from old titles recognized as belonging to indigenous groups, are still present in some Páramo areas. Those relatively large portions of forest on the outer slopes of the Andes with no visible land uses have had strong use limitations imposed by the State since the 1960s. The political leadership of Venezuela by Andean military forces, the boom of Venezuela as an oil exporting country and the international coffee price crisis, all in the early 20th century, promoted an exodus of Andean populations, heading to the oil industry and the large urban centres. This had an impact on wilderness areas, allowing for the return of natural succession to many areas of the Andes. Today, the population is growing and the economy is still based on horticulture, cattle ranching, educational services (higher education institutions) and tourism. Adjacent lowland areas have been incorporated into the Andean economy, mainly based on cattle ranching, plantain crop and diverse intensive tropical crops, managed mainly by Andean people (Méndez and Méndez, 1996).

Soil conservation became a major focus of the newly trained professionals working for government agencies since the 1940s. By that time, the recently established schools of forestry and agriculture started to influence political decisions. This was a period of political instability, shifting between autocracies to democracy. Nevertheless a common sign was the priority given to technical solutions to social problems. Soil conservation was perceived as a social problem, and successful programmes were implemented in rural areas, mainly in the Andes, in order to implement techniques for erosion prevention. In this context the

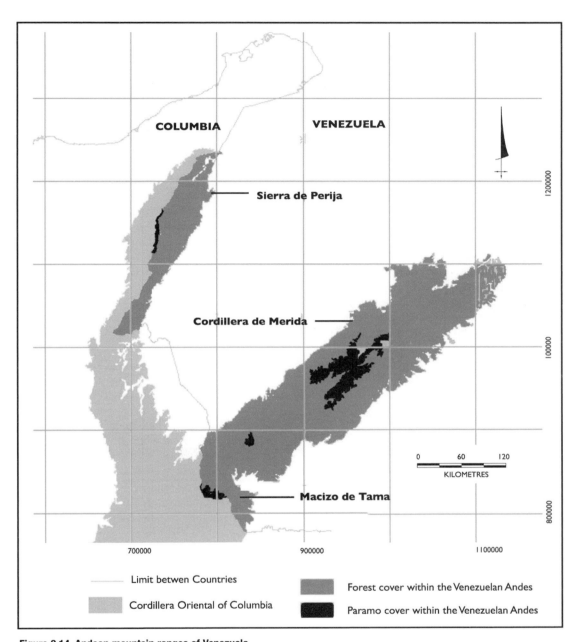

Figure 8.14 Andean mountain ranges of Venezuela

first Andean national park (Sierra Nevada National Park) was established in 1952. Democracy was established in 1958, and the continuity of such policies led to the subsequent designation of Yacambú and Terepaima National Parks. By 1983, a land-use planning law (Ley Orgánica para la Ordenación del Territorio) came into force, thus making national parks key instruments in the national land-use policy. A systemic vision of protected areas was adopted. Within this vision, protection of watersheds for hydroelectric and irrigation projects, for urban supply and for

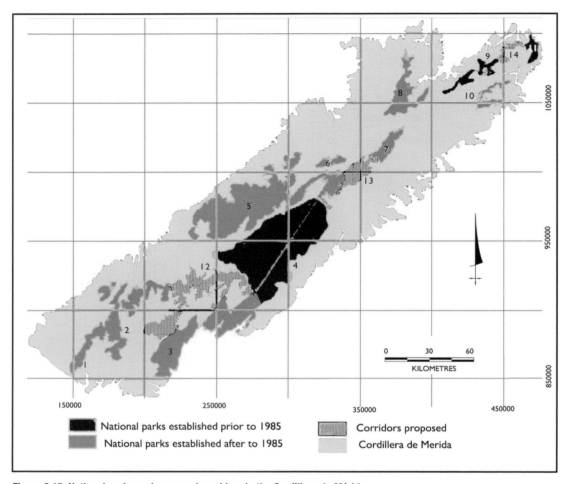

Figure 8.15 National parks and proposed corridors in the Cordillera de Mérida

tourism and cultural values, as well as protection of biodiversity, became objectives for a developing national system of protected areas. A step toward this system was taken in the Andes, incorporating connectivity conservation as a way to improve the viability of endangered biodiversity within protected areas. The new sciences of conservation biology and geography were thus incorporated in practice in protected areas planning.

Conservation concerns shifted from those of the elite in the 1950s, to a more general and widespread public interest in modern Venezuelan society. Nevertheless, political decisions regarding land use and conservation generally had not been taken in a participatory manner. This does not

mean that such decisions were not socially accepted; the general perception is that they were generally accepted as positive. This is understandable given that the urban population is a vast majority (around 80 per cent) in Venezuela and that urban sprawl has been a non-stop process since the 1930s. Most decisions regarding the allocation of areas for conservation purposes were taken via a top down approach, where politicians, scientists and technicians proposed and took actions with little participation of the general public or directly affected local people and communities. This was the process until 1987. That year, a general ruling on national parks policies, deriving from the 1982 Land Use Planning

Law, established participation mechanisms involving local people affected by protected areas designation and management. The outcome was the alleviation of conflicts with communities (Reyes and López, 1995) and the proposal and implementation of new protected areas. The technical boom in protected areas planning came to an end by 1993/1994, when a new administration came to power. A political shift towards one not favouring protected areas policies turned into institutional instability and the near collapse of the Venezuelan National Park Service and the Environment Ministry itself. This new paradigm has deepened since then, which has prompted reactions from non-governmental entities, organized citizens and universities, trying to overturn that political tendency. Although not having yet enough political power, these actors are now pushing to continue the planning and implementation of an interconnected system of protected areas in the Venezuelan Andes, now with a bottom-up approach.

The connectivity conservation initiative

By 1986, it was clear to park planners at the Venezuelan National Park Service that effective biodiversity conservation in the Venezuelan Andes could not be achieved within only a medium-sized park and a couple of small, isolated parks at the extreme of the cordillera (see 4, 9 and 11, Figure 8.15). On the other hand, several hydropower and irrigation projects already under construction or expansion were jeopardized since their upper watersheds were not properly protected. It was also acknowledged that Páramo ecosystems are essential to provide water to irrigation systems that fuel Andean agriculture and to the adjacent lowland. International and national tourism had become an important economic activity, mainly attracted by Andean natural landscapes. It was then evident for planners that conserving Andean natural or wilderness areas, based on a connectivity conservation scheme, could integrate watershed, landscape and biodiversity approaches, to achieve land-use planning, conservation and economy goals (Yerena, 1994). This required a vision of an interlinked protected areas system (Figure 8.16).

It was also clear that biological criteria should be incorporated to encompass all of the above objectives (Yerena and Torres, 1994). One approach was to plan for the needs of a species or biological group that was dependent on large-scale landscapes, where such planning also could benefit most of the biodiversity: an umbrella species approach. Such a species, with a large home range, low density and moving all along the cordillera and up and down its altitudinal gradient, could be

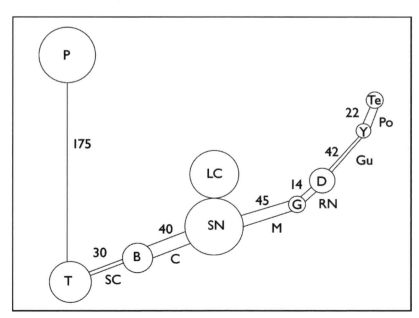

Figure 8.16 Schematic representation of the interconnected protected areas system for the Venezuelan Andes as envisaged by Yerena (1988)

Notes: Circle sizes represent system nuclei and are in proportion to areas sizes. Bars represent corridors and are proportional to width and distance. Numbers refer to distance in Km. Letters refer to areas in Figure 8.15 as follows: Te = Terepaima (11); Po = Terepaima–Yacambú Corridor (14); Y = Yacambu (9); Gu = Guache (10); D = Dinira (8); RN = Guache–Yacambú Corridor; G = Guaramacal (7); M = Ramal de Calderas Corridor (13) and Guirigay (6); SN = Sierra Nevada (4); LC = Sierra de La Culata (5); C = Tapo Caparo (3) and Pueblos del Sur Corridor (12); B = Páramos del Batallón y La Negra (2); SC = Chorro El Indio (1)

useful for such a purpose. The Andean bear (*Tremarctos ornatus*), the largest mammal of the tropical Andean ecosystems and a bear endemic to South American Andes, was an ideal candidate for this approach. Extensive fieldwork was conducted to determine its real distribution and to understand the basics of its natural history. Its distribution proved to match that of remnant natural and wilderness areas (Yerena and Torres, 1994).

A key moment in the planning process occurred when it became evident that the largest of the existing parks (Sierra Nevada National Park) was not big enough to maintain a viable bear population. If a protected areas system is to serve such a species, then connectivity conservation between protected core habitats should be sought. That is why a map of all natural and wilderness areas was needed in order to identify those areas that could be cores of the system, and those serving as connectors or corridors between them. This made evident that Sierra Nevada National Park and the adjoining Sierra de La Culata National Park were the only large core areas for inclusion in such a system, even through they alone would be insufficient to sustain a viable bear population. Every intact landscape radiating from this nucleus was needed in order to conserve enough habitat for the species. Such branches spatially matched upper watersheds, which were key to hydropower and irrigation systems such as Uribante-Caparo, Santo Domingo, Bocono-Masparro and Yacambú (see 2, 12, 3, 4, 6, 13, 7 and 9 in Figure 8.15). This meant that not only the cores, but also the corridors were necessary, and that only a whole interlinked system could contribute to sustain a viable Andean bear population. Within this vision, corridors were needed not only as dispersal media but also as habitat itself. Therefore, corridors and cores (except the large Sierra Nevada National Park and Sierra de La Culata National Park cores) might be performing the same function. More than a system of cores interlinked by corridors, it could be conceived of as a chain of small- and medium-sized cores, adjacent one to another, including some bottlenecks where corridors may be the only means of dispersal. Within this framework was applied an 'include as much natural areas as

you can' policy, giving priority to corridors containing bear habitat.

Two types of corridors were considered: habitat corridors and dispersal corridors. By habitat corridors, we refer to those that can provide habitat continuity, in different widths, between two already existing protected core areas. By dispersal corridors, we refer to areas that do not provide continuity since they are visibly impacted (mainly by agriculture) but that could provide ways of dispersal for bears, to move from one habitat patch to another. Habitat corridors require protection management in order to prevent habitat loss. Protection to the standards of IUCN Categories II or III is appropriate for such corridors. They might be designated with new names (such as Guirigay, see Table 8.3) or as extensions of already existing protected areas (such as Yacambú–Terepaima corridor, see Table 8.3). Category I does not exist in Venezuelan legislation. Dispersal corridors require management in order to restore habitat in key points and not to allow for additional habitat loss. IUCN categories IV or V better allow for this kind of management. They may contain coffee plantations, within a matrix of forest and agriculture patches (such as Yacambú–Guache corridor, see Table 8.3).

Habitat corridors are used frequently, seasonally or year round, by bears. They also might include areas with potential habitat despite the fact that there is no conclusive evidence of bears actually using the area. Secondary growth vegetation with no current human activity could be included as well as high risk areas for human settlement, such as those with very steep slopes or landslide risk. The key criteria here is the existence of vegetation continuity – allowing the possibility of small gaps of a few hundred metres – without human activity, linking existing protected areas. The width of such vegetation corridors may be variable; however, the wider they are the better.

From a management planning perspective, the whole of the interconnected system was envisaged as part of the national parks system. Alternatives were considered, such as a mix of different management categories; for instance, IUCN categories II (national park) and III (natural monument) as core areas plus IV (wildlife reserve) or V (special protective zone) as corridors. This option was kept open, but the government agency in charge of wildlife management showed little interest in designating areas within the Andes. Its priorities were focused on lowland wetlands. Also, Venezuelan legislation did not allow regional or local governments, or private agencies, to designate or manage protected areas. Because of this, and given the urgency to take advantage of the political opportunities, the Venezuelan National Park Service decided to incorporate every possible area suitable for the system into the national park system. This resulted in criticism, but proved to be strategically positive since many key areas for the system were incorporated in a timely fashion. Nevertheless there are some corridors within the system that do not contain mature habitat, and would be better managed under a category V or VI scheme. An updated synopsis of the system is presented in Table 8.3.

Given this, the next step was to find out and promote initiatives to conserve areas that were needed to form the system. Surprisingly, it was found that several petitions to protect areas coming from local concerned citizens and NGOs were on the desk of the Environment Ministry (see 1, 2, 5, 6, 7, 8 and 10 in Figure 8.15), and they matched some of those areas detected by the Venezuelan National Park Service as required to be part of the system. In an unorthodox initiative, the Venezuelan National Park Service made contact with such groups and started to provide technical and political support to them so they could reach high political decision levels, both formally and informally. This effort yielded the first good results when Guaramacal National Park was officially designated in 1988. From then on, a chain reaction was unleashed, which led to the designation of seven new national parks (see 1, 2, 3, 5, 6, 8 and 10 in Figure 8.15) and the expansion of one existing one (Yacambú National Park). A major achievement within this process was the designation of Sierra de La Culata National Park, which integrates the main core of the system by matching its physical and legal boundary with that of Sierra Nevada National Park (through a Páramo bridge, the only natural linkage between them).

Sustainable institutions and organizations are essential for the viability of such a system. This includes protected areas themselves, as well as government and citizens' organizations. In times of political instability, institutions become weak and unable to attend to their missions. A key turning point was year 1994, when a new administration was inaugurated. There is a general perception that conservation and land-use planning institutions were stronger before that year, and from then on significant erosion began. The 1994 to 1999 administration was focused on orthodox development policies, considering conservation and particularly protected areas to be antagonistic to such goal. Throughout 1999 to 2006, this administration deepened such focus, incorporating a de facto policy that led to de-gazetting protected areas by allowing colonization and extractive uses within them. This situation unfolded within a so-called revolutionary process, where legislation established prior to 1999 was considered inappropriate. This was in sharp contrast to the new 1999 Constitution, which elevated protected areas to the apex of the constitutional hierarchy, granting them the highest political protection. The *in situ* management practices and the constitutional mandates clearly showed opposite directions.

Connectivity conservation management

Establishing such a system takes more than a single decision taken at a particular time. Whether undertaken by institutions or individuals, promoting a system of interconnected protected areas requires a special leadership, with a strong long-term commitment. In our study case the Venezuelan National Park Service took the lead for a significant period, as did individuals linked to universities and NGOs. After the Venezuelan National Park Service was no longer capable of doing so, individuals helped by NGOs kept the idea alive and continued pursuing its accomplishment.

Two kinds of leadership might be identified: visionary leadership and implementation leadership. Individuals with little influence on decision-making levels might find it useful to take the lead on the vision, moving public opinion and grass roots organizations, while institutions or organizations linked to political levels might do better at implementing the system (designation and management). Respected scientists, planners

Table 8.3 Current units of the Cordillera de Mérida's protected area interconnected system

Unit/number (see Figure 8.15)	Size (km²)	Type of connectivity	IUCN category (existing or proposed*)	Current status (designation year)	Management viability
Terepaima[11]	187	Habitat corridor	II	Designated (1976)	Good
Terepaima–Yacambú Corridor[14]	150	Habitat corridor	II*	Designed and proposed as extension of Terepaima	Good
Yacambu[9]	296	Habitat corridor	II	Designated (1962)	Good
Guache–Yacambú Corridor	86	Dispersal corridor	V	Designed and partially designated	Fair
Guache[10]	122	Habitat corridor	II	Designated (1992)	Fair
Yacambu–Dinira Corridor	29	Dispersal corridor	V*	To be assessed	Poor
Dinira[8]	420	Habitat corridor	II	Designated (1988)	Good
Dinira–Guaramacal Corridor	14	Dispersal corridor	V*	To be assessed	Poor
Guaramacal[7]	215	Habitat corridor	II	Designated (1988)	Good
Ramal de Calderas Corridor[13]	412	Habitat corridor	II*	Designed but update needed	Good
Guirigay[6]	190	Habitat corridor	III	Designated (1996)	Good
Sierra de La Culata[5]	2004	Habitat corridor	II	Designated (1989)	Good
Sierra Nevada[4]	2764	Habitat corridor	II	Designated (1952)	Good
Guirigay–Sierra Nevada Corridor	22		III* or V*	Designed but update needed	Poor
Tapo Caparo[3]	2050	Habitat corridor	II	Designated (1993)	Fair
Pueblos del Sur Corridor[12]	950	Habitat corridor	II*	Designed but update needed	Fair
Páramos del Batallón y La Negra[2]	925	Habitat corridor	II	Designated (1989)	Good
Chorro El Indio[1]	64	Habitat corridor	II	Designated (1989)	Good

Sources: Yerena, 1994; Medina, 2006

and promoters linked to universities and NGOs have been good at the first kind of leadership, promoting the concept and giving focus to the effort. Implementation requires the adoption of policies by political institutions. This might be difficult, depending on the big picture political framework.

Once leadership to promote the vision has been effective, it might trigger the social actors necessary for implementation. NGOs linked to environment and rural social development, as well as grass roots organizations, are some of the key actors at this stage. When they exert pressure on local and regional governments, and on water management agencies, the process to activate the top decision level may be quite effective. Such an interlinked system must, at a minimum, be based on geographical representation. A strategic plan for its configuration and implementation will ensure the best possible outcomes. This should be the result of an interdisciplinary approach, with an emphasis on social, political and biological inputs. A ranking of the areas to be incorporated into the system, from political and geographical perspectives, is helpful.

The implementation of such a system may be perceived by some as extremely difficult. A key strategy is to promote critical public support for the idea. This requires committed leadership and a force of convinced supporters. Many participants might be more motivated by finding a solution to their local problem by means of a local conservation management plan, rather than in the success of a larger interlinked system. The bigger picture is of more interest to environmental NGOs and universities. By building upon multiple local interests, it is possible to accomplish the larger goal. It is also important that each supporting actor, whether a grass roots organization, a local NGO or a regional government, expresses its support formally and publicly. Also very important is the support of local and regional political leaders, particularly those sympathetic to green political ideas, especially when they are democratically elected. They may be good catalysts to precipitate support at higher government levels. At least one important regional political leader per state is needed. Vision leadership should focus on these actors.

Community or grass roots organizations may easily be convinced of the real benefits of protected areas functioning as corridors, especially by focusing on enhanced water quality. It is important to provide local actors with advice and tools to understand the concept and to exert more efficiently their pressure on appropriate decision levels, and also to make them take actions to protect those areas themselves. This means they need to know how to use appropriate legal mechanisms and procedures so they can activate the protection of such areas in their own interest. As well, they need to know how to make their current social and economic activities sustainable. Fostering local efforts that effectively demand action from authorities and help to switch their own activities towards sustainable uses are major strategies for successful implementation. It is necessary to include within the effort at least one grass roots organization per watershed.

Umbrella species used as flagship species are essential to marketing an interlinked connectivity conservation system – flagship species are those having a particular public appeal that helps to rally support for a conservation goal. Target audiences for outreach efforts are the general public, politicians and planners working at all levels and government agencies related to environment, land use and water management. Through the flagship species, emphasis must be put on the social benefits to be derived from the interlinked system. Water production and protection is the essential environmental service provided by the interlinked system required by the flagship species. In this case, maintaining natural landscapes as a resource for tourism activities proved to be another successful argument. The conservation of expensive and strategic hydroelectric dams and infrastructure by means of minimizing erosion levels within the watersheds was an effective argument at higher political levels.

A flagship species is essential to get the attention and support from urban audiences, the vast majority of the country in this case. The Andean bear was an excellent umbrella/flagship. To achieve this, mass media need to be provided with good information, always promoting the link between the needs of bears and social benefits. The corridor concept itself is a key message. It is a very appealing and intuitive concept easily understood by many people and attractive to journalists and reporters, as well as to grass roots organizations. Therefore it deserves to be explained and given thorough publicity.

Going door to door to promote the concept of connectivity conservation is particularly efficient in rural communities, while using mass media is efficient for urban audiences, by means of special reports, particularly targeted to cities in the Andean region. Person to person interaction is particularly effective with politicians, and is even better if accompanied by visits and meetings with grass roots leaders and organizations that may build bridges among them.

Scientists are needed as conceptual leaders, but most of them may not feel comfortable doing public, decision-maker and media outreach. However, gathering data that helps to define or redefine the geographical configuration of the system and its functioning, as well as the implementation strategy, are roles they can play. Updated land-cover and vegetation maps in detailed scale, temporal changes and evolution of socio-economic variables are critical data that can be provided by these experts.

In this case, drastic shifts in government policies regarding protected areas have been a major setback for the implementation of the conservation system. We believe such changes come from major factors affecting political stability, including sociological tendencies favouring populism and authoritarianism. These are issues more dependent on the modernization and social evolution of nations. It is foreseeable that such tendencies may fade away in the medium and long term. Within this scenario, the key issue is to keep the corridors idea alive through leadership. This can be done by strengthening institutions and organizations and individuals within them. We believe this approach is essential, since land-use patterns and major development projects can be modified in order to fit with the connectivity conservation concept as long as there are the right individuals and institutions involved in land-use and protected areas planning and policy implementation. While there are no positive advances towards the implementation of the system, the leadership has to be reinforced. Monitoring the proposed geographical configuration of the interconnected system, finding better data to support planning and assessing the management effectiveness of already protected areas are important tasks that must be undertaken.

From an overall perspective regarding this initiative, we believe that despite the political setbacks, the concept has been kept alive, and small but significant advances have been achieved since 1994.

Benefits and accomplishments

The benefits from this interconnected system are summarized in Table 8.4. The most obvious of these come from watershed protection. Protected areas always contribute to sound water management, but the geographical configuration of an interconnected protected areas system where connectivity is essential makes it possible to

provide such benefit to virtually all human communities living on the foothills, mid-slopes and adjacent lowlands of the cordillera. Five out of 40 major rivers born in the cordillera generate 918 million m^3 of water/year; and a larger potential exists. Four major cities in the region having a combined population of more than 1.2 million people are direct beneficiaries of the water protection gains from a protected areas system and three major hydroelectric facilities with a potential productivity of 5760 gigawatt hours (Maraven, 1991, 1993) are fed by watersheds protected under the interconnected protected areas system and have their infrastructure protected from sedimentation and erosion. This is enough to provide electricity to five million people. Seven large dams fed by the system provide irrigation to the best agricultural land in western Venezuela. The interconnected protected areas system assures the basis for a sustainable economy.

Lessons learned

The nature of landownership is a key factor

Land in the Venezuelan Andes is divided into small parcels owned by individual families. Applying conservation connectivity tools and policies in such circumstances was extremely challenging. At the same time, large areas of land had been managed with great restrictions on land uses, preserving the opportunity for conservation management.

Political support is essential

As the Venezuelan national government shifted from a democratic to a repressive regime in the 1990s, support for progress toward a national parks network disappeared. This caused the near collapse of bureaucratic mechanisms and systems that were focused on park establishment and management.

Popular support also is necessary

The objectives of the interconnected system may also match those related to major social needs, providing a concept to unify different interests. The connectivity conservation concept is appealing to ordinary people, and if properly marketed it can be accepted by most social actors. A charismatic umbrella species, used also as flagship species

Table 8.4 Some of the major benefits of specific units of the interconnected protected area system

Unit/number (see Figure 8.15)	Water for urban consumption	Water for hydroelectric power plants	Water for major irrigation systems	Landscape within current tourism areas
Terepaima[11]	•		•	
Terepaima–Yacambú corridor[14]	•		•	•
Yacambu[9]	•		•	•
Guache–Yacambú corridor	•		•	
Guache[10]	•		•	
Yacambu–Dinira corridor			•	
Dinira[8]			•	•
Dinira–Guaramacal corridor				•
Guaramacal[7]	•	•	•	•
Ramal de Calderas corridor[13]		•	•	•
Guirigay[6]			•	•
Sierra de La Culata[5]	•	•	•	•
Sierra Nevada[4]		•	•	•
Guirigay–Sierra Nevada corridor		•		•
Tapo Caparo[3]		•		
Pueblos del Sur corridor[12]		•	•	•
Páramos del Batallón y La Negra[2]	•	•	•	•
Chorro El Indio[1]	•			•

Source: Updated from Yerena, 1988

may provide strength to biodiversity conservation objectives, as well as to public support.

Cores and corridors often are indistinguishable

Sometimes a given piece of landscape must act both as core habitat and a connecting corridor. In this case, the core national parks in the system were of insufficient size to support a viable Andean bear population. Only an interlinked and appropriately managed system of cores and corridors would provide enough habitat to ensure the survival of a healthy population. Within this vision, corridors were needed as dispersal pathways and also as habitat itself. Therefore, corridors and cores might be performing the same function.

Protected core areas are a prerequisite to connectivity conservation

In Venezuela, the creation of protected areas in this landscape had started decades ago. Three national parks in the cordillera provided the anchors of a larger vision for landscape connectivity.

Umbrella species can help plan for an effective conservation network

Some species have such a wide range of life needs that providing enough secure habitat for their long-term survival will also protect a large number of other species. In such a fashion, planning for the conservation of these focal species acts as an umbrella that shelters many other elements of biodiversity in the system. In this case, the Andean bear provided an excellent planning tool. Research demonstrated that its distribution matched that of remnant natural and wilderness areas in the cordillera.

Long-term commitment is necessary for success

It is feasible to bring such a system into reality but it requires long-term leadership and commitment, mainly from proactive individuals and institutions. Its implementation has to be understood as a process, where grass roots organizations are primary key actors. A major obstacle may come from weak governmental institutions and policies. Strengthening such organizations and individuals working within them is essential. In this case, an unusual partnership between the government agency, the National Park Service and NGOs helped to convince politicians to create new national parks. Government decisions to formally incorporate areas into the system may need to be based upon data with some degree of uncertainty. The precautionary principle fully applies here.

Biodiversity, social and economic rationales can support connectivity conservation

The impetus to craft a vision for connected landscapes between the protected areas in the cordillera arose from a confluence of factors. The protection of watersheds was necessary for the successful management and operation of new hydroelectric power installations. Downstream irrigators and farmers also were dependent upon water catchment areas in the Páramo ecosystems to fuel Andean agriculture and to supply the adjacent lowland. International and national tourism had become an important economic activity, mainly attracted by Andean natural landscapes. It was then evident for planners that conserving Andean natural or wilderness areas, based on an interconnection scheme, could integrate watershed, landscape and biodiversity approaches, to achieve land-use planning, conservation and economy goals. This required a vision of an interlinked protected areas system.

9

Palaearctic Connectivity Initiatives

The Palaearctic is the largest biogeographical realm, and includes Europe, Asia north of the Himalaya, northern Africa, and the northern and central parts of the Arabian Peninsula. There are many mountain ranges, with the Himalayan Mountains forming the boundary between the Palaearctic and Indomalayan realms. The Caucasus Mountains, which run between the Black Sea and the Caspian Sea, incorporate important temperate forests. The Palaearctic contains significant freshwater areas, including the rivers of Europe and Russia that flow into the Arctic, Baltic, Black and Caspian seas, and Siberia's Lake Baikal, the oldest and deepest lake on Earth. The Palaearctic includes many protected areas, and 0.72 per cent of its area has been inscribed as world heritage. This chapter presents six connectivity conservation case studies from the Palaearctic.

Pasterze Glacier, near Heilingenblut, Hohe Tahern National Park, Austria

Source: Graeme L. Worboys

Altai Mountain Knot: Between conservation and development[1]

Yuri P. Badenkov

Setting

The Altai is a mountainous region located in the core of the Eurasian continent. It includes the highest mountain of the region (Mt Belukha, 4506m) and a vast glaciated area. The region is identified as one of World Wildlife Fund's 200 major world ecoregions (Altai-Sayan), which is of crucial importance for understanding the history of Asian ecosystems during the Holocene era. Run-off from the Altai Mountains endows two of the major Asian rivers: the Ob and the Irtysh. In 1998, UNESCO acknowledged the global significance of the region by including three Altai clusters in the world natural heritage list.

This small landscape of about 15,000ha is located at the junction of the borders of four countries: Kazakhstan, China, Mongolia and Russia, and forms the so-called Altai Knot (Figure 9.1). Before the demise of the USSR in 1991, large herds totalling over 500,000 animals (primarily sheep and goats) were shepherded across this territory from Mongolia through the Ukok Upland Plateau, which is a world heritage site, to slaughtering and meat processing plants in eastern Kazakhstan. Currently, the border between Mongolia and Kazakhstan is interrupted by 67km of Russian territory (the Altai Republic), and this channel of economic and cultural connection has been lost.

Altai is a crossroads of the world's major cultures and religions: Buddhism, Islam, Christianity (Orthodox) and Shamanism. Followers of Russian theosophist and artist Nikolas Roerich believe that the Altai Mountains shelter the mystical Shambala – sacred Buddhist country. Altai is world renowned for its archaeological findings made in the last half of the 20th century and especially in the early 1990s: human mummies 2000–2500 years old with well-preserved fragments of skin and tattoos were discovered in permafrost layers in burial mounds on the Ukok Plateau. Pieces of silk cloth and other artefacts found there and in other burial mounds in the Altai point to the existence of active cultural and humanitarian connections in the region since ancient times. Frozen tombs have been located in a broad area in the Altai (in all four countries).

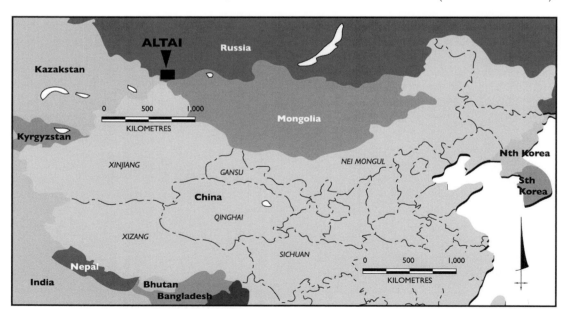

Figure 9.1 The Altai Knot in the core of Eurasia

---

1   This case study derives from material published by the author in Harmon and Worboys (2004).

This phenomenon has made the region very attractive for protection and conservation.

In light of potential climate change impacts, there is a great risk of loss of these semi-artificial human-nature memorials. A number of Russian and foreign scholars and NGOs have proposed to nominate these archaeological sites to the UNESCO world heritage site culture list. If this is successful, it would be the first mixed 'nature-culture' site in Russia.

The population of the Altai frontier regions is mostly represented by indigenous ethnic minorities of semi-nomadic stockbreeders: Kazakhs, Altais (Telenghets), Tuvins, Dyurbets and Uygurs. Some regions of Russia, Kazakhstan and China have a Russian population, which migrated here in the early and middle 19th century in search of the legendary 'belovodye' (white waters) – an area of abundant land and woods, with rivers full of fish, and a life of happiness and honesty. The immigrants – 'starovers' ('old believers') – held onto traditional orthodox beliefs and were persecuted in their motherlands. In Altai, their settlement areas were always associated with mountain-forest ecosystems (for example, the Ust-Koksa district).

Throughout the Altai region, the most pressing issues are those peculiar to the majority of the world's mountainous regions: poverty, unemployment and out-migration. Many settlements and cabins have no electricity or communication facilities; in winter they are cut off from the rest of the world. It is generally true that mountain frontier regions are 'twice marginalized': they exist in a marginal location at the periphery of their political states (save for Kazakhstan) and are socially and economically marginal, being the poorest among other regions.

At the same time, frontier regions have high biological, ecosystem and ethno-cultural diversity. The Altai region still has many rare species, such as the snow leopard (*Uncia uncia*). The latter makes these regions attractive for numerous environmental initiatives and for the development of ecotourism. The challenge is to integrate regional economic and social development projects with the conservation of biological diversity.

In 1996, China announced an ambitious development project for the East-Central Asian Economic Zone, incorporating China's Xinjiang-Uygur autonomous region, regions of western Siberia (Russia), eastern Kazakhstan and north-western Mongolia. According to the expectations of Chinese scientists, in mid-21st century this Asian region will represent a world centre of economic activity and development. The proposed transportation corridor – called 'the great Eurasian bridge' – will represent the spine of this region. This rail line will connect to the Trans-Siberian Railway in the north to the Silk Road in its new railway embodiment.

In 2006, the Russian president, implementing his energy security doctrine during his visit to China, announced a proposed Altai gas pipeline by Gazprom (the Russian national energy company) and the Chinese oil company to transport gas from western Siberia to Xinjiang, China. Considering that the border in the Altai between Russia and China is only 56km long with only two passes available for a pipeline crossing, there is a real threat of disturbance to the Ukok Plateau, one of three clusters of the Golden Mountains of Altai UNESCO world heritage site. Proposed initiatives for the future transportation corridor will traverse the transborder remote highlands of the Central Altai and will significantly change the life of local people, as well as local and regional environments and biodiversity.

In general, the Altai-Sayan ecoregion is located at the intersection of the Central Asian and Siberian faunal provinces. The foothill steppes in the northern part of the region differ little from the steppes of western Siberia and Kazakhstan. Among the dominant animals are small rodents such as ground squirrels, hamsters and field voles. Hares and badgers are also found. Typical taiga inhabitants such as brown bear (*Ursus arctos arctos*), wolverine (*Gulo gulo*), lynx (*Lynx lynx*), sable (*Martes zibellina*) and chipmunk (*Tamias sibiricus*) are widely represented in the mountain forests. There are also typical eastern Siberia species such as musk deer (*Moschus moschiferus*), Siberian maral deer (*Cervus canadensis sibiricus*) and big forest mouse (*Apodemus sylvaticus*). Almost 300 bird species have been observed in this region, the most common of which are the wood grouse (*Tetrao urogallus*), hazel grouse (*Bonasa bonasia*), black grouse (*Tetrao tetrix*), northern hawk owl

(*Surnia ulula*), Tengmalm owl (*Aegolius funereus*), Eurasian three-toed woodpecker (*Picoides tridactylus*) and crossbill (*Loxia curvirostra*).

In the very peculiar Uvs Nuur Hollow (or Depression), surrounded by high mountains, both the Central Asian and Siberian species can be observed. For example, sable (*Martes zibellina*), squirrel (*Eutamius sibiricus*) and elk (*Cervus canadiensis sibiricus*) inhabit the mountain taiga, while Dzeren antelope (*Procapra gutturosa*), tolai hare (*Lepus tolai*) and the long-eared hedgehog (*Hemiechinus auritus*) inhabit the steppe zone representing the species of the Mongolian semi-deserts. The rivers of the hollow are inhabited by central Asian fish species such as osman (*Diptychus dybowskii*) and thick-lipped mullet (*Chelon labrosus*).

Mountain goat (*Capra sibirica*), argali mountain sheep (*Ovis ammon ammon*) and the snow leopard represent the alpine fauna. The two latter species can be considered special symbols of the Altai-Sayan ecoregion, as the world community has regarded them as two of the most charismatic species for global biodiversity conservation. The snow leopard (also called 'irbis', the Mongolian word for snow) is the only large wild cat in the world that lives in high mountains. Occupying the

highest trophic level in the high mountain ecosystem, irbis represents the most significant species in the entire ecoregion. However, at the same time, the snow leopard also is one of the rarest and most vulnerable species of the Altai-Sayan mountain region. The total area of potential habitat for the snow leopard constitutes approximately 6,000,000ha. The total number of irbis in Russia is estimated to be between 150 and 200 cats (Kokorin, 2001). In Mongolia, data on the total number of snow leopards varies from several hundred to as many 4000.

Although the network of protected areas in the Altai-Sayan ecoregion is well developed (Figure 9.2), only a small portion of the irbis habitat is covered. In Russia only six to seven per cent of potential irbis habitat is located within the boundaries of nature reserves. In the Altai that rises to around 11 per cent. In Mongolia, the situation is the same: 19 protected areas cover no more than 20 per cent of the snow leopard's habitat. The problem is even more aggravated by the illegal export of leopard bones to China, where they are used in traditional medicine. Unfortunately, habitat expansion is especially unlikely due to the climate change impacts of forest

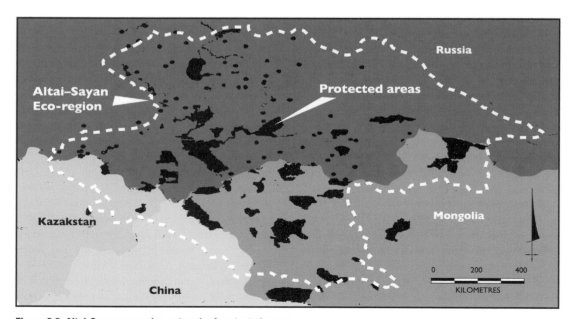

Figure 9.2 Altai-Sayan ecoregion network of protected areas

expansion and an increase in winter precipitation. Thus, conservation management especially is needed for high mountain populations in snow-less slopes.

The connectivity conservation initiative

As recommended in the Irbis Conservation Strategy developed by World Wildlife Fund, a new Katunskiy Biosphere Reserve as well as a trans-boundary (with Mongolia) Sailugemskiy Biosphere Reserve could help to increase the connectivity between these disparate protected areas.

In 1998, the International Conference *Strategic Considerations on the Development of Central Asia* held in Urumqi, Xinjiang, passed the Altai Declaration (Protocol of Intentions). It proposed transboundary cooperation in the area of biodiversity conservation and sustainable development. In addition, the Conference proposed to initiate the development of a legal act in the form of an Altai Convention on Regional Cooperation. The initiatives included the proposed creation of a transboundary biosphere territory 'Altai', comprising the frontier territories of four countries

and the protected territories within them. It is expected that this arrangement will meet the principles of the Seville strategy for UNESCO's biosphere reserves. The key objective in creating such an international structure is the establishment of legal and institutional mechanisms integrating the interests of various stakeholders in the conservation of biological diversity and in economic and regional development.

Under the United Nations Development Programme/Global Environment Facility Altai-Sayan (B) project, the concept of transboundary protected areas in this region was analysed and developed. Nine key areas were proposed and ranked for inclusion in the next full phase of UNDP/GEF project implementation in 2006–2009 (Figure 9.3).

The feasibility study for a transboundary biosphere territory in the Altai Mountains was realized in 2003–2005 with the sponsorship of Germany (German Federal Ministry of Cooperation and Development) in partnership with the Russian Academy (Siberian branch) and the governments of Kazakhstan and Mongolia. The key approach used in this project was

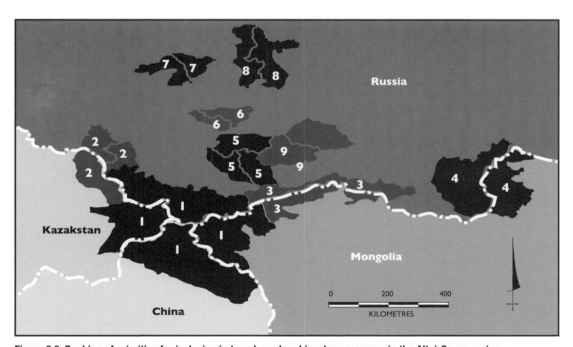

Figure 9.3 Ranking of priorities for inclusion in transboundary biosphere reserves in the Altai-Sayan region

reconciling development and conservation by delineating a future biosphere reserve under the UNESCO Man and the Biosphere (MAB) banner. The impact of the proposed Siberia–China linear transportation route on the world heritage site Ukok Plateau was not assessed in depth due to a lack of baseline information that continues to the present day.

In 2005, a proposal was initiated to create a transboundary biosphere reserve between Russia (Katunskiy Biosphere Reserve) and Kazakhstan (Katon-Karagai National Park). The Ministry of Natural Resources of the Russian Federation and the Russian MAB Committee supported this initiative. The next practical steps in this direction need to be taken by Kazakhstan authorities and its national MAB Committee.

Connectivity conservation management

In a political context, connectivity issues in the Altai region can be seen in the activity of an inter-parliamentary association known as 'Altai our common home'. This innovative cultural initiative was created in 2000 by interested members of regional parliaments – Altai Province and the Altai Republic in Russia, eastern Kazakhstan Hakumat (parliament) in Kasakhstan, Hovd and Bayan-Olgy aimaqs (provinces) in western Mongolia and representatives of Xinjiang autonomous province in China. The association 'Altai our common home' plays a significant role in regional cooperation and development issues: most of all in economic and cultural exchange programmes – and less in conservation and ecological themes.

Lessons learned

The story of the creation of a transboundary biosphere reserve in Altai began more than ten years ago. Many studies have been done and events have occurred since then but there are no tangible results yet. One could say the soil has been prepared for cultivation rather well. What lessons could be learned? From the 'top-down' level, the process of international negotiations and consultations was not adequate to the scale and significance of proposed initiatives. Not all interested stakeholders and actors were involved in the process and representatives of state institutions,

particularly, were absent. At the 'grass roots' level, managers of transboundary protected areas were not involved in the process. The leading role was played by international NGOs and funders. Overall, the general concept was not clearly formulated or developed.

Overview of connectivity projects in the European Alps and adjacent mountains

Barbara Ehringhaus

Setting

The Alps stretch primarily in an east–west direction from western Switzerland to Vienna, Austria, and bend southwards roughly at their highest summit (4810m) to continue to the Mediterranean Sea between Nice, France and Genova, Italy. This mountain chain constitutes a huge barrier to north–south connectivity for both seasonal animal migrations as well as for human traffic between northern and Mediterranean regions. Westward, in the French Massif Central and Cevennes, lie various potential stepping stones for connectivity towards the Pyrénées. Further west, in Spain, stretches the Cantabrian cordillera. The Carpathian Mountains extend eastward of the Alps, separated only by the Danube valley. Similar in size and population numbers and almost of symmetrical shape, the Carpathians form a complementary arch to the Alpine arch, although considerably lower in elevation.

The Apennine mountain chain runs from north to south along the Italian peninsula and onto Sicily. It has close natural connectivity with the Alpine arch through the Ligurian Alps (now used again by wolves (*Canis lupus lupus*) in dispersal to the Alps). Other middle mountains complete the alpine outskirts: Jura, Vosges-Black Forest north-west of the Alps, the half-circle of Krknose (transfrontier National Park and Biosphere Reserve) and Giant Mountains link with the Carpathians, which in turn are linked to the entire Balkan Peninsula from Croatia to southern Greece. The Caucasus range stretches at the easternmost edge of Europe between the Black Sea and the Caspian Sea and is linked to mountains in Turkey and Iran.

The Alps have been inhabited and shaped into cultural landscapes for thousands of years with many similarities between countries and cultures (such as multi-functional agriculture and forestry, grazing and transhumance, exposure to high natural risks and labour-intensive work), but also with high diversity between their northern and southern side, between German-speaking and Romance language countries and between almost all valleys and slopes respectively. On the other hand, a high mobility between different altitudes and also across the highest mountain ridges for trade and summer pastures has promoted cooperation and solidarity. Collaborative campaigns against mega-projects like hydroelectric dams, tunnels and ski areas with their respective mass residences, perceived as attacks on the integrity of alpine landscapes, often paved the way for the promotion of larger interconnected protected areas in spite of political borders. Such was the case with the creation of Austria's Hohe Tauern National Park after 70 years of lobbying and land acquisition by conservationists. Resistance to a wave of new protected areas from the 1970s onwards has diminished, because alpine people now hope for alternatives to the agonizing mountain agriculture, the disappearance of industry in their valleys and to the skiing boom, which is declining visibly due to climate change.

Anthropogenic pressure from surrounding cities and populous European countries on the species rich and diverse but fragile ecosystem of the Alps has been increasing continuously over the last 50 years. The slowly growing number of protected areas has not been able to slow down significantly the resulting fragmentation and species loss. The majority of them have proved to be too small and covering the territory irregularly without sufficient representation of key features and without linkages between many of them. On the contrary, these protected areas mostly protect islands of unfertile altitudes (without the interspersed valleys), often created by arbitrarian politics rather than an integrated vision of dynamic ecological systems and processes. Nevertheless, brown bears (*Ursus arctos arctos*) and wolves have expanded their realm of migration across the Alps. Accelerated climate change demands all the more for protection of the remaining glaciers and of high-altitude habitats for highly specialized resident and migrating fauna and flora.

The regained peace, mobility and freedom after the fall of the Iron Curtain offered the opportunity to convert formerly inaccessible border territories and military sites into protected areas (for example, the GreenBelt project and the Carpathian Network of Protected Areas, discussed below). At the same time, modern infrastructure rapidly threatened to cut well preserved areas into pieces too small for biodiversity conservation.

After the break-up of the Hungro-Austrian monarchy in World War I and the long continuation of violent protest in southern Tyrolia against their forced attachment to Italy, this alpine region has now developed peaceful cooperation in conservation management with Austria on one hand and with other Italian provinces on the other as a model for protected area connectivity. Spain, and in particular Catalunya, hastened to make up for the lack of coherent conservation initiatives under Franco by protecting especially well its part of the Pyrénées (complementary to the French side) and its other mountain ranges (Figure 9.4).

The main threats to alpine connectivity come from transportation infrastructure, unsustainable tourism and declining mountain agriculture with its corollary of out-migration and loss of biodiversity (particularly in subalpine meadows). Transportation infrastructure, both the alpine resort traffic and the growing trans-European heavy truck traffic, increase fragmentation and air pollution. The goal of the Alpine Initiative for ten years has been to mobilize a majority of Swiss citizens against this threat and to promote other NGOs to take up this cause in other alpine and Pyrénéan countries. Climate change poses threats of more natural risks with unviability of ski resorts in lower altitudes. This leads to increased use of artificial snow with its respective consequences. In spite of visible climate change, too many ski resorts still invest in enlarging their terrain and most push for interconnections between them, even across nature reserves and fragile ecological terrain. Regarding mountain agriculture, farmers tend to abandon the work in the species-rich highland forests, pastures and meadows for easier

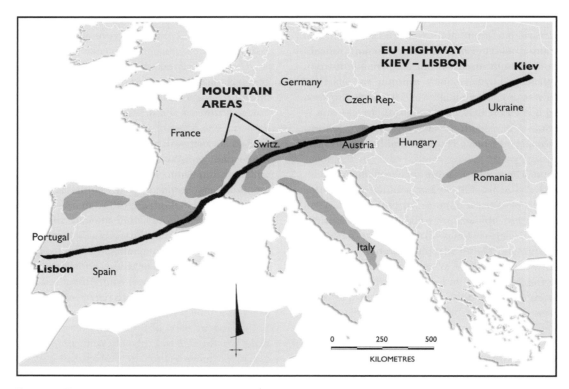

Figure 9.4 European mountains connectivity conservation initiatives

and better paid jobs in the plains. The unilateral support of industrialized agriculture by the European Union (EU) has increased this threat, even in neighbouring countries. Amenity migration is beginning to threaten conservation goals in some tourism hot spots like Chamonix and St. Moritz.

Connectivity conservation initiatives

While the Alpine biogeographic region includes the Carpathians and Pyrénées in addition to the Alps themselves, no overall vision has yet been publicly pronounced of a continental continuum from Cantabria (in north-west Spain and Portugal) to the Carpathians in eastern Europe (Cantabria to Carpathians), where large barriers of river valleys with heavy infrastructure will have to be overcome. Cantabria to the Carpathians form a predominantly east–west chain, although both the Carpathians and the Alps assume a north–south direction at their external ends, and

the link between the western Alps and the Pyrénées will run mainly diagonally through the French Massif Central and Cevennes.

Distinct from the wars and political fragmentation of the 20th century and before, since the 1950s Europe has evolved towards a broader vision of cooperation, complementarity and joint progress, such as the EU and its predecessors, the Council of Europe and the European Community (Council of Europe, 1996). Far from the hostile nations created in the 19th century, Europe now aims for greater power and influence through joint economic and political development, but also through becoming a model for environmental solutions, for transfrontier regional development and for the conservation of its diverse cultural landscapes. These different objectives often are in conflict; for example, the priority of long-distance transport and trade versus the conservation of biodiversity and connectivity of habitats.

One obvious region to protect from further threats of fragmentation and loss of species is the Alps, the highest mountain chain in the middle of densely populated Europe. However, the Commission Internationale pour la Protection des Alpes struggled for 40 years to secure in 1991 the signature of the eight alpine states (Austria, Slovenia, Italy, Germany, Switzerland, France, Liechtenstein and Monaco) and the EU to the Alpine Convention, and the ratification of some protocols is still ongoing. Nonetheless, the Convention has been legally binding since 2002, the International Year of the Mountains. The Convention is framed around eight thematic protocols intended to promote sustainable development in a clearly defined space of almost 200,000km^2 with a population of 14 million people. The protocol on Nature and Landscape Protection includes a commitment to create an ecological network, which remains high on the agenda until 2012.

As the first and most visible institution of the Alpine Convention, France and its partners created the Alpine Network of Protected Areas (AlpArc) in 1995, which encompasses all protected areas larger than 100ha within the Alps, almost 21 per cent of its territory. This network has strengthened the institutional, scientific and personal cooperation between those protected areas, especially among the dozens of bigger national parks, and promotes joint research, training and management programmes.

Under the Alpine Convention presidency of Germany in 2003/2004, it was charged to undertake an inventory of existing and potential ecological corridors with the goal of implementing an ecological network that would guarantee connectivity and halt the loss of biodiversity in the Alps. The study concentrates on eight model areas throughout the Alps using primarily the existing national parks as significant core areas to be enlarged towards adjacent habitats. In order to start implementing at least one of the model networks, the AlpArc has joined forces with Commision Internationale pour la Protection des Alpes, WWF (which produced a map of alpine hot spots of biodiversity) and the International Scientific Committee on Research in the Alps for further study and application on the ground with

the necessary political and financial support from the Alpine Convention, including the EU.

Despite these international agreements and institutions, so far no concrete decisions on implementing connectivity conservation have been made. This is due primarily to diffuse local fear of future development restrictions and also because of low engagement by states and the EU. There is a controversial discussion going on in most European countries about the rigorous restrictive use of national parks (especially in centralized states like France) and the intensive use and fragmentation throughout the rest of the landscape, which potentially might be worthy of better protection with the active involvement of the local authorities. Alpine protected areas enter into conflict especially with ski areas and their plans of interconnection, while they are scarcely usable in summer and constitute rather an asset for sustainable tourism.

The initiative to improve connectivity in the Alps needs to be seen in its wider geographical and political context. Both the Council of Europe, including almost all European states, and the EU, had been promoting ecological networks for decades. Examples are the PanEuropean Biological and Landscape Diversity Strategy, the subsequent Réseau Ecologique Paneuropéen and EEconet by the Council of Europe, and Natura 2000, a patchwork of protected areas that is intended to represent all typical habitats of the EU (based on its earlier directives on flora/fauna and birds). With the enlargement of the EU, especially after the fall of the Berlin Wall, these programmes have been extended through funding to the new central and east European countries. The GreenBelt project, for instance, is supposed to create a trans-European north–south ecological corridor along the former Iron Curtain, including several mountainous areas between northern Germany and the Balkans. The Carpathians, the mountain range east of the Alps and similar in shape, extension and population size, but much lower and with different socio-cultural and recent political context, gained special attention from the EU and the UN Development Programme for their high biological diversity and populations of brown bear, wolf and lynx. In analogy to the Alpine Convention, a Carpathian Convention was signed in 2003 by the seven Carpathian countries, five of which now belong to the EU. In close Alpine–Carpathian cooperation, a Carpathian Network of Protected Areas was created at the same time in order to stimulate cooperation among the members of that network as well as with those of its relative, AlpArc to share experience in managing, for example, large carnivores, sustainable tourism and staff exchange.

Mountain connectivity conservation links into the primarily mountainous Balkan countries, especially into the higher ranges of Bulgaria, are also being developed, including transfrontier protected areas between former socialist countries and EU–Greece, for instance. Three of the eight alpine signatories, namely Switzerland, Liechtenstein and Monaco, also are not yet EU members, which raises certain funding and technical problems. However, Switzerland has developed its own very detailed *réseau écologique national* (national ecological network) and its WWF Emerald ecological patchwork is analogous to Natura 2000.

UNESCO's World Heritage Centre has been encouraging alpine countries to collaborate on serial or clustered world heritage site nominations of unique global value across the Alps. This effort will fail so long as each country insists on separate proposals and no common criteria have been articulated. The existing and future natural and mixed world heritage sites will contribute significantly to alpine connectivity conservation.

Although within the same country and with many national and regional parks and nature reserves and although a Convention of the Appenines was signed in 2006, the envisaged great connectivity along the backbone of the Italian peninsula (*Appennino Parco d' Europa* or APE) still has not been implemented. But wolves have found their way through natural corridors up to the Alps and even to their central parts in recent years, which created an opportunity for enhanced learning and management cooperation between Appenine conservationists and their French and Swiss partners.

Besides large alpine mammals (ibex (*Capra ibex*), chamois (*Rupicapra rupicapra*), bear, wolf (*Canis lupus lupus*) and lynx (*Lynx lynx*), alpine connectivity also will benefit birds (such as capercaillie (*Tetrao urogallus*) and hazelhen (*Tetrastes bonasia*)) and flora. A bearded vulture (*Gypaetus barbatus*) reintroduction project successfully has been conducted from various centres in the Alps for 20 years and the royal eagle (*Aquilla chrysaetos*) is being monitored throughout the AlpArc network. Brown bears are most frequent in the Carpathians, and also occur in the Slovenian and Italian Alps as well as in the Cantabrian chain with only sporadic interconnection. Slovenian bears have been reintroduced to the Pyrénées, but there are no trans continental migration routes.

Maintenance of the alpine cultural landscape is crucial for the perception by residents and tourists alike. The mowing of alpine meadows has increased biodiversity and the mosaic of rock walls, forests, pastures and meadows is deliberately maintained by special funds for landscape gardening.

After years of parallel work and a certain green isolation, partnerships are now growing among conservation agencies, such as the joint efforts of the AlpArc, Commision Internationale pour la Protection des Alpes, WWF-Alpine programme and the International Scientific Committee on Research in the Alps to lobby the Alpine Convention states and the EU to implement corridors. But partnerships with administrators, business, local stakeholders and NGOs from outside the (small and often powerless) conservation community are still rare. Therefore, the Commision Internationale pour la Protection des Alpes and the Alpine Convention have created the Alliance des Alpes, a trans alpine network of mountain municipalities that pledge their commitment to sustainable development and to carry out specific projects toward that goal. The frequent exchange of their challenges and opportunities is appreciated by all members, who are as yet unevenly distributed (for example, there is none in France). In order to better involve the towns and their decision makers, the honourable title of the Alpine City of the Year has been conferred throughout the Arch.

A recent product of the Alpine Convention and the Commision Internationale pour la Protection des Alpes is the Via Alpina, a hiking trail from one end of the Alps to the other, which invites all stakeholders along several alternative routes to develop specific cultural, economic and environmental offerings wherever it passes by. The latest attempts to establish closer links with other stakeholders are the Commision Internationale pour la Protection des Alpes recent local initiatives of sustainable resource use and development projects in the Alps. Although it has signed the Alpine Convention and recently ratified some of its protocols (but not the crucial one about transport), the EU has not been a strong advocate for alpine conservation. However, it has been fostering transfrontier and inter-regional cooperation in general and in 2000 launched INTERREG III (a programme to stimulate inter-regional cooperation in the EU) specifically for the Alps. No major corridors have been implemented yet. International pressure seems to be a more effective force than lobbying by local scientists and protected area managers, or at least complementary to both.

Connectivity conservation management

Alpine protected area managers are now aware of their key role in a future ecological network and convinced of the importance of the best possible internal management of their respective parks. However, the political support of different levels of government for implementation of corridors is still weak or non-existent and times does not seem favourable for the creation of large new protected areas. That is perhaps why the proposed AlpArc enlargements and corridors are conspicuously modest in scope and rather pragmatically reaching out from existing parks without daring to embrace larger spaces including potential new areas. And perhaps smaller pilot cases of successful corridors will convince politicians of the need for and the benefits of larger connectivity. However, the objective of large-scale permeability in length and height must be kept in mind.

Conservation leadership has expanded from northern alpine countries towards the south. Thus the Commision Internationale pour la Protection des Alpes gained hold in the Bavarian Alps, Germany, and now has the support of the southern alpine countries (although a certain difference in eco-mentality persists – see above).

Inside and outside the AlpArc (especially in its bigger protected areas) and in specialized research institutions, there is a huge amount of relevant research available. The partnership between the International Scientific Committee on Research in the Alps and universities aims to tackle the difficult task of its promotion among decision makers, the media and the general public. The Commision Internationale pour la Protection des Alpes has launched a research project on knowledge management in order to find and promote innovative sustainable development options for the alpine future.

Benefits and accomplishments

The first AlpArc study of potential corridors is a very valuable and thorough start towards better connectivity. However, it does not yet adequately reflect the diversity of ecosystems and landscapes in the entire Alpine arch including non-protected areas. For example, it does not intend to provide a grand vision of the best possible connectivity network for future ecological dynamics and processes. It also has not taken into account either the multitude of current protected area initiatives or the existing and future natural world heritage sites. It further ignores the concrete large conservation project Espace Mont-Blanc, the crucial missing link between the protected area cluster in the Italo-French western Alps and the more dispersed, but growing, Swiss conservation network/protected area cluster.

While an overall vision of continental-scale connectivity and a vision of the ecologically optimal alpine connectivity are still lacking, the pragmatic approach of first enlarging existing protected areas wherever politically feasible is certainly the most realistic start. Cooperation with potential stepping stones or support for better connectivity conservation, for instance with private landowners, with local, national or international business companies and with government departments outside those responsible for nature protection is still extremely rare. There have been impressive initiatives of cooperation among parks, even across national borders (for example, AlpiMaritime/Italy and Parc National Mercantour/France), but it is not yet common for protected area managers to connect with other land uses in the broader surrounding landscape towards shared stewardship of nature and its processes.

Currently there is a general disillusion with the EU because of the enormous difficulties with a joint constitution, with rapid growth and with a growing bureaucracy, without enough visible benefits, which does not foster large-scale ecological solutions either. Thanks to the intensive networking of the AlpArc, park managers and staff now are well aware of the crucial role their territory plays within the larger ecological dynamics and processes. The existing protected areas benefit greatly from the close and continuous cooperation of their transalpine network and are encouraged to explore and lobby for links beyond their limited territory. Their good example now also helps to protect more efficiently and cooperatively the parks in the Carpathian Arch and even beyond to the Balkans and the Caucasus.

The implementation of Natura 2000 is still very slow and some countries remain resistant, although it definitely has resulted in an enthusiastic application in others. The Pan-European Biodiversity and Landscape Strategy has gradually developed further and resulted, for instance, in corresponding detailed national ecological network tools as in Switzerland and Italy. The networking of the Alpine Alliance of Municipalities helps small mountain communities to face and compare similar choices of development. Its members are now well above 100. The Via Alpina is only starting to build local and regional links on the ground around the skeleton of the trail traced through hundreds of alpine valleys and heights, before it becomes the intended joint marketing tool.

The Carpathian Convention is supposed to produce more socio-economic benefits to the former socialist countries, for example by the promotion of ecotourism, of biological agriculture and of wise traditional resource use. The same is intended for the Balkan mountain areas.

The Appenine Park of Europe project is trying to benefit the disadvantaged Appenine economy and the social coherence in this naturally rich, but threatened mountainous backbone of Italy.

In spite of fear and outright opposition to brown bear and wolf conservation by a large part of the European population and by sheep breeders, one spontaneous bear migrant from Italy into the Swiss National Park resulted in a ten fold increase of tourists in 2005. Another bear was shot in 2006 while roaming around in the Tyrolian and German Alps without fear of humans and domes-

tic animals. The compensation to be paid for wolves killing sheep is still a controversial matter of negotiation and acceptance in some areas where they are found.

Lessons learned

The commitment of individual managers is critical to success

Close cooperation among protected area managers and researchers from a large mountain range over a decade in spite of strong cultural diversity has paved the way for connectivity conservation on the ground, at least between members of the network. Such networking may be transferred and multiplied to other more or less similar (mountain) areas with the respective regional adaptation. In order to open a political chance for actual connectivity according to an overall ecological strategy, however, close cooperation with other stakeholders (NGOs, scientists, governments, businesses and local stakeholders) is indispensable.

The loss of traditional mountain livelihoods can facilitate connectivity conservation outcomes

Joint fights against mega-projects like hydropower dams, tunnels and ski areas with their respective mass residences, perceived as attacks on the integrity of alpine landscapes, often paved the way for the creation of larger interconnected protected areas in spite of political borders. Such was the case with the creation of Austria's Hohe Tauern National Park after 70 years of lobbying and land acquisition by conservationists. Resistance to a wave of new protected areas from the 1970s onwards diminished, because alpine people hope for alternatives to the agonizing mountain agriculture, the disappearance of industry in their valleys and to the skiing boom, which is declining visibly due to climate change.

It is important to communicate early and clearly the nature of activities that are compatible with connectivity conservation to avoid resistance due to unfounded fears

Diffuse local fear of future development restrictions, and also a low level of engagement by states and the EU, hampered connectivity conservation efforts in the Alps. Throughout the European conservation community there persists a debate about the rigorous restrictive use of national parks (especially in centralized states like France) and the intensive use and fragmentation throughout the rest of the landscape, which potentially might be worthy of better protection with the active involvement of the local authorities.

Changing habits is hard

There have been impressive initiatives of cooperation among parks, even across national borders (such as AlpiMarittime/Italy and Parc National Mercantour/France). However, it is not yet common for protected area managers to connect with other land uses in the broader surrounding landscape toward shared stewardship of nature and its processes.

Sometimes animals lead the way

Wolves found their way through natural corridors up to the Alps and even to their central parts in recent years, which created an opportunity for enhanced learning and management cooperation between Appenine conservationists and their French and Swiss partners. Brown bears also have expanded their realm of migration across the Alps.

Multiple jurisdictional responsibilities hamper connectivity conservation efforts

In a continent with many different nations sharing the same mountain ranges, it is extremely difficult to implement a vision or even conventions of connectivity conservation in space and time. Within each of the European countries and mountain ranges, it is not easy to carry out well-prepared large-scale connectivity conservation, as efforts in the Apennines and the Pyrénées confirm. Typically for pan-European cooperative efforts and for the regionalism within each country, there is little coordination between different initiatives and layers of decision making. Thus the network of regional parks in France works on its own connectivity conservation concepts alongside similar initiatives of the AlpArc. The often small Natura 2000 sites are not yet sufficiently integrated with EUROPARC (Federation of European Parks) and other pan-European networks. The joint world heritage approach throughout the Alps, as suggested by UNESCO–

IUCN, seems currently out of reach due to nationalistic ambitions. While the Catalan Pyrénées envisage extensive corridors westward towards Cantabria and eastwards towards the Alps, there is hardly any cooperation between the north (France) and the south (Spain) in the management of the only transfrontier world heritage site in the Pyrénées and so far in the European mountains as a whole.

International and inter-regional cooperative arrangements create opportunities for large-scale connectivity conservation initiatives

International pressure (World Summit on Sustainable Development, Rio 92, the Brundtland Report, etc.) and topicality help to raise awareness among decision makers to eventually overcome obstacles to connectivity conservation. If EU resources are available for focused action, there is a greater chance of eventual implementation, although the processes have been very slow (such as Natura 2000). Local forces and national/international ones are necessary and complementary in promoting a strategy of connectivity conservation and its implementation on the ground. Historical cultural links help (such as former Austrian Empire, common language, similar transhumance economy and pilgrimage trails). New trails like Via Alpina might help to link local development with larger scale geographical visions (for example, several regional projects like Innsbruck links to Via Alpina.)

Among legal experts, the Alpine Convention is considered a model of international environmental law and thus is being used as a model not only in the Carpathians, but also in the Caucasian and Himalayan mountain regions. But the lack of participation of local inhabitants in its initial concept has turned out to be a strong obstacle to its swift ratification and application on the ground.

Linked tourism/cultural products often help to draw attention to and support connectivity conservation efforts along mountain ranges

A recent product of the Alpine Convention and the Commision Internationale pour la Protection des Alpes is the Via Alpina, a hiking trail from one end of the Alps to the other, which invites all stakeholders along several alternative routes to develop specific cultural, economic and environmental offerings wherever it passes by.

Tri-national Mont Blanc Massif: A crucial link in European alpine connectivity

Barbara Ehringhaus

Setting

This is a case of transboundary conservation and regional connectivity in the politically contested and densely populated heart of Europe. The transfrontier Espace Mont-Blanc around the roof of the European Alps represents a crucial link between the existing and future protected areas of the surrounding countries and thus belongs to any vision of continental connectivity conservation in the European mountains (Figure 9.5).

Mont Blanc, the highest summit of the Alps and of the EU (4810m), is shared by Italy and France. The whole mountain range with the surrounding valleys and mountain balconies is divided among France, Italy and Switzerland. The region includes different habitats from very dry slopes to permanent snow. There are 30 summits above 4000m, a high diversity of glaciers with all exposures and gradients, most of the geological formations of the Alpine arch, a convergence of different climate zones and atmospheric currents, an altitudinal span of 4000m and the respective biodiversity at all those levels.

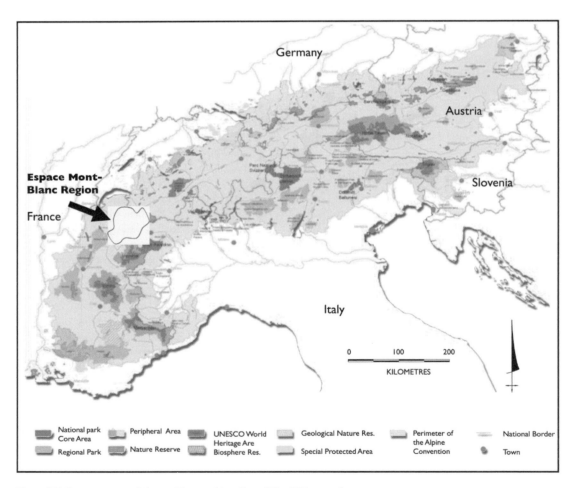

Figure 9.5 European mountain corridors and location of Mont Blanc region

Located at the hinge where the Alpine arch bends from a north–south to an east–west direction, Mont Blanc constitutes a biogeographic cross road and a potential buffer for climate change in the surrounding Mediterranean countries, since it is also the water catchment area for major headwaters of both the Po and the Rhône rivers.

The Mont Blanc Massif hosts most of the characteristic species of both the central and western Alps, such as roe deer (*Capreolus capreolus*), ibex (*Capra ibex*), chamois (*Rupicapra rupicapra*), lynx (*Lynx lynx*), wolf (*Canis lupus*) and avifauna like bearded vulture (*Gypaetus barbatus*) and capercaillie (*Tetrao urogallus*), and offers the highest potential refuge for fauna and flora from accelerating climate change. The longest gradient of glaciers (almost 4000m) of Europe can be found both north and south of the central hub, which is the most dramatic example of the geological Alpine uprising. And yet there are vineyards closer to glaciers here than anywhere else – and all this is easily accessible from a densely inhabited area in the middle of Europe.

In spite of its division among three countries and of its high mountain barriers, cultural connections abound within the Mont Blanc region. Thanks to their common history, religion and language (French and similar local dialects), humans have been raising cattle here in transhumance systems for centuries and share the respective cultural traditions of cheese-making, wine-growing and cow fights. After centuries of tough manual work and out-migration towards urban centres, the last four or five decades have brought a certain prosperity with increasing winter tourism, although this is very unevenly distributed throughout the area.

Wine production in Aosta Valley, with view to Mont Blanc

Source: Barbara Ehringhaus

While only 20 per cent of the territory within Espace Mont-Blanc is permanently inhabited, major impacts to the landscape have occurred. Traditional mountain agriculture and transhumance pastures have shifted towards more sheep and less cattle raising. Most significantly, land use has transitioned towards tourism (summer and winter) with a corresponding real estate boom (especially in Chamonix and Courmayeur) and increasing road and mountain infrastructure. In the central hub, the primary activities (France 80 per cent, Italy 15 per cent and Switzerland 5 per cent) are limited to mountaineering and skiing. However, the surrounding lower mountain ranges, the so-called balconies, are still used as summer pastures – especially on the Swiss and Italian side – and therefore host higher biodiversity. No road connection is available to drive around Mont Blanc, but there is a road and a train connection between Chamonix, France, and Martigny, Switzerland, and the sadly notorious tunnel underneath the summit connecting Chamonix and Courmayeur, Italy, which in turn are both reached by large motorways.

According to the European commission for transport, the heavy truck transport between the east and west of the continent, that is, on the European highway between Lisbon and Kiev, will pass, of all places, precisely through the tunnel underneath Mont Blanc. While local and national associations on both sides of that tunnel are fighting for security and environmental reasons against the heavy truck traffic through that much too narrow road corridor, they and ProMONT-BLANC favour, at the same time, the other more healthy and sustainable connectivity of 'green infrastructure', and thus the recognition as a significant stepping stone of European mountain corridors.

Since 1786, Mont Blanc has been the cradle of mountaineering and mountain research and to this day remains an icon for mountaineers, artists and scientists. Despite this history it still lacks appropriate conservation. During the last 30 years, decades after Italy's older Alpine national parks (Gran Paradiso and Stelvio), France created three national parks, four regional nature parks and a series of nature reserves throughout the French Alps, including several nature reserves opposite

Mont Blanc. The highest massif of the Alps itself, however, has remained only weakly protected in spite of strong worldwide demand (from the worldwide mountaineering community at the bicentennial of the first ascension in 1986 and four different IUCN resolutions since 1993) and in spite of the 1991 promise of an international park by the environment ministers of France, Italy and Switzerland.

Mer de glace glacier on Mont Blanc, Chamonix Valley

Source: Barbara Ehringhaus

The connectivity conservation initiative

Over the past 15 years, local and regional authorities from these three countries have announced their intention to balance conservation and economic development within a tri-national territory, called Espace Nature Mont-Blanc. An action plan to implement this initiative finally was released in 2006. Among its 55 transfrontier action projects and its 150 corresponding national projects, there are a number of internal corridors between the three countries and between different valleys that would permit connectivity with the surrounding protected areas and with other valuable alpine habitats in the three countries.

Although the three states initially had responded to the worldwide demand for protection by promoting an international park, decisions now are being made at the local and tri-regional level, interspersed with occasional consultations with local populations and with some stakeholders. Transboundary projects find funds more easily from the INTERREG programme of the EU (a programme to stimulate inter-regional cooperation in the EU), although it does not primarily favour conservation objectives. International conservation agreements like the Alpine Convention, the Pan-European Ecological Network and the respective Landscape Strategy did not significantly influence local decision makers.

There is potentially high connectivity within the western Alps of Espace Mont-Blanc thanks to the relative density of protected areas in the French and Italian Alps in the south (Figure 9.5) and the growing Swiss protected areas network of the central Alps in the north. Also, farther east from the Mont Blanc region in Italy, parts of Switzerland and especially Austria, large protected area networks are being established. In fact, without the crucial stepping stones of Espace Mont-Blanc, the extraordinary biodiversity of the Swiss Alps will remain largely disconnected from other Alpine corridors and even within its own protected areas patchwork. But for the moment, important parts of the Espace Mont-Blanc, with all of its environmental and cultural assets, still lack sufficiently strong protection to overcome the threat of increasing fragmentation and loss of cultural landscape. There remain large expanses of relative wilderness (by European standards) on all three sides, but they risk fragmentation from growing infrastructure both in the urbanized valleys as well as in the upper levels where skiing areas tend to interconnect even more. Therefore, the international umbrella NGO ProMONT-BLANC, which coordinates 30 environmental organizations and alpine clubs from the three countries and beyond as well as local organizations of the three regions, has been lobbying for a tri-national management plan and for a stronger linkage between the Mont Blanc area and other protected areas in the Alps, most notably through the creation of a world heritage site at Mont Blanc as well as a series of other protected areas.

Espace Mont-Blanc is surrounded by some valleys with heavy individual or transit traffic and by intensively frequented skiing areas. But the Swiss Rhône valley, the Italian Dora Baltica valley and the French Arve valley would eventually allow for green bridges as ecological corridors. While some migration corridors towards other protected areas are less threatened by tourism and transport in winter because the roads are closed (for example, Grand St. Bernard), heavy ski tourism (especially around Petit St. Bernard) might even increase disturbances in winter.

Except for the national parks, which are under national administration, protected areas in the Mont Blanc region are managed by the respective three regional administrations. An efficient transboundary leadership, which would also closely cooperate with the AlpArc, is crucially lacking. Strategic planning by the Alpine Convention, for instance, has only just started to consider ecological connectivity throughout the Alpine arch and the national networks, such as those of French and Italian regional parks, are also solicited, but the coordination between all these and other leading players is still insufficient.

Though originally considered as enemies, ProMONT-BLANC and some of its associations are now respected, although financially weak, partners of Espace Mont-Blanc. Hiking associations from the three countries launched the very popular Tour du Mont Blanc (trail networks linking Mont Blanc to the Matterhorn) two decades ago and are welcome helpers for the creation and upkeep of hiking trails.

While many scientists work on their respective national sides of Mont Blanc, only ProMONT-BLANC has involved those from all three countries in common projects. In spite of the geographical vicinity to the IUCN headquarters, there has been almost no contact notwithstanding several attempts by IUCN France. Therefore, state-of-the-art management standards are rare. Public–private partnership is only incipient: while there are few companies in the immediate surroundings, the multinational group Montblanc (pens and luxury goods) has refused to assume any commitment for the snow-capped mountain of its successful logo.

Benefits and accomplishments

In spite of the high degree of mutual intention and joint regional planning since 1991, there has been only slow progress regarding the conservation of the Mont Blanc Massif. Widespread distrust towards national politicians on one hand, and towards conservationists on the other, adds to the administrative and legal disparities between the three countries. The regional setting varies from strong autonomy in the Italian Val d'Aosta and relative cantonal self-determination in the Swiss Valais to the two Departments (Savoie and Haute Savoie) in the rather timid process of French decentralization.

The lack of political will of local politicians remains the main obstacle to implementing conservation projects, while the national governments increasingly have withdrawn from any active commitment.

While the current conditions for conservation connectivity within and beyond Espace Mont-Blanc are favourable, they will be even better in the future if transborder management can improve coordination on the ground between different protected areas categories and between administrative levels. The Espace Mont-Blanc vision has not yet actively assumed its potential role as the crowning completion of the series of French–Italian protected areas and as a crucial link with protected areas in the central Alps – neither within its territory nor beyond it. Nor have the international protected area networks in Europe incorporated connectivity conservation within and around Mont Blanc into their lobbying efforts.

Within Espace Mont Blanc, protected area connectivity is uneven and also poorly documented in the tri-national region, although there is a more complex set of protected areas in its French part (Figure 9.6). However, these are disconnected from Mont-Blanc's central hub, which is weakly and unevenly protected by different categories. Although the Swiss part is less urbanized and hosts both alpine wilderness and well-preserved cultural landscapes, there are only small areas of minor legal protection within its part of Espace Mont-Blanc.

The tri-national Espace Mont-Blanc Sustainable Development Plan represents an effort to plan development and conservation jointly in a large tri-national area, including its protected areas. While advancement to effective connectivity conservation is hampered by complex regional and national political processes and development interests, the Sustainable Development Plan nevertheless represents a key starting point for the integration of the Mont Blanc area with conservation corridors in the Alps.

On its three external borders, the vast Espace Mont-Blanc almost links up with the two national parks in the south, Gran Paradiso in Italy and Vanoise in France, as well as with the largest Swiss nature reserve Haut Val de Bagnes, in the north. The recently gazetted large territories in the western Swiss Alps, the world heritage site Jungfrau-Aletsch-Bietschhorn and the biosphere reserve Entlebuch are still too far away to provide effective connectivity, whereas south of the French national park, Vanoise, other large protected areas are relatively close (Figure 9.5). In the south-east the smaller nature reserve Grand Sassière in France and the hunting reserve Val Grisenche in Italy almost touch Espace Mont-Blanc as stepping stones towards the two national parks.

In order to turn the connectivity potential of Espace Mont-Blanc into reality, ProMONT-BLANC has been advocating that the following measures be implemented:

- a joint tri-national management plan and a subsequent transborder world heritage site nomination, possibly within a series or cluster of world heritage sites in the western Alps;
- a tri-national biosphere reserve surrounding the central hub to facilitate connectivity conservation between existing and future protected areas in the three countries;
- better integration of Natura 2000 sites (the European ecological network) in France and Italy with the respective Emerald Network sites in Switzerland;
- interconnectivity across all altitudinal layers for potential up-migration of species in time of acute climate change;
- coordination with the AlpArc and integration of scientific expertise;
- concretely designated conservation corridors within and beyond Espace Mont-Blanc.

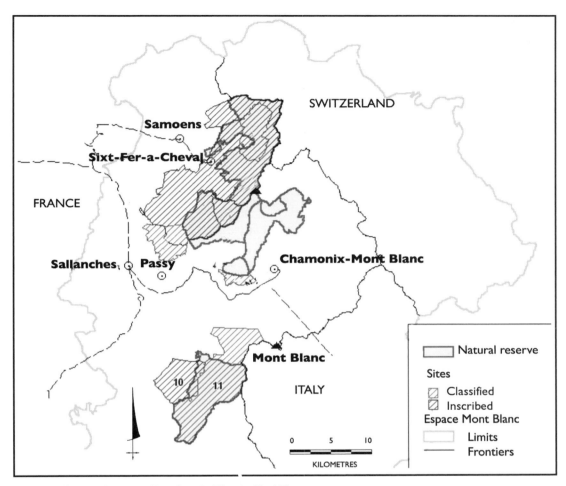

Figure 9.6 Protected areas on French part of Espace Mont-Blanc

Although scientifically evaluated and included within the national and transfrontier projects of its sustainable development plan, Espace Mont–Blanc has not yet outlined the necessary expansion of protected areas, the creation of new and stronger ones and the corridors within its territory. In particular, the summit and the central hub of Mont-Blanc need to become more strictly and more coherently protected in order to apply for tri-national natural world heritage site status. Around this core zone, those cultural landscapes that have avoided the impacts of mass tourism could unite in a tri-national biosphere reserve. Around Espace Mont Blanc, especially among the

series of Italian and French protected areas in the western Alps, the potential for connectivity conservation is very high, as the respective study of the AlpArc points out (Kohler and Plassman, this chapter). Although hardly mentioned in this study, the potential tri-national Mont Blanc area nevertheless represents an important missing link in the protected areas network of the western Alps and has an important connectivity role to play both in the south, as the crowning completion of the bi-national series of national and regional parks, and in the north with Switzerland linking up to a still scant but increasing protected area network.

With a new Swiss law on large protected areas that introduces the concept of regional parks and new national parks, Switzerland will finally overcome its mere patchwork of small protected sites and thus allow for the implementation of several protected area projects adjacent or in the vicinity of Espace Mont-Blanc.

In addition, there are also extensive well preserved adjacent areas in Italy and France, both within Espace Mont-Blanc and beyond, with the potential to close the remaining connectivity gaps to the south and east. As shown in the Figure 9.6, the opportunities for a closely knit network of different protected areas around the tri-national Roof of the Alps are extremely favourable, especially once the tri-national world heritage site and a transboundary biosphere reserve become a reality.

Sustainable tourism is starting to accrue as confidence increases in the potential benefit of contiguous intact and well preserved areas for nature tourism and consequently for the local economy. For instance, the Tour du Mont Blanc now explores more sustainable variations of trails. But mountaineers have also threatened to avoid the prestigious Mont Blanc area altogether, unless the growing fragmentation, destruction and pollution are stopped. Thematic circuits for smaller walks and longer hikes have been marked in each municipality and published in a guide with valuable information on natural and cultural heritage. Local artisans and farmers have united in order to jointly market their regional products, which are not published in the advertisements of tourist offices of the region.

Lessons learned

While connectivity conservation initiatives must have regard to large-scale conservation needs, implementation requires local cooperation and support

Cultural similarity facilitates connectivity on the ground, even across national boundaries, but it is not sufficient to guarantee a concrete system of corridors between protected areas without a recognized authority (such as a state or commission). Conservation efforts and Alpine corridors today will remain insufficiently implemented unless short-term economic and political benefits

can be demonstrated to local decision makers. Ecological connectivity may, in turn, benefit from ongoing social, economic or political cooperation, if the conservation of natural heritage can prove to be complementary to local development. Concrete local problems (such as excessive truck traffic through narrow tourist valleys and respective local uprising like the one after the tunnel accident in 1999) may eventually lead to more general environmental awareness and to the linkage with others about the same issue beyond national boundaries.

Connectivity conservation efforts are characterized by complexity

Progress in large-scale connectivity conservation is all the more difficult when several countries are involved and when existing protected areas are to be linked to those in the planning stages.

Connectivity conservation efforts must be broadly based

Initiatives for large-scale connectivity conservation, starting primarily from established protected areas management and from their networks, risk the exclusion of crucial missing links, unless they integrate initiatives that do not focus only on conservation objectives. Only if all levels – from local decision makers to national and international conservation agencies and organizations – share a vision and complement each other in promoting large-scale connectivity in the Alps and in the European mountains is there potential for implementation on the ground. The creation of Espace Nature Mont-Blanc as such does not warrant connectivity between protected areas within and outside its territory.

Ecological network of protected areas in the European Alps

Yann Kohler and Guido Plassmann

Setting

With summits above 4000m and an area of 25,000,00ha, the Alps are the most important mountain chain in central Europe. Because of significant climatic differences, the Alps shelter a large number of different natural and semi-natural habitats. They contain a rich diversity of land-scapes, which provide habitats for a large number of plants and animals. About 30,000 animal species and 13,000 plant species are found in the Alps. Several of these species are endemic (Pawlowski, 1969). The protected areas of the Alps (Figure 9.5) make an important contribution to the protection and preservation of this biodiversity and offer a refuge to wildlife. This case study will examine the prospect of establishing an ecological network of protected areas across the Alps.

The specific features of the alpine region contribute to the creation of an alpine identity that requires a supra national protection. The Alpine Convention (2003) is a framework agreement for the protection and sustainable development of the European alpine region. It was signed by Austria, France, Germany, Italy, Switzerland, Liechtenstein, Slovenia, Monaco and the EU and entered into force in March 1995.

Exploitation by human beings increasingly is threatening the alpine region and its environment. To address these threats, the Alpine Convention aims to balance economic and environmental interests. The objectives of the convention are the long-term protection of the natural ecosystems of the Alps and the promotion of sustainable development, considering the economic interests of local populations and establishing the principles that will encourage transboundary cooperation among the alpine countries. To achieve these objectives, contracting parties to the Convention are requested to develop appropriate measures with respect to matters such as population and culture, spatial planning, nature conservation and landscape planning, mountain farming, mountain forests, soil conservation, tourism, energy and transport. For each of these matters, an executing protocol is expected to be developed. At the time of writing, nine executing protocols had so far been approved and signed.

The key protocol for the work of the AlpArc is the Nature Conservation and Landscape Planning protocol. This protocol requires that the actual state of protection and conservation of natural values and landscapes be described and that programmes and/or plans be established with a view to identifying the needs and measures required for their conservation. Protected areas are

a major element of this protocol. Existing protected areas are to be maintained, managed and, where necessary, expanded. Where possible, new conservation areas such as national parks will be established. The aim is to connect conservation areas to form national and trans national ecological networks.

Article 12 of the protocol requires:

contracting parties [to] take adequate measures to establish a network of existing national and trans-boundary protected areas, of biotopes and other protected elements or those to be protected. They commit themselves to harmonize the objectives and applicable measures in transboundary protected areas.

The connectivity conservation initiative

The AlpArc was established in 1995 by France as a contribution to the implementation of the Alpine Convention. The network is designed to contribute to the nature conservation and landscape planning protocol and also to the strengthening of protected areas within the convention and domestic policies. The objectives of the network are: (i) the promotion of protected area management that is directed towards the conservation of biodiversity; (ii) the enhancement of the cultural heritage of the Alps; and (iii) the strengthening of sustainable development. Activities used to address these objectives include exchange of knowledge and expertise, the creation of an ecological network and a wide engagement with the general public.

Transboundary protected areas and the creation of spatial connections (common boundaries and ecological corridors) between the protected areas of the Alps play a major role in the implementation of the nature conservation and landscape planning protocol. Several articles refer directly or indirectly to such connections between protected areas (such as Articles 3, 11 and 12). Article 12 foresees the creation of an ecological network. In this context, the AlpArc was commissioned by the 27th Alpine Conference in February 2004 to undertake a feasibility study on how to create a transboundary ecological network.

In the Alps, ecological fragmentation caused by human settlement, roads, intensive agriculture and industrial activity, particularly in the valleys, has continuously reduced and isolated the habitats available for native plant and animal species. Scientists agree that only large and ecologically connected protected areas can ensure the sustainable and long-term protection of the biotic and abiotic natural resources of the Alps and guarantee the continuation of natural processes. Therefore large protected areas need to be created beyond national borders. This could be done by connecting existing protected areas in different states across frontiers. Another possibility is the creation of large complexes inside the different alpine states through spatial connections between the protected areas where these links are of ecological importance and in accordance with the technical and social conditions. Through these connections the protected areas would not be isolated islands, but allow for the exchange of individuals between

each other. Natura 2000 sites (Figure 9.7) as well as the effective protection of the priority areas identified by the WWF (Figure 9.8) in cooperation with other institutions (the AlpArc, the Commision Internationale pour la Protection des Alpes and the International Scientific Committee on Research in the Alps) can help to create such connections. The Natura 2000 network could be completed and a network of contiguous areas between the current protected areas could be developed.

Large protected areas and contiguous clusters of areas with different protection status are important. They will represent the core zones of an alpine network and are the shelter for wildlife. But the network cannot be based only on protected areas or single elements as nodes between ecological corridors. The permeability of the cultural land between the biotopes is also an important

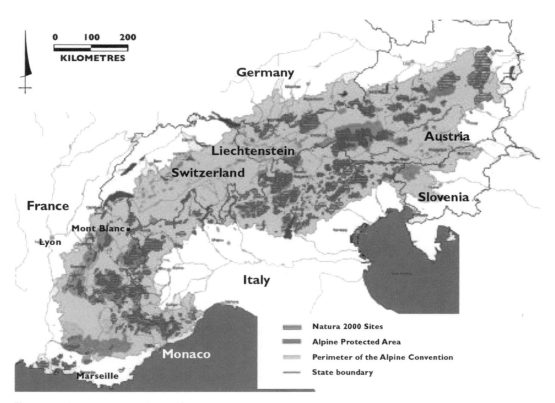

Figure 9.7 Natura 2000 sites in the Alps

element of the network to allow movements of the flora and fauna. Therefore sustainable and ecologically adapted land use (using adaptive land-use and landscape planning methods) is important to create effective connectivity between the nodes.

As well as a high level of natural diversity, the Alps also possess important cultural diversity, often expressed through traditional lifestyles and practices. Many of the traditional structures and land uses have given rise to habitats and to specially adapted species. As well as being of value in their own right, traditional land-use practices should therefore be regarded as providing opportunities to secure connectivity conservation.

Each country has a range of different measures and programmes that offer opportunities to improve the connectivity of habitats. These measures and programmes – for example in agriculture,

forestry and infrastructure development – need to be applied more efficiently. This means for example, that the measures should be regrouped by local or regional initiatives and projects to improve the interactions between the areas and to manage efforts in a coordinated way. Furthermore, the different strategies have to be coordinated internationally. Cooperation can be based on a particular theme with defined aims such as, for example, the protection of a certain species or sustainable regional development.

The design of a protected area network has to take into account the current spatial distribution of protected areas. In the Alps a considerable number of associations of protected areas can be detected: complexes of two or more transboundary areas, associations of two or more national areas and also large protected areas with a rigorous protection policy and an area of at least 1000ha

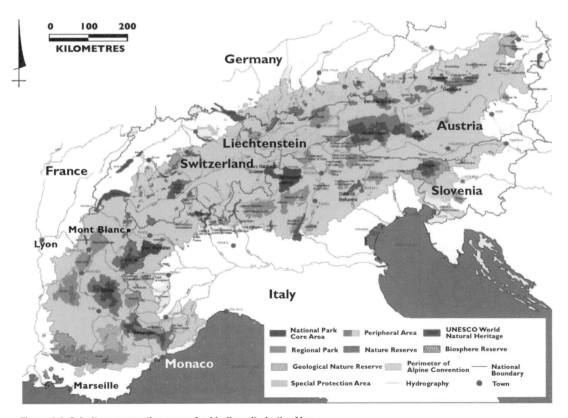

Figure 9.8 Priority conservation areas for biodiversity in the Alps

(Figure 9.9). These existing elements play an important role in connectivity conservation. The established connections and the common action programmes between such complexes can serve as basis for further national and especially international cooperation and facilitate the migration and exchange between habitats even across international borders.

Also of importance is assessment of current habitats, their quality and the existing connections between them. This can be done using satellite images, aerial photographs and geographic information system (GIS) methods, in combination with national and regional inventories of flora and fauna, the knowledge of biologists and naturalists and the ground-truthing of preliminary results. This method was used for the detection of corridors and continuums for the National Ecological Network in Switzerland (Berthoud, 2001).

This method makes the detection of existing continuums easier and, even more importantly, identification of isolated areas where these continuums are interrupted and where measures have to be taken to improve connectivity. Knowledge concerning established wildlife corridors as well as information on statistics of accidents caused by animals, obvious barriers in the landscape and areas of special biodiversity also must be taken in account.

If detailed analysis using satellite images or aerial photographs is not possible, areas can also be evaluated by using indicators or criteria. Because of time restrictions and the large area that had to be covered (the whole area covered by the Alpine Convention), the AlpArc chose this approach for identifying an ecological network. Indicators such as area and altitude of protected areas, density of habitants, land-use type, infra-

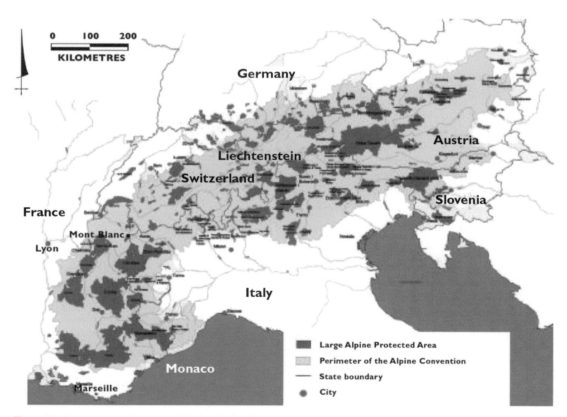

Figure 9.9 Large protected areas (> 1000ha) in the Alps

structure density and so on can allow some inter-pretation of the ability of a landscape to fulfil the role of a corridor. After a general evaluation of the situation by this method, different zones where particular problems have been identified may need to be analysed more in detail, in order to find solutions at a local level. The practical work of establishing corridors and creating connections between habitats has to be done at a local scale, by defining projects for a determined zone, species or habitat. By initiating the gover-nance and financial basis for such local projects and by sustaining and helping the stakeholders in their approach, the first step towards a coherent network can be made.

Lessons learned

Connectivity conservation initiatives require long-term commitment

The successful creation of a network of protected areas with ecological connectivity is a long-term endeavour. The general aim is to create a dynamic network across different protection areas and zones that has a beneficial impact across the whole landscape. Existing protected areas have to be grouped and connected in small associations to create larger units of wildlife refuge.

Innovative approaches may be necessary to ensure management for connectivity conservation

Since the creation of new large protected areas is not likely due to the political and economic circumstances in the Alps, existing areas have to be connected using informal means and other land-use categories. Article 12 of the Alpine Convention requires a network on a national and a transboundary level. This means that connec-tions are needed between protected areas and other areas that are not under protection but are important for the network. It is important to recognize that experience in protected areas in the fields of species management and measures of sustainable development of land use and coopera-tion between different stakeholders can be useful in non-protected areas and contribute to the creation of an ecological network.

International protocols can help push connectivity conservation efforts forward

Further efforts are required for the long-term implementation of the aims of the Alpine Convention. First of all, the existing measures and planning instruments in the different alpine coun-tries have to be synchronized. This can only be realized in large spatial units to reduce the expanding fragmentation and to reinstall a living landscape. The different protocols of the Alpine Convention constitute a potentially effective mechanism to engender the necessary coopera-tion across the whole alpine territory, inside and outside of protected areas. Such initiatives need to be undertaken in conjunction with national and regional legislation and associated general direc-tives for nature conservation.

Non-governmental organizations can help to further the connectivity conservation agenda

The AlpArc promotes the creation of an alpine ecological network between protected areas by proposing potential corridors based on criteria such as wildlife migration routes, geographic proximity, land use and low human impact. Efforts should focus on these zones, concentrating the application of measures and programmes and using Natura 2000 site protection programmes to establish the network.

Cantabrian Mountains– Pyrénées–Massif Central– Western Alps Great Mountain corridor

Josep M. Mallarach, Miquel Rafa and Jordi Sargatal

Setting

The purpose of this conservation initiative is to rebuild the ecological linkages between four of the main western European mountain ranges: the Cantabrian Mountains, the Pyrénées, the Massif Central and the Alps (Table 9.1 and Figure 9.10). The project emerged from the recommendations of the IUCN's 2003 World Parks Congress held in Durban. These mountain ranges are located in northern Spain, southern France and north-west-ern Italy. The maximum length of this initiative is

Table 9.1 Mountain ranges included in the Cantabrian–Pyrénées–Alps initiative

Mountain range	Area (km²)	Highest peak	Countries	Regions
Cantabrian Mountains	31,800	Torre Cerredo: 2648m	Spain and Portugal	6
Pyrénées	33,650	Aneto: 3404m	Spain, France and Andorra	6
Massif Central	43,940	Puy de Sancy: 1886m	France	5
Western Alps-Jura	52,370	Mont Blanc: 4807m	France, Italy and Switzerland	7
TOTAL	161,780		6	24
Linkage between mountain ranges	**Area (km²)**			
Cantabrian Mts–Pyrénées	8160			
Pyrénées–Massif Central	4450			
Massif Central–Western Alps	6500			
TOTAL	19,110			

about 1300km, while its total area is 16,178,000ha. Linkages between mountain ranges encompass some 1,900,000ha.

The European continent, especially western Europe, is one of the more intensively humanized areas of the planet. High mountain ranges, found mainly in its southern part, are an exception where outstanding scenic and ecological values persist. They include relatively intact landscapes, with glaciers, alpine pastures and subalpine forests, providing the last stronghold for some flagship species like brown bear (*Ursus arctos arctos*), chamois (*Rupicapra rupicapra* and *R. pyrenaica*), ibex (*Capra ibex*), lammergeier (*Gypaetus barbatus*) or capercaillie (*Tetrao urogallus*). The Cantabrian Mountains, the Pyrénées, Massif Central and the Alps conserve a natural and cultural heritage of unique significance within the EU context.

Mountain morphology is made up of glacier circus, rocky outcrops and cliffs and U-shaped valleys, some of which can be more than 2000m deep. There are thousands of mountain lakes and a large variety of wetlands, some of them located near the Mediterranean Sea. Ecosystem and vegetation integrity is high and includes a large number of both endemic and extremely rare species. The landscape of the valleys, which is

Forest trail, Parc Natural de la Muntanya de Montserrat, Cantabrian Mountains–Western Alps Great Mountain corridor, Spain

Source: Graeme L. Worboys

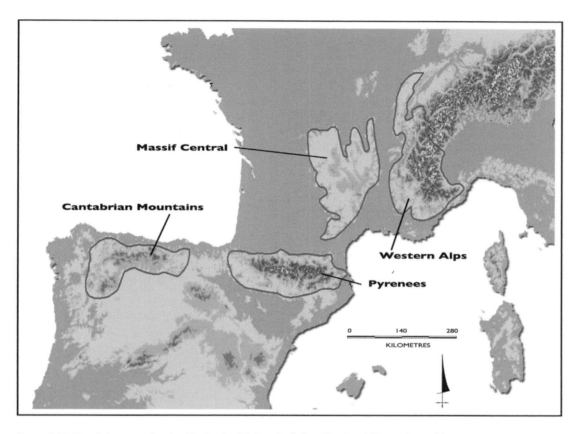

Figure 9.10 Mountain ranges involved in the Cantabrian–Pyrénées–Alps Great Mountain corridor

often the result of a historical interaction between natural vegetation and human intervention, has a great aesthetic and cultural value.

Mountain wildlife is very significant at both global and regional scales: endemic species, such as the broom hare (*Lepus castroviejoi*), alpine field mouse (*Apodemus alpicola*), Pyrenean frog (*Rana pyrenaica*), Pyrenean salamander (*Euproctus asper*) and alpine salamander (*Salamandra atra*); relicts from the last glacial age, such as boreal owl (*Aegolius funereus*) and ptarmigan (*Lagopus mutus*); threatened species in Europe, such as lammergeier (*Gypaetus barbatus*), cinereous vulture (*Aegypius monachus*) and European otter (*Lutra lutra*); and large mammals that have become regionally scarce, such as brown bear, lynx (*Lynx lynx*), wolf (*Canus lupus*), ibex and Chartreuse chamois (*Rupicapra rupicapra cartusiana*).

The human heritage of this mountainous region is very rich, including a great variety of cultural landscapes, among them several types of terraced croplands, alpine and subalpine pasturelands and dehesas (sparsely wooded pastures made up principally of holm and evergreen cork oak). Over centuries, these inhabited landscapes have evolved several types of communal governance systems that have provided good levels of conservation, such as *terrains sectionaux* in Massif Central, *comunals* in Catalonia, *quarts* in Andorra and *parzonerías* in Navarra and the Basque Country.

Cultural heritage is also abundant in these regions, with thousands of prehistoric sites, megalithic remnants, medieval villages, castles, monasteries, churches and hermitages, as well as a dense network of historic trails and paths, some of them over two millennia old. A few of these outstanding cultural monuments have been declared cultural world heritage sites, such as the medieval churches of Vall de Boí in the Catalan Pyrénées. The Way of Saint James, a set of pilgrimage trails to Saint James of Compostela across the Pyrénées and Cantabrian Mountains and surrounded by medieval buildings, was the first trail in the world to be declared a world heritage site.

Intangible cultural heritage is also very diverse, including a large variety of traditional festivals and dress and pastoral transhumant cultures. Up to nine different languages are still spoken in these mountain communities, the primary ones being Spanish, French, Italian, Catalan, Occitan and Basque, the last being the oldest living language of Europe.

Over time, the land-use and landscape history in these mountain ranges has been the object of many research studies. In general, it is quite well known from the time of the last glacial age, around ten thousand years ago, and with much greater detail from the time of the Roman Empire – that is during the last 25 centuries. Population, forest exploitation and pastoralism reached their peak during the late 19th century, as the demand for natural resources from the industrial towns increased. During the 1950s and 1960s, the combined impact of heavy modern machinery, fossil fuels, long-distance commerce and agricultural policies aimed towards intensification caused the abandonment of many mountain settlements, the decline of extensive pastures and the spontaneous expansion of different types of forest cover as a result. In the last two decades, these processes have become even more apparent.

Regional populations tend to be concentrated among and around mountain ranges. Within the mountain ranges and massifs, most towns and villages are located in valley bottoms, usually below 1500m. Small villages are the most common type of settlement in mountain areas. The economies of mountain communities tend to combine pastoral, forest and craft activities with several types of tourism, from mass tourism related to ski resorts and second homes to more diffuse and sustainable ecotourism models. Amenity migration is becoming significant in certain areas, especially where modern communication technologies allow alternative lifestyles.

This initiative is spread across six countries (Spain, France, Italy, Portugal, Switzerland and Andorra), and 24 different administrative regions, autonomous communities or cantons. Of these,

over half have full political responsibility concerning land-use planning, agriculture, forestry, nature conservation and infrastructure (Table 9.2 and Figure 9.11). Thus, the power to make decisions related to land-use and environmental policies are held by a variable number of administrative levels, from three to six, depending on the political structure and the degree of decentralization of each country. Another factor that contributes to the complexity of existing decision-making processes is the degree of public participation allowed in different regions, which has been increasing at strategic levels during the last years due to EU directives and regulations, mainly the requirement to assess the impact of plans and programmes.

Ecosystem, landscape and habitat fragmentation and the associated reduction of habitat quality has been one of the main causes of biodiversity losses in western Europe. The types of threat have changed dramatically during the last few decades. They are very different inside mountain ranges than between them. Hence, they will be discussed separately. Inside the mountain ranges:

- rural depopulation accompanies traditional agriculture landscape abandonment, expansion of forestlands and cultural impoverishment;
- the most popular protected areas are overcrowded during holidays;
- despite their dubious economic viability, large ski resorts are one of the main impacts, and many of them recently have undergone major redevelopment and expansion;
- urban sprawl associated with mountain recreation is creating environmental degradation and local population disturbances in a number of valleys.

Between the mountain ranges:

- road and railway networks are fragmenting the landscape (Figure 9.12);
- irrigation works, intensive agricultural uses and forestry plantations are transforming the remaining semi-natural habitats;
- urban and industrial development is spreading artificial areas, creating new barriers for wildlife.

Table 9.2 Political/administrative jurisdictions of the Cantabrics to Alps initiative

Political and/or administrative units	Area (ha²)	Massif (rounded to '000km²)
Asturias (Spain)	439,300	
Cantabria (Spain)	312,300	
Basque Country (Spain)	4200	
Castilla y León (Spain)	1,881,700	
Galicia (Spain)	488,200	
		Cantabrian mountains
Bragança (Portugal)	57,100	3,180,000
Auvergne (France)	1,559,600	
Rhône-Alpes (France)	620,500	
Limousin (France)	361,200	
Midi-Pyrénées (France)	1,064,500	
		Massif Central
Languedoc-Roussillon (France)	787,800	4,394,000
Aquitaine (France)	200,300	
Midi-Pyrénées (France)	777,700	
Languedoc-Roussillon (France)	347,700	
Aragón (Spain)	897,900	
Catalunya (Spain)	890,600	
Andorra (Andorra)	45,400	
		Pyrénées
Navarra (Spain)	205,000	3,365,000
Franche-Comte (France)	462,900	
Valais (Switzerland)	2000	
Rhône-Alpes (France)	2,222,000	
Piemonte (Italy)	614,800	
Génève (Switzerland)	800	
Valle d'Aosta (Italy)	2600	
Provence-Alpes-Cote d'Azur (France)	1,825,200	
		Occ. Alps-Jura
Liguria (Italy)	106,600	5,237,000

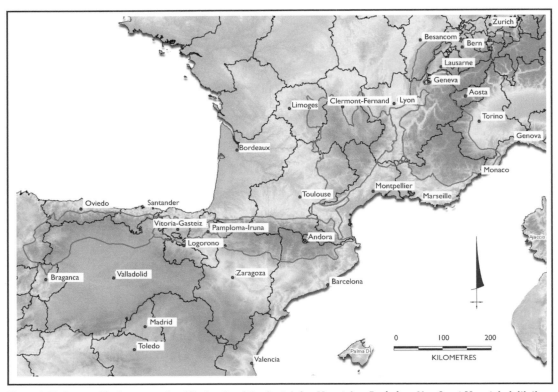

Figure 9.11 Geographical scope and political units of the Cantabrian Mountains–Pyrénées–Alps Great Mountain initiative

In both cases, lack of political cooperation between adjacent regions and/or countries increases the potential impacts and reduces the effectiveness of some measures. In addition, potential climate change effects include noticeable impacts on some of the most fragile species and communities, especially those occurring in the highest alpine ecosystems.

At the policy level during the last decade, the EU and the Council of Europe made significant steps towards recognizing the role of ecological connectivity in biodiversity conservation. Among the most important policy initiatives are: the 1995 Pan-European Biological and Landscape Diversity Strategy; the 1998 European Community Biodiversity Strategy; the 2000 General Guidelines for the Development of the Pan-European Ecological Network; and the 2003 Declaration of the Fifth Ministerial Conference on the Environment for Europe, Kiev. Ministers attend-

ing this last conference also issued the 'Message from Malahide', in which the EU countries committed themselves to halt biodiversity losses by the year 2010.

There are also other positive tendencies that deserve mention. Protected areas have significantly increased, covering 24 per cent of the project area. However, heterogeneity of legal protection categories (over 30 different types), weak integration of sectoral policies and little international coordination are reducing conservation effort effectiveness. Following the 1979 and 1992 directives on birds and habitats conservation, respectively, the EU promoted the Natura 2000 network, based on a bioregional analysis and prioritization, which is now in the stage of adoption and implementation by the concerned countries. Natura 2000 will increase protected area coverage to about 38 per cent of the initiative area (Figure 9.13). In addition to the existing system of protected areas, there exist

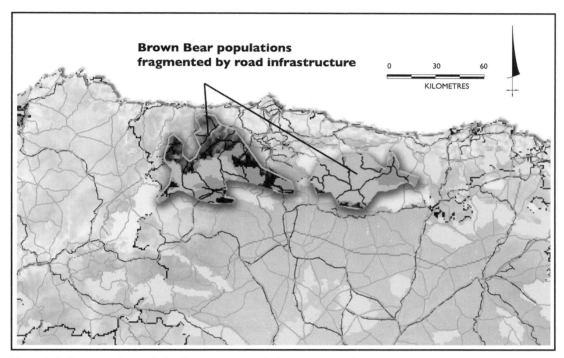

Figure 9.12 Fragmentation analysis of brown bear populations in the Cantabrian Mountains

a large number of community conserved areas, which might encompass 30–50 per cent of the mountain areas that are not formally protected. Transitional areas between these four mountain ranges have fewer protected areas, being more vulnerable to new threats.

Forestland expansion, cropland reduction and rural depopulation inside most mountain ranges are increasing ecological permeability for forest species, including large mammals. Ungulate reintroduction, restocking and natural population growth provide the necessary preys for large carnivore recovery, which is already taking place. The spontaneous wolf and lynx expansion and the recovery of the Cantabrian brown bear population are among the best examples. Movements of large carnivores, such as wolves, suggest the natural scope of this initiative. Wolves recolonized the western Alps in the 1990s, and some individuals have been recently sighted in the Massif Central and the Pyrénées, having travelled from the Alps. The lynx was reintroduced into the Alps and is currently increasing its range. In addition, efforts to reintroduce other flagship species, like the lammergeier, the cinereous vulture and the Spanish wild goat (*Capra pyrenaica pyrenaica*), are improving their regional status.

The last opportunity that deserves mention is the increasing influence of conservationist and ecologist NGOs. Their involvement has three main components:

- the management and protection of natural areas, through acquisition of land or land stewardship agreements;
- the vision for proposing new policies, programmes or plans, in partnership with public powers;
- the 'watchdog' function towards public administrations and the justice courts, to promote the application of the vast body of existing regulations.

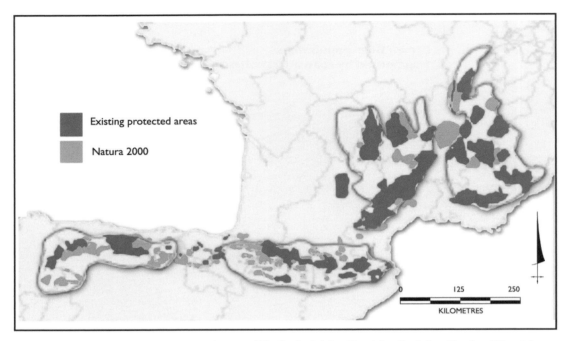

Figure 9.13 Existing and proposed protected areas within the Cantabrian Mountains–Pyrénées–Alps Great Mountain initiative

The connectivity conservation initiative

The goal of the Cantabrian Mountains–Pyrénées–Alps Great Mountain corridor is the establishment of a functional ecological network inside and between the main mountain ranges of western Europe. This initiative should continue towards central and eastern Europe, in order to ensure ecological and landscape connectivity between the Alps and the Apennines to the Balkan Mountains and the Carpathians.

To identify the geographical scope of the initiative and its ecological viability, a GIS-based analysis was done using the best data available at the European level, consistent with the *Indicative map of the Pan-European Ecological Network* (Jongman et al, 2005) and included:

- the European Environmental Stratification map (Metzger et al, 2005);
- the Corine Land Cover map;
- topographical information, including digital elevation models, hydrology, towns and cities, roads and railways.

This allowed the delimitation of the subject mountain ranges and the ecological linkages between them. A further analysis identified fragmentation processes and human-made barriers both within the mountain ranges and between them, to identify the critical points. Ecological and landscape permeability is higher in the corridor between the Cantabrian Mountains and the Pyrénées (Basque linkage) than the two other linkages. Regarding fragmentation, the linkage between the Massif Central and the Pyrénées is the most intact, followed by the linkage between the Basque and the Rhône valley, which joins the Massif Central and the Alps.

The next step was an analysis of the distribution of existing internationally and nationally protected areas, and the proposed Natura 2000 network sites, which are in different stages of implementation, depending on the counties and regions (Figure 9.13). This study concluded with a SWOT (strengths, weaknesses, opportunities and threats) analysis, which allowed the identification

Native Forest, Parc Natural de la Muntanya de Montserrat, Cantabrian Mountains–Western Alps Great Mountain corridor, Spain

Source: Graeme L. Worboys

of the opportunities and the main threats, including the critical points, at the local level. The primary conservation and restoration efforts over the coming years will focus both at the ecological and landscape levels.

Connectivity conservation management

The leadership for this initiative comes from the Fundació Territori i Paisatge, the main nature conservation foundation that purchases and manages land for nature conservation in Spain, created in 1997 and funded by Caixa Catalunya Savings Bank. The initiative has been included under the auspices of the Council of Europe, and has received initial support from the IUCN, the World Commission on Protected Areas Mountains Biome, the Europarc Federation, Eurosite, European Commission's DG-XI, the regional governments of Catalonia and Asturias, the

Provincial Government of Alava and the municipality of Vitoria (in the Spanish Basque County), the Fundación Oso Pardo and others.

The initiative of the Cantabrian to Alps mountain corridor was first announced at the World Commission on Protected Areas' 2004 International Mountain Corridors Conference in Banff, Canada. It since has been presented at several international events.

This international mountain connectivity initiative was officially launched at the 2005 WCPA Mountains Biome Conference, in the Catalan Pyrénées, by means of the *Declaration of Les Planes de Son*. The Declaration was translated into five languages (Basque, Catalan, French, Italian and Spanish) and received an initial support from representatives of over 20 public institutions and NGOs from nine different countries, particularly Spain, France, Italy and Switzerland (Fundació

Territori i Paisatge, 2006). Later, it received official endorsement from the Autonomous Government of Catalonia and the Provincial Government of Alava (Spanish Basque Country), both in October 2006.

Press releases that followed the launching of this initiative resulted in a number of news reports and interviews in Spanish national and regional media. The documents prepared by the Fundació Territori i Paisatge included a technical report, a shorter descriptive document aimed at policy makers and a conference poster. A website on the initiative was under preparation in 2006.

Since the launch of this initiative, several regional and autonomous communities in Spain presented ecological connectivity strategies that are consistent with the objectives of the corridor: Catalonia (Mallarach and Germain, 2006), the Basque Country (Gurrutxaga, 2005), Asturias (García Manteca and González Taboada, 2005) and the Province of Alava (Mallarach et al, 2005).

Additionally, regional land-use plans have been approved in 2006 in Asturias and the Catalonian Pyrénées region, including a sound system of ecological corridors (Generalitat de Catalunya, 2006). Moreover, the network of protected areas of the French Massif Central has undertaken a significant process of cooperation to promote and conserve ecological corridors among them, creating the largest group of protected areas of western Europe (Ipamac, 2005).

Finally, this initiative has stimulated new research projects, for instance for assessing the significance of the biological connectivity between mountain ranges by means of key mammal species, or to reconnect the two separated populations of brown bears in the Cantabrian mountain ranges, the last promoted by the Fundación Oso Pardo.

Benefits and accomplishments

Between the initiative's launch in October 2005 and the time of writing (November 2006) most of the identified benefits have been instrumental, such as:

- fostering the interest and commitment of several public agencies at different levels: international, European, national, regional and local;

- reassessing priorities for conservation planning and strategies, such as in the province of Alava, as the linkage between the Cantabrian Mountains and the Pyrénées;
- increasing cooperation beyond boundaries between public and private actors at the landscape scale (particularly in the Cantabrian Mountains and the Massif Central of France);
- promoting a specific conservation project aimed at restoring brown bear population viability, which is threatened by fragmentation caused by a corridor of infrastructures in the Spanish Cantabria and Asturias autonomous communities;
- promoting new research on ecological connectivity, mainly at the ecosystem and landscape levels.

Lessons learned

Inclusive approaches lead to better results

There is a need to adopt a wide multi-scale and multi-sectoral approach, aimed towards all sectors that have an impact on ecological connectivity, from local to international levels, avoiding a narrow conservation biology focus.

Nature is resilient

Despite centuries of destructive and fragmenting activities in western Europe's Alps and Cantabrian mountains, the opportunity to reconnect large areas and restore native wildlife populations remains promising.

Thinking at a large scale provides new opportunities

The power of 'thinking big', based in bioregional and ecosystem criteria, helped to overcome proposals constrained by political and administrative barriers, which are very narrow in south-western Europe.

NGOs can lead the way

Civil society and private organizations, when they have the support of key international organizations, have the ability to promote and lead international initiatives that are then followed by both public powers and private organizations.

Turn barriers into opportunities

The existence of political and administrative barriers can be seen, in this context, as an opportunity for increasing international and inter-regional cooperation, based on new priorities derived from large-scale ecosystem and bioregional assessments.

Large-scale thinking promotes new opportunities

The initiative provides an exciting framework for promoting new and stronger cooperation projects both at national an international levels, either between regions or countries, aimed toward rebuilding a 'green infrastructure' of continental significance.

The Apennines (European Alps to the Mediterranean)

Bernardino Romano

Setting

In the Apennines social and economic problems have major implications for environmental and ecosystem integrity. These mountains, like much of south Italy over the past few decades, have experienced increasing transportation costs, declining population and an employment crisis.

In some southern areas of the country, economic support from the European Community was withdrawn in recent years because some regions have been removed from the 'Objective 1' list that identifies socio-economically disadvantaged territories. Where European funds had been used to support unsustainable activities, the withdrawal of these subsidies has had a benefit for conservation. On the other hand, new development policies are resulting in increased environmental impacts. These development policies are concentrated, in particular, on improvement in transportation infrastructure and on supporting the productive and commercial utilities.

The goal of these new economic ventures is to reduce travel times between the main urban and productive centres and their hinterlands and to reduce the economic isolation of internal and marginal areas. In tandem with these initiatives, the tension between different political ideas about territorial and environmental governance has

diminished. Although the improvement of the road system and economic development are the main goals, approaches to these have evolved in a manner that also meets ecological objectives.

The awareness within mountain communities of the impacts of development policies on the environment, particularly when such impacts are more visible and urgent and when knowledge about their potential effects on human health is heightened, is much greater than it was in the 1980s and 1990s. In the last two decades, protected areas in mountain regions like Italy's Apennines have greatly expanded in number and area. In 1997, 1.25 million ha, about 26 per cent of the total Apennines surface, were encompassed within protected areas. However, the ecological connectivity between these has been severed due to the construction of roads, highways and other productive structures in the intermountain basins.

These developments are potentially fatal for the conservation of many faunal species of international conservation importance that now are still present in Apennine source areas, such as the brown bear (*Ursus arctos arctos*), wolf (*Canus lupus*) and lynx (*Lynx lynx*). The fragmenting impacts of development can quickly isolate populations leading to the possible extinction of some species, such as the brown bear, whose population already is greatly diminished in numbers. As of the time of writing, there was no national Italian legislation that mandates the protection of biodiversity or the establishment of a national ecological network. However, in some regions, Toscana for example, there is biodiversity protection legislation. In 2003, the Umbria region established the Regional Ecological Network by means of a regional planning tool – the Urban Territorial Plan.

Other regional initiatives are in development, such as those in the Marche and Veneto regions. About 20 Italian provinces have incorporated ecological networks or 'environmental continuity systems' into their coordination plans, but the effectiveness of these tools is very limited for achieving strategic results. While the rationales and structure of ecological networks are derived from WWF activities and from the work of some universities or research units, the interests and priorities of local administrators limit their application on the ground.

A workshop held in conjunction with the 2003 IUCN World Parks Congress in Durban, South Africa, publicized data on the state of connectivity conservation in the Appenines, using the concept of biopermeability (Romano, 2000; Gambino and Romano, 2004). Subsequently, with the support of WWF Italy, further research was conducted that has promoted an ecoregional approach to analysing national biodiversity values in the region (Bulgarini et al, 2004).

Additional research is ongoing to understand the relationship between urban settlement and biogeographical features. However, these efforts have had little impact on land-use decision making. In this regard, political and market trends are more determinative of the future improvement of ecological connectivity in the Apennines, while important risks are created by current infrastructure policies.

The connectivity conservation initiatives

The previous Italian government implemented new infrastructure legislation (called the Objective Law). The current government's priorities also seek to expand low cost production standards. The resultant infrastructure developments are forecast to interfere considerably with 'large cohesion environmental units' (Ferroni et al, 2006), where these units are defined as natural landscapes not fragmented by urbanization or other intensive productive activities (Table 9.3). Such units are characterized by their unfragmented nature with respect to potential biological flows. Within the Italian peninsula, ten large intact natural areas cover about 8,819,861ha (Pungetti and Romano, 2004). Moreover, the Objective Law infrastructures fragment 6 per cent of Italian Natural Sites of European Community Interest (SCIs) (about 136 of 2330 SCIs affecting 611,000 of 4,422,000ha) and 5 per cent of protected areas (60 out of 1147 affecting 956,522 of 6,703,300ha).

For the reasons outlined above, there are three possible territorial and political futures for the Apennines, a fundamental ecological linkage between the Mediterranean mountains and those of central Europe (Romano and Thomasset, 2003).

Scenario 1 – Culturally separate Apennines

The Apennines maintains its current identity and relative importance within the national scheme. The urbanization of coastal areas and the infrastructure linking them expand. The characteristics of coastal areas are distinguished from those of the Apennines. The Apennines offer a different model where a better quality of life with more connection to the natural world can be found and where people are willing to sacrifice economic and lifestyle amenities in return. Current levels of road density are maintained. No new inter-regional road networks are created. Investment is limited to local improvements. Sustainable policies govern commercial activities. Environmental projects and activities favour the spontaneous renaturalization of regional landscapes. While an economic gap exists between coastal areas and the Apennines, in the latter this is offset by a higher level of environmental quality. Economic investments are predicated on maintaining or improving environmental standards.

Scenario 2 – Culturally integrated Apennines

A political commitment is made to raise the socio-economic character of the Apennines to that of the coastal areas. Communications capacity is enhanced and an inter-regional road network is established. The goal is to reduce the costs to coastal residents by taking advantage of the cheaper production costs in the interior. Policies promote increased infrastructure, in particular by increasing highway capacities and expanding east–west transportation facilities. Because of infrastructure improvements, ecological fragmentation within the Apennines increases. The importance of existing protected areas is enhanced. Accessibility of coastal residents to interior tourist natural parks and reserves increases. Economic investments are focused on improving the ecological and functional performance of protected areas, and countering the trend toward their insularization. Efforts are aimed at increasing the social, economic and, potentially, demographic equivalency between mountain and coastal areas.

Table 9.3 Environmental cohesion units in Italy

1   Alpi Marittime e Cozie, Val Sesia, Val d'Isere (1,072,021ha) (Parco Regionale dell'Argentera, Parco Regionale Orsiera-Rocciavrè, Parco Regionale Monte Avic, Parco Nazionale Ecrins, Parco Nazionale della Vanoise, Parco Nazionale del Gran Paradiso)

2   Alpi Pennine e Lepontine, Alpi Bernesi (574,851ha) (Riserva Naturale di Grimsel, Parco Nazionale della Val Grande)

3   Alpi Orobiche, Alpi Retiche, Valtellina, Val Venosta (1,649,142ha) (Parco Regionale delle Orobie, Parco Regionale Adamello-Brenta, Parco Gruppo di Tessa, Parco Regionale Alto Garda Bresciano, Parco Nazionale dello Stelvio, Parco Nazionale dell'Engadina)

4   Dolomiti, Alpi Aurine (1,020,854ha) (Parco Nazionale delle Dolomiti Bellunesi, Parco di Paneveggio-Pale di S.Martino, Parco dello Sciliar, Parco Puez-Odle, Parco Fanes-Sennes-Braies, Parco Vedrette di Ries, Parco delle Dolomiti di Sesto, Parco delle Dolomiti d'Ampezzo)

5   Alpi Carniche, Alpi Giulie, Slovenia (603,970ha) (Parco Regionale delle Prealpi Carniche, Parco Regionale delle Alpi Giulie, Parco Regionale Dolomiti di Sesto-d'Ampezzo, Parco Nazionale di Triglavski)

6   Appennino Ligure (513,982ha) (Parco Regionale del Magra, Area Protetta del Bric-Tana, Monte di Portofino, Monte Antola)

7   Appennino Emiliano-Toscano (667,145ha) (Parco Regionale delle Alpi Apuane, Parco Regionale dell'Alto Appennino Reggiano)

8   Appennino Toscano–Umbro–Marchigiano–Abruzzese–Laziale–Molisano (2,977,830ha) (Parco Nazionale delle Foreste Casentinesi, Parco Nazionale dei Monti Sibillini, Parco Nazionale Laga-Gran Sasso d'Italia, Parco Nazionale della Majella, Parco Nazionale d'Abruzzo, Parco Regionale del Sirente-Velino, Parco Regionale dei Simbruini-Ernici, Parco Regionale Monte Cucco, Parco Regionale Monte Subasio, Parco Regionale Monti Lucretili, Parco Monti del Matese)

9   Promontorio del Gargano (176,847ha) (Parco Nazionale del Gargano)

10   Appennino Campano (464,265ha) (Parco dei Monti Picentini)

11   Murge (219,397ha)

12   Appennino meridionale Lucano-Calabrese (1,018,396ha) (Parco Nazionale del Cilento-Vallo di Diano, Parco Nazionale del Pollino)

13   Appennino Calabrese (432,401ha) (Parco Nazionale della Calabria)

14   Appennino Calabrese (304,619ha) (Parco Nazionale dell'Aspromonte)

15   Sicilia (499,402ha) (Parco Regionale dell'Etna, Parco Regionale delle Madonie, Parco Regionale dei Nebrodi)

16   Sardegna (1,941,821ha) (Parco Nazionale del Gennargentu)

17   Maremma Tosco-Laziale (787,385ha)

18   Valle di Mazara (183,542ha)

Source: PLANECO, 2000

Scenario 3 – Ecologically connected Apennines

The Apennine backbone becomes source area of natural quality that is exportable to other degraded spaces. The peninsular Italian mountains are recognized as internationally significant for their natural, bio–ecological, cultural, artistic and historical values. This scenario is not exclusive of the ones illustrated above, but is a model that considers the environmental structure as the fundamental one to obtain ecological, and also social and economic, results. The primary principle governing the design and construction of the transportation system is to minimize fragmentation and restore connectivity. A significant restoration effort is required along coastal areas. The new road network would be very compact, reducing the fragmentation effect by means of mitigation projects. Moreover, other and alternative transport forms are needed for the Apennines. Natural and landscape restoration and actions of environmental and ecological engineering would be the 'nodes' of the environmental policies in this scenario in concert with large ecosystem units, biogeographical cohesion features, river belts and lakes. An investment along the lines just listed should be relevant and linked to economic results with strong environmental protection policies. The aims of this scenario are the following: ecological connectivity conservation; international natural and cultural tourism; urban settlement with high quality of life; and preservation of traditional agricultural activity.

Lessons learned

Connectivity conservation opportunities for Italy

As we have seen, there are still real opportunities to implement connectivity conservation in Italy. Taking advantage of them will require a renewed commitment to dynamic environmental analyses and legislative tools. To achieve these results, the participation of scientists and other specialists is needed to recommend new plans and programmes that explore the relationships between natural and human systems. New indicators and indexes able to reduce conflicts between urban settlement and ecosystem are also necessary (Biondi et al, 2003).

A need for improved land-management policies

In Italy the better goal is a connectivity conservation policy applied to the control of land management. This hypothesis is not new, but we can find it in various publications (Gambino, 1992; Finke, 1996), although its pursuance is

difficult because it involves the local governance capabilities of local communities (Diamond, 2005). The problem occurs both at the strategic (regional) and the municipal urban level. At the local level, decision making has both regional and longer term impacts.

Provide a higher planning status for ecosystem values

Connectivity conservation means considering the ecological system as a 'first among equals' compared to the other systems that constitute the territorial 'networked' structure and, in this case, using the concept of 'network perspective' in planning (Dematteis and Emanuel, 1994).

A need to use an ecosystem mapping tool

One of the instruments available to facilitate the dialogue between territorial and ecological knowledge is the ecosystem map, which could contain the multi disciplinary information necessary to provide the territorial government with eco-sustainable choices. For example, we know that some animal and plant species are environmental indicators able to detect miniscule natural modifications due to urban development. However, the links between eco-biogeographical indexes and urban settlement indexes have not been fully explored, although there is beginning to be some studies in this direction (Battisti and Romano, 2005). An ecosystem map can provide an opportunity where environmental knowledge can be used to prepare future scenarios and provide support to decision making. Moreover these scenarios are requested by the European Community evaluation procedures such as VIA (environmental impact evaluation), VAS (strategic environmental evaluation) and VINCA (incidence environmental evaluation).

Acknowledgements

The author would like to thank Serena Ciabò and Mauro Fabrizio for their contribution to this case study through the development of GIS data.

10

Themes and Lessons from Global Experience in Connectivity Conservation

Graeme L. Worboys and Wendy L. Francis

In Chapters 4 to 9, leaders and managers offered their understanding, insights and lessons learned from 25 connectivity conservation case studies. In this chapter, we add to these lessons by presenting information generated by connectivity managers attending the IUCN World Commission on Protected Areas (Mountains Biome) workshop held in Papallacta, Ecuador in November 2006 (Figure 10.1). We then offer, as a second part to this chapter, an overview of the main themes to emerge from all of the cases and lessons, thereby establishing an empirical basis for a new connectivity conservation management framework presented in Chapter 11.

Figure 10.1 Papallacta workshop logo

Source: Linda McMillan

Lessons from the Papallacta workshop

The information generated by managers attending the IUCN workshop complement the case study lessons. Workshop participants were asked to provide lessons they had learned in managing areas for connectivity conservation. Here we synthesize these contributions to the major themes raised and provide some analysis. For each topic area, lessons are presented as bullet points, followed by a brief discussion.

Ecological information

- Connectivity conservation design is, in large part, a technical and scientific matter, and must be based on the best available Western and traditional ecological knowledge.
- Don't rely only on professional information, use amateur naturalists, local communities and indigenous knowledge in the management of the connectivity initiative.
- There is a need to assess the condition of landscape, the way in which it is used by focal species, location of sources and sinks, where additional core areas need protection and where linking corridors need to be identified and secured.
- Advanced models for forecasting species, habitat and climate interactions are required.
- A determination of the ecological function of a connectivity conservation area is needed.
- Research and monitoring is critical to determine the final matrix of connectivity areas that is needed to fulfil species' needs.
- Monitoring and research are needed to identify the ecological roles of the connectivity conservation area.

The lessons highlight the complexity and careful thought needed for the design of connectivity areas. Science information is needed for contemporary species conservation responses, for corridor design and for identifying future connectivity management needs in a climate change impacted world. In Chapter 2, we identified four types of connectivity conservation that needed consideration. All of these considerations need quality contextual information. In addition, any appreciation of the nature context for connectivity conservation may be completed as part of systematic conservation planning (Bottrill and Pressey, 2009).

Social and cultural context

* Determine social and cultural issues that influence connectivity conservation, positively or negatively.

* The needs of local communities are a vital consideration for connectivity conservation managers.
* Connectivity conservation managers need to work with local communities to help achieve sustainable use of natural products.
* The future sustainable use of natural products will need to be assessed in a context of human population growth (and needs) and biome shifts caused by climate change.
* For natural connectivity lands there is a need to negotiate with landowners on how plant and animal species can be conserved and how movement of species between protected areas can be achieved in a context of human use.
* Connectivity conservation areas are not possible without building the capacity of connectivity conservation staff and local communities.

Papallacta workshop participants

Source: Linda McMillan

The lessons focus sharply on the realities of human uses, needs and capacities within a connectivity conservation area. The areas may provide all or some of the basic needs of people. For many indigenous peoples, peoples undertaking transhumance, rural communities and others, this may include shelter, clean water, plant products including fuel for cooking fires, bushmeat or other natural area food sources, animal products such as feathers, teeth and fur, and mineral and soil materials that may be used for medicines or for ceremonial occasions. Such use may be for 12 months of the year, or it may be seasonal and linked to transhumance and seasonal grazing of domestic livestock. The rights, aspirations and needs of these peoples are critically important. Ecologically sustainable-use management will be critical, as will the special needs of ecosystems and habitats as climate change causes biome shifts and changes to the availability of resources.

Cultural and spiritual values

- Use traditional routes, new trail networks, road and aquatic routes to link cultural and natural attractions in connectivity conservation areas to provide tangible benefits, cultural relevance and tourism value, and aid in public understanding of the values of the areas.
- The Appalachian Trail and Pacific Rim-John Muir Trail in North America; the Inca Trail, Chilean Trail, and Mesoamerican Trail of Central and South America; the Australian Alps Walking Track and the Bicentennial National Horse Trail in Australia; and the Silk Route and Trans-Himalayan trading routes of Central Asia are examples of how cultural values and recreational opportunities can become important contributions to a connectivity conservation area.

People have special values for lands and places and this needs to be understood and dealt with sensitively when attempting management. The lessons learned focus on the relationship between cultural heritage and opportunities to present these values to the public. However, there are other considerations. Such values may include a 'sense of belonging' and importance that a large natural area and its culturally significant sites may have to

individuals and communities. Values like this have been identified for the Alpine Hinge area of Europe and natural lands within the Yellowstone to Yukon corridor. In the Cantabrian Mountains–Pyrénées–Massif Central–Western Alps Great Mountain corridor of Europe for example, there are pre-existing social and cultural ties to connectivity conservation lands that relate to Romanesque architecture, traditional songs and a harvest festival, and the Santiago de Compostela pilgrimage route. These provide opportunities for culturally resonant walking trails that can support the case for conservation. Spiritual values of natural lands are especially important: sacred sites, pilgrim trails, sacred pathways, dreaming tracks and ancient routes such as the Gran Ruta Inca along the Andes of South America need to be recognized. Ancient Aboriginal pathways and dreaming tracks in Australia can cut across natural connectivity areas or run parallel to them, and are characteristically linked to sacred sites and dreamtime stories that may be as old as 40,000 years. These traditional routes can play a critical role on communicating the social, cultural and natural importance of connectivity areas.

Economic considerations

- The benefits of high quality and reliable water need to be emphasized.
- The economic benefits of connectivity conservation to local communities and other key stakeholders should be recognized.
- Economic rewards for retaining naturalness such as financial returns for water catchment yields, for retaining stored carbon and for providing ecotourism destinations to natural sites will become increasingly important.
- Ecotourism is an important potential source of income.
- Establishment and management costs associated with the connectivity conservation initiative should be estimated.

The lessons focused on economic return from natural settings. Water catchment values and carbon sequestration and storage values (green carbon) for example are of particular importance. In an emerging carbon economy there may be opportunities for landowners to be rewarded for retaining carbon stored on natural lands (Mackey et al, 2008). New work functions in the connectivity area may become more important for local people. There may be an entirely new stewardship and protection role for connectivity lands. Connectivity conservation staff salaries may become an important component of local and regional economic activity.

Community support

- Establishing connectivity conservation is always easier where you have community support.
- The absence of active community support for connectivity conservation is not necessarily a veto. There may be unvoiced support.
- Accept that there will be some opposition. Stand your ground.
- Support from the broader world can sometimes be as important as local community support.
- Communities are not uniform, and support may vary tremendously across a region according to the social conditions.
- With the passage of time community support can change, due to raising awareness, capacity building, and employment opportunities being created.
- Avoid the 'decide, announce, defend' trap. Engage the community wherever possible in designing the connectivity conservation area.

Working with communities in connectivity areas is very important and the lessons identified provide a rich cross section of advice. Achieving and managing connectivity initiatives are directly related to support from the community. The importance of this should not be underestimated. The constant sharing of quality, accurate information about a connectivity area, its importance, and the scientific basis for its establishment is critical. The capacity to constantly provide such information through field days, print, electronic and other media is also important.

Political considerations

- Politicians need to see the connectivity conservation concept as a winner and that it is new and innovative.

- Sometimes 'the big idea' can engage the highest level of political support.
- Politicians need to be rewarded for their support and it's often helpful to have a formal 'launch' or to release a declaration.
- There is a need to determine which political levels are necessary for success including potentially sub-national, national and international levels.
- It is important to engage in policy work at all scales, local to international.
- Connectivity conservation areas can contribute to peace processes between countries.

Politicians and political considerations play a critical role in the future of connectivity conservation. The lessons provide firm advice about collaborative partnerships and providing positive recognition for politicians. They need to be well informed, to have access to the best scientific information and they need to have long-term rewards and benefits if they are to support corridor concepts. Many corridors extend beyond one nation, and dealing with international politics is important. Protected areas on international borders, such as the Waterton (Canada) Glacier (US) International Peace Park, and transboundary protected areas around the world (Ali, 2007) have gained special attention for how they can be managed. Connectivity conservation areas may interconnect with protected areas at borders, or simply with an extension of the corridor on the other side of a border. A shared connectivity conservation vision by politicians and communities on both sides of the border is very important for such a connectivity area.

Legislation and international agreements

- Legislation that supports the conservation and protection of native plants and animals and cultural heritage on all land tenures is critical for facilitating connectivity conservation.
- Legislation that specifically provides for connectivity conservation and its management does not exist in most countries and is formative in others: considerable additional work needs to be undertaken by most countries to develop and support such legislation.

- Legislation permitting formal recognition of conservation easements and areas on private lands may need to be developed.
- Legislation that enables or facilitates financial resourcing for natural lands stewardship needs to be further developed, particularly with respect to potential returns from water and carbon markets.
- The Convention on Biological Diversity's Programme of Work on Protected Areas specifically recognizes connectivity conservation as a major initiative for 2015 and this can be used as a major incentive for action.
- International migratory bird agreements (such as those entered into between Mexico, US and Canada) can inspire connectivity conservation actions.

Legislation specifically designed for achieving and managing connectivity conservation exists in some countries, but it is in its infancy. However, there is growing interest by nations in this approach. Importantly, other legislation such as native wildlife protection legislation that applies to all land tenures has provided opportunities for government and non-government organizations to facilitate connectivity conservation. International agreements and commitments, such as the *Convention on Biological Diversity* and its Programme of Work on Protected Areas (Dudley et al, 2005), Agenda 21 from the Rio De Janeiro Earth Summit, or internationally recognized designations such as UNESCO's Man and the Biosphere reserves or world heritage sites can provide important 'hooks' for engaging governments and funding agencies in connectivity conservation. The adequate, long-term protection of world heritage sites, for example, may require connectivity conservation of surrounding landscapes.

Governance

- Connectivity conservation governance will generally be multi-level – effective governance will generally require connection and communication between local, sub-national, national and international institutions.
- For a connectivity conservation initiative, it is generally best to work with existing conservation groups, other NGOs and funding institutions and partners rather than starting a new group with separate governance structures and competitive financial demands.
- Joint fund-raising can help reduce friction: competition for funds between (for example) large international NGOs can undermine aspects of social capital such as trust and connectivity between organizations.
- Connectivity conservation initiatives do not necessarily need a statutory framework to implement the concept, but they must have an effective and enforced legal framework in place for protected areas.

Being well organized is critical if an initiative is to succeed. Connectivity conservation is an inter-generational action, it directly involves people and it is subject to the range of political influences from local, to national and international. Clarity and commitment to a shared vision is perhaps the strongest and most cohesive force for connectivity conservation organizations, which may include a loose alliance of multiple small community based organizations across a nation and internationally. Flexibility is another critical trait. The governance model chosen needs to be financially sustainable and it needs to be able to endure time with its predictable cycle of connectivity champions and opponents.

Partnerships

- Look for opportunities to join forces with allies who can benefit from land conservation, such as recreationists, hunters, aboriginal peoples and industry leaders.
- Several case studies stress the importance of bringing together land and protected area managers from different jurisdictions to get to know each other and to build camaraderie. This personal connection helps to build a commitment to collaborative efforts and approaches.
- Connectivity conservation has often been more successful when managers on the ground see the value of collaboration.
- Collaborative arrangements can be used between a range of institutions to exchange information about the connectivity conservation initiative and to achieve publicity with the broader community.

- Collaborative planning helps develop an ecological network as part of spatial planning with government.
- Protected area managers and technical teams need to be brought together regularly to discuss successes and failures, and to plan together – building friendships is critical.
- Connectivity corridors often get environmental NGO groups into areas that are outside their realm of expertise, and capacity building and partnerships are needed to deal with aspects such as economic considerations and development planning.
- A shared capacity building across agencies dealing with connectivity conservation leads to consistent management.
- There can be different policy contexts in different countries that can drive the conservation strategies. This may lead to a slightly disjointed overall corridor 'vision', which is less effective than a single, shared vision.

Social interactions between connectivity champions, land managers, property owners and individuals and groups in the community are important and underpin the success of connectivity areas. It is the basis for collaborative projects and partnerships across the landscape. With connectivity areas interlinking protected areas, there may also be opportunities to involve protected area managers as advisors and mentors for connectivity planning and management. Similarly, there may be professional managers within the connectivity lands (such as foresters and farmers) who can assist. Where connectivity areas transcend political boundaries, there may be opportunities to develop social networks well beyond local communities to help achieve connectivity management.

The vision

- There is a need for a bold vision that can be conceptualized in simple and inspirational language. For example, the connectivity initiatives described as 'Yellowstone to Yukon', the 'Sacred Himalayan Landscape', 'Espace Mont-Blanc', 'Gondwana Link' and the 'Australian Alps to Atherton' define geographic areas that are easy to conceptualize and with which

people can quickly identify. Geographic identity can also be supplemented by focal species that can be used to capture public, media and decision maker attention, for example the grizzly bear (*Ursus arctos horribilis*) in the Yellowstone to Yukon connectivity corridor, and the snow leopard (*Panthera uncia*) in the Sacred Himalaya Landscape.
- There is a need for a vision in which all of the people who depend upon the landscape for their livelihood can identify a place for themselves.

The vision is critical. It needs to be clear and meaningful to all concerned. It needs to be developed by the community and 'owned' by them. A connectivity vision that is implemented by individual property owners and local communities (a bottom-up approach) will need to be flexible. The 'big picture' goals will be more important than the detail of how connectivity conservation management is implemented. Being well organized to implement a connectivity initiative needs very careful planning. A vision for connectivity conservation aims to inspire, mobilize and focus people, communities and organizations, and their skills and capacities to help achieve better futures for a connectivity conservation area.

Leadership

- There needs to be a lead institution and a lead individual with clear responsibility for a major connectivity corridor initiative to succeed.
- Connectivity leaders need to define the (broad) connectivity conservation concept early and clearly; otherwise opponents may try to define it in order to modify or stop it.
- Enlist the support of champions and opinion makers.
- Many initiatives started with a big idea and the scientific justification was developed later; use expert opinion and intuition to get the ball rolling.

Many of the great connectivity corridors described in Chapters 4 to 9 owe their existence to visionary and determined individuals and groups who are committed to a better Earth for their children and grandchildren. Good leadership is the difference between a vision for connectivity conservation being achieved or not being achieved. Effective leadership ensures that the vision is clear, that people and communities are involved, that excellent plans are developed, that people are well organized and that the plans are implemented to the fullest extent possible despite potential opposition that may be mounted. This leadership may be grass roots, or government. Leadership may be exhibited in many different ways and by many different individuals acting in their own right or on behalf of a group. Local leadership is very important. Regardless of how much influence there is from IUCN, the United Nations and governments, it is local organizations (and individual people) who will make connectivity conservation happen. Local leadership can be in the form of traditional leadership from an indigenous community, local government leaders, civil institutions, landowners or local NGOs. The Papallacta participants recognized three broad stages in the establishment of connectivity conservation areas, and each stage has different leadership needs.

Stage one. This is the stage where the formative ideas for a connectivity conservation initiative are developed. Often, the key leaders in this stage are NGOs and scientists (groups and/or individuals) but such leaders can come from any sector. NGOs and scientists also usually lead during the idea and vision development stage. This input helps to identify the landscape as having a geographical, cultural, geological, aquatic, social, cultural and ecological unity. The benefits of integrated planning and management are recognized and a focus for research and planning is created. Usually further consultation should include the spiritual or inspirational attributes of the proposed connectivity conservation area.

Stage two. This is the 'planning' stage. It is the stage where a feasibility analysis is conducted to see if the 'connectivity ideas' can be implemented. It is a diagnostic and early analytical stage. It is where governments, state institutions and NGOs play a large role, especially in the planning process. The approach typically includes negotiations, debates and workshops.

Stage three. This is the 'implementation' stage. It is the stage where the idea has been planned and

is being implemented on the ground. The leaders are typically local actors including private landowners, public land managers, private citizens, small NGOs and local government administrators.

Planning

- The planning objectives must be clear from the outset.
- The area subject to planning should be large scale to permit conservation of the four types of connectivity (Chapter 2). It may extend across jurisdictional and land-tenure boundaries.
- A 'least cost approach' should be used to determine the most socially acceptable configuration of core areas (protected areas) and connectivity corridors.
- Connectivity conservation initiatives must be inter-generational (very long term).
- An issues management strategy is important and could include a 'responses to frequently asked questions' statement.
- Local engagement in planning is essential if a connectivity conservation area is to be well supported.
- It is good to have government decision makers, protected areas planners and other land-use planners involved in planning.
- Collaborative planning with government and development planning agencies helps build capacity to be able to examine the full range of issues and needs.
- Connectivity conservation needs to build consensus among diverse actors and this takes time.
- In a landscape where there are threats from industrial, commercial or intensive recreational activities, the emphasis will be on securing policy, legislative, zoning, land acquisition and on communication to a broad general public.
- In a landscape where there are threats due to subsistence activities like securing fuel, growing crops or grazing animals, the emphasis will be on capacity building and communication with local communities, changing individual actions and facilitating alternative opportunities.

Questions such as the nature and scope of the planning exercise, the skills and expertise of the planners, achieving clarity of purpose, being absolutely clear and consistent with terms used and identifying and responding to the social context within which the planning is to be undertaken need to be clearly addressed. Many of these are standard planning considerations (Lockwood, 2006). What distinguishes planning for connectivity conservation is that it is very long term (inter-generational) and may transcend a range of traditional planning boundaries, including national and sub-national jurisdictional borders. Planning will also need to be situational relative to nature, people and management considerations as well as to threats to connectivity conservation.

Communication

- Dissemination and diffusion of information about connectivity conservation is critical.
- There is a need to explain the basics such as: 'What is a connectivity conservation area?'
- A lot of time is needed to share information in networks and across regions and issues.
- An issues management strategy is important and could include a 'responses to frequently asked questions' statement.

Good communication is an art as well as a science. There are a variety of potential audiences for a connectivity conservation effort, including local communities, NGO partners, landowners, government agencies, political decision makers and the media. For each audience, a sophisticated approach will require the development of appropriate messages, messengers and communications tools.

Instruments

- Planning should take advantage of statutory instruments and other land-use management tools that include in-perpetuity conservation agreements, stewardship agreements, easements and zoning.
- Implementation of connectivity conservation management is a social and political question that will involve a number of tools ranging from legislation and policy to individual tools used by land managers and owners.

- The creation of incentives for connectivity conservation is a helpful potential policy option for governments.
- Tax incentives for land set aside from agricultural production are important instruments, as is tax-deductible status for NGOs.
- The reserve system for a nation may be further developed by private investments where it is otherwise impossible for some lands of high conservation value to be protected. Connectivity conservation lands provide a strategic focus for such investments.

There may be a range of incentives that can help people and communities retain the natural environments of connectivity areas. These include local government and municipality schemes that provide rate relief, national (and state) taxation benefit schemes and incentive payments from external parties. In addition, the retention of natural lands for commercial reasons such as ecotourism is a major incentive. Big private game parks such as the natural game reserves adjacent to (and interconnected with) the Kruger National Park in South Africa have successfully maintained natural landscapes as a commercially successful ecotourism destination (Eagles and McCool, 2002).

Finance

- Governments and philanthropic organizations often provide funding for the restoration of catchments and habitats and for responding to pest animal and plant threats. Rather than a dispersed allocation of funds, connectivity conservation areas provide strategic opportunities for such investments and provide greater opportunities for species conservation.
- Carbon trading schemes have made investments in connectivity conservation such as buffer zones around protected areas.
- Reforestation and forest retention projects have been partially funded by companies to offset their carbon emissions.
- Once agreements are reached between countries to collaborate on transboundary conservation initiatives, large organizations such as the IUCN, WWF, Global Environment Facility and others can become significant funders for nations.

- Payments for ecosystem services can be a major source of connectivity conservation funds.
- It is very important to have a local partner to ensure continuity for investment schemes.
- Do not wait for money to get started – the idea can attract resources.
- Commitment from signatories of a Memorandum of Agreement can guarantee that funds support implementation of a programme's agreed tasks.
- It is often useful to have NGO and specific corridor project funding that can complement government funding, overcome government funding bottlenecks and push forward corridor agendas when governments are not proactive.

Effective connectivity conservation management will require a range of support to deal with the situational needs of people and communities, and such needs will change over time. Financial investment is often needed for the active stewardship of connectivity conservation lands and this could come from philanthropic payments, special grants or works, or even larger government management actions such as introduced species control programmes that extend across a landscape. People who own lands within connectivity conservation areas may need financial benefits from these lands, and this could be in the form of resource payments for water and potentially payment for carbon credits in the new carbon economy. Understanding available opportunities is important contextual information.

Implementation

- A programme of work can be a very useful tool for institutional coordination.
- Connectivity management implementation is achieved by maintaining conservation goals, while implementing them through diverse, multi-scale and multi-sectoral approaches, including the use of different tools, and undertaking different activities.
- Restoring or rehabilitating natural environments and reintroduction of species can be critical strategies when designing connectivity.

An effective organization includes the use of a range of implementation tools and systems. For very large organizations, this may include standard information technology systems and frameworks such as The Nature Conservancy's Conservation Action Framework for project management, or the IUCN's Management Effectiveness Evaluation Framework. For smaller organizations, it may simply mean the use of spreadsheets to manage finances and standardized project management arrangements based on Margoluis and Salafsky's (1998) *Measures of Success* or reporting frameworks such as those developed by the World Bank or NGOs. Strategic plans and operational work plans are also very useful organizational tools.

Evaluation

- Do not measure your successes in short-term increments only: change takes time – yet you should celebrate short-term successes.
- Failures are rarely shared – there is a tendency to focus on best practice, but connectivity conservation champions often learn more from their mistakes.
- Monitoring is critical including funding, community dynamics and appropriate payments such as the opportunity costs associated with retaining natural lands.

Evaluation involves assessing the performance of connectivity conservation management initiatives against the vision (including identifying outputs and outcomes achieved) and against the stated objectives for a range of strategic, tactical and operational actions. The process of achieving these results may also be evaluated. The implementation of connectivity conservation management needs to be evaluated for both management effectiveness and political reasons. Evaluation information that is collected needs to be carefully considered, especially in terms of cost, and who is to receive the information and how it is to be used. Adaptive connectivity management responses may originate from such monitoring work.

From practice to conceptual framework

The 25 case studies in Chapters 4 to 9 and the lessons learned from Papallacta (Chapter 10, first section), which we collectively call 'case material', provide evidence for a significant new global land-use phenomenon called 'connectivity conservation'. They identify that the concept is widely recognized as an appropriate response to the crises of biodiversity loss and climate change and is being implemented in myriad of ways in many locations. However, we have also identified (from the literature) that there are questions about connectivity conservation management that are unanswered even though work is happening on the ground. This situation may be acceptable for experienced managers, but there can be a high social and environmental cost associated with trial and error management by others, especially when this approach is repeated across many different connectivity areas.

A number of important questions need to be answered to provide on-the-ground guidance for managers. The questions can be elicited from the case material and include:

1   How does the management of connectivity conservation work?
2   What are the connectivity conservation management functions?
3   What is the process of connectivity conservation management?
4   What are the important connectivity conservation tasks?

These are very basic and practical questions and if they can be answered they will provide an input to a new framework for connectivity conservation management. Such input could be the difference between ad hoc management and a more ordered process to achieve connectivity conservation goals. In the following section we complete a preliminary analysis of the rich case material in relation to these four questions. Our aim was to identify basic building blocks for connectivity conservation management that could then be further developed in Chapter 11.

How does the management of connectivity conservation work?

It is clear from the case material that initiating, planning and implementing a large-scale connectivity conservation initiative is both a complex and a long-term venture. It works best when people want it to work and, as stated for the European Alps, 'only if all levels – from local decision makers to national and international conservation agencies and organizations – share a vision and complement each other in promoting large-scale connectivity in the Alps and in the European mountains is there potential for implementation on the ground' (European Alps, Chapter 9).

A variety of elements are essential to success, one of the most important of which is an inspirational and inclusive vision. Most, if not all, of the initiatives described above (such as Gondwana Link, Chapter 5; northern Sumatra, Chapter 6; and southern Appalachians, Chapter 7) rely on a grand vision that unites iconic landscape elements and is easy to communicate to the community. Such a vision is indispensable to inspire necessary public support for the project to leverage political and landowner engagement. The vision serves as a unifying element that organizes and focuses the many tasks and activities necessary to bring about connectivity conservation on the ground.

The case material also identifies that connectivity conservation works by pursuing multiple strategies that achieve implementation at different spatial scales. The vision and the science that guide the project must occur at a large or 'coarse' scale. This means that a landscape-scale governance approach is needed to set the large-scale and long-term goals for the initiative and to identify the region over which connectivity conservation activities must be coordinated. The ecological approach to connectivity conservation in the Andes needed to use this approach and 'a multi-disciplinary, large-scale approach facilitates connectivity conservation' (Andean Páramo corridor, Chapter 8).

At the same time, many of the actions that will implement the vision occur at the local scale. Changed land use and industrial practices, mitigation of the impacts of transportation corridors, improved protected areas management and altered community behaviours toward wildlife are just some of the ways in which connectivity conservation is implemented at the local level. Professionals in the northern Appalachians observed that connectivity conservation will occur at the local level and stated it will require the conservation of many kinds of lands (wild reserves, sustainable forests and nature-friendly agriculture) (northern Appalachians, Chapter 7).

At this local level, engendering local landowner, tenant farmer and community support for conservation outcomes and the actions needed to bring them about are a huge but necessary challenge for connectivity conservation. When working with the Mesoamerican biological corridor, it was found that connectivity conservation was not effective without an inclusive approach of all sectors of society and 'involving local communities was very important (Mesoamerican biological corridor, Chapter 8). It was also found that connectivity management works by being implemented at different spatial scales by many different individuals and organizations and that management must occur at the appropriate scale (Mesoamerican biological corridor, Chapter 8).

Based on this type of experience, large-scale connectivity conservation management works because of a compelling and shared vision. It is achieved through the active involvement of people from international, national and local scales. The local level is especially critical because connectivity conservation is a shared management approach across many different land tenures and by many peoples.

What are the connectivity conservation management functions?

The case material provides solid guidance for five connectivity conservation management functions.

Understanding the context was an important management function since connectivity management was undertaken in a broad range of landscapes, social and political contexts and situational challenges. This situational context needs to be understood by management. In some regions, challenges relate to the very survival of local human populations dependent on resources from natural lands. In others, armed conflict between

peoples and countries greatly hindered connectivity conservation efforts. In still other countries, challenges are related to large-scale industrial resource extraction activities and transportation and utility networks. The management responses to these different contexts are diverse. Gathering background (contextual) information about a connectivity area was recognized as an important and ongoing task. It is ongoing because local areas are dynamic environments, and new information about the context is constantly needed. There was also a focus on the collection of biotic information as indicated by some of our Papallacta participants who stated 'a basic knowledge and understanding of the ecological values of connectivity conservation corridors is needed'.

People and community contextual information were also very important, including identifying people's values, issues and needs. The views held by the community were considered to be variable depending on geography and were dynamic over time. As stated by our Papallacta participants 'communities are not uniform, and support may vary tremendously across a region according to the social conditions' and 'with the passage of time community support can change, due to raising awareness, capacity building and employment opportunities being created'.

The management environment was also important, especially matters such as legislation and internationally significant sites. Understanding the legal, political, planning and administrative context was considered important and our Papallacta participants stated that knowledge of 'legislation that supports the conservation and protection of native plants and animals … is critical'.

Of course, these different contexts do not exist in isolation, and our case study authors also recognized that an integrated approach to understanding and working with people, nature and management contexts was important. Comments made by two of our authors reinforced this. One from Venezuela stated that 'biodiversity, social and economic rationales can support connectivity conservation' (Venezuelan Andes, Chapter 8); and the second, from Brazil stated that 'linking ecological and cultural values can strengthen conservation efforts' (Serra do Espinhaço, Chapter 8).

Leading was the second important management function identified. It was considered critical for success, was given a high profile in the case material and was identified as occurring in many different ways in connectivity conservation. Its importance was identified from at least three biogeographic realms of Earth including: strong leadership is essential to success (northern Sumatra, Chapter 6); NGOs can lead the way (Cantabrian Mountains–Alps corridor, Chapter 9); identify local champions and persevere (Yellowstone to Yukon, Chapter 7); the commitment of individual managers is critical (European Alps, Chapter 9); government leadership is important (Australian Alps to Atherton, Chapter 5); and political will is essential (Bhutan, Chapter 6).

Successful connectivity initiatives benefit from leadership from a connectivity management organization (where it exists). In some of the cases, the connectivity initiative is led by one or more NGOs. In others, it is government agencies that have begun the process of collaboration and implementation while in others again, the involvement of both NGOs and government agencies has been a key to success. In several cases, large-scale connectivity conservation efforts have occurred because of preliminary work done by dedicated volunteers of non-profit conservation organizations. Leadership at a range of spatial scales is critical to connectivity conservation success.

Planning was a third management function that was important. It was critical to help coordinate and integrate many stakeholders, to provide clear direction, to recognize potential futures and to help establish firm priorities. Clarity of purpose was critical as identified for the southern Appalachians where clear goals and objectives enable the incorporation of new opportunities into connectivity conservation strategies (southern Appalachians, Chapter 7).

Implementing was the fourth function. A key lesson from the case material was that there was no standard way to undertake the management of connectivity conservation. The nature of the activities, the management structure, the nature and location of the leadership and the involved parties vary significantly from situation to situation and in nearly all cases are context specific. Implementation approaches identified included responding to threats (including climate change), the importance of managing for four types of connectivity conservation (Chapter 2), the pace at which connectivity conservation is implemented and the significance of coordinated approaches. How connectivity conservation was implemented was important as identified in the South Africa case where connectivity practitioners learnt that the pace of progress toward connectivity conservation outcomes must match the capacity of participants (Cederberg Mountains–Cape Floristic Region, Chapter 4). Working cooperatively with others was also critical as identified in the Himalayas where managers stated a coordinated approach fosters effective actions (Sacred Himalayan Landscape, Chapter 6).

Evaluating was the fifth management function identified. It was seen as being important for projects that were supported by external funding, as well being central to identifying the long-term success of a connectivity conservation area. The Australian Alps managers identified a need to: ensure regular reporting on projects (Australian Alps, Chapter 5). Above all, connectivity conservation management was seen to address biological imperatives. At the end of the day success needed to be measured by whether or not the long-term future of target species had been assured or improved. Over years of hard work to build widespread support, it could be easy to lose sight of this 'biological bottom line' and to compromise on difficult issues in order to avoid opposition. The most successful connectivity conservation endeavours find innovative ways to continue building support while keeping the biological imperative at the forefront of their efforts. Evaluation is needed to demonstrate performance against this imperative.

Five important functions of management were therefore identified for connectivity conservation: understanding the context, leading, planning, implementing and evaluating.

What is the process of connectivity conservation management?

While individual organizations have their own processes of management, the case material (and literature review) did not identify any specific process of management or management framework developed for large-scale connectivity conservation. This is a gap in connectivity management literature and points to a need for such a framework to be developed.

What are the important connectivity conservation tasks?

From the case material we identified a series of important connectivity conservation management tasks.

Undertake feasibility and scoping studies

Identifying and establishing a connectivity conservation area is a technical and scientific matter. It also needs the participation of the community. The case material identifies an early (formative) planning stage where a connectivity conservation area is first conceptualized, and the first semblance of a conservation vision established. This (very) preliminary work would normally be completed before involving the community. This early planning may be guided by an area being a large-scale natural area such as along a mountain chain; it may involve key species; and it would involve interconnecting (and potentially embedding) protected areas. Maps are very important to provide visual representation of the concept. Relevant comments were made in several of the case studies:

> 'Species' needs provide a rationale for connectivity conservation' (Greater Virunga landscape, Chapter 4) and 'umbrella species can help plan for an effective conservation network' (Venezuelan Andes, Chapter 8).
> 'Mountainous, transboundary regions provide many opportunities for conservation' (Sacred Himalayan Landscape, Chapter 6).
> Protected areas are a prerequisite for connectivity conservation (Venezuelan Andes, Chapter 8).
> Size (large-scale) matters and thinking at a large scale provides new opportunities (Australian Alps to Atherton, Chapter 5).

Establish a community vision

Community support for connectivity conservation was considered to be essential. Connectivity conservation would just not work without the involvement of local people and communities. It was identified that a vision for connectivity conservation needed to be the community's vision, and that it needed to be bold and inspiring. The importance of the vision was discussed by the case material including Gondwana Link, Chapter 5, Yellowstone to Yukon, Chapter 7, and, by the Papallacta workshop participants: 'There is a need for a bold vision that can be conceptualized in simple and inspirational language.'

Undertake pre-planning and establishment work

It takes time and effort to consolidate and move a connectivity conservation concept forward. The case material was very clear that many inputs were needed to initiate a connectivity area, such as where boundaries may be, what design weaknesses exist, what the special values are, what the people's needs are, what threats exist, what the capacities of implementing organizations are, how the area will be managed and other considerations. Some of the case material considerations included:

> 'A science-based approach is required for effective corridor design' (Bhutan, Chapter 6) and 'corridor design is a technical and scientific question' (Papallacta participants).
> 'A basic knowledge and understanding of the ecological values of connectivity conservation corridors is needed' (Papallacta participants).
> 'The needs of local communities are a vital consideration' (Papallacta participants).
> 'Determine social or cultural issues that influence connectivity conservation positively or negatively' (Papallacta participants).

Establish governance and administration

There was strong agreement that a coordinating organization was needed for the conservation management of a connectivity area:

> 'There needs to be a lead institution and a lead individual with clear responsibility for a major connectivity corridor to succeed' (Papallacta participants) and 'a coordinating actor is necessary' (Mesoamerican biological corridor, Chapter 8).

There were a range of views about how the lead organization should be structured, which identified there may be many different (situational) models for governance that could be used for connectivity areas:

> 'A bottom-up approach can facilitate connectivity conservation success'
> (Greater Virunga Landscape, Chapter 4).
> 'Establish a governance mechanism under common law, which facilitates citizen-driven connectivity conservation' (Yellowstone to Yukon, Chapter 7).
> 'A combination of top-down and bottom-up approaches can provide the greatest protection for connectivity' (Bhutan, Chapter 6).

Once established, there were also clear views about implementing the governance of connectivity areas, including the degree of difficulty for some administratively complex areas:

> 'Coordination between responsible managers across departmental boundaries is essential' (Vilcamba-Amboró, Chapter 8) and 'multiple jurisdictional responsibilities hamper connectivity conservation efforts' (European Alps, Chapter 9).

Establish strategic management priorities and requirements

Strategic considerations not only focused on the clarity of objectives and prioritizing tasks, it identified that there may be some 'non-traditional' actions such as support of spiritual and cultural practices that may be taken to help achieve connectivity conservation outcomes. Case study authors also identified that connectivity conservation is a long-term investment, that it is dynamic, and that action may need to happen when an opportunity presents itself:

> 'The planning objectives must be clear from the outset' (Papallacta participants).
> Implementing connectivity conservation management at a large scale is a long-term endeavour (southern Appalachians, Chapter 7; Venezuelan Andes, Chapter 8).
> 'Establish priorities for action' (Yellowstone to Yukon, Chapter 7); but 'strategic opportunism is important' (Gondwana Link, Chapter 5).

> 'Spiritual and cultural practices can support conservation efforts' (Sacred Himalayan Landscape, Chapter 6).

Manage financial resources, human resources and assets

The need for managing funding resources for a connectivity management organization was emphasized. Once funds were secured, it permitted staff to be employed and assets to be purchased. Different sources of potential funding were identified such as from philanthropic investments: 'Partnerships with philanthropic organizations were a key factor of success' (Yellowstone to Yukon, Chapter 7).

Deploy instruments that support connectivity management

A number of leading-edge approaches were described by case study authors that rewarded local people and local land managers for improved management practices. Increasingly, governments, communities and citizens are gaining an appreciation of the many values of intact natural systems. Clean water, productive soils, flood mitigation, clean air, carbon storage and opportunities to experience and enjoy the natural world are just some of the benefits that flow from connectivity and other natural areas. At the forefront of many landscape-scale conservation efforts, mechanisms to financially reward and compensate landowners and occupiers for maintaining ecological goods and services were identified (Papallacta participants; Yellowstone to Yukon, Chapter 7; Mesoamerican biological corridor, Chapter 8; Munchique–Pinche macro-corridor, Chapter 8; Llanganates–Sangay ecological corridor, Chapter 8). These economic instruments go a long way towards reducing local fears and increasing support for conservation projects.

Manage for threats

Threats to the conservation values of connectivity areas were an issue. Mitigation of threats was an important basis for connectivity management, with responses being recommended for both the symptoms of a threat and the root cause. Different types of threats were recognized depending on the development status of the country concerned:

'*Connectivity conservation initiatives must address root causes of ecosystem decline*' (Andean Páramo corridor, Chapter 8).

'*In a landscape where threats are from industrial, commercial or intensive recreational activities, the [management] emphasis will be on securing policy, legislative, zoning and land acquisition and on communication to a broad general public*' (Papallacta participants).

'*In a landscape where there are threats due to subsistence activities, like securing fuel, growing crops or grazing animals, the emphasis will be on capacity-building and communication with local communities, changing individual actions and facilitating alternative opportunities*' (Papallacta participants).

Undertake management operations

There were a range of management operations for connectivity areas such as restoring connections by re-establishing native vegetation, constructing connections over or under transportation barriers, dealing with threats, and anticipating and preparing for incidents. A programme of work was considered important, and there was advice about conducting operations at a pace suitable for all of those concerned with the operation, and in a coordinated (planned) manner.

Strive for sustainable resource use

Local communities may use the resources of connectivity areas and sustainable use is a key aspect of management. There are both sustainable development opportunities and a need to manage for sustainability:

'*Connectivity conservation offers opportunities for sustainable development*' (Serra do Espinhaço, Chapter 8).

'*Connectivity conservation managers need to work with local communities to help achieve sustainable use of natural products*' (Papallacta participant).

Manage for restoration

Restoration was considered to be a critical strategy for large-scale connectivity conservation areas, where habitat fragmentation and damage has impacted the landscape:

'*Restoring natural environments are a critical strategy when designing connectivity*' (Papallacta participants).

'*It [a connectivity conservation area] will require restoration or rewilding*' (northern Appalachians, Chapter 7).

Manage research

Research was identified as being an important task, for often there were critical gaps in information needed for connectivity management. Particular reference was made to the use of scientific models that help to forecast future environments at a time of climate change:

Science is an essential tool for connectivity conservation management (Llanganates–Sangay ecological corridor, Chapter 8) and '*a mobilized, supportive and integrated research contribution is critical*' (Yellowstone to Yukon, Chapter 7).

'*Advanced models for forecasting species, habitats and climate interactions are required*' (Papallacta participants).

Work with partners and with stakeholders

Collaboratively working with multiple stakeholders is normal practice for a connectivity area and is relevant for all tasks completed (it is a cross-cutting issue). Often this collaboration goes further by establishing formal partnerships. This was a very prominent issue for the case material (with 20 items raised) and it recognized actions such as planning, negotiation, capacity building and the involvement of people from local to international levels. Some of the matters raised included:

'*A stakeholder involvement strategy must be established as soon as possible*' (Maloti-Drakensberg, Chapter 4).

'*A cooperative approach that welcomes diverse actors has multiple management benefits*' (Cape Floristic Region, Chapter 4).

The involvement of local communities is critical to success, and multiple organizations and agencies must be involved from the outset (Sacred Himalayan Landscape, Chapter 6).

Building a broad base of support … can lead to long-term benefits and recruiting young people can help to ensure the future (southern Appalachians, Chapter 7).

'*Involving indigenous people in planning helps ensure positive outcomes*' (Vilcamba–Amboro conservation corridor, Chapter 8).

'*Local capacity building can help ensure appropriate management for conservation*' (Munchique–Pinche macro-corridor, Chapter 8).

'*International and interregional cooperative arrangements create opportunities for large-scale connectivity conservation initiatives*' (European Alps, Chapter 9).

'*The support of international agencies is often necessary for successful outcomes*' (Bhutan, Chapter 6).

Communicate

Communication was seen as a vital part of connectivity management. It applies to all of the tasks identified (it is another cross-cutting task), and nine separate matters were identified. The issues raised included the importance of education, the accessibility of information and the time-consuming nature of communication:

'*An informed, inspired and supportive community is a powerful ally*' (Yellowstone to Yukon, Chapter 7).

'*Knowledge and information sharing facilitate landowner engagement*' (Cape Floristic Region, Chapter 4).

'*Success depends on good communication*' (Australian Alps, Chapter 5).

'*Publicly accessible information facilitates connectivity conservation*' (Serra do Espinhaço, Chapter 8).

'*Outreach and education are critical*' (Mesoamerican biological corridor, Chapter 8).

'*A lot of time is needed to share information in*

networks and across regions and issues' (Papallacta participants).

Conclusion

In this chapter we have moved from describing lessons learned at the Papallacta workshop to analysing the rich case material information generated by the case study authors. In this preliminary analysis we responded to four questions, which were: How does the management of connectivity conservation work? What are the connectivity conservation management functions? What is the process of connectivity conservation management? What are the important connectivity conservation tasks? Our analysis identified the importance of a unifying and motivating vision for a connectivity area, and that connectivity management was undertaken in a complex, multi-sectoral landscape by many different organizations and at many different spatial scales. We identified five connectivity management functions (understanding context, leading, planning, implementing and evaluating), and also noted an absence of a unifying framework for connectivity conservation management. In responding to the fourth question, we identified important connectivity management tasks that were being undertaken by practitioners from around the world. These findings help us to take our next step. Our aim for Chapter 11 is to analyse the case material further and to bring forward a (new) conceptual framework for connectivity conservation management as well as to describe, relative to a process of management, the actions that constitute the key connectivity management tasks.

Part III

Synthesis

11

Connectivity Conservation Management Framework and Key Tasks

Graeme L. Worboys and Michael Lockwood

Large-scale connectivity conservation areas need to be actively managed. Threats such as habitat destruction, development, pollution, unsustainable use, invasive species and climate change effects need active and continuous responses. There is broad consensus that connectivity areas need to be established and:

> *most conservation biologists and practitioners agree that this [connectivity conservation] is the only viable way to combat the devastating process of fragmentation – which is threatening species, habitats, ecosystems, and ecological processes throughout the globe* (Anderson and Jenkins, 2006, p79).

For connectivity areas to be successful, effective and systematic management is also needed to help conserve species, ecosystems and habitats in a world that is being increasingly impacted by human-caused changes. The nature conservation benefits of effective connectivity initiatives include the maintenance of ecosystems and ecosystem functions, retention of habitats, protection of wild species, securing animal migration routes, and provision of opportunities for species to seek suitable habitat in response to climate change. Benefits to people include access to valued places that would otherwise be subject to transformative development, securing the supply of ecosystems service such as clean water and crop pollination, sustainable use of resources, and long-term local development opportunities including direct employment in connectivity conservation and sustainable resource-based industries and income from incentive and stewardship payments.

Large-scale connectivity conservation areas involve a complex of uses and land tenures, and their management needs to be ordered and systematic, while also having a capacity for innovation and evolution. A framework for connectivity conservation management can assist by providing a unifying conception of connective conservation management and guide its initiation, design and implementation. In this chapter, we use our reading of the literature, experience as managers, and the examples and insights offered by the case material and lessons from Chapters 4 to 10, to construct a connectivity conservation management framework. A draft of the framework was reviewed by 32 connectivity conservation practitioners and scientists at an IUCN-ICIMOD workshop in Dhulikhel, Nepal in 2008. We applied a 'Strength, Weakness, Opportunity, Threat' (SWOT) analysis to the alternatives suggested at Dhulikel to derive the framework presented in this chapter. We then employ this framework to explicate the management tasks identified in Chapter 10.

Components of a management framework

It is evident from the case material that a critical function of management is to research and develop an understanding of the context in which connectivity conservation management takes place, and continually review and update this understanding to inform policy, planning and the implementation of management. We have classified the required understanding into three contextual domains: nature, people and management. A guiding vision for a connectivity area was also seen by practitioners as central to all connectivity management functions. Also apparent is that leadership, while important in any conservation management endeavour, is particularly crucial in the establishment and ongoing performance of a connectivity conservation initiative.

Understanding context

Understanding the context for a connectivity area is a central function for connectivity management. Contemporary connectivity management involves conserving nature at a time of climate change, changing environments and biome shifts. It involves people, their needs, aspirations and livelihoods in a context of a rapidly increasing human population; and it involves a land-use management setting that is subject to government policies, changing politics, competing needs and different demands for skills, tools and financial resources. Natural environment changes (for example) may interact with people, and people respond and influence the nature of the political (management) context.

From the case studies (Chapters 4 to 9), the lessons learned (Chapter 10) and the literature, it is clear that researching and thoroughly understanding the key contexts of nature, people and management is critically important for the success of connectivity management. One-off, one-dimensional contextual assessments are not enough: the three contexts interact with each other, thus potentially generating more complex outcomes that need to be understood and managed. Climate change, for example, will cause biome shifts, and species and habitats will be different for a fixed site over time (Mansergh and Cheal, 2007). This means that some species will move to survive, and the natural characteristics of a connectivity area will be critical to facilitate such movement. Climate change will affect the nature context of many, many areas, with flow-on impacts to people. There may be less (or more) water in streams, there may be large carnivores or mammals present where there had not been before, and there may be new government policies introduced and

new management environments created because of such changes (Welch, 2005; Worboys, 2005b).

The nature context

The nature context is the principal driver for initiating and maintaining connectivity conservation. It is important to consider the four types of natural connectivity discussed in Chapter 2 – that is, habitat, ecological, landscape and evolutionary process connectivity, and their dynamic inter-relationships. The nature context does not function in isolation; it is dynamic and interactive with people and this may have resultant management implications. The nature context as a dynamic setting influences all four types of connectivity, as is illustrated in Figure 11.1.

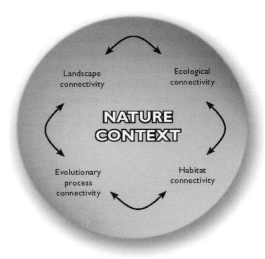

Figure 11.1 The nature context sphere and key research considerations

While scientific surveys and analyses will typically form the backbone of actions designed to understand the nature context of a connectivity area, local knowledge can also be a rich source of information. American Wildlands, for example, undertook, in cooperation with local landowners and government agencies, a rapid assessment of key wildlife connectivity areas for the southern area of the Yellowstone to Yukon Connectivity Initiative. Their work identified over 250 priority

---

Box 11.1 Prioritizing connectivity conservation project areas

Maintaining ecological connections or wildlife linkage areas between major wildlife habitats is one of the most pressing conservation challenges in the northern Rockies of USA. National parks, refuges, wilderness and roadless areas that are not connected can potentially isolate populations of a wide range of species such as the grizzly bear (*Ursus arctos horribilis*) and wolverine (*Gulo gulo*). American Wildlands, a conservation group based in Bozeman Montana, and primarily involved in maintaining and conserving habitat connectivity, needed to prioritize its efforts to efficiently use its available resources. A survey to identify the most important connectivity areas was completed. The assessment focused on ecological quality, threats and 'opportunity for conservation', and the data were collected using expert-opinion interviews with locals with a focus on public lands. The information was scored in a database linked to spatial GIS data, and over 250 major linkage areas were identified for eight species. These assembled data can be analysed further (for example) to estimate conservation needs for individual properties or organizations, to assess where wildlife/transport conflicts occur (or could occur), and which linkages are used by highly specialized species.

Source: Johnston and Olimb, 2008

---

wildlife linkages across the northern Rockies in Montana and Idaho as a result (Box 11.1).

The people context

People live in, utilize, care about and manage connectivity conservation areas. For protected areas, on many occasions in the past, conservation actions have been taken with too little involvement of local people. These were formative times for protected areas and their management, and approaches have changed (Phillips, 2003; McNeely et al, 2006). At the beginning of the 21st century, there are new, progressive, *Convention on Biological Diversity*-driven initiatives that aim to achieve conservation beyond protected area boundaries and at a landscape scale help to conserve the integrity of natural landscapes and their embedded, interconnected protected areas (Ervin et al, 2009). Large-scale connectivity conservation is one of these initiatives and because it involves lands of multiple tenures and diversity of sectoral interests, people are naturally involved as part of achieving conservation management. Understanding the context of people within a connectivity conservation area is fundamental.

The dynamic people context and its key contextual information needs are represented in Figure 11.2. Contemporary information about this context needs to be constantly available. Researching the people context should address all the social, economic and cultural considerations

discussed in Chapter 3, including peoples' needs, aspirations and values. It should identify what people care about, their concerns and preferences. It will typically include an assessment of community knowledge, views and attitudes about connectivity conservation in general and the effect of a particular initiative. Threats to people and from people need to be understood, as well as the dynamics of people in the landscape. Migration of people is a major reality for many natural areas. Such migration may be caused by displacement due to conflict or environmental events including

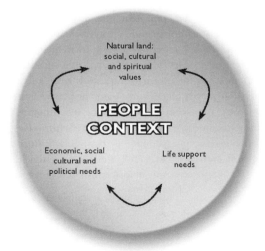

Figure 11.2 The people context sphere and key research considerations

---

Box 11.2 Amenity migration

Around the world there is a growing migration of people to mountain (and other) areas to benefit from their remaining natural areas and distinct cultures. This 'amenity migration' is recognized as migration to places that people perceive as having greater environmental quality and a more 'rural' culture. Amenity migration is the outcome of a complex web of many dynamic motivation factors including superior natural environment, leisure and learning, economic gain, and flight from large cities. It is also helped by many factors such as discretionary time and wealth, access-facilitating technology, and comfort amenities (such as paved roads, water, electricity, waste management, medical care and fire support services). However future higher energy costs such as aviation fuel will be a constraint.

Amenity migration induced population change in mountains is considerable, rapid and characteristically stressful for residents and newcomers. It can create a complex, turbulent and, at times, unexpected mix of animosities and conflicts, convergences and alliances. In the USA for example, this may witness rancher and environmentalist in conflict or collaboration, and newcomers for and against local 'growth' or 'development'. Newcomers may lack attachment to a local area. Locals may be displaced by an increase in price of goods and services; however, the newcomers also help create wealth and jobs in the mountains. The natural environments sought are those that are found in natural connectivity conservation areas, with the consequent conflict with natural lands that this urbanization brings. Issues such as the reduction of habitat area, increasing fragmentation, wildlife harassment, weeds, impacts on streams and an increased fire hazard are some of the problems that accompany amenity migration.

Source: Moss, 2006

---

drought, fire, storms, floods or tsunami. There are also economic migrants and a newly recognized phenomenon of 'amenity migration' (Box 11.2).

The management context

Researching the management context involves identification of how land is legally and institutionally organized, planned and managed. It includes the laws and policies of governments, plans of organizations, authorities and companies, and the tenure and planning status of land. The management of a typical connectivity conservation area will be guided and influenced by a wide range of treaties, conventions, agreements, policies, legislation and plans. At the international level, for example, instruments such as the *Convention on Biological Diversity* provide broad direction for the conservation of species and ecosystems.

National and sub-national laws concerning protected areas, threatened and vulnerable species and ecosystems, forestry, water, agriculture, mining and tourism will often apply. At least three countries in Asia, for example (Bhutan, India and South Korea), have specific legal instruments that provide for the establishment of connectivity areas, and other counties, including Argentina, Brazil, Canada

and South Korea, have enabling instruments (IUCN, 2007). Local land-use plans must also be taken into account. Current policy and management instruments such as education programmes, economic incentives or voluntary management agreements may assist or inhibit achievement of connectivity conservation outcomes. Many people – technical experts, local communities, NGO workers and government agency staff – will possess knowledge that can inform the management of a connectivity conservation area. The capacity of land managers and local communities needs to be understood. As with nature and people, this dynamic management context and its key information needs are presented as a sphere (Figure 11.3).

Context: A management function with three priority inputs

Each of the three contexts has its own internal dynamic and contextual interactions that influence management (Figure 11.4). All three contexts interact with each another and create an even more complex dynamic. These outcomes need to be constantly monitored and analysed in order to ensure that management is appropriate and effective.

Figure 11.3 The management context sphere with key research considerations

Leading

Leading is perhaps the most critical management function for connectivity conservation. It may be exhibited in many ways. A charismatic leader may champion the cause of conserving a connectivity area. A national government may provide leadership by transforming the legislative and policy environment and it may provide resources in support of connectivity conservation. A farmer may demonstrate leadership by pioneering new ways of conserving habitat within a connectivity area.

A major challenge for leadership is to be truly collaborative and not dominated by one or a few individuals or organizations. Sustained leadership from all levels is needed, and empowerment needs to occur across all spatial scales. Leaders involved at different scales need to participate in idea development, planning and implementation. Where leadership is concentrated in a small number of individuals, or in one or two organizations, building the capacity of others to assume leadership roles will be important.

Implementing the management of connectivity conservation requires leadership, constant vigilance and good information to ensure that adequate responses are made to critical issues. The attributes of an individual connectivity conserva-

tion leader identified by Papallacta Workshop participants included:

- being a visionary and having a consistency of vision;
- having a deep understanding of the connectivity concept (philosophy) and perspectives on development held by others;
- being an innovative thinker;
- being flexible;
- having a responsible outlook;
- having an ability to take the initiative;
- having the ability to access, analyse and synthesize information;
- leading by example;
- having the courage and ability to take action;
- having the ability to change the status quo and develop new approaches that can further a connectivity vision (such as off-reserve land use changes) (IUCN WCPA, 2006).

Planning

In essence, planning is concerned with the future and, in particular, future courses of action. Planning is a process for determining 'what should be' (usually defined by a series of objectives), and for selecting actions that can help achieve these objectives:

> *Improved conservation outcomes will not occur on non-protected areas by accident. Rather, careful long-term planning is an imperative. Planning for the long-term conservation of biodiversity must assume worst-case scenarios and take an unashamedly cautionary approach* (Soulé et al, 2006, p666).

Planning can occur at various geographic scales. Land-use planning is the process of deciding in a broad sense which areas of land will be used for what purpose, including which areas will be identified as connectivity conservation areas. Such processes may include a scientifically based selection procedure, as well as many other elements that provide for community involvement, effective decision making and implementation. Area management planning is concerned with how to manage these areas once their land-use designation has been determined, including definition of core, corridor and buffer zones (Lockwood, 2006). Planning is also required to

Figure 11.4 The context management function that includes three dynamic and interacting inputs

ensure that systems and process designs are appropriate to management needs and directions.

The function of planning is commonly undertaken at three levels of detail. Organizational goals are often translated into strategic plans that, as they pass down the hierarchy, are translated initially into a series of tactical and then operational plans (Worboys and Winkler, 2006a). To achieve its principal purpose, an organization identifies what major strategic goals must first be attained, and the ways to achieve these goals. Such plans have ramifications for the whole of an organization and have a long-term time frame. A strategic management plan is important for connectivity

conservation since it articulates planning for an entire landscape or landscapes within a connectivity area. It should identify the purpose of the connectivity conservation initiative; it should establish priorities and provide a framework for more detailed tactical and operational plans. Examples of strategic planning also include: corporate planning; organizational policies; organizational planning and budget systems and business planning; management effectiveness evaluation systems including monitoring; organizational baseline sustainable performance measures; and operational procedural systems and statements.

Tactical plans set tactical goals that help in the implementation of a strategic plan. They typically prescribe how parts of an organization's strategic plan are to be achieved. Tactical plans establish a set of steps to achieve each tactical goal. Good tactical planning ensures efficient and effective allocation of an organization's internal resources. Operational plans are directed towards actions and short-term goals derived from the strategic and tactical plans. Operational plans may be developed as a consequence of tactical plans. As such, they contribute to achieving tactical goals (Worboys and Winkler, 2006a).

Implementing

Implementation involves carrying out management of the productive processes that convert inputs into goods and services – that is, deploying and putting into practice those inputs, processes and systems that directly contribute to the achievement of conservation outcomes. Undertaking connectivity conservation management actions is critical if the vision is to be achieved. Management actions may be implemented by many different organizations and individuals, and at many different spatial scales.

Evaluating

Evaluating the effectiveness of connectivity conservation management is critical for success. Judgement of success in the long term should be based on whether the vision has been achieved and whether or not more species, ecosystems and habitats have been conserved than would have otherwise been the case. An important task will be to develop a plan for managing evaluation (Margoluis and Salafsky, 1998), which will help identify the evaluation subjects to be assessed (Worboys, 2007), the nature of the information to be collected and used, and the indicators that may be used (Hockings et al, 2006). This will not be easy in a dynamic management environment of a connectivity area, and the plan may need to be regularly improved and updated. Tracking the 'big picture' of the change in condition (from a known baseline) of the corridor environments, as part of achieving the vision, will also be important. Anderson and Jenkins (2006, p46) reinforce this point:

because corridors and other landscape elements are dynamic, it will be necessary to define and monitor a few strategic indicators relevant to corridor integrity – especially those corresponding to connectivity and habitat quality – as a basis for making future adjustments to corridor design.

The vision

A connectivity conservation vision was identified in the case material as a critical part of management and is necessarily part of any management framework for a connectivity area. It needs to be owned by the communities who live in the area encompassed by an initiative, as well as non-local stakeholders. The vision is the 'glue' that provides guidance for multiple individual stakeholders implementing management actions across a range of landscapes and scales. It is a central, guiding force for connectivity management. It is the bold, big idea that unites many people to strive for better futures. A vision should be compelling and motivating. It should tap into people's 'hearts and minds' and inspire enthusiasm and energy to achieve the conservation of the connectivity area. It should offer a view of the future that is clearly better than not undertaking action, it should fit the times and circumstances and it should reflect the uniqueness of the organization. People also need to believe the vision is attainable. It should be challenging but 'doable'. The visions that work best are those that have powerful imagery and are easily grasped and accepted (Robbins et al, 2003). One example of a vision statement is that of the Yellowstone to Yukon (Y2Y) initiative:

Combining science and stewardship, Y2Y seeks to ensure that the wilderness, wildlife, native plants, and natural processes of the Yellowstone to Yukon region continue to function as an interconnected web of life, capable of supporting all of the natural and human communities that reside within it, for now and for future generations (Y2Y, 2007).

The management framework

Management of connectivity conservation needs to be planned and implemented in a systematic manner, especially given the complexity and dynamic nature of connectivity areas. The vision provides clarity of direction and purpose for managing connectivity conservation areas, but what is the most appropriate sequence for undertaking the management functions? Does it actually matter? Or is some form of order and sequencing of events useful? Connectivity conservation is different from managing a single land-use type by a single organization. A connectivity management organization may, for example, comprise a single authority, a coordinating body representing a consortium of other organizations, or multiple organizations acting in partnership. It may be accountable for coordinating and facilitating the work of multiple individuals and organizations all of whom have their own management systems and management processes. Given this variability of management approaches and the multiple separate

management actions, a broad management framework that provides guidance for a systematic approach is likely to be helpful.

Responding to this need, we have prepared a management framework that incorporates the five management functions identified above – understanding context, leading, planning, implementing and evaluating – structured according to a familiar process of management and directed by a guiding vision (Figure 11.5). The context management function is located centrally and provides and receives information with each of the four management process functions. Connectivity leadership is given primacy and helps drive a management cycle of planning, implementation and evaluation functions that are directed towards fulfilment of the vision.

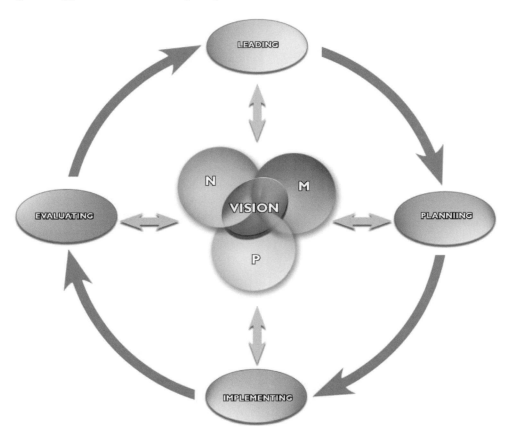

Figure 11.5 Management framework for connectivity conservation management

Notes: M = Management Content
N = Nature Content
P = People Content

Given its critical importance and role, we have placed the vision at the heart of the framework. A vision is not an active management function. It guides management by describing the purpose and desired future for a connectivity area. It is located centrally to emphasize that it is the guiding and driving influence for all aspects of connectivity management. As noted above, it is the 'glue' that holds connectivity conservation management together in an operating environment that is geographically large scale, complex, involves multiple stakeholders and is dynamic.

The context function is centrally positioned in the framework along with the vision. It is made up of three parts, the nature, people and management contexts and provides vital information for leadership, planning, implementation or evaluation management functions. The spherical presentation of the three contexts identifies that they are a dynamic environment in their own right, and their overlap identifies that they interact with each other. The context function aims to capture relevant and important information from the dynamic world of the connectivity area. The framework illustrates this information flow with arrows that lead from context to each of the management functions. The two-way arrows identify that there is contextual information flowing back from the process of implementing management.

The two-way arrows also identify that there may be an iterative process between the different management functions as a basis for achieving the overall broad process (cycle) of management. This cycle is represented as interconnected management functions (using broad clockwise arrows), which start at leading, and then flow to planning, implementing and then evaluating. A well informed leader (for example) using contextual information would inspire action to deal with a management task. The action would be planned, implementation would occur, and the results of the management intervention would be evaluated. Midway though the management process, evaluation may take place, more planning completed and the implementation refined. The conceptual management framework therefore represents a dynamic, potentially iterative, but broadly ordered process of management for a connectivity conservation area.

Spatial scales

Connectivity management may be implemented at a number of different spatial scales. These include a whole of connectivity area level (such as a multi-country mountain chain), national, landscape, transboundary and site-level spatial scales (Figure 11.6). The management framework works effectively for each of these scales.

Connectivity conservation management tasks

In Chapter 10, we identified a set of broad tasks that are deemed important by connectivity conservation practitioners. These tasks address the initiation and delivery of connectivity conservation management, as well as crucial engagement work:

Foundational tasks

1 Undertake feasibility and scoping studies.
2 Establish a community vision.
3 Undertake pre-planning.
4 Establish governance and administration.
5 Establish strategic management priorities and requirements.

Delivery tasks

1 Manage finances, human resources and assets.
2 Deploy instruments.
3 Manage for threats.
4 Assist management of incidents.
5 Strive for sustainable resource use.
6 Rehabilitate degraded areas.
7 Provide and manage research opportunities.

Cross-cutting tasks

1 Work with partners.
2 Work with stakeholders.
3 Undertake communication.

In organizing the tasks in this way, we do not mean to imply that they are or should be undertaken in any particular sequence. While some 'foundation' tasks, such as undertaking a feasibility study, will logically need to occur at an early stage and may be 'one-off', others such as those addressing governance and strategic management are likely to be ongoing and include review and improvement

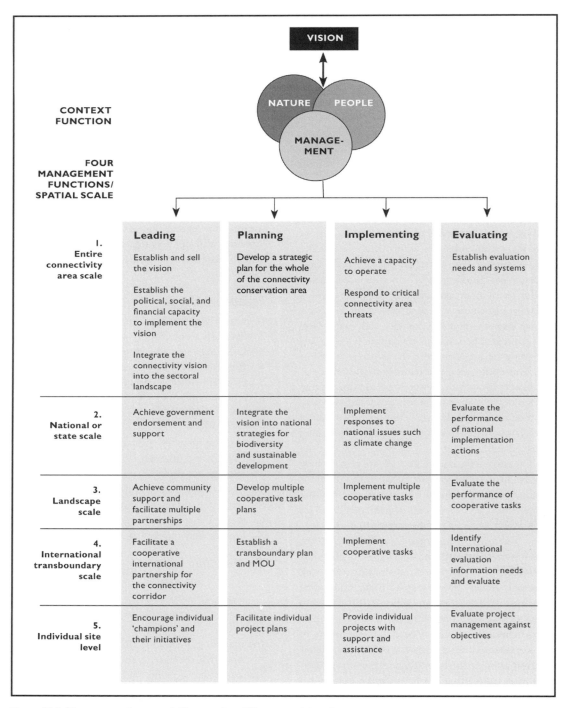

Figure 11.6 Management framework illustrated at different spatial scales

processes. Some 'delivery' tasks, such as deployment of incentive instruments, may already be being undertaken, and can be immediately integrated into a connectivity conservation initiative, possibly with some modifications to their focus and design. Others such as managing assets or rehabilitating areas are likely to commence following the initial establishment of a governance and administration capability, and proceed on an ongoing basis thereafter. 'Cross-cutting' tasks will generally be ongoing throughout both the initial establishment and ongoing delivery phases.

In this section, we consider each of the 15 management tasks in relation to the framework of management. For each task, we suggest a series of actions that will typically be required to fulfil the five management functions of understanding context, leading, planning, implementing and evaluating. Again, listing the management functions in this order is not to suggest that actions are undertaken sequentially: understanding context, leading and planning, for example, may occur concurrently in the early stages of undertaking a task, and continue throughout the process. Some implementation may begin before planning is complete. Evaluation may be most evident following completion of key phases of a task, but can also be undertaken on a more continuous basis, especially where a process for achieving a task needs refining. We also exemplify some actions by providing cross-references to case studies from Chapters 4 to 9.

Foundation tasks

Undertake feasibility and scoping studies

This task involves researching the desirability and viability of establishing a connectivity conservation area, broadly defining the location and boundaries of the area, and establishing a preliminary vision and broad purposes for the area. These foundational activities will generally be initiated and implemented by the organization or consortium, whether government, private, NGO or community-based, that is driving the initiative. At this early stage, this organization may be acting unilaterally, but as with all other tasks, initial studies can be strengthened by beginning the process

of building partnerships, engaging stakeholders and communicating intentions (the three cross-cutting tasks).

Desirability and viability assessments, preliminary examination of the spatial location and extent of the connectivity area, and setting preliminary direction through draft vision and purpose statements, all require an understanding of the natural, social and managerial context. Successful implementation of these actions will require strong leadership from, and effective planning by, key personnel within the initiating organization. Suggestions for the specific management actions needed to fulfil this task are given in Table 11.1.

Establish a community vision

A draft vision has been developed as part of the previous task. This initial specification will largely reflect the views, values, concerns and aspirations of the initiating organization. However, there may be a big difference between a group of professionals and local conservation champions envisioning a preferred future, and achieving wider community support for the direction and purposes of a connectivity conservation area. As the case examples show, the communities living within and potentially affected by a connectivity conservation area should be co-architects of the vision. The environmental planning, management and governance literature also emphasizes the ethical and practical importance of community ownership of conservation initiatives (see for example, Healey, 1997; Wondolleck and Yaffe, 2000; Webler et al, 2001; Borrini-Feyerabend, 2004).

To develop a vision that has wide and deep community ownership and support, the contextual understanding established under the previous task will probably need to be further developed, refined and in some cases substantially modified. Essential scientific data regarding species distributions and so on should be complemented by affective expressions 'from the heart' – such feelings, which often reflect a strong sense of place (Chapter 3), play an important motivating role. Senses, personal experiences and personal interactions are all important in establishing a vision.

A walk in the forest; a swim in a mountain stream; the aroma of new rain on damp ground; and, count-

Table 11.1 Actions for connectivity conservation feasibility and scoping studies

Management task	Description	Notes
Understanding context		
Document the key natural, social and managerial contexts relevant to the broad region being considered for the connectivity conservation area	Undertake literature reviews, interviews with key informants and stakeholders, and perhaps some primary data gathering, to identify the important context topics and develop a preliminary understanding of each of them	Topics likely to be of importance include: the distribution, requirements and threats to significant animal and plant species and ecosystems; identifying the significance, values and needs of connectivity conservation (Langhammer et al, 2005); international status (see the Sacred Himalayan Landscape, Chapter 6, and the Munchique–Pinche macro-corridor of Colombia, Chapter 8) (Brooks et al, 2006); current land uses, tenures and governance arrangements (Kormos 2008); and socio-economic and cultural conditions, values, concerns and aspirations of people living in and around the region – dynamic influences such as fires, human conflict, pollution and climate change also need to be considered
Leading		
Drive and sustain initial efforts to assess and gather support for the connectivity initiative	Mobilize the commitment and resources needed for foundational tasks	Leadership during this early phase of the initiative can harness community support, but also may have to acknowledge and address scepticism and opposition – demonstrating scientific, social and economic credibility is likely to be a key strategic requirement
Planning		
Develop processes for the efficient and effective delivery of the four implementation actions	Identify who will undertake the implementation tasks, the methods to be used, time frames, budgets and deliverables	The initiating organization may not have the capacity to undertake the implementation actions, and so planning may have to include capacity building and partnership development
Implementing		
Assess the desirability and viability of the initiative	Use the understanding of the context to assess whether the initiative should proceed – there is no standard method for conducting such an analysis: an expert panel, peer review and community forum are some of the possible approaches – of course negative results in the assessment would suggest that it is not wise to proceed with the initiative	Factors to consider include the strength of any political or local community resistance, the extent of land and resource use changes that are likely to be required, and the magnitude of the benefits expected to arise from the initiative

Table 11.1 Continued

Management task	Description	Notes
Identify a potential location and approximate boundaries for the connectivity conservation area	Use the understanding of the context to identify a 'fuzzy' boundary for the connectivity conservation area – conservation planning techniques such as that illustrated in Box 11.3 can assist this identification process	The connectivity conservation area should, as far as practicable, encompass the key natural features to be conserved, including consideration of animal migration patterns (Mackinnon et al, 1986) and long-term ecosystem dynamics and shifts associated with, for example, climate change, and should take into account current land uses and tenures – 'umbrella' species have also been used to help identify a connectivity conservation area (see the Venezuelan Andes, Chapter 8)
Develop a draft vision statement	Use the understanding of the context to develop a draft vision – at this stage the vision will primarily reflect the aspirations and analyses of those leading the connectivity initiative	The draft vision should include aspirations for the natural features of the area, and may also address social, cultural and economic matters (see Yellowstone to Yukon, Chapter 7, and Vilicamba–Amboro conservation corridor, Chapter 8)
Develop a draft list of primary purposes for the initiative	Use the understanding of the context to develop a draft list of primary purposes – these directional statements will primarily reflect the aspirations and analyses of those leading the connectivity initiative	The draft purposes elaborate the broad direction given in the vision, and articulate the goals of the initiative, which will address the key nature conservation issues and aspirations, and may, as appropriate, also include social, cultural and economic goals
	Evaluating	
Assess the adequacy and utility of contextual information	Review the needs, processes and systems for collecting and utilizing contextual information, and identify additional information needs	If the evaluation uncovers major information deficiencies, further data gathering may be required, and some planning and implementation actions may need to be repeated
Assess each of the four implementation products	Review the viability conclusions, draft boundaries, vision and purposes – this assessment could be done by peer review, and may also include stakeholders' views	If the evaluation uncovers major concerns, some revision may be required to one or more of the implementation products

less fleeting sounds and sights of magnificent wildlife all heighten your senses to the special values of an area. Participating in cultural ceremonies, listening to stories of the past and experiencing special cultural sites add to this appreciation. The stories of scientists are remarkably rich. Just listening to how wildlife migrate and disperse, which species survive and thrive and what populations are in trouble and why; they are all fascinating. At some stage, there may be a dawning of a collective 'heart and mind' apprecia-

tion of conservation needs at a grand scale, and with it, a resolve to work with many people to ensure such grand wild lands are retained. It is perhaps the beginning of a vision for conservation of grand natural landscapes. It is appreciated that others have already taken such grand steps such as the inspirational large-scale conservation work to help the Tiger in the Terai Arc of Nepal. Motivated by opportunity, appreciation and admiration, my creative ideas for landscape-scale conservation evolve. A Google Earth

Box 11.3 Assessing the viability of target areas for conserving biodiversity

Assessing the viability of areas being considered for biodiversity conservation is a key step in nearly all conservation planning processes (Margules and Pressey, 2000). This holds true for the process of integrating protected areas into the broader landscape, as the extent and distribution of viable populations of focal species and intact ecosystems form the cornerstone of a functioning ecological network. Species viability is defined as the extent to which a population can maintain its vigour, and maintain its ability to adapt and evolve over time (Soulé, 1987). Ecosystem integrity, a related concept, is the degree to which an ecosystem has the full range of elements, such as species, communities and structures, and the full range of naturally occurring processes such as biotic interactions, disturbance regimes and nutrient and energy flows (Groves, 2003).

In many conservation planning processes, species viability assessments focus primarily on three indicators: size (that is, the population size or size of the ecosystem patch); condition (that is, the quality of the species habitat); and immediate landscape context (that is, the condition of land and water surrounding the habitat patch) (Groves, 2003). They are less likely to focus on connectivity aspects in their viability analyses. One of the challenges to conservation planners is the difficulty in combining rankings of size, condition and landscape context to arrive at an overall ranking for viability. The matrix in Figure 11.7 shows one method of integrating these three factors.

Source: TNC, 2006

Overall Viability Summary

East Molokai – Hawaii

Conservation Targets	Landscape Context	Condition	Size	Viability Rank
1. North Shore Forests and cliffs	Fair	Good	Fair	Fair
2. Montane Wet Forest	Fair	Very Good	Fair	Good
3. South Slope Mesic Forest & Shrubland	Poor	Good	Poor	Fair
Overall Biodiversity Health Rank				Fair

Figure 11.7 Matrix method for assessing ecological viability of areas

Source: Adapted from Ervin et al, 2009

computer scan of the local landscape from forest patches to its continental scale mountain range, a debate about landscape conservation opportunities with colleagues, and finally an emergence of firmer ideas for a visionary large-scale connectivity conservation area. How it fits into the larger vision for biodiversity conservation for a landscape and establishing its principle purpose are critical checks and help to refine an early, un-articulated vision further. The motivation to start creating a conservation future for this special area is confirmed.

These fictionalized reflections of one person's experiences and influences illustrates that a vision is not always a grand flash of inspiration. It may evolve steadily and in many different ways, over time, and be influenced by many people and encounters.

Another important consideration in developing a vision is the meaning of 'community'. Communities can be identified according to cultural and spiritual beliefs and practices, socioeconomic commonalities, connection to a particular locality (sense of place), and/or a common interest in nature conservation, for example, or in a particular resource sector (agriculture, forestry, fishing, mining or tourism). This diversity of meanings suggests that there is no 'one community' that will be concerned about a connectivity conservation area. Given the spatial extent of a typical connectivity initiative, a 'local' community is unlikely to be homogenous and is probably actually comprised of multiple, overlapping communities. To add to this complexity, 'communities of interest' will not be confined to the connectivity area. Nature conservation stakeholders, for example, form a community of interest that is scattered throughout the world. People far removed from a connectivity conservation area will have legitimate interests in and claims to the visioning process (and indeed to connectivity conservation decision-making processes more generally): local interests, while important, do not automatically 'trump' non-local interests. Nonetheless, some communities will have stronger interests than others, and there will be practical limits to how many groups and individuals can be included in engagement processes. All this suggests that connectivity conservation leaders and managers need to think carefully about with which communities they need to engage and how this best might be accomplished. In some initiatives, attempting to develop a 'community' vision may be their first exposure to such matters, and there are likely to be many opportunities to learn from this experience.

Suggested actions to secure a 'community' vision are given in Table 11.2. In pursuing these actions, care must be taken that approval of the draft vision developed in the previous task is not seen as fixed, and that it does not become the agenda behind community engagement – stakeholders must have a genuine opportunity to influence and shape a vision for the connectivity area that is meaningful for them. It is also possible to envisage cases where the community vision may have little in common, or major points of conflict, with the draft vision put forward by an initiating organization. In such cases the initiating organization can set aside its own vision and support the community view, extend the engagement in an attempt to reach a compromise or consensus, or withdraw from the initiative. Forcing an unpopular vision onto communities is neither a viable nor appropriate option.

Undertake pre-planning

Pre-planning includes providing input to assessment of reserve adequacy and encouraging and facilitating reserve establishment, delineating the broad connectivity conservation area, identifying critical connectivity linkages (especially between protected areas), identifying choke points, progressively refining the connectivity conservation purposes, identifying key threats, identifying information management needs and urgent research, and identifying a preferred governance model. These actions (Table 11.3), which are spread across the context, planning, implementation and evaluation functions, generate the need for additional associated actions, and provide the knowledge and direction needed to build effective and appropriate organizational structures and capacities.

Under this task, the crucial design work for the connectivity conservation area is undertaken. This planning identifies key habitats within connectivity conservation areas – large-scale connectivity corridors that embed protected areas also include other tenures with important species habitats (Bennett, 2003). Many parts of large-scale connectivity areas include habitat that is critical for the conservation of species, even though it is not possible for these areas to be part of the protected area system. The conservation needs of keystone and umbrella species and potential focal species, patterns of movement (migration) and dispersal, preferred habitat and niches, population dynamics, predator–prey relationships, and evolutionary and adaptation forces can all inform the

Table 11.2 Actions for establishing a community vision

Management action	Description	Notes
	Understanding context	
Research stakeholder aspirations and preferences and test the acceptability of the draft vision	Build on the context understanding already obtained to more fully identify stakeholder aspirations and preferences – this information could be obtained by community surveys, in-depth interviews, community meetings and discussions	As noted above, care must be taken not to bias the process in favour of the draft vision, but use the draft as an important input into an open and deliberative process
	Leading	
Initiate the process to achieve a community vision	Identify relevant communities, and commission a plan for the visioning process	Considerable stakeholder liaison may be required to ensure that a visioning process is supported by, and inclusive of, relevant communities (see comments above concerning different types and locations of communities)
	Planning	
Plan the process of establishing a vision	Identify which communities to include; suitable engagement methods; how to share information; how the draft vision statement is to be used, developed and amended; and how the final vision statement(s) will be determined	The process to develop a community vision should be transparent, inclusive and, where necessary and appropriate, allow for multiple (nested) visions to emerge from different communities or locations, which are broadly consistent with an overarching vision
	Implementing	
Implement the process for establishing a community vision	A typical process is likely to involve: providing information to communities about the draft vision, the values of the connectivity area, and threats to these values; offering opportunities for involvement; facilitating the development of draft visions; and assisting convergence to final vision statement(s)	In some cases the initiating organization may 'host' the process – however, it may be beneficial if the process is run by a community leader or independent facilitator
		People may be inspired by the vision, and opportunities need to be available for how they can contribute to connectivity conservation (see Yellowstone to Yukon, Chapter 7)
	Evaluating	
Assess the effectiveness of the development and engagement process	Identify the strengths and weaknesses of the engagement processes – assessment methods could involve interviews with and/or surveys of key stakeholders at local, national and possibly international levels	Lessons from this evaluation can inform the design of future engagement processes – widespread concern about the process amongst stakeholders would suggest a need to use a different approach and potentially undertake a second round of engagement
Assess the effectiveness of the vision statement(s)	Market the vision statement(s), and undertake research to determine its impact and support	If the results of the effectiveness assessment show a low level of knowledge about the initiative, or luke-warm support for the vision, further engagement work may be required

process of designing connectivity areas. Co-nnectivity-related ecological process issues that may need to be researched include:

- critical species interactions, migrations and dispersal patterns;
- potential refugia for species;
- movements of species in and out of the connectivity area (permeability);
- hydro-ecological processes that underpin landscape primary productivity and habitats;
- human-caused barriers to natural flows and movements of species and materials;

- conditions necessary for continuing evolution, particularly the potential for adaptation and speciation (Soulé et al, 2006).

As the planning and design work identifies long-term conservation characteristics and needs, it ideally would involve climate change modelling to identify future scenarios. Climate change will bring biome shifts and habitat changes. Modelling these changes will help with an analysis of a connectivity area design, including what management objectives have priority and what new threats may be anticipated.

Table 11.3 Preplanning actions

Management action	Description	Notes
	Understanding context	
Undertake detailed mapping of natural features and conditions, together with current land uses, tenures and ownership	Produce or access high-resolution digital map overlays of ecosystems, habitats, significant species, degree of naturalness, land uses and governance	Some of this work may have already been completed in earlier action, and in some areas these data may be available from governments or NGOs – for most areas, collecting and maintaining the currency of this base information will be an ongoing requirement (see Bhutan biological corridors, Chapter 6)
Identify key threats	Document threats to achievement of the purposes of the connectivity conservation area – methods may include document analyses (of media statements, policies, legislation and so on), stakeholder and key informant interviews, community attitude surveys and literature reviews	Threats may stem, for example, from current and proposed land uses, ongoing dispersal of non-local flora and fauna, altered fire or hydrological regimes, climate change, aspirations of pro-development, pro-resource extraction or anti-conservation proponents, and inadequate or poorly conceived policies and legislation
Identify potential governance models	Undertake a literature review and key informant consultations to document alternative governance models for the initiative – some general possibilities are indicated in Box 11.4	This exploratory work ensures that a wide range of possible governance models is considered, including options that may shift power and responsibility away from the initiating organization
	Leading	
Ensure participants maintain motivation and focus	Provide direction, support and encouragement to the people tackling the complex of actions that comprise the pre-planning task	Leaders of the connectivity conservation initiative may need to counteract negative influences (sceptics, political opposition, uncooperative governments and communities), and ensure that a coherent direction is maintained

Table 11.3 Continued

Management action	Description	Notes
	Planning	
Delineate the general boundary of the connectivity conservation area and identify critical connectivity linkages and choke points	Use the digital mapping (see above) to delineate current and aspirational connectivity linkages, choke points, wildlife use areas and potential areas for restoration – tools that may assist with this action include C-Plan (Linke et al, 2008), MARXAN (UQ, 2008), RESNET (Fuller et al, 2006), and the 'Priority Linkage Assessment Process' (Johnston and Olimb, 2008)	This action establishes a general boundary and design for the connectivity area, and clarifies the spatial relationships between the linking natural lands, disturbed lands and embedded protected areas (see Vilicamba–Amboro conservation corridor, Chapter 8) – some design considerations are given in Box 11.5
Refine the purposes of the connectivity conservation area	Consistent with the community vision, and utilizing the understanding of threats, level of disturbance and natural values, establish goals for the connectivity area that provide specific guidance and direction for managing the initiative – the process for developing these goals should in general combine scientific and expert knowledge with community aspirations	The purpose influences the key management objectives, management priorities, the nature of actions and what information is collected for evaluation – the conservation of assemblages of plants and animals including some keystone and/or flagship species are typically a priority purpose, and goals may also be developed for cultural, social and economic aspects of management (see Cederberg-Cape Floristic Region connectivity conservation, Chapter 4)
	Implementing	
Provide input to assessment of reserve adequacy and encourage reserve establishment	Support ecological gap assessments comparing what exists with what is needed and promote the establishment of a nation's comprehensive, adequate and representative reserve system together with the use of a systematic conservation planning process (Box 11.6)	As protected areas will in general form the core of a connectivity conservation area, it is important that this core adequately protects a representation of a regions' species and ecosystems – systematic conservation planning processes provide a formal structure for the design of such a protected area network
	Evaluating	
Identify urgent research	Assess the adequacy of the contextual data for underpinning pre-planning actions and prioritize research needs	This assessment may reveal data inadequacies – ideally such inadequacies should be dealt with by urgent actions that augment or repeat previous contextual research, so that pre-planning actions are supported by robust information
Identify and assess potential information management systems	Review systems being used by other protected area and connectivity area organizations, and identify features of these systems that may match the context and requirements of different models for information management	In a complex and data-intensive endeavour such as connectivity conservation, an effective information management system is critical – assessing potential systems should consider information needs, integration, acquisition, verification, storage, retrieval and utilization

Table 11.3 Continued

Management action	Description	Notes
Identify a preferred governance model	Assess each of the potential governance models (see above) and select a preferred model – a suitable assessment method might include soliciting key informant, partner and stakeholder responses to each option, and/or a multi-criteria analysis (see Lahdelma et al (2000) for an overview)	Two broad assessment criteria might be: (i) fitness for purpose (whether the model will work in the environment in which it is operating, and whether it will have the capacity to address the purposes of the connectivity conservation area); and (ii) quality (the extent to which the model satisfies the principles of legitimacy, transparency, accountability, inclusion, fairness, connectedness and resilience (Chapter 3))
Assess the above planning actions	Review the design and purposes of the connectivity conservation area – scientific, economic and community-based methods could be used	Ideally, the results from the planning actions above should be tested for their scientific merit and community acceptability – potentially a cost–benefit analysis could also be conducted to identify their economic implications

Establish governance and administration

Governance addresses who in an organization makes the decisions and how. It is about power, relationships, responsibility and accountability within and between organizations. It is about who has influence, and who makes the decisions (Borrini-Feyerabend et al, 2006). It has been defined as:

> the interactions among structures, processes and traditions that determine how power is exercised, how decisions are taken on issues of public concern, and how citizens or other stakeholders have their say (Graham et al, 2003, pp2–3).

Effective governance is critical for the management of a connectivity area. In a previous action (Table 11.3), a preferred governance model for the connectivity conservation area was identified. This task involves implementing this preferred model and establishing the associated administrative processes and capabilities that will make the connectivity organization or network functional. The core areas of administrative capacity are finance, human resources, information and assets. Suggested actions to establish the required governance and administration institutions and processes are given in Table 11.4.

Establish strategic management priorities and requirements

Strategic management deals with the big-picture responses needed for a connectivity conservation management. Guided by the vision, strategic management sets measurable objectives and identifies and prioritizes actions that can meet these objectives (Table 11.5). These objectives and actions may focus on linking areas and degraded zones, as well as cross-boundary matters related to embedded protected areas and the lands adjacent to the connectivity conservation area. Strategic management of the core protected areas is generally dealt with by separate governance bodies and is subject to their own planning, implementation and evaluation processes, many of which are detailed in Lockwood et al (2006).

For the connectivity area, many objectives and actions will involve establishing partnerships, engaging with landholders and providing incentives for land-use and behavioural change:

> By its nature, most 'link habitat' is owned by someone else and is most likely managed for objectives other than conservation. Maintaining it, and to an even greater extent improving it, for conservation is therefore usually a matter of negotiation and trade-offs (Dudley and Rao, 2008, p13).

Box 11.4 Six potential governance models for a connectivity conservation area

The following six models indicate some of the possible governance arrangements for a connectivity conservation area. Many other variations are also possible.

1   *Single 'top-down' organization.* An organization with wide ranging powers and/or resources – such as a government, an authority established and appointed by government or (rarely) a large international NGO, may assume sole governance responsibility for a connectivity conservation initiative. This is a 'top-down' model in that the ultimate power to determine processes and reach decisions is held within the organization, which are then passed down to or imposed on local-level actors. The top-down nature of such arrangements may be moderated by engagement processes initiated by the governing organization – however, the ultimate authority still resides with that organization. This model may be popular in jurisdictions where strong central government is the norm. It may also be used in the early phases of an initiative, particularly when the government or NGO is the initiator. At the moment, for example, the Alps to Atherton initiative in Australia (Chapter 5) is being led by a government agency, the New South Wales Department of Environment and Climate Change. However, it is likely that as this initiative matures, another governance model will be adopted that is less 'top-down'. The Y2Y effort is led by a single NGO that establishes multiple ground-level partnerships to deliver implementation actions.

2   *Single 'bottom-up' organization.* A local indigenous or community-based organization may initiate and assume sole governance responsibility for a connectivity conservation area. However, given their spatial extent, most initiatives would encompass multiple indigenous lands and local communities, so that a multi-community 'bottom-up' model along the lines of options 4, 5 or 6 is likely to be required.

3   *Decentralized authority.* Decentralization of government responsibilities and, on occasion, powers, is a feature of contemporary environmental governance. In a connectivity conservation context, a government may, for example, devolve responsibilities to a regional (landscape-level) authority. Many variations are possible in the make-up of such an authority – office bearers for example may be elected by a regional constituency or appointed by a government minister. The degree of autonomy granted to an authority can also vary considerably. At one extreme, a government may limit the devolved powers by, for example, making funding conditional on the organization pursing a particular strategic direction and adopting approved processes. At the other extreme, a government may grant an authority full independence.

4   *Representative authority.* A 'local government' model for a connectivity conservation organization is one in which its authority and office bearers are legitimized though an electoral process. The constituency for such an organization might be the residents of a defined geographic area encompassed by, and perhaps adjacent to, a connectivity conservation area.

5   *Representative federation.* Several organizations can come together and create a federation that represents each of their interests. Under such a federation, each member organization influences policy and direction, leaving day-to-day management to a secretariat lead by a director or general manager. The federation may be formalized through articles of association, Memorandum of Understanding (MOU) or contract. Members may include governments, NGOs, private companies and community-based organizations.

6   *Loose confederation.* Several organizations can come together in a partnership focused around the vision for a connectivity area. Under this model, there is no secretariat to coordinate and implement the initiative. Each partner undertakes actions according to their own interpretation of what is required and using their own capacities, perhaps supplemented by any additional resources brought in by confederation. The Andean Páramo connectivity corridor (Chapter 7) is an example where partnerships have been established between four countries, (and within each country, from site- to national-level involvement) to help conserve the transboundary Páramo ecosystem.

Issues that may require action include urbanization and development, transportation, energy, tourism, wildlife use, agriculture and grazing, forestry and agroforestry, freshwater resource management, waste management, invasive species management, climate change, the legal and judiciary environment, inter-sectoral communication and conflict (Ervin et al, 2009). The ecosystem

Box 11.5 Connectivity conservation area design considerations

1 Small or isolated protected areas cannot accommodate climatically driven biome shifts: 'Large contiguous areas are needed to accommodate essential movements and flows' (Soulé et al, 2006, p655) and 'conservation of large tracts of high-quality habitat in landscape corridors provides the best hedge against climate change impacts' (Anderson and Jenkins, 2006, p35).

2 Connectivity conservation areas provide opportunities for species to move and to survive and 'without the ability to move as connectivity is lost, climate disruption will have a profound and negative consequence on the diversity of life on Earth' (Bennett et al, 2006, p678).

3 Habitat connectivity is characteristic of natural environments and 'protection and restoration of connectivity is not an artificial change to the landscape; rather, it is the loss of connectivity and the isolation of natural environments that is an artefact of human land use' (Noss, 1991, cited in Bennett, 2003, p63.).

4 Connectivity conservation provides opportunities for interconnected systems of habitats and 'by increasing the flow of organisms and continuity of processes between parts of the landscape mosaic, there is potential to build habitat networks that integrate conservation efforts at multiple levels, including local, landscape, regional, continental and even global scales' (Bennett et al, 2006, p682).

5 Large-scale connectivity conservation areas are important for conserving a range of species 'when the movement of entire assemblages is considered and/or when little is known of the biology of the species concerned, and/or the corridor is intended to function over decades, the appropriate width must be measured in kilometres' (Harris and Scheck, 1991, p204).

approach provides a useful framework for action (Box 11.7).

Delivery tasks

Manage finances, human resources and assets

Managing the financial and human resources and assets needed for connectivity conservation management is a basic but critical task. Management of staff, finances and assets lies at the heart of a connectivity conservation organization's capacity to operate. Finance needs to be secured and managed. Staff and contractors need to be hired and paid, and volunteers and partners supported and mobilized. These personnel may need a base from which to operate – offices and workshops may need to be purchased, constructed or leased. People need to be mobile and to have access to equipment and materials. This may require the use, hire or purchase of transport, vehicles, heavy construction plant and other equipment. Assets include constructed items such as roads, sewer lines, bridges, buildings, trails and various cultural heritage structures, as well as tools, vehicles and intellectual property. Asset manage-

ment systems are needed so that managers can predict when assets will need to be refurbished or replaced ('maintenance cycles') and can allow for these expenses in their annual budget. Staff and volunteers also need a supportive operating framework, which ranges from employment contracts to workplace safety rules and skills training. Systems need to be in place to evaluate and monitor the staff's performance so that professional standards remain high. Numerous routine administrative tasks and systems are needed to support the conservation of a connectivity area. Well-designed administration systems help to manage these needs (Worboys and Winkler, 2006b).

At the same, time, depending on the governance model and capacity base, the extent of 'professionalization' within connectivity organizations will vary. Community-based and local NGO led initiatives may not be able to afford, and indeed may not need, all the administrative and management apparatus of a large professional organization. Nonetheless, the actions in Table 11.6 are broadly indicative of the requirements for effective financial, human resource and asset management.

Box 11.6 Systematic conservation planning

Systematic conservation planning involves the use of explicit and often quantitative objectives, which means that planners and managers must be clear about what they intend to achieve and be accountable for decisions that should make progress toward their objectives. It also involves the principle of complementarity, where systematic methods have identified systems of conservation areas that are complementary to one another in achieving conservation objectives. It usually involves working through a structured, transparent and defensible process of decision making and achieves an integrated system of conservation areas. The approach is used for a broad range of spatial scales from ecoregions, countries, provinces, states and local government areas. Bottrill and Pressey (2009) describe 11 broad stages of planning for conservation, each of which can be unpacked further. They advise that not all steps will be relevant to all regions, and that it is not necessarily a linear process. The 11 steps are:

1   scoping and costing the planning process;
2   identifying and involving stakeholders;
3   Identifying the context for conservation areas – assess the social, economic, and political context for the planning process, and assess the constraints for establishing conservation areas;
4   identifying conservation goals – refine the values of stakeholders from a broad vision statement to specific qualitative goals;
5   collecting data on threats and socio-economics – collecting and evaluating spatially explicit data on tenure, extractive uses, costs, threats and existing management as a basis for planning decisions;
6   collecting data on biodiversity and other natural features – collecting and evaluating spatially explicit data on biodiversity pattern and process, ecosystem services and previous disturbance to potential conservation areas;
7   setting conservation targets – translating goals into quantitative targets that reflect the conservation requirements of biodiversity and other natural features;
8   reviewing target achievement in existing conservation areas – assessing the achievement of targets in different types of conservation areas;
9   selecting additional conservation areas – with stakeholders, design an expanded system of conservation areas that achieves targets while integrating commitments, exclusions and preferences;
10 applying conservation actions in selected areas – applying effective conservation actions to areas identified in the conservation plan;
11 maintaining and monitoring established conservation areas – applying and monitoring long-term management in established conservation areas.

Table 11.4 Governance and administration actions

Management action	Description	Notes
Understanding context		
Review potential administration systems	From the literature and consultations with peers, identify the governing organization's requirements for administration systems	The review will help establish appropriate administration systems for the managing organization
Leading		
Achieve recognition of the connectivity conservation area	Engage with politicians, senior government officials and community leaders to achieve recognition for a connectivity conservation area	In its developmental phase, the survival of an initiative may depend on generating recognition, if not support, from governments, major NGOs and community leaders

Table 11.4 Continued

Management action	Description	Notes
Oversee the establishment of governance and administration	Initiate and guide the establishment process, and ensure that any legal and procedural requirements are met	Attention to legal and procedural detail is important to protect the developing organization from unnecessary conflicts and sanctions
Planning		
Develop governance and administration protocols	Develop protocols for matters such as board, committee and staff appointment procedures, financial management, and project management	Good governance requires that these procedural matters pay attention to principles of fairness, transparency and accountability
Implementing		
Establish the preferred governance model	Set up any necessary legislation, contracts, agreements, MOUs and electoral processes; establish any boards and committees and appoint office bearers	The specific mechanisms required to implement a governance model will vary widely – co-governance partnerships are likely to be a feature of many connectivity initiatives (see Australian Alps national parks, Chapter 5)
Establish a supporting 'secretariat'	Appoint staff or identify volunteers who are charged with implementing decisions made by office bearers, boards and committees, and resource this secretariat	Staffing and resourcing will vary widely depending on the stage of maturity of the initiative, local economic and political circumstances, and so on – a staff 'wish list' might include a general manager, administration staff (reception, records management and finance), technical staff (such as a GIS professional), media and communications manager, and project implementation staff; an assets 'wish list' might include an office, information technology systems and vehicles
Establish the preferred information management system	Put into place the staff, processes and technology needed to make functional the information system identified under a previous action (Table 11.3)	Systems are likely to vary widely depending on priorities and available resources – in some circumstances, a connectivity conservation organization may be able to 'outsource' the information capability they need, or access services from a partner organization; where they have the need and capacity to build their own system, approaches such as that described by Sallans (2006) may provide helpful guidance
Evaluating		
Assess the performance of the governance body and secretariat	Prepare an annual report that could include subjects such as output (task) reporting, outcome (performance against the objectives) reporting, process reporting (such as engagement activities, staff capacity to operate and efficiency of achieving tasks against industry benchmarks), as well as human resource management and financial reporting	Reporting of organizational performance is important for transparency and accountability, and can also support continuous improvement processes

Table 11.5 Strategic management actions

Management action	Description	Notes
Understanding context		
Identify natural, social and management factors that will shape strategic management	Undertake a SWOT analysis	A strength is an internal aspect that can improve an organization's competitive situation; a weakness is an internal aspect where the organization is potentially vulnerable to a competitor's strategic moves; an opportunity is an environmental condition that can significantly improve an organization's situation relative to that of competitors; and a threat is an environmental condition that can significantly undermine an organization's competitive situation (Bartol et al, 1998)
Leading		
Initiate and oversee the design of strategic planning	Establish a planning team and guide the planning process	Strategic planning for a connectivity corridor will require a clear brief for what is expected, and processes for decision making and engagement that should meet the requirements for good governance, particularly accountability, transparency, inclusion and fairness and connectedness – a balance also needs to be achieved between strategic planning and on-ground performance (see Cederberg Mountains-Cape Floristic Region, Chapter 4)
Planning		
Plan for the strategic planning project	Develop a project plan that: describes the task objectives and requirements; indicates how the strategic plan relates to other plans and policies; specifies the methods to be used, including engagement approaches; and details resources, budget, milestones and evaluation process and criteria	An endorsed project plan: helps planners to be organized, achieve milestones and to remain strategic; is a basis for conducting evaluation of the planning project; and enables transparency and accountability
Implementing		
Set strategic direction	Identify strategic management objectives and their relative priorities	Objectives should be consistent with higher-level visions and goals, and ideally also be measurable, realistic yet challenging (so not a 'wish list'), and achievable within the planning period (Lockwood, 2006) – see Bhutan biological corridors, Chapter 6
Identify strategic initiatives	For each objective, identify associated actions	Actions should be specified in sufficient detail to ensure predictable outputs, while allowing for the initiative and professional judgement of those implementing the actions

Table 11.5 Continued

Management action	Description	Notes
	Evaluating	
Assess the efficacy of the planning process	Evaluate the quality of the strategic plan and the process used to develop it – assessment methods could include peer review and stakeholder surveys or interviews	This assessment can confirm the planning process or lead to recommendations for improvement, given that strategic planning is not a 'one-off' event but needs to be repeated at least every five years
Assess performance against the plan	Assess the outputs and outcomes from implementing the strategic plan – guidelines for undertaking such an evaluation are offered in Box 11.8	Measurable objectives will allow an assessment of the extent to which they have been achieved, and establish a basis for adaptive management – that is, adjusting actions based on experience and new knowledge in an attempt to better meet objectives (Box 11.9)

Box 11.7 The ecosystem approach

Both the introduction and Target 1.2 of the *Convention for Biological Diversity* Protected Area Programme of Work specifically mention the use of the ecosystem approach when integrating protected areas into the wider landscape, seascape and relevant sectors. The *Convention* describes this approach as the primary framework for action. The ecosystem approach provides a framework within which the relationship of protected areas to the wider landscape and seascape can be understood, and the goods and services flowing from protected areas can be valued (CBD, 2008). The ecosystem approach is primarily about linking people with nature at various spatial and temporal scales, and is therefore well suited to connectivity conservation areas. The ecosystem approach has 12 principles (CBD, 2008):

1 The objectives of management of land, water and living resources are a matter of societal choice.
2 Management should be decentralized to the lowest appropriate level.
3 Ecosystem managers should consider the effects (actual or potential) of their activities on adjacent and other ecosystems.
4 Recognizing potential gains from management, there is usually a need to understand and manage the ecosystem in an economic context. Any such ecosystem management programme should reduce those market distortions that adversely affect biological diversity, align incentives to promote biodiversity conservation and sustainable use, and internalize costs and benefits in the given ecosystem to the extent feasible.
5 Conservation of ecosystem structure and functioning, to maintain ecosystem services, should be a priority target of the ecosystem approach.
6 Ecosystems must be managed within the limits of their functioning.
7 The ecosystem approach should be undertaken at the appropriate spatial and temporal scales.
8 Recognizing the varying temporal scales and lag-effects that characterize ecosystem processes, objectives for ecosystem management should be set for the long term.
9 Management must recognize that change is inevitable.
10 The ecosystem approach should seek the appropriate balance between, and integration of, conservation and use of biological diversity.
11 The ecosystem approach should consider all forms of relevant information, including scientific and indigenous and local knowledge, innovations and practices.
12 The ecosystem approach should involve all relevant sectors of society and scientific disciplines.

Source: Adapted from Ervin et al, 2009

Box 11.8 Guidelines for undertaking a performance evaluation in the context of a strategic plan

IUCN's framework for assessing the effectiveness of management of protected areas (Hockings et al, 2006) is a useful guide for how a connectivity area strategic plan could be evaluated. This IUCN best practice guideline describes a recommended method for assessing management performance. While it assesses performance against an IUCN framework for protected area management, the process of evaluation considerations are essentially the same for connectivity conservation management. The process recognizes four phases (adapted from Hockings et al, 2006).

Phase I identifies the assessment objectives. It helps define a clear purpose for the evaluation and to what extent, at what level (quick or in-depth) and how often it is conducted. This is a very practical step that concerns itself about matters such as cost, time availability and the purpose of the evaluation. The connectivity conservation plan identifies a vision (with its associated goals) and major tasks, all of which may be subject to evaluation. More specific aspects such as the implementation of individual projects may also be assessed. How well connectivity management is being undertaken as a process using the framework of management may be an additional assessment. The purpose for doing all or some of these evaluations may be for adaptive management, resource allocation, accountability or for building support. This phase should also identify exactly what evaluation information is needed and what it is to be used for.

Phase II identifies that an evaluation method needs to be chosen. The actual method for conducting an evaluation should be guided by the purpose and scale at which it is to be conducted, but it should be cost-effective, replicable, robust and statistically valid, simple, field-tested, documented, credible, congruent (between management and community expectations), efficient and adaptable. The data collected should directly serve the information that is needed. An analysis of the evaluation information needed by different levels of connectivity area management (such as site level and landscape level) may lead to efficiencies in how evaluation data is collected (Worboys, 2007). Decisions also need to be made about who conducts the evaluation, and who is involved, and typically a plan would be prepared for actually conducting the evaluation.

Phase III is the implementation of the assessment, and it would normally be based on an approved plan. It includes the collection of data and its responsible storage.

Phase IV involves analysing the data, the preparation of evaluation information and recommendations and the reporting of results. The recommendations would be crafted clearly and carefully, and the process of reporting the information would also be conducted carefully.

Box 11.9 Adaptive management

Adaptive management systematically tests options and assumptions in order to learn and thereby improve outcomes. Management is treated as an iterative process of review and revision, not as a series of fixed prescriptions to be implemented. Management interventions are seen as a series of successive and continuous adaptations to variable conditions. The approach is experimental and emphasizes flexibility, requires willingness to learn through experience, and may require sacrificing present or short-term gains for longer term objectives (Briassoulis, 1989). The emphasis is on learning how the system works through management interventions that are both issue-oriented and experimental. Adaptive management recognizes that there is often considerable uncertainty about the outcomes of any particular action. This uncertainty is built into plans so that information about the actual results of actions is used to inform and where necessary modify management practices (Salafsky et al, 2001). Adaptive management:

- integrates contributions from both the natural and social sciences;
- recognizes uncertainty, complexity and long time scales;
- acknowledges that management interventions are essentially experimental, and while directed towards improving environmental and human conditions, also allows for testing and improving understanding and capabilities along the way;
- provides for wide inclusion of stakeholders in a purposeful and structured fashion;
- designs mechanisms to allow feedback and communication between theory, policy and practice (Dovers, 1998).

Measurable outcomes (as distinct from outputs), and clear processes that link outcome assessment to practice change, are essential elements in effective adaptive management.

Table 11.6 Management actions for finances, human resources and assets

Management action	Description	Notes
Understanding context		
Identify potential funding sources	Research opportunities to access funds from governments, philanthropic organizations and individuals, private companies, as well as 'beneficiary pays' and 'polluter pays' mechanisms	Sustainable conservation financing requires accessing funds from a diversity of sources (Emerton et al, 2005), and exploring innovative funding options such as obtaining payments for the ecosystem services provided by a connectivity conservation area (Box 11.10) – see Yellowstone to Yukon, Chapter 7
Leading		
Keep the organization 'on track' while also paying attention to management details	Ensure that a balance is achieved between effectively managing staff, finance and assets, and achieving strategic outcomes	Systems, processes and protocols for managing staff, finance and assets are important, but these should not get in the way of, nor deflect too much energy from, undertaking substantive connectivity actions
Planning		
Identify asset management requirements	Develop an asset management plan, which includes an inventory of assets, their condition and maintenance requirements	This action ensures that the inventory of assets is kept current, and the information is available for financial management and for maintenance and replacement programmes – asset management should be part of an integrated management system that includes programmes for development projects, annual maintenance programmes, performance review and assessment, and financial management
Provide a framework for safety and integrity in the workplace	Identify and, where necessary, develop finance, human resource and asset standards and policies	Relevant policies and standards might include: design standards for construction and equipment; corporate standards for such things as letterheads and signs; codes for staff appointment, employment conditions and workplace relations; occupational health and safety codes; financial and accounting protocols; contract management manuals and leasing and licensing manuals
Support implementation of the strategic plan	Develop a 'business plan' for the connectivity area that includes a financial plan	A business plan for a connectivity area might include: the vision and goals; identification of the services and activities that will be provided and undertaken; a marketing strategy that identifies strategic alliances and explains how the business will position and promote itself and distribute its services and activities; an indication of the organizational structure, staff, assets and decision-making structures needed to implement the business plan; and a financial plan
		A financial plan sets indicators that: will be used to track performance; determine the amount and timing of funding required to achieve management goals; and identify income sources to meet short, medium, and long-term needs

Table 11.6 Continued

Management action	Description	Notes
Implementing		
Manage staff, finance and assets	Implement the asset management plan and business plan, and follow codes, protocols and standards	These actions will usually be the responsibility of the general manager or equivalent, but will require the active support and cooperation of all staff and office bearers
Implement the financial plan	Make the applications, develop the partnerships and enter into the contacts needed to finance the initiative	Strong partnerships with governments and international NGOs can extend the capacity of a single connectivity organization to seek and acquire funding
Evaluating		
Assess the utility and efficacy of the asset management plan, business and financial plans, and codes, protocols and standards	Undertake an internal evaluation of staff, business and asset management processes – this will typically be led by a general manager or management board and should involve all staff, partners and volunteers	The evaluation should examine the justification for each plan and process, how well they are being observed and implemented, whether any further plan or procedure development is required or conversely whether some rationalization is desirable, and how well the plans and procedures contribute to achieving the organization's strategic goals

---

Box 11.10 Payments for ecosystem service provision: An example from Quito, Ecuador

An ecosystem service fund known as the Water Conservation Fund or 'Fondo para la Conservacion del Agua' was formally launched in Quito in 1998 as a result of collaborative work by The Nature Conservancy and Fundación Antisana, an Ecuadorian NGO, with support from USAID. The fund relates to the domestic water supply for Quito, the capital of Ecuador, and the source of this water in protected areas in the neighbouring high Andes. The Condor Biosphere Reserve, which includes the Antisana and Cayambe-Coca ecological reserves and the Cotopaxi and Llanganates national parks, forms an important part of the water catchment area of Quito. There were threats to these catchments from unregulated developments and consequent degraded water quality, and active management was needed. There were insufficient funds for adequate protected area management. A proposal for a water consumption fee to pay for improved management of the watersheds was accepted after negotiations. The fees were paid into a trust fund and managed by an experienced asset management company to ensure financial stability and to generate revenue from interest from investments. The fund also solicits additional support from national and international entities. Based on the experience learned from establishing this (water) ecosystem service fee, a number of key lessons were identified:

- choose a site of biological and hydrological importance;
- employ a coordinator;
- identify key design criteria for the mechanism;
- identify the water users and key stakeholders;
- develop a well-communicated, clear message and sell the idea;
- be timely – carefully choose the moment for the pitch;
- integrate the financial mechanism into the overall conservation strategy for an area;
- develop an economic valuation study;
- persevere!

Source: Echavarria and Arroyo, 2004

Deploy instruments; manage threats, incidents and degraded areas; and strive for sustainable resource use

In this section, we address the complex of delivery tasks that together form the actions by which a connectivity conservation organization achieves the 'on-ground' outcomes (objectives) specified in its strategic plan.

There is typically a suite of management *instruments* that managers can use to achieve their strategic objectives (Chapter 3). Regulatory instruments include legislation designed to protect species or areas, prohibit or restrict activities and set standards and limits on resource extraction. Economic instruments include creating markets for natural resources such as water, or for trading the rights to produce externalities such as greenhouse gases, offering incentives for reducing environmental degradation, and placing financial burdens on resource users. Voluntary measures such as codes of practice and management agreements rely on voluntary action and self-regulation to achieve conservation objectives. Education can be used to enhance awareness of values and problems, as well as informing about potential solutions and appropriate courses of action.

In 2005, the findings of 1360 experts from 95 countries advised that human activities were causing environmental damage on a massive scale (MEAB, 2005; Chapter 1). They confirmed the underlying *threats* posed by humans to the environment, and reinforced a common sense view that the capacity of Earth to absorb human-induced change was finite. Population growth and material aspirations drive unsustainable natural resource consumption. Inadequate legal and political systems fail to secure environmental protection .Corruption leads to failures in governance, enforcement and management. Inequitable distributions of benefits and costs lead to civil unrest and dysfunctional social, cultural and political relations Poverty constrains or precludes options to adopt sustainable practices. War and civil conflict impair the capacity to manage. Knowledge and education deficiencies impair the capacity to identify and implement solutions. The threat of climate change is now well known.

Inappropriate land-use decisions cause habitat destruction and fragmentation. Expansion of human settlements impacts on habitats and natural ecosystems. Polluted air and water, and introduced plants and animals, damage species and ecosystems and reduce landscape productivity (Worboys et al, 2006). While many of these threats may be beyond the capacity and authority of connectivity conservation managers to solve, there are actions they can take to mitigate some of their impacts.

It is inevitable that large-scale connectivity areas will be affected by *incidents*. Few connectivity conservation management organizations will have a direct involvement in dealing with these events, as this will usually be the responsibility of one or more organizations such as: fire brigades (fire and pollution incidents); police (conflict, major transport accidents, search and rescue); ambulance (health and accidents); wildlife management (rogue animal incidents); agriculture (animal diseases); emergency services (earthquakes, storms, fires, tsunami, floods and mass wasting); and the military (civil conflict). For some large incidents, the control and management may be integrated to involve multiple organizations. This usually means that a single emergency controller will be appointed with (often) formidable delegated powers. There is great potential for incident-response impacts to occur in the 'heat of the moment' during these large events and connectivity conservation leaders need to anticipate, plan and prepare for incidents to help prevent this.

Many people who own and occupy lands within connectivity conservation areas rely on these natural and semi-natural lands for food, shelter, water and grazing for domestic animals. Often this use extends (in forest areas for example) to logging for timber and clearing for enhanced grazing or cash crops. Economic returns may also be funded from ecotourism to these natural sites. The natural and semi-natural condition of many of these areas is a positive testimony to their conservation stewardship of lands. Retention of natural habitats is an important goal for connectivity areas, and helping people strive for *sustainable use* of resources is a key task of management. There are many programmes and instruments that promote and enable land stewardship for connectivity conservation. Connectivity conservation managers can support existing initiatives and take action to assist the development and implementation of new initiatives.

Parts of many connectivity conservation areas may have been disturbed by clearing and fragmentation, and there may be a need to *restore* parts or all of these modified areas. Restoration work may be an important task for connectivity areas, and there may be a focus on strategic sites such as choke points or key areas that have been disconnected.

In Table 11.7, we suggest some of the actions that are likely to be important in undertaking delivery tasks to protect lands within the connectivity area and manage threats, incidents, restoration and sustainable resource use.

Table 11.7 Actions to deliver 'on-ground' outcomes

Management action	Description	Notes
Understanding context		
Identify instruments that may be useful to support delivery of actions	For each strategic management goal concerning an on-ground outcome, identify any potentially useful regulatory, economic, voluntary or educational instruments available from external 'providers'	The research should be cross-sectoral and cross-scalar: useful instruments may be sourced from sectors such as agriculture, forestry, fisheries, catchment and water management or tourism, conservation and protected areas, and from governments and other authorities at the local, sub-national, national and international levels
Reassess threats	Review and update identification and status of threats	A previous action in understanding context involved a threat assessment to inform strategic planning – the currency of this assessment needs to be checked and if necessary amended
Research effective threat responses and restoration methods	Review the literature and engage with conservation practitioners to identify good practice response options for dealing with particular threats and undertaking restoration works	Good practice examples can be obtained from protected area, forestry, water, agriculture, fishing, mining and tourism literatures and practitioners
Identify regulatory requirements for undertaking operations	Identify and document any regulations, protocols and standards associated with implementing on-ground actions	Management operations may deal with the relocation or killing of pest animals, the use of herbicides and other tasks that may be regulated or be subject to safety or other protocols
Leading		
Address inadequacies in the legislative, policy or instrument base	Where necessary and appropriate, lobby governments to introduce legislative and policy reforms and instrument development	Leaders may need to take the initiative and lobby senior government officials, politicians and other key stakeholders to achieve improvements
Align operations with the vision and strategic plan	Direct (when the connectivity organization has the authority) or guide and advise (when it does not) the implementation of operations according to strategic directions and priorities	Many organizations and individuals may be undertaking actions under the auspices of a connectivity conservation organization – it may be a significant task for connectivity leaders to guide these diverse actions towards achieving strategic goals

Table 11.7 Continued

Management action	Description	Notes
Attempt to influence landholders' and rights-holders' resource management practices	Where necessary and appropriate, engage and negotiate with community, industry and government agency leaders to seek alignment of their practices with the connectivity conservation vision	Over time, connectivity conservation leaders may be able to exert influence on landholders and industries, mitigating the threats that they pose to the connectivity area, and encouraging environmentally, economically and socially sustainable practices
Provide input during incidents	Providing timely and constructive counsel to positively influence incident-management decisions	Leaders may need to proactively contribute in an emergency response situation to ensure that connectivity conservation objectives are not unnecessarily impacted

	Planning	
Identify which instruments will be accessed or employed for what purposes	From the relevant 'understanding context' research, analyse and select those instruments that can usefully contribute to strategic objectives, and develop a tactical plan for deploying or encouraging the use of these instruments	Connectivity conservation managers and their partners may be able to directly deploy some instruments, such as incentives, to achieve on-ground change – they can also encourage others to access and deploy instruments in a manner consistent with the connectivity vision
Identify how on-ground actions will be managed	From the relevant 'understanding context' research, and consistent with the strategic plan, prepare tactical plans that detail area-specific outcomes and actions for managing threats and incidents and supporting sustainable use	This action involves the detailed planning required to direct on-ground operations – using the overarching strategic plan as a starting point, detailed objectives, actions, milestones, accountabilities, risk management strategies and assessment criteria can be developed for particular places and issues within the connectivity area – for example a plan may be developed for the removal of an invasive species in a linking corridor, or for the restoration of a particular area of degraded land
Identify how on-ground actions will be implemented	For each tactical plan prepare an associated operational plan that specifies the logistical details needed to implement the actions	These plans specify the deployment of staff, volunteers, partners, finance and equipment

	Implementing	
Use and/or promote conservation covenants, land purchase and rolling funds	As directed by strategic and tactical plans, purchase or covenant lands with high current or potential conservation values, and/or encourage others to do likewise	Land in important connectivity conservation locations may, by agreement, be purchased, with the property title then amended to include a conservation covenant to permanently protect lands – purchased and covenanted lands can then be resold with the legal protection in place, freeing up funds for additional purchases
Provide and/or promote financial and other incentives	As directed by strategic and tactical plans, deliver incentives for land managers to protect lands, mitigate threats and restore lands, and/or encourage them to take up incentives offered by others	Incentives may take the form of cash payments that cover all or part of the costs of conservation works, and secured by a contractual agreement, or in-kind contributions towards conservation works (labour, materials or equipment)

Table 11.7 Continued

Management action	Description	Notes
Use and/or promote financial compensation schemes	Make payments for conservation opportunity costs and wildlife damage	Compensation payments for damage caused by wildlife or the opportunity costs of not extracting resources help people with recouping costs, minimize social and political fall-out, and help prevent unlawful taking of wildlife
Promote market trading schemes	Show landholders and managers how trading in biodiversity offsets, carbon or some other environmental good can both generate economic benefits and lead to conservation outcomes	Carbon trading offers potential to earn revenue from carbon offsets through carbon sequestration in natural forests – payments for maintaining sequestered carbon may also offer opportunities for financial returns as climate change mitigation 'insurance'
Promote payment schemes for ecosystem services	Show landholders and managers how they might benefit form conserving lands by accessing payments for the ecosystem services they provide	Payments for clean water and other ecosystem services can provide an incentive to landholders to conserve lands and/or manage them more sustainably
Undertake and/or encourage action to mitigate threats	As directed by strategic and tactical plans, undertake threat mitigation actions and/or encourage other land managers do to so	Actions range from participation in land-use planning processes in an attempt to prevent unsustainable or anti-conservation decisions, through to works such as spraying weeds or stabilizing soils to control erosion
Respond to incidents	Initiate and/or provide assistance in response to floods, fires, civil conflict, drought or other incidents	Anticipate the inevitable – partnerships, education, training and equipment purchase and other preparations can provide a response capability that, as far as possible, enables a connectivity organization to help deal with the incident and ensure connectivity conservation objectives are not compromised (Worboys and Winkler, 2006c)
Undertake and/or encourage restoration	As directed by strategic and tactical plans, undertake restoration works and/or encourage other land managers to do so	Connectivity design and strategic planning should have identified parts of the connectivity conservation area to be targeted for such works – these may involve replanting with native vegetation, fauna reintroductions, soil stabilization, removal of structures, streamside and wetland rehabilitation
Evaluating		
Evaluate the implementation of tactical and operational plans	Prepare a report that identifies the extent to which the outcomes and outputs specified in the various tactical and operational plans have been achieved	Typically the reporting is for performance against the objectives, and provides output and outcome reporting (Hockings et al, 2006) and these can form the basis for an adaptive management response – project evaluation reports may also be required for grant donors and government organizations
Evaluate the tactical and operational plans	Prepare a report that assesses the utility of the plans and the efficacy of the processes that were used to develop them	This review should include an examination of the performance assessment, and where necessary recommend changes to plan objectives, actions or processes

Table 11.7 Continued

Management action	Description	Notes
Conduct and participate in incident-management evaluations	Conduct an internal evaluation of an incident and its impacts on the connectivity area, and identify any changes needed to strategic, tactical or operational plans; participate in an attempt to influence the outcomes of any external reviews	The internal evaluation for a connectivity organization would help review incident decisions and help initiate follow-up actions such as restoration, capacity building and education, as well as informing plan modification; participation in any external review would ensure the interests of the connectivity conservation area are represented

Weed spraying unit, Kosciuszko National Park, A2A connectivity corridor, Australia

Source: Graeme L. Worboys

Provide and manage research opportunities

Research can identify and assesses the presence, significance, functioning and interdependence of natural, cultural, social and economic features and resources. Such information is needed to ensure business, strategic, tactical and operational plans address the most important tissues, set meaningful directions, prescribe actions that are likely to yield the intended outcomes and allow for monitoring and evaluation of change. Given the need to understand and manage across natural, human and managerial contexts, many discipline-based specialists have a contribution to make: geologists, geomorphologists, hydrologists, botanists, zoologists, ecologists, conservation biologists, biogeographers, anthropologists, ethnographers, historians, archaeologists, cultural heritage specialists, sociologists, cultural and economic geographers, rural development and health specialists, engineers, economists, financial and business experts, political scientists and legal experts. The cross-disciplinary expertise of environmental science, environmental studies and social science experts can synthesize and integrate critical knowledge, and offer methods for acquiring and analysing cultural-socio-economic data.

Some connectivity conservation managers may have such experts working within their organization, undertaking research that aims to fill knowledge gaps and helping to design and implement monitoring and evaluation programmes. However, for many areas, managers will need to build partnerships with external research providers – universities, specialist institutes, NGOs and government agencies – in order to acquire the knowledge they need to effectively manage a connectivity area. Volunteer and community groups can also provide research support and the private sector may sponsor research programmes. Managers should be at the forefront of introducing ways in which experts from different organizations can be helped to conduct applied research in connectivity areas. For example, managers may be able to facilitate permits and provide technical or logistical assistance. Importantly, by establishing a track record of working together, managers and researchers are likely to enhance their competitiveness when seeking external research funding. Highlighting opportunities to do 'cutting-edge' work that may have significant practical importance can also be a strong attractor for researchers.

In general, connectivity managers do not take the lead in managing the research itself – that is generally done by the organization for which the expert works, and by the experts themselves. Rather, connectivity managers need to work with partners to facilitate and provide research opportunities that address important management questions and needs, and take steps to ensure that the knowledge generated is integrated into management processes. Some of the actions that might constitute this role are indicated in Table 11.8.

Cross-cutting tasks

Work and communicate with partners and stakeholders

A vast body of research literature supports the need for environmental managers to apply well-developed, continuous and broadly based engagement and communication programmes

Table 11.8 Actions for providing research opportunities

Management action	Description	Notes
Understanding context		
Help identify knowledge gaps	Work with experts to identify strategic gaps in connectivity conservation management knowledge	This information would be used to prepare a list of priority research areas
Identify potential research providers	Develop a register of potential research providers and their areas of expertise	The information would be used to identify potential partnerships with researchers
Leading		
Initiate research partnerships	Communicate research opportunities to potential providers, and where appropriate initiate partnership agreements	Leaders need to deal directly with research institutions and individual researchers, using the prospectus (see below) to identify what the connectivity organization can offer to researchers, and the questions for which they are seeking answers – note that researchers should also be given room to pursue their own interests
Planning		
Establish a research prospectus	Using the 'understanding of context', produce a research prospectus that identifies priority areas for research and specifies the types of support that the connectivity organization can offer	Support may include technical and logistical capability, funding, availability of volunteer assistance, help with permits and cooperation with local communities
Integrate research programs into plans	Using adaptive management principles, build a research component, where appropriate, into business, strategic, tactical and operational plans	This helps ensure that research is effectively integrated with management, and that planning is in place to take advantage of, and learn from, new knowledge (Biggs and Rogers, 2003)

Table 11.8 Continued

Management action	Description	Notes
Implementing		
Establish and support research partnerships	Enter into agreements (formal or informal) with research providers and implement these by supplying support services to researchers	While some research will be directed towards strategic 'one-off' outcomes, agreements should also encourage and support long-term programmes along the lines of the Global Observation Research Initiative in Alpine Environments (Grabherr, 2008), the Global Mountain Biodiversity Assessment (Spehn and Körner, 2005), and the Global Change in Mountain regions research strategy (Gurung, 2008)
Employ new knowledge	Using an adaptive management approach, integrate new knowledge into activities and plans	Planning and project management processes should provide clear pathways for translating knowledge into practice
Evaluating		
Review research partnership arrangements	Assess partnerships in terms of their strategic targeting of research needs, performance of researchers, and efficiency and appropriateness of support provision	This review might reveal a need to adjust current agreements or seek new partners, reform the types of support and/or the ways in which support is delivered
Review processes for translating knowledge into practice	Assess the extent to which knowledge products are utilized in planning and on-ground actions	This review may reveal a need to reform management processes, or suggest that a reorientation is required in research planning and/or the targeting of research partnerships

(Chapter 3). This conclusion is clearly supported in a connectivity conservation context by the Chapter 4 to 9 case studies and the Papallacta workshop (Chapter 10).

Partnerships are widely regarded as a key strategy to mobilize resources and expertise for conservation initiatives (De Lacy et al, 2002; Stubbs et al, 2005), stimulate innovation (Tremblay, 2000), moderate power inequalities, foster collaborative decision making and conflict resolution (Leach and Pelkey, 2001) and help coordination and improve understanding (Davidson and Lockwood, 2008). For example, important outcomes identified by Moore et al (2008b) for tourism-protected area partnerships included mutual economic gains, improved information availability, adoption of innovative approaches to

problems solving, improved understanding of protected area values, enhanced conservation outcomes and increased local community engagement.

From a pragmatic point of view, *engagement* is particularly critical for connectivity managers because, in many cases, they do not have direct authority to take measures to protect lands or undertake on-ground action, and must rely on others – government agencies, NGOs, landholders, resource users – to cooperate with their plans. This requires managers to develop partnerships with such individuals and organizations at the international, national, sub-national and local levels. From an ethical and good governance point of view too, connectivity managers must respect the rights and values of the diverse communities

Climate change research, Victoria Alpine National Park, A2A connectivity corridor, Australia

Source: Graeme L. Worboys

of place and interest by taking seriously their needs and aspirations and incorporating them into planning and action. For these reasons, we have identified engagement tasks as 'cross-cutting', in that they span the entire domain of governance, planning and action that forms the 'business' of connectivity management.

Informing stakeholders (especially communities) about the vision, purpose and management of a connectivity conservation area is an essential task. There has been very little research on the effectiveness of different *communication* channels (such as print media, radio, television, newsletters, Internet and direct contact) and the types of messages that might best suit the interests, abilities and requirements of each stakeholder. We do know, however, that 'stakeholder segments' differ

in their attitudes, beliefs and values, and these are likely to influence what messages have the most resonance (Morrison et al, 2008). Furthermore, people differ in terms of their awareness of the engagement opportunities on offer, their understanding of the purposes, benefits and costs of connectivity conservation, and their confidence in connectivity managers – such characteristics will determine whether communication should focus on creating awareness, providing information, arguing the wisdom of participation, dealing with concerns or building trust (Ki and Hon, 2007).

In Table 11.9 we indicate some of the partnership, stakeholder and communication actions that might contribute to fulfilling the task of engagement for connectivity conservation.

Table 11.9 Engagement actions

Management action	Description	Notes
	Understanding context	
Identify and understand stakeholders	Scan across international, national, sub-national and local scales to identify potential stakeholders, and attempt to determine their values, attitudes, aspirations, concerns and preferences – useful methods for the latter action include interviews with organizational and community leaders, and surveys designed to understand a representative sample of particular stakeholder groups	An understanding of stakeholder characteristics can inform all aspects of engagement and increase management effectiveness: for example, connectivity instruments such as economic incentives, covenants, contracts, certifications and management agreements differ in their acceptability to various stakeholders (Curtis et al, 2001) – in marketing terms, there are different 'segments' within stakeholder populations, some responsive to most instruments, some with strong preferences for a particular kind of approach, and others may be difficult to involve with any of the instruments currently on offer (Morrison et al, 2008) – such information can assist managers to design and target instruments for maximum effect
Identify partnership requirements and opportunities	From the strategic and business plans, identify actions that could be progressed though partnerships, and scan across international, national, sub-national and local scales to locate potential partners	Potential partners are likely to include government agencies, local community-based organizations, NGOs, universities and businesses
Identify target audiences for communications	Regularly update stakeholder identity and contact information	This information may identify audiences for specialist communications (such as researchers, educators and planners) as well as general community contacts
Research target audience needs and preferences	Undertake surveys to identify the preferred communication media and messages for particular audiences	This research will help match media and message with audience – for example, some landholders might be best reached through local community newsletter articles that emphasize the ecosystem service and production benefits of connectivity conservation
	Leading	
Initiate partnerships	Make contact with potential partners with a view to establishing partnership agreements	Initial contact coming from a connectivity conservation leader indicates to a partner the importance of the approach – securing high-level support from governments, for example, may be a long process and require considerable perseverance from the connectivity leadership
Ensure community and partner engagement is given a high strategic priority	Communicate with, and where necessary convince, office bearers, staff and volunteers about the importance of establishing and maintaining stakeholder engagement and strategic partnerships	Some office bearers, staff and volunteers may be strongly focused on aspects of research, planning and delivery that are of particular interest to them – leaders may need to reinforce the cross-cutting importance of community engagement

Table 11.9 Continued

Management action	Description	Notes
Planning		
Develop a partner engagement plan	Draw on the understanding of partnership requirements and opportunities to identify strategies for partner engagement	In developing and implementing partnership plans, managers should take account of characteristics known to be important for successful partnerships: direct involvement of decision makers; commitment of time and resources by all partners; good communication; clear objectives, shared purpose and a written agreement; and an understanding of each partner's aspirations and constraints (Moore et al, 2008b)
Develop a stakeholder engagement and communications plan	Draw on the understanding of community values, attitudes, aspirations, concerns and preferences to identify strategies for community engagement and communication	The plan should tailor engagement objectives, methods and actions to particular communities and stakeholder 'segments' (see above), and in particular take into account the particular needs and interests of local and indigenous communities – on the other hand, large numbers of people can be influenced by using high profile 'champions of connectivity areas' such as sports stars and media celebrities to deliver messages especially crafted to win hearts and minds
Implementing		
Undertake actions in accordance with the partner engagement plan	Work with partners on site-level activities – local communities, businesses, government and NGOs are likely to be the main partners in such work	Local-level actions with partners may include: articulating a community connectivity area vision; training and capacity building; protection of particular properties through reservation, purchase or covenant; threat mitigation such as removal of weeds; and restoration works such as tree planting or erosion control
	Work with partners on landscape-level activities – local and regional (sub-national) communities, government agencies and larger NGOs and businesses are likely to be the main partners in such work	Landscape-level actions with partners may include: articulating a connectivity area vision; influencing land-use planning processes; coordinating and implementing wildlife management; dealing with threats such as pest animals, weeds and fire; offering stewardship incentives; and implementing ecosystem payment schemes – protected area managers may have a particularly important role (Box 11.11)
	Work with partners on national-level activities – government agencies, large NGOs and businesses are likely to be the main partners in such work	National-level actions with partners may include: seeking reform or effective enforcement of conservation, natural resource and planning laws; enhancing the policy context for connectivity areas, including climate-change policy; securing investment; and educating the wider community about connectivity conservation

Table 11.9 Continued

Management action	Description	Notes
	Work with partners on international-level activities – governments, international NGOs and United Nations agencies are likely to be the main partners in such work	International-level actions with partners may include: negotiation of transboundary agreements (Box 11.12; Sandwith and Lockwood, 2006); securing finance; providing input to international meetings such as IUCN world conservation congresses and international instruments such as the *Convention on Biological Diversity*; and contributing to informal voluntary networks of connectivity conservation practitioners
Undertake actions in accordance with the stakeholder engagement and communications plan	Communicate and engage and with local, sub-national, national and international stakeholders	Communication and engagement actions may include: informing stakeholders about the significance, values and management of connectivity areas; building community and political support for connectivity conservation; attempting to change behaviours that are threatening connectivity conservation areas (such as unsustainable resource use); and encouraging stakeholders to become partners
Evaluating		
Evaluate the quality of engagement plans	Undertake a review of the plans and the processes that were used to develop them, and as necessary implement process and/or plan revisions	Plan review could be done internally amongst the connectivity organization's office bearers and staff – however, external commentary on plan quality and appropriateness can also yield valuable process or content improvements
Assess engagement performance	Identify the extent to which the outcomes and outputs specified in the partner, stakeholder and communication plans have been achieved, and as necessary identify new or remedial actions	Output assessment identifies the extent to which actions have been carried out according to the plan; outcome assessment identifies the extent to which objectives have been achieved

Box 11.11 Opportunities for protected area managers to engage with connectivity initiatives

Protected areas are an integral and essential part of connectivity conservation areas. A typical large-scale connectivity area will include an archipelago of protected areas, giving the managers of these reserves important roles in considering the wider conservation context of their own management, as well as supporting conservation initiatives in the surrounding connectivity landscape. Here we suggest some of the opportunities for protected area managers to take action in relation to the second of these roles.

Lead or contribute to the establishment of large-scale connectivity conservation areas

Establishing connectivity conservation areas may be a delicate political issue because of their multi-tenure status. The nature and extent of participation by protected area managers is therefore situational. Some governments may require their protected area agency to provide cooperative leadership in the development of connectivity areas. Others may organize this leadership to be vested in a planning authority or other government department. Another (common) option is for government to abstain from the connectivity initiative process in favour of a community group or NGO taking the lead. Anxiety by many local peoples concerning historical land-acquisition processes for protected areas may drive this sensitivity. Integrating protected areas into the wider landscapes is a key target for the *Convention on Biological Diversity* Programme of Work on Protected Areas (Ervin et al, 2009).

Participate in governance

Protected area managers are key stakeholders in the management of connectivity areas and it would be normal for a representative to be part of the governance arrangements for a connectivity area management organization. This has two-way benefits. The protected area manager has the opportunity to influence connectivity area stewardship priorities and the connectivity management organization can benefit from cross-boundary cooperation on issues such as fire and wildlife management and control of introduced species.

Provide expertise

Protected area managers usually possess multiple years of land management experience; they are often highly trained, and some possess specialist expertise in the management of species and other heritage. This can be of great value for connectivity conservation management and could, by mutual agreement, be made available for connectivity areas that interconnect with the protected areas. Dealing with wildlife issues is particularly relevant, though the rehabilitation of degraded ecosystems (such as catchments) is also an important opportunity.

Provide management information

Information, which may include fire weather, snow deposition, water yield and visitor-use data, is commonly collected in protected areas for routine operations. Other data may be linked to research, and specifically adaptive management for threats, endangered species management and visitor-use management. Once analysed, these data are useful information for people and organizations in the surrounding landscape and especially connectivity areas. There are a number of potential benefits from such information services. First, there may be the immediate benefit of receiving up-to-date information on matters such as fire weather and snow conditions. Second, longer-term trend data can support connectivity planning. Third, the potential power of long-term data sourced from multiple collection points in the landscape from an archipelago of protected areas that include large latitudinal or longitudinal ranges may enable tracking of climate change effects and biome shifts.

Provide services

A protected area agency may be contracted by a connectivity management organization to undertake conservation works within a connectivity area. Specialist land management support services may include the provision of GIS capability, remote sensing for performance evaluation or support logistics such as helicopter operations.

Box 11.11 Continued

Engage in cooperative activities

Joint-educational information, shared web sites, hosted functions, joint tourism marketing and other cooperative actions may be undertaken by protected area managers to help connectivity conservation stewardship. A coordinated effort facilitated by the connectivity area's archipelago of protected areas provides powerful opportunities for this work. Partnerships between protected area and connectivity conservation managers can strengthen capacity to deal with visitor management, introduced animal and pest plant control, fire management and human–wildlife interactions across entire landscapes.

Develop capacity

Training and educational services are routine business for protected area organizations, and many of them have well-developed capability in this area. A cooperative educational programme for the entire connectivity conservation area, for example, could involve multiple protected area staff strategically selected for participation from the connectivity area's archipelago of protected areas.

Provide grants and resourcing

Governments and other donors may provide grants to assist connectivity conservation, and protected area organizations, because of their immediate proximity, may facilitate these investments. In addition, protected area managers may resource cooperative cross-boundary conservation stewardship initiatives.

Box 11.12 Types of transboundary agreements

Using experience gained from transboundary protected areas, there are a number of different levels of formalizing transboundary agreements available. Cross-border sensitivities may preclude any agreements, but where it is possible there are a range of options that may be suitable:

- a formal agreement or bilateral or multilateral agreement to bind the parties to long term and accountable co-operation;
- administrative instruments such as a MOU developed between key agencies, departments or ministries;
- a more limited agreement to address specific issues, such as protocol or contingency plans for dealing with emergencies or incidents like oil spills, fire, pest control or search and rescue control;
- informal agreements used by managers to promote cooperative friendly relations where the situation is not favourable to more formal arrangements;
- representation provided on each other's advisory or management bodies;
- potential establishment of a transboundary connectivity conservation area policy advisory committee which would include stakeholders, especially local community members.

Source: Sandwith et al, 2001

12

Challenges and Opportunities for Connectivity Conservation

Graeme L. Worboys, Michael Lockwood and Wendy L. Francis

Climate change, human population growth and habitat destruction and fragmentation are directly and indirectly contributing to the sixth great extinction event in Earth's history. Overexploitation and clearing for timber extraction, mining, agriculture (including palm-oil plantations) and tourism has caused major problems (as exemplified by the Sumatran (Chapter 6) and Appalachian (Chapter 7) case studies). The last great natural areas are being irreversibly altered; this trend will cause the extinction of multiple species, damage ecosystem services and, ultimately, threaten the health of humans. Many people have responded to these challenges. Individuals, community groups, NGOs and government organizations are contributing to conserving the last large-scale natural lands. The expansion in the number of protected areas from approximately 40,000 in 1980 (Chape et al, 2008) to more than 114,000 in 2008 (UNEP-WCMC, 2009) represents the greatest land use achievement of recent times. An integrated landscape conservation and sustainable use ethic, notably expressed in the 1992 United Nations Conference on the Environment and Development (Dresner, 2002) and the associated Agenda 21, has also driven significant changes in land management practices outside protected areas. Also important has been the establishment, by 2009, of 531 world biosphere reserves in 105 countries (UNESCO, 2009). Despite these successes, they are not in themselves enough to

prevent or minimize species extinctions (Chapter 1). The prognosis is bleak, the rapidity of change great, and more needs to be done. Big thinking and big responses are needed.

Large-scale connectivity conservation is one big thinking response that has emerged. The origins of connectivity conservation areas are linked to the conservation of species in an environment of rapid destruction and fragmentation of natural habitats, climate change and a realization that protected areas, as islands in a modified landscape, cannot adequately achieve species conservation. Large-scale connectivity conservation includes protected areas interconnected and embedded within larger essentially natural landscapes that may have dimensions measured in hundreds or even thousands of kilometres. These large-scale natural lands may extend over many degrees of latitude, may transcend national and international boundaries, may include an archipelago of protected areas and may provide opportunities for some species to move, adapt, evolve and survive when otherwise there would be no opportunities. Across such lands, communities, landowners, NGOs and governments work to plan and implement measures aimed at securing landscape-scale conservation stewardship of lands (see, for example, the Cape Floristic region case study in Chapter 4). Connectivity conservation provides for a more adequate reserve system, especially at a time of climate change. It provides opportunities for fixed geographic features such as national parks, world heritage sites, biosphere reserves and Ramsar wetlands to maintain many of their values at a time of dynamic ecosystem change and biome shifts.

We need to manage through a period of major change while the level of greenhouse gases in the Earth's atmosphere is stabilized and then reduced. This may take hundreds of years. From a species conservation perspective, many critical actions are needed. The completion of adequate and representative national reserve systems is one. Connectivity conservation is another. The focus of this book is on strategically important, large-scale connectivity conservation areas that interconnect and embed protected areas within a continuum of natural and semi-natural lands. The numerous case examples it contains are pioneering initiatives to establish and effectively manage large-scale connectivity areas. Often these initiatives have been the result of courageous leadership from individuals and NGOs, even though, in some cases, they received little government support. Others are linked to outstanding politicians and governments who have pioneered a new type of land use for conserving species and ecosystem services. Large-scale connectivity conservation is shaping better futures and providing hope and inspiration for many people.

How are these large-scale connectivity conservation areas to be managed? This question was the basis for IUCN convening a workshop of connectivity conservation professionals in Papallacta, Ecuador, in November 2006. The workshop participants responded by offering a wealth of case-based examples (Chapters 4 to 9), as well as insights from their experience as connectivity managers and experts (Chapter 10). The Papallacta participants also identified the key challenges facing connectivity conservation to be: establishing a global connectivity conservation agenda; securing and maintaining broad-based support; dealing with conflict; securing and sustaining financial support; providing strong long-term leadership; and establishing and maintaining good governance and planning.

Apart from demonstrating that high-level professional skills and insights are available to achieve large-scale connectivity conservation management, the Papallacta workshop also provided a rich source of empirical data from which to construct a draft framework for connec-

tivity conservation management. This is a significant undertaking. A framework can provide a unifying conception for connectivity conservation management, and guide its initiation, design and implementation. The diversity of land uses, governance authorities and aspirations within a typical connectivity conservation area means that existing frameworks, such as those for protected area management for example, are not adequate. A draft framework was develop as part of the process of writing this book, and presented to a group of connectivity management experts at a second IUCN workshop held in Dhulikhel, Nepal, in November 2008.

Inputs from Dhulikhel substantially progressed the thinking about an appropriate form for, and representation of, the connectivity management framework – thinking that was further refined by discussions and peer review to produce the framework presented in Chapter 11. This framework establishes an understanding context function with three themes – nature, people and management – that continually influence a cycle of leadership, planning, management and evaluation functions, which are guided by an integrating vision. This is not to suggest that this management cycle proceeds in a strictly sequential fashion – rather that there is a continual interplay and feedback between the functions.

Effective connectivity conservation also requires that managers attend to a set of priority tasks, addressing: contextual knowledge; vision, purpose and design; governance and administration; strategic planning; engagement; communication; resourcing; instruments; threats; operations; sustainable resource use; and restoration. In Chapter 11, we apply the framework to these tasks and offer indicative connectivity management practices for each of them. Together, the framework, tasks and practices provide a conceptual basis for connectivity conservation management that is intended to assist the initiation and implementation of strategic connectivity initiatives around the world. The framework also orders and scopes connectivity practice in a way that, we hope, might assist managers to meet the challenges indicated above.

We also take the opportunity here to draw together the literature, empirical results and conceptual material presented in this book and fashion some summative statements that, for us, capture important norms and guidance for effective and principled connectivity conservation management:

1   The primary function of connectivity conservation management should be to help conserve species and to maintain ecological functions and services since 'the weight of evidence shows that isolation of populations and communities, through loss of intervening habitat, has a detrimental effect' (Bennett, 2003, p63). Fulfilling this primary function is motivated by the aim of simultaneously sustaining the intrinsic value of wild nature, which is also a critical component of our common humanity, while supporting the well-being of human communities through the maintenance of ecosystems services, uses and products.

2   Effective connectivity conservation generally demands action at a large scale since 'linkages that maintain the integrity of ecological processes and continuity of biological communities at the biogeographic or regional scale have a more significant role than those operating at localised levels' (Bennett, 2003, p170).

3   A clear, widely supported community vision should guide the purpose, establishment and management of connectivity conservation areas. This does not imply that all stakeholder communities of place or interest will be unanimous in their support of the vision – that, of course, is unrealistic. Rather, connectivity conservation needs to be supported and sustained by a vision that expresses the joint aspirations of leaders, managers and participants in the initiative, without closing off avenues for constructive debate and disputation.

4   Connectivity conservation areas should serve multiple land-use objectives, which alongside nature conservation (which should always underpin a connectivity initiative), will often include protection of cultural and spiritual places and practices. They may also include: the maintenance of agricultural, forestry and fisheries productivity; water supply; carbon storage; and provision of recreation and tourism opportunities.

5   Connectivity conservation areas should be designed to have an adaptive role in countering climate change, interconnecting and embedding protected areas in order to maximize the resilience of the present conservation network (Bennett, 2003).

6   The conservation and production values of connectivity conservation areas and their needs are situational and 'each site will have its own peculiar ecological, physical, economic and social circumstances which dictate the steps required to secure the site as a functional [connectivity] corridor' (Hilty et al, 2006, p236).

7   Protected areas should form a core component of all connectivity conservation areas, as 'tracts of natural vegetation have greater conservation potential as linkages than comparable areas of land that require partial or major restoration of their vegetation' (Bennett, 2003, p173). The management of protected areas needs to be improved through quality management plans, sufficient resources and on-ground management capability, so that they can provide effective core natural areas within connectivity conservation areas. However, most connectivity conservation areas will also contain semi-natural and disturbed lands under various tenures and uses. All these lands need to be jointly managed in a manner consistent with the vision of a spatially defined connectivity conservation area.

8   Good governance practice is essential for principled and effective connectivity conservation. Institutions and decision makers should have legitimacy, be accountable and transparent. All stakeholders, local and non-local, should have an opportunity to be heard and represented in decisions. A special effort may need to be made to engage marginalized people. The design, establishment and implementation of connectivity conservation management should be both a community activity and a government activity. The distributional effects of decisions and actions – who gains and who may be disadvantaged – should be taken into account. Local communities

need to obtain economic benefits from connectivity conservation management. Planning needs to integrate vertically between geographical and geopolitical levels, horizontally within each level, and thematically between issues and sectors. For many connectivity initiatives, networked institutions, partnerships and cross-scalar (local, sub-national, national and international) connections will be vital, as will an ability to adapt to changing political, social, economic and environmental circumstances. This will require multi-centred governance involving coordinating bodies, devolution to local authorities and constructive linkages with national governments. Devolution of power to local authorities makes it important to find ways to make the broader context of connectivity conservation areas relevant at the local scale. At the same time, connectivity management works best when it is guided by a lead coordinating and facilitation organization.

Environmental refugees and conflicts over increasingly scarce resources such as water and oil will be a growing challenge for effective conservation collaboration. International and national treaties and conventions for connectivity conservation areas are needed to deal with conflicts over infrastructure and resource development projects that have impacts across borders. Given that security issues, population pressures and resource shortages will make cooperation increasingly difficult and complex, connectivity conservation areas (such as 'peace parks') can play a role in promoting cooperation between regions and countries. Connectivity conservation management may assist with reducing tensions and facilitating cooperation across borders, and may contribute to peace outcomes.

9 Connectivity conservation leaders and managers need to gain an understanding of the aspirations, motivations, values and capacities of the communities with which they work. Effective social science research should therefore be part of every connectivity conservation initiative. Given an increasingly urbanized world that removes many people from contact with wild nature, and the degree to which people are viewing the world through virtual representations, we cannot assume people have some familiarity with and affection for nature – sustained and innovative efforts to engage people with nature are needed. There is a need to get environmental issues into the national education curriculum and maintain funding for environmental education over the long term. Widespread community support and forceful argument, supported by powerful media images and messages are needed to shift the thinking of community leaders and decision makers. Biological, social and economic concepts of connectivity conservation need to be 'mainstreamed' through formal education programmes, skill training for conservation agency staff and efforts to influence key target audiences including government and business leaders, engineers, planners and private sector developers. Networks of connectivity professionals and supporters are needed to raise awareness of connectivity issues and build bridges across sectors, disciplines and cultural and institutional divides. Building trust and establishing robust connections with local, national and international communities is critical.

10 Connectivity conservation champions and sustained leadership are vital for achieving a connectivity conservation vision. Leadership capability needs to be dispersed across all levels and sectors and include 'top-down' and 'bottom-up' leadership – at the same time, fragmented, competitive and uncoordinated leadership should be avoided. Current leaders need to invest in developing the next generation of leaders, including mentoring and inclusion of young professionals in meetings and decision-making processes. Leadership needs to be committed for the long term, and to build support for sustained efforts to plan and implement connectivity conservation initiatives. Connectivity leadership needs to challenge and shift the short-term thinking of most politicians. Leaders must continuously monitor and identify threats to connectivity conservation and adopt innovative responses. Leaders need to identify how to deal more

effectively with large infrastructure and development projects that impact connectivity conservation areas. Leaders need to forge an effective union of conservation and development within connectivity conservation areas, including specification of meaningful goals and realistic strategies.

11 Connectivity conservation needs long-term commitment and sustained effort. Connectivity conservation actions need to occur at site, landscape, national and international levels. Local people and local actions are critical to the long-term success of connectivity conservation areas. Equally, governments, for example, need to participate actively in connectivity initiatives. Innovators and innovation at all levels needs to be encouraged and facilitated.

Connectivity conservation management is a relatively new land use, and the need for managing large landscapes for the conservation of connectivity has never been more urgent. It is also a new social phenomenon, for the act of conserving these lands directly involves and empowers people and provides opportunities for them to directly contribute to grand, national landscape-scale responses to global change. Designed with a clear purpose and functional boundaries, connectivity areas can include landscape, habitat, ecological and evolutionary connectivity conservation functions within a landscape that supports a complex of tenures and sectoral interests. This will not be easy, but the end result is too important for us not to succeed. It is an opportunity for governments, NGOs, communities and individuals to work together for the long-term benefit of nature and people.

Connectivity areas include some of the last large-scale natural areas of Earth. They are multi-purpose areas of immense value to people and other species and typically they are: highly aesthetic; destinations for recreation; of great value as water catchments; and offer temporary or permanent habitats for species and opportunities for their movement. However, outside of the legally conserved core protected areas, they are highly vulnerable to a tyranny of small development decisions that incrementally could mean protected areas become isolated in a modified landscape. Concerted action involving many people and governments will be needed to retain these naturally interconnected lands for the long term.

Connectivity conservation management is needed in the face of forecast futures. This simple challenge is not an over reaction. Without intervention, the reality of past and forecast human behaviour identifies the inevitable fragmentation and loss of natural lands and their ecosystem services. The end result would be an unhealthy and less diverse world. For many areas of Earth, however, we still have a choice: a worldwide network of large-scale natural connectivity conservation lands with their associated interconnected and embedded protected areas would constitute an investment in the survival of many species and a better future for the planet and the people who live on it. The case studies, management framework and practices presented in this book aim to facilitate this work.

References

AALC (Australian Alps Liaison Committee) (2004) *Australian Alps National Parks Co-operative Management Program, Strategic Plan 2004–2007*, Australian Alps Liaison Committee, Canberra

AALC (2005) *Alps Walking Track Brochure*, Australian Alps Liaison Committee, Canberra

AALC (2006) *Australian Alps Statement of Values*, Submission to the Australian Heritage Council, Australian Alps Liaison Committee, Canberra

Acha, M. O. (2003) 'Wirikuta: The Wixarika/Huichol sacred natural site in the Chihuahuan Desert, San Luis Potosi, Mexico', in Harmon, D. and Putney, A. (eds) *The Full Value of Parks: From Economics to the Intangible*, Rowman & Littlefield, Lanham, MD

Adams, W. M. and Hutton, J. (2007) 'People, parks and poverty: Political ecology and biodiversity conservation', *Conservation and Society*, vol 5, pp147–183

Adger, W. N., Brown, K. and Tompkins, E. L. (2005) 'The political economy of cross-scale networks in resource co-management', *Ecology and Society*, vol 10, no 2, www.ecologyandsociety.org/vol10/iss2/art9/

Alpine Convention (2003) *Alpenkonvention – Nachschlagewerk*, Alpensignale 1, Permanent Secretariat of the Alpine Convention, Innsbruck

Alroy, J. (2001) 'A multi-species overkill simulation of the end-Pleistocene megafaunal mass extinction', *Science*, vol 292, pp1893–1896

Agrawal, A. and Gupta, K. (2005) 'Decentralization and participation: The governance of common pool resources in Nepal's Terai', *World Development*, vol 33, pp1101–1114

Alcorn, J. B. (1993) 'Indigenous Peoples and Conservation', *Conservation Biology*, vol 7, no 2, pp424–427

Ali, S. H. (ed) (2007) *Peace Parks. Conservation and Conflict Resolution*, MIT Press, London

Allan, C. and Curtis, A. (2005) 'Nipped in the bud: Why regional scale adaptive management is not blooming', *Environmental Management*, vol 36, pp414–425

Anderson, A. B. and Jenkins, C. N. (2006) *Applying Nature's Design: Corridors as a Strategy for Biodiversity Conservation*, Columbia University Press, New York

Anderson, C., Locker, L. and Nugent, R. (2002) 'Microcredit, social capital and common pool resources', *World Development*, vol 30, pp95–105

Anhalzer, J. J. (1998) *Llanganati*, Imprenta Mariscal, Quito

Anonymous (2002) *Biodiversity Action Plan for Bhutan*, Ministry of Agriculture, Royal Government of Bhutan, Thimphu

Araujo, N., Muller, R., Nowicki, C. and Ibisch, P. (in press) *Analisis de Vacios de Representatividad del Sistema Nacional de Areas Protegidas*, Editorial FAN, Santa Cruz

Ashwell, A., Sandwith, T. S., Barnett, M., Parker, A. and Wisani, F. (2006) *Fynbos Fynmense: People Making Biodiversity Work*, SANBI Biodiversity Series Occasional Report No 4, South African National Biodiversity Institute, Pretoria

Backus, P. (2007) 'Grizzly shot in Selway-Bitterroot', *The Missoulian*, 12 September 2007, Missoula MT

Baillie, J. E. M., Hilton-Taylor, C. and Stuart, S. M. (eds) (2004) *IUCN Red List of Threatened Species: A Global Species Assessment*, IUCN, Gland and Cambridge

Bajaña, F. and Viteri, X. (2002) *Plan Preliminar de Manejo del Corredor Ecológico Llanganates Sangay*, Fundación Natura, WWF and Ministerio del Ambiente, Quito

Balasinorwala, T., Kothari, A. and Goyal, M. (2004) *Participatory Conservation: Paradigm Shifts in the International Policy*, IUCN, Gland, Cambridge and Kalpavriksh

Balslev, H. (2001) 'Vascular plants on Volcán Chiles and Páramo del Angel, Ecuador – a preliminary list', in Ramsay, P. M. (ed) *The Ecology of Volcán Chiles: High Altitude Ecosystems of the Ecuador-Columbian Border*, Pebble & Shell, Plymouth, UK, p1

BAPPENAS (1993) *Biodiversity Action Plan for Indonesia*, National Development Planning Agency, Ministry of Development Planning, Jakarta

Barber, C.V., Miller, K. R. and Boness, M. (eds) (2004) *Securing Protected Areas in the Face of Global Change: Issues and Strategies*, IUCN, Gland and Cambridge

Barrett, T. (2005) 'C-Plan', in Worboys, G. L., Lockwood, M. and De Lacy, T. (eds) *Protected Area Management, Principles and Practice*, Second Edition, Oxford University Press, Melbourne, p146

Barrett, T. (2009) *Report: Population within 100 kilometres of the Great Eastern Ranges Connectivity Corridor and East of the Great Dividing Range*, Department of Environment and Climate Change, NSW Government, Queanbeyan

Bartol, K., Martin, D., Tein, M. and Mathews, G. (1998) *Management: A Pacific Rim Focus*, Second Edition, McGraw-Hill, Sydney

Bass, Q. (2000) Archeologist, Cherokee National Forest, Cleveland, TN, personal communication to Hugh Irwin, Southern Appalachian Forest Coalition, Asheville, NC

Battisti, C. and Romano, B. (2005) *Parametri Eco-Biogeografici e Urbanistici di Diversità, Area, Isolamento, Interferenza: Confronto e Possibili Applicazioni in Paesaggi Frammentati*, Atti Convegno Internazionale Biodiversità, dinamica del paesaggio e gestione delle aree montane, Stelvio settanta, Rabbi 8–11 Settembre 2005

Bauer, M. W. (2002) 'The EU "partnership principle": Still a sustainable governance device across multiple administrative arenas?', *Public Administration*, vol 80, pp769–789

Beier, P. and Noss, R. F. (1998) 'Do habitat corridors provide connectivity?', *Conservation Biology*, vol 12, no 6, pp1241–1252

Bengtsson J., Angelstam P., Elmqvist T., Emanuelsson U., Folke C., Ihse M., Moberg F. and Nyström M. (2002) 'Reserves, resilience, and dynamic landscapes', *Ambio*, vol 32, issue 6, pp389–396

Beniston, M. and Fox, D. G. (1996) 'Impacts of climate change on mountain regions', in Watson, R. T., Zinyowera, M. C. and Moss, R. H. (eds) *Climate Change 1995: Impacts, Adaptations, and Mitigation of Climate Change: Scientific–Technical Analyses*, Contribution of Working Group II to the Second Assessment Report, pp191–214, Cambridge University Press, New York

Benítez, V., Sánchez, D. and Larrea, M. (2000) 'Evaluación ecológica rápida de la avifauna del Parque Nacional Llanganates', in Vázquez, M. A., Larrea, M and Suárez, L. (eds) *Biodiversidad en el Parque Nacional Llanganates: Un Reporte de Las Evaluaciones Ecológicas y Socioeconómicas Rápidas*, EcoCiencia, Ministerio del Ambiente, Herbario Nacional del Ecuador, Museo Ecuatoriano de Ciencias Naturales y Instituto Internacional de Reconstrucción Rural, Quito, pp67–108

Bennett, A. F. (2003) *Linkages in the Landscape. The Role of Corridors and Connectivity in Wildlife Conservation*, IUCN, Gland and Cambridge

Bennett, A. F., Crooks, K. R. and Sanjayan, M. (2006) 'The future of connectivity conservation', in Crooks, K. R. and Sanjayan, M. (eds) *Connectivity Conservation*, Cambridge University Press, Cambridge

Bennett, G. (ed) (2004) *Integrating Biodiversity Conservation and Sustainable Use: Lessons Learned From Ecological Networks*, IUCN, Gland and Cambridge

Bennett, G. and Mulongoy, K. J. (2006) *Review of Experience with Ecological Networks, Corridors and Buffer Zones*, Technical Series No 23, Secretariat of the Convention on Biological Diversity, Montreal

Bennett, S., Brereton, R. and Mansergh, I. (1992) *Enhanced Greenhouse and the Wildlife of South Eastern Australia*, Technical Report No 127, Arthur Rylah Institute for Environmental Research, Melbourne

Berger, J. (2004) 'The last mile: How to sustain long-distance migration in mammals', *Conservation Biology*, vol 18, no 2, p320

Berkes, F., Folke, C. and Colding, J. (eds) (1998) *Linking Social and Ecological Systems. Management Practices and Social Mechanisms for Building Resilience*, Cambridge University Press, Cambridge

Berkes, F., Colding, J. and Folke, C. (eds) (2002) *Navigating Social-Ecological Systems: Building Resilience for Complexity and Change*, Cambridge University Press, Cambridge

Bernbaum, E. (1997) *Sacred Mountains of the World*, University of California Press, Berkeley and Los Angeles

Berthoud, G. (2001) *Les Corridors Ecologiques en Isère, Projet de Réseau Ecologique Départemental de L'Isère (REDI)*, Conseil général de l'Isère, Grenoble, France

Beukering, P., van Herman, J. H., Cesar, S. J. and Janssen, M. A. (2003) 'Economic valuation of the Leuser National Park on Sumatra', *Ecological Economics*, vol 44, pp43–62

Bhutan Nature Conservation Division (2005) *Tiger Action Plan for Bhutan 2006–2015*, Nature Conservation Division, Department of Forests, Thimpu

Biggs, H. C. and Rogers, K. H. (2003) 'An adaptive system to link science, monitoring and management in practice', in Du Toit, J. T., Rogers, K. H. and Biggs, H. C. (eds) *The Kruger Experience. Ecology and Management of Savanna Heterogeneity*, Island Press, Washington DC

Biondi, M., Corridore, G., Romano, B., Tamburini, P. and Tetè P. (2003) *Evaluation and Planning Control of the Ecosystem Fragmentation due to Urban Development*, ERSA 2003 Congress, Agosto 2003, Jyvaskyla

Bischoff, N. T. and Jongman, R. H. G. (1993) *Development of Rural Areas in Europe: The Claim for Nature*, Preliminary and background studies, no v79, Netherlands Scientific Council of Government Policy, SDU Publishers, The Hague

BOM (Bureau of Meteorology) (2008) *Trends in Annual Total Rainfall, 1950–2007 (mm/10 years)*, Australian Bureau of Meteorology, Canberra, www.bom.gov.au

Borrini-Feyerabend, G. (2004) 'Governance of protected areas, participation and equity', in *Biodiversity Issues for Consideration in the Planning, Establishment and Management of Protected Areas Sites and Networks*, Convention on Biological Diversity, Technical Series 15, Secretariat of the Convention on Biological Diversity, Montreal

Borrini-Feyerabend, G., Kothari, A. and Oviedo, G. (2004) *Indigenous and Local Communities and Protected Areas: Towards Equity and Enhanced Conservation*, IUCN, Gland and Cambridge

Borrini-Feyerabend, G., Johnson, J. and Pansky, D. (2006) 'Governance', in Lockwood, M., Worboys, G. L. and Kothari, A. (eds) *Managing Protected Areas: A Global Guide*, Earthscan, London, pp116–144

Bottrill, M. and Pressey, R. L. (2009) *Designs for Nature. Regional Conservation Planning, Implementation and Management* (in press), Best Practice Protected Areas Guidelines Series, IUCN, Gland

Bouwma, I. R. and Jongman, R. H. G. (2006) 'Methodology to identify the Pan-European Ecological Network for Western Europe', draft document, Methodology of the indicative map of the Pan-European Ecological Network for Western Europe, version 2

Bradby, K. (1991) 'A data bank is never enough: The local approach to Landcare', in Saunders, D. and Hobbs, R. (eds) *Nature Conservation 2 – The Role of Corridors*, Surrey Beatty and Sons, Sydney, pp377–385

Brechin, S. R., Wilshusen, P. R., Fortwangler, C. L. and West, P. C. (2002) 'Beyond the square wheel: Toward a more comprehensive understanding of biodiversity conservation as a social and political process', *Society and Natural Resources*, vol 15, pp41–64

Breckenridge, L. P. (1998) 'Nonprofit environmental organizations and the restructuring of institutions for ecosystem management', *Ecology Law Quarterly*, vol 25, no 4, pp692–701

Briassoulis, H. (1989) 'Theoretical orientations in environmental planning: An inquiry into alternative approaches', *Environmental Management*, vol 13, pp381–392

Brinkerhoff, J. (2002) 'Assessing and improving partnership relationships and outcomes: A proposed framework', *Evaluation and Program Planning*, vol 25, pp215–231

Brooks, T. M., Mittermeier, R. A., da Fonseca, G. A. B., Gerlach, J., Hoffmann, M., Lamoreux, J. F., Mittermeier, C. G., Pilgrim, J. D. and Rodrigues, A. S. L. (2006) 'Global biodiversity conservation priorities', *Science*, vol 313, no 5783, pp58–61

Buckley, R., Sander, N., Ollenburg, C. and Warnken, J. (2006) 'Green change: Inland amenity migration in Australia', in Moss, L. A. (ed) *The Amenity Migrants. Seeking and Sustaining Mountains and their Cultures*, CABI, Oxfordshire

Bulgarini F., Teofili C. and Bologna G. (2004) *Global 200 ERC-Ecoregional Conservation, Il Processo di Conservazione Ecoregionale e La Sua Applicazione in Italia*, WWF, New York

Buytaert, W., Célleri, R., De Bièvre, B., Cisneros, F., Wyseure, G., Deckers, J. and Hofstede, R. (2006) 'Human impact on the hydrology of the Andean Páramos', *Earth-Science Reviews* vol 79, nos 1–2, pp53–72

Canova, L. (2006) 'Protected area and landscape conservation in the Lambbardy plain (north Italy): An appraisal', *Landscape and Urban Planning*, vol 74, pp102–109

Castaño, C. (ed) (2002) *Páramos y Ecosistemas Alto Andinos de Colombia en Condición Hotspot y Global Climatic Tensor*, IDEAM, Bogotá

CBC Television (1997) *The Nature of Things with David Suzuki: Yellowstone to Yukon*, Toronto

CBD (Convention on Biological Diversity) (2008) *CBD Ecosystem Approach*, Secretariat of the Convention on Biological Diversity, Montreal, www.cbd.int/ecosystem/description.shtml

CCAD (Comisión Centroamericana de Ambiente y Desarrollo) (2002) *Proyecto para la Consolidación del Corredor Biológico Mesoamericano El Corredor Biológico Mesoamericano: Una Plataforma para el Desarrollo Sostenible Regional/ Proyecto para la Consolidación del Corredor Biológico Mesoamericano*, 1a ed, Proyecto Corredor Biológico Mesoamericano, Managua

CCAD (2003) *The Central American Protected Areas System (SICAP): A Key Arena for Conserving Biological Diversity*, Regional Report, Guatemala

Center for Transportation and the Environment (2006) *Wildlife Crossing Structures Field Course, Banff*, North Carolina State University, Raleigh www.itre.ncsu.edu/cte/gateway/banff_classroom.asp

CEPF (Critical Ecosystem Partnership Fund) (2001) *Perfil del Ecosistema: Ecosistema Forestal de Vilcabamba Amboro del Área Prioritaria de Conservación de la Biodiversidad en los Andes Tropicales de Perú y Bolivia*, Washington DC

CEPF (2005) *Ecosystem Profile: Indo-Burman Hotspot, Eastern Himalayan Region*, WWF-US Asian Program, Washington DC

CEPF and CI (Conservation International) (2003a) *Estrategia Básica de Implementación del Corredor de Conservación Vilcabamba – Amboró*, Critical Ecosystem Partnership Fund and Conservation International, Lima

CEPF and CI (2003b) *Informe Final: Mitigación de las Amenazas a la Biodiversidad por las Actividades Mineras en el Corredor de Conservación Vilcabamba Amboro*, Critical Ecosystem Partnership Fund, Washington DC

Chadwick, D. (2000) *Yellowstone to Yukon*, National Geographic Society, Washington DC

Chape, S., Spalding M. and Jenkins., M. (eds) (2008) *The World's Protected Areas: Status, Values and Prospects in the 21st Century*, University of California Press, Berkeley, CA

Chapin, M. (2004) 'A challenge to conservationists', *Worldwatch,* November/December, vol 17, no 6, pp17–31

Chapman, J., De Lacy, T. and Whitmore, M. (2006) 'Sustainability practice and sustainable use', in Lockwood, M., Worboys, G. L. and Kothari, A. (eds) *Managing Protected Areas: A Global Guide*, Earthscan, London, pp377–405

Chassot, O., Monge-Arias, G. and Jiménez, V. (2005) *Corredor Biológico San Juan – La Selva*, Centro Científico Tropical, San José

Chauvin, L. O. (2003) 'Peru natural gas pipelines, plant ignite controversy: Critics fear damage to jungle, tribes along route', *San Francisco Chronicle*, 5 August, San Francisco

Chester, C. C. (2006) *Conservation Across Borders: Biodiversity in an Interdependent World*, Island Press, Washington DC

Chettri, N. and Sharma, E. (2005) 'Transboundary landscapes for protected areas and conservation corridors', in *Transboundary Landscape for Protected Areas and Conservation Corridors, Hindu Kush-Himalayan Biodiversity Conservation E-Conference*, 29 August to 4 September, www.mtnforum.org/E-Consultation05/backgroundpapers.htm

Chettri, N. and Sharma, E. (2006) 'Prospective for developing a transboundary conservation landscape in the eastern Himalayas', in McNeely, J. A., McCarthy, T. M., Smith, A., Whittaker, O. L. and Wikramanayake, E. D. (eds) *Conservation Biology in Asia*, Society for Conservation Biology, Asia Section and Resources Himalaya Foundation, Kathmandu

CI (Conservation International) (2004a) *Perfil de Ecosistema. Región Norte del Hotspot de Biodiversidad de Mesoamérica: Belice, Guatemala, México*, Critical Ecosystem Partnership Fund, Washington DC

CI (2004b) *Conserving the Earth's Living Heritage: A Proposed Framework for Designing Biodiversity Conservation Strategies*, Conservation International, Washington DC

CI (2005) *Refining Biodiversity Conservation Corridors: Executive Summary of Workshop Proceedings*, Conservation International, Washington DC

CI (2006a) *Memoria del Taller sobre IIRSA, Carretera InterOceanica Sur y Otros Megaproyectos*, Conservation International, La Paz

CI (2006b) *Fortalecimiento a la Planificación Territorial y Gestión Ambiental Apolo*, Conservation International, La Paz

Clark, T., Paquet, P. and Curlee, A. P. (1996) 'Large carnivore conservation in the Rocky Mountains', *Conservation Biology*, vol 10, issue 4, p936

Commander, S. and Peek, P. (1986) 'Oil exports, agrarian change and the rural labor process: The

Ecuadorian Sierra in the 1970s', *World Development*, vol 14, no 1, pp79–96

Commonwealth of Australia (2002) *Australia's Natural Resources: 1997 to 2002 and Beyond*, National Land and Water Resources Audit, Canberra

Community Development Resource Association (2006) *Review of the Functioning of the Greater Cederberg Biological Corridor's Steering Committee*, unpublished report, Community Development Resource Association, Cape Town

Cork, S. J. and Shelton, D. (2000) 'The nature and value of Australia's ecosystem services: Framework for sustainable environmental solutions', in *Sustainable Environmental Solutions For Industry And Government*, Proceedings of the 3rd Queensland Environmental Conference, Institution of Engineers, Australia and Queensland Chamber of Commerce and Industry, Brisbane

Costa Rica Network of Private Reserves (2006) www.reservasprivadascr.org

Costanza, R., D'Arge, R., de Groot, R., Farber, S., Grasso, M., Hannon, M., Limburg, K., Naeem, S., O'Neill, R. V., Pauelo, J., Raskin, R., Sutton, P. and Van Den Belt, M. (1997) 'The value of world's ecosystem services and natural capital', *Nature*, vol 387, pp253–260

Council of Europe (1996) *The Pan-European Biological and Landscape Diversity Strategy. A Vision for Europe's Natural Heritage*, UNEP, European Centre for Nature Conservation, Netherlands, Tilberg

Coyne, P. (2001) *Protecting the Natural Treasures of the Australian Alps*, a report to the Natural Heritage Working Group of the Australian Alps Liaison Committee, Canberra, www.australianalps.deh.gov.au/publications/natural-treasures/pubs/natural-treasures.pdf

CPAWS (Canadian Parks and Wilderness Society) (2006) *Only We Can Protect Nahanni Forever*, campaign brochure, Canadian Parks and Wilderness Society, Ottawa, ON

Crabb, P. (2003) *Managing the Australian Alps: A History of Cooperative Management of the Australian Alps National Parks*, Australian Alps Liaison Committee and Australian National University, Canberra

Crooks, K. and Sanjayan, M. (eds) (2006) *Connectivity Conservation*, Cambridge University Press, New York

Cropper, S. (1996) 'Collaborative working and the issue of sustainability', in Huxham, C. (ed) *Creating Collaborative Advantage*, Sage, London, pp80–100

Cuatrecasas, J. (1958) 'Aspectos de la vegetación

natural de Colombia', *Revista de la Academia Colombiana de Ciencias Exactas y Físicas*, vol 10, no 40, pp221–264

Curtis, A. and Lockwood, M. (2000) 'Landcare and catchment management in Australia: Lessons for state-sponsored community participation', *Society and Natural Resources*, vol 13, no 1, pp61–73

Curtis, A., Lockwood, M. and MacKay, J. (2001) 'Exploring landholder willingness and capacity to manage dryland salinity in the Goulburn Broken Catchment', *Australian Journal of Environmental Management*, vol 8, pp20–31

DAFF (Department of Agriculture Fisheries and Forestry) (1999) *Regional Forest Agreement for the Eden Region of New South Wales between the Commonwealth of Australia and the State of New South Wales*, Department of Agriculture Fisheries and Forestry, Commonwealth of Australia, Canberra

Damschen, E. I., Haddad, N. M., Orrock, J. L., Tewksbury, J. J. and Levey, D. J. (2006) 'Corridors increase plant species richness at large scales', *Science*, vol 313, no 5791, pp1284–1286

D'Arcy, W. G. (1977) 'Endangered landscapes in Panama and Central America: The threat to plant species', in Prance, G. T. and Elias, T. S. (eds) *Extinction is Forever*, New York Botanical Garden, Bronx, pp89–104

Davidson, J. and Lockwood, M. (2008) 'Partnerships as instruments of good regional governance: Innovation for sustainability in Tasmania', *Regional Studies*, vol 24, no 5

Davidson, J., Lockwood, M., Curtis, A., Stratford, E. and Griffith, R. (2006) *Governance Principles for Regional Natural Resource Management, Report No 1*, Pathways to good practice in regional NRM governance project, University of Tasmania, Hobart

Davies, J. (1986) *The Australian Alps National Parks Co-operative Management, Proceedings of a Working Meeting of Officers from Management Agencies*, Howmans Gap, Victoria, 28–31 October 1986, Report Series No 7, Canberra Australian National Parks and Wildlife Service, Canberra

Dawson, M. (2005) *The Population Ecology of Feral Horses in the Australian Alps Management Summary*, Australian Alps Liaison Committee, Canberra, www.australianalps.deh.gov.au/publications/feral-horses/pubs/feral-horses.pdf

De Lacy, T., Battig, B., Moore, S. and Noakes, S. (2002) *Public–Private Partnerships for Sustainable Tourism: Delivering a Sustainability Strategy for Tourism Destinations*, CRC for Sustainable Tourism, Gold Coast

De Oliveira, J. A. P. (2002) 'Implementing environmental policies in developing countries through decentralization: The case of protected areas in Bahia, Brazil', *World Development*, vol 30, pp1713–1736

Dean, C. (2006) 'Research shows that plants like a path to biodiversity', *New York Times*, 5 September 2006, New York

Dearden, P. and Rollins, R. (2002) *Parks and Protected Areas Management in Canada*, Second Edition, Oxford University Press, Ontario

DECC (Department of Environment and Climate Change, NSW) (2008) *The Great Eastern Ranges Initiative from the Australian Alps to Atherton and Beyond: Business Plan, 2008–2009*, Sydney

DECC (2009) *Biobanking*, www.environment.nsw.gov.au/biobanking/

Dematteis, G. and Emanuel, C. (1994) 'La diffusione urbana, interpretazioni e valutazioni', in: Dematteis, G. (ed) *Il Fenomeno Urbano in Italia: Interpretazioni, Prospettive, Politiche*, Angeli ed, Milano

Dephutbun (Kantor Wilayah Kehutanan dan Perkebunan) (1999) *Potensi dan Distribusi Sumberdaya Kehutanan dan Perkebunan di Daerah Kabupaten/Kota Se-Propinsi Riau*, Kantor Wilayah Departemen Kehutanan dan Perkebunan Propinsi Riau, Pekanbaru

D'Huart, J. P. (1989) *Bases for the Development of a Coordinated Management of Contiguous Protected Areas in Zaïre and Uganda*, unpublished report cited by Andrew Plumptre, Wildlife Conservation Society, New York

Diamond, J. (2005) *Collapse: How Societies Choose to Fail or Succeed*, Penguin, New York

Dinerstein, E., Olson, D., Graham, D., Webster, A., Primm, S., Bookbinder, M. and Ledec, G. (1995) *A Conservation Assessment of the Terrestrial Ecoregions of Latin America and the Caribbean*, The International Bank for Reconstruction and Development/The World Bank, Washington DC

DLIA (Discover Life in America) (2007) *The All Taxa Biodiversity Inventory in Great Smoky Mountains National Park*, www.dlia.org/atbi/new_science/index.shtml

DLUPC (The Dehcho Land Use Planning Committee) (2006) *Respect for the Land: The Dehcho Land Use Plan*, Dehcho First Nations, Fort Simpson, www.dehcholands.org/home.htm

Dobson, A., Ralls, K., Foster, M., Soulé, M. E., Simberloff, D., Doak, D., Estes, J. A., Scott Mills, L., Mattson, D., Dirzo, R., Arita, H., Ryan, S., Norse, E. A., Noss, R. F. and Johns, D. (1999)

'Connectivity: Maintaining flows in fragmented landscapes', in Soulé, M. E. and Terborgh, J. (eds) *Continental Conservation: Scientific Foundations of Regional Reserve Networks*, Island Press, Washington DC

Dourojeanni, M. J. (2006) *Estudio de Caso sobre la Carretera Interoceanica en la Amazonia Sur del Peru*, SERVIGRAF EIR, Lima, Peru

Dovers, S. R. (1998) *Public Policy and Institutional Research and Development for Natural Resource Management: Issues and Directions for LWRRDC*, Report to the Land and Water Resources Research and Development Corporation, Centre for Resource and Environmental Studies, Australian National University, Canberra

Downer, C. (1996) 'The mountain tapir, endangered flagship species of the high Andes', *Oryx*, vol 30, no 1, pp45–58

Dresner, S. (2002) *The Principles of Sustainability*, Earthscan, London

Dricuru, M. (1999) *The Lions of Queen Elizabeth National Park, Uganda: Their Demographic and Health Status and Relationships with People*, unpublished MSc Thesis, Institute of Environment and Natural Resources, Department of Wildlife and Animal Resource Management, Makerere University, Kampala

Driver, A., Cowling, R. M. and Maze, K. (2003) *Planning for Living Landscapes: Perspectives and Lessons from South Africa*, Center for Applied Biodiversity Science at Conservation International, Washington DC, Botanical Society of South Africa, Cape Town

Dudley, N. (ed) (2008) *Guidelines for Applying Protected Area Management Categories*, IUCN, Gland

Dudley, N. and Stolton, S. (2003) *Running Pure: The Importance of Forest Protected Areas to Drinking Water*, World Bank-WWF Alliance for Forest Conservation, Washington DC

Dudley, N. and Parish, J. (2005) *Closing the Gap, Creating Ecologically Representative Protected Area Systems. A Guide to Conducting Gap Assessments of Protected Area Systems for the Convention on Biological Diversity*, Technical Series No 24, Secretariat of the Convention on Biological Diversity, Montreal

Dudley, N. and Rao, M. (2008) *Assessing and Creating Linkages. Within and Beyond Protected Areas: A Quick Guide for Protected Area Practitioners*, The Nature Conservancy, Arlington

Dudley, N., Mulongoy, K. J., Cohen, S., Stolton, S., Barber, V. and Gidda, S. B. (2005) *Convention on Biological Diversity Programme of Work on Protected*

Areas, Technical Series No 18, Secretariat of the Convention on Biological Diversity, Montreal, Montreal

Duellman, W. and Wild, E. (1993) *Anuran Amphibians from the Cordillera Huancabamba, Northern Peru: Systematics, Ecology, and Biogeography*, Occasional Papers of the Museum of Natural History, vol 157, The University of Kansas, Lawrence

Dunleavy, P., Margetts, H., Bastow, S. and Tinkler, J. (2006) 'New Public Management is dead: Long live digital era governance', *Journal of Public Administration Research and Theory*, vol 16, pp467–494

Eagles, P. F. J. and McCool, S. F. (2002) *Tourism in National Parks and Protected Areas: Planning and Management*, CABI, New York

Ecclestone, K. and Field, J. (2003) 'Promoting social capital in a "risk society": A new approach to emancipatory learning or new moral authoritarianism?', *British Journal of Sociology of Education*, vol 24, pp267–282

Echavarria, M. and Arroyo, P. (2004) 'FONAG: A water-based finance mechanism for the Condor Biosphere Reserve in Ecuador', in Harmon, D. and Worboys, G. L. (eds) *Managing Mountain Protected Areas: Challenges and Responses for the 21st Century*, Andromeda Editrice, Colledara

Eckholm, E. P. (1975) 'The deterioration of mountain environments', *Science*, vol 189, pp764–770

El Comercio (2006) 'La afluencia de turistas al teleférico disminuyó', newspaper article published 20 October, Redacción Sociedad

Ellenberg, H. (1979) 'Man's influence on tropical mountain ecosystems in South America', *Journal of Ecology*, vol 67, pp401–416

Emerton, L., Bishop, J. and Thomas, L. (2005) *Sustainable Financing of Protected Areas: A Global Review of Challenges and Options*, IUCN, Gland and Cambridge

Epps, C. W., Palsboll, P. J., Wehausen, J. D., Roderick, G. K., Ramey, R. R. and McCullough, D. R. (2005) 'Highways block gene flow and cause a rapid decline in genetic diversity of desert bighorn sheep', *Ecology Letters*, vol 8, no 10, pp1029–1038

Ervin, J. (2007) *Assessing Protected Area Management Effectiveness. A Quick Guide for Protected Area Practitioners*, The Nature Conservancy, Arlington, VA

Ervin, J., Game, E., Gidda, S., Lawrence, K., Mulongoy, K. J., Rao, Madhu and Wong, G. (2009) *Connecting the Dots. A Guide to Integrating Protected Areas into Wider Landscapes, Seascapes and Natural Resource Sectors*, draft Version 2, The Nature Conservancy, Arlington, VA

Etter, A. (1998) *Mapa General de Ecosistemas de Colombia*, Instituto Alexander von Humboldt, Bogotá

Etter, A. and van Wyngaarden, W. (2000) 'Patterns of landscape transformation in Colombia, with emphasis in the Andean Region', Royal Swedish Academy of Sciences, *Ambio*, vol 29, pp432–43

Etter A., McAlpine, C., Wilson, K., Phinn, S. and Possingham, H. (2006) 'Regional patterns of agricultural land use and deforestation in Colombia', *Agriculture, Ecosystems and Environment*, vol 114, pp369–386

Fadli, N. (2006) *The Root Causes of Elephant–Human Conflict*, WWF Riau Elephant Conservation Program, WWF-US, Washington DC

Faith, D. P. (2005) 'Global biodiversity assessment: Integrating global and local values and human dimensions', *Global Environmental Change*, vol 15, pp5–8

Faith, D. P. and Walker, P. A. (2002) 'The role of trade-off in biodiversity conservation planning: Linking local management, regional planning and global conservation efforts', *Journal of BioScience*, vol 27, no 2, pp393–407

Falk, I. and Kilpatrick, S. (2000) 'What is social capital? A study of interaction in a rural community?', *Sociologia Ruralis*, vol 40, no 1, pp87–110

Fandiño-Lozano, M. and van Wyngaarden, W. (2005) *Prioridades de conservación Biológica para Colombia*, Grupo ARCO, Bogotá

Ferroni, F., Filpa, A. and Romano, B. (2006) 'Le opere della legge obiettivo versus aree protette, reti ecologiche e conservazione ecoregionale: Elementi per un bilancio', in AA.VV., *La Cattiva Strada, La Prima Ricerca Sulla Legge Obiettivo, Dal Ponte Sullo Stretto alla Tav*, WWF, Gland, pp43–62

Finke, L. (1996) 'Ecologia del paesaggio e pianificazione degli spazi aperti', *Urbanistica*, vol 107, INU, Roma

Fleck, L., Amend, M., Painter, L. and Reid, J. (2006) *Beneficios Económicos Regionales Generados por La Conservación: El Caso Del Madidi*, Conservation Strategy Fund, La Paz

Flores, M. (2007) Land Use Consultant, Conservation International, personal communication to Jordi Surkin, La Paz, Bolivia

Folke, C., Carpenter, S., Elmqvist, T., Gunderson, L., Holling, C. S., Walker, B., Bengtsson, J., Berkes, F., Colding, J., Danell, K., Falkenmark, M.,

Gordon, M., Kasperson, R., Kautsky, N., Kinzig, A., Levin, S., Mäler, K. G., Moberg, F., Ohlsson, L., Olsson, P., Ostrom, E., Reid, W., Rockström, J., Savenije, H. and Svedin, U. (2002) *Resilience and Sustainable Development: Building Adaptive Capacity in a World of Transformations*, scientific background paper on resilience for the process of The World Summit on Sustainable Development, on behalf of The Environmental Advisory Council to the Swedish Government, Stockholm

Folke, C., Hahn, T., Olsson, P. and Norberg, J. (2005) 'Adaptive governance of social-ecological knowledge', *Annual Review of Environment and Resources*, vol 30, pp441–473

Fonseca, R. M., Carrera, J. P., Enríquez, D., Lasso, O., Pinto, M., Tello, S., Novoa, J. and Viteri, X. (2003) 'Identificación preliminar de un corredor ecológico para mamíferos entre los Parques Nacionales Llanganates y Sangay', *Revista de la Pontificia Universidad Católica del Ecuador*, no 71, pp201–216, Quito

Foreman, D. (2004) *Rewilding North Amercia: A Vision for Conservation in the 21st Century*, Island Press, Washington DC

Forest Watch Indonesia (2001) *The State of the Indonesian Forest Report (draft)*, Expert Review Workshop, 29–30 June 2000, Bogor

Forman, R. T. T. (1991) 'Landscape corridors: From theoretical foundations to public policy', in Saunders, D. A. and Hobbs, R. J. (eds) *Nature Conservation 2: The Role of Corridors*, Surrey Beatty and Sons, Chipping Norton, NSW

Forno, E., Ponce, C., Telesca, A., Espinel, L., Mendoza, E. and Bensted-Smith, R. (2006) 'Vilcabamba-Amboro: Transboundary collaboration from the Andean Peaks to the Amazon Basin', in Mittermeier, R. A., Kormos, C. F., Mittermeier, C., Robles Gil, P., Sandwith, T. and Besancon, C. (eds) *Transboundary Conservation: A New Vision for Protected Areas*, Cemex, Bogotá

Francis, W. L. (2003) Acting Executive Director, Yellowstone to Yukon Conservation Initiative, personal communication to Harvey Locke, Toronto

Franklin, J. F. (1993) 'Preserving biodiversity: Species, ecosystems, or landscapes?', *Ecological Applications*, vol 3, pp202–205

Franklin, J. F. and Lindenmayer, D. (2009) 'Importance of matrix habitats in maintaining biological diversity', *Proceedings of the National Academy of Sciences of the United States of America*, vol 106, pp349–350

Frome, M. (1989) *Conscience of a Conservationist*, UT Press, Knoxville, TN

Fundació Territori i Paisatge (2006) *Mountain Corridors in the Pyrenees. International Conference on Mountain Corridors Proceedings*, CD edition, Fundació Territori i Paisatge, Barcelona

Fuller, T., Munguia, M., Sanchez-Cordero, V. and Sarkar, S. (2006) 'Incorporating connectivity into conservation planning: A multi-criteria case study from central Mexico', *Biological Conservation*, vol 133, pp131–142

Gambino, R. (1992) 'Reti urbane e spazi naturali', in Salzano, E. (ed) *La città sostenibile*, delle Autonomie, Roma

Gambino, R. and Romano, B. (2004) 'Territorial strategies and environmental continuity in mountain systems: The case of the Apennines (Italy)', in Harmon, D., Worboys, G. L. (eds) *Managing Mountain Protected Areas: Challenges and Responses for the 21st Century*, IUCN, Andromeda Editrice, Colledara

García, V. R. (1996) *Propuesta Técnica de Ordenamiento Territorial con Fines de Conservación de Biodiversidad en Costa Rica: Proyecto GRUAS*, Working Paper No10, Wildlife Conservation Society, New York

García Manteca, P. and González Taboada, F. (2005) *La Red de los Espacios Naturales Protegidos en Asturias. Análisis GAP y corredores ecológicos*, INDUROT y Univ de Oviedo, Oviedo

Generalitat de Catalunya (2006) *Pla Territorial Parcial de l'Alt Pirineu i Aran*, Dept de Politica Territorial i Obres Públiques

Gentry, A. H. (1982) 'Neotropical floristic diversity: Phytogeographical connections between Central and South America, Pleistocene climatic fluctuations, or an accident of the Andean orogeny?', *Annals of the Missouri Botanical Gardens*, vol 69, pp557–593

Georgieva, K., Pagiola, S. and Deeks, P. (2003) 'Paying for the environmental services of protected areas: Involving the private sector', Paper presented at the Vth IUCN World Parks Congress Sustainable Finance Stream, Durban, IUCN, Gland

Gibbs, R. (1993) *Australian Alps National Parks Horse Riding Management Strategy*, Australian Alps Liaison Committee, Canberra

Gibbs, R. and Mackay, J. (1994) *Australian Alps National Parks Tour Operators' Manual*, Australian Alps Liaison Committee, Canberra

Gill, A. M., Good, R., Kirkpatrick, J., Lennon, J., Mansergh, I. and Norris, R. (2004) *Beyond the*

Bushfires 2003, Environmental Issues in the Australian Alps, Australian Alps Liaison Committee, Canberra

Gisbert, E. F. (2007) Director, Conservation International Bolivia, personal communication to Jordi Surkin, La Paz, Bolivia

Gitay, H., Brown, S., Easterling, W. and Jallow, B. (2001) 'Ecosystems and their goods and services', in McCarthy, J. J., Canziani, J. J., Leary, O. F., Dokken, D. J. N. A. and White, K. S. (eds) *Climate Change 2001: Impacts, Adaptation, and Vulnerability*, Contribution of Working Group II to the Third Assessment Report of the Intergovernmental Panel on Climate Change, Cambridge University Press, New York, pp237–342

Giulietti, A. M., Menezes, N. L., Pirani, J. R., Meguro, M. and Wanderley, M. G. L. (1987) 'Flora da Serra do Cipó, Minas Gerais: Caracterização e lista das espécies', *Bol. Botânica*, University São Paulo, vol 9, pp1–151

Godoy, J. C. and Cardona, J. (1996) *Propuesta Técnica para Desarrollar el Sistema Guatemalteco de Áreas Protegidas y sus Corredores Ecológicos. Informe de país. Proyecto Sistema Regional Mesoamericano de Areas Protegidas, Zonas de Amortiguamiento y Corredores Biológicos*, RLA/95/G41, PNUD, Guatemala

Grabherr, G. (2008) *GLORIA – The Global Observation Initiative in Alpine Environments. Background Information Brochure*, Department of Conservation Biology, Vegetation and Landscape Ecology, University of Vienna, Austria, Gulger, Melk

Grabherr, G., Gottfried, M. and Pauli, H. (1994) 'Climate effects on mountain plants', *Nature*, vol 369, no 6480, p448

Graham, J., Amos, B. and Plumptre, T. (2003) *Governance Principles for Protected Areas in the 21st Century*, Institute on Governance, Ottawa

Grandia, L. (2007) 'Between Bolivar and bureaucracy: The Mesoamerican Biological Corridor', *Conservation and Society*, vol 5, pp478–503

Grayson, D. (2001) 'Did human hunting cause mass extinction?', *Science*, vol 294, pp1459–1462

Green Mountain Club (2006) *The Long Trail*, www.greenmountainclub.org

Groves, C. (2003) *Drafting a Conservation Blueprint*, Island Press, Washington DC

Gunderson, L. H. and Holling, C. S. (eds) (2002) *Panarchy: Understanding Transformations in Human and Natural Systems*, Island Press, Washington DC

Gunderson, L. H., Holling, C. S. and Light, S. S. (eds) (1995) *Barriers and Bridges to the Renewal of Ecosystems and Institutions*, Columbia University Press, New York

Gurrutxaga, M. (2005) *Red de Corredores Ecológicos de la Comunidad Autónoma de Euskadi*, Informe Técnico, IKT – Gobierno de Euskadi

Gurung, C. P., Maskay, T. M., Poudel, N., Lama, Y., Wagle, M. P., Manandhar, A., Khaling, S., Thapa, G., Thapa, S. and Wikramanayke, E. D. (2006) 'The Sacred Himalayan Landscape: Conceptualizing, visioning, and planning for conservation of biodiversity, culture and livelihoods in the eastern Himalaya', in McNeely, J. A., McCarthy, T. M., Smith, A., Whittaker, O. L. and Wikramanayake, E. D. (eds) *Conservation Biology in Asia*, Society for Conservation Biology, Asia Section and Resources Himalaya Foundation, Kathmandu

Gurung, G. S. (2008) *Terai Arc Nepal*, presentation to the IUCN WCPA Mountains Biome Transboundary Protected Area and Connectivity Conservation Workshop, Kathmandu (Dhulikhel), 11–15 November 2008, WWF-Nepal, Kathmandu

Hagan, J. M., Irland, L. C. and Whitman, A. A. (2005) *Changing Timberland Ownership in the Northern Forest and its Implications for Biodiversity*, Manomet Center for Conservation Sciences, Report #MCCS-FCP-2005-1, Brunswick, ME

Hall, M. H. P. and Fagre, D. B. (2003) 'Modelled climate-induced glacier change in Glacier National Park, 1850–2100', *Bioscience*, vol 52, no 2, pp131–140

Hamilton, L. S. (2000) 'Some guidelines for managing mountain protected areas having spiritual or cultural significance', *Parks*, vol 10, no 2, pp26–29

Hamilton, L. S., Askew, B. and Odell, R. (1982) 'Forest History, Report No 1', *New York State Forest Resources Assessment*, New York State Department of Environmental Conservation, Albany, NY

Hansen, A. J., Rasker, R., Maxwell, B., Rotella, J. J., Johnson, J. D., Parmenter, A. W., Langner, U., Cohen, W. B., Lawrence, R. L. and Kraska, M. P. V. (2002) 'Ecological causes and consequences of demographic change in the new west', *BioScience*, vol 52, no 2, pp151–162

Hanski, I. (1998) 'Metapopulation dynamics', *Nature*, vol 396, pp41–49

Harmon, D. and Worboys, G. L. (eds) (2004) *Managing Mountain Protected Areas: Challenges and Responses for the 21st Century*, Andromeda Editrice, Colledara

Harper, S. (2007) *Canada's New Government Announces the Expansion of Nahanni National Park Reserve*, press release, 8 August 2007, Canadian

Government, North West Territories, Fort Simpson

Harris, L. D. (1984) *The Fragmented Forest: Island Biogeography Theory and the Preservation of Biotic Diversity*, University of Chicago Press, Chicago, IL

Harris, L. D. and Scheck, J. (1991) 'From implications to applications: The dispersal corridor principle applied to the conservation of biological diversity', in Saunders, D. A. and Hobbs, R. J. (eds) *Nature Conservation 2: The Role of Corridors*, Surrey Beatty and Sons, Chipping Norton, pp189–220

Hatley, T. (2001) 'American Indian History', in Irwin, Hugh, Andrew, S. and Bouts, T. (eds) *Return the Great Forest: A Conservation Vision for the Southern Appalachian Region*, Southern Appalachian Forest Coalition, Asheville, NC, pp15–17

Hayes, G. (1995) 'Co-operative pest species management in the Australian Alps', Paper presented at an IUCN Trans-border protected area workshop, Jindabyne, cited in Crabb, P. (2003) *Managing the Australian Alps: A History of Cooperative Management of the Australian Alps National Parks*, Australian Alps Liaison Committee and the Australian National University, Canberra

Haynie, M. L., Brant, J. G., Mcaliley, L. R., Carrera, J. P., Revelez, M. A., Parish, D. A., Viteri, X., Jones, C. and Phillips, C. J. (2006) 'Investigations of a natural corridor between two national parks in Central Ecuador: Results from the Sowell Expedition', *Occasional Papers*, Museum of Texas Tech University, Lubbock, TX

Hazelton, V. and Keenan, W. (2000) 'Social capital: Reconceptualizing the bottom line', *Corporate Communications*, vol 5, no 2, p81

Healey, P. (1997) *Collaborative Planning: Shaping Places in Fragmented Societies*, Macmillan Press, London

Hebda, R. (2004) Schools of Earth and Ocean Sciences and Environmental Studies, University of Victoria, personal communication to H. Locke, Sydney, BC

Heller, N. E. and Zavaleta, E. (2009) 'Biodiversity management in the face of climate change: A review of 22 years of recommendations', *Biological Conservation*, vol 142, pp14–32

Hernández-Camacho, J., Hurtado-Guerra, A., Ortíz-Quijano, R. and Walschburger, T. (1992) 'Unidades biogeográficas de Colombia, La diversidad biológica de iberoamérica', *Acta Zoológica Mexicana*, Volumen Especial, Xalapa, Mexico

Hervas Ordoñez, T. (1994) 'Llamas, llama production and llama nutrition in the Ecuador highlands', *Journal of Arid Environments*, vol 26, pp67–71

Hess, C. G. (1990) 'Hacia arriba-hacia abajo: Un bosquejo de sistemas de producción en el Páramo del Ecuador', *Revista Geográfica de Ecuador*, vol 29, pp65–81

Hess, K. (2001) 'Parks are for people – but which people?', in Anderson, T. L. and James, A. (eds) *The Politics and Economics of Park Management*, pp159–181, Rowman & Littlefield, Lanham, MD

Heuer, K. (2002) *Walking the Big Wild*, McClelland and Stewart, Toronto

Hilty, J. A., Lidicker, W. Z. and Merenlender, M. A. (2006) *Corridor Ecology: The Science and Practice of Linking Landscapes for Biodiversity Conservation*, Island Press, Washington DC

HMGN-MFSC (His Majesty's Government of Nepal-Ministry of Forests and Soil Conservation) (2002) *Nepal Biodiversity Strategy*, Ministry of Forests and Soil Conservation, Government of Nepal, Kathmandu

HMGN-MFSC (2005) *Proceedings of the National Stakeholders' Consultation on Sacred Himalayan Landscape in Nepal*, Ministry of Forests and Soil Conservation, Government of Nepal, Kathmandu

Hobbs, R. J. and Hopkins, A. J. M. (1991) 'The role of conservation corridors in a changing climate', in Saunders, D. A. and Hobbs, R. J. (eds) *Nature Conservation 2: The Role of Corridors*, Surrey Beatty, Chipping Norton, pp281–290

Hockings, M., Stolton, S., Leverington, F., Dudley, N. and Corrau, J. (2006) *Evaluating Effectiveness: A Framework for Assessing Management Effectiveness of Protected Areas*, Second Edition, International Union for the Conservation of Nature, Gland

Hodge, I. (1991) 'Incentive policies and the rural environment', *Journal of Rural Studies*, vol 7, no 4, pp373–384

Hofstede, R. G. M. (1995) *Effects of Burning and Grazing on a Colombian Páramo Ecosystem*, PhD dissertation, Universidad of Amsterdam, Amsterdam

Hofstede, R. (2006) 'The ecosystem approach applied to the conservation of the Páramo ecosystem in Colombia', in Price, M. (ed) *Global Change in Mountain Regions*, Sapiens Publishing, Duncow, pp237–238

Hofstede, R. and Mujica, E. (2002) 'Birth of the Páramo Group: An international network of people, institutions, and projects working on páramo', *Mountain Research and Development*, vol 22, no 1, pp83–84

Hofstede, R., Coppus, R., Mena, P., Segarra, P., Wolf, J. and Sevink, J. (2002) 'The conservation status of tussock grass Páramo in Ecuador', *Ecotropicos*, vol 15, no 1, pp3–18

Hofstede, R., Segarra, P. and Mena, P. (2003) *Los Páramos del Mundo*, Global Peatland Initiative, Ecociencia, International Union for the Conservation of Nature, Quito

Holling, C. S. (2001) 'Understanding the complexity of economic, ecological, and social systems', *Ecosystems*, vol 4, pp390–405

Hopper, S. D. and Gioia, P. (2004) 'The southwest Australian floristic region: Evolution and conservation of a global hotspot of biodiversity', *Annual Review of Ecology and Systematics*, vol 35, pp623–650

Hopper, S. D., van Leeuwen, S., Brown, A. P. and Patrick, S. J. (1990) *Western Australia's Endangered Flora and Other Plants Under Consideration for Declaration*, Department of Conservation and Land Management, Perth

Hopper, S. J., Harvey, M. S., Chappill, J. A., Main, A. R. and Main, B. Y. (1996) 'The Western Australian biota as Gondwanan heritage: A review', in Hopper, S. J., Chappill, J. A., Harvey, M. S. and George, A. S. (eds) *Gondwanan Heritage: Past, Present and Future of the Western Australian Biota*, Surrey Beatty and Sons, Chipping Norton, pp1–46

Hosking, J., Sainty, G. and Jacobs, S. (2006) *Alps Invaders: Weeds of the Australian High Country*, Second Edition, Australian Alps Liaison Committee, Canberra

Hough, J. (2006) 'Developing capacity', in Lockwood, M., Worboys, G. L. and Kothari, A. (eds) *Managing Protected Areas: A Global Guide*, IUCN, Earthscan, London, pp164–184

Howlett, M. and Rayner, J. (2006) 'Convergence and divergence in "new governance" arrangements: Evidence from European integrated natural resource strategies', *Journal of Public Policy*, vol 26, pp167–189

Hughes, C. J. (2002) 'After 2,169 miles, what's another 690?' *New York Times*, 27 September, D 1-2, New York

Hull, R. B., Lam, M. and Vigo, G. (1994) 'Place identity: Symbols of self in the urban fabric', *Landscape and Urban Planning*, vol 28, nos 2–3, pp109–120

IBGE (Instituto Brasileiro de Geografia e Estatística) (2000) *Demographic Census 2000*, Ministério do Planjamento, Orçamento e Gestào, Brasilia

Ibisch, P. L. and Choquehuanca, J. (2003) 'Uso de la biodiversidad en el contexto de servicios ambientales', in Ibisch, P. L. and Mérida G. (eds)

Biodiversidad: La Riqueza de Bolivi. Estado de Conocimiento y Conservacion, editorial, Ministerio de Desarrollo Sostenible y Planificación, Santa Cruz

Ibisch, P. L., Araujo, N. and Nowicki, C. (eds) (2007) *Vision de la Conservacion de la Biodiversidad en el Corredor Amboro-Madidi*, editorial, FAN, Santa Cruz

Igoe, J. and Brockington, D. (2007) 'Neoliberal conservation: A brief introduction', *Conservation and Society*, vol 5, pp432–449

Interamerican Development Bank (2001) *El Corredor Biológico Mesoamericano como un eje de Desarrollo Sostenible para la Región: Perspectiva del Financiamiento Internacional*, Madrid

Ipamac (2005) *Parcs Naturels du Massif Central. Une mise en reseau exemplaire*, Rapport d'activité 2000–2005

IPCC (Intergovernmental Panel on Climate Change) (1996) *Working Group II, Summary for Policymakers: Scientific-Technical Analyses of Impacts, Adaptations and Mitigation of Climate Change*, www.ipcc.ch/pub/sarsum2.htm

IPCC (2001) *Climate Change 2001: Impacts, Adaptation, and Vulnerability*, Contribution of Working Group II to the Third Assessment Report of the Intergovernmental Panel on Climate Change, Cambridge University Press, Cambridge

IPCC (2007a) *IPCC Third Assessment Report*, www.ipcc.ch

IPCC (2007b) *Climate Change 2007: Synthesis Report*, Contribution of Working Groups I, II and III to the Fourth Assessment Report of the Intergovernmental Panel on Climate Change, IPCC, Geneva

IPCC (2007c) *Climate Change 2007: Impacts, Adaptation and Vulnerability*, Contribution of Working Group II to the Fourth Assessment Report of the Intergovernmental Panel on Climate Change, Cambridge University Press, Cambridge

IUCN (International Union for the Conservation of Nature) (1998) *Economic Values of Protected Areas: Guidelines for Protected Area Managers*, IUCN, Gland

IUCN (2005) *Proyecto Gestión Participativa de Áreas Protegidas*, boletín número 2, Gland

IUCN (2006) *2006 IUCN Red List of Threatened Species*, www.iucnredlist.org

IUCN (2007) *Connectivity Conservation: International Experience in Planning, Establishment and Management of Biodiversity Corridors*, IUCN Regional Protected Areas Programme, Asia, Bangkok

IUCN WCPA (World Commission on Protected Areas) (2005) *IUCN WCPA 2005–2012 Strategic Plan*, IUCN, Gland

IUCN WCPA (2006) *Attributes of a Connectivity Conservation Leader*, minutes of the IUCN WCPA Papallacta meeting, Ecuador, November 2006, www.mountains-wcpa.org

IUCN WCPA (2008) *IUCN WCPA Members Guide January 2008*, IUCN, Gland

Iverson, L. R., Prasad, A. M., Hale, B. J., and Sutherland, E. (1999) *Atlas of Current and Potential Future Distributions of Common Trees of the Eastern United States*, General Technical Report NE-265, USDA Forest Service, Washington DC

Jackson Hole Chamber of Commerce (2006) *Power of Place*, www.jacksonholechamber.com

Jennings, R. (2006) Rancher in southern Alberta, personal communication to H. Locke, Waterton Lakes National Park

Jha, A. (2002) 'Ecological prudence for the Lepchas of Sikkim', *Tigerpaper*, vol 29, no 1, pp27–28

Johnson, D. (2004) *The Geology of Australia*, Cambridge University Press, Cambridge

Johnson, J. (2004) *The Economic Implications of Expanding Waterton Glacier International Peace Park*, Canadian Parks And Wilderness Society, Vancouver

Johnston, A. E and Olimb, S. (2008) *Prioritising Connectivity Conservation Project Areas*, American Wildlands, Bozeman, MT

Jongman, R. H. G. (2004) 'The context and concept of ecological networks', in Jongman, R. and Pungetti, G. (eds) *Ecological Networks and Greenways. Concept, Design and Implementation*, Cambridge University Press, Cambridge

Jongman, R. H. G. and Troumbis, A. Y. (1995) *The Wider Landscape for Nature Conservation: Ecological Corridors and Buffer Zones*, MN2.7 Project-report 1995, submitted to the European Topic Centre for Nature Conservation in fulfilment of the 1995 work programme, ECNC, Tilburg

Jongman, R. H. G and Pungetti, G. (eds) (2004a) *Ecological Networks and Greenways. Concept, Design and Implementation*, Cambridge University Press, Cambridge

Jongman, R. H. G. and Pungetti, G. (2004b) 'Introduction: Ecological networks and greenways', in Jongman, R. and Pungetti, G. (eds) *Ecological Networks and Greenways. Concept, Design and Implementation*, Cambridge University Press, Cambridge

Jongman, R. H. G., Bouwma, I. M. and van Doorn, A. (2005) *Indicative Map of the Pan-European Ecological Network for Western Europe*, technical background document, Alterra-Technical Report, Alterra, Wageningen

Jorgensen, B. S. and Stedman, R. C. (2001) 'Sense of place as an attitude: Lakeshore owners attitudes toward their properties', *Journal of Environmental Psychology*, vol 21, pp233–248

Jørgensen, P. and Ulloa, C. (1994) *Seed Plants of the High Andes of Ecuador: A Checklist*, AAU Reports no 34

Julius, S. H. and West, J. M. (2008) *Preliminary Review of Adaptation Options for Climate-Sensitive Ecosystems and Resources*, Final Report, Synthesis and Assessment Product 4.4, U.S. Climate Change Science Program and the Subcommittee on Global Change Research, Washington DC

Kaiser, J. (1999) 'Great Smokies species census under way', *Science*, vol 284, no 5421, pp1741–1748

Kattan, G., Díaz, D., Hernández, O. L., Yerena, E., Viteri, X., Corrales, E. and Arancibia, D. (2000) *Complejo Ecorregional de los Andes del Norte: Hacia Una Visión de la Biodiversidad*, FUDENA, WWF, Fundación Natura

Kattan, G., Hernández, O. L., Goldstein, I., Rojas, V., Murillo, O., Gómez, C. Restrepo, H. and Cuesta, F. (2004) 'Range fragmentation in the spectacled bear *Tremarctos ornatus* in the northern Andes', *Oryx*, vol 38, no 2, pp155–163

Kaufman, R. (2002) *Australian Alps Mining Heritage Conservation and Presentation Strategy*, Australian Alps Liaison Committee, Canberra, www.australianalps.environment.gov.au/publications/mining-report/pubs/mining-report

Kay, J. J., Regier, H. A., Boyle, M. and Francis, G. (1999) 'An ecosystem approach for sustainability: Addressing the challenge of complexity', *Futures*, vol 31, pp721–742

Ki, E.-J. K. and Hon, L. C. (2007) 'Testing the linkages among the organization-public relationship and attitude and behavioural intentions', *Journal of Public Relations Research*, vol 19, no 1, pp1–23

Klyza, C. M. and Trombulak, S. C., (1999) *The Story of Vermont: A Natural and Cultural History*, University Press of New England, Hanover, NH

Kokorin, A. (2001) *Climate Passport. Ecoregional Climate Change and Biodiversity Decline: Altai-Sayan Ecoregion*, WWF, Moscow

Konstant, W. R., Locke, H. and Hanna, J. (2005) 'The Waterton Glacier International Peace Park: The first of its kind', in Mittermeier, R. A., Kormos, C. F., Mittermeier, C. G., Robles Gil, P.,

Sandwith, T. and Besancon, C. (eds) *Transboundary Conservation: A New Vision for Protected Areas*, Cemex-Agrupacion Sierra Madre-Conservation International, Mexico City, pp71–82

Kormos, C. (ed) (2008) *A Handbook on International Wilderness Law and Policy*, Fulcrum Publishing, Golden, CO

Körner, C. (2000) 'The alpine life zone under global change', *Gayana Botanica*, vol 57, no 1, www.scielo.cl/scielo.php?pid=S0717-66432000000100001&script=sci_arttext

Kothari, A. (2006) 'Community conserved areas', in Lockwood, M., Worboys, G. L. and Kothari, A. (eds) *Managing Protected Areas: A Global Guide*, Earthscan, London, pp528–548

La Marca, E. (1997) *Origen y Evolución Geológica de la Cordillera de Mérida, Andes de Venezuela*, Cuadernos de la Escuela de Geografía, No 1, Universidad de Los Andes, Mérida

Lachapelle, P. R. and McCool, S. F. (2005) 'Exploring the concept of "ownership" in natural resource planning', *Society and Natural Resources*, vol 18, pp279–285

Lægaard, S. (1992) 'Influence of fire in the grass Páramo vegetation of Ecuador', in Balslev, H. and Luteyn, J. L. (eds) *Páramo: An Ecosystem Under Human Influence*, Academic Press, London

Lahdelma, R., Salminen, P. and Hokkanen, J. (2000) 'Using multicriteria methods in environmental planning and management', *Environmental Management*, vol 26, no 6, pp595–605

Laliberte, A. S. and Ripple, W. J. (2004) 'Range contractions of North American carnivores and ungulates', *Bioscience*, vol 54, pp123–138

Lambert, J. D. and Carr, M. H. (1998) 'The Paseo Pantera Project: A case study using GIS to improve continental-scale conservation planning', in Savitsky, B. G. and Lacher, T. E. Jr (eds) *GIS Methodologies for Developing Conservation Strategies: Tropical Forest Recovery and Wildlife Management in Costa Rica*, Columbia University Press, New York, pp138–147

Langhammer, P. F., Bakarr, M. I., Bennun, L. A., Brooks, T. M., Clay, R. P., Darwall, W., De Silva, N., Edgar, G., Eken, G., Fishpool, L., da Fonseca, G. A. B., Foster, M., Knox, D. H., Matiku, P., Radford, E. A., Rodrigues, A. S. L., Salaman, P., Sechrest, W. and Tordoff, A. (2005) *Guidelines for the Identification and Gap Analysis of Key Biodiversity Areas as Targets for Comprehensive Protected Area Systems*, Conservation International, Washington DC

Lanjouw, A., Kayitare, A., Rainer, H., Rutagarama, E., Sivha, M., Asuma, S. and Kalpers, J. (2001) *Beyond Boundaries: Transboundary Natural Resource Management for Mountain Gorillas in the Virunga-Bwindi Region*, Biodiversity Support Program, World Wildlife Fund, Washington DC

Lavergne, S., Thuiller, W., Molina, J. and Debussche, M. (2005) 'Environmental and human factors influencing rare plant local occurrence, extinction and persistence: A 115-year study in the Mediterranean region', *Journal of Biogeography*, vol 32, no 5, pp799–811

Leach, W. D. and Pelkey, N. W. (2001) 'Making watershed partnerships work: A review of the empirical literature', *Journal of Water Resources Planning and Management*, vol 127, no 6, pp378–385

Leach, W. D. and Sabatier, P. A. (2005) 'Are trust and social capital the keys to success? Watershed partnerships in California and Washington', in Sabatier, P. A., Focht, W., Lubell, M., Trachtenbert, Z., Vedlitz, A. and Matlock, M. (eds) *Swimming Upstream: Collaborative Approaches to Watershed Management*, MIT Press, Cambridge, MA, pp233–258

Lebel, L., Anderies, J. M., Campbell, B., Carl Folke, C., Hatfield-Dodds, S., Hughes, T. P. and Wilson, J. (2006) 'Governance and the capacity to manage resilience in regional social-ecological systems', *Ecology and Society*, vol 11, no 1, art 19, www.ecologyandsociety.org/vol11/iss1/art19/

Lennon, J. (2006) 'Cultural heritage management', in Lockwood, M., Worboys, G. and Kothari, A. (eds) *Managing Protected Areas: A Global Guide*, Earthscan, London

Lennon, J. and Mathews, S. (1996) *Cultural Landscape Management: Guidelines for Identifying, Assessing and Managing Cultural Landscapes in the Australian Alps National Parks*, Australian Alps Liaison Committee, Canberra

León, C. (2002) 'Diagnóstico socioeconómico en el Corredor Ecológico Llanganates Sangay', in Viteri, X. (ed) *Corredor Ecológico entre Los Parques Nacionales Llanganates y Sangay: Un Informe de Los Estudios Biológicos y Sociales*, Fundación Natura and World Wildlife Fund, Quito, pp76–115

Lindenmayer, D. (2007) *On Borrowed Time. Australia's Environmental Crisis and What We Must Do About It*, CSIRO Publishing, Penguin Books, Camberwell

Lindenmayer, D. and Burgman, M. (2005) *Practical Conservation Biology*, CSIRO Publishing, Collingwood

Lindenmayer, D. and Fischer, J. (2006) *Habitat Fragmentation and Landscape Change: An Ecological and Conservation Synthesis*, CSIRO Publishing, Melbourne

Linke, S., Norris, R. H. and Pressey, R. L. (2008) 'Irreplaceability of river networks: Towards catchment-based conservation planning', *Journal of Applied Ecology*, vol 45, pp1486–1495

Llambi, L. D., Smith, J. K., Pereira, N., Pereira, A. C., Valero, F., Monasterio, M. and Davila, M. V. (2005) 'Participatory planning for biodiversity conservation in the high tropical Andes: Are farmers interested?', *Mountain Research and Development*, vol 25, no 3, pp200–205

Loaiza, J. M. and Morales, G. (2002) 'Evaluación y análisis para la identificación de un corredor ecológico entre los parques nacionales Llanganates y Sangay: Una prueba de hipótesis con aves', in Viteri, X. (ed) *Corredor Ecológico Entre los Parques Nacionales Llanganates y Sangay: Un Informe de Los Estudios Biológicos y Sociales*, Fundación Natura and World Wildlife Fund, Quito, pp41–75

Lochner, P., Weaver, A., Gelderblom, C., Peart, R., Sandwith, T. and Fowkes, S. (2003) 'Aligning the diverse: The development of a biodiversity strategy for the Cape Floristic Region', *Biological Conservation*, vol 112, pp29–43

Locke, H. (1994) 'The Wildlands Project and the Yellowstone to Yukon Biodiversity Strategy: Preserving the wild heart of North America', *Borealis*, issue 15, pp18–24

Locke, H. (1997) 'The role of Banff National Park as a protected area in the Yellowstone to Yukon Mountain Corridor of western North America', in Nelson, G. and Serafin, R. (eds) *National Parks and Protected Areas: Keystones to Sustainable Development*, NATO Series G: Ecological Sciences, Springer, Berlin, pp117–124

Locke, H. and Dearden, P. (2005) 'Rethinking protected area categories and the new paradigm', *Environmental Conservation*, vol 32, no 1, pp1–10

Lockwood, M. (2006) 'Management planning', in Lockwood, M., Worboys, G. L. and Kothari, A. (eds) *Managing Protected Areas: A Global Guide*, IUCN, Earthscan, London, pp292–327

Lockwood, M. and Kothari, A. (2006) 'Social context', in Lockwood, M., Worboys, G. L. and Kothari, A. (eds) *Managing Protected Areas: A Global Guide*, Earthscan, London, pp41–72

Lockwood, M. and Quintella, C. E. (2006) 'Finance and economics', in Lockwood, M., Worboys, G. L. and Kothari, A. (eds) *Managing Protected Areas: A Global Guide*, Earthscan, London, pp328–358

Lockwood, M., Worboys, G. L. and Kothari, A. (eds) (2006) *Managing Protected Areas: A Global Guide*, Earthscan, London

Lockwood, M., Davidson, J., Curtis, A., Stratford, E. and Griffith, R. (2009) Governance principles for natural resource management, *Society and Natural Resources* (in press)

Low, G. (2003) *Landscape Scale Conservation: A Practitioner's Guide*, The Nature Conservancy, www.conserveonline.org/coldocs/2003/09/Landscape_Practitioners_Handbook_July03_New.pdf

Lowenthal, D. (2000) *George Perkins Marsh, Prophet of Conservation*, University of Washington Press, Seattle, WA

Lundblad, J. P. (2003) 'A review and critique of Rogers' diffusion of innovation theory as it applies to organizations', *Organization Development Journal*, vol 21, no 4, pp50–64

Luteyn, J. L. (1992) 'Páramos: Why study them?', in Balslev, H. and Luteyn, J. L. (eds) *Páramo: An Andean Ecosystem Under Human Influence*, Academic Press, London, pp1–14

Luteyn, J. L. (1999) 'Páramos: A checklist of plant diversity, geographic distribution and botanical literature', *Memoirs of The New York Botanical Garden*, vol 84, 278pp

MacArthur, R. H. and Wilson, E. O. (1967) *The Theory of Island Biogeography*, Princeton University Press, Princeton, NJ

Macbeth, J., Carson, D. and Northcote, J. (2004) 'Social capital, tourism and regional development: SPCC as a basis for innovation and sustainability', *Current Issues in Tourism*, vol 7, no 6, pp502–522

Macdonald, P. and Haiblen, J. (2001) *Mountains of Science, Volume 1: A Thematic Interpretation Strategy for Scientific Sites of Cultural Heritage in the Australian Alps*, report to the Australian Alps Liaison Committee, Canberra

Mackey, B. (2007) 'Climate change, connectivity and biodiversity conservation', in Taylor, M. and Figgis, P. (eds) *Protected Areas: Buffering Nature Against Climate Change*, Proceedings of a WWF and IUCN World Commission on Protected Areas Symposium, 18–19 June 2007, Canberra, WWF-Australia, Sydney

Mackey, B. G., Soulé, M. E., Nix, H. A., Recher, H. F., Lesslie, R. G., Williams, J. E., Woinarski, J. C. Z., Hobbs, R. J. and Possingham, H. P. (2007) 'Applying landscape-ecological principles to regional conservation: The Wildcountry Project in Australia', in Wu, J. and Hobbs, R. J. (eds) *Key Topics in Landscape Ecology*, Cambridge University Press, Melbourne

Mackey, B. G., Keith, H., Berry, S. L. and Lindenmayer, D. B. (2008) *Green Carbon. The Natural Role of Forests in Carbon Storage. Part 1: A Green Carbon Account of Australia's South-Eastern Forests, and Policy Implications*, The Fenner School of Environment and Society, The Australian National University, Canberra

Mackey, B. G., Watson, J. and Worboys, G. L. (2009) *Connectivity Conservation and the Great Eastern Ranges Corridor*, NSW Department of Environment and Climate Change, Queanbeyan

MacKinnon, J., MacKinnon, C., Child, G. and Thorsell, J. (1986) *Managing Protected Areas in the Tropics*, IUCN, United Nations Environment Programme, Gland

Mallarach, J. M. and Germain, J. (eds) (2006) *Bases per a Les Directrius de Connectivitat Ecològica de Catalunya*, Departament de Medi Ambient i Habitatge, Barcelona

Mallarach, J. M., Comas, E. and López, C. (2005) *Conectividad Ecológica y Paisajística del Territorio Histórico de Álava. Delimitación de Espacios y Elaboración de una Estrategia de Conservación y Restauración*, Diputación Foral de Álava (unpublished technical report), Barcelona

Mansergh, I. and Cheal, D. (2007) 'Protected area planning and management for eastern Australian temperate forests and woodland ecosystems under climate change: A landscape approach', in Taylor, M. and Figgis, P. (eds) *Protected Areas: Buffering Nature Against Climate Change*, WWF-Australia, Sydney

Manson, S. M. (2001) 'Simplifying complexity: A review of complexity theory', *Geoforum*, vol 32, pp405–414

Maraven (1991) 'Región Los Andes: Estado Táchira', *Serie Estudios Regionales Sistemas Ambientales Venezolanos, No 7*, Ediciones Maraven, Caracas

Maraven (1993) 'Región Los Andes: Estados Mérida y Trujillo', *Serie Estudios Regionales Sistemas Ambientales Venezolanos, No 8*, Ediciones Maraven, Caracas

Margoluis, R. and Salafsky, N. (1998) *Measures of Success. Designing, Managing and Monitoring Conservation and Development Projects*, Island Press, Washington DC

Margules, C. R. and Pressey, R. L. (2000) 'Systematic conservation planning', *Nature*, vol 45, pp243–253

Mariaca, M.R. (2007) Communications Coordinator, Landscape Conservation Programme, Conservation International Bolivia, personal communication to Jordi Surkin, La Paz

Marsh, G. P. (1864) [1965] *Man and Nature*, Belknap Press of Harvard University Press, Cambridge, MA

Mattews, E. (ed) (2002) *The State of the Forest: Indonesia*, World Resources Institute, Washington DC

McCarthy and Salas (2003) 'Desafío de la gestión ambiental, Estudio sobre caracterización del Corredor Biológico Mesoamericano en su configuración geográfica actual', in *Segundo informe sobre Desarrollo Humano en Centroamérica y Panamá'*, United Nations Development Programme, New York

McDougal, C. and Tshering, K. (1998) *Tiger Conservation Strategy for the Kingdom of Bhutan*, Nature Conservation Division, Forestry Services Division, Ministry of Agriculture and WWF Bhutan Program, Thimphu

McLaughlin, K. and Osborne, S. P. (2002) 'Current trends and future prospects of public management', in McLaughlin, K., Osborne, S. P. and Ferlie, E. (eds) *New Public Management: Current Trends and Future Prospect: A Guide*, Routledge, London

McNeely, J. A. (2004) 'Sustainable landscape: Linking conservation and production', in Joe, D. (ed) *Millennium Development Goals and Conservation: Managing Nature's Wealth for Society's Health*, International Institute for Environment and Development, London

McNeely, J. A., Lockwood, M. and Chapman, J. (2006) 'Building support for protected areas', in Lockwood, M., Worboys, G. L. and Kothari, A. (eds) *Managing Protected Areas: A Global Guide*, IUCN, Earthscan, London

MDBC (Murray-Darling Basin Commission) (1990) *The Murray*, Murray-Darling Basin Commission, Canberra

MEAB (Millennium Ecosystem Assessment Board) (2005) *Millennium Ecosystem Assessment Report*, www.millenniumassessment.org

Medina, R. (2006) *Evaluación del Paisaje Para La Interconexión de Los Parques Nacionales Yacambu y El Guache, Sierra de Portuguesa, Andes de Venezuela*, Trabajo Especial de Grado de Licenciatura en Biología, Universidad Simón Bolívar, Caracas

MEF (Ministry of Environment and Forests, India) (2004) *Securing India's Future: The National Biodiversity Strategy and Action Plan (Draft)*, Government of India, New Delhi

Mena, P. (2002) *Lecciones Aprendidas en las Alturas: Una Sistematización del Proyecto Páramo*, Abya Yala/Proyecto Páramo, Quito

Méndez, E. and Méndez, J. (1996) *Mérida en la Perspectiva del Siglo XXI*, Centro Iberoamericano de Estudios Provinciales y Locales, CIEPROL, Mérida

Mendieta, A. and Vinocour, A. C. (2000) *Corredor Biológico Mesoamericano: Del Paseo Pantera a un Modelo de Desarrollo Sostenible. Datos Relevantes para una Estrategia de Comunicación*, Comisión Centroamericana del Ambiente y Desarrollo (CCAD), Banco Mundial (Proyecto RUTA III), San José

Merrill, T. (2005) *Grizzly Bear Conservation in the Yellowstone to Yukon Region*, Technical Report No 6, Yellowstone to Yukon Conservation Initiative, Canmore

Messick, R. (2000) *Old-Growth Forest Communities in the Nantahala-Pisgah National Forest*, Western North Carolina Alliance, Asheville, NC

Messick, R. (2004) *High Quality Reconnaissance and Verification in Old Growth Forests of the Blue Ridge Province*, Southern Appalachian Forest Coalition, unpublished report, Asheville, NC

Metzger, M. J., Bunce, R. G. H., Jongman, R. H. G., Muncher, C. A. and Watkins, J. W. (2005) 'A climatic stratification of the environment of Europe', *Global Ecology and Biogeography*, vol 4, pp549–563

Millennium Ecosystem Assessment (2005) *Ecosystems and Human Well-being Synthesis*, Island Press, Washington DC

Miller, K., Chang, E. and Johnson, N. (2001) *Defining Common Ground for the Mesoamerican Biological Corridor*, World Resources Institute, Washington DC

Ministerio de Economía y Finanzas de Peru (2001) *Hacia La Búsqueda de un Nuevo Instrumento de Focalización para La Asignación de Recursos Destinados a La Inversión Social Adicional en El Marco de La Lucha Contra La Pobreza*, Ministerio de Economía y Finanzas, Lima

Ministerio del Medio Ambiente (2000) *Relación de Talleres Regionales de Gestión de Ecorregiones Estratégicas*, Bogotá

Mitchell, J. G. (2006) 'Conservationists thinking big to save the last great places', *Environment Yale*, vol 5, no 1, pp4–11

Mittermeier, R., Myers, N. and Mittermeier, C. G. (1999) *Hotspots: Earth's Biologically Richest and Most Threatened Ecoregions*, CEMEX, Mexico City and Washington DC

Mittermeier, R. A., Mast, R. B., del Prado, C. P. and Mittermeier, C. G. (1997) 'Peru', in Mittermeier, R. A., Robles Gil, P. and Mittermeier, C. G. (eds) *Megadiversity: Earth's Biologically Wealthiest Nations*, CEMEX, Monterrey

Mittermeier, R. A., Gils, P. R., Hoffman, M., Pilgrim, J., Brooks, T., Mittermeier, C. G., Lamoreaux, J. and da Fonseca, G. A. B. (eds) (2004) *Hotspots Revisited: Earth's Biologically Richest and Most Endangered Terrestrial Ecoregions*, CEMEX, Mexico City and Washington DC

Monasterio, M. (1980) *Estudios Ecológicos en Los Páramos Andinos*, Universidad de los Andes, Mérida

Moore, S. A., Severn, R. C. and Millar, R. (2006) 'A conceptual model of community capacity', *Geographical Research*, vol 44, no 4, pp361–371

Moore, S. A., Weiler, B., Lockwood, M., Wegner, A., Laing, J., Pfueller, S., Croy, G., Lee, D. and Macbeth, J. (2008a) *Protected Area – Tourism Partnerships: What Makes Them Tick?*, Paper presented to the First Australian Protected Area Congress (APAC), Sunshine Coast, Queensland Environment Protection Authority, Brisbane

Moore, S. A., Weiler, B., Croy, G., Laing, J., Lee, D., Lockwood, M., Pfueller, S. and Wegner, A. (2008b) *Tourism – Protected Area Partnerships in Australia: Designing and Managing for Success*, Paper presented at the Annual Parks and Visitor Services Workshop, WA Department of Conservation and Land Management, Perth

Morrison, P. (2001) Personal communication to Hugh Irwin, Pacific Biodiversity Institute, Winthrop, WA

Morrison, M., Durante, J., Greig, J. and Ward, J. (2008) *Encouraging Participation in Market Based Instruments and Incentive Programs*, Land and Water Australia, Canberra

Moss, L. A. G. (2006) *The Amenity Migrants: Seeking and Sustaining Mountains and their Cultures*, CABI, Cambridge, MA

Mulvaney and Kamminga, J. (1999) *Prehistory of Australia*, Allen and Unwin, St Leonards

Muskwa-Kechika Management Board (2006) www.muskwa-kechika.com/management-area

Myers, N., Mittermier, R. A., Mittermier, C. G., da Fonseca, G. A. B. and Kent. J. (2000) 'Biodiversity hotspots for conservation priorities', *Nature*, vol 403, pp853–858

Nampindo, S. and Plumptre, A. J. (2005) *A Socioeconomic Assessment of Community Livelihoods in Areas Adjacent to Corridors Linking Queen Elizabeth National Park to Other Protected Areas in Western Uganda*, unpublished report, prepared for

Conservation International, Wildlife Conservation Society, New York www.jgiuganda.org/pdf/Conserving_Corridors_Around_QENP.pdf

Nampindo, S., Plumptre, A. and Victurine, R. (2006) *Increasing the Functionality of the Kyambura–Kasyoha–Kitomi Corridor and Mpanga Falls Area in the Greater Virunga Landscape: Management Options and Cost Implications*, Final Report prepared for Conservation International, Wildlife Conservation Society, New York www.jgiuganda.org/pdf/Kymabura_Kasyoha_Kitomi_Corridor%20final.pdf

Naveda, J. (2005) *Algunos Lineamientos Teóricos y Metodológicos para un Plan Nacional de Ordenación del Territorio: Una Aproximación a Través de La Ciencia de Los Paisajes y la Sustentabilidad Ambiental*, Trabajo Especial de Grado de Maestría en Ordenación Territorial y Ambiente, Universidad de Los Andes, Mérida

NCD (Nature Conservation Division) (2005) *Tiger Action Plan for the Kingdom of Bhutan*, Department of Forests, Royal Government of Bhutan, Thimpu

Negret A J. (1990) *Propuesta para el Establecimiento de un Corredor de Las Selvas Humedas del Pacifico Colombiano*, Universidad del Cauca-Inderena, Popayán

Nelson, J. G., Day, J. C., Sportza, L. M., Loucky, J. and Vasquez, C. (eds) (2003) *Protected Areas and the Regional Planning Imperative in North America*, University of Calgary Press and University of Michigan Press, Calgary

NFA (Northern Forest Alliance) (2005) *The Northern Forest Fiscal Year 2005 Report*, Montpelier, VT

NFCT (Northern Forest Canoe Trail) (2006) *Northern Forest Canoe Trail*, www.northernforestcanoetrail.org

Nielsen, E. A. (2006) *Dimensions of Public Participation in Community-based Conservation Projects: Methods, Processes, Hope and Empowerment*, PhD Thesis, University of Idaho, Moscow, ID

Nixon, A. and Mackay, J. (1995) *Australian Alps National Parks Back Country Recreation Strategy*, Australian Alps Liaison Committee, Canberra

NLWRA (National Land and Water Resources Assessment) (2002) *Australian Terrestrial Biodiversity Assessment*, Commonwealth of Australia, Canberra

Noss, R. F. (1991) 'Landscape connectivity: Different functions at different scales', in Hudson, W. E. (ed) *Landscape Linkages and Biodiversity*, Island Press, Washington DC, pp27–39

Novoa, J. (2002) 'Uso de un sistema de información geográfica como herramienta para identificar un corredor ecológico entre los Parques Nacionales Llanganates y Sangay', in Viteri, X. (ed) *Corredor Ecológico Entre Los Parques Nacionales Llanganates y Sangay: Un Informe de Los Estudios Biológicos y Sociales*, Fundación Natura and World Wildlife Fund, Quito, pp116–137

NPA (National Parks Association of NSW) (2002) *Connect to Protect: Eastern links: A Proposal to Establish an Eastern Highlands Conservation Corridor*, National Parks Association of NSW, Sydney

NPS (National Park Service) (2006) *Yellowstone National Park Historical Annual Visitation Statistics*, US Department of Interior, National Parks Service, www.nps.gov/yell/parkmgmt/historicstats.htm

Nunes, P. A. L. D., van den Bergh, J. C. J. M. and Nijkamp, P. (2003) *The Ecological Economics of Biodiversity: Methods and Policy Applications*, Edward Elgar, Cheltenham

O'Donnell, M., Allan, C. and Peetz, D. (1999) *New Public Management and Workplace Change in Australia*, University of NSW, Sydney

O'Phelan Guachilla, M. C. and Argandoña Zegada, J. (2001) *Metodologia: Medicion de la Efectividad de Manejo del SNAP (MEMs)*, SERNAP, La Paz

Ochoa, G., Hoffman, J. and Tin, T. (2005) *Climate: The Force that Shapes Our World – and the Future of Life on Earth*, Rodale, London

Ollier, C. D. (1982) 'The Great Escarpment of Eastern Australia: Tectonic and geomorphic significance', *Journal of the Geological Society of Australia*, vol 29, pp431–435

Olson, D. M. and Dinerstein, E. (1998) 'The Global 200: A representative approach to conserving the Earth's distinctive ecoregions', *Conservation Biology*, vol 12, pp502–515

Olson, D. M. and Dinerstein, E. (2002) 'The Global 200: Priority ecoregions for global conservation', *Annal Missouri Botanical Gardens*, vol 89, pp199–224

Ortega, L. A. and Gomez, A. (1998) 'Propuesta conservación de la cuenca alta del rio Guapi', *Biopacifico/CRC*, Popayán

Ostrom, E. (1990) *Governing the Commons: The Evolution of Institutions for Collective Action*, Cambridge University Press, Cambridge

Palminteri, S., Powell, G. and Naranjo, L. G. (2001) 'Visión de la Biodiversidad de los Andes del Norte', *CD-ROM*, FUDENA, Fundación Natura, World Wildlife Fund, New York

Pant, R. (2002) *Customs and Conservation: Cases of Traditional and Modern Law in India and Nepal*, Community Based Conservation in South Asia No 7, Kalpavriksha

Pastor, C. (2003) *Chalalan: Un Modelo Ecoturistico con Vision Comunitaria*, Conservation International, La Paz

Pastor, C. (2007) Manager, Landscape Conservation Programme, Conservation International Bolivia, personal communication to Jordi Surkin, La Paz

Pawlowski, B. (1969) 'Der Endemismus in der Flora der Alpen, der Karpaten und der balkanischen Gebirge', in *Verhaeltnis zu den Pflanzengesellschaften*, Mitteilungen der Ostalpin-Dinarischen pflanzensoziologischen Arbeitsgemeinschaft, Heft 9, Internationale Vereinigung für Vegetationskunde, Ostalpin-Dinarische Sektion, Camerino

PC (Parks Canada) (1997) *Banff National Park Management Plan*, Canadian Heritage, Hull, Quebec

PC (2000) *Unimpaired for Future Generations? Protecting Ecological Integrity with Canada's National Parks: Vol 2 – Setting a New Direction for Canada's National Parks*, Parks Canada, Ottawa

PC (2004) *Highway Mitigation Research in the Mountain Parks*, www.pc.gc.ca/pn-np/ab/banff/docs/routes/chap1/sec1/routes1b_e.asp

PC (2007a) *The Banff Wildlife Crossings Project Report, 2002*, www.pc.gc.ca/pn-np/ab/banff/docs/routes/chap3/sec1/routes3b_E.asp

PC (2007b) *Banff National Park of Canada, Fact Sheet: Visitation*, Parks Canada, www.pc.gc.ca/banff

Pei, S. and Sharma, U. R. (1998) 'Transboundary biodiversity conservation in the Himalayas', in *Ecoregional Cooperation for Biodiversity Conservation in the Himalayas*, United Nations Development Programme, New York

Pennington, M. (2000) *Planning and the Political Market: Public Choice and the Politics of Government Failure*, Athlone Press, London

Peters, R. L. (1992) 'Conservation of biological diversity in the face of climate change', in Peters, R. L. and Lovejoy, T. E. (eds) *Global Warming and Biodiversity*, Yale University Press, New Haven, pp15–30

Peters, G. and Pierre, J. (2004) 'Multi-level governance and democracy: A Faustian bargain?', in Bache, I. and Flinders, M. (eds) *Multi-level Governance*, Oxford University Press, Oxford, pp75–89

Peterson, A. T. (2003) 'Projected climate change effects on Rocky Mountain and Great Plains birds: Generalities of biodiversity consequences', *Global Change Biology*, vol 9, no 5, pp647–655

Phillips, A. (2003) 'Turning ideas on their head: The new paradigm for protected areas', in Jaireth, H. and Smyth, D. (eds) *Innovative Governance: Indigenous Peoples, Local Communities and Protected Areas*, Ane Books, New Delhi

Pirot, J. Y., Meynell, P. J. and Elder, D. (2000) *Ecosystem Management: Lessons from Around the World – a Guide for Development and Conservation Practitioners*, IUCN, Gland

Pittillo, J. D., Hatcher, R. D. Jr and Buol, S. W. (1998) 'Introduction to the environment and vegetation of the Southern Blue Ridge province', *Castanea*, vol 63, pp202–216

PLANECO (2000) *Planning in Ecological Networks*, Italian Ministry of University and Scientific Research, University of L'Aquila, L'Aquila

Plumptre, A. J., Behangana, M., Ndomba, E., Davenport, T., Kahindo, C., Kityo, R., Ssegawa, P., Eilu, G., Nkuutu, D. and Owiunji, I. (2003) *The Biodiversity of the Albertine Rift*, Wildlife Conservation Society, Albertine Rift Technical Reports No 3, www.albertinerift.org/media/file/AlbertineRiftBioD1.PDF

Plumptre, A. J., Kujirakwinja, D., Treves, A., Owiunji, I. and Rainer, H. (2007) 'Transboundary conservation in the Greater Virunga Landscape: Its importance for landscape species', *Biological Conservation*, vol 134, no 2, pp279–287

Poncelet, E. C. (2004) *Partnering for the Environment: Multistakeholder Collaboration in a Changing World*, Rowman & Littlefield, Lanham, MD

Porter, D. (2002) *Speech on Behalf of the Kaska Nation to the Yellowstone to Yukon Conservation Initiative*, www.kaskadenacouncil.com/speeches.html

Pounds, J. A., Fogden, M. P. L. and Campbell, J. H. (1999) 'Biological response to climate change on a tropical mountain', *Nature*, vol 398, pp611–615

Pressey, R. L., Watts, M. E., Barrett, T. W. and Ridges, M. J. (2009) 'The C-Plan Conservation Planning System: Origins, applications and possible futures', in Moilanen, A., Wilson, K. A. and Possingham, H. (eds) *Spatial Conservation Prioritisation, Quantitative Methods and Computational Tools*, Oxford University Press, London

Pretty, J. (2003) 'Social capital and the collective management of resources', *Science*, vol 302, pp1912–1914

Pretty, J. and Ward, H. (2001) 'Social capital and the environment', *World Development*, vol 29, pp209–227

Pretty, J. and Smith, D. (2004) 'Social capital in biodiversity conservation and management', *Conservation Biology*, vol 18, pp631–638

Proshansky, H. M., Abbe, K. F. and Kaminoff, R. (1995) 'Place-identity: Physical world socializations of the self', in Groat, L. (ed) *Readings in Environmental Psychology: Giving Places Meaning*, Academic Press, London, pp87–113

Prowse, T.D. (2004) Research Chair, Water and Climate Impacts Research Centre, University of Victoria, personal communication to H. Locke, Sydney, BC

Pulsford, I., Worboys, G. L., Gough, J. and Shepherd, T. (2004) 'The Australian Alps and the Great Escarpment of Eastern Australia conservation corridors', in Harmon, D. and Worboys, G. L. (eds) *Managing Mountain Protected Areas: Challenges and Responses for the 21st Century*, Andromeda Editrice, Colledara, pp106–114

Pungetti, G. and Romano, B. (2004) 'Planning the future landscapes between nature and culture', in Jongman, R. and Pungetti, G. (eds) *Ecological Networks and Greenways*, Cambridge University Press, Cambridge, pp107–127

Purchase, E. (1999) *Out of Nowhere: Disaster and Tourism in the White Mountains,* Johns Hopkins University Press, Baltimore, MD

Putnam, R. (1993) 'The prosperous community: Social capital and public life', *The American Prospect*, vol 13, pp35–42

Putnam, R. (2000) *Bowling Alone: The Collapse and Revival of American Community*, Simon and Schuster, New York

Putney, A. (2003) 'Introduction: Perspectives on the values of protected areas', in Harmon, D. and Putney, A. D. (eds) *The Full Value of Parks*, Rowman & Littlefield, Lanham, MD

Quinby, P., Trombulak, S., Lee, T., Long, R., MacKay, P., Lane, J. and Henry, M. (2000) 'Opportunities for wildlife habitat connectivity between Algonquin Provincial Park and the Adirondack Park', *Wild Earth*, vol 10, no 2, pp75–81

Rai, S. C., Sharma, E. and Sundriyal, R. C. (1994) 'Conservation in the Sikkim Himalaya: Traditional knowledge and land use of the Mamlay watershed', *Environmental Conservation*, vol 15, pp30–35

Ramakrishnan, P. S. (1996) 'Conserving the sacred: From species to landscape', *Nature and Natural Resources*, UNESCO, Paris

Ramón, G. (2000) *Cambios Históricos en el Manejo de Los Suelos Serranos, Manejo, Recuperación y Conservación de Los Suelos Serranos*, CAMAREN, Quito

Ramsay, P. (1992) *The Páramo Vegetation of Ecuador: The Community Ecology, Dynamics and Productivity*

of Tropical Grasslands in the Andes, PhD Dissertation, University of Wales, Bangor

Rasker, R. and Alexander, B. (1998) *The New Challenge*, Yellowstone to Yukon Conservation Initiative, Canmore, Alberta

Rasker, R. B., Alexander, B., van den Noort, J. and Carter, R. (2004) *Prosperity in the 21st Century West*, Sonoran Institute, Bozeman, MT

Rastogi, A., Shengi, P. and Amatya, D. (1997) *Regional Consultation on Conservation of the Kangchenjunga Mountain Ecosystem*, International Centre for Integrated Mountain Development, Kathmandu

Raven (2005) *The Shining Mountains*, Raven HD Productions, Banff, Alberta

Recharte, H. and Gearheard, J. (2001) 'Los páramos altamente diversos: Ecología política de una ecorregión', in Mena, P., Medina, G. and Hofstede, R. (eds) *Los Páramos del Ecuador: Particularidades, Problemas y Perspectivas*, Abya Yala/Proyecto Páramo, Quito

Recher, H. F. (2004) 'WildCountry', *Pacific Conservation Biology*, vol 10, pp221–222

Reichel-Dolmatoff, G. (1982) *Colombia Indígena, Manual de la Historia de Colombia*, Procultura, Bogotá

Reining, C., Beazley, K., Doran, P. and Bettigole, C. (2006) *From the Adirondacks to Acadia: A Wildlands Network Design for the Greater Northern Appalachians*, Wildlands Project Special Paper No 7, Richmond, VT

Relph, E. (1976) *Place and Placelessnes*, Pion Limited, London

Relph, E. (2008) 'A pragmatic sense of place', in Vanclay, F., Higgins, M. and Blackshaw, A. (eds) *Making Sense of Place*, National Museum of Australia Press, Canberra

Reyes, S. and López, I. (1995) 'Sierra Nevada National Park: Cooperation with traditional inhabitants', in Amend, S. and Amend, T. (eds) *National Parks Without People?: The South American Experience*, IUCN, Parques Nacionales y Conservación Ambiental, No 5, Quito, pp438–443

RGB (Royal Government of Bhutan) (1999) *Bhutan 2020, A Vision for Peace, Prosperity and Happiness*, Planning Commission, The Royal Government of Bhutan, Thimphu

RGB (2002a) *Biodiversity Action Plan for Bhutan*, Ministry of Agriculture, The Royal Government of Bhutan, Thimphu

RGB (2002b) *9th Plan Main Document 2002–2007*, The Royal Government of Bhutan, Thimphu

Ribot, J. C. (2002) *Democratic Decentralisation of*

Natural Resources: Institutionalising Popular Participation, World Resources Institute, Washington DC

Ridler, K. (2007) 'Grizzly bear search planned for north-central Idaho, W. Montana', *Deseret News*, 25 November

Rijavek, F. (2002) *A Million Acres a Year*, Snakewood Films in association with SBS Independent, Sydney

Rittel, H. W. J. and Webber, M. M. (1973) 'Dilemmas in a general theory of planning', *Policy Sciences*, vol 4, pp155–169

Robbins, S. P., Bergman, R., Stagg, I. and Coulter, M. (2003) *Foundations of Management*, Pearson Education Australia, French's Forest

Roberts, N. (2000) 'Wicked problems and network approaches to resolution', *International Public Management Review*, vol 1, pp1–19

Robinson, C. J. (1997) *Integrated Vegetation Management Plan for Fitzgerald Biosphere Reserve Zone of Cooperation*, commisioned report to Environment Australia, Canberra

Rodríguez, C. M. (2006) Reflexiones a modo de conclusión, Presidente Protempore. Discurso de Cierre de la Conferencia de Socios y Donantes de la Iniciativa del Corredor Biológico Mesoamericano, www.ccad.ws/noticias/2002/4o/reflexiones.htm

Rodriguez, J. (ed) (1998) *Estado del ambiente de los recursos naturales en Centroamérica 1998*, CCAD (Comisión Centroaméricana de Ambiente y Desarrollo), San José

Rodríguez, N., Armenteras, D., Morales, M. and Romero, M. (2004) *Ecosistemas de los Andes Colombianos*, Instituto de Investigación de Recusos Biológicos Alexander von Humboldt, Bogotá

Romano, B. (ed) (2000) *Environmental Continuity, Planning for the Re-organisation of Territory*, Andromeda, Teramo

Romano, B. and Thomasset, F. (2003) 'I sistemi ambientali e le aree protette', in Gambino, R. (ed) *APE, Appennino Parco d'Europa*, Ministero dell'Ambiente e della Tutela del Territorio, Alinea Ed, Firenze, pp26–36

Rosenberg, D. K., Noon, B. R. and Meslow, E. C. (1997) 'Biological corridors: Form, function, and efficacy', *BioScience*, vol 47, no 10, pp677–687

Rouget, M., Richardson, D. M., Cowling, R. M., Lloyd, J. W. and Lombard, A. T. (2003) 'Current patterns of habitat transformation and future threats to biodiversity in terrestrial ecosystems of the Cape Floristic Region', *Biological Conservation*, vol 112, pp63–85

Roy, M. S., Cardoso da Silva, J. M., Arctander, P., García-Moreno, J. and Fjeldså, J. (1997) 'The speciation of South American and African birds in montane regions', in Mindell, D. P. (ed) *Avian Molecular Evolution and Systematics*, Academic Press, New York, pp325–343

Runte, A. (1987) *National Parks: The American Experience*, University of Nebraska Press, Lincoln, NE

Sack, R. D. (1992) *Place, Modernity, and the Consumer's World: A Relational Framework for Geographic Analysis*, Johns Hopkins University Press, Baltimore, MD

Sader, S. A., Hayes, D. J., Irwin, D. E. and Saatchi, S. S. (2000) *Preliminary Forest Cover Change Estimates for Central America (1990s), With Reference to the Proposed Mesoamerican Biological Corridor*, www.gis.usu.edu/docs/protected/procs/aprs2001/Proceed/00135.pdf

Salafsky, N., Margoluis, R. and Redford, K. (2001) *Adaptive Management: A Tool for Conservation Practitioners*, World Wildlife Fund, Washington DC

Salas Chavez, J., Sanchez Huaman, S., Ponce del Prado, C. and Alfaro Lozano, L. (eds) (2006) *Los Áreas Naturales Protegidas del Perú*, ALPECO, Lima

Salinas, E. (2006) *Documento de Sistematización de Información sobre las Lecciones Aprendidas en la Planificación y Desarrollo del Corredor de Conservación Vilcabamba-Amboro*, Conservation International, La Paz

Sallans, S. (2006) 'Tasmanian Parks and Wildlife Service Information Management System, Australia', in Lockwood, M., Worboys, G. L. and Kothari, A. *Managing Protected Areas: A Global Guide*, Earthscan, London, pp274–276

SAMAB (Southern Appalachian Man and the Biosphere) (1996) *The Southern Appalachian Assessment Report*, five volumes, US Department of Agriculture, Forest Service, Southern Region, Atlanta, GA

Sanderson, E. W., Jaiteh, M., Levy, M. A., Redford, K. H., Wannebo, A. V. and Woolmer, G. (2002a) 'The human footprint and the last of the wild', *BioScience*, vol 52, no 10, pp891–904

Sanderson, E. W., Redford, K. H., Vedder, A., Coppolillo, P. B. and Ward, S. E. (2002b) 'A conceptual model for conservation planning based on landscape species requirements', *Landscape and Urban Planning*, vol 58, issue 1, pp41–56

Sandwith, T. and Lockwood, M. (2006) 'Linking the landscape', in Lockwood, M., Worboys, G., L. and Kothari, A. (eds) *Managing Protected Areas: A*

Global Guide, IUCN, Earthscan, London, pp574–601

Sandwith, T., Shine, C., Hamilton, L. and Sheppard, D. (2001) *Transboundary Protected Areas for Peace and Co-operation*, Best Practice Protected Area Guidelines Series No 7, IUCN World Commission on Protected Areas, Gland, Switzerland and Cambridge

SASEC (South Asia Sub-Regional Economic Cooperation) (2004) *South Asia Sub-Regional Economic Cooperation Tourism Development Plan*, Asian Development Bank, Manilla

Sattler, P. and Glaznig, A. (2006) *Building Natures Safety Net: A Review of Australia's Terrestrial Protected Area System, 1991–2004*, WWF-Australia, Sydney

Sawchuk, W. (2004) *The Muskwa-Kechika: Wild Heart of Canada's Northern Rockies*, Peace photoGraphics, Dawson Creek, British Columbia

Schjellerup, I. (1992) 'Pre-Columbian field systems and vegetation in the jalca of northeastern Peru', in Balslev, H. and Luteyn, J. L. (eds) *Páramo: An Andean Ecosystem Under Human Influence*, Academic Press, London, pp137–150

Schnelling, D., Nash, C., Underwood, J., Taylor-Ide, D. and Underwood, J. (1992) 'Appalachians', in Stone, P. (ed) *State of the World's Mountains*, Zed Books, London, pp300–358

Schuchmann, K., Weller, A. and Heynen, I. (2001) 'Systematics and biogeography of the Andean genus *Eriocnemis* (Aves: Trochilidae)', *Journal fur Ornithologie*, vol 142, pp433–481

Schulz, F. (2005) *Yellowstone to Yukon: Freedom to Roam*, Mountaineers Books, Seattle, WA

Scott, J., Michael, F. W., Davis, R., McGhie, G., Wright, R. G., Groves, C. and Estes, J. (2001) 'Nature reserves: Do they capture the full range of America's biological diversity?', *Ecological Applications*, vol 11, no 4, pp999–1007

SERNAP (Servicio Nacional de Áreas Protegidas) (2002) *Guía para la Elaboración de Planes de Manejo para Áreas Protegidas en Bolivia*, MAPZA-GTZ, La Paz

Sharkey, M. J. (2001) 'The all-taxa biological inventory of the Great Smoky Mountains National Park', *Florida Entomologist*, vol 84, no 4, pp556–564

Sharma, E. (1997) 'Socio-economic issues related to conservation of the Khangchendzonga mountain ecosystem', in Rastogi, A., Shengji, P. and Amatya, D. (eds) *Proceedings of a Workshop on Conservation and Management of Khangchendzonga Mountain*

Ecosystem, International Centre for Integrated Mountain Development, Kathmandu

Sharma, E. and Acharya, R. (2004) 'Summary report on mountain biodiversity in the convention on biological diversity (CBD)', *Mountain Research and Development*, vol 24, no 3, pp63–65

Sharma, E. and Chettri, N. (2005) 'ICIMOD's Transboundary Biodiversity Management Initiative in the Hindu Kush-Himalayas', *Mountain Research and Development*, vol 25, no 3, pp280–283

Sheppard, D. (2000) 'Conservation without frontiers: The global view', *The George Wright Forum*, vol 17, no 2, pp70–80

Sherpa, L. N., Peniston, B., Lama, W. and Richard, C. (2003) *Hands Around Everest: Transboundary Cooperation for Conservation and Sustainable Livelihoods*, International Centre for Integrated Mountain Development, Kathmandu

Sherpa, M. N., Wangchuk, S. and Wikramanayake, E. (2004) 'Creating biological corridors for conservation and development: A case study from Bhutan', in Harmon, D. and Worboys, G. L. (eds) *Managing Mountain Protected Areas: Challenges and Responses for the 21st Century*, Andromeda Editrice, Colledara

Shoo, L. P., Williams, S. E. and Hero, J. (2006) 'Detecting climate change induced range shifts: Where and how should we be looking?', *Austral Ecology*, vol 31, no 1, pp22–29

Shrestha, T. B. and Joshi, R. B. (1996) *Rare, Endemic, and Endangered Plants of Nepal*, WWF-Nepal, Kathmandu

SICAP (The Central American Protected Area System) (2003) *2003 Regional Report: Progress with Complying with the Convention on Biological Diversity*, Guatemala

Simberloff, D. and Cox. J. (1987) 'Consequences and costs of conservation corridors', *Conservation Biology*, vol 1, no 1, pp63–71

Simberloff, D., Farr, J. A., Mehlman, D. W. and Cox, J. (1992) 'Movement corridors: Conservation bargains or poor investments?', *Conservation Biology*, vol 6, no 4, pp493–504

Simpson, B. B. (1986) 'Speciation and specialization of *Polylepis* in the Andes', in Vuilleumier, F. and Monasterio, M. (eds) *High Altitude Tropical Biogeography*, Oxford University Press and the American Museum of Natural History, New York

Sklenar, P. and Ramsay, P. M. (2001) 'Diversity of zonal Páramo plant communities in Ecuador', *Diversity and Distributions*, vol 7, no 3, pp113-124

Sklenar, P., Luteyn, J. L., Ulloa, C., Jørgensen, P. M. and Dillon, M. (2005) 'Flora genérica de los Páramos – Guía ilustrada de las plantas vasculares', *Memoirs of The New York Botanical Garden*, New York

Smith, B. D. (1992) *Rivers of Change: Essays on Early Agriculture in Eastern North America*, Smithsonian, Washington DC

Smith, J. M. B. and Cleef, A. M. (1988) 'Composition and origins of the world's tropicalpine floras', *Journal of Biogeography*, vol 15, pp631–645

Smith, R. D. and Maltby, E. (2003) *Using the Ecosystem Approach to Implement the Convention on Biological Diversity: Key Issues and Case Studies*, IUCN, Gland and Cambridge

Soriano, R., Arze, M. and Behoteguy, M. (eds) (2006) *Ecoturismo en Bolivia: Construyendo una Agenda Nacional*, Comité Nacional de Apoyo al Ecoturismo, La Paz

Soulé, M. E. (1987) 'Where do we go from here?', in Soulé, M. E. (ed) *Viable Populations for Nature*, Cambridge University Press, Cambridge

Soulé, M. E. and Terborgh, J. (1999) *Continental Conservation: Scientific Foundations of Regional Reserve Networks*, The Wildlands Project and Island Press, Washington DC

Soulé, M. E., Mackey, B. G., Recher, H. F., Williams, J. E., Woinarski, J. C. Z., Driscoll, D., Dennison, W. G. and Jones, M. E. (2004) 'The role of connectivity in Australian conservation', *Pacific Conservation Biology*, vol 10, pp266–279

Soulé, M. E., Mackey, B. G., Recher, H. F., Williams, J. E., Woinarski, J. C. Z., Dennison, W. C. and Jones, M. E. (2006) 'The role of connectivity in Australian conservation', in Crooks, K. R. and Sanjayan, M. (eds) *Connectivity Conservation*, Cambridge University Press, Cambridge

Spehn, E. and Körner, C. (2005) *Global Mountain Biodiversity Assessment of DIVERSITAS*, Institute of Botany, University of Basel, Basel

Stattersfield, A. J., Crosby, M. J., Long, A. J. and Wege, D. C. (1998) *Global Directory of Endemic Bird Areas*, BirdLife International, Cambridge

Still, C. J., Foster, P. N. and Schneider, S. H. (1999) 'Simulating the effects of climate change on tropical montane cloud forests', *Nature*, vol 398, no 6728, pp608–610

Stoker, G. (1998) 'Governance as theory: Five propositions', *International Social Science Journal*, vol 50, pp17–28

Stokols, D. and Shumaker, S. A. (1981) 'People in places: A transactional view of settings', in Harvey, D. (ed) *Cognition, Social Behavior, and the Environment*, Erlbaum, Hillsdale, NJ, pp441–488

Stubbs, B. J. and Specht, R. L. (2005) *Lamington National Park and Binna Burra Mountain Lodge, Queensland: Partners in Conserving Rainforest*, Paper presented at 6th National Conference of the Australian Forest History Society, Millpress, Rotterdam

Surkin, J. (2006) *Memoria del Taller sobre IIRSA, Carretera InterOceanica Sur y Otros Megaproyectos*, Andes, Conservation International, La Paz

Suzuki, D. and Dressel, H. (2002) *Good News for a Change*, Douglas and MacIntyre, Vancouver

Swyngedouw, E. (2005) 'Governance innovation and the citizen: The Janus face of governance-beyond-the-state', *Urban Studies*, vol 42, pp1991–2006

Tabor, G. M. and Locke, H. (2004) 'Yellowstone to Yukon Conservation Initiative', in Harmon, D. and Worboys, G. L. (eds) *Managing Mountain Protected Areas: Challenges and Responses for the 21st Century*, Proceedings of the IUCN Mountain Protected Areas Workshop, Fifth World Parks Congress, South Africa, Andromeda Editrice, Colledara

Tarquino, R. (2006) *Manual de Uso de la Carpa Verde*, Conservation International, La Paz

Taylor, D. E. (2000) 'The rise of the environmental justice paradigm', *American Behavioral Scientist*, vol 43, no 4, pp508–580

Tewksbury, J. J., Levey, D. J., Haddad, N. M., Sargent, S., Orrock, J. L., Weldon, A., Danielson, B. J., Brinkerhoff, J., Damschen, E. I. and Townsend, P. (2002) 'Corridors affect plants, animals, and their interactions in fragmented landscapes', *PNAS* 99, no 20, pp12923–12926

Thackway, R. and Cresswell, I. D. (eds) (1995) *An Interim Biogeographic Regionalization for Australia: A Framework for Setting Priorities in the National Reserves System Cooperative Program*, Version 4.0, Australian Nature Conservation Agency, Canberra

The Allen Consulting Group (2005) *Climate Change Risk and Vulnerability: Promoting an Efficient Adaptation Response in Australia*, Report to the Australian Greenhouse Office, Department of Environment and Heritage, Australia

TNC (The Nature Conservancy) (2003) *The Cumberlands and Southern Ridge and Valley Ecoregion: A Plan for Biodiversity Conservation*, The Nature Conservancy, Arlington, VA

TNC (2004) *A Guide to the Nature Conservancy's Natural Areas and Projects in Vermont*, updated 2006 (personal communication), Arlington, VA

TNC (2006) *The Matrix Method for Assessing Ecological*

Viability of Areas, The Nature Conservancy, Arlington, VA

TNC (2007) *Conservation Action Planning Handbook: Developing Strategies, Taking Action and Measuring Success at any Scale*, The Nature Conservancy, Arlington, VA

TNC and SAFC (The Nature Conservancy and Southern Appalachian Forest Coalition) (2000) *Southern Blue Ridge Ecoregional Conservation Plan: Summary and Implementation Document*, The Nature Conservancy, Durham, NC

Tompkins, E. L. and Adger, N. W. (2004) 'Does adaptive management of natural resources enhance resilience to climate change?', *Ecology and Society*, vol 9, no 2, art 10, www.ecologyandsociety.org/vol9/iss2/art10/

Tremblay, P. (2000) 'An evolutionary interpretation of the role of collaborative partnerships in sustainable tourism', in Bramwell, B. and Lane, B. (eds) *Tourism Collaboration and Partnerships: Politics, Practice and Sustainability*, Channel View, Clevedon, pp314–332

Tscharntke, T., Klein, A. M., Kruess, A., Steffen-Dewenter, I. and Their, C. (2005) 'Landscape perspective in agriculture intensification and biodiversity-ecosystem service management', *Ecology Letters*, vol 8, pp857–874

Tuan, Y. F. (1977) *Space and Place*, University of Minnesota Press, Minneapolis, MN

Udvardy, M. D. F. (1975) *A Classification of the Biogeographical Provinces of the World*, IUCN Occasional Paper No 18, prepared as a contribution to UNESCO's Man and the Biosphere Programme, Project No 8, International Union for the Conservation of Nature and Natural Resources, Morges

UN Millennium Project (2005) *Investing in Development: A Practical Plan to Achieve the Millennium Development Goals*, Millennium Project, New York, www.unmillenniumproject.org

UNEP (United Nations Environment Programme) (2002) *Global Environmental Outlook 3: Past, Present and Future Perspectives*, United Nations Environment Programme and Earthscan, Nairobi and London

UNEP (2007) *GEO 4 Global Environment Outlook: Environment for Development*, UNEP, Nairobi

UNEP-WCMC (2009) *World Data Base on Protected Areas Statistics for January 2008*, www.UNEP-WCMC.org/wdpa/mdgs/WDPAPAstats_Jan08

UNESCO (United Nations Educational, Scientific and Cultural Organization) (1995) *The Seville Strategy for Biosphere Reserves*, www.unesco.org/mab/BRs/offDoc.shtml

UNESCO (2006) *Man and the Biosphere, Biosphere Reserve Directory 2006*, www.unesco.org

UNESCO (2009) *Man and The Biosphere Programme*, www.unesco.org

UNESCO-MAB (United Nations Educational, Scientific and Cultural Organization, Man and the Biosphere Programme) (1979) *Resolucion de declaracion de la Reserva de la Biosfera Constelación del Cinturon Andino*, PNN Nevado del Huila, Purace y Cueva de los Guacharos en Colombia, París

UQ (The University of Queensland) (2008) *Marxan*, www.uq.edu.au/marxan/index.html?page=77644

US Department of Transportation (2002) *A Hallmark of Context-Sensitive Design*, www.tfhrc.gov/pubrds/02may/02

US Fish and Wildlife Service (2006) *Cabinet Yaak, Grizzly Bear Recovery Home Page*, www.r6.fws.gov/endspp/grizzly

van Bueren, E. M., Klijn, E.-H. and Koppenjan, J. F. M. (2003) 'Dealing with wicked problems in networks: Analyzing an environmental debate from a network perspective', *Journal of Public Administration Research and Theory*, vol 13, pp193–212

Van der Hammen, T. and Cleef, A. M. (1986) 'Development of the high Andean Páramo flora and vegetation', in Vuilleumier, F. and Monasterio, M. (eds) *High Altitude Tropical Biogeography*, Oxford University Press and the American Museum of Natural History, New York, pp153–201

van der Linde, H., Oglethorpe, J., Sandwith, T., Snelson, D. and Tessema Y. (2001) with contributions from Anada Tiéga and Thomas Price, *Beyond Boundaries: Transboundary Natural Resource Management in Sub-Saharan Africa*, Biodiversity Support Program, World Wildlife Fund, Washington DC

Vanclay, F. (2008) 'Place matters', in Vanclay, F., Higgins, M. and Blackshaw, A. (eds) *Making Sense of Place*, National Museum of Australia Press, Canberra

Vaske, J. J. and Kobrin, K. C. (2001) 'Place attachment and environmentally responsible behavior', *Journal of Environmental Education*, vol 32, pp16–21

Verweij, P. (1995) *Spatial and Temporal Modelling of Vegetation Patterns. Burning and Grazing in the Paramo of Los Nevados National Park, Colombia*, PhD Dissertation, University of Amsterdam and International Institute for Aerospace Survey and Earth Sciences ITC, Enschede

Viteri, X. (ed) (2004) *Caracterización Ecológica y Socioeconómica de las Ecorregiones: Bosques Montanos de la Cordillera Real Oriental y Páramos de los Andes del Norte con Especial Referencia a los Parques Nacionales Llanganates y Sangay y al Corredor Ecológico Llanganates Sangay, Ecuador*, Fundación Natura, World Wildlife Fund, Quito

Wallington, T. J. and Lawrence, G. (2008) 'Making democracy matter: Responsibility and effective environmental governance in regional Australia', *Journal of Rural Studies*, vol 24, pp277–290

Wang, S. (ed) (2008) *Linking Up With the World. Proceedings of the International Workshop on Protected Area Management and Biodiversity Conservation, East Asia, 2–3 September 2008*, Department of Geography, National Taiwan University, Taipei

Watson, J. W. (1967) *North America, Its Countries and Regions*, F. A. Praeger Press, New York

Watson, J. E. M., Fuller, R. A., Watson, A. W. T., Mackey, B. G., Wilson, K. A., Grantham, H. S., Turner, M., Klein, C. J., Carwardine, J., Joseph, L. N. and Possingham, H. (2009) 'Wilderness and future conservation priorities in Australia', *Diversity and Distributions*, vol 15, pp1028–1036

WCS (Wildlife Conservation Society) (2006) *Plan de Manejo de la Reserva de la Biosfera-Tierras Comunitarias de Origen Pilón Lajas*, Wildlife Conservation Society, La Paz

Wear, D. N. and Greis, J. G. (eds) (2002) 'Southern forest resource assessment', *General Technical Report, SRS-53*, Southern Research Station, Forest Service, US Department of Agriculture, Asheville, NC

Webler, T., Tuler, S. and Krueger, R. (2001) 'What is good public participation process? Five perspectives from the public', *Environmental Management*, vol 27, no 3, pp435–450

Welch, D. (2005) 'What should protected area managers do in the face of climate change?', *The George Wright Forum*, vol 22, no 1, pp75–93

Wells, M. and McShane, T. O. (2004) 'Integrating protected area management with local needs and aspirations', *Ambio*, vol 33, pp513–519

Western Cape Department of Environmental Affairs and Development Planning (2005) *Western Cape Provincial Spatial Development Framework, 2005*, www.capegateway.gov.za/eng/pubs/guides/W/120505

White, M. E (1994) *After the Greening, the Browning of Australia*, Kangaroo Press, Sydney

Whitten, T., Damanik, S. J., Anwar, J. and Hisyam, N. (1997) *The Ecology of Sumatra*, Periplus, Jakarta

Wikipedia (2007) *John Birch Society*, Wikipedia, the free encyclopaedia, http://en.wikipedia.org/wiki/John_Birch_Society

Wikramanayake, E. (2005) *A Biological Assessment and Overview of the Sacred Himalayan Landscape, with Conservation Targets*, unpublished report, WWF-Nepal, Kathmandu

Wikramanayake, E., Dinerstein, E., Loucks, C., Olson, D., Morrison, J., Lamoreux, J., McKnight, M. and Hedao, P. (2001) *Terrestrial Ecoregions of the Indo-Pacific: A Conservation Assessment*, Island Press, Washington DC

Wildlands Network (2009) www.twp.org/cms/page1090.cfm

Wilkie, D. S., Hakizumwami, E., Gami, N. and Difara, B. (2001) *Beyond Boundaries: Regional Overview of Transboundary Natural Resource Management in Central Africa*, Biodiversity Support Program, World Wildlife Fund, Washington DC

Willcox. L., Robinson, B. and Harvey, A. (1998) *A Sense of Place: An Atlas of Issues, Attitudes and Resources in the Y2Y Ecoregion*, Yellowstone to Yukon, Canmore, Alberta

Wille, M., Hofstede, R., Fehse, J., Hooghiemstra H. and Sevink, J. (2002) 'Upper forest line reconstruction in a deforested area in northern Ecuador based on pollen and vegetation analysis', *Journal of Tropical Ecology*, vol 18, pp409–440

Williams, D. R. and Vaske, J. J. (2003) 'The measurement of place attachment: Validity and generalizability of a psychometric approach', *Forest Science*, vol 49, no 6, pp830–840

Williams, K. J, Faith, D. P., Ford, A., Metcalf, D., Pert, P., Rosauer, D., Slatyer, C., Ferrier, S., Cogger, H., Margules, C., James, R. and Williams, S. (2006) *Progress in Defining the Status and Extent of a Global High Biodiversity Hot Spot in Eastern Australia*, unpublished project update, 21 August 2006, sourced from NSW Department of Environment and Climate Change, Queanbeyan

Wilson, E. O. (2001) *The Future of Life*, Knopf, New York

Wilson, J. (1902) *Message From the President of the United States Transmitting a Report of the Secretary of Agriculture in Relation to the Forests, Rivers, and Mountains of the Southern Appalachian Region*, Government Printing Office, Washington DC

Wing, L. D. and Buss, I. O. (1970) 'Elephants and forests', *Wildlife Monographs*, vol 19, pp1–92

Wiratno, I. (2002) *Forest Policy Summary*, unpublished document, Conservation International, Indonesia, Jakarta

Wiratno, I. (2006) *Strategic Planning for Leuser National Park (2006–2010)*, unpublished document, Medan

Wondolleck, J. M. and Yaffe, S. L. (2000) *Making Collaboration Work: Lessons From Innovation in NRM*, Island Press, Washington DC

Worboys, G. L. (1996) *Conservation Corridors and the NSW Section of the Great Escarpment of Eastern Australia*, Paper presented at the IUCN World Conservation Congress, 13–23 October 1996, Montreal

Worboys, G. L. (2003) 'A brief report on the Australian Alps bushfires', *Mountain Research and Development*, vol 23, no 3, pp294–295

Worboys, G. L. (2005a) 'The South East Forest National Park of NSW', in Worboys, G. L., Lockwood, M. and De Lacy, T. (2005) *Protected Area Management, Principles and Practice*, Second Edition, Oxford University Press, Melbourne, p25

Worboys, G. L. (2005b) *Climate Change and Protected Area Managers: Some Contributions That can be Made to Reduce the Effects of Climate Change*, IUCN WCPA (Mountains Biome), www.mountains-wcpa.org

Worboys, G. L. (2007) *Evaluation Subjects and Methods Required for Managing Protected Areas*, PhD Thesis, Griffith University, Gold Coast

Worboys, G. L. and Winkler, C. (2006a) 'Process of management', in Lockwood, M., Worboys, G. L. and Kothari, A. (eds) *Managing Protected Areas: A Global Guide*, IUCN, Earthscan, London, pp146–163

Worboys, G. L. and Winkler, C. (2006b) 'Managing staff, finances and assets', in Lockwood, M., Worboys, G. L. and Kothari, A. (eds) *Managing Protected Areas: A Global Guide*, IUCN, Earthscan, London, pp359–376

Worboys, G. L. and Winkler, C. (2006c) 'Incident management', in Lockwood, M., Worboys, G. L. and Kothari, A. (eds) *Managing Protected Areas: A Global Guide*, IUCN, Earthscan, London, pp474–496

Worboys, G. L., Lockwood, M. and De Lacy, T. (2005) *Protected Area Management: Principles and Practice*, Second Edition, Oxford University Press, Melbourne

Worboys, G. L., Winkler, C. and Lockwood, M. (2006) 'Threats to protected areas', in Lockwood, M., Worboys, G. L. and Kothari, A. (eds) *Managing Protected Areas: A Global Guide*, IUCN, Earthscan, London, pp223–261

World Bank (1998) *Corredor Biológico del Atlántico*, www.gefweb.org/Outreach/outreach-PUblications/Project_factsheet/Panama-atla-1-bd-wb-spa-ld.pdf#search=%22corredor%20biologico%20mesoamericano

%20fondos%20totales%20US%24%22

WWF (World Wide Fund for Nature) (2001) *Tiger Conservation in Bhutan*, WWF-Bhutan Report submitted to WWF-US, New York

WWF and ICIMOD (International Centre for Integrated Mountain Development) (2001) *Ecoregion-based Conservation in the Eastern Himalaya: Identifying Important Areas for Biodiversity Conservation*, WWF-Nepal, Kathmandu

WWF and IUCN (International Union for the Conservation of Nature) (1995) *Centres of Plant Diversity: A Guide and Strategy for their Conservation. Vol 2: Asia, Australasia, and the Pacific*, IUCN, Cambridge

WWF and World Bank (1996) *Ecoregiones Prioritarias para America Latina y el Caribe*, World Bank Report, Washington DC

Xu, J. and Melic, D. R. (2007) 'Rethinking the effectiveness of public protected areas in Southwestern China', *Conservation Biology*, vol 21, no 2, pp318–328

Xu, J., Ma, E. T., Tashi, D., Fu, Y., Lu, Z. and Melick, D. (2005) 'Integrating sacred knowledge for conservation: Cultures and landscapes in southwest China', *Ecology and Society*, vol 10, no 2, www.ecologyandsociety.org/vol10/iss2/art7/

Y2Y (Yellowstone to Yukon Conservation Initiative) (2002) *Strategic Plan 2000–2005* (unpublished), Y2Y Board of Directors, Yellowstone to Yukon Conservation Initiative, Canmore, Alberta

Y2Y (2006) *Conservation Action – Critical Cores and Corridors*, www.y2y.net

Y2Y (2007) *Yellowstone to Yukon Conservation Initiative*, www.y2y.net/overview/default.asp

Yerena, E. (1988) 'Planning for spectacled bear conservation in Venezuela', in Rosenthal, M. (ed) *Proceedings of the First International Symposium on the Spectacled Bear*, Lincoln Park Zoo, Chicago, pp44–59

Yerena, E. (1994) 'Corredores ecologicos en Los Andes de Venezuela', in Amend, S. and Amend, T. (eds) *No 4, Serie Parques Nacionales y Conservacion Ambiental*, Fundacion Polar, Editorial Torino, Caracas

Yerena, E. and Torres, D. (1994) 'Spectacled bear conservation and dispersal corridors in Venezuela', *Int Conf Bear Research and Management*, vol 9, no 1, pp169–172

Yonzon, P., Pradhan, S., Bhujel, R., Khaling, S., Lachungpa, U. and Lachungpa, C. (2000) *Kanchenjunga Mountain Complex. Biodiversity Assessment and Conservation Planning*, WWF-Nepal, Kathmandu

Yost, E. C., Johnson, K. S. and Blozan, W. F. (1994) *Old Growth Project: Stand Delineation and Disturbance Rating*, Technical Report NPS/SERGSM/NATR, National Park Service, Great Smoky Mountains National Park, Gatlinburg, TN

Young, M. D., Gunningham, N., Elix, J., Lambert, J., Howard, B., Grabosky, P. and McCrone, E. (1996) *Reimbursing the Future: An Evaluation of Motivational, Voluntary, Price-based, Property Right, and Regulatory Incentives for the Conservation of Biodiversity*, Department of the Environment, Sport and Territories, Canberra

Young, M. D., Proctor, W. and Qureshi, M. E. (2006) *Without Water. The Economics of Supplying Water to 5 Million more Australians. National Research Flagships – Water for a Healthy Country Flagship Report*, CSIRO, Canberra

Index